11th Conferencia Iberoamericana en Software Engineering (CIbSE 2008)

Pernambuco, Brazil
13-17 February 2008

Editors:

Maria Lencastre
Antonio Valecillo
Joao Falcao e Cunha

ISBN: 978-1-5108-4066-9

Printed from e-media with permission by:

Curran Associates, Inc.
57 Morehouse Lane
Red Hook, NY 12571

Printed by Curran Associates, Inc. (2017)

CIbSE - IberoAmerican Conference on Software Engineering
c/o Luca Cernuzzi
Universidad Católica "Nuestra Seóra de la Asunción",
Campus Universitario, Asunción
Barrio Santa Ana, C.C.1683, C.P. 1364
Asunción - Paraguay

Phone: +595 21 334650
Fax: +595 21 310587

lcernuzz@uca.edu.py

Additional copies of this publication are available from:

Curran Associates, Inc.
57 Morehouse Lane
Red Hook, NY 12571 USA
Phone: 845-758-0400
Fax: 845-758-2633
Email: curran@proceedings.com
Web: www.proceedings.com

TABLE OF CONTENTS

Discovering service compositions that feature a desired behaviour*

Fabrizio Benigni, Antonio Brogi, Sara Corfini

Department of Computer Science, University of Pisa, Italy
{benigni,brogi,corfini}@di.unipi.it

Abstract. Web service discovery is one of the key issues in the emerging area of Service-oriented Computing. In this paper, we present a complete composition-oriented, ontology-based methodology for discovering semantic Web services, which exploits functional and behavioural properties contained in OWL-S service advertisements to satisfy *functional* and *behavioural* client queries. To this aim, we build on top of the results contained in two recent articles, where we presented (1) a suitable data structure (viz., a dependency hypergraph) to collect functional information of services, and (2) a suitable notion of behavioural equivalence for Web services. We also discuss the architecture and the main implementation choices of the matchmaking system applying such a methodology.

Keywords: Service-oriented computing, Web service discovery, OWL-S.

1 Introduction

Service-oriented Computing (SoC) [1] is emerging as a new promising computing paradigm that centers on the notion of service as the fundamental element for developing distributed software applications. In this setting, Web service discovery is a major issue of SoC, as it allows developers to find and re-use existing services to rapidly build complex applications.

The standard service description language (WSDL) provides services with purely syntactic descriptions, not including neither behavioural information on the possible interaction among services, nor semantics information to describe the functionality of services. Yet, both behavioural and semantic information may be necessary, for example, to satisfy complex queries that require to compose the functionalities offered by different services, as well as to automatise the processes of service discovery and composition.

During the last years, various proposals have been put forward to feature more expressive service descriptions that include both semantics (viz., ontology-based) and behaviour information about services. One of the major efforts in this direction is OWL-S [2], a high-level ontology-based language for describing services. In particular, OWL-S service descriptions include a list of semantically

* Research partially supported by EU FP6-IST STREP 0333563 SMEPP and MIUR FIRB TOCAI.IT.

annotated functional attributes of services (the *service profile*), and a declaration of the interaction behaviour of services (the so-called *process model*).

In this paper, we present a composition-oriented, ontology-based methodology for discovering OWL-S described services. In particular, we employ semantic information to select available services that can be exploited to satisfy a given query, and we employ behaviour information to suitably compose such services to achieve the desired result.

The methodology integrates the results recently presented in [3, 4]. In [3] a suitable data structure (viz., a dependency hypergraph) to collect relationships among ontology-annotated inputs and outputs of services (i.e., semantic information) was introduced. It is important to stress that the construction of such a hypergraph does not affect the query answering time, as it is built off-line and updated whenever a new service is added to the local service repository. In [4] we defined a suitable notion of behavioural equivalence for Web services. Such a notion allows to establish whether two services, described by means of a simple variant of standard Petri nets, are behaviourally equivalent, i.e., such that an external observer can not tell them apart. An interesting feature of this methodology is the ability of addressing both *functional* and *behavioural* queries, i.e., respectively, queries specifying the functional attributes of the desired service, and queries also requiring a specific behaviour of the service to be found. In particular, in case of a behavioural query, the methodology – besides satisfying the query functional requirements – guarantees that the returned service features the desired behaviour.

In this paper we also present a system – called SAM, for Service Aggregation Matchmaking – implementing the discovery methodology here introduced. The main features of the new version of SAM can be summarised as follows:

- *Composition-oriented matching* – that is, the capability of discovering service compositions. When no single service can satisfy the client query, SAM checks whether the query can be fulfilled by a suitable composition of services.
- *Ontology-based matching* – that is, the ability of "crossing" different ontologies and performing flexible matching automatically. Given that different services are typically described in terms of different ontologies, SAM determines relationships between concepts defined in separate ontologies, so to establish functional dependencies among services.
- *Behaviour-aware matching* – that is, the ability of guaranteeing behavioural properties. Given a query synthetising the behaviour of a service, SAM searches for (compositions of) services which are behaviourally equivalent to the query. Each matched service (composition) can be used interchangeably with the service described by the query.

It is also worth observing that, with respect to its first version described in [5], SAM is now capable of properly coping with the problem of "crossing" different ontologies (thanks to the introduction of the hypergraph), as well as of suitably addressing behavioural queries.

The rest of the paper is organized as follows. Section 2 describes the composition-oriented, ontology-based methodology for discovering services. Section 3 is devoted to discuss the architecture, the main implementation choices, and possible future extensions of the system applying such a methodology. Finally, some concluding remarks are drawn in Section 4.

2 A Methodology for a Composition-oriented Discovery

In this Section, we present a methodology for discovering compositions of semantic Web services which takes into account both *semantic* and *behavioural* information advertised in the OWL-S service descriptions. In particular, we employ "semantics", namely all those ontological information regarding the functional attributes (i.e., inputs and outputs) of services, to select services with respect to "what they really do", and we employ "behaviour", namely, information concerning the order with which messages can be received or sent by each service, to guarantee some useful properties of selected services. Before presenting the discovery methodology, we describe hereafter the data structures and formalisms we employ to summarise service descriptions.

2.1 The internal Representation of Services

As briefly mentioned in the Introduction, the complete behaviour of a service is described by the OWL-S process model, which may include conditional and iterative constructs. Hence, a service may behave in different ways and feature different functionalities. We say that a service may have different *profiles*, each of them requiring/providing different inputs/outputs. Hence, as one may expect, we represent each service with two distinct items: a *set of profiles*, to summarise the different sets of functional attributes employed by each profile of the service, and a *Petri net*, to model the whole service behaviour.

More precisely, a profile S_n represents a dependency between the set of the inputs and the set of the outputs employed by the specific behaviour n of a service S. Service profiles are collected into a hypergraph, whose nodes correspond to the functional attributes of the service profiles, and whose hyperedges represent relationships among such attributes. It is worth observing that each node v of the hypergraph, that is, each functional attribute, is associated with a concept, which is defined in one of the ontologies referred by the service employing v. The hypergraph also includes equivalent and sub-concept relationships among nodes, viz., among ontology concepts. (A formal definition of the hypergraph and the algorithms for its construction can be found in [3, 6].)

Example. Let us consider the simple service T, defined as a choice of two atomic operations. The former inputs a *zipCode* (*Z*) and returns the corresponding *geographicCoordinates* (*GC*), and the latter inputs a *location* (L) and a *date* (*D*), and returns the computed *wheatherInformation* (*W*). The service T has hence two profiles, T_1 and T_2, represented by the hyperedges $\{Z\} \xrightarrow{T_1} \{GC\}$ and $\{L, D\} \xrightarrow{T_2} \{W\}$, respectively. Consider next the service S, which inputs a *city* (C) and a *nation* (*N*), and returns the corresponding *zipCode* (*Z*). Service S exposes a single profile S_1 represented by the hyperedge $\{C, N\} \xrightarrow{S_1} \{Z\}$. The hypergraph including profiles S_1, T_1, T_2 is illustrated in Figure 1. Note the equivalent relationship linking together *state* (ST) and *nation* (viz., ST and N are synonyms), as well as, the sub-concept relationship linking *geographicCoordinates* and *geographicLocation* (GL) (viz., GC is a sub-concept of GL).

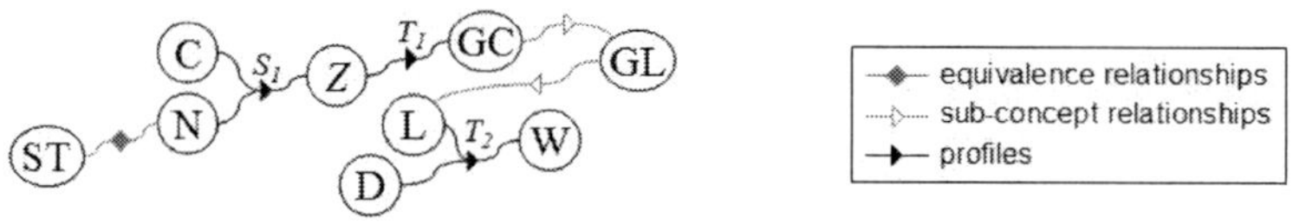

Fig. 1. A simple hypergraph.

While a profile describes a particular behaviour of a service from a functional point of view, the complete interaction behaviour of a service is represented by an OCPR net. OCPR nets (for Open Consume-Produce-Read nets) [4] are a simple variant of the standard Condition/Event Petri nets, designed to naturally model the behaviour of services, and in particular the persistency of data (i.e., once a data has been produced by some service operation, it remains available for all the service operations that input it). Briefly, an OCPR net is equipped with two disjoint sets of places, namely, control and data places, to properly model the control flow and the data flow of a Web service, and with an interface, which establishes those data places that can be observed externally. Hence, whilst control places can be produced and consumed, data places can be read, produced but not consumed. We formally defined OCPR nets in [4], where a mapping from OWL-S process models to OCPR nets is also presented. Intuitively speaking, transitions map (OWL-S) atomic operations, while data places and control places respectively model the availability of data and the executability of atomic operations. It is worth observing that when a service is translated into an OCPR net, all the data places of the net are externally observable by default.

Example. Figure 2 (which will be explained in more detail later) illustrates four simple OCPR nets, where rectangles, circles and diamonds respectively represent transitions, data places and control places. The initial control place i as well as the final control place f of each net are emphasised in light gray. Furthermore, each net is delimited by a box which represents the net interface, namely, the set of places which can interact with the environment. Hence, those data places that lie on the box are the ones that can be observed externally.

2.2 Discovering Compositions of Services

So far, we have introduced the internal representation of services that we use to store them in a local repository. We can now propose a complete composition-oriented methodology for discovering services. The methodology takes as input the so-called *behavioural queries*, that is, queries specifying both the inputs and outputs, as well as the expected behaviour of the service to be found. A behavioural query, for example, can be expressed in terms of the OWL-S process model describing the desired service. The set of the functional attributes of the query can be easily retrieved by its OWL-S process model, which can be in turn suitably translated into an OCPR net [4]. Hence, we can assume that a query consists of two parts: a couple (I, O) and an OCPR net, respectively describing the set of the inputs and outputs, and the behaviour of the service to be found.

The discovery methodology we are going to propose consists of two main phases: a *functional analysis* and a *behavioural analysis*, that we describe below.

Functional Analysis

This first phase consists in a sort of *functional filter*, indeed, services are selected according to their functional attributes only. More precisely, the functional analysis focuses on the first functional part of the query (viz., the couple (I, O) of inputs and outputs), and returns those set of services which satisfy the functional requirements of the query. Hence, for each set of services S passing the functional filter: (1) all the query outputs are provided by the service in S, (2) all the inputs of the services in S are provided by the query (or they can be produced by some service in S).

As described in the previous subsection, we summarise functional information of the services stored in the repository in an hypergraph. The functional analysis hence consists of a visit of the hypergraph. It is worth noting that by exploring *profiles*, we address the discovery of sets of services, as well as by exploring *sub-concept* and *equivalent* relationships we properly reason with (different) ontologies. In particular, the functional analysis explores the hypergraph starting from those nodes corresponding to the query outputs, and it continues by visiting backwards the hyperedges until reaching, if possible, the query inputs. The profile-labelled hyperedges which take part in an hyperpath from the query outputs to the query inputs determine a set of service profiles satisfying the query. A detailed discussion of the algorithm for visiting the hypergraph can be found in [6]. Furthermore, it is also worth noting that we have enriched the functional analysis with a *minimality check* [5], in order to avoid constructing non-minimal sets of service, that is, sets containing (at least) a service not strictly necessary to satisfy the query.

Example. Consider the simple hypergraph illustrated in Figure 1, and the query taking as input a *city* (C) and a *state* (ST) and providing as output the corresponding *geographicLocation* (GL). The functional analysis visits the hypergraph starting from the query output GL. Then, by exploring the sub-concept relationship $\{GC\} \rightarrow \{GL\}$ and the profile T_1, it reaches the node Z. Next, by visiting the profile S_1 and by crossing the equivalence relationship $\{ST\} \rightarrow \{N\}$, it reaches both the query inputs $\{C, ST\}$. Hence, the set of profiles $\{S_1, T_1\}$ satisfies (the functional requirements of) the query.

Behavioural Analysis

As previously described, every set of profiles determined by the functional analysis satisfies the query from a functional perspective. Consider now a specific set P of profiles. The behavioural analysis checks whether the services included in the set, and suitably composed together, are *behaviourally* equivalent to the client query. The behavioural analysis consists of the following two main steps.

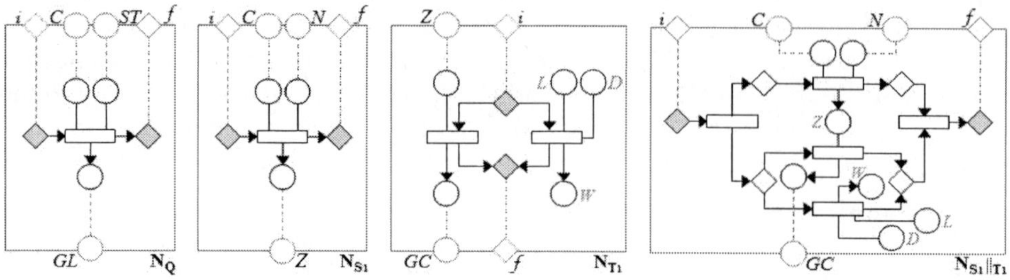

Fig. 2. OCPR nets.

(1) Constructing the composite service. The objective of this step is to construct the OCPR net modelling the parallel composition of the service profiles included in P. Firstly, for each service profile S_n in the set, we retrieve from the local repository the OCPR net modelling the complete behaviour of the corresponding service S. As described in subsection 2.1, all the data places of an OCPR net are externally observable by default (viz., all the data places of the net belong to the net interface). Yet, a profile identifies a specific portion (i.e., behaviour) of the service, which may partially employ the inputs and outputs of the whole service. Hence, let S_n be a profile of a service S, and let N_S be the OCPR net modelling S. Then, we remove from the interface of N_S those data places which do not belong to the inputs and outputs of the profile S_n.

We can now construct the composite OCPR net $N_{\|}$ modelling the parallel composition of the OCPR nets $N_{S_1}, \ldots, N_{S_n}$ associated to the profiles $S_1, \ldots, S_n$ belonging to the set P. Note that, if the set of profiles returned by the functional analysis contains n profiles of the same service S, we insert into the composite net n copies of the OCPR net modelling S, each of them typically providing a different interface. In other words, we are considering multiple executions of the same service.

As stated before, the data places which belong to the net interface are the only ones that can interact with the external environment. Consequently, in order to compose OCPR nets, we have to operate on their interfaces. To build $N_{\|}$ we first perform the disjoint union of the transitions, data places and control places of the nets $N_{S_1}, \ldots, N_{S_n}$. Next, we collapse those data places which are equivalent and which occur in the interfaces of $N_{S_1}, \ldots, N_{S_n}$. It is worth noting that we qualify as equivalent data places, those data places which are syntactically and/or semantically equivalent. For example, we collapse two data places corresponding to two syntactically different, yet synonyms concepts. Moreover, in order to perform the parallel composition of $N_{S_1}, \ldots, N_{S_n}$, we add to $N_{\|}$ the necessary additional transitions and control places, according to the OCPR mapping of the parallel composition (viz., the OWL-S `split+join` construct) given in [4]. It is important to observe that the initial control places as well as the final control place of an OCPR net are externally observable by default. The interface of the resulting composite net $N_{||}$ is the union of the interfaces of the nets $N_{S_1}, \ldots, N_{S_n}$. Finally, before verifying the equivalence of the composite net with the behavioural query, we have to properly revise the interface of the composite net. Indeed, the interface of $N_{||}$ may contain some data places with do not belong to the interface of the query net. We do not need to observe those data places, which, hence, have to be removed from the interface of $N_{||}$.

Example. Let us continue the example previously introduced. For each profile included in the set $\{S_1, T_1\}$ returned by the functional analysis, we consider its OCPR net representation. The OCPR nets N_{S_1}, N_{T_1}, respectively representing the profiles S_1, T_1, are illustrated in Figure 2. While all the data places of N_{S_1} belong to the net interface (as they belong to the single profile S_1 of S), the interface of N_{T_1} contains only the data places employed by the profile T_1. We perform next the parallel composition of the two nets N_{S_1} and N_{T_1}. The resulting net $N_{S_1||T_1}$ is depicted in the right part of Figure 2. Finally, note that we removed Z from the interface of $N_{S_1||T_1}$, since it does not belong to the query.

(2) Analysing the service behaviour. The second step of the behavioural analysis checks whether the composition of those services previously selected during the functional analysis is capable of satisfying the query from a behavioural perspective. Let N_Q denote the net representing the behavioural query. Namely, this step checks whether N_Q and $N_{||}$ are equivalent, that is, whether they are externally indistinguishable.

To this end, we defined in [4] a suitable notion of behavioural equivalence for Web services, which features *weakness*, as it equates structurally different yet externally indistinguishable services; *compositionality*, as it is also a congruence; and *decidability*, as the set of states that an OCPR net can reach is finite. More precisely, a state of an OCPR net is the marking of its observable places. In the initial state only the initial control place contains a token, while all the other places belonging to the net interface are empty. Then, in each state, an OCPR net can execute two types of actions, namely, it can put a token in one of the data places of its interface, or it can perform τ-transitions (i.e., it can fire transitions not requiring any additional token). Hence, intuitively speaking, in order to verify whether N_Q and $N_{||}$ are equivalent, the second step of the behavioural analysis checks whether for each state s of N_Q: (1) there exists a state t of $N_{||}$ which can perform all the actions executable by s; (2) for each state s' reachable from s by executing the action a, t can reach a state t' by executing the same action a, such that s' and t' are equivalent. It is important to observe that if s reaches s' by performing a single τ-transition, t can reach a state t' equivalent to s' with one or more τ-transitions. Dually, this step checks whether similar conditions hold for each state of $N_{||}$. If so, the query and the composite net are equivalent, that is, the found service composition fully satisfies the query.

Example. Consider the nets N_Q and $N_{S_1||T_1}$, illustrated in Figure 2, and respectively representing the client query and the previously built composite service. According to [4], the nets N_Q and $N_{S_1||T_1}$ are equivalent. In particular, note that if we add a token in C and ST (namely, N, since ST and N are equivalent), N_Q reaches the final state in a single τ-transition, while $N_{S_1 \| T_1}$ needs of performing four τ-transitions.

3 Implementation of the Methodology

We discuss below the architecture and the main implementation choices of the system (viz., SAM) applying the discovery methodology described in Section 2.

Architecture
Figure 3 illustrates the overall architecture of the matchmaking system implementing the proposed discovery methodology. The system – available as Web service – is designed to cope with two classes of users, *clients* and *providers*, which, mainly, can query the system, and add a new service to the system, as reflected by the WSDL interface depicted in Figure 3.

The client queries are handled by the *search engine* core component, which consists of two building blocks, namely, the *functional analyser* and the *behavioural analyser*, respectively implementing the functional analysis and the behavioural analysis of the discovery methodology described in subsection 2.2. In particular, functional queries can be satisfied by the functional analyser only, while behavioural queries need of the joint work of both functional and behavioural analysers. It is worth noting that the implementation of the *behavioural analyser* makes use of the algorithm presented by Fernandez and Mounier in [7] for verifying the bisimilarity of two systems. Clients can also list available services and ontologies: the *service browser* component satisfies these requests.

When a provider adds a new service to the system, the *hypergraph builder* and the *OWL-S2PNML* components translate the service into the internal representation described in subsection 2.1. The hypergraph builder determines the profiles of the service. Moreover, it exploits SemFiT [8], a tool for "crossing" different ontologies, to establish the semantic (viz., equivalence and sub-concept) relationships among ontology concepts. In particular, the hypergraph builder determines the relationships concerning those concepts defined in the new ontologies employed by the service to be added, and those concepts which belong to the ontologies previously registered to the system. A more detailed description of the behaviour of the hypergraph builder component is available in [6].

OWL-S2PNML translates the OWL-S process model of the service into an OCPR net, which is described by a corresponding PNML file. The Petri Net Markup Language[1] (PNML) is a XML-based and customizable interchange format for Petri nets. We employ PNML in order to enhance the modularity and portability of the system. Providers can also add single ontologies: in such a case, the hypergraph builder component suffices to update the hypergraph.

It is also worth noting that, before adding a new service as well as a new ontology, a provider has to login the system. The authentication service is managed by the *account manager* component.

[1] `http://www2.informatik.hu-berlin.de/top/pnml/about.html`

Service internal descriptions (i.e., profiles and semantic relationships, and PNML files), ontologies and account information are stored in the *local registry*. All system components can access the local registry by means of a suitable *registry manager*.

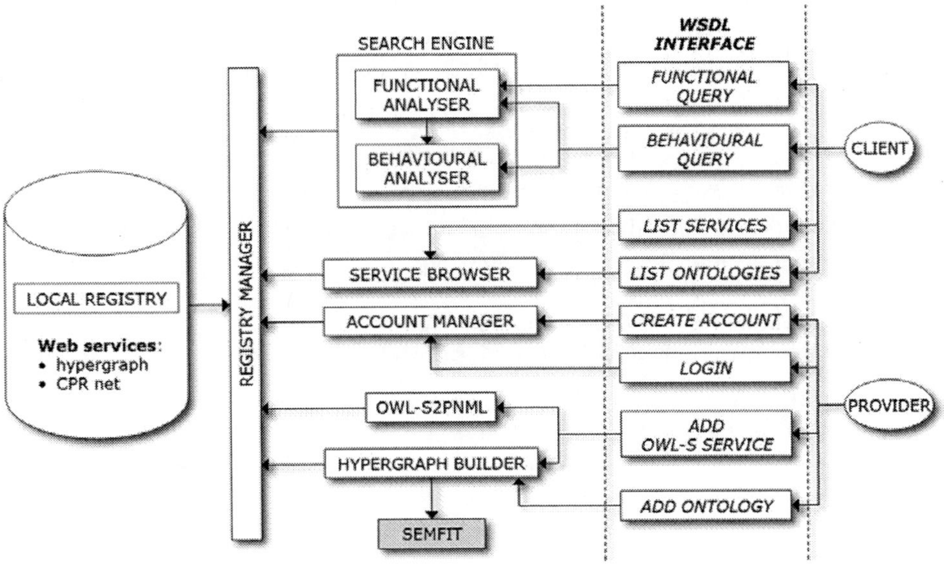

Fig. 3. System architecture.

Implementation

We discuss hereafter the main implementation aspects of SAM, the matchmaking system previously described in Section 2. In particular, the implementation of SAM has been conditioned by the following requisites.

- *Portability* – the system consists of Java packages, each of them wrapped in a standard Java EE 5 component. SAM is accessible as a Web service, described by a standard WSDL interface as well as by an OWL-S advertisement.
- *Extensibility* – SAM is deployed as a multitiered Java enterprise application, which allows for high levels of modularization and ease of substitute/add logic components (e.g., the integration with SemFiT, remotely accessed by its WSDL interface). Furthermore, the use of Java language allows us to employ many existing Java libraries and tools (e.g., OWL-S parsers).
- *Scalability* – Java EE platform natively guarantees suitable performance and scalability to component-based and multitiered applications.
- *Use of standards* – Besides the use of Java EE platform, the system implementation relies on other standard languages and well-known technologies:
  - PNML, to describe OCPR nets by means of standard XML files,

- javaDB, to deploy the database (which is accessible via JDBC API directly by the Java EE component containers),
- Mindswap OWL-S API, to validate, marshal/unmarshal OWL-S descriptions,
- PNML framework API, to marshal/unmarshal PNML descriptions.

The domain logic of SAM is implemented by three Java libraries: SamFeedLogics, which implements the *OWL-S2PNML* and *hypergraph builder* components of Figure 3, SamFunctionalLogics, that implements the *functional analyser* component, and SamBehaviouralLogics, which implements the *behavioural analyser* component. It is worth noting that each library is connected to the rest of the architecture by facade EJB (Enterprise Java Beans) components, that automatically retrieve other components' references by Java EE server injection. Hence, each functional component is totally independent from the overall architecture, and it can be tested in a Java SE 5 environment by employing suitable stubs and drivers. Furthermore, facade components declaratively instruct the application server (by means of Java 5 annotations included in the class files) to expose relevant methods as (WSDL described) Web services.
The implementation of SAM is completed by the following Java EE components.

- SamPersistence – which, by abstracting from the actual data representation, provides two interfaces to respectively view and modify (only upon authorization) the data contained in the local registry of SAM.
- SamDBBrowser – which implements a simple database browsing tool (viz., the *service browser* component).
- SamAccountMgmt – which grants (or denies) access to SamFeedLogics component. In particular, the current security management allows only registered users to submit new OWL-S descriptions and new ontologies. Moreover, it keeps trace of every submission to discourage any abuse. Future improvements of security management may be implemented in order to prevent possible leaks in quality of service.
- SamGWTServlet – which provides SAM with a friendly Web interface, developed with the Google Web Toolkit.

Extending the Implementation
For testing the system concisely presented in this section, we manually produced several OWL-S service descriptions. Although the behaviour of each single part of the system has been properly checked, currently, we are not able to provide a serious experimental assessment of the system. Please, note that no standard test collection for OWL-S service retrieval does exist, yet. To be more exact, by accurately scanning the Web, we found two OWL-S repositories[2], both generated with semi-automatic WSDL annotators. However, as one may expect, WSDL annotators generate very simple OWL-S process models, typically a list of atomic operations, as no behavioural information is available in WSDL descriptions. Obviously, such process models are not useful for testing the system.

[2] `http://moguntia.ucd.ie/repository/owl-ds.html`
`http://www-ags.dfki.uni-sb.de/ klusch/owls-mx/index.html`

To overcome this problem, a brute force (time-consuming and error-prone) solution could be to manually create a test collection of OWL-S services. Yet, given that WS-BPEL [9] has been recently approved as an OASIS standard, we plan to extend our system in order to cope with WS-BPEL services. For instance, a possible solution is to translate BPEL processes into OWL-S services, by plugging into the system the BPEL*2*OWL-S [3] translator developed by Aslam et al. in [10]. Yet, there is still a prominent problem, namely, the lack of ontological information in WS-BPEL descriptions. Hence, when a provider adds a WS-BPEL process into the system, firstly, the WS-BPEL process is translated into a "rough" OWL-S service, and secondly, the provider is asked to complete the OWL-S description, by annotating the service parameters with ontology concepts (e.g., by employing some friendly ontology editor, such as Protégé (`http://protege.stanford.edu`). The new OWL-S service can be then registered into the system as described in the previous subsections.

Finally, given the high computational (viz., exponential) complexity of the functional and behavioural analysers, another important line for future work is to develop indexing and/or ranking techniques (as search engines do for Web pages) in order to sensibly improve the efficiency of the discovery methodology.

4 Concluding Remarks

In this paper, we have introduced an automated composition-oriented, ontology-based methodology for discovering (semantic) Web services. We have also presented a matchmaking system, called SAM, which prototypically implements such a methodology. SAM is the first matchmaker – at the best of our knowledge – that takes properly into account functional, semantic and behaviour information provided by service descriptions. More precisely, given as input a query specifying inputs, outputs and expected behaviour of the service to be found (viz., a *behavioural* query), SAM returns an ordered list of (compositions of) services, each of them (1) requiring as input a subset of the query inputs, (2) providing as output all the query outputs (or more), (3) featuring a behaviour equivalent to the query. In particular, it is important to observe that feature (3) makes our system suitable to be employed to address emerging issues of the Service-oriented Computing area, such as service replaceability.

Recently, automatic matchmaking of Web services has gained prominent importance and new approaches are frequently introduced. For the lack of space, we briefly discuss hereafter only some of the widely known approaches.

The first effort towards the automation of Web service discovery has been put forward by some of the authors of OWL-S in [11]. Their algorithm performs a functionality matching between service requests and service advertisements described as DAML-S (the predecessor of OWL-S) service profiles. This approach was the first at introducing the notion of an automatic and flexible matching by suitably considering subsumes and plug-in relationships among the ontology-annotated attributes of services and service requests. Yet, the algorithm proposed

[3] `http://bpel4ws2owls.sourceforge.net`

in [11] does not deal with the ontology crossing problem, that is, it is not able to determine relationships between attributes annotated with concepts of separate ontologies. To this aim, it is worth mentioning the service matchmaking approach presented by Klusch et al. in [12], which employs both logic based reasoning and IR techniques to properly relate concepts of different ontologies.

A common drawback of [11, 12] is that they search for a *single* service capable of satisfying a client query by itself. However, as previously described, composing functionalities of different services may be necessary to satisfy a query. An approach to a composition-oriented discovery is presented by Benatallah et al. in [13], where the matchmaking problem is reduced to a best covering problem in the domain of hypergraph theory.

With respect to the approach presented in this paper, it is important to stress that none of the mentioned proposals takes into account behavioural aspects of services. Indeed, our matchmaker – differently from [11, 13, 12] – is capable of solving behavioural queries, guaranteeing, as well, some behavioural properties of the returned (compositions of) services.

Behavioural aspects of services are partially taken into account by the approach of Agarwad and Studer, that proposed in [14] a new specification of Web services, based on description login and π-calculus. Their algorithm consider semantic and temporal properties of services, yet, their matchmaking approach is limited to a single service discovery.

References

1. Papazoglou, M.P., Georgakopoulos, D.: Service-Oriented Computing. Communications of the ACM **46**(10) (2003) 24–28
2. OWL-S Coalition: OWL-S: Semantic Markup for Web Service (2004) `http://www.ai.sri.com/daml/services/owl-s/1.2/overview/`.
3. Brogi, A., Corfini, S., Aldana, J., Navas, I.: Automated Discovery of Compositions of Services Described with Separate Ontologies. In Dan, A., Lamersdorf, W., eds.: ICSOC 2006. *LNCS* 4294, Springer (2006) 509–514
4. Bonchi, F., Brogi, A., Corfini, S., Gadducci, F.: A behavioural congruence for Web services. In Arbab, F., Sarjani, M., eds.: Fundamentals of Software Engineering, *LNCS* (To appear), Springer (2007)
5. Brogi, A., Corfini, S.: Behaviour-aware discovery of Web service compositions. International Journal of Web Services Research **4**(3) (2007) *To appear*.
6. Brogi, A., Corfini, S., Aldana, J., Navas, I.: A Prototype fot Discovering Compositions of Semantic Web Services. In Tumarello, G., Bouquet, P., Signore, O., eds.: Proc. of the 3rd Italian Semantic Web Workshop. (2006)
7. Fernandez, J.C., Mounier, L.: "On the Fly" verification of behavioural equivalences and preorders. In Larsen, K., Skou, A., eds.: Computer Aided Verification, *LNCS* 575, Springer (1992) 181–191
8. Navas, I., Sanz, I., Aldana, J., Berlanga, R.: Automatic Generation of Semantic Fields for Resource Discovery in the Semantic Web. In Andersen, K.V., Debenham, J.K., Wagner, R., eds.: DEXA 2005. *LNCS* 3588, Springer (2005) 706–715
9. BPEL Coalition: WS-BPEL 2.0 (2006) `http://docs.oasis-open.org/wsbpel/2.0/wsbpel-v2.0.pdf`.

10. Aslam, M.A., Auer, S., Shen, J., Herrmann, M.: Expressing Business Process Models as OWL-S Ontologies. In Eder, J., Dustdar, S., eds.: Business Process Management Workshops. *LNCS* 4103, Springer (2006) 400–415
11. Paolucci, M., Kawamura, T., Payne, T., Sycara, K.: Semantic Matchmaking of Web Services Capabilities. In Horrocks, I., Hendler, J., eds.: 1st Int. Conf. on The Semantic Web, *LNCS* 2342, Springer (2002) 333–347
12. Klusch, M., Fries, B., Sycara, K.: Automated semantic web service discovery with OWLS-MX. In: AAMAS'06, ACM (2006) 915–922
13. Benatallah, B., Hacid, M.S., Léger, A., Rey, C., Toumani, F.: On automating Web services discovery. VLDB J. **14**(1) (2005) 84–96
14. Agarwal, S., Studer, R.: Automatic Matchmaking of Web Services. In: IEEE Int. Conference on Web Services, IEEE Computer Society (2006) 45–54

Using Refinement Checking as System Testing

Cristiano Bertolini and Alexandre Mota

Federal University of Pernambuco, Centre of Informatics, P.O.Box 7851, Cidade Universitária, CEP 50732-970, Recife, PE, Brazil
cbertolini,acm@cin.ufpe.br

Abstract. Software testing is an expensive and time-consuming activity; it is also error-prone due to human factors. But, it still is the most common effort used in the software industry to achieve an acceptable level of quality for its products. An alternative is to use formal verification approaches, although they are not widespread in industry yet. This paper proposes an automatic verification approach to aid system testing based on refinement checking, where the underlying formalisms are hidden from the developers. Our approach consists in using a controlled natural language (a subset of English) to describe requirements (where it is automatically translated into the formal specification language CSP) and extracting a model directly from a mobile phone using a developed tool support; these artifacts are normalized in the same abstraction level and compared using the refinement checker FDR. This approach is being used at Motorola; the source of our case study.

Key words: System Testing, Refinement Checking, CSP

1 Introduction

Although formal methods are considered difficult to be used in practice, formal models are a current trend in the software industry. These models are used, for instance, in analysis, design and testing. In software testing, many approaches are using formal models to automate test case generation [1] as well as to improve the quality of the process of testing itself [2].

This work is the result of a research partnership between Motorola and the Centre of Informatics. We are using the formal language CSP (Section 2.1); a language primarily designed to model concurrent and distributed systems. Also, we use automatic verification based on refinement checking [3] (Section 2.2) using hidden formal models. That is, developers keep using their traditional artifacts and get the expected results without knowing that internally formal models are being handled. The main motivation of our approach is to avoid human errors (increase quality level) as well as to increase productivity (minimize effort).

A general overview of our approach (Section 3) is shown in Figure 1. We consider two inputs: a requirements document written in a Controlled Natural Language—CNL[1] (a subset English), where we reuse the work reported in [4]

[1] The reason to use CNL instead of a graphical language, say UML, is related to the artifacts used at Motorola; they are written in English.

to generate a CSP specification from that document (Section 3.1), and a mobile phone, where we developed a tool called BxT (Section 3.2) to extract a CSP specification from the phone automatically using the source code of a Motorola proprietary test framework called PTF [5]. With both models available, we adjust their abstraction levels (Section 3.3), because the implementation model has more details than the requirement model, and apply a proposed algorithm based on refinement checking, performing a kind of conformance testing, to analyze and report the problems found (Section 3.4). Note that, the whole approach hides the formalisms from the developers.

Although we have focused on mobile phones, any application could be used.

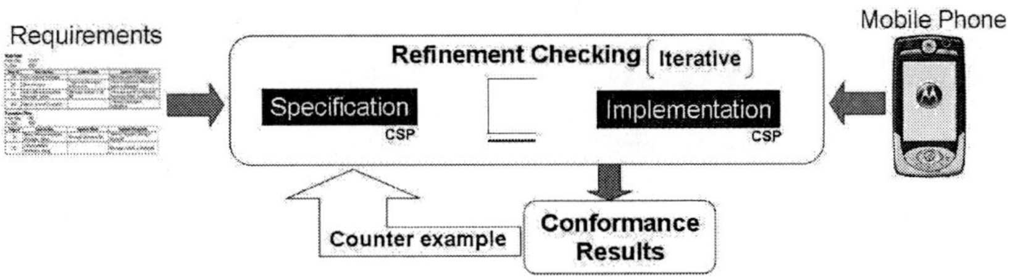

Fig. 1. Approach Overview.

Finally, to show the advantage of the proposed approach, we present a case study (Section 4) based on a real mobile application. Also, we consider some related work (Section 5), conclusions and future works (Section 6).

Therefore, the main contributions of this paper are:

- Propose an automatic approach to improve the quality of system testing in the context of mobile applications;
- Develop a tool (BxT) to extract the behavior of the mobile phones as a CSP formal specification;
- Show how to adjust the different abstraction levels of the requirement and implementation specifications to allow a correct refinement checking;
- Present an algorithm based on refinement checking to capture all faults found between requirements and implementation in the style of a testing approach.

2 Background

In this section we give an overview of model checking and the language CSP.

2.1 CSP Overview

The basic idea of CSP is to represent a system as a set of processes interacting with each other using actions (events). The alphabet of a process P, represented as αP, is the set of events this process uses. To use CSP in practice, we have to use its machine-readable version named CSP_M; all CSP elements used in this paper use the CSP_M version. Once we have a CSP_M specification, we can apply the model checker FDR [6] (Failures-Divergences Refinement).

We use the following CSP specification from our case study to introduce CSP.

```
SysImpl = P1_Hiding ; SysImpl
P1_Hiding = P1 \ {|goto.DTGOT_SCREEN.(IDLE_SCREEN,{}),
goto.DTGOT_MENU.(MAIN_MENU,{})|}
P1 = steps -> goto.DTGOT_SCREEN.(IDLE_SCREEN,{}) ->goto.DTGOT_MENU.
(MAIN_MENU,{}) -> start.DTSTA_APPLICATION.(IM_APPLICATION,{})
-> (P2 [] PA1)
P2 = steps -> login.DTLOG_APPLICATION.(IM_SERVER_APPLICATION,{})
-> (P3 [] SKIP)
P3 = steps -> select.DTSEL_LISTITEM.(CONTACT_ITEM,{}) -> P4
P4 = steps -> start.DTSTA_LISTITEM.(CONVERSATION_ITEM,{}) -> SKIP
PA1 = steps -> goto.DTGOT_LIST_ITEM.(SAVED_CONVERSATION_FOLDER,{})
-> SKIP
```

This CSP specification captures the behavior of the implementation of a real mobile phone. It starts with the description of the main process `SysImpl`. This process represents a sequential composition (;) between the process `P1_Hiding` and itself. Thus `SysImpl` behaves like `P1_Hiding` until a successful termination occurs (we explain this below). In this case, it becomes `SysImpl` again.

The hiding operator (\) is used to abstract some details of a process. For instance, the process `P1_Hiding` hides the events `goto.DTGOT_SCREEN.(IDLE_SCREEN,{}),goto.DTGOT_MENU.(MAIN_MENU,{})` from the process `P1`.

A prefix (`a -> P`) combines an event and a process to produce a new process; a linear behavior. In `steps -> goto.DTGOT_SCREEN.(IDLE_SCREEN,{}) ->...`, after `steps` occurs, the `goto` event is the first event of the resulting behavior.

When we have an external choice (`[]`), it determines a choice between two processes. The environment decides on which process to engage. For instance, in `( P2 [] PA1 )` the environment can choose process `P2` or `PA1`.

The process `Skip` means a successful termination. And the process STOP means a problematic behavior; a deadlock. It can also serve to other purposes (see Section 3.4).

Three complementary semantic models describe the semantics of CSP: traces, failures and failures-divergences [3]. This work uses the traces model to describe process behavior. It is the simplest of all models and captures what a process can do in the form of a set of sequences of events. Thus, for any CSP process `P`, the function $\mathcal{T}$`(P)` gives its traces.

A non-deterministic choice between two CSP processes is represented as `P |~| Q`. In the traces model, we cannot capture non-determinism because $\mathcal{T}$`(P [] Q)` $=$ $\mathcal{T}$`(P |~| Q)` $=$ $\mathcal{T}$`(P)`$\cup$$\mathcal{T}$`(Q)`. This is useful for this work because test cases are very similar to traces and then the traces model is sufficient.

Having the traces of a processes, we can check their relation via refinement. Let P and Q be two CSP processes, then $P \sqsubseteq_T Q =_{def} \mathcal{T}(Q) \subseteq \mathcal{T}(P)$ that is, Q is better than P if Q has less than or the same possible behaviors of P.

Furthermore, CSP processes can also be represented semantically (using its operational semantics) in terms of LTS (Labelled Transition Systems); a kind of labelled graph (see Figure 5(a) for an example of LTS).

2.2 Model and Refinement Checking

Model checking is an automatic technique to check whether a given model satisfies a given desired property. Usually, model checking is used on hardware design, but currently it is being used on software as well [7]. Properties are written as temporal logic formulas (for example, CTL or LTL [8]) and models in some concurrent specification language (for example, CSP and PROMELA [9]). Then, given a temporal logic formula f and a model M, model checking, which is represented as $M \models f$, means checking whether M satisfies f. In practice, this checking involves representing M and f as LTS (Labelled Transition Systems), a kind of graph, and performing a search using these structures. The essence about this is that model checking is exhaustive (it uses the entire structure if it is necessary [10]) and it obviously needs that such structures be finite.

A special kind of model checking, called refinement checking, uses two models written in the same concurrent specification language instead of temporal logics. Its goal is to check whether a model Q is better than another model P in the sense that all properties of P are preserved by Q. Formally, given models P and Q, one says that Q refines P whether $P \sqsubseteq Q$ holds. To connect this new view with the previous one, we can think that P is a model that is already known to have a certain property given by formula f. Thus, $Q \models f \Leftrightarrow P \sqsubseteq Q$.

In our approach, we have the requirements of an application as well as its implementation. We could think of using traditional model checking by means of PROMELA instead of CSP and SPIN [9] instead of FDR [6], but refinement checking is the most natural choice to check whether an implementation conforms to its specification.

Currently, many approaches are using model checking to aid testing with respect at generating test cases. Although refinement checking can also be used in this sense [11], we use it here in its essence. That is, instead of extracting parts os a specification (tests) to execute in an implementation, we simply check whether the implementation model conforms to the specification model.

3 The Proposed Approach

The proposed approach (see Figure 1) consists in checking the conformance (refinement) between requirements, say `SysSpec`, and its implementation, say `SysImpl`. As it is usual in the literature [8], we also assume that `SysSpec` is correct but `SysImpl` can have problems (that is, it might not conform to `SysSpec`). To apply refinement checking we need two formal models capturing the requirements and implementation behaviors. And as formal languages are not widespread in industry, we hide the formalisms to the developers to obtain a better acceptance of our approach.

3.1 From Requirements to its Formal Model

To deal with requirements formally but in a hidden way we use a CNL [4]. It is a subset of English that does not introduce ambiguities and syntactic problems. In our Research Project at Motorola, we already have a CNL. It was developed to generate test cases automatically [11]. For example, a simple CNL sentence is "*Select phonebook application*".
Were a requirements document is seen as a set of CNL sentences. A simplified view of the syntax of the CNL we use here is:

```
sentence ::= verb nounPhrase
nounPhrase ::= preposition article modifier noun modifier
               | article modifier noun modifier
               | modifier noun modifier
               | modifier noun
               | noun modifier
               | noun
verb ::= send | call | select ... article ::= the | a | an
preposition ::= from | to ... modifier ::= at least | protected ...
noun ::= phone | folder ...
```

For example, Figure 2 describes part of the feature used in our case study (Section 4). As observed in Figure 2, there are two flows: the main flow and the exception flow; for each flow we have a step description, a system state that complements the steps and the system response. The exception flow is related with some step of the main flow (*From Step:*). The `Step ID` is used to make each step unique in the use case. For instance, `UC_01_1M` is the first step in the `Main Flow` use case. From `UC_01_1M`, we can follow the current main flow. But note that in the `Alternative Flows` use case, the `From Step:` indicates the step `UC_01_1M`. Thus, the flow in the step `UC_01_1A` is an alternative for `UC_01_1M`.

From a CNL use case, we can use the CNL engine to obtain CSP processes. In Figure 3(a), we have the CNL Engine that consists of:

- CNL Sentences: requirements are written in a Microsoft Word document based on a specific template (Figure 2);
- CNL processing: translates each sentence into a CSP event (see Figure 3(b)) and the use case as a whole in a CSP specification.
- CSP alphabet: is formed by all CSP events extracted from the use case;
- CSP process: is the output of the CNL processing and represents the CNL use case described as a CSP specification.

Main Flow
From Step: START
To Step: END

Step Id	User Action	System State	System Response
UC_01_1M	Start IM application.		The IM application is displayed.
UC_01_2M	Log in the IM Server.		The user is logged in.
UC_01_3M	Select a contact. Start a conversation.		The conversation screen is displayed. There is no IM message in the Conversation Screen. The im editor is empty.

Alternative Flows
From Step: UC_01_1M
To Step: END

Step Id	User Action	System State	System Response
UC_01_1A	Go to Saved Conversations folder.		Saved Conversations folder is displayed.

Fig. 2. Use Case written in CNL.

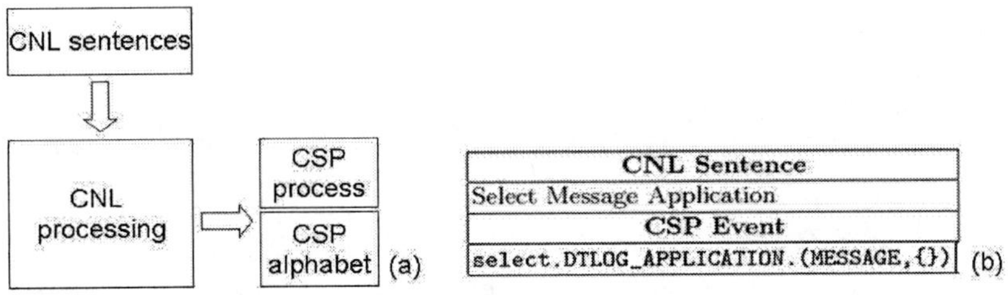

Fig. 3. CNL engine.

The CNL engine checks for some inconsistencies. When a grammar error is reported, the user must adjust the corresponding CNL sentence in the use case. The other case occurs when a word is not found in the CNL database. Here the user can change the word for a synonymous already available or store the new word in the database.

3.2 From an Implementation to its Model

To obtain a CSP specification of a mobile phone application, we implemented a tool called BxT–Behavior Extractor Tool. It obtains all relevant paths of a mobile phone application by analyzing the source code of a Motorola proprietary test framework called PTF (Phone Test Framework) [5]. This framework gives us access to all mobile phone functions. Furthermore, to produce a model towards a specific objective, BxT was designed to allow the user to guide the model generation. It suffices to enter an objective (for example, an application or a set of menu names) and the model is generated toward such an objective. It is worth noting that BxT extracts a high-level behavior from the source-code, that is, a functional behavior related mainly to navigational aspects.

Another important aspect of this generation is reusing the module of CNL processing to obtain a compatible alphabet between the requirement and implementation models. This is accomplished by writing sequences of PTF method calls using CNL sentences. For example, the navigation corresponding to Figure 4(b) is expressed in CNL as "Select Message".

These are the main reasons our implementation models are closer to our requirement models as will be discussed in Section 3.3.

Given a mobile phone application, BxT assumes that the initial state is idle (the initial screen of the phone) and using the PTF structure of method calls it gets all paths of a specific application. BxT yields a CSP specification as output but can also output a log of PTF method calls.

Figure 4(a) shows the BxT engine: for each screen, the phone captures all its components using the corresponding PTF of the source code. The components are the screens, buttons, labels, pictures, panels, etc. For each component, a set of properties can be captured like text, state, color, position, etc. BxT captures the components for the navigation.

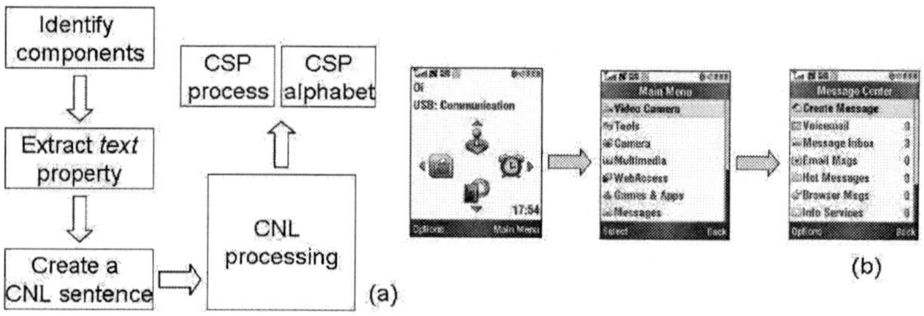

Fig. 4. BxT engine and mobile phone screens.

Figure 5(a) corresponds to the use case of Figure 2 as an LTS. And Figure 5(b) to the CSP implementation model of Section 2.1. By a careful observation of these models, we can note that Figure 5(b) almost contains Figure 5(a). The difference between these two models comes from two sources: low-level navigation events (for example, Go to main menu) and extra transitions not allowed by the requirements. The former are natural and related to the artifact used to generate the model: the implementation. The later, however, are problematic because they express behaviors not allowed and thus are considered errors in our approach.

3.3 Dealing with different Abstraction levels

When we first met these two models, requirements and implementation, we thought that the behavioral difference between them would be enormous because of the usual semantic gap between them. However, once the BxT tool

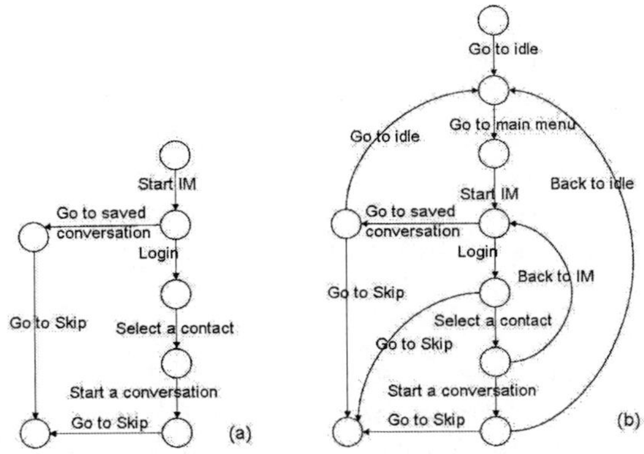

Fig. 5. Implementation (a) and specification (b) in LTS representation.

captures the navigational (or system) behavior based on the PTF framework, it only adds details necessary to achieve a certain objective. Thus, while requirements capture more objective oriented behaviors, the implementation behavior complements such a behavior with detailed navigational transitions.

Thus, from the previous observation about Figures 5(a) and 5(b), to do a correct comparison between requirements and implementation, we need to hide all events of `SysImpl` that do not occur in `SysSpec` (the additional navigation details). This corresponds to the following refinement relation:

$$\texttt{SysSpec} \sqsubseteq_T \texttt{SysImpl} \setminus \texttt{Impl\_Details}$$

where

$$\texttt{Impl\_Details} = \alpha\texttt{SysImpl} \setminus \alpha\texttt{SysSpec}$$

3.4 Conformance Results

With the previous refinement relation available, we just have to perform a verification using the model checker FDR to obtain two possible situations: everything is all right and thus the implementation satisfies the requirements, or there is a conformance problem and FDR generates a counter-example. This counter-example is very similar to a failing test case. Thus we need to collect all possible counter-examples to adjust the implementation accordingly, following a traditional testing process. As the model checker provides only one counter-example for each verification (the shortest possible path), to discover of them we must propose an iterative procedure to gradually find the next counter-example.

The key idea to collect all counter-examples of the previous refinement relation is based on the properties of two basic elements of CSP: the traces of an external choice and the definition of traces refinement. Suppose that we have the refinement relation `SysSpec` $\sqsubseteq_T$ `SysImpl` and such a refinement produces a trace s as a counter-example. Recall from Section 2.1 that SysSpec $\sqsubseteq_T$ SysImpl means $\mathcal{T}$(SysImpl) $\subseteq \mathcal{T}$(SysSpec) and that $\mathcal{T}$(P [] Q) $= \mathcal{T}$(P) $\cup\mathcal{T}$(Q). Thus, to find the next possible counter-example we update the specification SysSpec with the choice of performing the counter-example s as a CSP process.

To build a process from a given trace we introduce the MakeCSPProcess function which takes as input a trace $< e_1, \ldots, e_n >$ and produces as output the process e_1->...->e_n-> STOP as follows:

MakeProcess($< e_1, \ldots, e_n >$) $=$ e_1->...->e_n-> STOP

The function MakeProcess produces a process ended in STOP because T(STOP)={<>}, which does not interfere in the refinement relation. Therefore, the refinement SysSpec $\sqsubseteq_T$ SysImpl becomes SysSpec [] F $\sqsubseteq_T$ SysImpl, after the update of SysSpec, where F=MakeProcess(s), for a counter-example s.

Algorithm 1 Conformance procedure.

input: CSP specifications SysSpec, SysImpl, N is the maximum number of counter-examples of interest
output: The set *Res* of counter-examples found
$s \leftarrow$ SysSpec $\sqsubseteq_T$ SysImpl;
If ($s \neq$<>)
then {
  while ((s $\neq$<>)*and*(#Res < N)) do {
    Res$\leftarrow$ Res $\cup$ <s>;
    F $\leftarrow$ MakeProcess(s);
    SysSpec $\leftarrow$ SysSpec [] F;
    s $\leftarrow$ SysSpec $\sqsubseteq_T$ SysImpl;
  }
} else {
    println("No counter-example was found.");
}

From the previous discussion, we propose the Algorithm 1 which yields the set Res of all counter-examples found. That is, if the refinement relation between SysSpec and SysImpl does not hold (SysSpec $\not\sqsubseteq_T$ SysImpl), then a counter-example s is generated and included in the set Res. The counter-example s becomes the process F using the function MakeProcess, and thus it is combined with the process SysSpec using an external choice. The refinement (SysSpec $\sqsubseteq_T$ SysImpl) is repeated until it holds (in this case s = $\langle\rangle$).

An observation about Algorithm 1 is that it can run indefinitely. To deal with this problem the parameter N is used to collect only N (#Res<N) counter-examples.

Another important contribution is using our navigation oriented analysis for investigating parts of the mobile device considered critical by experienced test designers. This is a step forward in the analysis because it can take less time to be accomplished as well as analyze exactly those parts historically known as problematic. In particular, the models presented in this paper followed such a directive using as objective the parts of the mobile phone related to the feature of messaging.

4 Case Study: Mobile Application

In this section, we apply our proposed approach in a real case study: a mobile phone application of Motorola.

This case study is simple to save space. However, it is a real scenario in the development of a mobile application. Its simplicity comes from the fact that we have used our navigation-oriented analysis to analyze just those parts of the application related to the feature of messaging.

The first effort in the direction of analyzing the conformance between requirements and implementation of our mobile application is to obtain the formal specifications of both specification and implementation. Thus, applying the following CNL processing engine in the use case description of Figure 2 we obtain the CSP specification.

```
SysSpec = UC_01_1M ; SysSpec
UC_01_1M = steps -> start.DTSTA_APPLICATION.(IM_APPLICATION,{})
-> isstate.DTISS_APPLICATION_STATEVALUE.(IM_APPLICATION,{}).
(DISPLAYED_VALUE,{}) -> (UC_01_2M [] UC_01_1A)
UC_01_2M = steps -> login.DTLOG_APPLICATION.
(IM_SERVER_APPLICATION,{}) -> UC_01_3M
UC_01_3M = steps -> select.DTSEL_LISTITEM.(CONTACT_ITEM,{})-> SKIP
UC_01_1A = steps -> goto.DTGOT_LIST_ITEM.
(SAVED_CONVERSATION_FOLDER,{}) -> SKIP
```

Furthermore, using our BxT engine (Figure 4(a)) in the real mobile device under analysis we obtain the CSP specification shown on Section 2.1.

To generate the requirements model we assume that the model is written correctly and it take few seconds to extract the formal model CSP. In other hand, the model from implementation took about 3 minutes to BxT extract the formal model CSP.

With these two formal models we can make a series of classical (basic) analysis such as deadlock, livelock and non-determinism. These classical concurrent properties are interesting to be analyzed because, in general, the specification as well as the implementation are intended to be free of these problems. If one finds such problems these artifacts can be immediately adjusted (if necessary[2]).

Figure 6(a) shows the results of using the FDR model checker: both requirements and implementation are deadlock and livelock free as well as deterministic.

[2] Sometimes a deadlock situation (a device has broken) is intentional and thus the specification can be maintained as it is.

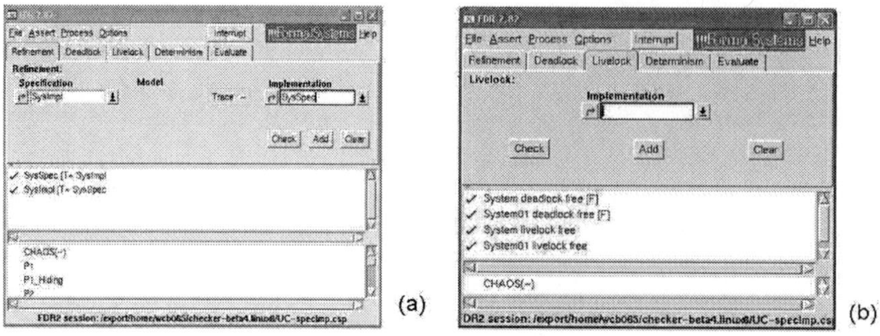

Fig. 6. Classical properties and refinement checked.

After the previous basic analysis, we can start our conformance checking by executing Algorithm 1 until the refinement relation between requirements and implementation be satisfied.

When an error is found, this means an implementation bug. By asking FDR for the counter-example, we get the sequence of events presented in Figure 7. This trace shows a sequence of events that is possible to be performed by the implementation model but not by the requirements model. Therefore, this is the implementation bug.

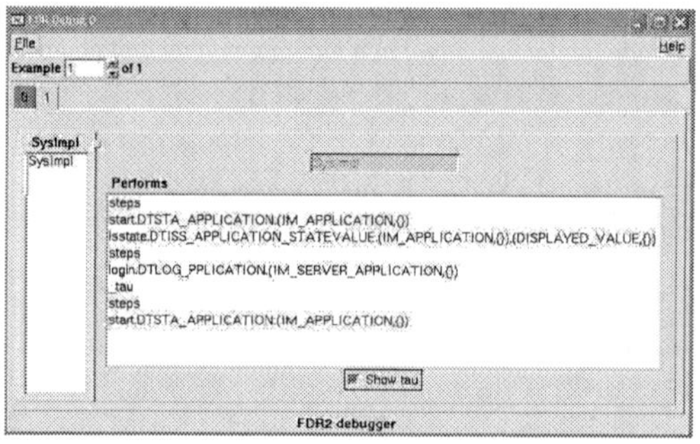

Fig. 7. Counter-example.

With this counter-example at hand and following the proposed algorithm, we store this counter-example and use it to obtain a new CSP requirement specification (presented below). A new refinement checking uses this new requirement specification by also following Algorithm 1. As this last refinement checking does not produce any counter-example; the algorithm finishes successfully.

```
SysSpec = UC_01_1M ; SysSpec [] F UC_01_1M = ...
F = steps -> start.DTSTA_APPLICATION. (IM_APPLICATION,{}) ->
isstate. DTISS_APPLICATION_STATEVALUE.(IM_APPLICATION,{}).
(DISPLAYED_VALUE,{}) -> steps -> login.DTLOG_APPLICATION.
(IM_SERVER_APPLICATION,{}) -> steps ->
start.DTSTA_APPLICATION.(IM_APPLICATION,{}) -> STOP
```

Because BxT is based on PTF, the counter-example of Figure 7 could be easily rewritten as a Motorola PTF automatic test case.

An observation, depicted in Figure 6(b), is because the abstraction level between requirements and implementation in our context (black-box view of mobile phone applications) is very close, we indeed have an equivalence relation between requirements and implementation when the implementation conforms to the specification. That is, both refinement relations $\texttt{SysSpec} \sqsubseteq_T \texttt{SysImpl}$ and $\texttt{SysImpl} \sqsubseteq_T \texttt{SysSpec}$ are satisfied ($\texttt{SysSpec} \equiv_T \texttt{SysImpl}$).

To give an idea of the effort spent to perform the approach proposed here, we have used a PC with 1GB and 1,7MHZ. The requirements in CSP were obtained instantaneously, although we have used about 3 hours to understand the feature and write its CNL. The BxT produced the model in 5 min, and Algorithm 1 took another 50 sec. That is, the effort needed to use our approach is basically associated to understand the feature in question.

5 Related Work

The most related works to testing and software model checking are associated to classical model checking [12, 13]. Usually, the properties are described in some temporal logic (like LTL) and the model of the implementation is described in some formal method (like automaton, state machines, *etc*), then each property is checked into the model. Concerning refinement checking, both properties and model are represented in the same language; in our case CSP.

Testing Graphical User Interfaces (GUI) involves dealing with models. There are approaches to generate test cases automatically, select test cases and ripping tools for GUI testing [14]. Thus, our approach is similar to GUI testing but differs in the fact that we extract our models using the proprietary testing framework of Motorola PTF [5]. Thus, we can extract as much information as we need, whereas by extracting from the GUI we are limited by what is offered to interact with.

Doron, Vardi, and Yannakakis [15] proposed an approach combining model checking and testing: black box checking. Their approach tests whether an implementation satisfies some given properties. It assumes that the structure of the implementation is unknown and there is incomplete information to perform model checking directly. Thus, the specification model is adjusted using a learning approach based on Angluin's algorithm. The black box checking approach is characterized as a problem and several algorithms are proposed to solve it. A variation of the black box checking is the Adaptive model checking [12]. This approach considers an incorrect but not obsolete model and explores it by learning the incorrect model to construct the correct model adapting black box testing and machine learning techniques together. In this context, our approach assumes that the requirements are trustable such that any problem must be related to the implementation. Thus we do not need a learning approach to improve our requirements model.

Considering the specification and implementation models, the approach of Güldali [13] uses both models to do a coverage-driven model checking. In this case, model checking performs automatic testing. In addition, the approach generates test cases through model checking [13]. In both approaches, a motivation to incorporate model checking is to test case generation. Differently from that, we are interested on when we can use model checking instead of testing.

Other approaches combining model checking and software testing have been proposed with different purposes and applicability. Godskesen and Skou propose algorithms to generate test for embedded systems combining the fault model of the system [16]. Vlad, Herv and Thierry presented a combination of verification techniques and conformance testing with a test case generation algorithm [17]. Both works are related to test case generation; they suggest the use of model checking to automate the test case generation.

6 Conclusions

Usually, testing just covers a set of critical situations due to time and cost restrictions. Therefore, sometimes the experience of test designers can leave certain situations uncovered and this can result in serious problems.

The approach presented in this paper proposes an alternative way, than testing, to improve quality by only requiring that the test team writes the requirements in a CNL and plug the phone in a computer; the CNL engine and the BxT tool do the rest. After obtaining both models, we simply have to execute Algorithm 1 to obtain the set of test cases that fails. Although this work have focused on mobile phones, any application seen abstractly (by a navigational point of view) can benefit from it.

Because BxT is based on PTF, it represents a PTF extension to generate CSP models to a specific mobile application. Thus, we can easily rewritten the counter-example of Figure 7 as a Motorola PTF automatic teste case. A set of generated test cases based on counter-examples could be applied as a good regression test suite.

Although the literature reveals some works relating model checking with software testing [12, 13], we argue that refinement checking is more appropriate to our context because we simply need a refinement theory to compare requirements with corresponding implementation. The generation of test cases is a natural consequence of the refinement theory, we did not need to focus on test case generation as long as our purpose is simply to check whether the implementation conforms to its corresponding specification. We have used the traces model to perform our analysis because it is directly related to testing. Using the traces model can be seem fragile because the process STOP refines any process P (for any process `P`, $\texttt{T(STOP)} = \{\langle\rangle\} \subseteq \mathcal{T}(\texttt{P})$). Therefore, if the implementation model has fewer events than the requirements model we cannot detect this. To overcome this we may use other semantic models, such as the failures model.

Although the current version of the BxT tool is already useful, it has some limitations: behaviors that need specific data (for instance, passwords) occur state related information (for example, empty email) and non functional requirements like performance are not captured. Therefore, as future work we intend to improve BxT to deal with such situations.

References

1. Rajan, A.: Automated Requirements-Based Test Case Generation. SIGSOFT Softw. Eng. Notes **31**(6) (2006) 1–2
2. Drabick, R.D.: Best Practices for the Formal Software Testing Process: A Menu of Testing Tasks. Dorset House Publishing Company (2003)
3. Roscoe, A.W.: The Theory and Practice of Concurrency. Prentice Hall PTR, Upper Saddle River, NJ, USA (1997)
4. Cabral, G., Sampaio, A.: Formal Specification Generation from Requirement Documents. In: Brazilian Symposium on Formal Methods, Natal, Brazil, ENCS (2006)
5. Esipchuk, I., Validov, D.: PTF-based Test Automation for JAVA Applications on Mobile Phones. In: Proceedings of the IEEE 10th International Symposium on Consumer Electronics (ISCE). (2006) 1–3
6. Systems, F.: (FDR2 Model-Checker.) http://www.fsel.com/.
7. Group, S.: (BANDERA Model-Checker.) http://bandera.projects.cis.ksu.edu/.
8. Clarke, E.M., Grumberg, O., Peled, D.: Model Checking. The MIT Press (2000)
9. Barland, I.: (Promela and SPIN Reference.) http://www.spinroot.com/.
10. Andersen, H.R.: Partial Model Checking. In: LICS '95: Proceedings of the 10th Annual IEEE Symposium on Logic in Computer Science, Washington, DC, USA, IEEE Computer Society (1995) 398
11. Nogueira, S.: Automatic CSP Test Case Generation Guided by Purposes. (In Portuguese). Master's thesis, Federal University of Pernambuco, Brazil (2006)
12. Groce, A., Peled, D., Yannakakis, M.: Adaptive Model Checking. In: Tools and Algorithms for the Construction and Analysis of Systems : 8th International Conference, TACAS 2002, Held as Part of the Joint European Conference on Theory and Practice of Software, ETAPS 2002, Grenoble, France, LNCS (2002)
13. Güldali, B.: Model Testing Combining Model Checking and Coverage Testing. Master's thesis, University of Paderborn, Germany (2005)
14. Xie, Q., Memon, A.M.: Designing and Comparing Automated Test Oracles for GUI-Based Software Applications. ACM Transactions on Software Engineering and Methodology **16**(1) (2007)
15. Peled, D., Vardi, M.Y., Yannakakis, M.: Black Box Checking. J. Autom. Lang. Comb. **7**(2) (2001) 225–246
16. C. Godskesen, B.N., Skou, A.: Connectivity Testing through Model-Checking. In: International Conference on Formal Techniques for Networked and Distributed Systems (FORTE), Madrid, Spain (2004)
17. Vlad, R., Herv, M., Thierry, J.: Automatic Verification and Conformance Testing for Validating Safety Properties of Reactive Systems. In Fitzgerald, J., Tarlecki, A., Hayes, I., eds.: Formal Methods 2005 (FM05). LNCS, Springer (2005)

Modelado de sistemas P2P con control de excepciones

Antonio Brogi[1], Francisco Gutiérrez[2], Pablo López[2], Ernesto Pimentel[2] y Razvan Popescu[1]

[1] Dipartimento di Informatica, Universitá di Pisa, Italia
[2] Departamento de Lenguajes y Ciencias de la Computación, Universidad de Málaga, España

Resumen. En este trabajo se introduce un modelo orientado a servicios para el desarrollo de sistemas P2P (peer-to-peer) con control de excepciones. Las características básicas del modelo son las nociones de grupos, pares y servicios (que son ofrecidos por los propios pares o por los grupos que los hospedan), así como la existencia de aspectos no funcionales como calidad de servicios, niveles de seguridad, credenciales, etc. Al intercambio de mensajes por invocación directa o envío de eventos, se une la posibilidad de controlar las situaciones excepcionales, de particular importancia en este tipo de sistemas.

1 Introducción

Los sistemas P2P (*peer-to-peer*) son sistemas distribuidos donde todos los elementos de la red actúan tanto como consumidores de servicios (o clientes) como proveedores. Además, la mayoría de los mecanismos de comunicación P2P no están basados en infraestructuras preexistentes, sino más bien en redes ad-hoc dinámicas entre pares [12].

Los sistemas P2P empotrados (EP2P) [5] representan un nuevo reto en el desarrollo de software para sistemas distribuidos. Un sistema EP2P es un sistema P2P donde pequeños dispositivos empotrados de bajo coste y potencia cooperan intercambiando y procesando información por medio de canales inalámbricos. Los sistemas EP2P pueden emplearse en diversas áreas de aplicación con resultados prometedores, como la telefonía móvil, los hogares inteligentes y la monitorización ambiental. Este tipo de sistemas presentan un alto grado de heterogeneidad (las aplicaciones pueden ejecutarse en dispositivos de distinta naturaleza, desde PDAs a nodos en una red de sensores, presentando ancho de banda y potencia de cómputo muy diferentes) y autonomía (las componentes entran y salen del sistema de forma autónoma, causando frecuentemente reorganizaciones de los sistemas). Estos elementos involucran retos tecnológicos importantes, como la descentralización, la existencia de enlaces con comunicaciones transitorias (se pueden producir conexiones y desconexiones de forma frecuente e impredecible), y la gestión de topologías de interconexión en constante cambio.

Una de las claves del éxito de este tipo de sistemas es la posibilidad de abstraerse de todos los problemas anteriores por medio de la construcción de capas intermedias (*middleware*) apropiadas. Sin la existencia de un middleware (incluyendo el soporte de herramientas formales y metodologías de desarrollo), la definición, creación y mantenimiento de una aplicación se hace costosa y propensa a errores, teniendo que enfrentarse a los problemas propios de los sistemas EP2P en cada prototipo. Un middleware adecuado debería ocultar la complejidad de la infraestructura subyacente, al tiempo que proporciona a terceros interfaces abiertas para el desarrollo de aplicaciones.

El desarrollo de un middleware como el que describimos resulta, por tanto, de una importancia trascendental, ya que muchos requisitos críticos deben tenerse en cuenta: movilidad, nuevos problemas de seguridad, protocolos de localización y descubrimiento, o nuevos criterios de calidad del software.

El desarrollo de un middleware seguro para sistemas P2P empotrados — Secure Middleware for Embedded Peer-To-Peer Systems (SMEPP) — es, precisamente, el objetivo de un proyecto europeo en el que los autores están involucrados, y que persigue la construcción de un middleware que sea seguro, genérico, configurable y adaptable a diferentes dispositivos (desde PDAs y los teléfonos móviles de nueva generación hasta los sistemas de redes de sensores) y dominios de aplicación (desde sistemas críticos hasta aplicaciones de entretenimiento).

Entre los objetivos concretos de SMEPP está el proporcionar un modelo orientado a servicios de alto nivel de abstracción para programar la interacción entre pares, ocultando de este modo los detalles de bajo nivel propios de la infraestructura de soporte. El lenguaje resultante se denomina SMOL (SMEPP MOdelling Language).

En este trabajo, presentamos el conjunto de primitivas diseñadas para constituir el modelo SMEPP, de forma que satisfacen los requisitos identificados por el proyecto. Las características básicas del modelo son la noción de *grupo* de pares, la noción de *servicio* ofrecido por pares (o por grupos), y lo concerniente a la *seguridad*.

La base del modelo orientado a servicios toma prestado conceptos del estado del arte de las tecnologías de los servicios Web. Por un lado, nosotros modelamos contratos de servicios utilizado un lenguaje de marcas (*eXtensible Markup Language*), basado en esquemas XML [13] y, en particular, modelamos las signaturas de los servicios de forma similar a como lo hacen los lenguajes de descripción de servicios, como WSDL [14], y los lenguajes que proporcionan información ontológica de los servicios Web, como OWL [11]. El modelo, asimismo, soporta operaciones entre servicios de un solo sentido y esquemas de comunicación basados en petición-respuesta. Por otro lado, modelamos el comportamiento de los servicios de forma similar a como lo hace BPEL [3] (*Business Process Execution Language*). Por último, el modelo emplea primitivas de comunicación para invocar operaciones, para recibir mensajes y eventos, así como para dar respuesta a las invocaciones. Una primera versión de este lenguaje fue presentado en [4] y ha ido evolucionando hasta incluir un mecanismo sofisticado para el tratamiento de excepciones. En efecto, las operaciones en este tipo de sistemas pueden provocar excepciones debido a la ocurrencia de situaciones anómalas que aparecen con cierta frecuencia debido a la movilidad de los dispositivos, su disponibilidad, el ruido del entorno, etc. Por lo tanto, es necesario que el lenguaje que modele estos sistemas disponga de un mecanismo de control de excepciones, que constituye uno de los objetivos del presente trabajo.

Después de introducir la sintaxis de las primitivas de SMOL (Sec. 2), presentamos una semántica abstracta para un cálculo simple definido sobre dichas primitivas (Sec. 3.1). La semántica permite establecer formalmente si un conjunto de procesos (código ejecutándose en pares o servicios) pueden interactuar sin bloquear, y proporciona una base sólida para el desarrollo de herramientas de análisis, verificación y simulación de especificaciones SMOL.

2 Primitivas abstractas

Comenzaremos ofreciendo una descripción informal de los conceptos clave de SMOL (Subsec. 2.1), seguida de una descripción breve de las primitivas (Subsec. 2.2).

2.1 Conceptos clave

Los **pares** son contenedores de servicios. Un par tiene asociado un programa (o código) de par y puede ofrecer uno o más servicios.[3]

Los **servicios** tienen contratos e implementaciones. Por un lado, un contrato facilita una descripción formal —y procesable de forma automática— de un servicio. Por otro lado, la implementación es un ejecutable (por ejemplo, un servicio Java). Un contrato describe lo que el servicio ofrece (la signatura del servicio) y cómo puede ser invocado por los clientes (vinculación de servicios). También puede incluir otras propiedades del servicio (vg. calidad) y descripciones ontológicas. Los servicios son de dos tipos: con y sin comportamiento. Los contratos de los servicios sin comportamiento no deben revelar ningún comportamiento, puesto que sus operaciones pueden ser invocadas varias veces y en cualquier orden. Los servicios sin comportamiento son similares a los servicios WSDL [14]. Los servicios con comportamiento deben facilitar el comportamiento (parcial) de su protocolo de interacción. La invocación de sus operaciones está sujeta a las restricciones impuestas por la descripción del comportamiento. Se puede considerar a los servicios con comportamiento como procesos BPEL [3].

Las **operaciones de servicio** son una representación abstracta de unidades de trabajo. Por ejemplo, una operación se puede referir a un método Java o a una operación de un servicio web. La comunicación entre entidades consiste,

[3] Utilizaremos *par* para referirnos tanto al *contenedor del par* como al *código de par*, según el contexto. Utilizaremos *entidad* para referirnos a los *pares* y a los *servicios*.

básicamente, en paso de mensajes a través de la invocación de operaciones: una entidad invoca una operación ofrecida por otra entidad. Las operaciones son de dos clases: síncronas (entrada"/salida) y asíncronas (sólo entrada). El invocador de una operación síncrona se bloquea hasta que la correspondiente invocación ha terminado. Por el contrario, la invocación de una operación asíncrona no bloquea a la entidad invocadora. Cada entidad en una invocación puede ser tanto un proveedor (que ofrece una o más operaciones) como un cliente (que requiere una o más operaciones).

Los **eventos** son una forma de comunicación entre las entidades. Por simplicidad, modelaremos los eventos como operaciones, de manera que lanzar un evento es similar a invocar una operación, mientras que esperar a un evento es similar a esperar a la invocación de una operación. A diferencia de las operaciones, una entidad que lanza un evento no tiene que esperar a que otra entidad (suscrita a ese evento) lo reciba.

2.2 Descripción informal

Uno de los objetivos principales de SMOL es la definición de un conjunto de primitivas que serán implementadas por uno o más APIs. Tales primitivas son los componentes básicos del código que se encarga de la interacción entre los pares y los servicios. Las primitivas tienen la siguiente forma: *output primitiveName(*$input_1$*, ..., *$input_N$*) throws exception* donde los parámetros opcionales están seguidos de '?'.

peerId ***new****(credentials?) throws exception*
Excepciones: invalidCredentials, invalidCall.
Los programas invocan a la primitiva *new* para convertirse en pares. El parámetro opcional *credentials* sirve para autenticar al par. La primera invocación de *new* devuelve un nuevo identificador de par único *peerId*. Las siguientes invocaciones devuelven el mismo *peerId*. Invocar a alguna otra primitiva antes de invocar a *new* provoca una excepción *invalidCall*. Si el par no puede ser autenticado, se eleva una excepción *invalidCredentials*. Puesto que los pares son contenedores de servicios, a los servicios no se les permite generar nuevos pares y por lo tanto no pueden invocar a *new*. Si un servicio invoca a *new* se elevará una excepción *invalidCall*.

groupId ***createGroup****(groupName, securityLevel?) throws exception*
Excepciones: permissionDenied, invalidCall.
Los pares invocan a *createGroup* para crear un nuevo grupo llamado *groupName*. La primitiva *createGroup* devuelve un nuevo identificador de grupo único, *groupId*. El grupo existe mientras contenga al menos un miembro. En adelante, nos referiremos a los miembros de un grupo mediante la lista *Pares*, que contendrá al par creador de cada grupo. Si a un par no le está permitido crear un grupo con cierto nivel de seguridad dado (*securityLevel*), se elevará

una excepción *permissionDenied*. Hay que destacar que un servicio de un par[4] no puede invocar a *createGroup*, puesto que esto podría suponer ofrecer otros servicios del par como servicios del grupo. Por lo tanto, tales invocaciones elevarán una excepción *invalidCall*. Por motivos similares, las primitivas *joinGroup*, *leaveGroup*, *publish* y *unpublish* (descritas más adelante) elevarán la excepción *invalidCall* cuando sean invocadas por un servicio.

void ***joinGroup****(groupId, credentials?) throws exception*
Excepciones: accessDenied, invalidGroupId, invalidCall.
Los pares pueden unirse a un grupo mediante la primitiva *joinGroup*. El parámetro *groupId* identifica el grupo del que el par desea formar parte, mientras que el parámetro *credentials* permite validar el par; es decir, comprobar que le está permitido unirse al grupo. Un par puede unirse a varios grupos. Apuntarse a un grupo varias veces no genera ninguna excepción. Sin embargo, si las credenciales facilitadas por el par (*credentials*) no satisfacen el nivel de seguridad del grupo (*securityLevel*), se eleva una excepción *accessDenied*. Por otra parte, invocar a *joinGroup* con un identificador de grupo (*groupId*) no válido genera una excepción *invalidGroupId*.

void ***leaveGroup****(groupId) throws exception*
Excepciones: invalidGroupId, peerNotInGroup, invalidCall.
Los pares utilizan la primitiva *leaveGroup* para abandonar un grupo identificado por *groupId*. Cada grupo almacena una lista *Servicios* de servicios de par publicados (ver la primitiva *publish*) como servicios de grupo. Cada elemento de la lista *Servicios* es una terna <*peerId, peerServiceId, groupServiceId*> donde *peerId* identifica al par que publicó el servicio de par *peerServiceId* como servicio de grupo *groupServiceId*. Cuando un par *peerId* abandona un grupo *groupId* (o cuando *peerId* termina inesperadamente), *peerId* se eliminará de la lista *Pares*, y todos los servicios publicados por *peerId* en *groupId* (es decir, todas las ternas de la forma <*peerId, *, **>)) se eliminarán de la lista *Servicios* de *groupId*.[5]

<*groupServiceId, peerServiceId*> ***publish****(groupId, serviceContract) throws exception*
Excepciones: invalidService, invalidGroupId, peerNotInGroup, invalidCall.
Los pares ofrecen sus servicios desde un grupo *groupId* a través de la primitiva *publish*. Como mencionamos, el contrato *serviceContract* facilita tanto información abstracta (signatura, comportamiento, ...) como concreta (vinculación) del servicio. La primitiva *publish* devuelve una pareja <*groupServiceId, peerServiceId*>, cuya primera componente identifica el servicio como servicio de grupo, y la segunda se refiere al servicio como servicio de par. El middleware se encarga de añadir una terna <*peerId, peerServiceId, groupServiceId*> a la lista *Servicios* del grupo *groupId*, donde *peerId* identifica al par que publicó el servicio. Los clientes del servicio pueden utilizar *groupServiceId* para invocar

[4] En adelante utilizaremos *servicio* para referirnos tanto a un *servicio de par* como a un *servicio de grupo*, según el contexto. Cuando sea necesario, utilizaremos los nombres completos.
[5] Utilizaremos "*" como cuantificador universal sobre los identificadores de servicio.

un servicio de grupo de forma transparente (es decir, sin especificar un proveedor concreto), o bien el *peerServiceId* para invocar un servicio de par concreto. Es importante destacar que si diferentes pares publican servicios con el mismo contrato (*serviceContract*) en el mismo grupo (*groupId*), entonces todos reciben el mismo *groupServiceId* y diferentes *peerServiceIds*.

Una invocación a *publish* eleva una excepción *invalidService* si *serviceContract* no se refiere a un servicio válido, o una excepción *invalidGroupId* si *groupId* no corresponde a un grupo. Además, se genera una excepción *peerNotInGroup* si el invocador no pertenece al grupo *groupId*.

void ***unpublish***(*peerServiceId*) *throws exception*
Excepciones: invalidService, invalidGroupId, peerNotServiceOwner, invalidCall.
Los pares dejan de ofrecer servicios en un grupo retirándolos del mismo mediante *unpublish*. Retirar un servicio supone eliminar la terna <*peerId, groupServiceId, peerServiceId*> de la lista *Servicios* del grupo correspondiente. *peerId* es el par que invocó *unpublish*, y que anteriormente publicó (como <*groupServiceId, peerServiceId*>) el servicio. La primitiva *unpublish* eleva las mismas excepciones que *publish*.

<*groupId, groupServiceIdid, peerServiceId*>*[]* ***getServices***(*groupId?, peerId?, serviceContract?, maxResults?*) *throws exception*
Excepciones: invalidGroupId, invalidPeerId, invalidService.
La primitiva *getServices* permite descubrir servicios publicados. La salida consiste de una lista de ternas que contienen identificador de grupo, identificador del servicio en el grupo e identificador del servicio en el par.

Los parámetros de entrada *groupId* y *peerId* (opcional) restringen la búsqueda de servicios al grupo *groupId* y al par *peerId*, respectivamente. Se puede limitar aún más la búsqueda indicando el máximo número de resultados que se desean (*maxResults*). Cuando el grupo, el par o el contrato facilitados como entrada no sean válidos, se elevará la correspondiente excepción.

La salida proporcionada por *getServices* puede tomar las siguientes dos formas:

- si el servicio descubierto no tiene comportamiento, entonces *getServices* devuelve su *groupServiceId*. Por lo tanto, los clientes pueden usar este servicio de forma transparente: dos invocaciones del servicio podrían ser atendidas por distintos proveedores del mismo (en el caso de que existieran varios pares que hubieran publicado el mismo contrato). En este caso, es responsabilidad del middleware determinar el proveedor que atenderá cada invocación.

- si el servicio descubierto tiene comportamiento, entonces *getServices* devuelve el *peerServiceId* que corresponde a un proveedor concreto. Todas las llamadas realizadas a través de este *peerServiceId* serán por lo tanto atendidas por el mismo servicio de par.

El proceso de descubrimiento de servicios compara el contrato del servicio demandado (*serviceContract*) con los contratos de los servicios publicados. La correlación entre dos contratos puede hacerse a varios niveles: sintáctico (comprobando si el servicio publicado ofrece las operaciones demandadas), de comportamiento (comprobando si el comportamiento del servicio publicado es similar al comportamiento solicitado) o basado en la calidad (comprobando si el servicio publicado satisface los criterios de calidad requeridos). Además, el proceso de descubrimiento podría aprovechar la información ontológica de los contratos para mejorar sus resultados.

*output? **invoke**(entityId, operation, input?) throws exception*
Excepciones: invalidServiceId, invalidPeerId, invalidOperation, invalidInputParameter, invalidOutputParameter, accessDenied.
La primitiva *invoke* permite invocar una operación (*operation*) de una entidad identificada por *identityId*, ya sea un *groupServiceId* o un *peerServiceId*. Es importante destacar que tanto el invocador como el proveedor invocado deben pertenecer al mismo grupo. Como se mencionó, las invocaciones pueden hacerse de forma transparente sobre un *groupServiceId* o bien sobre un *peerServiceId* particular. El parámetro *input* facilita la entrada para la operación invocada, mientras que *output* representa su salida. El tipo de operación determina el tipo de invocación, que puede ser síncrona o asíncrona. En ambos casos, la primitiva *invoke* bloquea al invocador hasta que se produce el correspondiente *receiveMessage* (ver más adelante) en el proveedor. En las invocaciones asíncronas, el cliente (invocador) realiza un *invoke* y el proveedor (invocado) realiza un *receiveMessage*. Por el contrario, en las invocaciones síncronas, el cliente debe realizar un *invoke*, mientras que el proveedor debe ejecutar primero un *receiveMessage* y después un *reply* (descrito más adelante). La primitiva *invoke* eleva excepciones cuando se le facilitan identificadores de par o servicio que no son válidos. Se elevará una excepción *accessDenied* si el cliente y el proveedor no pertenecen al mismo grupo. Además, la excepción *invalidOperation* indica que el proveedor o bien no soporta la operación solicitada o bien no puede realizar el correspondiente *receiveMessage* en ese momento. También se elevarán excepciones cuando los parámetros reales no se correspondan con los formales.

*void **event**(eventName, input?) throws exception*
Excepciones: invalidEvent.
La primitiva *event* lanza —es decir, notifica al middleware— un evento *eventName*. El parámetro opcional *input* sirve para especificar datos asociados al mismo. Las invocaciones a *event* realizadas desde un servicio suponen la publicación previa de un contrato de servicio que incluya *eventName* en su signatura (sin embargo, las invocaciones a *event* realizadas desde un par no están sujetas a esta restricción). Aunque se debe invocar a *receiveEvent* (descrito más adelante) para esperar notificaciones de eventos, la invocación a *event* no es bloqueante; es decir, *event* no se bloquea a la espera de que los suscriptores (ver *subscribe*) invoquen *receiveEvent*. Es tarea del middleware almacenar los eventos lanzados y distribuirlos a los suscriptores. Los eventos lanzados son reenviados a todos los suscriptores de *eventName* que pertenezcan al mismo grupo que el lanzador del evento. Si *eventName* no estaba definido en el contrato del servicio invocante, se eleva una excepción *invalidEvent*.

<callerId, input?> ***receiveMessage****(operationName) throws exception*
Excepciones: invalidOperation, invalidInputParameter.
<callerId, input?> ***receiveEvent****(eventName) throws exception*
Excepciones: invalidEvent, invalidInputParameter.
La primitiva *receive* tiene dos formas —*receiveMessage* y *receiveEvent* — que permiten esperar invocaciones de servicios y notificaciones de eventos, respectivamente. En el primer caso, las invocaciones a *receiveMessage* suponen la publicación previa de un servicio que ofrezca la operación *operationName*. En el segundo caso, las invocaciones a *receiveEvent* suponen una suscripción previa del invocador a recibir notificaciones del evento *eventName* (ver primitiva *suscribe*). En ambos casos, la salida de *receive* contiene el identificador del invocador *callerId*, que puede ser un *peerId* o un *peeServiceId*. Además, la salida contiene los datos de entrada de la operación o los datos asociados al evento. El invocador de *receive* puede enviar información al cliente (*callerId*) a través de *invoke*, *event*, o *reply* (descrita más adelante). La primitiva *receiveMessage* eleva la excepción *invalidOperation* si la operación *operationName* no está definida en el contrato del invocador; mientras que *receiveEvent* eleva *invalidEvent* si el invocador no está suscrito al evento. Además, se eleva una excepción *invalidInputParameter* cuando los parámetros reales y formales no se corresponden.

void ***reply****(callerId, operation, output?) throws exception*
Excepciones: invalidServiceId, invalidPeerId, invaildOperation.
Un *reply* señala la terminación de una operación síncrona. Por lo tanto, el invocador de *reply* debe haber invocado previamente el correspondiente *receiveMessage* sobre la misma operación. Cuando se ejecuta *reply*, el invocador (cliente) de la operación se desbloquea. La salida de la operación se facilita en el parámetro *output*. Las excepciones de *reply* son similares a las de *invoke*.

void ***subscribe****(eventName?, groupId?) throws exception*
Excepciones: invalidGroupId, callerNotInGroup.
Los servicios utilizan *subscribe* para suscribirse a:

- los eventos *eventName* lanzados en un grupo *groupId*

- los eventos *eventName* lanzados en todos los grupos a que pertenezca el invocador

- todos los eventos lanzados en un grupo *groupId*

- todos los eventos lanzados en todos los grupos a que pertenezca el invocador

según la combinación de sus dos parámetros opcionales. Si el identificador de grupo *groupId* no es válido, se eleva una excepción *invalidGroupId*. Además, se elevará una excepción *callerNotInGroup* cuando el servicio invocador no sea miembro del grupo *groupId*.

void ***unsubscribe****(eventName?,groupId?) throws exception*
Excepciones: invalidGroupId, callerNotInGroup, notSubscribed.
Las subscripciones realizadas se pueden anular mediante *unsubscribe*. Aunque *unsubscribe* requiere una suscripción previa, los parámetros del *subscribe* correspondiente no tienen por qué coincidir. Por ejemplo, *unsubscribe(eventName,*

groupId) puede cancelar una suscripción realizada mediante *subscribe(eventName)*. En este caso, el invocador no será notificado cuando se lance un evento *eventName* en el grupo *groupId*. Un *unsubscribe* sin parámetros anula las suscripciones a todos los eventos en todos los grupos a los que pertenezca el invocador (sólo un grupo en el caso de un servicio, puesto que cada publicación de un servicio en grupos distintos es diferente). Si no existe una suscripción previa que se ajuste a los parámetros de *unsubscribe*, se eleva una excepción *notSubscribed*. El resto de excepciones son similares a las de *subscribe*.

3 αSMOL: Un lenguaje de modelado abstracto

El lenguaje SMOL define la conducta (parcial) del código de un par o un servicio de una manera abstracta. Sin embargo, el nivel de abstracción de SMOL aún retiene muchos detalles que no son relevantes desde el punto de vista de la interacción. Por ello, para razonar sobre cuestiones de comunicación, se hace necesario abstraer aún más algunas características de SMOL. Con este propósito definimos el lenguaje αSMOL (*abstract SMEPP modelling language*).

Así, αSMOL puede ser considerado como una versión abstracta de SMOL. Por ejemplo, no modelaremos explícitamente aspectos de seguridad (como los parámetros relativos a *credenciales*, *niveles de seguridad* o *calidad del servicio* del grupo de primitivas). Por otro lado, la salida de algunas primitivas también se ha simplificado debido al uso de localizadores (MURL) para identificar los servicios tanto en pares como en grupos. En cualquier caso, ninguna de estas simplificaciones afecta a la expresividad del lenguaje.

3.1 Un cálculo para primitivas SMOL

Sean $\mathcal{P}$ y $\mathcal{S}$ un conjunto de identificadores para pares y servicios respectivamente. Consideremos también un conjunto de identificadores para grupos, $\mathcal{G}$, que incluye un símbolo especial 0 para denotar el llamado grupo *universal*. Para identificar las entidades del sistema usaremos direcciones (*MURL*) tomadas del conjunto formado por $\mathcal{G} \times \mathcal{P} \times \mathcal{S}$, donde $g.p.s$ identifica un servicio s en un par p publicado en un grupo g (le llamaremos *localizador*). Cuando g y s son 0, el localizador denota el código ejecutable del propio par.

Un grupo se define por una terna etiquetada $\langle P, Sr, Sb \rangle_g$ consistente en un conjunto $P \subseteq \mathcal{P}$ de identificadores de pares (que representan los *miembros* del grupo), un conjunto Sr que contiene información sobre los *servicios proporcionados* por el grupo y un conjunto Sb de suscripciones de entidades a eventos proporcionados por otros servicios en el grupo. El conjunto de servicios proporcionados por el grupo aparecen en un conjunto de tuplas, $Sr \subseteq \mathcal{S} \times \mathcal{C} \times \mathcal{P}$, donde la primera componente es el identificador del servicio, la segunda es el contrato expuesto por el servicio y la última es el identificador del par que proporciona ese servicio. El conjunto de suscripciones a eventos es un conjunto de ternas, $Sb \subseteq MURL \times MURL \times \mathcal{O}$, donde la primera componente denota la localización de la entidad suscriptora, la segunda es la localización del servicio al que se suscribe y la tercera representa la signatura del evento suscrito.

3.2 Sintaxis abstracta de αSMOL

Un par ejecuta un programa y puede ofrecer uno o más servicios, también definido por programas. Un programa o agente tiene la siguiente sintaxis:

$$\begin{array}{ll} \mathsf{Prg} & ::= x = new().\mathsf{Code} \\ \mathsf{Code} & ::= 0 \mid a.\mathsf{Code} \mid \mathsf{Code} \parallel \mathsf{Code} \mid \mathsf{Code} \oplus \mathsf{Code} \mid \mathsf{Code@Excs} \mid D(\vec{x}) \\ \mathsf{Excs} & ::= [] \mid \sum_i b_i.\mathsf{Code}_i : \mathsf{Excs} \qquad\qquad D(\vec{y}) \stackrel{def}{=} \mathsf{Code} \end{array}$$

- donde a representa una de los siguientes primitivas: $x = \mathsf{createGroup}()$, $\mathsf{joinGroup}(g)$, $\mathsf{leaveGroup}(g)$, $\mathsf{unpublish}(m)$, $x = \mathsf{publish}(g, cs)$, $\mathsf{event}(m?, op, in)$, $x? = \mathsf{invoke}(m, op, in)$, $x = \mathsf{getServices}(m, cs)$, $\langle x, y? \rangle = \mathsf{receiveMessage}(op)$, $x = \mathsf{receiveEvent}(op)$, $\mathsf{reply}(m, op, out)$, $\mathsf{subscribe}(op, m)$, $\mathsf{unsubscribe}(op, m)$.
- b representa $\mathsf{catch}(e, in)$.

En las primitivas, x, $\vec{x}$ y $\vec{y}$ son nombres de variables, g representa un *identificador de grupo*, cs es un *contrato de servicio*, m un localizador en *MURL*, op una *operación*, in una *entrada*, out una *salida*, e un *nombre de excepción* y 0 es un programa vacío.

Los programas pueden crearse usando el prefijo (.), la composición paralela ($\parallel$), la elección no determinista con guardas ($\oplus$) y la construcción para el manejo de excepciones (@).

Internamente, el lenguaje αSMOL extiende los programas definidos anteriormente como sigue:

$$\mathsf{Prg}^\star ::= \mathsf{Prg} \mid [\mathsf{Code}]_{MURL}$$

donde a definida en Code incluye además los siguientes comandos: $\mathsf{excep}(e, in)$, $\mathsf{dispatch}(e, n, in)$, $x = \mathsf{suspend}(n)$. Aquí, n es el *nombre de una operación*, in es una *estrada* y e es un *nombre de excepción*.

3.3 Un ejemplo de aplicación

Con objeto de ilustrar el uso del modelo propuesto para definir servicios en una arquitectura P2P, consideramos el ejemplo de la Fig. 1 que pretende gestionar un proveedor de temperaturas leídas desde un dispositivo externo, y un servicio que mantiene la media de todas las lecturas efectuadas. Para ello, definiremos programas sobre dos pares diferentes. El primero, `TempPeer`, será el encargado de crear un grupo y publicar un servicio descrito por el contrato `TempServCS`. Después de procesar otras tareas, el par publicará el servicio. Una implementación simplificada de los contratos `TempPeer` y `TempServCS` se muestra en la parte superior de la Fig. 1, donde o bien se recibe una señal de terminación o la temperatura es leída desde algún dispositivo externo y es comunicada a cualquier subscriptor del evento `"Temperature"`. La parte inferior de la figura define el comportamiento de un par (que haría las veces de un cliente en este caso), `PeerClient`, cuyo cometido es descubrir el servicio `TempServCS` en algún grupo y unirse al mismo, antes de publicar un

```
TempPeer =
  p=new().
  g=create().
  s=publish(g,TempServCS).
  // Processing other tasks
  // Now invoke TempServ of p
  invoke(g.p.s,"Terminate").
  unpublish(g,TempServCS).
  0
```

```
TempServ =
  // temp=...
  event("Temperature",temp).
  TempServ.
  +
  receiveMessage("Terminate").
  0
```

```
PeerClient =
  p=new().
  g.q.s=getServices(*.*.*,TempServCS).
  join(g).
  s'=publish(g,TempServInvokerCS).
  invoke(g.p.s',"Start",g.q.s).
  // Processing other tasks
  avg=invoke(g.p.s',"GetAverage").
  invoke(g.p.s',"Terminate").
  unpublish(g,TempServInvokerCS).
  // Processing the average avg
  0
  @ catch(invalidGroupId,g).
    // The service does not exist
    ...
```

```
TempServInvoker =
  id=receiveMessage("Start").
  subscribe(id,"Temperature").
  AverageTemp(0,0,id)

AverageTemp(a,n,id) =
  t=receiveEvent("Temperature").
  // a'=a + t, n'=n + 1
  AverageTemp(a',n',id)
  +
  id'=receiveMessage("GetAverage").
  // avg = n==0?ERROR:a/n
  reply(id', "GetAverage", avg).
  AverageTemp(a,n,id)
  +
  receiveMessage("Terminate").
  unsubscribe(id,"Temperature").
  0
```

Fig. 1. Dos pares que proporcionan servicios complementarios.

nuevo servicio, `TempServInvokerCS`, que es el que computa la media de las temperaturas. Tras esto, se invocan las operaciones `"Start"` y `"GetAverage"` sobre ese servicio, de forma que se transfiere el localizador del servicio a `TempServInvokerCS` y se obtiene la media. Si no hay ningún servicio con contrato `TempServCS`, la primitiva getServices devolverá el localizador 0.0.0 y al intentar unirse al grupo 0 se lanzará una excepción invalidGroupId. Para tratar esta excepción se añade al final de `PeerClient` la cláusula catch correspondiente. Obsérvese que estamos utilizando cadenas de caracteres para denotar nombres de operaciones y el símbolo + para representar $\oplus$.

3.4 Programas, entornos y ejecuciones

Un programa αSMOL puede ser un código etiquetado ($[\text{Code}]_{MURL}$) cuando lo ejecuta un par ya identificado por el middleware, o un código no etiquetado (Prg) cuando el programa está esperando a que el par se registre en el middleware.

Para simplificar la semántica introducida a continuación, asumiremos que cualquier programa está afectado por un manejador de excepciones (posiblemente vacío). Definimos la semántica de estos programas introduciendo proposiciones de la forma:

$$\Theta\,;\Gamma \leadsto \Pi$$

donde Γ es un conjunto de grupos (es decir, ternas etiquetadas) llamada el *entorno* (denotaremos por *Env* el conjunto de entornos) y Π es un conjunto de programas (Prg*). Denotaremos por *Prog* el conjunto de conjunto de programas. Por otro lado, $\Theta \subseteq \mathcal{E} \times MURL \times MURL \times \mathcal{O}$ (donde $\mathcal{E}$ es un conjunto de identificadores de eventos) denota el conjunto de eventos pendientes de procesar por parte de los receptores y que llamaremos *contexto de eventos pendientes* (*polling context*) (denotaremos con *Context* el conjunto de los contextos de eventos pendientes). Así, cada vez que un servicio $g.p.s$ produce un evento $n \in \mathcal{O}$, se genera un elemento en Θ de la forma $(e, g'.p'.s', g.p.s, n)$ para cada entidad $g'.p'.s'$ suscrita. Todas las tuplas correspondientes al mismo evento están identificadas por único identificador compartido $e \in \mathcal{E}$.

La intención de las proposiciones introducidas es la de que los programas en Π pueden ejecutarse concurrentemente hasta su terminación, comenzando desde el entorno Γ, es decir, estos juicios expresan *terminación*.

La semántica se describe por medio de reglas de inferencia de la forma:

$$\frac{Pr \qquad \Theta\,;\Gamma \leadsto \Pi}{\Theta'\,;\Gamma' \leadsto \Pi'} \qquad (\textsc{Name})$$

donde la proposición situada en la parte superior de la línea es la hipótesis, la de la parte inferior es la conclusión y *Pr* es una premisa que condiciona la aplicación de la regla.

Para cada construcción de un programa —acciones primitivas y operadores de composición— disponemos de reglas de inferencia que describen su semántica. El estilo de las reglas consideradas es similar al presentado en [4] con la salvedad de que los programas en las reglas (Π) pueden tomar la forma *A@Ls* donde *A* es el programa y *Ls* una lista de manejadores de excepciones. Cada elemento de *Ls* (*E* : *Es* en las reglas de la Fig. 2) define un ámbito de captura de excepciones, de forma que una excepción producida en *A* puede ser tratada por el primer nivel de ámbito *E* (regla ExcCatch) si dispone del tratamiento adecuado, o propagarse al resto de niveles, *Es* (regla ExcPropagation).

$$\frac{E = \mathsf{catch}(e,x).A \oplus E' \qquad \Theta\,;\Gamma \leadsto [A\{in/x\}@Es]_{g.p.s}, \Pi}{\Theta\,;\Gamma \leadsto [\mathsf{excep}(e,in).0@E : Es]_{g.p.s}, \Pi} \qquad (\textsc{ExcCatch})$$

$$\frac{E \neq \mathsf{catch}(e,x).P \oplus E' \qquad \Theta\,;\Gamma \leadsto [\mathsf{excep}(e,in).0@Es]_{g.p.s}, \Pi}{\Theta\,;\Gamma \leadsto [\mathsf{excep}(e,in).0@E : Es]_{g.p.s}, \Pi} \qquad (\textsc{ExcPropagation})$$

Fig. 2. Reglas para el tratamiento de excepciones.

Operacionalmente, la ejecución abstracta de un programa se realiza comenzando con una proposición formada por el contexto inicial y el propio programa, y se procede aplicando las reglas de inferencia de abajo hacia arriba hasta que se alcance la terminación (ejecución finita con éxito), o una proposición donde ninguna regla es aplicable (bloqueo).

4 Agradecimientos

Este trabajo ha sido parcialmente financiado por el proyecto SMEPP (EU-FP6-IST 0333563) y además, Gutiérrez, López y Pimentel han sido apoyados por los proyectos TIC2250 (Junta de Andalucía) y TIN07-67134 (MEC, España).

5 Conclusiones y trabajo futuro

En este trabajo hemos presentado un conjunto de primitivas que caracterizan un modelo para arquitecturas P2P seguras. Nuestro objetivo ha sido proporcionar un modelo orientado a servicios, con un alto nivel de abstracción, capaz de especificar la interacción entre pares, así como definir una semántica sencilla que permita el razonamiento sobre especificaciones abstractas de sistemas P2P. Con este objetivo, hemos definido una semántica basada en un cálculo donde las reglas (*judgements*) representan ejecuciones concurrentes controladas por un middleware (que se modela explícitamente por medio de dos componentes, el *entorno* y el *contexto*). La idea que subyace a la existencia de una semántica de estas características es hacer posible la construcción de un entorno de verificación para analizar propiedades como la ausencia de bloqueos, la terminación correcta, etc.

Aunque la aplicación real del modelo de servicios en sistemas empotrados es uno de los objetivos básicos del proyecto SMEPP, el modelo propuesto puede emplearse para especificar sistemas P2P generales (es decir, no necesariamente empotrados). El carácter empotrado se recogerá en la arquitectura software y a nivel de implementación mediante el despliegue de prototipos del middleware para dispositivos con diferentes capacidades de cómputo (desde portátiles a teléfonos inteligentes, pasando por ordenadores de bolsillo).

Es oportuno comentar que se han propuesto otros modelos de interacción y servicios para el modelado de sistemas EP2P. Algunos de ellos están inspirados en el paradigma de arquitecturas orientadas a servicios (por ejemplo, [6, 10]), otros están basados en JXTA [8] o lo extienden (por ejemplo, [1, 2]), mientras que otros son modelos de coordinación orientados a datos (por ejemplo, [7, 9]). Sin embargo, como ya se ha mencionado, los modelos de interacción basados en servicios existentes o bien no tienen en cuenta requisitos fundamentales como la seguridad ligada a grupos, la comunicación basada en eventos e invocación síncrona y asíncrona de mensajes, el establecimiento de contratos de servicios, o no proporcionan un lenguaje formal abstracto con excepciones que pueda ser utilizado para el desarrollo de prototipos y la simulación y verificación del comportamiento de pares y servicios, y su interacción.

Como trabajo futuro, hemos de explorar la expresividad del modelo, especificando casos de estudio reales y más complejos, para validarlo sobre dominios específicos tales como la monitorización ambiental en plantas industriales, y la telefonía móvil. Además, el modelo ha de ser soportado por medio de herramientas de verificación basadas en una extensión de las reglas presentadas en [4] y sobre las que nos encontramos actualmente trabajando.

References

1. Sascha Alda and Armin B. Cremers. Towards composition management for component-based peer-to-peer architectures. *Electr. Notes Theor. Comput. Sci.*, 114:47–64, 2005.
2. Mario Bisignano, Giuseppe Di Modica, and Orazio Tomarchio. Jmobipeer: A middleware for mobile peer-to-peer computing in manets. In *ICDCS Workshops*, pages 785–791. IEEE Computer Society, 2005.
3. BPEL4WS Coalition. Business Process Execution Language for Web Services (BPEL4WS) Ver. 1.1, 2003. ftp://www6.software.ibm.com/software/developer/library/ws-bpel.pdf.
4. Antonio Brogi, Razvan Popescu, Francisco Gutiérrez, Pablo López, and Ernesto Pimentel. A Service-Oriented Model for Embedded Peer-to-Peer Systems. In Pascal Poizat Carlos Canal and Mirko Viroli, editors, *Foundations of Coordination Languages and Software Architecture (FOCLASA'07)*, ENTCS. Springer, 2007. To appear.
5. Paolo Costa, Geoff Coulson, Cecilia Mascolo, Gian Pietro Picco, and Stefanos Zachariadis. The runes middleware: A reconfigurable component-based approach to networked embedded systems. In *Proceedings of the 16th Annual IEEE International Symposium on Personal Indoor and Mobile Radio Communications (PIMRC'05)*, Berlin (Germany), September 2005.
6. G. Gehlen and L. Pham. Mobile web services for peer-to-peer applications. In *Proceedings of the Consumer Communications and Networking Conference 2005*, pages 427–433, 2005.
7. Radu Handorean, Rohan Sen, Greg Hackmann, and Gruia-Catalin Roman. Supporting predictable service provision in manets via context aware session management. (3):1–26, 2006.
8. JXTA homepage. http://www.jxta.org/.
9. Roberto Lucchi and Gianluigi Zavattaro. Wssecspaces: a secure data-driven coordination service for web services applications. In Hisham Haddad, Andrea Omicini, Roger L. Wainwright, and Lorie M. Liebrock, editors, *SAC*, pages 487–491. ACM, 2004.
10. P. Maheshwari, S.S. Kanhere, and N. Parameswaran. Service-oriented middleware for peer-to-peer computing. In *3rd IEEE International Conference on Industrial Informatics (INDIN '05)*, pages 98–103, 2005.
11. D.L. McGuiness and F. van Harmelen (Eds). Web Ontology Language (owl) Overview, 2004. Web guide. http://www.w3.org/TR/owl-features.
12. Sylvia Ratnasamy, Paul Francis, Mark Handley, Richard M. Karp, and Scott Shenker. A scalable content-addressable network. In *SIGCOMM*, pages 161–172, 2001.
13. W3C. Extensible Markup Language (XML) 1.0 (second edition), 2000. http://www.w3.org/TR/2000/REC-xml-20001006.
14. W3C. Web Service Description Language (WSDL) version 1.1. http://www.w3.org/TR/wsdl.

Inteligencia Ambiental: Protegiendo a los Usuarios Finales de Ellos Mismos[1]

Carlos Cetina, Vicente Pelechano, Sonia Montagud

Departamento de Sistemas Informáticos y Computación,
46022 Camino de Vera s/n, Universidad Politecnica de Valencia, España.
{ccetina, pele, smontagud}@dsic.upv.es

Abstract. Tradicionalmente los usuarios han demandado cierto nivel de personalización en los sistemas software para adaptarlos a sus gustos. Con el tiempo se ha incrementado el nivel de integración de estos sistemas en la vida cotidiana de los usuarios, a la vez que han crecido las exigencias de personalización. Hoy en día, con sistemas que envuelven completamente a los usuarios, podemos hablar del concepto de sistemas de usuarios para usuarios. Sistemas que por su naturaleza, es el propio usuario el que desde el diseño especifica los servicios que espera obtener. Los sistemas de Inteligencia Ambiental son un claro ejemplo de este tipo de sistema. De igual modo que los usuarios son los más indicados para configurar sus propios sistemas, son los menos indicados para evaluar su corrección. Por ello debemos ofrecerles mecanismos que les permitan expresar sus necesidades sin comprometer por ello la calidad.

Keywords: Ambient Intelligent, software-product lines, MDD, software factories, End User Development.

1 Introducción

Las exigencias de personalización por parte de los usuarios se incrementan proporcionalmente a la penetración de los sistemas en sus vidas cotidianas. Para maximizar el nivel de satisfacción de los usuarios debe contemplarse esta característica desde las fases iniciales de producción. Para ello, los métodos de producción debe contemplar la figura del usuario final bajo el rol del propio diseñador del sistema. Por ejemplo en [20] se describe la experiencia de aplicar esta idea a los servicios electrónicos del e-government, donde con las herramientas adecuadas los expertos del dominio, que no son programadores, pueden construir sus propios sistemas.
Feature Oriented Programming (FOP) es un paradigma para líneas de producto software donde los programas son sintetizados por composición de características [1].
Model Driven Development (MDD) es un paradigma para desarrollo de software en

[1] Este trabajo ha sido desarrollado con el soporte del MEC bajo el proyecto SESAMO TIN2007-62894 y cofinanciado por FEDER, dentro del programa de becas FPU.

el que los modelos se convierten en el artefacto principal [17]. Ambos paradigmas proponen especificar los sistemas utilizando niveles de abstracción mayores que los utilizados por los leguajes de programación clásicos. Pero no sólo es necesario elevar el nivel de abstracción de los lenguajes de especificación para que los usuarios puedan formar parte del proceso de desarrollo. Debemos evitar utilizar conceptos generalistas y proporcionarles conceptos cercanos a su entendimiento. Sin por ello descuidar la validez de las especificaciones realizadas por estos usuarios finales.

En este artículo planteamos una propuesta para facilitar la incorporación de los usuarios de los sistemas a la especificación de los mismos. Para ello proponemos acomodar el lenguaje de especificación a sus habilidades. Proporcionando mecanismos para garantizar ciertos aspectos sobre sus especificaciones. Además aplicaremos estas ideas a un método de producción de sistemas de inteligencia ambiental fundamentado en MDD y líneas de producto software.

2 Contexto

Existe una gran diversidad de técnicas para proporcionar la especificación de un sistema. La elección de una técnica u otra se verá condicionada por diversos criterios como: potencia expresiva, capacidad para razonar, simplicidad o adecuación al problema, entre otros.

En el caso de las líneas de producto, contamos con técnicas tan variadas como: perfiles de UML, lenguajes de dominio específico, modelos de características o wizards. La técnica de modelos de características cuenta de una gran aceptación por parte de la comunidad. La propuesta inicial FODA [15], fue presentada en 1990 y le siguieron: FORM [16], FeatureRSEB [12], Generative Programing [9], PLUSS [10], Riebisch et al. [23, 24], van Gurp et al. [13], van Deursen et al. [8], Czarnecki et al. [6, 7], Batory [2] y Benavides et al. [3]. Free Features Diagrams [22] es una propuesta orientada a generalizar la sintaxis de las distintas propuestas de modelos de características.

En el caso de Model Driven Development las técnicas empleadas suelen dividirse en dos grandes grupos, emplear un lenguaje multipropósito como UML o utilizar lenguajes de dominio específico (DSL). Ambos grupos cuentan con fuertes comunidades que los respaldan y existen alternativas dentro de cada uno de ellos. En el grupo de UML, se han definidos múltiples perfiles para precisar el significado del lenguaje. Por otro lado, en el grupo de los DSL de forma natural han surgido distintos lenguajes para cada dominio que se pretende especificar.

Contamos con múltiples técnicas y diversos lenguajes para afrontar la tarea de especificar un sistema. Todas ellas ofrecen beneficios que las caracterizan y están respaldadas por grandes comunidades. En la siguiente sección presentaremos un método de producción de sistemas de inteligencia ambiental en el que se utiliza un DSL para especificar los sistemas. Será sobre este método donde aplicaremos nuestra propuesta para acercar a los usuarios del sistema a su especificación.

3 Producción de sistemas de Inteligencia Ambiental

Los sistemas de Inteligencia Ambiental tienden cada vez más a incrementar su extensión y complejidad. Resultando necesario disponer de métodos de producción y herramientas de soporte para abordar su desarrollo. Pervasive Modeling Language (PervML) es un lenguaje de especificación de este tipo de sistemas, utilizado en un método de producción de servicios pervasivos para entorno ubicuos presentado en [18]. Este método sigue el enfoque de desarrollo de software dirigido por modelo (DSDM) en el cual los sistemas son especificados utilizando modelos de alto nivel de abstracción que posteriormente son transformados para obtener el código de implementación del sistema. Este método se apoya en las propuestas de Arquitectura Dirigida por Modelos (MDA) [21] promovida por la OMG y en las Fábricas de Software [11] promovidas por Microsoft.
Los sistemas que pueden ser desarrollados utilizando este método están formados por una serie de servicios heterogéneos que son ofrecidos a los usuarios de un entorno físico concreto. Estos servicios son implementados por dispositivos situados en el entorno, pero también por componentes software.

3.1 Desarrollo Dirigido por Modelos

De acuerdo a la estrategia propuesta en DSDM, los modelos PervML se utilizan para generar el sistema final y no sólo para generar la documentación o asistir en el proceso de desarrollo. Con este fin el método de producción viene complementado de una serie de artefactos que hacen de esta propuesta una realidad:

- **Lenguaje de dominio especifico PervML.** Utilizando una notación gráfica basada en UML, determina los sistemas que pueden ser producidos.
- **Arquitectura de implementación.** Embebe aquellos aspectos invariantes a los distintos sistemas que pueden ser especificados.
- **Reglas de transformación.** A partir de los modelos PervML generan el código que instancia la arquitectura de implementación.
- **Herramienta de modelado y generación.** Proporciona soporte al proceso de desarrollo, desde la especificación del sistema a la generación de código, en [5] se describe de forma detallada.

Mediante la conjunción de todos estos artefactos es posible abordar de una forma sistemática la producción de este tipo de sistemas. En el siguiente apartado llevaremos un paso más allá las ideas de reutilización subyacentes al método de producción presentado.

3.2 Líneas de Producto Software

El método descrito propone especificar los sistemas utilizando PervML y generar a partir de estas especificaciones el código de implementación. Aplicando este método en un caso de estudio como [19] detectamos que al fijar el dominio de aplicación se incrementan las similitudes entre las especificaciones de los sistemas. En concreto en el dominio de los sistemas domóticos detectábamos que en cada hogar digital

contaban con servicios comunes, como iluminación o seguridad, aunque presentaban pequeñas diferencias en el comportamiento de los mismos.
Con el fin de explotar sistemáticamente la reutilización, aplicamos la metáfora de los bloques de construcción a las especificaciones de PervML. Identificando dos tipos de bloques: (1) los componentes, que se corresponden con los conceptos de *servicio* y *proveedor de enlace* existentes en PervML y (2) los de comportamiento, que se corresponden con los conceptos de *interacción* y *disparador* existentes en PervML. En la Fig. 1 se presenta el metamodelo de PervML, además de la relación entre los bloques y el lenguaje.

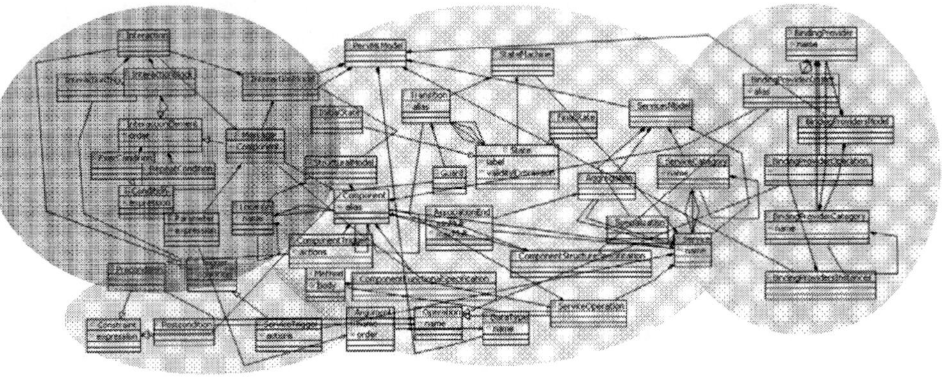

Fig. 1. Abstracción de bloques en PervML.

Aplicando esta metáfora de bloques de construcción obtenemos un conjunto de activos reutilizables en futuros desarrollos. De este modo la producción de un nuevo sistema domótico se convierte en un ensamblado de estos activos. A lo largo de las siguientes secciones describiremos como especificar los activos que han de ensamblarse para producir un nuevo sistema.

4 Desarrollo dirigido por los usuarios

Los activos reutilizables son los elementos clave en las Líneas de Producto Software. Sus distintas combinaciones determinarán aquellos productos que es posible obtener. El ensamblado de estos activos se realiza de acuerdo a una especificación que recoge las características que contemplará el producto final. Los Modelos de Características es el actual estándar de facto para realizar este tipo de especificaciones. En ellos se formaliza las posibles características con las que es posible dotar a un producto, así como las relaciones entre estas, siendo las de dependencia y exclusión las más utilizadas.
En la Fig. 2 mostramos un subconjunto del modelo de características que representaría la familia de productos inspirada en el caso de estudio [19], desarrollado con PervML. En este ejemplo los elementos circulares se corresponden con las posibles características del sistema. Las relaciones entre características decoradas con

un circulo blanco representan opcionalidad en la subcaracterística, mientras que las decoradas con uno negro representan obligatoriedad. Por otro lado, aquellas relaciones unidas entre sí por una línea recta indican que debe seleccionarse entre las subcaracterísticas implicadas.
Los Modelos de Características no son los únicos dotados con la expresividad suficiente para expresar este tipo de información. Existen diversas alternativas como: (1) modelos de UML etiquetados para concretar sus conceptos, (2) Lenguajes de Dominio Específico construidos para disponer únicamente de los conceptos necesarios o (3) asistentes con una expresividad limitada pero muy intuitivos.

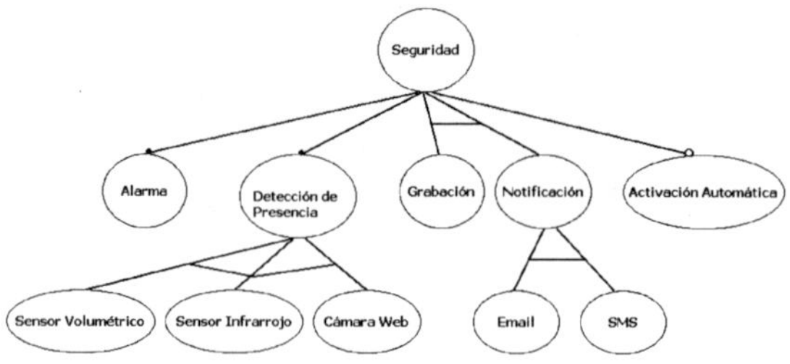

Fig. 2. Modelo de Características de un sistema domótico.

Para definir un producto, es posible utilizar tanto los Modelos de Características como las alternativas anteriormente mencionadas. Algunos de estos productos podríamos denominarlos como "de usuarios para usuarios". Son productos que, por su naturaleza, es deseable que sean los propios usuarios los que especifiquen que servicios esperan obtener. Un claro ejemplo son los sistemas domóticos.
Promover los usuarios al rol de diseñadores de sus propios sistemas, plantea una serie de nuevos desafíos a nivel de especificación. A continuación, enumeramos los principales problemas que identificamos del uso de los lenguajes de especificación más populares.

- Los lenguajes de especificación populares no han sido concebidos para usuarios sin conocimientos en ingeniería del software. Es por ello que los conceptos presentes en estos lenguajes se alejan de los conceptos que utilizan los usuarios de los productos.
  Ejemplo/ Los conceptos nativos de UML, como la agregación o los clasificadores, pertenecen a un nivel de abstracción distinto al de conceptos como servicio o dispositivo, más propios de un usuario de un sistema domótico.
- Abordar el desarrollo de sistemas complejos, suele implicar la participación de distintas Líneas de Producto. La especificación de los distintos productos del sistema, no necesariamente, ha de hacerse siguiendo el mismo lenguaje de especificación. Este escenario plantea un esfuerzo extra por parte de los usuarios para traducir los conceptos entre lenguajes.
  Ejemplo/ Es posible encontrar en distintas propuestas de Modelos de características que conceptos comunes, cardinalidad o dependencia, toman distintas representaciones gráficas.

- La elección de cualquier lenguaje de especificación implica renunciar a buenas propiedades de otros lenguajes.
  Ejemplo/ Decantarnos por los modelos de características nos permitirá beneficiarnos de todo el trabajo realizado por la comunidad de Líneas de Productos, pero perderemos la extrema sencillez de los asistentes o las buenas propiedades de un estándar como UML para interoperar.

Motivados por los problemas detectados, vamos a presentar a lo largo de las siguientes subsecciones una propuesta que pretende acercar los lenguajes de especificación a los usuarios de los sistemas, sin perder por ello rigurosidad a nivel de especificación.

4.1 Conceptos de los lenguajes de especificación

En esta sección, vamos a presentar aquellos conceptos relacionados con los lenguajes de especificación que utilizaremos. Todo lenguaje cuenta con unas estructuras internas utilizadas por la máquina para almacenar sus elementos, el conjunto de estructuras se conoce como la sintaxis abstracta. A estas estructuras se les asocia una representación gráfica o textual que les permita ser fácilmente manipulables por humanos. Son estas metáforas gráficas o representaciones textuales lo que se conoce como sintaxis concreta del lenguaje. La sintaxis concreta persigue que el uso del lenguaje sea intuitivo, pero es posible que surjan distintas interpretaciones por parte de los usuarios. Por ello, es necesario proporcionar una formalización de la semántica del lenguaje.

Proporcionar la semántica del lenguaje no es una tarea sencilla, no es suficiente con proporcionar un metamodelo de la sintaxis concreta, acompañado de restricciones o con describir el comportamiento. En [14] se propone formalizar un dominio semántico y definir relaciones de los elementos de la sintaxis concreta a los del dominio semántico.

Íntimamente ligado al concepto de semántica encontramos el de expresividad. Considerando el dominio semántico del lenguaje como el conjunto (A) y la sintaxis concreta como el conjunto (B). La expresividad de un lenguaje viene determinada por el subconjunto (C) formado por todos los elementos de (A) que tienen una relación con elementos de (B). De este modo, diremos que un lenguaje tiene más riqueza expresiva cuantos más elementos de su dominio semántico formen parte del subconjunto (C).

En torno a los conceptos de expresividad y semántica articularemos durante el resto de secciones nuestra propuesta para acercar la figura de diseñadores del sistema a los usuarios finales.

4.2 Generalización de la expresividad

Existen distintas alternativas para describir un producto centrándonos en sus características. Es posible utilizar modelos de características, modelos de UML etiquetados, wizards e incluso lenguajes de dominio especifico. En esencia, todos ellos expresan las características del producto, así como las relaciones entre ellas.

Estas relaciones se representan de distinta forma según sea el lenguaje escogido, así por ejemplo si utilizamos un lenguaje de dominio especifico veremos conceptos propios del dominio, mientras que con UML utilizaremos conceptos multipropósito, como las clases o las asociaciones. Nuestro objetivo es abstraer el conjunto minimal para describir las características de un producto.

A diferencia de los lenguajes de especificación mencionados no pretendemos un lenguaje manipulable por humanos, sino que buscamos un lenguaje de bajo nivel procesable por máquinas. En los lenguajes orientados a humanos podemos identificar dos tipos de constructores: (1) los destinados a dotar al lenguaje de más expresividad y (2) los orientados a compactar la notación. Estos últimos, son comúnmente conocidos como azúcar sintáctico y se caracterizan porque pueden ser substituidos por constructores del tipo (1).

Para ilustrar la diferencia entre los dos tipos de constructores, utilizaremos un ejemplo basado en los lenguajes de programación. En este caso utilizaremos el lenguaje C# y sus constructores *foreach* y *for*. En la columna de la izquierda de la Fig. 3, se muestra un bucle que recorre todos los elementos de una colección utilizando el constructor *foreach*. El uso de este constructor nos facilita de forma transparente el incremento de una variable contador, así como la asignación de la variable que visita la colección. En la columna central de la imagen se muestra un código equivalente sin hacer uso del constructor *foreach* y en la columna de la derecha otro equivalente a los dos anteriores utilizando el constructor *while*. En el caso del lenguaje C# los constructores *foreach* y *for* son del tipo (2) ya que pueden rescribirse por constructores del tipo (1) como *while* con un resultado equivalente.

```
foreach (figura i in lienzo)
{
   i.pintar();
}
```

```
for(int i = 0; i < lienzo.Length; i++)
   {
      lienzo[i].pintar();
   }
```

```
int i = 0;
while (i<lienzo.Length)
      {
         lienzo[i].pintar();
         i++;
      }
```

Fig. 3. Fragmentos de C# equivalentes.

Como se observa en el ejemplo de la Fig. 3, sustituir en un lenguaje los constructores de tipo (2) por constructores de tipo (1) tiene un efecto directo: disminuye el número de constructores del lenguaje con la contrapartida de una notación más densa. En lenguajes orientados a humanos, los constructores de tipo (2) resultan de vital importancia, pero en un lenguaje de bajo nivel orientado a maquinas podemos prescindir completamente de ellos.

Generalizando la expresividad de los distintos lenguajes utilizados para especificar características y prescindiendo de constructores destinados a compactar la notación, obtenemos un lenguaje de bajo nivel que comprende el conjunto minimal que buscábamos. En la Fig. 4 se presenta el metamodelo de su sintaxis concreta. El concepto principal del lenguaje es la característica que puede explotar en subcaracterísticas y sobre estas pueden definirse relaciones. En la próxima sección describiremos de forma precisa la semántica de los conceptos de este lenguaje.

Con esta generalización se consigue un lenguaje de bajo nivel que puede servir como origen o destino común para realizar traducciones entre distintos lenguajes de especificación. Pero hemos de recordar que las especificaciones utilizando este lenguaje están orientadas a ser procesadas por máquinas, por lo que resultan complejas y poco entendibles por humanos.

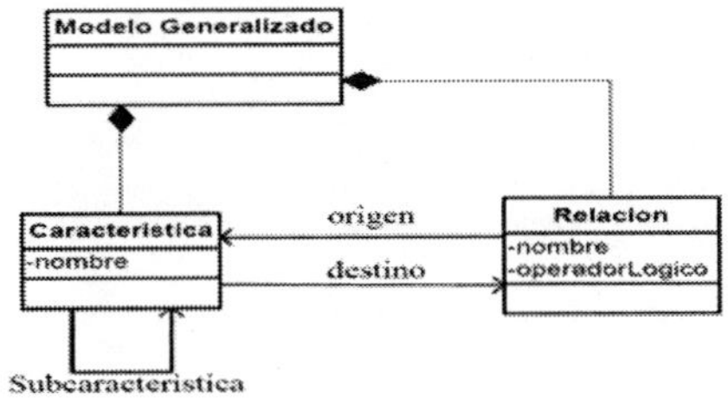

Fig. 4. Metamodelo del lenguaje de bajo nivel.

4.3 Formalización de la semántica

En la sección anterior, hemos propuesto una generalización de distintos lenguajes para especificar características de un producto. En la Fig. 4, presentamos su sintaxis concreta por medio de un metamodelo. Únicamente proporcionando el metamodelo de un lenguaje pueden surgir distintas interpretaciones de su semántica. Modelos conformes a su metamodelo garantizan que sintácticamente están bien formados, pero no necesariamente serán interpretados de la misma forma por distintas personas. Para evitar que surjan distintas interpretaciones de un mismo modelo hemos de formalizar correctamente la semántica del mismo.

Para formalizar la semántica definiremos el dominio semántico y estableceremos relaciones con los conceptos de la sintaxis concreta como se propone en [14]. Para definir el dominio semántico es posible utilizar desde lenguaje natural a las matemáticas. En nuestro caso, utilizaremos una aproximación mixta, para el concepto principal de característica utilizaremos un incremento en la funcionalidad del producto. Para las relaciones entre estas características definiremos dos tipos, (1) una composicional, para indicar qué subcaracterísticas forma una característica y (2) una relación basada en los operadores lógicos de las matemáticas. Mediante los operadores lógicos podremos simular relaciones de dependencia, exclusividad u otros tipos de relaciones más complejas.

Una vez definido el dominio semántico, hemos de establecer las relaciones entre este y la sintaxis concreta del lenguaje. Para formalizar estas relaciones utilizaremos el concepto matemático de función, para ello definimos relaciones R entre la sintaxis concreta S y el dominio semántico D; R: S -> D:

- **R1: Metaclase Característica -> Característica.** Relacionamos la zona sombreada con líneas verticales de la Fig. 5 con el concepto de característica como un incremento en la funcionalidad.
- **R2: Relación -> Operadores Lógicos.** Relacionamos la zona sombreada con líneas oblicuas de la Fig. 5 con los operadores lógicos de las matemáticas.

- **R3: SubCaracterística -> Relación Composicional.** Relacionamos la zona sombreada con puntos de la Fig. 5 con el concepto de relación composicional.

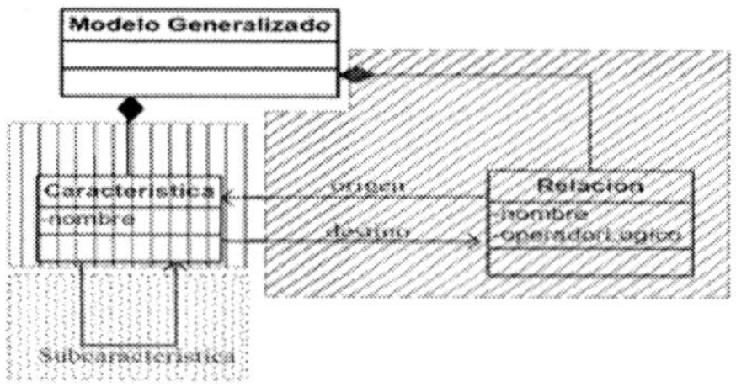

Fig. 5. Metamodelo sombreado del lenguaje de bajo nivel.

Una vez formalizada la semántica, contamos con un lenguaje de bajo nivel que puede ser utilizado como origen o destino para realizar transformaciones entre distintos lenguajes. Por ejemplo, podemos definir mappings entre un perfil de UML o lenguajes de dominio específico.
Definir mappings entre distintos lenguajes y nuestra generalización de la expresividad, proporciona dos beneficios directos: (1) por un lado somos capaces de representar los mismos conceptos con distintos lenguajes y (2) por otro podemos formalizar transitivamente la semántica de otros lenguajes. La generalización de la expresividad actuaría como dominio semántico y los mappings como la relación entre la sintaxis concreta y el dominio específico. De este modo, se formalizaría parcialmente la semántica de los lenguajes con los que estableceríamos mappings.

4.4 Potencia expresiva

En la sección anterior hemos propuesto una generalización de la expresividad para definir las características de un producto. Para definir la equivalencia entre otros lenguajes y nuestra generalización de la expresividad, nos serviremos de transformaciones entre modelos. Hemos identificado cuatro tipos de transformaciones de acuerdo a los conceptos presentes en estos lenguajes:

- **Características y subcaracterísticas.** Es el concepto principal en este tipo de lenguajes. En torno a él giran el resto de transformaciones.
- **Atributos de las características.** Las características de un producto pueden ser complementadas con atributos. Estos atributos pueden utilizarse únicamente para describir las características o como base para definir restricciones complejas.
- **Restricciones de cardinalidad.** Determinan si las características se encuentran o no presentes de forma obligatoria en el producto, así como su valor mínimo o máximo.
- **Restricciones de dependencia y exclusividad.** Entre las relaciones que podemos definir entre características, es común encontrar soporte a este tipo de restricciones. Estas relaciones suelen definirse entre dos características y se expresan directamente con la sintaxis del lenguaje.

- **Restricciones complejas.** En este apartado recogemos todas aquellas restricciones más sofisticadas que se presentan de forma puntual en los lenguajes. No suelen embeberse en la sintaxis del propio lenguaje, sino que se suele recurrir a un lenguaje específico de restricciones como Object Constraint Language.

De acuerdo a los cuatro tipos de transformaciones que hemos identificado, todavía nos encontramos evaluando la potencia expresiva de la generalización propuesta. Algunas transformaciones que hemos definido vienen impuestas por nuestro objetivo de obtener transformaciones bidireccionales. Otras transformaciones se obtienen de forma directa mediante los operadores lógicos. También, hemos detectado transformaciones que, como esperábamos, su resultado es complejo y únicamente aceptable en un lenguaje de bajo nivel no orientado a humanos. A continuación vamos a describir nuestra experiencia con cada uno de los 4 tipos de transformaciones detectadas:

- **Características y subcaracterísticas.** En la transformación de origen-destino evitamos la creación de características sintéticas, con el objetivo de preservar la capacidad de poder aplicar la transformación inversa destino-origen y obtener un resultado equivalente al inicial.
- **Atributos de las características.** Respecto a los atributos es posible proporcionar un soporte inicial para aquellos atributos destinados únicamente a describir las características. Actualmente no hemos explorado la posibilidad de utilizar los atributos para definir restricciones sobre ellos.
- **Restricciones de cardinalidad.** Es en este tipo de transformaciones donde hemos detectado la mayor diversidad de patrones. Algunas restricciones como las de existencia, tienen una representación directa en los operadores lógicos, mientras que las relacionadas con restricciones de cardinalidad mínimas y máximas sobre conjuntos, son las que requieren de patrones más complejos. Este tipo de transformaciones es sin duda en el que más esfuerzos estamos dedicando para explorar la expresividad de nuestra propuesta.
- **Restricciones de dependencia y exclusividad.** Contamos con operadores lógicos que simulan de forma muy cercana este tipo de restricciones, pero debemos analizar más escenarios con el fin de identificar posibles disimilitudes y complementar nuestros patrones de traducción.
- **Restricciones complejas.** A priori son las restricciones más complejas pero se presentan en ocasiones puntuales. Actualmente, es el tipo de restricciones que menos hemos explorado, originalmente se expresan con lenguajes específicos muy potentes, pero esperamos poder encontrar patrones que nos permitan simularlas mediante el uso de los operadores lógicos.

Para los distintos tipos de transformaciones, hemos identificado múltiples patrones de traducción, pero somos conscientes de la envergadura del trabajo restante. No sólo proponer patrones de traducción para los conceptos ya identificados, sino explorar más escenarios y detectar nuevos conceptos que traducir.

5 Acomodando el lenguaje a la audiencia

La generalización de la expresividad propuesta constituye un marco común para los distintos lenguajes de especificación de productos. Permitiendo trasladar los conceptos relacionados con las características a las distintas representaciones de cada lenguaje. De este modo, entramos en un paradigma en el que independizamos la especificación de las características de un lenguaje en concreto, permitiendo seleccionar el lenguaje más apropiado a las habilidades del diseñador. Con la aparición de los usuarios finales de los productos como diseñadores de los mismos, debemos ofrecer lenguajes de especificación sencillos y cercanos a su entendimiento. Por otro lado, no debemos olvidar que ya sean expertos diseñadores o usuarios finales, debemos garantizar que los productos especificados sean válidos y libres de inconsistencias.
Al desvincularnos de un lenguaje de especificación concreto podemos explotar las buenas características de cada uno de ellos:

- **Lenguajes de dominio específico.** Al ser lenguajes construidos para modelar un dominio muy concreto es posible utilizar conceptos cercanos a los usuarios.
- **Wizards.** Presentan de forma intuitiva la información mientras asisten al usuario con información contextual.
- **Modelos de características**. Disponen de operaciones que permiten razonar sobre ellos, indicando información relativa a la validez de un producto o posibles inconsistencias.
- **UML.** Estándar promovido por el Object Management Group (OMG) como lenguaje de modelado. Al contar con el respaldo tanto de la OMG, como de una gran parte de la comunidad, se convierte en un lenguaje muy apropiado para interoperar.

Nuestros esfuerzos persiguen unificar todas estas características en un único proceso de producción, de modo que el usuario se vea beneficiado de las buenas propiedades de cada lenguaje sin ser consciente de los cambios entre lenguajes. De este modo, utilizaría durante la etapa de especificación los wizars que, de forma sencilla, le guiarían por las características del producto. Para aquellas características que requirieran mayor nivel de detalle se recurriría a lenguajes de dominio específico. Como hemos de garantizar que se especifique un producto válido, libre de ambigüedades, utilizaríamos la potencia de los modelos de características para razonar [4]. Finalmente, conscientes que los desarrollos de software no se realizan de forma aislada, proporcionaríamos UML como un lenguaje mediante el cual el usuario pudiera exportar las configuraciones de los productos.

5.1 Aplicación practica

Con el fin de experimentar empíricamente nuestra propuesta hemos aplicado nuestras ideas al método de producción de sistemas de inteligencia ambiental que da soporte a PervML. Como hemos presentado en la sección 3, PervML es un lenguaje para especificar sistemas de Inteligencia Ambiental a partir del cual derivamos automáticamente el código de implementación. La herramienta que da soporte a este método, PervGT [5], hace uso de la plataforma Eclipse y sus plugins de modelado.

Para crear nuevos sistemas utilizando PervML seguimos la metáfora de los bloques de construcción, de modo que de acuerdo a las características del sistema se ensamblan unos bloques u otros. Utilizando el plugin de Eclipse Graphical Modeling Framework, GMF, hemos definidos las vistas que abstraen los bloques de construcción sobre los modelos de PervML. En la zona A de la Fig. 6 se representa de forma intuitiva la abstracción de los bloques de construcción, con el objetivo de situar este paso dentro de la propuesta completa.

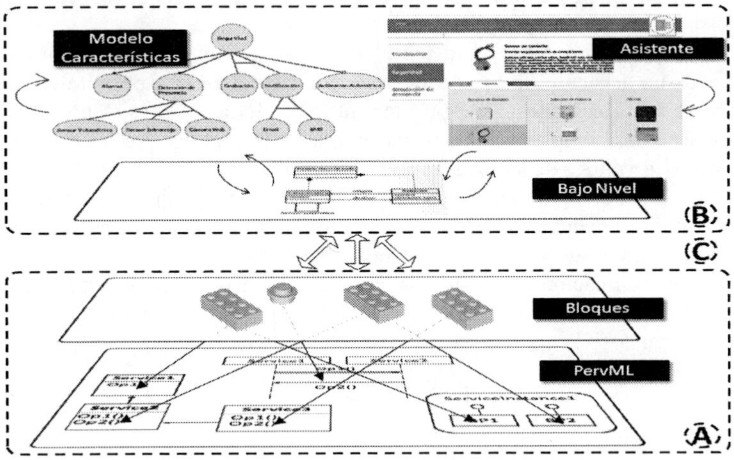

Fig. 6. Visión Global de la propuesta.

Para que un usuario final pueda seleccionar las características que configurarán su sistema hemos utilizado como lenguajes de especificación (1) la implementación de modelos de características propuesta por Benavides [4] y (2) un asistente desarrollado a mano por nosotros. Este asistente presenta de forma sencilla las características de un producto organizándolas en distintos pasos. Para implementar el lenguaje de bajo nivel hemos utilizando Ecore. Ecore es el lenguaje utilizado por el plugin Eclipse Modeling Framework, EMF, que proporciona a partir de un modelo Ecore las clases Java que lo representan. Finalmente utilizando Atlas Transformation Language, ATL, hemos definido transformaciones entre estos lenguajes y nuestro lenguaje de bajo nivel. Es en la zona B de la Fig. 6 donde situamos este paso dentro de la propuesta.

Una vez seleccionadas las técnicas para especificar las características del sistema, zona B, y abstraídos los bloques, zona A, es necesario formalizar que bloques soportaran cada característica. Para ello hemos utilizado un modelo de enlace entre el lenguaje de bajo nivel y los bloques de construcción. Mediante el plugin Atlas Model Weaving, AMW, utilizando un modelo *c* es posible expresar las relaciones entre dos modelos *a* y *b*. Siendo *a* un modelo creado con nuestro lenguaje de bajo nivel donde se expresan todas las posibles características del sistema y *b* el conjunto de bloques abstraído de los modelos de PervML. Será en la zona C de la Fig. 6 donde, mediante un modelo de enlace, se establecen las relaciones entre bloques y características.

5.2 Experiencia

Estas ideas las hemos aplicado a un caso de estudio de un sistema domótico descrito en [19]. Para especificar las características de los sistemas inicialmente utilizamos un modelo de características. Al representar sistemas complejos utilizando estos modelos aparecen múltiples elementos y relaciones de composición, dependencia o exclusividad sobre ellos. Conforme se incrementa la complejidad de los sistemas también se incrementa el número de elementos y las relaciones, dejando de ser atractivos para los usuarios finales.

Con el objetivo de acercar el diseño de estos sistemas a los usuarios finales, introdujimos un asistente de diseño del sistema. Este asistente permite especificar el sistema mediante elecciones de respuesta múltiple. Mediante el asistente acercamos el diseño de sistemas complejos a los usuarios finales, a costa de perder la capacidad de razonar sobre la validez de los mismos.

Al aplicar la idea propuesta de alternar entre lenguajes de especificación, conservamos la capacidad de razonar sobre los sistemas, mientras ofrecemos una técnica fácil para su especificación. Como fruto de este trabajo hemos permitido acercar la especificación de sistemas concretos a los propios usuarios de estos sistemas, mientras los protegemos de malas decisiones de diseño que conduzcan a sistemas incorrectos.

6 Conclusiones

Conscientes de que la figura del usuario final del sistema cada vez reclama más protagonismo en el diseño del mismo, hemos presentado una propuesta para permitir que los usuarios finales tomen el rol de diseñadores sin perder la rigurosidad a nivel de especificación.

Para ello, proponemos independizar el lenguaje de especificación del método de producción, utilizando un lenguaje de bajo nivel que sirva como marco para establecer relaciones entre distintos lenguajes.

Nuestros esfuerzos persiguen ofrecer al diseñador el lenguaje de especificación más adecuado a sus necesidades sin perder los beneficios de otros lenguajes. A nivel teórico hemos propuesto la primera versión del lenguaje de bajo nivel, formalizado su semántica así como definidos varios patrones de traducción. Finalmente, contamos con implementaciones muy preliminares sobre las que realizar nuestros experimentos. Somos conscientes del largo trabajo que queda por delante, tanto a nivel de formalización de nuevos patrones como identificación de nuevos conceptos a traducir.

Referencias

1. Batory, D., Sarvela, J.N., A. Rauschmayer.: Scaling Step-Wise Refinement. IEEE TSE (2004)
2. Batory, D.S.: Feature Models, Grammars and Propositional Formulas. In: Obbink and Pohl, pp. 7--20

3. Benavides, D., Trinidad, P., CortCs, A.R.: Automated Reasoning on Feature Models. In: Pastor, 0., Cunha, J.F. (eds) CAiSE, vol. 3520 of Lecture Notes in Computer Science, pp. 491--503 (2005)
4. Benavides, D., Segura, S., Trinidad, P., Ruiz-Cortés, A.: FAMA: Tooling a Framework for the Automated Analysis of Feature Models. First International Workshop on Variability Modelling of Software-intensive Systems (VAMOS) (2007)
5. Cetina, C., Serral, E., Muñoz, J., Pelechano, V.: Tool Support for Model Driven Development of Pervasive Systems. MOMPES (2007). To be Published
6. Czarnecki, K., Helsen, S., Eisenecker, U.: Staged Configuration Using Feature Models. Software Process Improvement and Practice, special issue on Software Variability: Process and Management, pp. 143--169 (2005)
7. Czarnecki, K., Helsen, S., Eisenecker, U.W.: Formalizing cardinality-based feature models and their specialization. Software Process: Improvement and Practice, pp. 7--29 (2005)
8. Van Deursen, A., Klint, P.: Domain-Specific Language Design Requires Feature Descriptions. Journal of Computing and Information Technology, pp.1--17 (2002)
9. Eisenecker, U.W., Czarnecki, K.: Generative Programming: Methods, Tools, and Applications. Addison-Wesley (2000)
10. Eriksson, M., Borstler, J., Borg, K.: The PLUSS Approach - Domain Modeling with Features, Use Cases and Use Case Realizations. In: Obbink and Pohl, pp 33--44
11. Greenfield, J., Short, K., Cook, S., Kent, S.: Software Factories. Wiley Publising Inc. (2004)
12. Griss, M., Favaro, J., dlAlessandro, M.: Integrating Feature Modeling with the RSEB. In: Proceedings of the Fifth International Conference on Software Reuse, pp. 76--85, Vancouver, BC, Canada (1998)
13. Van Gurp, J., Bosch, J., Svahnberg, M.: On the Notion of Variability in Software Product Lines. In: Proceedings of the Working IEEEPFIP Conference on Software Architecture
14. Harel, D., Rumpe, B.: Meaningful Modeling: What's the Semantics of "Semantics"? IEEE Computer, pp. 64--72 (2004)
15. Kang, K., Cohen, S., Hess, J., Novak, W., Peterson, S.: Feature-Oriented Domain Analysis (FODA) Feasibility Study. Technical Report CMU/SEI-90-TR-21, Software Engineering Institute, Carnegie Mellon University (1994)
16. Kang, K.C., Kim, S., Lee, J., Kim, K.: FORM: A Feature-Oriented Reuse Method. In Annals of Software Engineering 5, pp. 143--168 (1998)
17. Mellor, S.J., Clark, A.N., Futagami, T.: Model-driven development - Guest editor's introduction. IEEE Software, pp. 14--18 (2003)
18. Muñoz, J., Pelechano, V.: Building a Software Factory for Pervasive Systems Development. In: CAiSE 2005, Porto, Portugal. LNCS, vol. 3520, pp. 329--343 (2005)
19. Muñoz, J., Pelechano, V., Cetina, C.: Implementing a Pervasive Meetings Room: A Model Driven Approach. IWUC 2006, Paphos, Cyprus (2006)
20. Lepouras, G., Vassilakis, C., Halatsis, C., Georgiadis, P.: Domain Expert User Development: The SmartGov Approach, CACM, pp. 79--83 (2007)
21. Object Management Group: Model Driven Architecture Guide (2003)
22. Schobbens, P.Y., Heymans, P., Trigaux, J.C.: Feature Diagrams: A Survey and a Formal Semantics
23. Riebisch, M.: Towards a More Precise Definition of Feature Models. Position Papel. In: Riebisch, M., Coplien, J.O., Streitferdt, D. (eds.) Modelling Variability for Object-Oriented Product Lines (2003)
24. Riebisch, M., Bollert, K., Streitferdt, D., Philippow, I.: Extending Feature Diagrams with UML Multiplicities. In: Proceedings of the Sixth Conference on Integrated Design and Process Technology (IDPT2002), Pasadena, CA (2002)

Introduciendo Conceptos de Metrología en el Diseño de Medidas de Software[1]

Nelly Condori-Fernández[1], Oscar Pastor[1], Alain Abran[2], Asma Sellami[2]

[1]Departamento de Sistemas Informáticos y Computación
Universidad Politécnica de Valencia, Camino de Vera s/n, 46022, Valencia.
{nelly, opastor}@dsic.upv.es
[2]École de Technologie Supérieure ETS
1100 Notre-Dame Ouest, Montreal, Canada H3C 1K3
alain.Abran@etsmtl.ca , asma.sellami@isimsf.rnu.tn

Resumen. Una revisión del vocabulario internacional de términos de metrología fue llevada a cabo con el fin de identificar los conceptos que debieran ser considerados en el diseño de las medidas de tamaño de software. Luego, un análisis es llevado a cabo sobre el diseño de un procedimiento de medición de tamaño funcional, llamado RmFFP. Los resultados muestran que RmFFP considera la mayoría de los conceptos de metrología en comparación con otras medidas definidas en base a otros estándares.

Palabras clave: metrología, medición de software, tamaño funcional, especificación de requisitos

1 Introducción

La unidad de longitud fue uno de los primeros descubrimientos de la medición hechos por el hombre, siendo el mismo cuerpo humano la base que facilitó su creación; tal como es el caso de la pulgada, la mano, el pie, y la yarda. Sin embargo, la carencia de uniformidad en estas unidades de medida, originó la necesidad por estandarizar las medidas, surgiendo la metrología como la ciencia de la medición preocupada por la definición de nuevos estándares de medición y el control de los mismos [1]. Así, con el transcurrir de los años, la metrología en constante evolución se ha ido extendiendo a nuevas áreas de tecnología, tales como los estándares eléctricos (1937), fotométricos (1937), de radiación por ionización (1960), estándares de medición en tiempo (1988) y estándares de medición en la química (2000) [5]. Sin embargo, su extensión a las tecnologías de la información aún no ha podido ser, a pesar de existir una gran cantidad de "métricas de software" en la literatura. Por consiguiente, surge la necesidad de analizar e identificar los conceptos de metrología que pudieran ser utilizados en la medición del software, ya sea por ingenieros de software interesados

[1] Este trabajo está subvencionado por el proyecto SESAMO con ref. TIN2007-62894 del Ministerio de Ciencia y Tecnología y parcialmente por el Programa Marie Curie del Sexto Marco de la Comunidad Europea con ref. MIF1-CT-2006-039212.

en el diseño de medidas de software; administradores de proyectos de software interesados en el uso coherente de estas medidas; etc.

El propósito del presente artículo es en primer lugar introducir los conceptos relevantes de metrología en el diseño de las medidas de tamaño de software. Luego un análisis, en base a estos conceptos metrológicos, es ilustrado en un procedimiento de medición de tamaño funcional, llamado RmFFP [2], [3]. Este procedimiento ha sido diseñado para medir automáticamente el tamaño funcional de las especificaciones de requisitos generadas con un método basado en la transformación de modelos, OO-Method [4].

Este artículo es organizado en seis secciones. En la sección 2 se describe los trabajos relacionados a la aplicación de la metrología en la medición del software. En la sección 3, un modelo de proceso de medición es introducido para describir en mayor detalle el diseño del procedimiento de medición RmFFP. En la siguiente sección se presenta los conceptos de metrología que están relacionados con el diseño de las medidas de tamaño del software. En la sección 5, un análisis metrológico del procedimiento RmFFP es ilustrado. Finalmente, se presenta las conclusiones y trabajos futuros.

2 Metrología y Medición de Software

El término "Metrología" es definido por la Organización Internacional de Metrología Legal (OIML) [5], en el Vocabulario Internacional de Términos en Metrología (VIM) [1], como la ciencia de la medición que abarca aspectos teóricos y experimentales a cualquier nivel de incertidumbre y cualquier campo de la ciencia o la tecnología. De este modo, el alcance de la aplicación de la metrología es ilimitado, ya que las nuevas áreas de estudio incitan algunas veces a la creación de nuevas unidades de medida e instrumentos de medición. Sin embargo, el VIM que se constituye en el consenso internacional sobre la terminología de metrología, ampliamente conocido en las ciencias físicas, químicas y sociales, actualmente es casi desconocido en la comunidad de "métricas de software".

El Instituto Nacional de Estándares y Tecnología de los EE.UU (NIST) tiene muchos años de experiencia en medir cantidades físicas, pero en lo que respecta a medición de la "tecnología de la información digital" su experiencia es relativamente nueva. El NIST identificó un conjunto de cambios, oportunidades y prioridades que surgen al intentar aplicar los conceptos de metrología a la Tecnología de la Información (TI) [6]. Ellos identificaron dos aspectos que distinguen a la "metrología de la tecnología de la información" de la "metrología física":

Primero.- las cantidades de la TI no son medibles usando un sistema de medición físico tal como es el Sistema Internacional de Unidades. De las siete unidades base solamente el "segundo" aparece como esencial para la TI.

Segundo.- los métodos existentes para calcular expresiones de incertidumbre en la metrología física no pueden ser aplicados fácilmente en la TI. La incertidumbre puede ser mucho más difícil de definir que de cuantificar. Los métodos estadísticos sobre repetibilidad y exactitud en la metrología física no se aplican con claridad en las mediciones llevadas a cabo en las TI.

Diferentes clasificaciones de métricas de software fueron propuestas con el fin de mejorar la selección adecuada de métricas para un determinado propósito; entre las taxonomías encontradas tenemos las de Peng y Wallace (1993) [8], Brito y Carapuca (1994) [9], Woodings (1995) [10] y Mendes et al. (2005) [11]. Sin embargo, todas estas métricas aún no han tenido una plena aceptación por los ingenieros del software. A pesar de que la ingeniería del software necesita ser soportada por medidas, métodos de medición y modelos cuantitativos y descriptivos bien probados [12].

Abran et al. afirman lo siguiente: "para que la ingeniería del software sea conocida como una disciplina de ingeniería legítima y una profesión reconocida, un consenso sobre una base del conocimiento es imperativo" [13]. Conscientes de este problema, una ontología de medición de software ha sido introducida por García et al. [14] con el fin de armonizar los diferentes estándares y modelos de medición existentes en la literatura de la ingeniería de software. Abran identificó algunas ambigüedades de alto nivel en el dominio de la medición del software y propuso un conjunto de recomendaciones para lograr una evolución de las métricas del software hacia la metrología del software [12]. Gray discutió la aplicabilidad de la Metrología a las Tecnologías de Información [15] y concluyó que no hay todavía las bases fundamentales en la medición del software que podrían ser aplicadas a los principios de la metrología; por ejemplo las líneas de código y los puntos de función tienen problemas con los principios de unidad, escala y medición de incertidumbre.

Una propuesta de Abran y Sellami introduce un modelo inicial de conceptos de medición del Vocabulario ISO de metrología [16]. Finalmente, un análisis del método estándar de medición COSMIC [17] y del reporte técnico de la ISO 9126-4 [18] fue llevado a cabo usando este modelo inicial de conceptos de metrología en [19] y [20] respectivamente.

Como el presente artículo se centra en el diseño de medidas de software, en la siguiente sección, introducimos el diseño de métodos de medición.

3 Diseño de Métodos de Medición

Jacquet y Abran definen un modelo de proceso de medición [22], identificando y definiendo un conjunto de pasos que guíen las fases de diseño, aplicación, análisis y utilización de resultados de la medición (Figura 1).

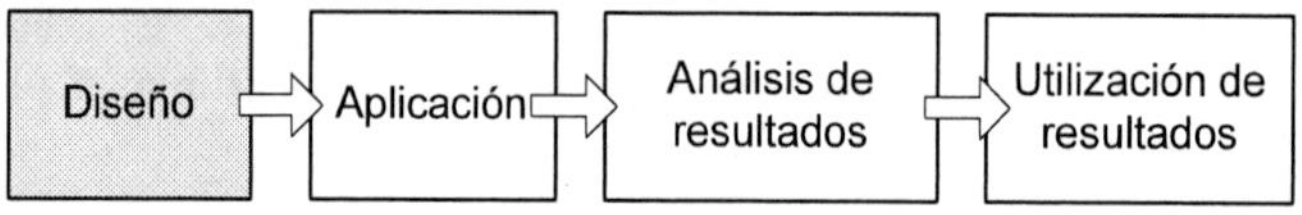

Fig. 1. Modelo de Proceso de Medición [22]

Según este modelo, el diseño de un método de medición se inicia con la *definición de objetivos*, paso donde definimos qué es lo que se desea medir, cuál es el punto vista de medición y cuál es la intención de uso. Luego *caracterizamos el concepto a ser medido*, mediante la identificación y definición del atributo a medir, (por ejemplo el tamaño, complejidad, cohesión, etc.). Teniendo en cuenta este atributo, un conjunto de conceptos, que permitan describir el software a medir, son seleccionados; este paso es llamado también *selección del meta-modelo del software*. Finalmente, un conjunto de *reglas de asignación numérica* son definidas con el fin de cuantificar el modelo de software a medir. La Figura 2 muestra esta secuencia de pasos necesarios para llevar a cabo el diseño de un método de medición.

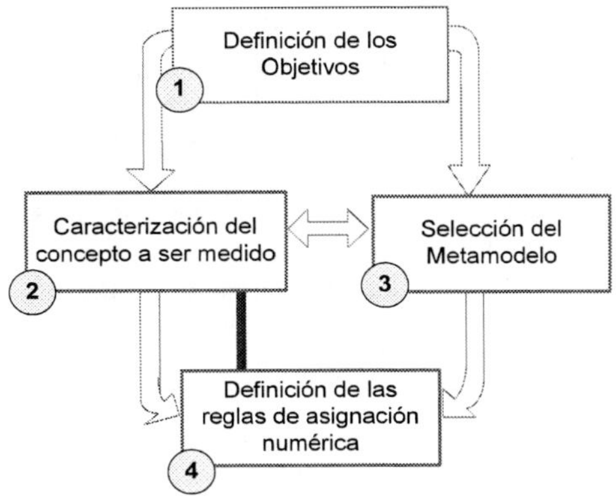

Fig. 2. Diseño de un Método de Medición [22]

A continuación, con el fin de ilustrar cada uno de los pasos de la fase de diseño del modelo de proceso de medición presentamos el diseño del procedimiento de medición RmFFP.

Definición de objetivo

Teniendo en cuenta la plantilla GQM (Goal/Question/Metric), el siguiente objetivo fue definido:

Definir	*un Procedimiento de medición*
Para el propósito de	*medir el tamaño funcional*
Con respecto a las	*especificaciones de requisitos funcionales*
Desde el punto de vista	*del analista*
En el contexto del	*Modelo de Requisitos de OO-Method.*

Caracterización del concepto a ser medido

A partir de nuestro objetivo, identificamos al tamaño funcional como el atributo a ser medido, el cual es definido, según el estándar ISO 14143-1[21], como el tamaño del software derivado por la cuantificación de los requisitos funcionales de usuario.

Sin embargo, esta definición, al ser muy general, necesita ser aclarada (qué entendemos por "cuantificación de los requisitos funcionales"). Para hacer esto, previamente nos apoyamos en el siguiente paso que es explicado a continuación.

Selección del metamodelo

El metamodelo a ser seleccionado debe ser acorde con el atributo a medir; en nuestro caso, como el atributo es el tamaño funcional, en la literatura existen varios metamodelos de métodos estándares candidatos, tales como IFPUG FPA, MARK II FPA, NESMA FPA y COSMIC. RmFFP fue diseñado conforme al método estándar COSMIC. Este estándar, a diferencia de los otros métodos estándares, se caracteriza por su capacidad de medir artefactos en diferentes dominios software, siendo esta una de las razones principales de nuestra elección.

El metamodelo del método estándar COSMIC fue elaborado con el fin de representar de manera más clara los diversos conceptos genéricos que son descritos en su manual de medición [25], así como también poder identificar las diferentes relaciones existentes entre dichos conceptos.

Teniendo en cuenta este conjunto relevante de conceptos, la "cuantificación de requisitos funcionales" es entendida como la cantidad de *movimientos de datos* identificados. Siendo un "*movimiento de dato*" el componente funcional básico de RmFFP.

Para facilitar la correcta identificación de este componente funcional, un conjunto de reglas fueron definidas para representar todos los conceptos del metamodelo de COSMIC en las primitivas relevantes del modelo de requisitos de OO-Method [27]. Este conjunto de reglas son presentadas detalladamente en [3] y [26]. La Tabla 1 resume esta correspondencia.

Tabla 1. COSMIC y el Modelo de Requisitos de OO-Method [3],[26]

Conceptos COSMIC		**Primitivas del Modelo de Requisitos**
Usuarios		Actores del diagrama de casos de uso
Frontera		Diagrama de casos de uso
Procesos Funcionales		Casos de Uso Primarios Casos de Uso Secundarios
Grupos de datos		Clases del diagrama de secuencia Actores diagrama de casos de uso
Atributos de datos		Atributos de Clase
Movimientos de Datos	Entrada	Mensaje de tipo Señal con valor Input
	Lectura	Mensaje de tipo Consulta Condición de Mensaje Precondición de Caso de Uso Condición de relación EXTEND Restricción de integridad
	Escritura	Mensaje de tipo Servicio con la propiedad: - New - Destroy - Update
	Salida	Mensaje de tipo Señal con valor Output

Definición de las reglas de asignación numérica

Para cuantificar el modelo de software a medir (instanciación del meta-modelo mediante la aplicación de reglas de representación previamente definidas), la *función de medición* del método estándar COSMIC fue considerado. Así mismo, con el fin de obtener el tamaño funcional de toda la especificación funcional del alcance de medición, un conjunto de reglas fue definido, las cuales fueron también presentadas en [3].

4 La Metrología en el Diseño de Medidas de Software

El VIM es un documento ISO que presenta 120 conceptos organizados en 6 categorías: cantidad y unidades, instrumentos de medición, estándares de medición, características de medición y resultados [1].

Antes de llevar a cabo el análisis metrológico de las medidas de software, primero, un modelo de los conceptos de alto nivel del VIM ha sido elaborado, Con el fin de enfatizar las relaciones identificadas entre estas categorías y facilitar su comprensión en la comunidad de ingeniería de software. Este modelo es presentado en la Figura 3.

Luego, dos preguntas fueron planteadas con la finalidad de introducir el VIM en la medición del software. Estas preguntas son:

Q1.- ¿Qué categorías del VIM debieran ser considerados durante la fase de diseño de los métodos de medición?

Q2.- ¿Qué conceptos de estas categorías debieran ser tomadas en cuenta en el diseño de las medidas de tamaño de software?

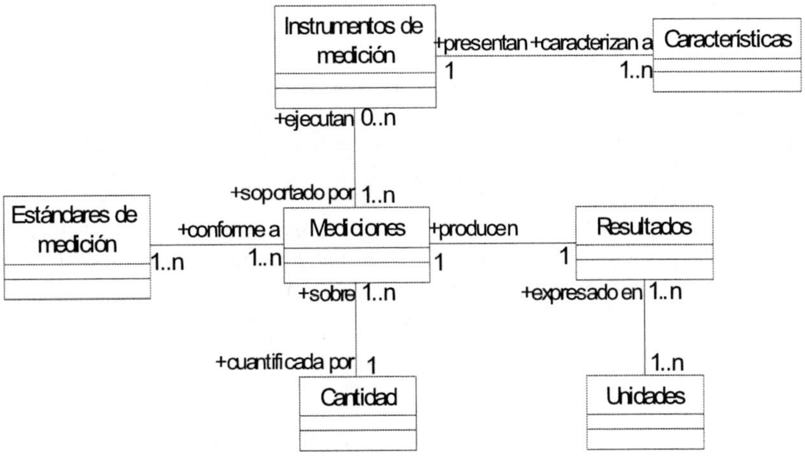

Fig. 3. Modelo de las categorías del VIM

Con respecto a la primera interrogante, partiendo del análisis inicial, llevado a cabo por Sellami y Abran [23], sobre la relación existente entre las categorías del VIM y las fases del Modelo de Proceso de Medición [21], consideramos que además de la categoría *"cantidades y unidades"*, las categorías *"medición"* y *"estándares de medición"* debieran ser también consideradas para la fase de diseño; ya que es necesario tener en cuenta sobre qué *fundamentos de medición* un método o procedimiento será diseñado. Además de que los diferentes tipos de *estándares de medición* debieran ser considerados a lo largo de todo el proceso de medición..
La Tabla 2 muestra la relación de las categorías del VIM que debieran ser consideradas en los respectivos pasos a seguir en el diseño de medidas de software.

Tabla 2. Relación entre categorías del VIM y los pasos de la fase de diseño

Fase de diseño según [22]	**Categorías del VIM**	
Paso1: Definición de objetivos		
Paso2: Caracterización de concepto a ser medido	- Medición: Fundamentos-Principio de la medición	Estándares de medición
Paso 3: Selección de meta-modelo	- Medición: Fundamentos-Método de medición - Cantidades	
Paso 4: Definición de las reglas de asignación numérica	- Cantidades y unidades	

Con respecto a la segunda interrogante, los conceptos que debemos de considerar de las categorías identificadas en la Tabla 2 son los siguientes:

- *Categoría "Medición"* incluye 2 sub-categorías: Fundamentos de Medición y la Medición propiamente dicha. Tal como se observa en la Tabla 2, hemos considerado únicamente los conceptos de la sub-categoría. Fundamentos de Medición: "Principio de Medición" y "Método de Medición" para el diseño de las medidas de software:

  1) *"Principio de medición"* que representa la base científica de una medición. Este concepto facilitará la caracterización del concepto o atributo a ser medido.

  2) *"Método de medición"* que representa una secuencia lógica de operaciones utilizada en una medición. Este concepto está relacionado directamente con el tercer paso de la fase de diseño, ya que el meta-modelo a seleccionar corresponde justamente al método de medición seleccionado.
- *Categoría "Cantidades y unidades",* los conceptos de esta categoría están organizados en cuatro sub-categorías: sistema de cantidades, dimensión, unidades de medición y valores (Vea Figura 4).

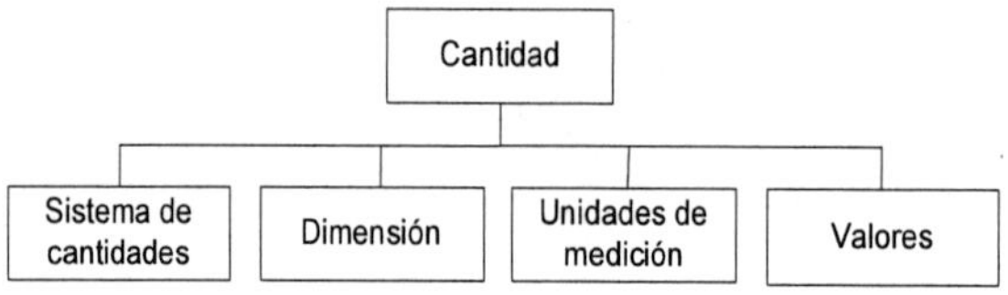

Fig. 4. Topología de alto nivel de la categoría "cantidad y unidades"

Tal como se observa en la Tabla 3, 17 conceptos están organizados dentro de estas subcategorías; de los cuales: 10 conceptos son apropiados para el análisis del diseño de medidas de tamaño. El concepto de "valor verdadero" fue considerado como indeterminado (I), debido a que no existe "medición perfecta", más aún, en la medición del software, donde intervienen varios factores externos que podrían afectar a la obtención de este "valor verdadero" (por ejemplo: la calidad de la documentación del software a ser medido). El resto de conceptos, que son definidos en el VIM [1], no fueron considerados para este tipo de medida, la razón es que la mayoría de estos conceptos se refieren a otro tipo cantidades y unidades que no corresponden a una medida de tamaño.

Tabla 3. "Cantidades y unidades": Conceptos del VIM para las medidas de tamaño

.Sistema de cantidades		**Unidad**	
Cantidad base	√	Símbolo de unidad	√
Cantidad derivada	X	Unidad base	√
Dimensión de una cantidad		Unidad derivada	X
Dimensión	√	Unidad coherente	X
Valores		Sistema de unidades	√
Valor verdadero	I	Sistema coherente de unid.	X
Valor verdadero convencional	√	Sistema internacional de unid.	X
Valor numérico	√	Sistema Off de unidad	X
Escala de referencia convencional	√	Múltiplos de una unidad	√
		Sub múltiplos de una unidad	√

- *Categoría "Estándares de Medición"*: este concepto es entendido en el VIM como un material de referencia o sistema de medición para definir, realizar, conservar o reproducir una unidad o uno o más valores de cantidad para servir como una referencia. Tal como se observa en la Tabla 2, los estándares de medición deben ser considerados en todos los pasos de la fase del diseño.

Teniendo en cuenta los conceptos seleccionados de estas tres categorías del VIM, a continuación presentamos el análisis del diseño de RmFFP.

5 Analizando Metrológicamente el Diseño de RmFFP

En la presente sección, presentamos el análisis del diseño del procedimiento RmFFP, introducido brevemente en la sección 3, en base a las categorías: fundamentos de medición, cantidades y unidades, y estándares.

5.1 Fundamentos de medición

RmFFP ha sido diseñado conforme al *principio de medición* del *método* estándar ISO/IEC 19761 [17] (Vea figura 5). Por consiguiente, RmFFP si considera los fundamentos de medición que establece el VIM: principio y método. Cabe mencionar que el conjunto de operaciones generales del método de medición ha sido adaptado para facilitar la medición del tamaño funcional de las especificaciones de requisitos.

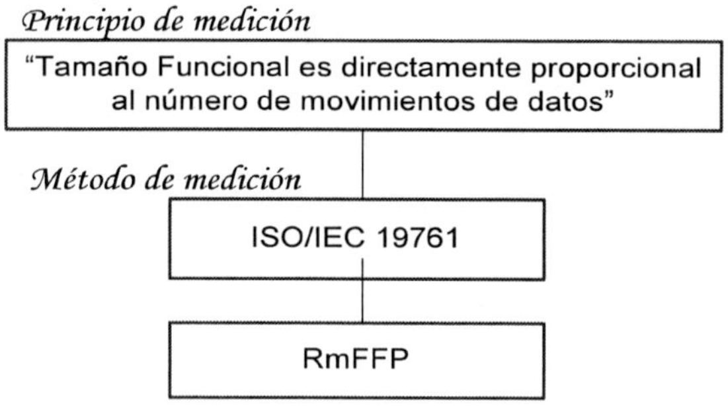

Fig. 5. RmFFP y los fundamentos de la medición

5.2 Cantidades y unidades

Teniendo en cuenta los 10 conceptos del VIM que fueron identificados como apropiados para el análisis de medidas de tamaño de software (Tabla 3), RmFFP considera lo siguiente:

En cuanto *al sistema de cantidades*, una "cantidad base" es convencionalmente aceptada como una cantidad independiente de cualquier otra cantidad. En RmFFP esta "cantidad base" es representado por el "tamaño funcional".

En cuanto a la sub-categoría *dimensión de una cantidad*, una "dimensión" es la expresión de una cantidad representada como un producto de potencias, cuyos factores son dimensiones de *cantidades base.* Por lo tanto, la dimensión del tamaño del software estaría conformada únicamente por un factor. Sin embargo, en RmFFP, para este concepto aún falta determinar su notación dimensional.

En cuanto a la *sub-categoría valores*, el concepto "valor verdadero convencional", en RmFFP viene a ser determinado por el valor obtenido por algún experto certificado en el estándar ISO/IEC 19761 [17] [24]. El concepto "valor numérico", en RmFFP este valor es obtenido aplicando la "función de medición", la misma que permite cuantificar el tamaño funcional, este valor pertenece al conjunto de números enteros positivos. El concepto "escala de referencia convencional", en RmFFP esta escala es dada por el conjunto de valores numéricos discretos, cuyo valor mínimo es 1 movimiento de dato y su valor máximo no es establecido. Actualmente RmFFP considera que esta escala es expresada únicamente en movimientos de "grupos de dato".

En cuanto a la sub-*categoría unidad de medición*, la "unidad base" de RmFFP es el movimiento de dato, cuyo "símbolo" es CFP (COSMIC Function Point). El concepto de "sub-multiplo" en RmFFP actualmente no ha sido posible definirlo, ya que la relación de equivalencia entre las diversas formas de expresar un dato es difícil de determinar (grupo de dato, atributo de dato), lo que impide fraccionar la unidad de RmFFP. Sin embargo, el concepto de "múltiplo" en RmFFP si es posible determinarlo, siempre y cuando se establezca previamente algún tipo de escalonamiento por convenio. El concepto de "sistema de unidades" que incluye el conjunto de unidades base y derivadas, en RmFFP es conformado únicamente por la unidad base: movimiento de dato; a pesar de existir unidades derivadas a partir del tamaño funcional (productividad).

Por lo tanto, de los 10 conceptos de esta categoría del VIM, que debieran ser considerados en el diseño de medidas de tamaño de software, 7 han sido tomados en cuenta en el diseño de RmFFP.

5.3 Estándares de medición

Con respecto a esta categoría, el manual de medición de COSMIC [25] ha sido utilizado para el diseño de RmFFP. Sin embargo, aún hace falta la definición de otros materiales de referencia que permitan la trazabilidad de las mediciones de tamaño del software [30].

6 Conclusión

En el presente artículo se ha introducido el Vocabulario Internacional de Metrología con el fin de identificar los términos o conceptos que debieran ser considerados al momento de diseñar medidas de tamaño de software. Para esto, se ha elaborado un modelo de conceptos de alto nivel (categorías) del VIM, identificando a las categorías: medición, cantidades y unidades, y estándares de medición.

Para la *categoría medición* se ha considerado únicamente los conceptos relacionados con los *fundamentos de medición*; los demás conceptos de esta categoría (operador, procedimiento, resultados, etc.) están más implicados con la aplicación de los métodos de medición.

Para la *categoría cantidades y unidades*, alrededor del 50% de los conceptos de esta categoría fueron considerados como apropiados para el diseño de medidas de tamaño de software (10 de 17 conceptos); ya que al ser el tamaño una cantidad base, varios conceptos de esta categoría no fueron consideradas por tratarse de cantidades y unidades derivadas.

Para la *categoría estándares de medición*, se identificó la necesidad de definir "materiales de referencia" con el fin de contribuir a la trazabilidad de las mediciones de tamaño funcional y a la conservación de los actuales métodos estándar (IFPUG FPA, MARK II FPA, NESMA FPA y COSMIC).

En base a los conceptos del VIM de estas tres categorías, identificados previamente como relevantes para la medición del software, un análisis metrológico de RmFFP fue llevado a cabo; en el cual se observó que RmFFP ha sido diseñado teniendo en cuenta la mayoría de estos conceptos. Actualmente el concepto de sub-múltiplo no ha sido todavía considerado en RmFFP, y el concepto dimensión de una cantidad tampoco ha sido contemplado ya que hace falta determinar su notación dimensional. Por lo tanto, en términos metrológicos, RmFFP resulta ser mejor en comparación con otras medidas de tamaño funcional, como los puntos de función que si tienen problemas con los principios de unidad y escala [28], [29].

Como trabajo futuro inmediato se plantea llevar a cabo un análisis del VIM para las fases de aplicación, análisis y utilización de los resultados. Además un estudio sobre la aplicación de ontologías en el análisis metrológico de las medidas de software también sería llevado a cabo.

Referencias

1. ISO/IEC, International Vocabulary of Basic and General Terms in Metrology (VIM), International Organization for Standardization, Geneva, Switzerland, 1993.
2. N. Condori-Fernández, S. Abrahão, O. Pastor, Towards a Functional Size Measure for Object-Oriented Systems from Requirements Specifications, Quality Software International Conference 2004, Braunschweig, Alemania, IEEE Computer Society, pp. 94-101.
3. N. Condori-Fernández, S. Abrahão, O. Pastor, On the Estimation of the Functional Size of Software from Requirements Specifications. Journal of Comput. Science and. Technoly, Springer, 22(3): 358-370 (2007)
4. O. Pastor, J. Molina, Model Driven Architecture in Practice, Springer Berlin Heidelberg, New York, 2007.
5. OIML: http://www.oiml.org última visita Diciembre 2007
6. Carnahan L., Carver G., Gray M., Hogan M., Hopp T., Horlick J., Lyon G., and Messina E., Metrology for Information Technology, Standard View, 5(3):103-109, 1997.
7. BIPM: http://www.bipm.org/ última visita Diciembre de 2007
8. Peng W., Wallace D., Software Error Analysis, NIST Special Publication, National Institute of Standards and Technology, Gaithersburg, MD, March 1993.
9. Brito F. and Carapua R., Candidate metrics for object oriented software within a taxonomy framework. Journal of Systems and Software, 26(1):87-96, July 1994.
10. Woodings, T L, A Taxonomy of Software Metrics, Software Process Improvement Network (SPIN), available from Comast Consulting, Perth, 1995.
11. Mendes E., Councell S., Mosley N., Towards a Taxonomy of Hypermedia and Web Application Size Metrics, International Conference on Web Engineering, Springer LNCS, Sydney, Australia, July , 2005, pp. 110-123.
12. Abran A., Software Metrics Need to Mature into Software Metrology (Recommendations)", presented in the NIST Workshop on Advancing Measurements and Testing for Information Technology (IT), Maryland, USA, 1998.
13. Abran A., Sellami A., Suryn W., Metrology, Measurement and Metrics in Software Engineering, Proceedings of the Ninth International Software Metrics Symposium, Sydney, Australia, 2003.
14. Garcia F., Bertoa M., Calero C., Vallecillo A., Ruiz F., Piattini M., Genero M., Towards a consistent terminology for software measurement. Journal on Information & Software Technology, Elsevier, 48(8): 631-644 (2006).
15. Gray M., Applicability of Metrology to Information Technology, Journal of Research of the National Institute of Standards and Technology, 4(3):103-109, 1999.
16. Abran A. and Sellami A., Initial Modeling of the Measurement Concepts in the ISO Vocabulary of Terms in Metrology, in Software Measurement and Estimation-

Proceedings of the 12th International Workshop on Software Measurement, Magdeburg-Germany, October 2002, Shaker Verlag, pp. 315.

17. ISO, "ISO/IEC 19761: 2003, Software Engineering: COSMIC-A Functional Size Measurement Method", International Organization for Standardization-ISO, Geneva, 2003.
18. ISO/IEC, ISO/IEC TR 9126-4: Software Engineering – Product Quality – Part 4: Quality in Use Metrics, International Organization for Standardization, Geneva, Switzerland, 2004.
19. Abran A. Sellami A., Analysis of Software Measures Using Metrology Concepts – ISO 19761 Case Study, International Workshop on Software Audits and Metrics, Porto, Portugal 2004.
20. Abran A., E. Al-Quatish, J. Cuadrado, Investigation of the Metrology Concepts in ISO 9126 on Software Product Quality Evaluation, In Proceedings of the 10th International Conference on Computers, Athens-Greece, July 2006, pp. 864-872.
21. ISO, ISO/IEC 14143-1- Information Technology - Software measurement-Functional Size Measurement. Part 1: Definition of Concepts, International Organization for Standardization, Geneva, Switzerland, 1998.
22. Jacquet J. P. and Abran A., "From Software Metrics to Software Measurement Methods: A Process Model", in International Software Engineering Standards Symposium and Forum, ISESS 97: IEEE-Computer Society Press, 1997, pp. 128-135.
23. Sellami A., Abran A., The contribution of metrology concepts to understanding and clarifying a proposed framework for software measurement validation, in International Workshop on Software Measurement , Montreal , Shaker-Verlag , 2003, pp.18-40.
24. COSMIC: http://www.cosmicon.com/ última visita Noviembre de 2007.
25. Abran A., J. M. Desharnais, S. Oligny, D. St-Pierre, and C. Symons, "COSMIC Measurement Manual – Version 3,0, The COSMIC Implementation Guide for ISO/IEC 19761:2003" École de technologie supérieure- ETS, Montreal (Canada) 2003. Available free at: http://www.gelog.etsmtl.ca/COSMIC/
26. N. Condori-Fernández, S. Abrahão, O. Pastor, El Problema de la Duplicidad de Movimientos de Datos en un Procedimiento de Medición, IDEAS 2006, Universidad de La Plata, Argentina 2006.
27. Insfran E., 2003. A Requirements Engineering Approach for Object-Oriented Conceptual Modeling, PhD Thesis, Valencia Polytechnic University.
28. Kitchenham B. Counterpoint: The Problem with Function Points, Status Report. IEEE Software, 1997, 14(2): 29-31.
29. Abran A., Pierre N. Function Points: A Study of Their Measurement Processes and Scale Trans-formations. Journal Systems and Software, 1994, 25(2): 171-184.
30. Khelifi, A., Abran, A., 'Design Steps for Development Software Measurement Standards Etalons for ISO 19761 – COSMIC-FFP', World Scientific and Engineering Academy and Society - WEAS 2007 Conference, Agios Nicolaos (Greece), July 26-28 2007, pp. 590-598.

ONTORMAS: Uma ferramenta dirigida por ontologias para a Engenharia de Domínio e de Aplicações Multiagente

Adriana Leite[1], Rosario Girardi[1]

[1]DEINF/GESEC – Universidade Federal do Maranhão (UFMA)
Av. dos Portugueses, s/n, Campus Bacanga, CEP 65080-040 – São Luís – MA – Brasil
adri07lc@gmail.com, rgirardi@deinf.ufma.br

Resumo. A aplicação de Ontologias na Egenharia de Software apresenta diversas vantagens. As ontologias permitem a representação formalizada e integrada de modelos e sua documentação em uma mesma base de conhecimento, tornando a seleção desses artefatos mais precisa através de inferências semânticas. Elas também são facilmente expansíveis e integráveis. Este artigo apresenta ONTORMAS, uma ferramenta dirigida por ontologias para o desenvolvimento de sistemas multiagente. Ela integra conceitos da Engenharia de Domínio e de Aplicações Multiagente seguindo as diretrizes das metodologias MADEM ("Multi-Agent Domain Engineering Methodology") e MAAEM ("Multi-Agent Application Engineering Methodology").

Palavras-chave: Reúso de Software, Ontologias, Sistemas Multiagente, Engenharia de Domínio, Engenharia de Aplicações.

1 Introdução

Uma ontologia é freqüentemente definida como a especificação de uma conceitualização [12]. A conceitualização refere-se à abstração de uma parte do mundo (um domínio) onde são representados os conceitos relevantes e seus relacionamentos. A especificação é formal e, portanto, processável por um sistema de computação.

As ontologias são geralmente formalizadas através de técnicas de representação do conhecimento como a lógica descritiva e os sistemas de frames. Um frame representa um conceito presente na ontologia e a cada frame são associados atributos ("slots") que representam características e relacionamentos entre conceitos [19].

As ontologias provêem uma terminologia não-ambígua que pode ser compartilhada por todos os envolvidos no processo de desenvolvimento de software. Elas podem ser tão genéricas quanto necessário permitindo o seu reúso e fácil extensão. Estas características tornam a ontologias úteis para representar o conhecimento das técnicas e metodologias para a Engenharia de Software e é um mecanismo de abstração apropriado para especificação de artefatos de software reusáveis de alto nível como modelos de domínio, frameworks e padrões de software [9] [10] [11][12].

Este trabalho descreve a ferramenta ONTORMAS, uma conceitualização da MADEM ("Multi-Agent Domain Engineering Methodology") [8] [10], uma metodologia de desenvolvimento de software para a Engenharia de Domínio Multiagente e da MAAEM ("Multi-Agent Application Engineering Methodology") [15] [16] [17], uma metodologia de desenvolvimento de software para a Engenharia de Aplicações Multiagente.

A Engenharia de Domínio, também chamada desenvolvimento PARA o reúso, é um processo para criação de abstrações de software reusáveis no desenvolvimento de uma família de aplicações em um determinado domínio de problema. A Engenharia de Aplicações ou desenvolvimento COM reúso é um processo para a construção de uma aplicação específica através do reúso das abstrações disponibilizadas pela Engenharia de Domínio.

A ONTORMAS é utilizada por ambas as metodologias para guiar a realização das suas tarefas de modelagem e para representação dos produtos gerados como instâncias da sua hierarquia de classes.

Este artigo está organizado da seguinte forma. A seção 2 apresenta uma visão geral das metodologias MADEM e MAAEM, descreve a ferramenta ONTORMAS e exemplifica a sua utilização. A seção 3 apresenta uma análise das ferramentas para desenvolvimento de aplicações multiagente. Na seção 4 são feitas as considerações finais sobre a ferramenta ONTORMAS e dos trabalhos que estão sendo desenvolvidos a fim de automatizar o processo de desenvolvimento no paradigma orientado a agentes.

2 A ferramenta ONTORMAS

A ONTORMAS é uma ferramenta dirigida por ontologias que representa uma conceitualização das metodologias MADEM e MAAEM. Nela foram expressas todas as diretrizes para o desenvolvimento de sistemas multiagente especificadas por essas metodologias.

A ontologia foi desenvolvida no ambiente de desenvolvimento de sistemas baseados no conhecimento Protégé [7], como um sistema de frames, no qual cada frame representa um conceito e os slots representam as características e relacionamentos entre esses conceitos. Uma notação gráfica foi definida para a representação dos conceitos presentes nos diferentes produtos das tarefas de modelagem. No desenvolvimento da ONTORMAS houve a integração da ONTOMADEM [9], uma ferramenta dirigida por ontologias para o desenvolvimento de artefatos para a Engenharia de Domínio Multiagente. A ONTOMADEM quando usada isoladamente é limitada, visto que não permite o desenvolvimento de aplicações específicas, somente de artefatos reusáveis.

2.1 Visão Geral das Metodologias MADEM e MAAEM

A MADEM é uma metodologia para o desenvolvimento de artefatos de software reusáveis integrantes de uma família de aplicações multiagente. Uma família de aplicações é definida como um conjunto de aplicações de software similares que compartilham algumas características em comum e outras específicas [4]. Para a especificação do domínio de problema a ser resolvido, a MADEM orienta a realização da modelagem de objetivos, papéis, interações de entidades de uma organização e prototipação da interface com usuário. As entidades possuem conhecimento e o usam para exibir comportamento autônomo. Uma organização é composta de entidades com objetivos geral e específicos que estabelecem o que a organização pretende alcançar. A execução dos objetivos específicos permite alcançar o objetivo geral da organização. Por exemplo, um sistema de informação pode ter o objetivo "satisfazer as necessidades de informação de uma organização" e os objetivos específicos de "satisfazer as necessidades de informação dinâmica ou em longo prazo". Os objetivos específicos são alcançados através da execução de responsabilidades que as entidades têm para a execução de papéis com certo grau de autonomia [9].

Os papéis têm destrezas sobre uma ou um conjunto de técnicas que suportam a execução de responsabilidades. Pré-condições e pós-condições podem necessitar serem satisfeitas para ou após a execução de uma atividade. Conhecimento pode ser requerido e produzido na realização de uma responsabilidade. Por exemplo, uma entidade pode atuar como o papel "recuperador" com a responsabilidade de executar atividades para satisfazer as necessidades de informações dinâmicas de uma organização. Outra entidade pode atuar como o papel de "filtrador" com a responsabilidade de executar atividades para satisfazer as necessidades de informações em longo prazo das organizações. Destrezas podem ser, por exemplo, as regras da organização que as entidades conhecem para acessar e estruturar suas fontes de informação. Algumas vezes, as entidades têm que se comunicar com outras entidades internas ou externas para cooperar na execução de uma responsabilidade. Por exemplo, uma entidade atuando como o papel de "filtrador" pode necessitar interagir com um usuário (entidade externa) para observar seu comportamento e requisitar a inferência do seu perfil de interesses de informação.

A fase de Análise de Domínio aborda a construção de um Modelo de Domínio, no qual são especificados os requisitos atuais e futuros de uma família de aplicações em um determinado domínio, considerando o conhecimento do domínio e as experiências de desenvolvimento extraídas a partir de especialistas e de aplicações já desenvolvidas nesse domínio. Padrões de Análise também podem ser reusados nessa tarefa de modelagem. Na fase de Análise de Domínio são realizadas as seguintes tarefas: Modelagem de Conceitos, onde é realizada uma "tormenta de idéias" sobre os conceitos do domínio e seus relacionamentos; Modelagem de Objetivos, na qual são identificados e representados os objetivos de uma família de aplicações, as entidades externas com as quais coopera e as responsabilidades necessárias para alcançá-los; Modelagem de Papéis, onde são associadas as responsabilidades identificadas na tarefa de Modelagem de Objetivos aos papéis que serão encarregados delas; Modelagem de Variabilidades, onde são distinguidas as características comuns das variáveis em uma família de aplicações multiagente; Modelagem de Interações entre Papéis, onde é identificado como as entidades externas e internas cooperam para alcançar um objetivo específico e a Prototipação da Interface com o Usuário, cujo objetivo é identificar as interações dos usuários com o sistema e construir um protótipo da interface. O produto desta fase é um Modelo de Domínio. A fase de Projeto de Domínio aborda o projeto arquitetural e detalhado de frameworks multiagente provendo uma solução aos requisitos de uma família de aplicações multiagente especificadas em um Modelo de Domínio. Esta fase possui três subfases: Modelagem do Conhecimento da Sociedade Multiagente, a qual identifica e representa semanticamente os conceitos compartilhados por todos os agentes em sua comunicação; Projeto Arquitetural, que estabelece um modelo arquitetural da sociedade multiagente incluindo seus mecanismos de coordenação e cooperação; e o Projeto do Agente, que define o projeto interno de cada agente, modelando sua estrutura e comportamento.

A fase de Implementação do Domínio aborda o mapeamento de modelos de projeto para agentes, comportamentos e atos de comunicação envolvidos no framework JADE [1], o qual tem sido adotado como plataforma de implementação. Um Modelo de Implementação da Sociedade Multiagente é construído como produto desta fase da MADEM, composto de um Modelo de Comportamentos e de um Modelo de Atos de Comunicação. Um resumo das tarefas realizadas, dos insumos requeridos e dos produtos obtidos em cada fase de desenvolvimento de uma aplicação multiagente seguindo as diretrizes da metodologia MADEM é descrito na Tabela 1.

A MAAEM é uma metodologia para a análise, o projeto e a implementação de aplicações multiagente através da reutilização de artefatos de software anteriormente produzidos na Engenharia de Domínio Multiagente. Sendo inspirada no desenvolvimento baseado em componentes, ela envolve a seleção, adaptação e composição desses artefatos para a construção de uma aplicação. Na fase de análise dos requisitos pretende-se identificar e especificar os requisitos de uma determinada aplicação, partindo de modelos de domínio, elaborados na fase correspondente da Engenharia de Domínio Multiagente. Desse modo, a tarefa central do desenvolvedor é reusar um conjunto de requisitos da família em um domínio. Tais requisitos específicos da aplicação, quando provenientes da família, são levantados a partir da seleção dentre os requisitos comuns ou variáveis no domínio.

Na fase de Projeto da Aplicação o desenvolvedor irá reutilizar algumas soluções de projeto relacionadas a uma família de aplicações e adaptá-la aos requisitos específicos da aplicação em desenvolvimento. Essa fase consiste de três tarefas: Modelagem do Conhecimento da Sociedade Multiagente, a qual representa os conceitos compartilhados por todos os agentes em sua comunicação; o Projeto Arquitetural, que estabelece um modelo arquitetural da sociedade multiagente incluindo seus mecanismos de coordenação e cooperação; e o Projeto do Agente, que define o projeto interno de cada agente da sociedade, modelando sua estrutura de conhecimento e seus comportamentos.

Na fase de Implementação da Aplicação, os agentes são identificados a partir do modelo de atividades da fase anterior, sendo associado a cada uma de suas responsabilidades comportamentos em uma determinada linguagem/plataforma de desenvolvimento de agentes, como o JADE. São ainda identificadas as interações entre agentes presentes no modelo de interações entre agentes, sendo estas mapeadas para uma determinada linguagem de comunicação entre agentes, como a FIPA_ACL [6]. O reúso, se dá através da complementação do código gerado, para a qual o programador utiliza agentes de software anteriormente implementados na fase de Implementação do Domínio. A seleção dos agentes ocorre conforme a semelhança de comportamentos e comunicações. A adaptação torna-se necessária em função dos detalhes que diferem de uma aplicação para outra.

Tabela 1 - Fases, Insumos, Tarefas e Produtos da metodologia MADEM

Fases	Insumos		Tarefas	Produtos		
Análise de Domínio	Conhecimento de Especialistas, Literatura no Domínio, Aplicações de Software Existentes.		Modelagem de Conceitos	Modelo de Conceitos		Modelo de Domínio
Análise de Domínio	Requisitos da família de aplicações		Modelagem de Objetivos	Modelo de Objetivos		Modelo de Domínio
Análise de Domínio	Modelo de Objetivos		Modelagem de Papéis	Modelo de Papéis		Modelo de Domínio
Análise de Domínio	Modelo de Objetivos Modelo de Papéis		Modelagem de Interações entre Papéis	Modelo de Interações entre Papéis		Modelo de Domínio
Análise de Domínio	Modelo de Interações entre Papéis Modelo de Objetivos Modelo de Papéis		Prototipagem da Interface com o usuário	Protótipo da Interface com o usuário		Modelo de Domínio
Projeto de Domínio	Modelo de Conceitos Modelo de Papéis		Modelagem do Conhecimento da Sociedade Multiagente	Modelo do Conhecimento da Sociedade Multiagente		Modelo do Framework Multiagente
Projeto de Domínio	Modelo de Papéis	Modelagem Arquitetural	Modelagem da Sociedade de Agentes	Modelo da Sociedade Multiagente	Modelo Arquitetural	Modelo do Framework Multiagente
Projeto de Domínio	Modelo da Sociedade Multiagente	Modelagem Arquitetural	Modelagem das Interações entre Agentes	Modelo de Interações entre Agentes	Modelo Arquitetural	Modelo do Framework Multiagente
Projeto de Domínio	Modelo da Sociedade Multiagente Modelos de Estados dos Agentes	Modelagem Arquitetural	Modelagem das Atividades	Modelos de Atividades	Modelo Arquitetural	Modelo do Framework Multiagente
Projeto de Domínio	Modelo de Objetivos (Requisitos Não-Funcionais) Modelo da Sociedade Multiagente Modelo das Interações entre Agentes	Modelagem Arquitetural	Modelagem dos Mecanismos de Cooperação e Coordenação	Modelo dos Mecanismos de Cooperação e Coordenação	Modelo Arquitetural	Modelo do Framework Multiagente
Projeto de Domínio	Modelo de Interações entre Papéis Modelo do Conhecimento da Sociedade Multiagente	Projeto do Agente	Modelagem do Conhecimento do Agente	Modelos do Conhecimento do Agente	Modelos do Agente	Modelo do Framework Multiagente
Projeto de Domínio	Modelo da Sociedade Multiagente Modelo de Interações entre Agentes Modelos de Atividades	Projeto do Agente	Modelagem dos Estados dos Agentes	Modelos de Estados do Agente	Modelos do Agente	Modelo do Framework Multiagente
Implementação de Domínio	Modelos de Atividades		Modelagem de Comportamentos	Modelo de Comportamentos		Modelo de Implementação da Sociedade Multiagente
Implementação de Domínio	Modelo de Interações entre Agentes		Modelagem de Atos de Comunicação	Modelo de Atos de Comunicação		Modelo de Implementação da Sociedade Multiagente
Implementação de Domínio	Modelo de Comportamentos Modelo de Atos de Comunicação		Implementação dos Agentes	Agentes de Software Executáveis		
Extração e Representação de Padrões	Experiências de Desenvolvimento e outras fontes disponíveis		Extração e Representação de Padrões	Padrões de Sistema e de Software		

Um resumo das tarefas realizadas, dos insumos requeridos e dos produtos obtidos em cada fase de desenvolvimento de uma aplicação multiagente seguindo as diretrizes da metodologia MAAEM está descrito na Tabela 2. Nessa tabela, temos além dos insumos presentes na Tabela 1, os produtos desenvolvidos pela metodologia MADEM.

Tabela 2 - Fases, Insumos, Tarefas e Produtos da metodologia MAAEM

Fases	Insumos	Tarefas		Produtos		
Análise dos Requisitos da Aplicação	Modelo de Conceitos Conhecimento de Especialistas, Literatura no Domínio, Aplicações de Software Existentes		Modelagem de Conceitos	Modelo de Conceitos		Especificação da Aplicação
	Modelo de Objetivos Requisitos da família de aplicações		Modelagem de Objetivos	Modelo de Objetivos		
	Modelo de Papéis Modelo de Objetivos		Modelagem de Papéis	Modelo de Papéis		
	Modelo de Interações entre Papéis Modelo de Objetivos Modelo de Papéis		Modelagem de Interações entre Papéis	Modelo de Interações entre Papéis		
	Protótipo da Interface com o usuário Modelo de Papéis Modelo de Interações entre Papéis		Prototipagem da Interface com o usuário	Protótipo da Interface com o usuário		
Projeto da Aplicação	Modelo do Conhecimento da Sociedade Multiagente Modelo de Conceitos Modelo de Papéis		Modelagem do Conhecimento da Sociedade Multiagente	Modelo do Conhecimento da Sociedade Multiagente		Arquitetura da Aplicação
	Modelo da Sociedade Multiagente Modelo de Papéis	Modelagem Arquitetural	Modelagem da Sociedade de Agentes	Modelo da Sociedade Multiagente	Modelo Arquitetural	
	Modelo de Interações entre Agentes Modelo da Sociedade Multiagente		Modelagem das Interações entre Agentes	Modelo de Interações entre Agentes		
	Modelos de Atividades Modelo da Sociedade Multiagente Modelos de Estados		Modelagem das Atividades	Modelos de Atividades		
	Modelo dos Mecanismos de Cooperação e Coordenação Modelo de Objetivos (Requisitos Não-Funcionais) Modelo da Sociedade Multiagente Modelo das Interações entre Agentes		Modelagem dos Mecanismos de Cooperação e Coordenação	Modelo dos Mecanismos de Cooperação e Coordenação		
	Modelos do Conhecimento do Agente Modelo de Interações entre Papéis Modelo do Conhecimento da Sociedade Multiagente	Projeto do Agente	Modelagem do Conhecimento do Agente	Modelos do Conhecimento do Agente	Modelos do Agente	
	Modelos de Estados do Agente Modelo da Sociedade Multiagente Modelo de Interações entre Agentes Modelos de Atividades		Modelagem dos Estados dos Agentes	Modelos de Estados do Agente		
Implementação da Aplicação	Modelo de Comportamentos Modelos de Atividades		Modelagem de Comportamentos	Modelo de Comportamentos		Modelo da Aplicação Multiagente
	Modelo de Atos de Comunicação Modelo de Interações entre Agentes		Modelagem de Atos de Comunicação	Modelo de Atos de Comunicação		
	Agentes de Software Executáveis Modelo de Comportamentos Modelo de Atos de Comunicação		Implementação dos Agentes	Agentes de Software Executáveis		

2.2 A hierarquia de classes da ONTORMAS

A ONTORMAS é formada por um conjunto de classes organizadas hierarquicamente, tendo como superclasses principais: “Variable Concepts”, “Modeling Concepts”, “Modeling Tasks” e “Modeling Products”. A superclasse “Variable Concepts” e suas correspondentes subclasses são utilizadas para especificar a variabilidade de uma família de aplicações multiagente (Figura 1). Isso é realizado através da definição de

"Pontos de Variação" e de "Variantes". Um ponto de variação é a representação de um conceito sujeito a variação. Uma variante representa uma variação do conceito propriamente dito. Uma variante poderá representar um grupo de variações alternativas ou opcionais. A superclasse "Modeling Concepts" especifica os conceitos fundamentais de modelagem presentes nas metodologias MADEM e MAAEM (Figura 1). Esses conceitos são básicos para o desenvolvimento de sistemas multiagente e estão especificados em níveis de abstração indo do nível mais abstrato (Fase de Análise dos Requisitos da Aplicação) ao mais concreto (Fase de Implementação). Os conceitos de modelagem podem ter entre si a relação de sinonímia, generalização ou especialização. Na ONTORMAS também podem ser representados conceitos específicos de uma plataforma de implementação de agentes, como o JADE, para possibilitar a geração automática de código.

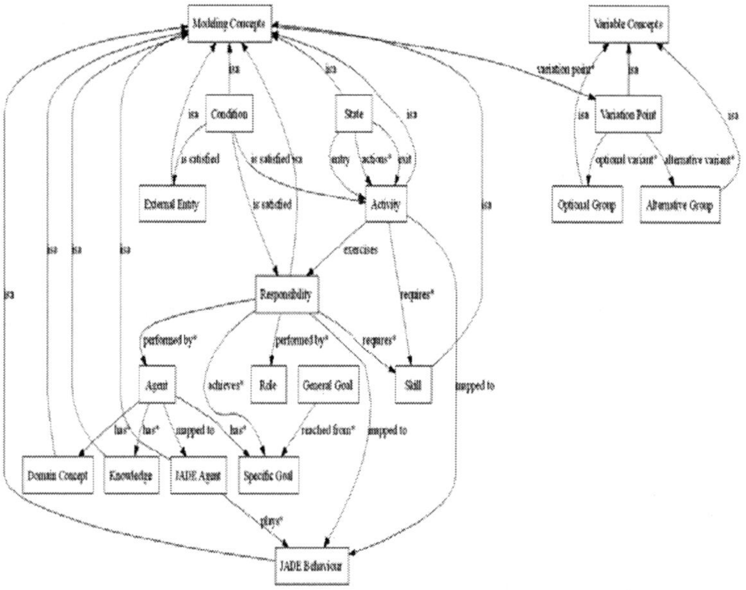

Fig. 1. Rede semântica com os principais conceitos de modelagem especificados pelas metodologias MADEM e MAAEM

Na superclasse "Modeling Tasks" e em suas correspondentes subclasses são definidas as tarefas de modelagem especificadas pelas metodologias MADEM e MAAEM. A figura 2 ilustra a representação das tarefas realizadas na fase de Análise de Domínio e na de Análise dos Requisitos da Aplicação. Essas tarefas são divididas em "Domain Engineering Tasks", cujas subtarefas são relacionadas à metodologia MADEM e "Application Engineering Tasks", relacionadas à metodologia MAAEM. Na superclasse "Modeling Products" estão definidas as classes que representam os possíveis produtos de modelagem produzidos através das metodologias MADEM e MAAEM. Alguns destes produtos como "Domain Model" são compostos por subprodutos, isso é especificado através do relacionamento "subproducts". Na figura

3 são ilustradas classes e instâncias do Modelo de Objetivo de ambas as metodologias.

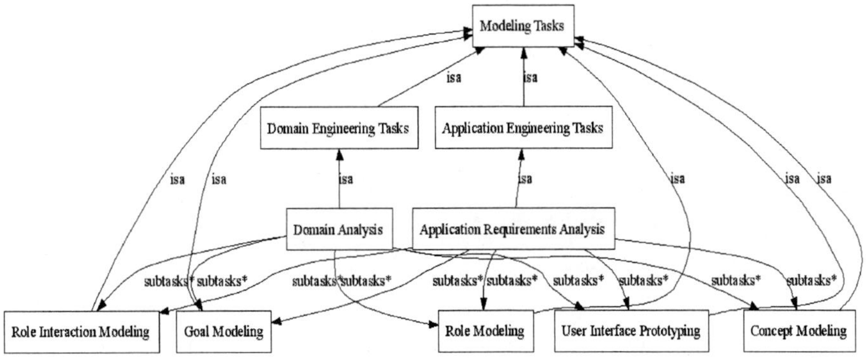

Fig. 2. Rede semântica das tarefas e subtarefas referentes à fase de Análise das metodologias MADEM e MAAEM

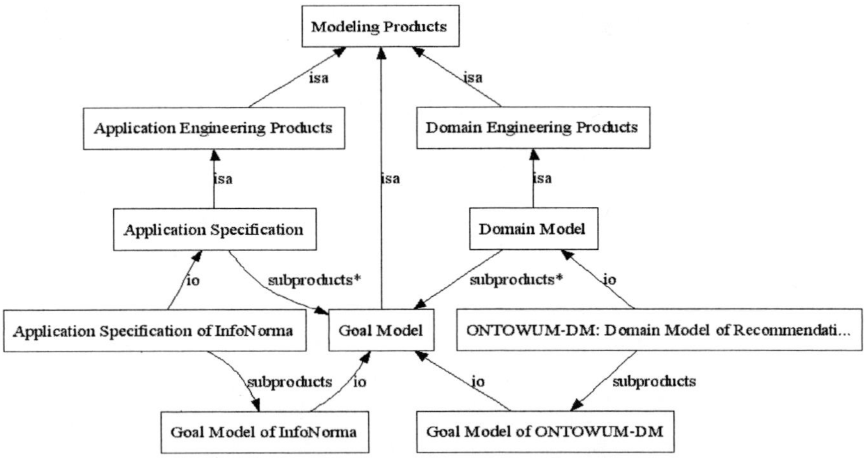

Fig. 3. Rede semântica exemplificando o relacionamento entre classes e instâncias de produtos presentes nas metodologias MADEM e MAAEM

A aplicação das metodologias MADEM e MAAEM e os produtos das mesmas são obtidos através da instanciação dos correspondentes conceitos na hierarquia de classes da ONTORMAS. A notação gráfica utilizada em todos os produtos presentes na ONTORMAS tem sido especificada nas metodologias MADEM e MAAEM, onde cada conceito possui uma representação gráfica particular. A Figura 4 ilustra a criação do modelo de domínio ONTOWUM-DM e seus respectivos subprodutos. ONTOWUM-DM [10] descreve os requisitos comuns e variáveis de uma família de aplicações multiagente para fornecer recomendações personalizadas através da Mineração de Uso. Na ONTORMAS, para criar um Modelo de Domínio é necessário a instanciação das classes que especificam suas tarefas de modelagem ("Concept Modeling", "Goal Modeling", "Role Modeling", "Role Interaction Modeling" e "User Interface Prototyping") e das que especificam os seus subprodutos ("Concept Model", "Goal Model", "Role Model", "Role Interaction Models" e "Prototype of the User Interface"). Uma vez que o Modelo de Domínio e seus respectivos subprodutos estejam instanciados, tornam-se parte da base de conhecimento da ONTORMAS, sendo então utilizados em consultas e inferências através de raciocínio lógico, facilitando o seu reúso.

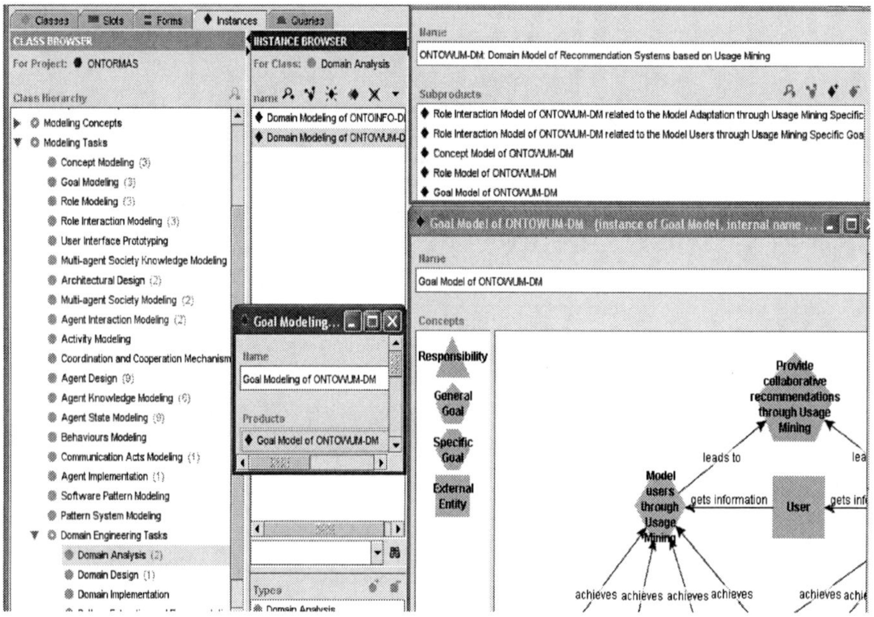

Fig. 4. Processo de Instanciação da ONTORMAS para criação de um Modelo de Domínio

2.3 O suporte à Engenharia de Domínio Multiagente

Na ONTORMAS são desenvolvidos artefatos de software multiagente com alto nível de abstração destinados ao reúso. Uma das atividades centrais no desenvolvimento desses tipos de artefatos é a modelagem de variabilidades, onde são definidas as características comuns e variáveis em uma família de aplicações multiagente.

A metodologia MADEM e a ferramenta ONTORMAS foram utilizadas para a modelagem de ONTOSERS-DM, um modelo de domínio que especifica os requisitos comuns e variáveis de uma família de Sistemas de Recomendações, baseados na tecnologia da Web Semântica, utilizando as seguintes abordagens de filtragem de informação: Filtragem Baseada no Conteúdo (FBC), Filtragem Colaborativa (FC) e Filtragem Híbrida (FH) [18]. No Modelo de Objetivos do ONTORSERS-DM (Figura

5) é especificado o objetivo geral da família de sistemas: "Provide recommendations using Semantic Web Technologies". Para alcançar esse objetivo geral são definidos três objetivos específicos: "Model Users", "Filter Information" e "Deliver recommendations" e as responsabilidades que precisam ser exercidas para alcançá-los. O modelo de objetivos (Figura 5) do ONTOSERS-DM tem no primeiro nível o objetivo geral, no segundo, a entidade externa, no terceiro, os objetivos específicos e, no último nível, as responsabilidades. Em um modelo de objetivos, o objetivo geral está sempre presente em todas as aplicações de uma família de aplicações multiagente. Os conceitos objetivo específico, entidade externa e responsabilidade podem possuir instâncias variáveis. Para esses conceitos é realizada a modelagem de variabilidades, onde são identificados os pontos de variação e classificadas as variantes em alternativas ou opcionais.

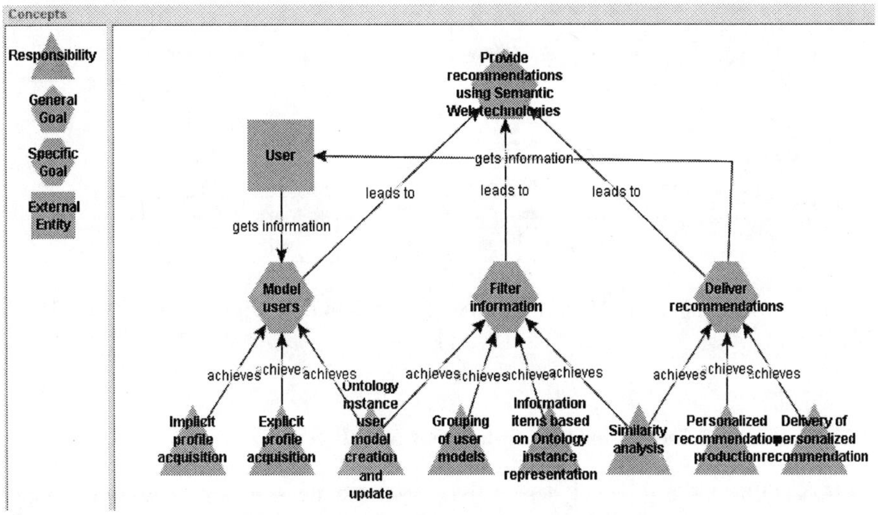

Fig. 5. Modelo de Objetivos do ONTOSERS-DM

Na Modelagem de Variabilidades do Modelo de Objetivos da ONTOSERS-DM (Figura 6), o objetivo específico "Model Users" tem como ponto de variação grupos de responsabilidades alternativas para a aquisição do perfil de usuário, sendo possível à escolha entre três variantes: "Implicit profile acquisition", "Explicit profile acquisition" ou os dois tipos de aquisição de perfis. A última responsabilidade "Ontology instance user model creation and update" é fixa, pois será requerida por todas as aplicações da família. O objetivo específico "Filter Information" possui um ponto de variação que tem como variantes alternativas a responsabilidade "Grouping of user models" que ocorre em sistemas que utilizam a FC e a responsabilidade "Information items based on Ontology instance representation" naqueles que utilizam a FBC. O objetivo específico "Deliver recommendations" não possui pontos de variação, pois as responsabilidades "Similarity analysis", "Personalized recommendation production" e "Delivery of personalized recommendation" são requeridas em todas as aplicações da família, sendo então parte fixa do modelo de objetivos.

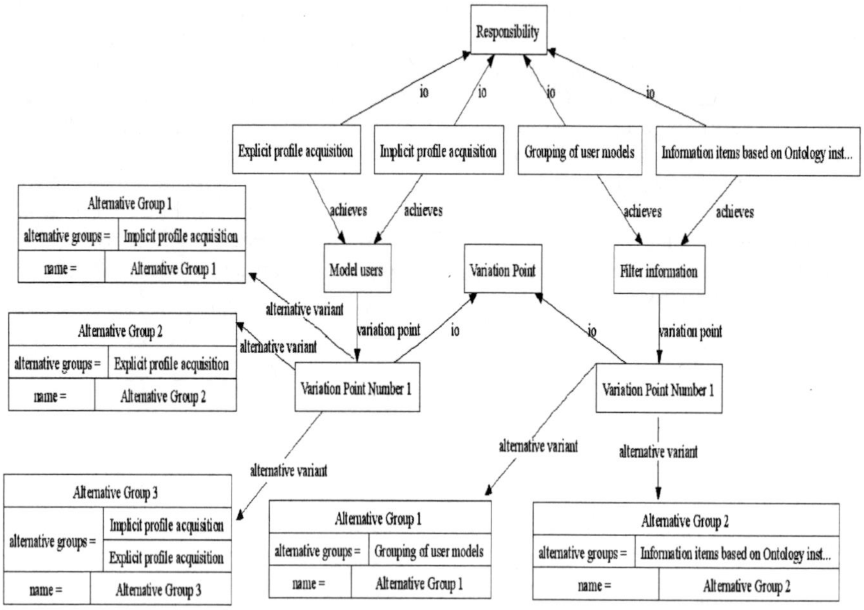

Fig. 6. Modelagem de Variabilidades do Modelo de Objetivos do ONTOSERS-DM

2.4 O suporte à Engenharia de Aplicações Multiagente

Na ONTORMAS é possível desenvolver artefatos de software reusando produtos genéricos desenvolvidos pela Engenharia de Domínio Multiagente através da seleção, adaptação e integração desses artefatos. A seleção é feita através de mecanismos de recuperação, onde o usuário faz uma consulta especificando as características do produto a ser reusado e obtém como retorno os artefatos disponíveis no repositório que satisfazem essa consulta. Após a seleção do artefato que mais se aproxime a sua necessidade, o usuário deverá verificar se este pode ser reusado integralmente ou se necessita realizar adaptações ou integrá-lo com outros artefatos.

Na ONTORMAS há três formas de recuperação de artefatos para o reúso: recuperação simples por palavras-chave, recuperação avançada através da Algernon Tab do Protégé ou por busca exploratória, através da hierarquia das correspondentes subclasses de "Modeling Products". Para fazer a recuperação por palavras-chave devem ser especificados na consulta os termos e em qual classe e slot esses termos possivelmente se encontrem. Na figura 7, é ilustrado um exemplo de uma busca por um objetivo específico relacionado a recomendações colaborativas através da mineração. A busca foi feita usando os termos "recommendation", "mining", "collaborative" na propriedade "name" e na classe "General Goal" tendo o obtido como resultado "Provide collaborative recommendations through Usage Mining".

Uma consulta avançada é expressa através da Algernon Tab (Figura 8). No exemplo, o objetivo da consulta é encontrar um padrão arquitetural que permita a representação da arquitetura multiagente em diferentes níveis de abstração. A consulta foi feita pelos termos "multi-agent" e "abstraction level" nos slots "context" e "problem" em instâncias da classe "Architectural Pattern", tendo como resultado o padrão arquitetural em camadas "Multi-agent Layer".

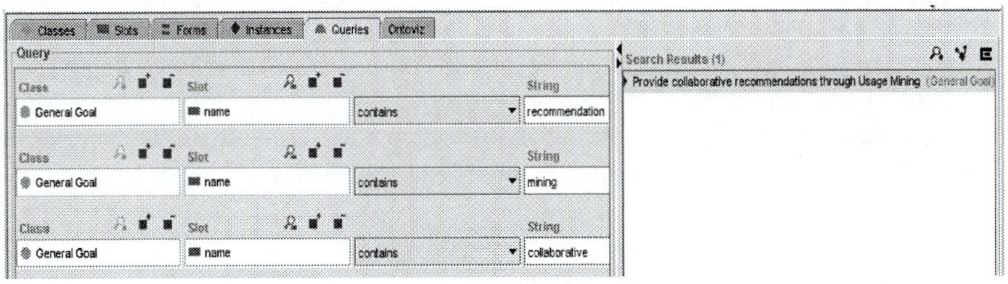

Fig. 7. Consulta simples por palavras-chave

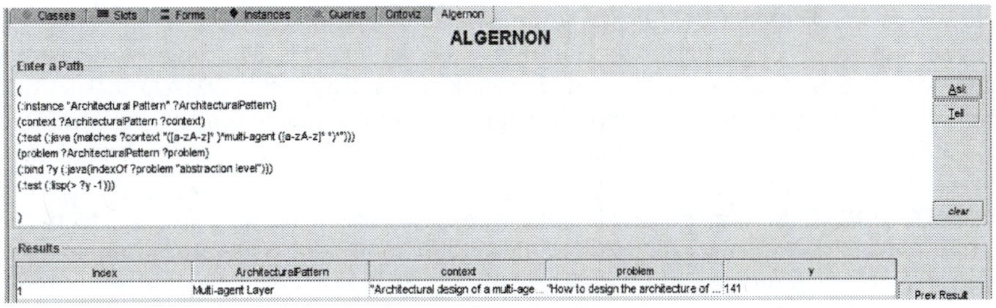

Fig. 8. Consulta avançada através do Algermon Tab

3 Trabalhos Relacionados

O processo de desenvolvimento de software é facilitado através do uso de ferramentas que permitam guiar e automatizar tarefas. Para o desenvolvimento de sistemas multiagente, já existem algumas ferramentas que auxiliam uma ou mais etapas do ciclo de vida de desenvolvimento desse tipo de sistemas [1][2][3][9][14].

A ferramenta TAOM4E "Tool for Agent Oriented Modeling" [2], um plug-in para a plataforma Eclipse, suporta as fases de análise e projeto da metodologia para desenvolvimento de agentes TROPOS [2]. Essa ferramenta, por sua integração com a plataforma JADE, permite testar os comportamentos dos agentes e, a partir de seus modelos da fase de projeto, gerar um esqueleto de código nessa plataforma. A metodologia PASSI "Process for Agent Societies Specification and Implementation" [3] é suportada pela ferramenta PTK (PASSI Toolkit) [3], um Add-in para a ferramenta CASE baseada em UML Rational Rose. A PTK possibilita o desenvolvimento dos cinco diagramas definidos pela PASSI, sendo alguns deles modelados manualmente pelo desenvolvedor, uns gerados automaticamente pela ferramenta e outros parcialmente gerados pela ferramenta e completados pelo desenvolvedor. Ela também possibilita a geração de grande parte do código a partir dos diagramas modelados. As principais características distintivas da ONTORMAS em relação às outras ferramentas existentes são:

- Suporte ao desenvolvimento de software multiagente com base no reúso, através da integração de conceitos da Engenharia de Domínio e da Engenharia de Aplicação.
- Por ser dirigida por ontologias, possui forte estruturação semântica, aumentando consideravelmente a precisão dos resultados do processo de seleção de artefatos reutilizáveis através de inferências semânticas.
- Integração com o editor de ontologias Protégé, a plataforma de implementação de agentes JADE e a linguagem de comunicação de agentes FIPA_ACL.

4 Conclusões e Trabalhos Futuros

Este artigo apresentou ONTORMAS, uma ferramenta dirigida por ontologias que oferece suporte a Engenharia de Domínio e de Aplicações Multiagente de forma integrada. A ONTORMAS é uma evolução da ferramenta ONTOMADEM [9] que apenas suportava o desenvolvimento de artefatos para a Engenharia de Domínio. Tem sido utilizada tanto no desenvolvimento de famílias de aplicações destinadas ao reúso [10] [18] quanto de aplicações individuais [5].

A ONTORMAS faz parte de um projeto para a melhoria das técnicas, metodologias e ferramentas de apoio ao desenvolvimento de sistemas multiagente. A partir da base de conhecimento fornecida pela ONTORMAS está sendo desenvolvido um sistema especialista, cujos principais objetivos são automatizar várias das tarefas especificadas pelas metodologias, melhorias na interação com o usuário-desenvolvedor e geração parcial de código.

A ferramenta ONTORMAS suporta atualmente o reúso composicional, baseado na seleção, adaptação e composição de artefatos. Uma abordagem gerativa [4] para o reúso tem sido explorada com a especificação da metodologia GENMADEM e da ferramenta ONTOGENMADEM [14]. GENMADEM fornece suporte para criação de Linguagens Específicas de Domínio a serem utilizadas na construção de aplicações específicas em um determinado domínio de problema. Como trabalho futuro, espera-se estender a ONTORMAS a partir da ONTOGENMADEM de forma a fornecer auxílio para o reúso gerativo na Engenharia de Aplicações Multiagente.

Referências

1. Bellifemine, F., Caire, G., Poggi, A., Rimassa, G.b.: JADE A White Paper. Exp v. 3 n. 3, Sept., (2003). http://jade.tilab.com/
2. Bertolini, D., Novikau, A., Susi, A., Perini A.: TAOM4E: an Eclipse ready tool for Agent-Oriented Modeling. Issue on the development process. Technical report, ITC-irst, (2006).

3. Cossentino, M., Potts, C.: A CASE tool supported methodology for the design of multi-agent systems. In: The 2002 International Conference on Software Engineering Research and Practice (SERP'02). June 24-27, Las Vegas (NV), USA.
4. Czarnecki, K., Eisenecker, U. W.: Generative Programming: Methods, Tools, and Applications. ACM Press/Addison-Wesley Publishing Co., New York, NY, (2000).
5. Drumond, L., Girardi, R., Lindoso A., L. Marinho.: "A Semantic Web Based Recommender System for the Legal Domain". Proc. of the European Conference on Artificial Intelligence (ECAI 2006) Workshop on Recommender Systems, pp. 81-83, Riva del Garda, Itália, (2006).
6. FIPA. ACL Message Structure Specification. Disponível em: <http://www.fipa.org/specs/fipa00061/SC00061G.html>. Acessado em: 30 Agosto 2007.
7. Gennari J. et al.: "The evolution of Protégé: An environment for knowledge-based systems development", tech. report SMI-2002-0943, (2002).
8. Girardi R., Lindoso A.: An Ontology-based Methodology for Multi-agent Domain Engineering, In: 3rd Workshop on Multi-Agent Systems: Theory and Applications (MASTA 2005) at 12th Portuguese Conference on Artificial Intelligence (EPIA 2005), Ed. IEEE, pp. 321-324. Covilhã, Portugal. December 05-08, (2005).
9. Girardi, R., Leite, A.: ONTOMADEM: An Ontology-driven Tool for Multi-Agent Domain Engineering, Proceedings of The Nineteenth International Conference on Software Engineering and Knowledge Engineering, Ed. Knowledge Systems Institute, pp. 559-564. July, (2007).
10. Girardi, R., Marinho, L.: A Domain Model of Web Recommender Systems based on Usage Mining and Collaborative Filtering, Requirements Engineering Journal, vol.12 n. 1, Ed. Springer-Verlag, pp. 23-40. London, (2007).
11. Girardi, R., Lindoso, A.: "An Ontology-based Knowledge Base for the Representation and Reuse of Software Patterns". ACM Software Engineering Notes, v. 31, n. 1, pp. 1-6. New York, (2006).
12. Girardi, R., Serra, I.: Using Ontologies for the Specification of Domain-Specific Languages in Multi-Agent Domain Engineering. Proceedings of the Sixth International Bi-Conference Workshop on Agent-oriented Information Systems (AOIS-2004) at The 16th International Conference on Advanced Information Systems Engineering (CAISE'04), Ed. Janis Grundspenkis and Marite Kirikova (Eds.), pp. 295-308. Riga, Latvia. June 07 -11, (2004).
13. Gruber, T. R.: "Toward Principles for the Design of Ontologies used for Knowledge Sharing", International Journal of Human-Computer Studies. Nº 43, pp. 907-928. 1995.
14. Jansen, M., Girardi, R.: GENMADEM: A Methodology for Generative Multi-agent Domain Engineering. In: The 9th International Conference on Software Reuse, 2006, Torino. Proceedings of the 9th International Conference on Software Reuse, Lecture Notes in Computer Science (LNCS), v. 4039, p. 399-402. Berlin: Springer-Verlag, (2006).
15. Lindoso, A.: Uma Metodologia Baseada em Ontologia para a Engenharia de Aplicações Multiagente. Dissertação de Mestrado. São Luís, (2006).
16. Lindoso, A., Girardi, R.: An Ontology-based technique for Framework and Pattern Reuse in Multi-agent Application Engineering, In: First Workshop on Software Engineering for Agent-oriented Systems (SEAS 2005), 19º Brazilian Symposium on Software Engineering (XIX SBES). Uberlândia, Minas Gerais, Brazil. Oct., (2005).
17. Lindoso, A., Girardi, R. The SRAMO Technique for Analysis and Reuse of Requirements in Multi-agent Application Engineering. IX Workshop on Requirements Engineering, Cadernos do IME, UERJ Press, v. 20, pp. 41-50. Rio de Janeiro, (2006).
18. Mariano, R., Girardi, R., Leite, A., Drumond, L.: Um Modelo de Domínio de Sistemas de Recomendações Baseado na Tecnologia da Web Semântica. (Artigo Submetido).
19. Russell, S., Norvig, P.: Artificial Intelligence: A Modern Approach. Prentice Hall, Englewood Cliffs, NJ, second edition, (2002).

Balanceando entre a sensibilidade à riqueza do campo e a praticidade do *design* de software

Genésio Cruz Neto[1], Alex SandroGomes[2], Jaelson Castro[2]

[1]Faculdade Integrada do Recife, Recife PE, Brasil, 50720-635

[2]Universidade Federal de Pernambuco, CIN, Recife PE , Brasil, 50732-970
genesio@fir.br, asg@cin.ufpe.br, jbc@cin.ufpe.br

Resumo. Abordagens etnometodológicas de estudos qualitativos do usuário propiciam uma descrição detalhada das práticas humanas, no entanto, o caráter retórico enfatizado pelas mesmas dificulta a integração com o *design* de software. Por outro lado, a argumentação contrária ao uso dos atuais métodos oferecidos por *designers* é a perda da sensibilidade aos dados do campo devido a análise ser "direcionada" por *frameworks* e modelos cognitivos (orientados a objetivos e processos). O presente artigo apresenta uma solução balanceada que usa o processo indutivo de análise de dados da *Grounded Theory* para construção de representações sociais baseadas na Teoria da Atividade e na técnica i*. Entre outros pontos, o trabalho apresenta como os aspectos não funcionais dos modelos i* podem ser elicitados a partir da incorporação de recentes re-formulações de conceitos da Teoria da Atividade e de atributos não funcionais qualitativos associados às ações humanas.

Palavras Chaves: Engenharia de Requisitos, Pesquisa Qualitativa, Teoria da Atividade, Modelagem Organizacional

1 Introdução

Teoria da Atividade [1],[2],[3] é um *framework* pós-cognitivista considerado como um possível ponto de partida para soluções que venham a promover um melhor balanceamento entre as abordagens etnometodológicas [4],[5] e as orientadas pelo *design* [6],[7]. No entanto, as atuais tentativas de operacionalização deste referencial ainda oferecem limitações que dificultam sua ampla utilização devido a dificuldades na manipulação de seus conceitos [3] e pela falta de integração com modelos e processos de Engenharia de Requisitos [8].

Na área de Engenharia de Requisitos, destaca-se atualmente a técnica i* ("i estrela") [9] que está há um passo a frente dos atuais modelos cognitivos por incorporar aspectos intencionais e de dependências sociais estratégicas aos elementos processuais dos sistemas de informações. No entanto, as metodologias atuais baseadas em i* [10] geralmente não tratam o problema de como os modelos iniciais são originados. Trabalhos recentes procuram abordar esta lacuna utilizando análises sociais baseadas em modelos cognitivos [11].

Neste contexto de integração de estudos de campo no *design*, um ponto importante é como garantir um processo qualitativo "valido" para obtenção de modelos que representem as práticas humanas observadas. Trabalhos que dão mais ênfase a estas questões metodológicas são encontrados em pesquisas qualitativas que se utilizam da *Grounded Theory* [12], um método indutivo para geração de teorias (ou explanações) sobre os fenômenos a partir de uma análise sistemática dos dados empíricos.

A solução advogada pelos autores para a realização e documentação de estudos sociais de campo voltados à elicitação de requisitos de sistemas baseia-se em um processo de pesquisa qualitativa que integra o uso de *Grounded Theory* [12], Teoria da Atividade [1],[2] e a Técnica i* [9]. O processo centra-se em um método sensível à riqueza dos dados para construção de representações válidas de práticas humanas que favoreçam tanto uma visão rica do papel da tecnologia, como sejam úteis para realização de análises transformacionais próprias do *design* de software.

Em recente publicação dois dos autores deste artigo apresentam como aliar o uso de *Grounded Theory* e da Teoria da Atividade para o melhor entendimento de práticas humanas [13]. O presente trabalho apresenta um versão mais atual deste processo que inclui a geração de modelos i* de *design* a partir deste entendimento. Entre outros pontos, é discutido como os aspectos não funcionais dos modelos i* (objetivos-soft) podem ser elicitados a partir da incorporação de re-formulações de conceitos da Teoria da Atividade e de atributos não funcionais qualitativos [14] associados às ações humanas.

O artigo está estruturado da seguinte forma: a seções 2 apresenta a Teoria da Atividade e o *framework* analítico baseado na mesma que é utilizado na abordagem proposta. O processo qualitativo que concilia o uso da *Grounded Theory*, da Teoria da Atividade e da técnica i* é apresentado na seqüência (seção 3). A seção 4, por sua vez, é dedicada a como os modelos i* são construídos a partir do entendimento das práticas humanas, com um foco especial na elicitação dos aspectos não funcionais. Uma discussão sobre a solução proposta em comparação com trabalhos relacionados é discorrida na seção 5. A última seção é reservada para algumas conclusões e diretivas de trabalhos futuros.

2 *Framework* Analítico baseado na Teoria da Atividade

Teoria da Atividade [1] é um referencial teórico que ajuda o pesquisador de campo a direcionar o foco de suas observações e análises, transformando um processo etnográfico aparentemente intuitivo e empírico, em um trabalho guiado por reflexões objetivas e sistemáticas [15]. Teoria da Atividade propicia o entendimento da estrutura, desenvolvimento e contexto social das atividades humanas através de um conjunto de princípios básicos [1] que são descritos a seguir (ver [3]).

1. Orientação a um Objeto: toda atividade é realizada por um sujeito em direção a um objeto, onde transformações mútuas ocorrem de cada lado.
2. Mediação: toda relação dos seres humanos com os objetos ao redor é mediada por ferramentas, podendo estas serem externas ou presentes na mente do sujeito. Ferramentas de mediação são usadas na transformação dos objetos, e evoluem com o tempo durante a prática da atividade.

3. Estrutura Hierárquica da Atividade: estabelece que a relação dos seres humanos com os objetos do mundo ocorre de forma hierárquica. Esta relação vai de um nível mais alto, associado à intencionalidade e motivações pessoais (nível de atividade), passando pelas as ações e sub-ações observáveis orientadas a um determinado objetivo consciente (nível intermediário de ação), chegando, por fim, as operações realizadas inconscientemente pelos sujeitos como respostas a certas condições do ambiente (nível de operação).
4. Desenvolvimento: a análise de qualquer tipo de fenômeno deve levar em consideração o contexto histórico. Todas as práticas são um resultado da resolução de contradições[1] ocorridas durante o desenvolvimento das mesmas.
5. Internalização-Externalização: internalizarão significa apropriação, por parte do sujeito, das informações do contexto social em que a pessoa está inserida. Já a externalização é o processo inverso, verificada através de como ações humanas transformam o ambiente ao seu redor. Esse processo é dialético e contínuo.

Através destes princípios, a Teoria da Atividade desperta o pesquisador para compreender a tecnologia como parte mediadora de um largo escopo de interações humano-mundo, onde estas interações envolvem motivações, ações, operações, internalizações, contradições, entre outros aspectos [3].

Desde a década de 90, inúmeros trabalhos têm demonstrado as vantagens do uso destes princípios para o *design* de software [3]. No entanto, as atuais tentativas de operacionalização deste referencial teórico, a maioria baseada no modelo de atividades de Engström [2], ainda apresentam restrições devido ao modelo citado muitas vezes dificultar um entendimento sobre questões associadas à intencionalidade [3],[13],[16], e devido a ausência de trabalhos que derivem modelos de *design* a partir das descrições de atividades [8] Outro ponto é que o uso dos diagramas de Engström pode induzir o *designer* à tentação de adotar as conceituações da estrutura e usá-las relativamente sem reflexão aos dados empíricos [15].

Objetivando trabalhar melhor questões associadas à intencionalidade e ao uso de múltiplos motivos, autores deste trabalho utilizaram-se de recentes re-formulações de conceitos da Teoria da Atividade para propor um *framework* analítico e novas formas de representação [13]. A representação mostrada na Figura 1 é usada para descrever graficamente as atividades. Ela utiliza-se do recente conceito de engajamento [16] e incorpora o uso de múltiplos motivos [3]. Segundo Gonzáles, Nardi e Mark (2007) um engajamento[2] *é "uma agregação de ações tematicamente conectadas, direcionadas a um propósito específico, e moldada por uma atividade orientada a um motivo".*

[1] Contradições são tensões ou problemas que impedem ou dificultam a evolução das atividades.

[2] Os autores do termo têm preferido atualmente usar a nomenclatura "essemble" para designar o mesmo conceito, que inicialmente foi publicado com o nome "engajamento" [3].

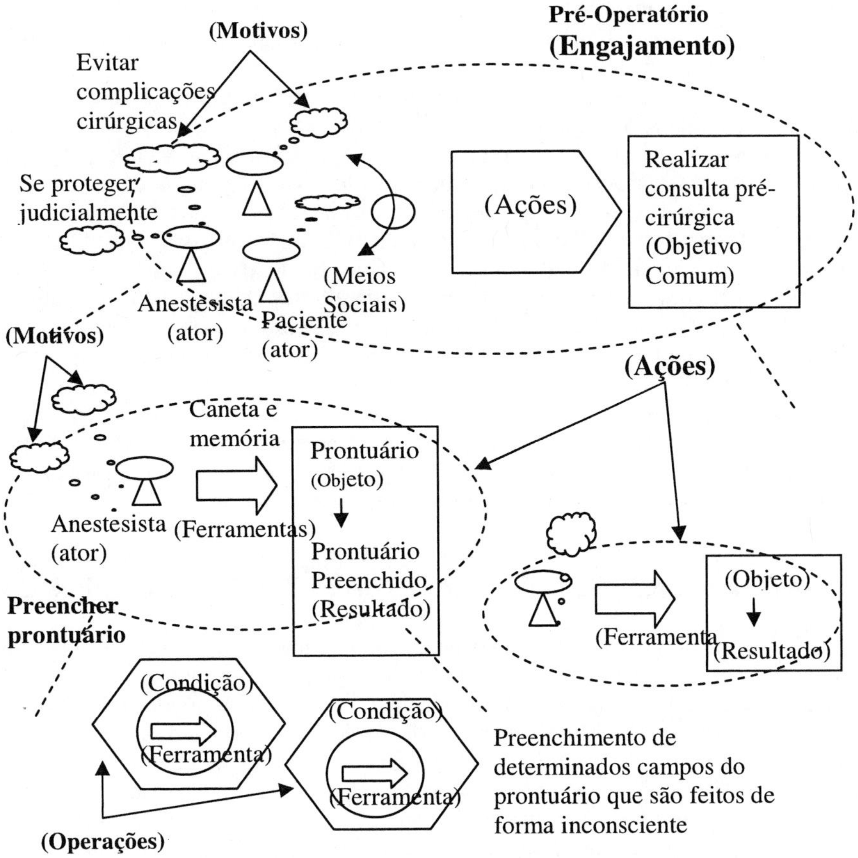

Fig. 1: Representação para as atividades humanas

A Figura 1 apresenta os conceitos usados da Teoria da Atividade aliados a descrição de um exemplo de uso de cada conceito oriundos do contexto de uso de prontuários de paciente por parte de profissionais de anestesia. A mesma descreve que um engajamento, tal como uma consulta pré-cirúrgica, é constituído por vários sujeitos (anestesista, paciente, enfermeira, etc.) que, através de meios sociais (divisão do trabalho, regras, mecanismos de coordenação, etc), realizam ações com um objetivo comum de realizar a consulta pré-anestésica.

Cada sujeito possui um ou vários motivos que são as razões pelas quais os engajamentos e ações são realizados. No exemplo usado, um anestesista possui entre outros motivos, os de "evitar complicações cirúrgicas" e o de "se proteger judicialmente". As ações são compostas por sujeitos que buscam transformar um objeto em um resultado mediado por ferramentas. O exemplo de ação descrita foi a de "preencher o prontuário". As ações podem ser sub-divididas em sub-ações até se chegar ao nível das operações, quando as mesmas já não são realizadas de forma consciente. Tais operações possuem associadas a ela a condição de sua realização, bem como a ferramenta envolvida na operação. Como exemplo de operação citado foi descrito o processo de "preenchimento de alguns campos do formulário" que é realizado sem que o anestesista objetive mentalmente esta tarefa.

Além das representações de atividades apresentadas, o *framework* analítico [13] enumera um conjunto de fatores contextuais pré-definidos *a* partir de uma compilação de trabalhos em análises de contexto de uso [7], teoria da atividade [1][2][3] e análises de dependências sociais [9] de modo a oferecer um guia para a observação e análise dos dados de campo. Tais fatores são agrupados em 6 dimensões de análise: sujeitos, ambientes físicos, motivos, engajamentos, ações e operações. Destaca-se aqui a inclusão também de atributos não funcionais qualitativos definidos pela norma ISO 9126 [14] como parte destes fatores para facilitar a elicitação dos aspectos não funcionais presentes nas atividades humanas. Tais fatores contextuais, no entanto, não são rígidos. Novos fatores podem ser identificados nos dados e classificados em um dos 6 níveis de análise.

Contudo, sabe-se o risco associado ao uso de referenciais teóricos é sempre deixar que os construtores "ceguem" a observação e a análise social, tornando o processo menos sensível a riqueza dos dados [15], [17]. Na próxima seção é demonstrado como o uso da *Grounded Theory* pode auxiliar a evitar que isto ocorra.

3 Processo que integra *Grounded Theory*,Teoria da Atividade e i*

A abordagem proposta neste trabalho para integração de estudos de campo qualitativos na Engenharia de Requisitos está centrada em um balanceamento entre uma postura sensível à riqueza dos dados, e um método útil à atividade de *design*. A solução pode ser descrita como uma metodologia com três elementos centrais:

1. Um processo indutivo de pesquisa qualitativa baseado nas etapas da *Grounded Theory* [12] para construção de representações sobre as práticas humanas que sejam baseadas na análise dos dados e validadas através do uso de princípios de pesquisa qualitativa interpretativa.
2. Uso do *framework* analítico apresentado na seção 2.
3. Guias para geração de modelos i* [9] de dependências sociais estratégicas a partir das descrições de atividades de modo a propiciar, além de uma visão do contexto social de um diferente ponto de vista, análises transformacionais que atendem as demandas dos engenheiros de software.

Como resultado de todo o processo qualitativo proposto temos um documento com descrições gerais das práticas que incluem representações de atividades e modelos i*. Tais gráficos são contextualizados no relatório através de uma narrativa que descreve uma estória central do estudo realizado, citando as categorias, representações e modelos construídos a partir dos dados empíricos. Desta forma, pretende-se gerar um artefato com uma descrição do contexto social que seja, tanto rica e detalhada para um melhor entendimento das práticas humanas, como útil para a natureza criativa da atividade de *design* de software.

1.1 Etapas da análise indutiva de dados

A idéia básica da *Grounded Theory* é ler (e re-ler) um banco de dados textuais (tais como, notas de observações de campo e/ou transcrições de entrevistas) para "descobrir" ou criar variáveis (chamadas categorias, conceitos e propriedades) que descrevem os fenômenos e seus relacionamentos.

O processo é composto das etapas de coleta de dados, codificação aberta, uso do *framework* analítico, geração de modelos i* e documentação dos resultados. A figura 2 apresenta graficamente as etapas, onde o fluxo das mesmas é mostrado de baixo para cima para enfatizar que as categorias, representações, modelos e documentação final vão sendo construídos a partir de uma análise indutiva.

Tais etapas seguem basicamente as fases de codificação aberta, codificação axial e codificação seletiva da *Grounded Theory*, com a diferença que a etapa de codificação axial é sub-dividida entre as etapas de uso do *framework* analítico (etapa 3) e geração dos modelos i* (etapa 4). Assim como na *Grounded Theory*, as etapas do processo não ocorrem de forma linear, ou seja, podem ocorrer ciclos para re-leitura dos dados e re-codificações durante qualquer etapa. Segue descrição de cada uma:

1. **Coleta de dados:** uso de diversos métodos para coleta dos dados de campo. A *Grounded Theory*, bem como o processo proposto, concentra-se firmemente na interpretação dos dados não importando como estes foram coletados [12]. As decisões sobre os dados a serem integrados e os métodos de coleta a serem utilizados baseiam-se na situação em mãos no momento.
2. **Codificação aberta**: referente à atribuição de conceitos livres para o fenômeno de interesse, onde esses conceitos significam idéias que emergem do texto. Essencialmente cada linha, sentença e parágrafo do texto é lida na busca de se responder uma questão central "*O que estas informações querem dizer?*", ou seja, o que está sendo tratado ou referenciado no texto e que explicações podemos dar daquilo [12]. Com isto, desperta-se no pesquisador a sensibilidade na busca do "novo" nos dados de modo a evitar que os construtores dos referenciais teóricos direcionem a análise inicial.
3. **Uso do *framework* analítico**: a segunda etapa utiliza o *framework* analítico citado para guiar o processo de criar relacionamentos e associações entre as conceituações livres realizadas durante a codificação aberta. Caso alguma categoria não se encaixe nos fatores pré-determinados, novos fatores podem ser associados ao *framework* analítico de modo a torná-lo flexível e não venha a dificultar o entendimento de situações inusitadas. Nesta etapa também são geradas, em paralelo, as representações gráficas que especificam as atividades.
4. **Geração dos modelos i*:** um conjunto de diretrizes de mapeamento são usadas para analisar as categorias e representações de atividades geradas visando a construção dos modelos i* do contexto social. Novas categorias neste instante podem ser criadas para nomear os elementos do modelo i* presentes nos dados. Mais informações na seção 4.
5. **Documentação dos resultados:** o passo final, chamado de codificação seletiva na *Grounded Theory* [12], identifica categorias chaves e as usa para realizar uma narrativa central do fenômeno, relacionando-as com as demais categorias identificadas. Gera-se um documento final com uma descrição sobre o fenômeno estudado que inclui a lista de categorias encontradas, exemplos retirados dos

dados empíricos, além de representações de atividades e modelos i* descrevendo o contexto social. Nesta etapa são realizadas codificações seletivas para escolha das categorias que irão se inseridas no relatório.

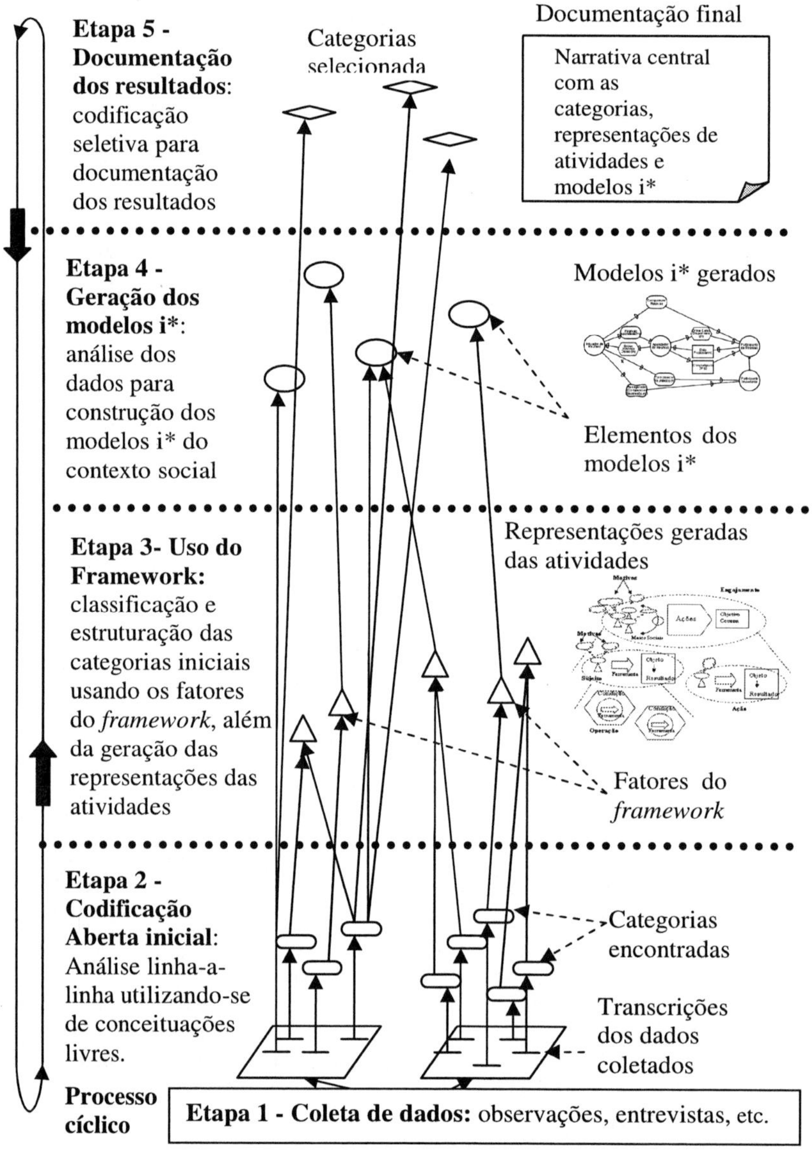

Fig. 2: processo que integra *Grounded Theory*, Teoria da Atividade e i*

Com a utilização de uma codificação inicialmente aberta e o uso de referenciais teóricos em uma etapa posterior do processo, a abordagem proposta dá preferência aos dados na busca por explanações e modelos que devam ser "descobertos" e formulados a partir de análise indutiva. Este procedimento tenta evitar que os referenciais teóricos usados (Teoria da Atividade e i*) deixe os pesquisadores menos sensíveis em relação aos aspectos inusitados do campo.

Ferramentas computacionais de análise qualitativa de dados são usadas para apoiar todas estas etapas permitindo que linhas ou trechos de entrevistas sejam associadas às categorias, criando ao final uma árvore hierárquica de conceitos [18]. A Figura 4 apresenta a utilização da abordagem através do uso ferramenta NVIVO [19] de análise de dados. O exemplo mostra a análise de uma entrevista com um profissional de anestesia relativa ao contexto de uso prontuário de paciente. Ao lado esquerdo, as categorias originadas na etapa 2 (segundo nível da hierarquia) são estruturadas segundo os fatores pré-determinados no *framework* de análise (etapa 3). Ao lado direito, encontra-se um trecho transcrito da entrevista que corresponde a categoria escolhida.

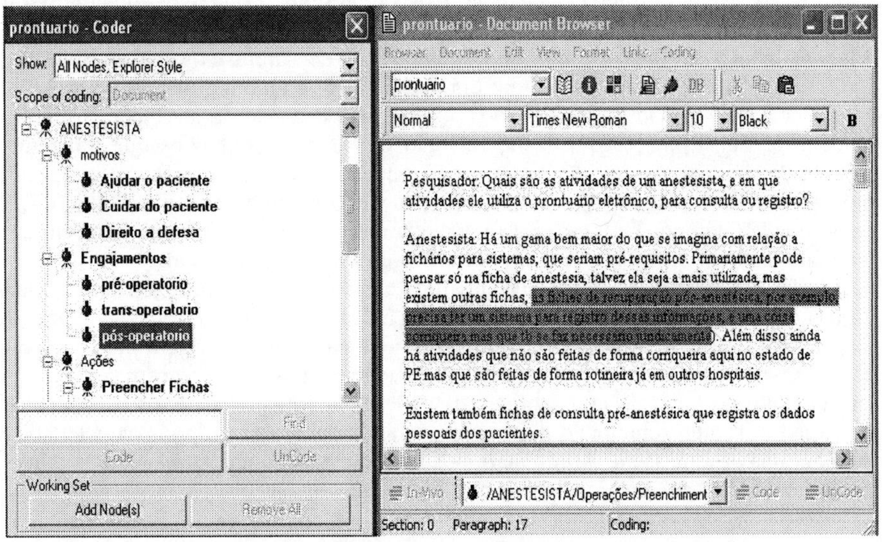

Fig. 4: Análise indutiva de dados através da ferramenta NVIVO

Ressalta-se aqui que o resultado do estudo qualitativo não se resume a um relatório. As próprias categorizações armazenadas na ferramenta podem ser usadas como "resultados", onde os projetistas podem navegar pelos textos que servem de base para os modelos criados, propiciando com isto uma rastreabilidade entre as interpretações construídas e os dados empíricos que as embasaram.

4 Construindo os modelos i*

A técnica i* [9] foi desenvolvida para a modelagem do ambiente organizacional e seus sistemas de informações. Ela oferece formas de especificar os relacionamentos de dependência entre os atores organizacionais e como eles internamente trabalham para satisfazer estes relacionamentos. Uma característica importante desta técnica para o *design* de software é sua capacidade de realizar re-engenharias organizacionais para simular o impacto de alternativas de produtos.

O *framework* i* consiste de dois tipos de modelos organizacionais: o Modelo de Dependências Estratégicas e o Modelo de Razões Estratégicas. O Modelo de Dependências Estratégicas é um grafo composto pelos atores do ambiente (incluindo também os sistemas de *software*) e suas relações de dependência. As relações de dependência modeladas podem ser de vários tipos, incluindo a dependência de objetivo, de objetivo-soft, de tarefa e de recurso.

Já o Modelo de Razões Estratégicas fornece uma visão complementar, através da descrição de como os atores são internamente estruturados de modo a satisfazer as relações externas de dependência especificadas no Modelo de Dependências Estratégicas. Além de oferecer elementos que representam objetivos, objetivos-soft, tarefa e recurso, o Modelo de Razões Estratégicas adiciona três novos tipos de relacionamentos: os Meio-Fim, os de Decomposição de Tarefa, e os de Contribuição.

Os autores deste artigo publicaram um método [20] com um guia passo a passo de como modelos i* podem ser elicitados a partir da descrição de atividades usando o modelo de Engström (1987). Como relatado em [3],[13], trabalhos que utilizam o modelo de Engström usualmente aplicam o conceito de atividade para especificar um processo colaborativo de produção, o que não necessariamente equivale à definição de atividade dada por Leont´ev [1] (associada aos motivos de formação de sentido). Este fato também ocorreu no trabalho dos autores anteriormente citado.

Tarefas colaborativas são melhor classificadas com o que Gonzáles, Nardi e Mark (2007) denominam de "engajamento" (ver seção 2). Desta forma, todas as regras de mapeamento presentes em [20] podem ser usadas na atual abordagem para construir os aspectos operacionais (funcionais) dos modelos bastando usar o conceito de engajamento no lugar do conceito de atividade. Consequentemente, os aspectos não funcionais de intencionalidade não são explorados devido às próprias características do diagrama de Engström. Apresentaremos na sequência como o *framework* analítico apresentado na seção 2 pode transpor esta limitação.

4.2 Elicitando aspectos não funcionais

Segundo classificação apresentada em [21] objetivos-soft presentes em modelos i* podem ser usados para definir os seguintes aspectos não funcionais: (1) um critério subjetivo para alcançar um determinado estado; (2) uma condição extra para alcançar determinado objetivo; (3) uma restrição adicional para realizar uma tarefa; e (4) uma propriedade adicional para um recurso ser aceitável.

Segue descrição de diretrizes que podem ser usadas para elicitação dos mesmos a partir de descrições de atividades. Ao final da sessão, a figura 4 apresenta um exemplo para melhor esclarecer o uso de cada diretriz apresentada. Nesta figura cada diretriz é demonstrada através do exemplo citado na figura 1, onde um médico anestesista realiza, durante uma consulta pré-operatória (engajamento), diversas ações que são energizadas por motivos e estão associadas a atributos não funcionais qualitativos. Na figura 4, para cada aspecto não funcional modelado é inserido ao lado a diretriz usada para sua elicitação.

Através da inclusão do conceito de engajamento como mais um nível intermediário da hierarquia da atividade (motivos, engajamentos, ações e operações), pesquisadores se tornam mais abertos a buscarem os múltiplos motivos que energizam suas ações e tarefas colaborativas. Assim, os motivos da hierarquia máxima da Teoria da Atividade são classificados como o tipo 1 de objetivos-soft da enumeração dada em [21]. Tais motivos são modelados a partir da diretriz abaixo:

Diretriz NF-1 (não funcional 1): Os motivos (nível mais alto da hierarquia da atividade) de um indivíduo são mapeados para objetivos-soft. Contudo, existem dois lugares onde estes objetivos-soft podem ser inseridos no modelo i*

NF-1.1: Quando para realização deste motivo o ator A depende de ações ou engajamentos a serem realizadas por um ator B, então o motivo é mapeado em um relacionamento de dependência de A (*depender* – dependente) para B (*dependee* – que gera a dependência). No exemplo da figura 4 temos o motivo do paciente de "voltar a ter saúde" que é dependente das ações do anestesista.

NF-1.2: Caso contrário o motivo é inserido como objetivo-soft dentro da área de delimitação do ator que possui o motivo. Relações de contribuição positiva são colocadas a partir dos engajamentos e ações para os objetivos-soft que representam os motivos que energizam tais engajamentos e ações. No exemplo, "evitar complicações cirúrgicas" é um motivo que o anestesista possui, no entanto ele não depende de outros atores no modelo para sua realização.

O *framework* analítico proposto associa aspectos não funcionais qualitativos, definidos pela norma ISO-9126 [14], aos diferentes níveis da hierarquia de atividades. Tais informações são usadas para a elicitação de objetivos-soft que representam restrições extras para alcançar um objetivo, realizar uma tarefa. Pretende-se com isto que a ênfase no papel mediador das tecnologias, proporcionada pela Teoria da Atividade, proporcione uma visão de que requisitos não funcionais possam ser elicitados a partir da análise dos atributos de qualidade das ações e engajamentos que serão apoiados (ou mediados) pelo futuro sistema.

Diretriz NF-2: caso sejam detectados nos dados restrições extras, classificadas pela norma ISO-9126 como não funcionais, associados a um motivo, engajamento, ação ou operação. Tais restrições são mapeadas para objetivos-soft, onde:

NF-2.1: Caso seja uma restrição a um motivo, então o objetivo-soft que representa o motivo (gerado na diretriz NF-1) terá um complemento no próprio nome do objetivo-soft indicando a restrição extra (nome = nome do motivo + complemento não funcional). No exemplo da figura 4, "sem sequelas" é um complemento inserido no motivo de "curar paciente".

NF-2.2: Caso seja uma restrição associada a um engajamento, ação ou operação, cria-se um objetivo-soft representando esta restrição como um sub-elemento (relação de decomposição) da tarefa que representa o engajamento, ação ou operação. Na figura 4, várias ações possuem as restrições extras de "rapidez" e "segurança" que são inseridas através de relacionamentos de decomposição.

Por fim, o conjunto de objetivos-soft criados pelas diretrizes NF-1 e NF-2 deve ser re-analisado com a intenção de identificar contribuições e conflitos entre os diferentes elementos intencionais. Esta análise pode ser feita de modo similar ao *framework* NFR [22].

Diretriz NF-3: caso existam evidências nos dados de que algum elementos i* modelado contribui (negativamente ou positivamente) para que determinado objetivo-soft seja satisfeito, cria-se relacionamentos do tipo meio-fim (tradução do inglês: "*means-end link*") entre o elemento que contribui e o objetivo-soft que recebe a contribuição. Esta diretriz pode, por exemplo, gerar relacionamentos de contribuição entre um atributo de "segurança" que incide negativamente sobre um atributo de "rapidez" como mostrado na figura 4.

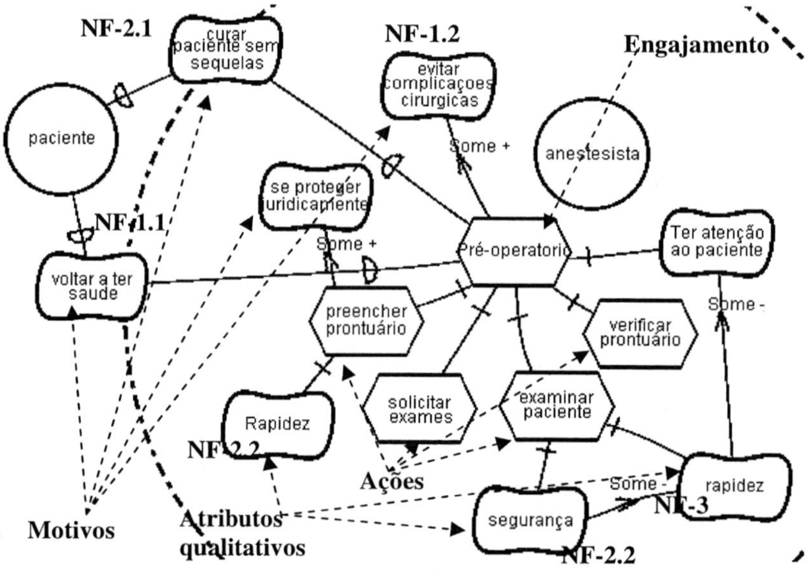

Fig. 4: Modelagem de aspectos não funcionais usando i*

5 Discussão

Em um trabalho com pretensões similares, Grau *et al.* (2005) [11] apresentam uma abordagem sistemática para geração de modelos i* a partir de estudos de campo centrados em análises cognitivas do trabalho. Na nossa opinião, o ponto negativo do trabalho citado está nas restrições dos modelos cognitivistas em descrever práticas humanas [3].

Usualmente os métodos cognitivos são orientados as tarefas, métodos e procedimentos; não levando muito em consideração as práticas humanas, os relacionamentos sociais e a coordenação através da qual as tarefas são realizadas. Outro ponto relevante é que a maioria dos trabalhos centrados em análises cognitivas focaliza-se na relação do usuário com o sistema, muitas vezes não abrindo o leque de análise para o ambiente, as demais ações humanas e os motivos que circundam e dão significados a esta relação [3].

Como exemplo de uma destas limitações, contata-se que o método proposto em [11] se lança de novas entrevistas com os usuários para propiciar a geração dos objetivos-soft do modelo intencional, devido possivelmente as restrições dos modelos cognitivos usados em fornecem tais informações [11].

É importante considerar que os modelos i*, apesar de incorporarem aspectos de intencionalidade aos elementos processuais cognitivos, não fornecem elementos suficientes para descrever os diversos fatores sociais existentes. Aspectos relativos ao ambiente físico (mobília, espaço físico, condições climáticas, etc.), características dos sujeitos (idade, limitações físicas e mentais, etc.), tensões na realização das atividades, perspectivas históricas do desenvolvimento das práticas, bem como fatores que descrevem atividades colaborativas (regras sociais, coordenação, divisão de trabalho, etc.) são exemplos de informações do contexto, presentes no *framework* analítico usado, que são difíceis de serem modelados usando apenas a técnica i*.

Temos uma série de trabalhos em etnografia que se baseiam no *framework* apresentado em [23] para estruturar os estudos etnográficos. Alguns fazendo uso inclusive de diagramas UML para representar as informações de modo mais compreensível aos *designers* [24]. O trabalho aqui apresentado tem como diferencial o uso da Teoria da Atividade e da técnica i* para tanto melhor entender o papel mediador da tecnologia nas práticas humanas, quanto apoiar a atividade criativa e transformacional de *design*.

Outro ponto relevante na proposta apresentada é um processo qualitativo para a geração de modelos "válidos" a partir dos dados. Em pesquisa qualitativa tem sido argumentado que uma forma de trabalhar a questão da validade dos resultados obtidos é através da exposição das fundamentações teóricas, escolhas e métodos qualitativos adotados durante o processo [12],[15]. No entanto, nas publicações atuais raramente se discute as bases teóricas do trabalho de campo ou o processo como ele foi conduzido em detalhes [5],[15].

Podemos encontrar na literatura alguns trabalhos atuais em *Grounded Theory* que chegam a oferecer "recomendações" para a elicitação de requisitos de sistemas [25] através do uso de um *framework* analítico com as dimensões social, política, simbólica e estrutural do trabalho. Contudo, tais soluções ainda não apresentam, por exemplo, como modelos possam ser gerados a partir dos dados.

Uma crítica associada ao uso de *Grounded Theory* é que ela auxilia o pesquisador a teorizar sobre o mundo do ponto de vista de quem está categorizando, ao invés de como os usuários enxergam aquela situação. Ou seja, os pesquisadores buscam um entendimento do mundo provindo dos dados, mas que tende a ser influenciado por bagagens culturais do pesquisador [17]. Mas neste contexto é preciso considerar a dificuldade em se garantir uma noção "pura" sobre o ponto de vista do usuário. Sabe-se, por exemplo, que todo pesquisador faz naturalmente "escolhas" sobre o que será observado [15], pois toda observação é uma observação de algum lugar [3].

Ressalta-se que no paradigma qualitativo não se procura uma representação exata da realidade. As representações construídas só valem para um determinado contexto. O objetivo é criar descrições da realidade no intuito de facilitar a partilha de significados e promover o diálogo na busca de um entendimento mais elaborado [25].

6 Conclusões e Trabalhos Futuros

Sabe-se que resultados puramente descritivos de práticas humanas são pouco usados no *design* pela dificuldade de se gerar generalizações sobre um número sem fim de dados retóricos [4],[3]. No outro lado na moeda, métodos orientados a modelos, incluindo aqui os atuais métodos que usam a técnica i*, são pouco sensíveis à riqueza dos dados. Este trabalho apresenta uma abordagem de compromisso, baseada no uso da *Grounded Theory*, Teoria da Atividade e da Técnica i*, para se obter resultados úteis ao *design* que sejam ao mesmo tempo sensíveis a leitura dos aspectos inusitados dos dados de campo.

Por delimitações de espaço, o presente artigo se ateu as argumentações teóricas essenciais para justificar a solução proposta. Um artigo que descreve a utilização do método em um estudo de caso passo-a-passo encontra-se em desenvolvimento. Um outro trabalho em andamento está sendo a elaboração de diretrizes de mapeamento para modelagem i* das ferramentas computacionais existentes no contexto social. Atualmente as diretrizes não englobam a especificação de um sistema já existente e como este sistema se relaciona com os demais atores. Também como um trabalho futuro que pode ser derivado seria a pesquisa sobre como os atributos não funcionais qualitativos elicitados possuem impacto na modularização do novo sistema utilizando abordagens orientadas a aspectos [26].

Um dos pontos negativos da solução apresentada, no entanto, é o elevado tempo consumido atualmente no processo de transcrição, análise e modelagem de dados. Um trabalho futuro que pode vir a sobrepor esta limitação será o desenvolvimento de ferramentas integradas de análise, modelagem e documentação de dados, específica para uso por profissionais de engenharia de requisitos. Outro ponto relevante associado seria a construção de tradutores semi-automáticos para a geração dos modelos i* a partir dos diagramas de atividades dentro da perspectiva de MDD (*Model Driven Development*) [27].

Referências

1. Leont´ev, A. N.: The Problem of Activity in Psychology. J. Werstch (Ed.): The concept of Activity in Soviet Psychology. Armonk, New York: M. E. Sharpe, inc. (1979).
2. Engeström, Y.: Learning by Expanding, Helsinki: Orienta-Konsultit (1987).
3. Kaptelinin, V. e Nardi, B. A.: Acting with Technology: Activity Theory and Interaction Design. MIT Press (2006)
4. Button, G. e Dourish, P.: Technometodology: paradox and possibilities. Human Factors in Computer Systems.CHI´96, ACM Press (1996) 19-26
5. Dourish, P.: Implications for Design. CHI – Human Factors in Computing Systems. Canada (2006)

6. Vicente, K.: Cognitive Work Analysis. Lawrence Erlbaum Associates (1999)
7. Maguire, M.: Context of Use within Usability Activities, International Journal of Human-Computer Studies, 55 (2001) 453-483
8. Souza, C. R. B.: Interpreting Activity Theory as a Software Engineering Methodology. European Conference on Computer Supported Cooperative Work (2003)
9. Yu, E.: Modelling Strategic Relationships for Process Reengineering, Tese de Doutorado, University of Toronto, Department of Computer Science (1995)
10. Castro, J., Kolp, M. e Mylopoulos, J.: Towards Requirements Driven Information Systems Engineering: The Tropos Project. Journal: Information Systems.27,(6) (2002) 365– 389
11. Grau, G., Franch, X., e Maiden, N.: A Goal Based Round-Trip Method for System Development. Eleventh International Workshop on Requirequirements Engineering: Foundation for Software Quality (REFSQ'05) (2005) 13-14
12. Strauss, A. e Corbin, J.: Basics of Qualitative Research: Techniques and procedures for developing grounded theory. Sage (1998)
13. Cruz Neto, G., Gomes, A., Oliveira, N.: Aliando Grounded Theory e Re-formulações de conceitos da Teoria da Atividade para o melhor entendimento de práticas humanas. Workshop on Perspectives, Challenges and Opportunities for Human-Computer Interaction in Latin America, Rio de Janeiro (2007)
14. ISO-9126: ISO/IEC 9126 – Information Technology, Software Product Evaluation, Quality, Characteristics and Guidelines for their use. International Standard Organization (1991)
15. Macaulay, C., Benyon, D. e Crerar, A.: Ethnography, Theory and System Design: From Intution to Insight. Journal of Human Computer Studies, 53, (2000) 35-60
16. González, V., Nardi, B., Mark, G.: Ensembles: Understanding the Instantiation of Activities, Submetido para o Scandinavian Journal of Information Systems (2007)
17. Crabtree, A., O'Brien, J., Nichols, D., Rouncefield, M. e Twidale, M.: Ethnometodologically informed ethnography and information system design. JASIST, vol. 51 (7), (2000) 666-682.
18. Richards, T. J. e Richards, L.: Using Computers in Qualitative Research. Denzin, N. K. and Lincoln, Y. S. (eds.): Collecting and Interpreting Qualitative Materials. Sage Publication (1998) 211-243.
19. Gibbs, G.: Qualitative Data Analysis: Explorations with Nvivo. Open University (2002)
20. Cruz Neto, G.G., Gomes, A.G. e Castro, J.B.: Mapping Activity Theory Diagrams into i* Organizational Models, Journal of Computer Science and Technology. Special Issue on Software Requirement Engineering. Vol. 5 – No. 2- Julho – ISSN 1666-6038 (2005) (selecionado a partir de artigos do WER 2004)
21. Grau, G., Franch, X., Mayol, E., Ayala, C.:RiSD: A Methodology for Building i* Stretegic Dependency Models. Seventeenth International Conference on Software Engineering and Knowledge Engineering (2005)
22. Chung, L., Nixon, B. Yu, E. e Mylopoulos, J.: Non-functional requirements in software engineering". Kluwer Academic (2000)
23. Hughes, J., O'Brien, J., Rodden, T. e Rouncefield, M.: Designing with Ethnography: A Presentation Framework for Design". ACM DIS (1997)
24. Viller, S. e Sommerville, I.: Social Analysis in the Requirement Enginnering Process: From Etnography to Method", 4th IEEE International Symposium on Requirement Engineering. Limerick, Ireland, IEEE Computer Society Press (1999) 6-13.
25. Ramos, I.:Aplicações das Tecnologias de Informação que suportam as dimensões estrutural, social, política e simbólica do trabalho. Tese de Doutorado. Univ. do Minho (2000)
26. Elrad, T., Filman, R. e Bader, A.:Aspect-Oriented Programming: Introduction, Communications of the ACM, v.44 n.10 (2001) 29-32.
27. Beydeda, S., Book, M. e Gruhn, V.: Model Driven Software Development. Springer (2005)

Evaluación del Desarrollo de Software Mediante una Herramienta MDA: Un Caso de Estudio

José María Duarte V.[1], Magalí González[1,2], Luca Cernuzzi[1], Oscar Pastor[2]

[1] Universidad Católica "Nuestra Señora de la Asunción", DEI
Campus Universitario, Asunción, Paraguay
joseph.duartev@gmail.com, {mgonzalez, lcernuzz}@uca.edu.py
[2]Universidad Politécnica de Valencia, DSIC
Valencia, España
opastor@dsic.upv.es

Resumen. Model Driven Architecture (MDA) surge a principios de esta década como una propuesta de estandarización del enfoque Model Driven Development (MDD). MDA adopta a los modelos como elementos esenciales de la cadena de producción de software, proporcionando un conjunto de lenguajes estándares para manejar eficientemente tales modelos. Según los creadores de MDA, la postura de mantener énfasis en la obtención de un grado satisfactorio de productividad, en depreciación de otras características como portabilidad, interoperabilidad, reusabilidad y mantenibilidad, es la que se pretende cambiar con la aplicación de MDA al desarrollo de los sistemas informáticos, independientemente del dominio específico del que se trate una aplicación. El objetivo de este trabajo es verificar la efectividad de tales características, a partir de la experiencia obtenida en el desarrollo de una aplicación real usando por un lado una herramienta MDA, contrastándola con el enfoque tradicional.

Keywords: Model Driven Architecture, Model Driven Development, Software Engineering, Web Engineering, code generation.

1 Introducción

Model Driven Architecture (MDA) surge a principios de esta década como una propuesta de estandarización del enfoque Model Driven Development (MDD) en el desarrollo de software. La regla principal de la propuesta MDA para poder cumplir sus objetivos es la de usar en lo posible estándares, por ello la base (*core*) de la arquitectura lo conforman estándares definidos por el OMG que permiten trabajar con modelos como componentes esenciales en el proceso de desarrollo de software [1]. MDA adopta a los modelos como elementos esenciales de la cadena de producción de software, proporcionando un conjunto de lenguajes estándares para manejar eficientemente los modelos. En particular se consideran dos principales modelos: el Modelo Independiente de Plataforma (PIM, por sus siglas en inglés), y el Modelo Dependiente de Plataforma (PSM, por sus siglas en inglés).

El PIM es el modelo con mayor nivel de abstracción. Describe la estructura, funcionalidad y restricciones del sistema, omitiendo detalles sobre cómo y dónde va a ser implementado.

En el PSM, además de contener la información del PIM, incluye los detalles relacionados a una plataforma de implementación dada (.NET, J2EE, etc.). Este modelo se obtiene partir del PIM por medio de la transformación que lleva a cabo la herramienta MDA teniendo en cuenta la plataforma seleccionada de destino y eventualmente algunos parámetros de ajustes que el desarrollador proporciona. Varios PSM's pueden ser generados a partir de un mismo PIM, cada uno describiendo al sistema desde una perspectiva diferente.

De todo esto podemos ver que un componente importante del enfoque MDA recae sobre una o varias herramientas MDA. En este proceso se intenta lograr el grado máximo posible de automatización de la construcción de los sistemas, haciendo uso intensivo de las transformaciones para una o más plataformas específicas de implementación.

Actualmente es posible contar con herramientas MDD, que ofrecen soporte para una plataforma o dominio de aplicación particular, permitiendo a los desarrolladores la construcción de software con cierta eficiencia y productividad notable en esos entornos. No obstante, la postura de mantener énfasis en la obtención de un grado satisfactorio de **productividad**, en depreciación de otras características como **portabilidad**, **interoperabilidad**, **reusabilidad** y **mantenibilidad**, es la que se pretende cambiar con la aplicación de MDA al desarrollo de los sistemas informáticos, independientemente del dominio específico del que se trate una aplicación. Sin embargo, en la literatura especializada no se cuenta con suficiente documentación de experiencias y casos de estudio que confirmen esta tendencia.

A raíz de la necesidad de poner a prueba el desarrollo de aplicaciones en MDA para determinar el alcance de la implementación actual de este nuevo enfoque en las herramientas que dicen conformarse al estándar MDA, surge este trabajo en el que se establecen dos propósitos principales. Por un lado, la verificación del desarrollo completo de una aplicación con una herramienta MDA concreta, en particular ArcStyler [6], seleccionada a partir de un proceso de evaluación entre un conjunto de herramientas (ArcStyler, Objecteering [11], Enterprise Architect [12], Model-In-Action Generation [13] y OlivaNova [14]). En dicho proceso de evaluación fueron considerados principalmente las siguientes prestaciones de cada herramienta: 1) que cumpla en lo posible con las especificaciones del estándar MDA , 2) que pueda disponerse de manera gratuita para un período razonable de tiempo para aprendizaje y evaluación, 3) que la generación automática cubra el mayor número posible de componentes de las capas de la aplicación: base de datos, lógica de aplicación y interfaz de usuario, y 4) que soporte más de una plataforma para la generación de aplicaciones.

Por otro lado, se pretende efectuar la comprobación y evaluación de las características obtenidas del producto realizado por el proceso de desarrollo MDA, contrastando con los resultados obtenidos por el método tradicional. Esto nos permite establecer el grado efectivo de satisfacción de las características afirmadas en el documento de especificación del estándar MDA (productividad, portabilidad, interoperabilidad, reusabilidad y mantenibilidad) [1], y en varias publicaciones de los distintos propulsores de esta iniciativa [2, 3, 5]. Para realizar el proceso de evaluación, se identificaron una serie atributos, y eventuales métricas que fueron aplicadas para cada una de las características afirmadas.

El documento se organiza de la siguiente manera: la sección 2 presenta el desarrollo de una aplicación utilizando una herramienta MDA; la sección 3 presenta el análisis de los resultados teniendo en cuenta las características consideradas como más importantes a la hora de aplicar el enfoque MDA al desarrollo de aplicaciones; finalmente, la sección 4 presenta las conclusiones y trabajos futuros.

2 Desarrollo de un sistema con una herramienta MDA

La herramienta **ArcStyler** [12] fue la escogida para trabajar y poner a prueba el desarrollo en MDA de un sistema real a modo de caso de estudio. Esta herramienta fue seleccionada por reunir mejor calificación de entre un grupo de herramientas pre-evaluadas como fue indicado en la Introducción del trabajo.

Una característica elemental de esta herramienta es la definición de su arquitectura, cuyos componentes centrales son los **cartuchos** o *MDA-cartridges*, que conforman el "motor" o *MDA-engine* de la herramienta. Además, ArcStyler permite que un usuario defina sus propios cartuchos, o extienda algunos de los proporcionados.

ArcStyler logra la transformación de modelos a código a partir de un PIM marcado y estereotipado con información de la plataforma de implementación.

La aplicación de caso de estudio seleccionada es una adaptación de un sistema empleado en un ambiente de trabajo real, que sirve de gestión y despliegue de información contable de los departamentos de una Facultad. Este sistema de gestión cliente-servidor llamado **Sistema de Rubros**, satisface las necesidades propias de determinación de gastos e ingresos y de información de ejecución presupuestaria de la Facultad de Ciencias y Tecnología de la Universidad Católica de Asunción. El desarrollo de este sistema originalmente se ha hecho siguiendo la técnica tradicional en el marco de procesos evolucionarios (*rapid prototyping)* o de crecimiento incremental, en el cual, a partir de diseños de las interfaces ajustadas a las necesidades y requerimientos de los usuarios, se van construyendo gradualmente todos los componentes restantes, haciendo el programador la codificación 'en duro' de la lógica de negocios, de disposición de los elementos de interfaz y de interacción con la base de datos. El tipo de interfaz empleado para esta aplicación es el de ventanas y diálogos típicos de un sistema *stand-alone*. A fin de dimensionar el sistema de rubros original, enumeramos a continuación los artefactos que componen al mismo: 13 entidades de lógica de negocios implementadas en 22 tablas de la base de datos, 50 pantallas de interfaces de usuario y las definiciones adicionales de la base de datos que abarcan 4 vistas, 12 *triggers* y 6 procedimientos almacenados. Estos elementos sirven de soporte para las 38 funcionalidades que ofrece el sistema a sus usuarios.

Para el desarrollo del sistema de caso de estudio planteado, se eligió implementar un número significativo de funcionalidades, las cuales suman 24 y representan las operaciones elementales que satisfacen los requisitos más importantes del sistema. Se decidió trabajar en el desarrollo de esta aplicación en la plataforma Java, específicamente J2EE. También optamos por brindar un entorno Web como interfaz de usuario, pues ese es el que dispone de un soporte pleno en la herramienta ArcStyler.

En la figura 1 se reúnen los diagramas del modelo de la aplicación necesarios en el desarrollo con la herramienta MDA ArcStyler, que deben contener las especificaciones apropiadas de los componentes implicados de lógica y presentación para poder ser interpretados por los cartuchos MDA correspondientes durante la etapa de generación de artefactos.

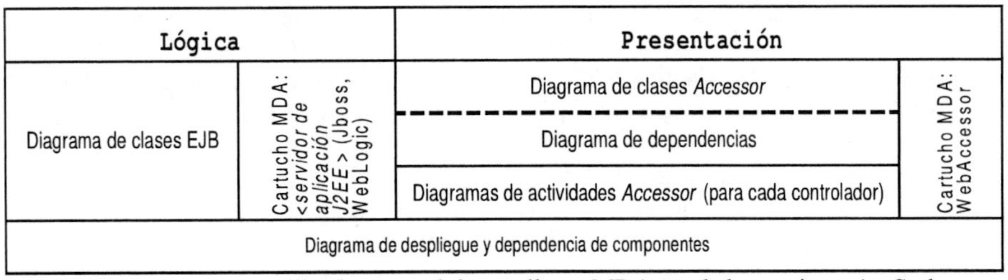

Fig. 1. Diagramas utilizados para el desarrollo en MDA con la herramienta ArcStyler

El modelo de la *Lógica de Negocio* con la herramienta ArcStyler consiste en el modelo de los componentes de la lógica de negocios en un diagrama de clases UML. Esta etapa es relativamente sencilla y permite al desarrollador ir notando la variedad y complejidad de los componentes básicos de la aplicación. Si bien, el enfoque de este diagrama es el de uno independiente de plataforma (PIM), por las características ya mencionadas de la herramienta se deben ir indicando con estereotipos y marcas MDA algunas propiedades distintivas de la plataforma de implementación, en éste caso J2EE.

El modelado de la capa de *Presentación* de la aplicación siguiendo el *framework Accessor* es el trabajo más costoso de todo el proceso de desarrollo en la herramienta ArcStyler. El *framework Accessor* [8] incorporado en ArcStyler provee un proceso bien definido para la construcción de la capa de presentación de las aplicaciones. En el modelo *Accessor*, se establecen el flujo de control y el flujo de datos de la capa de presentación de un modo abstracto. Un modelo *Accessor* es una instancia del metamodelo del mismo nombre: «Accessor», el cual es una extensión del metamodelo UML. El metamodelo *Accessor* resuelve los aspectos de Vista y Control del paradigma Modelo/Vista/Controlador (MVC). Este paradigma se usa para modelar las interacciones de la capa de presentación con la de lógica de negocio, que representa la parte de Modelo de MVC.

Aproximadamente el 80% del tiempo dedicado al modelado se insume en la capa de presentación. Explicando resumidamente, en esta etapa se proceden a identificar y especificar las vistas (*representers*), los controladores (*accessors*) y las transiciones entre las distintas vistas (interfaces) y las acciones esperadas entre cada una de ellas modeladas en un diagrama de estados extendido de UML por cada controlador.

En la etapa de *Generación de Código* del proceso de desarrollo de software en MDA se realiza la generación de código para la plataforma de implementación por medio de los módulos del Generador y los cartuchos MDA, los cuales permiten crear las secciones mayores de la infraestructura de despliegue, como también la preparación de los entornos de construcción (compilación) y *testing*, todos ellos a partir de los modelos UML.

La generación de código, si bien está disponible en cualquier etapa de desarrollo y puede hacerse para un solo elemento en particular, no es segura ni completa hasta no concluir la etapa del modelado de los componentes *desplegables*[1], en especial al primer componente esencial, el que contiene las entidades de la lógica de la aplicación. Además, como comprobación de la validez del modelo, es recomendable utilizar el verificador de modelos proporcionado por el cartucho MDA de la plataforma J2EE para el servidor de aplicaciones definido (JBoss, WebLogic, etc.).

En cuanto al aprendizaje en el manejo de la herramienta, podemos afirmar que ésta presenta una curva de aprendizaje de esfuerzo moderado, pues a pesar de constituir un entorno de desarrollo integrado, con una documentación incluida más o menos extensa, y con ejemplos de proyectos simples, es necesaria una cuidadosa lectura de cada parte de la documentación, y el ensayo con tutoriales para comprender tanto el entorno de trabajo como la serie de pasos que deben seguirse en cada fase de trabajo, ya que algunos detalles, aunque simples pero importantes en el proceso de desarrollo, no resultan demasiado obvios para el desarrollador principiante.

3 Análisis de los resultados

Aprovechamos la experiencia ganada en el desarrollo de dos sistemas que ofrecen un conjunto de funcionalidades equivalentes pero realizados por procesos diferentes para determinar el nivel de satisfacción de las cualidades seleccionadas para ambos procesos involucrados. En base a ello presentamos un análisis de las cualidades de la aplicación obtenida siguiendo el enfoque MDA con el apoyo de la herramienta ArcStyler, y además establecemos una comparación de los puntos principales del desarrollo de la aplicación de caso de estudio entre el sistema construido por el proceso tradicional y el sistema realizado con la herramienta MDA para éste trabajo. Es importante tener en cuenta que los resultados derivados de la evaluación del enfoque MDA en el desarrollo del sistema de caso de estudio corresponden a particularidades de las partes implicadas. Por un lado, el desarrollo hecho con el soporte de una herramienta específica está sujeto a la implementación propia de la herramienta ArcStyler del enfoque MDA y las prestaciones o funciones que ofrece a sus usuarios. Por otra parte, tenemos que la aplicación modelada y generada por la herramienta se trata de un sistema típico de información y gestión, en el que las tareas más realizadas se refieren a funciones *CRUD* (crear, recuperar, actualizar y borrar datos). Por lo tanto, las afirmaciones dadas en este análisis no necesariamente deben extenderse a otros tipos de sistemas más complejos o especiales (sistemas de tiempo real, sistemas embebidos, etc.), si bien los investigadores y expertos en la arquitectura MDA y la misma herramienta ArcStyler afirman poder aplicarse plenamente a la construcción de varios tipos de sistemas. No obstante, consideramos que los resultados hallados son de interés y relevancia para los desarrolladores y demás

[1] En una aplicación típica, usualmente se tendrán dos módulos componentes principales: el de la lógica de negocios y el de la capa de presentación. Este mismo enfoque es el aplicado para el modelado de los componentes desplegables en la herramienta.

personas involucradas en la industria del software, ya que gran parte de la demanda de software a medida son sistemas que contienen principalmente funciones *CRUD*.

En el siguiente cuadro se resumen las características y los atributos empleados en la evaluación de las cualidades obtenidas del sistema de caso de estudio desarrollado. Como fue mencionado en la introducción, estas características se definen a partir de las cualidades que el enfoque MDA pretende satisfacer, mencionados explícitamente en el documento de especificación [1], y también indicado por algunos autores que promueven la arquitectura [2, 3, 5]:

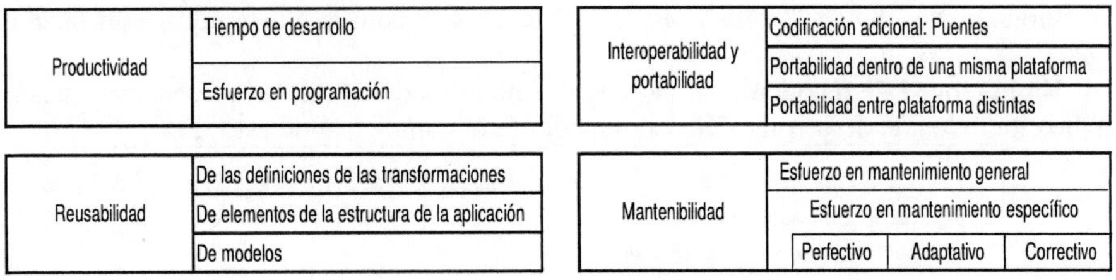

Fig. 2. Atributos de evaluación empleados en el caso de estudio.

Los atributos definidos por cada característica, fueron identificados a partir de lo siguiente:

- Selección de atributos que puedan ser fácilmente cuantificables a partir de métricas conocidas: tiempo de desarrollo, esfuerzo en programación, esfuerzo en mantenimiento general, codificación adicional de puentes.
- Atributos, que si bien no son cuantificables, son fácilmente comparables: los atributos definidos para la característica de reusabilidad y la portabilidad dentro de una misma plataforma.
- Atributos deseables para una característica en particular que pueden ser comparables de manera cualitativa: la portabilidad entre plataformas distintas, y los atributos indicados para el esfuerzo de mantenimiento específico.

La definición de las métricas y evaluación pretende más bien ayudar a analizar las características deseables, de una manera más bien cualitativa, utilizando, en aquellos casos en que fueron posibles, valores cuantitativos. Si bien, esta experiencia no representa un proceso totalmente riguroso de validación, consideramos que puede ser muy útil para realizar un análisis del grado de satisfacción de tales características.

3.1 Productividad

a. Tiempo de desarrollo

Con el desarrollo del sistema por el proceso enmarcado en la arquitectura MDA, pudimos notar que prácticamente todas las funcionalidades consideradas de la aplicación de caso de estudio pudieron lograrse eficazmente, previa definición de ajustes manuales en el código fuente. Por funcionalidad definimos como una tarea indivisible que debe llevar a cabo el sistema, pudiendo exactamente corresponder a un caso de uso, o formar parte de un conjunto de tareas que inscribe un caso de uso.

Con el fin de dimensionar el tamaño del sistema, utilizamos la métrica del número de funcionalidades que implementa la aplicación. Conociendo el tiempo empleado en implementar todas las funcionalidades, desde el inicio del desarrollo hasta la disposición de la aplicación para su comunidad de usuarios, podemos emplear otra métrica a la que llamaremos **índice de productividad** *p*, que es igual al la cantidad de funcionalidades ***F*** efectivas que presta la aplicación, dividido el tiempo total ***T*** de desarrollo e implementación: $p = F/T$.

Con los valores de ésta unidad correspondientes a los procesos de desarrollo tradicional y en MDA para el caso de estudio expuesto, podemos establecer una primera comparación objetiva para la característica de *productividad* en la elaboración de sistemas, y verificar la conformidad o no de ésta propiedad obtenida utilizando el enfoque MDA en el desarrollo, en confrontación con los métodos tradicionales de *Rapid Prototyping* / *Code and fix* (prototipado rápido / codificar y ajustar).

En la tabla 1 se recogen los datos de las métricas descritas arriba concernientes a ambos métodos de desarrollo del sistema adoptado como caso de estudio:

Método de desarrollo:	*Enfoque tradicional*	*Enfoque MDA*
Cantidad de funcionalidades (F)	24	
Tiempo total de desarrollo (días trabajados) (T)	90	15
Tiempo total de desarrollo (días calendario para referencia)	140 días [4 meses]	20 días [3 semanas]
Valor p = F/T	**0,267**	**1,6**
Tiempo de ahorro	---------	**600%**

Tabla 1. Tiempos de desarrollo del Sistema de Rubros FCyT

Otra observación importante es que las funcionalidades implementadas en el sistema original incluyen las tareas relativas a la validación de datos introducidos por el usuario, en todas las interfaces concernientes a la ejecución de una tarea, cuidados que no fueron incorporados en la aplicación desarrollada por el enfoque MDA, por tratarse meramente de un trabajo de codificación adicional, que no tiene contribución significativa en la satisfacción de los requisitos funcionales del sistema, claves para establecer criterios de comparación entre ambos métodos de desarrollo.

Como puede apreciarse, los tiempos insumidos en el desarrollo de ambos sistemas por una sola persona difieren significativamente, notándose una reducción de tiempo de desarrollo con el enfoque MDA de hasta 6 veces menos que el empleado sin utilizar enfoque alguno de MDD. Esta diferencia hallada, que muestra marcadamente un acentuado aumento en el índice de productividad del desarrollo de sistemas a favor del primer enfoque, no obstante puede ser matizado con otros factores relevantes del sistema hecho con la herramienta MDA tales como: la falta de tiempo consignado en tareas que confieren la adecuación de requisitos no funcionales de la aplicación como módulos de validación, ajustes manuales de las interfaces a requerimientos visuales, así como los entornos de presentación (entorno *stand-alone* en el sistema original vs. entorno *web* de la aplicación de caso de estudio en MDA).

El esfuerzo en el modelado incide mayormente en el componente de presentación, debido al número de elementos que deben diseñarse. De acuerdo a observaciones del desarrollo del sistema de caso de estudio, estimamos que el tiempo dedicado al modelado de este componente supera ligeramente el 80% del tiempo total de diseño y especificación, perteneciendo la fracción restante al modelado de la lógica de negocios, que no pasa el 20% del tiempo empleado. Estos datos sugieren que la lógica de negocio para este tipo de aplicaciones CRUD es relativamente simple y con un bajo grado de complejidad. Sin embargo, como se puede apreciar en el siguiente indicador, gracias al enfoque MDA es posible una fuerte reducción del esfuerzo manual de desarrollo de la lógica de negocio lo cual no deja de ser una ventaja significativa. En el modelado de la presentación, gran parte del trabajo es dedicado al diseño de las vistas, en donde se esbozan los elementos de interfaz de usuario y los atributos de los *representers*.

El tiempo total dedicado a la presentación, podría extenderse un poco más de lo indicado en la tabla anterior, ya que luego de la generación de las interfaces pueden requerirse ajustes manuales en la apariencia de algunas interfaces de usuario.

En la experiencia con la aplicación de caso de estudio, se determinó efectuar ciertos ajustes a determinadas interfaces que constituyen las esenciales para realizar las operaciones más importantes del sistema de rubros, conforme a las necesidades de los usuarios. Se editaron en total 12 vistas de interfaz, que incluyen 9 *webforms* y 3 reportes. Este conjunto permite realizar eficientemente 8 funcionalidades, de las 24 que implementa el sistema desarrollado en MDA. Los formularios web sirven de implementación a 5 funcionalidades, y cada uno de los reportes implementa una funcionalidad. El tiempo empleado en los ajustes de los formularios web fue de 3 horas, y de los tres reportes en total fue de 3 horas. Haciendo una estimación de lo que llevaría completar los ajustes en las interfaces relacionadas a las funcionalidades restantes (2/3), obtenemos que se necesitarían 12 horas adicionales para tener completo los ajustes más importantes de las interfaces (páginas web) de la aplicación de acuerdo a los requisitos de los usuarios. A una razón de 6 horas de trabajo en desarrollo por día, tenemos que se debe añadir 2 días de trabajo aproximadamente al tiempo expresado en la tabla 1, lo que nos da un valor de 17 días. Si consideramos esta cifra como nuevo tiempo total de desarrollo, tenemos que 3 de los 17 días, o el 17,6% del tiempo total de desarrollo correspondería a cambios manuales en los artefactos de interfaces generados automáticamente por la herramienta.

b. Esfuerzo en programación

Podemos determinar además otro índice de productividad utilizado desde los primeros tiempos de la aplicación de ingeniería de software: el número de líneas de código (***LOC***). Haciendo una adaptación para su empleo en el desarrollo con MDA, definimos la métrica que indica la cantidad de líneas de código efectivo generado por la herramienta, y la cantidad de código necesario que debe ser programado manualmente. De esta manera se puede obtener una estimación interesante del "*trabajo*" hecho por la herramienta y por el programador, esperando obtener como resultado una proporción de esfuerzo realizado en términos de línea de código mucho mayor para la herramienta que el producido por el programador, siguiendo las expectativas de MDA. En la tabla 2 se recogen los resultados del cálculo aplicado a los archivos fuentes indicados[2].

Como podemos apreciar en los datos, el esfuerzo en el código agregado manualmente, alcanza aproximadamente al 10% de todo el código fuente. Este esfuerzo (en programación) es modestamente superior cuando se toma en cuenta solo

---

[2] Las líneas de código consideradas sólo corresponden a los archivos fuentes en los que se definen clases e interfaces de la lógica de la aplicación. Por lógica de aplicación incluimos a las definiciones de las entidades del sistema, que para la plataforma J2EE son los *beans* y sus interfaces, además de la lógica de los controladores *accessors* del modelo web, que no abarcan a las clases *representers* que enmarcan las vistas o interfaces de usuario de la aplicación

los controladores de la capa de presentación, llegando cercanamente al 15% del código fuente correspondiente a los controladores de la arquitectura MVC de *Accessor*, que como sabemos, proporcionan la "inteligencia" o dinámica del sistema.

	Líneas de código (LOC)		
	Total	Manual	Generado
Lógica de negocios	5.289	152	5.137
	100%	2,87%	97,13%
Controladores de la lógica de presentación			
`Login`	551	42	509
`MenuPrincipal`	7.007	1.075	5.932
	7.558	1.175	6.441
	100%	14,78%	85,22%
Resumen de la aplicación			
Lógica de negocios	5.289	152	5.137
Controladores de la presentación	7.558	1.117	6.441
	12.847	1.227	11.620
	100%	9,55%	90,45%

Tabla 2. Resumen de la proporción de código generado y código programado

3.2 Interoperabilidad y Portabilidad

a. Codificación adicional: Puentes

El trabajo de las herramientas MDA no debería limitarse a transformar modelos y generar código sino también de generar pasarelas o puentes entre las diferentes capas de la aplicación para que puedan interoperar satisfactoriamente. A las conexiones entre los componentes de una aplicación componentes (base de datos, lógica de la aplicación, interfaz de usuario) se lo llaman "puentes", y son necesarios para completar la implementación de las funcionalidades elementales de la aplicación. En ArcStyler encontramos que el esfuerzo "manual", indispensable para tener listos los fuentes de la aplicación de manera a llevar a cabo la construcción completa e interoperable de la aplicación, concierne básicamente a la programación manual de esas conexiones o pasarelas, concretamente a las interconexiones entre las entidades (*EJB's* desplegados) del modelo de la lógica, y los elementos de interfaz de las vistas (páginas), coordinadas adecuadamente desde las operaciones de los controladores (*accessor*) pertinentes. Si bien se podría esperar algún grado mayor de generación automática de tales puentes haciendo uso del rico mecanismo de marcas y patrones de MDA, hallamos que la adición y edición de código es racionalmente manejable, ágil y sin mayores dificultades.

b. Portabilidad dentro de una misma plataforma

La portabilidad dentro de una misma plataforma como el caso de J2EE y sus distintos servidores de aplicaciones es coherentemente convincente y rápida, quizás considerando que los modelos definidos estén orientados a una misma definición de arquitectura (J2EE) y que el cambio de servidor de aplicación sólo conlleva a ajustes específicos de configuración propios del servidor de destino para el cual se elige la generación, mediante las marcas ofrecidas por el cartucho MDA del servidor J2EE elegido. Particularmente en esta investigación se ha trabajado con los servidores Jboss 4 y WebLogic 8.1, y en lo que respecta a la experiencia del desarrollo para estos productos con la herramienta ArcStyler podemos hacer las siguientes observaciones:

- El modelo de lógica de negocios que comprende la descripción completa de *beans* no sufre de alteraciones importantes cuando se trata del cambio de

proveedores de implementación J2EE. No obstante, el verificador de modelos avisa las incompatibilidades encontradas cuando no reconoce alguna especificación del modelo para el cartucho MDA del servidor de destino. Por ejemplo, las clases utilizadas como enumeraciones, modeladas adecuadamente con el estereotipo respectivo, no son soportadas por el servidor WebLogic 8.1, lo que hace que salte un aviso de error si existe en el modelo tal instancia. Sin embargo, en el servidor JBoss son reconocidas perfectamente.
De acuerdo a la misma documentación de ArcStyler [10], el modelo *Accessor* y su debido conjunto de artefactos generados, no es 100% compatible con los servidores distintos a WebLogic 8.1.

- El otro *framework* disponible en la herramienta para la presentación, *Struts,* no tiene un soporte completo y funcional como *Accessors*, ya que los artefactos generados están incompletos y requieren de mucho trabajo adicional en la manipulación de código. El modelado en *Struts* lleva aproximadamente el mismo tiempo de diseño que el realizado en su par *Accessor*, lo que determina un innecesario trabajo adicional si se escoge primeramente el *framework Struts* para el diseño de la capa de presentación, y luego se cambia por *Accessor* al ver que los artefactos generados para *Struts* son improductivos.
- El trabajo con una base de datos específica (distinta a la establecida por defecto en el servidor de aplicación) no requiere de cambios especiales en el modelo. Sólo se necesitan establecer en las marcas de la configuración de transformaciones los datos relativos al servidor de base de datos, como autenticación de usuario, ubicación y nombre de base de datos, *driver* JDBC, etc. No obstante, el tiempo necesario para llevar a cabo los ajustes del servidor J2EE con el servidor de base de datos específico varía según el motor de base de datos y de la experiencia del desarrollador en llevar a cabo dichos ajustes.

c. Portabilidad entre plataformas distintas

Por otra parte, viendo la portabilidad a otra plataforma distinta a Java, tenemos que la herramienta ofrece el soporte de modelado y generación de artefactos de la plataforma .NET y el lenguaje C# a través de los cartuchos MDA respectivos. De manera similar a la arquitectura J2EE, la generación de artefactos para la plataforma .NET está orientada a la arquitectura *enterprise* a través del modelado de los *Enterprise Distributed Objects* con la definición de las 4 capas de la arquitectura (*bussiness facade*, *bussiness rules*, *data access*, *common*), y la generación de los fuentes correspondientes. No obstante, el modelado y generación de la aplicación no se ha realizado para esta plataforma por lo que se encuentra fuera del alcance de los resultados analizados.

3.3 Reusabilidad

a. De las definiciones de las transformaciones

ArcStyler no sólo permite al usuario la elección de la plataforma de trabajo, y la selección de un proveedor *middleware*. Al no ser una herramienta "cerrada", el soporte para nuevas plataformas no depende exclusivamente del fabricante de la herramienta, sino del desarrollo de los mismos usuarios de nuevos cartuchos MDA (*MDA-Cartridge*) ó de la extensión de los cartuchos MDA ya existentes con el fin de adaptarlos a los requisitos específicos para luego utilizarlos en proyectos concretos.

Mediante la arquitectura CARAT [4, 7, 9] y un entorno de desarrollo exclusivo para la edición y creación de cartuchos brindados por la herramienta, se pueden definir nuevos cartuchos con los ajustes necesarios para realizar las transformaciones buscadas utilizando el mecanismo de herencia de cartuchos MDA. Estas tareas, aunque requieren un conocimiento profundo de la arquitectura CARAT, pueden proporcionar definiciones de transformación ajustadas a los requisitos comunes del dominio de los sistemas, como ser una empresa o una industria de software, en donde las aplicaciones desarrolladas presentan con regularidad patrones similares en funcionalidades y detalles de presentación. Dicha utilidad podría ser interesante si se aplica eficazmente en la construcción de sistemas, pues se puede llegar a ahorrar tiempo sustancial en el modelado y en la codificación manual de secciones comunes de la aplicación mediante la utilización de patrones por ejemplo.

b. De elementos de la estructura de la aplicación

Podemos señalar que como consecuencia del enfoque MDA y de su lógica subyacente que es la orientación a objetos, contamos con modelos y artefactos cuyos elementos son fácilmente reusables en distintas partes de la aplicación. Además, al momento de agregar código adicional para completar la implementación de funcionalidades, el esfuerzo del programador es mínimo ya que gran parte del código fuente es generado por la herramienta en base a reglas de transformación adecuados a estándares de plataformas y *frameworks* (como *Accessor* por ejemplo). Esta reducción de esfuerzo para el programador es debida fundamentalmente al mecanismo de generación (cartuchos MDA, generador), que reutiliza las definiciones de las transformaciones, por lo que contamos con artefactos que contienen porciones de código generado muy similares, observándose patrones de código a lo largo del código fuente (reusabilidad de definiciones de transformaciones). En el enfoque de desarrollo tradicional, la disponibilidad de elementos reusables depende de un mayor esfuerzo del desarrollador, quien es responsable del diseño e implementación de componentes reusables de la aplicación.

c. Reusabilidad de modelos

La reusabilidad de modelos en ArcStyler está disponible básicamente para la lógica de negocios en arquitecturas *enterprise*, como J2EE y .NET EDS, permitiendo en cualquier etapa de desarrollo la inclusión del cartucho MDA relativo a una plataforma específica en el proyecto de trabajo, y de ese modo consignar las marcas necesarias para la transformación a esa plataforma. Sin embargo, el modelo de la capa de presentación está orientado a un ambiente particular (web) y para una plataforma determinada como J2EE. Esta limitación nos demuestra que ArcStyler trabaja con modelos que son más dependientes de plataforma para la capa de presentación de una aplicación.

3.4 Mantenibilidad

a. Esfuerzo en mantenimiento general

El índice de productividad indicado en la sección 4.1 también nos sirve para hallar el costo de mantenimiento de agregar una nueva funcionalidad. Proponemos interpretar el valor obtenido de p=1,6 diciendo que se invierte en promedio 1 o 2 días a lo sumo para implementar una funcionalidad, que contempla desde el diseño, la generación, codificación manual y construcción de la aplicación actualizada que ofrece la nueva funcionalidad agregada.

b. Esfuerzo en mantenimiento perfectivo

Esta cualidad bien puede ser una de las ventajas más constatadas a lo largo del todo el trabajo de la aplicación de caso de estudio con la herramienta MDA ArcStyler, pues en todo el período de producción se ha realizado una implementación gradual de las funcionalidades. Dicha incorporación gradual de nuevas funcionalidades es posible gracias al mecanismo del generador de la herramienta, que permite mantener una consistencia entre los modelos y el código generado, de tal modo a que cualquier cambio hecho al modelo, como la creación de un nuevo elemento, o la eliminación de alguna pieza del modelo (tareas típicas de un mantenimiento perfectivo), queda reflejado en el código fuente generado, sea con la adición o eliminación de la porción de código correspondiente.

Los cambios manuales introducidos en el código fuente, son conservados en las sucesivas regeneraciones. A esta propiedad facilitada por la herramienta se le conoce con el nombre de "consistencia incremental". A menos que intencionalmente se eliminen uno o más archivos fuentes que contengan porciones de código escritos manualmente, tales modificaciones no son afectadas y son compiladas junto al código bruto generado por la herramienta, formando parte del módulo de ensamblado respectivo de la aplicación.

La aplicación constante de cambios en el modelo conduce a un ciclo de generación-construcción permanente, por lo que es importante mantener también una consistencia entre el código fuente y el código objeto compilado, a fin de que en la construcción se obtenga con certeza los componentes de despliegue correspondientes a la última generación de código. Para ello es necesario aplicar las tareas de "limpieza" de código compilado, que para la plataforma Java se trata de clases compiladas (.class), antes de cada inicio de secuencia de construcción de la aplicación, mediante la ejecución de la operación de limpieza facilitada por la herramienta de construcción ANT.

c. Esfuerzo en mantenimiento adaptativo

En cuanto al mantenimiento adaptativo de la aplicación, encontramos que este se realiza sobre todo en los elementos de la capa de presentación, es decir, controladores *accessor* y vistas o *representers*. La dedicación a ajustes en las interfaces, es decir páginas JSP-HTML, es inevitable si se requiere de una estructura apropiada de los elementos GUI o controles de los formularios web conforme a los intereses de los usuarios. En otros casos, la introducción de cambios manuales es imperativa porque el generador produce código incompleto como en la conversión de tipos de datos, en particular para el tipo fecha. Generalmente la aplicación de formato en la presentación de datos de cualquier tipo en las interfaces debe ser manejado manualmente en el código fuente. En la sección 4.1 pudo verse un detalle de los cambios aplicados en las interfaces generadas por la herramienta de la aplicación de caso de estudio. Otro aspecto referente al mantenimiento adaptativo tiene que ver con el trabajo de aplicar ajustes adicionales para un eventual cambio de plataforma, el cual se realiza de manera ágil y no involucra costo importante cuando se trata de cambios en una misma plataforma, ó entre plataformas diferentes pero dentro de una arquitectura *enterprise* (J2EE, .NET EDS), para el componente de lógica de negocios, tal como se ha mostrado en la sección 4.2.

d. Esfuerzo en mantenimiento correctivo

El código introducido por el programador en distintas partes del código fuente puede no estar exento de errores, lo que podría advertirse en tiempo de compilación o en tiempo de ejecución. Las habilidades del programador en la depuración de código entran en juego, porque facilitan la detección temprana de errores para su corrección adecuada, que pueden influir más o menos en los costos de mantenimiento correctivo del sistema. Los errores que pudieran contener los modelos suelen ser indicados en el momento de generación de artefactos o en la verificación de modelos, por lo que la probabilidad de trasladar errores desde el modelo al código fuente es relativamente menor que aquellos introducidos involuntariamente por el programador en la manipulación del código. Al centrarse más en los modelos el diagnóstico de errores posibles, se facilita considerablemente su corrección y se logra obtener un código fuente generado más fiable, puesto que antes de proceder a la generación de artefactos los eventuales errores son detectados y manejados apropiadamente en su gran mayoría.

Una propiedad deseable que debería soportar toda herramienta MDA es la **trazabilidad**, y se refiere a la capacidad de conocer el destino en el código generado de los elementos del modelo (seguimiento de una *traza*). Esta característica es útil para las tareas de mantenimiento porque contribuye en la optimización en el trabajo con el código fuente. Pero ArcStyler sólo permite ver detalles sobre el modelo indicando los diagramas que contienen un determinado elemento, como una clase o relación. La herramienta no facilita información que permita saber rápidamente y en cualquier momento el origen de los archivos fuentes o el destino en el código fuente de un elemento del modelo.

4 Conclusión

En este trabajo hemos comprobado el alcance de los beneficios planteados por el enfoque MDA con el desarrollo del sistema de gestión e información presentado en una herramienta particular como *ArcStyler*. Evidentemente, los resultados alcanzados son significativos para el ámbito de la herramienta utilizada y para el tipo de aplicaciones CRUD de pequeño tamaño y complejidad, como es el caso del sistema de rubros. Sin embargo, cabe mencionar que sistemas con estas características son bastante comunes en muchas organizaciones.

Analizando los resultados obtenidos, especialmente en lo que se refiere a ahorro de costos de producción, la experiencia ganada nos ha mostrado un índice de productividad obtenido muy ventajoso, ya que se ha llegado a ahorrar hasta seis veces el tiempo desarrollo para un sistema corriente de información y una importante reducción de esfuerzo en codificación siendo que el programador se ha ocupado sólo del 10% del código fuente de la aplicación. En cuanto al mantenimiento, se ha constatado como la facilidad en las tareas de mantenimiento perfectivo de la aplicación. No obstante, todavía hay aspectos que pueden mejorarse, principalmente los referidos a las propiedades cualitativas de una aplicación (como ser los requisitos no funcionales que incluyen robustez, seguridad, interfaz del usuario adaptable, etc.), y a las cuestiones de portabilidad entre distintas plataformas, ya que estas se aplican más bien al componente de lógica de negocios en arquitecturas Enterprise, como

J2EE y .NET EDS, y no tanto al modelo de la presentación, ya que estos son solo útiles para un entorno y plataforma específicos: aplicaciones Web basadas en Java. Es importante recordar que el logro de los beneficios planteados inicialmente en *MDA* no responde a un único factor, que es la herramienta *MDA*, el cual se considera uno de los más importantes dentro de este enfoque. Existen otros factores también valiosos que contribuyen a la satisfacción de los objetivos de *MDA* en el desarrollo de un producto, por lo que es importante mencionarlos: el manejo correcto de los lenguajes estándares *MDA* por los desarrolladores, así como los no estándares (por ejemplo, aquellos usados para la definición de transformaciones), el modelado adecuado (diagramas UML y otras extensiones de UML) y la completitud de las especificaciones, la habilidad en la aplicación de ajustes de configuración de las herramientas a las necesidades de un proyecto específico. La combinación apropiada de estos factores, junto con el soporte de una buena herramienta *MDA*, logrará finalmente la satisfacción plena de los objetivos planteados por *Model Driven Architecture* en cada proyecto de desarrollo de sistemas informáticos.

En futuros trabajos sería interesante profundizar aspectos tales como la ampliación de la experiencia a aplicaciones de otro dominio y mayor complejidad; la creación de un metamodelo para la capa de presentación, independiente de plataforma; y la aplicación del trabajo de evaluación con otras herramientas MDA (androMDA, Borland Together, etc.).

Referencias

1. Object Management Group. MDA Guide Version 1.0.1. (2003) www.omg.org/cgi-bin/apps/doc?omg/03-06-01.pdf
2. Kleepe, J. Warmer, W. Bast. MDA Explained. The Model Driven Architecture practice and promise. Addison-Wesley Pearson Education. (2003)
3. The Middleware Company. Model Driven Development for J2EE utilizing Model Driven Architecture (MDA) Approach. Productivity Analisis. (2003). www.omg.org/mda_files/MDA_Comparison-TMC_final.pdf
4. Marquina Muñoz, F. Arquitecturas de Transformación MDA: ArcStyler y OptimalJ. Proyecto Informático de Fin de Carrera. Departamento de Informática y Sistemas, Universidad de Murcia (España). (2005)
5. Rodríguez Vicente, J. Ingeniería de modelos con MDA: Estudio comparativo de OptimalJ y ArcStyler. Proyecto Informático de Fin de Carrera. Departamento de Informática y Sistemas, Universidad de Murcia (España). (2004)
6. ArcStyler (Interactive Objets). www.interactive-objets.com/products/arcstyler
7. Lasheras Velazco, J. Cartuchos MDA en ArcStyler 4.0. Curso de Doctorado: Arquitectura del Software. Universidad de Murcia (España). (2004)
8. Interactive Objects. ArcStyler Accessor Guide for ArcStyler Version 5.5. (2006)
9. Interactive Objects. ArcStyler Carat Guide for ArcStyler Version 5.5. (2006)
10. Interactive Objects. ArcStyler Release Notes for ArcStyler Version 5.5. (2006)
11. Objecteering (Objecteering Software). www.objecteering.com
12. Enterprise Architect (Sparx Systems). www.sparxsystems.com
13. Mia-Generation (Mia-Software). www.mia-software.com
14. OlivaNova (Care Technologies). www.care-t.com

Unifying Models of Test Cases and Requirements

Clélio Feitosa[1], Glaucia Peres[1] and Alexandre Mota[1]

[1] Centro de Informática – Universidade Federal de Pernambuco (UFPE)
Caixa Postal 7851 - 50732-970 – Recife – PE – Brazil
{cfs, gbp, acm}@cin.ufpe.br

Abstract. In industry, due to market pressures, it is common that the system requirements are out of date or incomplete for certain parts of the system. Nevertheless, we can always find up to date test cases which implicitly complements the related requirements. Therefore, instead of simply using test cases to detect software failures, in this paper we present an approach to update requirements using test cases. To accomplish this, we first assume that both requirements and test cases are formally documented; we reuse previous works that provide such models automatically as CSP formal specifications. Thus, we formally define a merge operation using the operational semantics of CSP. Finally, we use part of a real case study to experience the proposed approach.

Keywords: formal methods and models, CSP, CNL, modelling and unifying models.

1 Introduction

It is well-known from Software Engineering that a good requirements document is a required starting point to quality software development [1]. From requirements, one originates the architecture of the system, considers design decisions, builds the implementation, and specifies test cases among other tasks. For instance, inside the requirements document we can find the requirements specification (or model) which, in general, only considers the functional aspects of the product.

Unfortunately, in real (or industrial) software development, due to associated market pressures to release new product versions as soon as possible, some requirements are unavailable or out of date. But interestingly, as the product must be released, the implementations and test cases stay up to date. This situation is not so difficult to explain. Initially, we have an up to date requirements specification. Later, during development, it is sometime forgotten (the team has no time to update it), giving priority to what the market wants: software running (code) and quality (tests).

This work has been developed in the context of the CIn/BTC research project, which is sponsored by Motorola Inc. This project aims to improve the software testing process through automation.

In this paper we propose an approach to automatically update the (out of date) requirements specification using (up to date) test cases. To accomplish this, we reuse a controlled natural language---CNL (Section 2), developed in the context of the

CIn/BTC research project, to describe both requirements and test cases. Thus, we translate both documents into the process algebra CSP (Section 3), used as our formal basis, where we reuse the translation CNL-CSP and present one for test cases to CSP. Finally, we propose a merge operator (Section 5) using the operational semantics of CSP, which takes two CSP models and returns the unifying one. In Section 6 we show a tool support for our proposal and use it in a simple case study. Finally, we present our conclusions and future works in Section 7.

2 The Controlled Natural Language

Controlled Natural Language (CNL) is a processable version of English. The CNL grammar is a subset of the English grammar. Its sentences contain domain specific verbs, terms, and modifiers. The phrases are centered on the verb. Domain terms and modifiers are combined in order to take thematic roles around the verb [2]. This strategy is detailed in [3] where it has been used to translate test cases sentences into CSP constructions. Fig. 1 presents a simplified view of the syntax of the CNL. Thus a requirements document is seen as a set of CNL sentences.

```
sentence ::= verb nounPhrase
nounPhrase ::= preposition article modifier noun modifier
             | article modifier noun modifier
             | modifier noun modifier
             | modifier noun
             | noun modifier
             | noun
verb ::= send | call | select ...
article ::= the | a | an
preposition ::= from | to ...
modifier ::= at least | protected ...
noun ::= phone | folder ...
```

Fig. 1. BNF for the Controlled Natural Language

In Fig. 2, we observe an example of a use case where the fields `User Action` and `System Response` are written in the CNL. The example is a template of a use case document proposed by [4] and it is used to represent the use cases involved in our approach. There are two types of flows: the `Main Flow` and the `Alternative Flows`. For each flow we have the step description (represented by the field `User Action`), the `System State` that complements the steps and the `System Response`. Each alternative flow is related with some step of the `Main Flow` or with some step of another `Alternative Flow`, by the field `From Step`. The field `Step Id` is used to make each step unique in the use case. In our example, the step `UC_01_1M` represents the first step of the use case. The field `To Step` indicates which step follows the last step of its corresponding flow. For instance, the `To Step` of the last alternative flow in Fig. 2, filled with `SKIP`, says that after the step `UC_01_4A`, the execution of the flow is over. In this example the

Requirements Codes field is empty, meaning that the use case UC_01 is not related to other use cases.

UC 01 – Send and receive a SMS message

Related requirement(s)

Requirements Codes

Description

Verify if a SMS message is received after it had been sent.

Main Flow

From Step: START
To Step: END

Step Id	User Action	System State	System Response
UC_01_1M	Turn on the phone and go to the messaging application		The message box is shown on screen.
UC_01_2M	Create a SMS message with the fields: To: 555-5555 Fom: 555-5555, and CONTENT: Test.		All message fields are displayed with the information filled.
UC_01_3M	Send SMS message.		A screen is shown with a progress bar of sending.
UC_01_4M	Go to Message Center and verify if the sent SMS is there.		The message inbox is shown on screen.

Alternative Flows

From Step: UC_01_4M
To Step: UC_01_3M

Step Id	User Action	System State	System Response
UC_01_1A	The sent message is not in the inbox folder.		The message inbox is shown on screen, but there is not any message.
UC_01_2A	Verify if the phone number is correct.		

From Step: UC_01_1A
To Step: SKIP

Step Id	User Action	System State	System Response
UC_01_3A	The sent message is in the inbox folder.		The sent message is shown in the inbox folder.
UC_01_4A	Delete the sent message.		

Fig. 2. Example of a use case written in the CNL

Fig. 3 illustrates two examples of CNL sentences. The first one, Delete the sent message, is an imperative sentence that has the verb Delete and the term sent message. In this case, thematic roles are defined to the verb Delete in order to determine how the verb to delete is associated with terms. Thus, the positions of the terms in the sentence are also defined by the thematic roles. The same happens to the second sentence, All message fields are displayed, where thematic roles are also defined to the verb `to be` in order to validate the construction `<term> <verb> <modifier>`.

Delete (Verb) **the sent message** (Term)

All message fields (Term) **are** (Verb) **displayed** (Modifier)

Fig. 3. CNL sentences components

3 An Outline of CSP

The process algebra CSP [5] is a formal specification language specially designed to describe the behaviour of concurrent systems. However, CSP can also be seen as a mathematical theory to study processes, which interact with each other and their environments, using communications. CSP is based on a synchronous communication model. In practice, we use a machine-readable version of CSP called CSP_M [6]. It basically adds a functional language to CSP to deal with data aspects of a system as well as has an ASCII representation for all elements of CSP. CSP_M is used in the CSP model-checker FDR [7] and animator ProBE [8]. The former allows us to check properties, such as deadlock and refinements automatically, whereas the latter allows us to investigate the behaviour of a CSP model interactively.

The fundamental idea of CSP is a communication based on events; events are instantaneous (atomic) actions that a system can perform. Events are assumed to be drawn from a set Σ; the *alphabet* of a specification. Thus, the set Σ contains all possible communications a CSP specification can perform. In a specification, events are introduced by `channel` declarations; channels can be typed or untyped. Untyped channels (`turnOn`) are indeed events (or simply synchronization points), whereas typed channels (`send` and `receive`) are collection of events (also seen as vehicles to communicate data of the respective type). Types are built-in (`Int` for integers) or user-defined (`datatype` denotes enumerations and `nametype` abbreviations). The following fragment of CSP specification illustrates these elements.

```
datatype MESSAGES = SMS | EMS | MMS
nametype PHONE = Int
channel turnOn
channel send, receive: MESSAGES.PHONE
```

A typed channel `send` can communicate any data from the composed type `MESSAGES.PHONE`. Thus, an event from this collection is an element whose name is `send`, followed by (`.`) a value formed from the enumerated type `MESSAGES` (or an `SMS`, `EMS` or `MMS` message), followed by (`.`) a phone, specified by the type `PHONE` (or an integer). For instance, `send.SMS.1` defines the action of sending an SMS message to phone `1`. Typed events can be used to input or output data. To describe an input using the channel `receive` we write `receive?msg?phone`. This pattern introduces two variables msg and phone where their values are only determined after a communication has occurred successfully. In order to input or output data, synchronize communications and describe behaviours, CSP uses processes. A process is a behavioural unit. A BNF of a CSP process is.

```
P ::= STOP
| SKIP
| a -> P
| P |~| P
| P [] P
| P [|X|]P
| Q
```

In CSP, two basic processes deserve special attention: The first is the process STOP, which represents a broken machine (that is, a machine that is unable to communicate anything), and the second is the process SKIP used to denote a successfully terminated process. SKIP differs from STOP by simply performing a special event √ (tick) before terminating and behaving like STOP. The simplest behaviour apart from STOP and SKIP is given by the prefix (->) operator. The process e -> P offers the event e to its environment[1] and waits indefinitely for its occurrence. Once the event e occurs, the process e -> P behaves like P.

Alternative behaviour is characterized by two kinds of choice operators: The internal or non-deterministic choice (|~|) and the external or deterministic choice ([]). The process P |~| Q behaves like P or Q independent of the environment. So, the process P |~| Q passes to behave like P or Q and only after that the environment can interact with it. On the other hand, the process P [] Q can behave like P or Q but the choice is decided by the environment. If the environment is only able to interact with P, then P is chosen, otherwise Q is chosen.

Sometimes it is necessary to model independent machines that can eventually communicate to each other. Thus, the parallel ([|X|]) operator is used. The process P [|X|] Q can behave like P' [|X|] Q, in case P can evolve to P', and like P [|X|] Q', if Q can evolve to Q'. If both P and Q can evolve but the environment cannot distinguish which of them has evolved, then a non-deterministic behaviour occurs. These situations occur when P and Q cannot interact with each other. If they interact then the previous process behaves like P' [|X|] Q', that is, both processes must evolve simultaneously (synchronously).

A CSP process is defined by an equation, where the left-hand side has the name of the process with eventual parameters and the right-hand side has the process body, given by a composition of the previous operators. The following equation defines the process TEST_CASE_1 as a series of prefixes terminating successfully.

```
TEST_CASE_1 =
   setup -> goTo.MESSAGE_EDITOR.1 -> create.SMS.1 ->
   test -> send.SMS.1 -> receive?mesg.1 -> open.mesg ->
   cleanup -> delete.mesg -> goTo.IDLE -> SKIP
```

[1] A CSP environment is anything which can interact with a process.

To capture non-terminating behaviour, we simply use recursive processes. The last element of our BNF refers to a recursive process call (`Q`). This occurs when in the right-hand side of an equation, `P = ... Q`, the name of a process corresponds to the left-hand side of some (other or the same) equation (`Q = ...`). In this case, the behaviour is simply transferred to the right-hand side of the called process. Therefore, recursive behaviour allows infinite system modelling.

To state formally the meaning of a CSP process various semantics were proposed [5]. At least three distinct ways are proposed to gain a rigorous mathematical understanding of what a CSP program means. They are the operational, denotational, and algebraic semantics. In this paper, we consider the CSP operational semantics to propose the merge operator, described in Section 5.

4 CSP Models of Test Cases and Requirements

To unify documents automatically, an obvious starting point is that the artefacts (test cases and requirements) being written in a formal language. In this paper we use the process algebra CSP as this medium. Prior to present how the unification is performed we must present how our artefacts are generated in terms of CSP, which in general is a difficult task itself. In this work we show that this task is relatively easy to satisfy once we consider a specific domain, mobile phone applications.

Section 4.1 gives an overview of how the CSP model is generated from standard test cases, and Section 4.2 for models originated from system requirements.

4.1 From Test Cases to CSP Model

The generation of a CSP model from a set of test cases is performed automatically. First, each test case is translated to CSP and thus the various intermediate CSP representations (CSP test cases) are grouped using a CSP function. In what follows, we present a brief idea about this translation task.

In general, in industry, we have two kinds of test cases: one is informal and described in some natural language, and another is precise having a programming language as basis. Informal test cases are a central artefact for human beings but are not so useful for automatic testing. In this latter case, precise test cases are employed. A test script, or test case script, is a kind of precise test case defined by a series of steps based on some programming language. To ease the understanding of this translation process, we consider an instance of a test script (see Fig. 4) and its generated formal test case. The test script of Fig. 4 is related to the use case described in Fig. 2 and it is composed by three main parts: setup, test, and cleanup. Each part has a set of actions, where each action is described in a CNL (**description**), corresponding to its related use case's step. Each description represents a goal of a specific step (set of actions) of the test. Associated to each action, we have a sequence of script commands. The translation consists in taking each goal (**description** field) of the test described in CNL and generating a corresponding CSP event. In general terms, the translation CNL-CSP follows a natural language processing [3], where the verb of the sentence (main element) is converted to a typed CSP event or channel. The verbal complements mean the composed data of the typed channel, which are supposed to communicate. Beyond the generated CSP events, such translation is also responsible for generating all CSP header definitions, such as type, event and channel definitions, and so on. The detailed description of this translation task is out of the present work scope. For further details consider the work presented in [3].

A CSP test case is represented as a CSP trace, where each event corresponds to an action of the test case. In what follows, we show an instance of a CSP test case generated from the test script shown in Fig. 4. That is, we present the trace `TC_Send_SMS_Message` in terms of CSP. Such a representation is similar to any sequence in a functional language and thus dispenses further explanation.

```
TestCase TC_Send_SMS_Message :
  Setup :
      description("Turn on the phone and go to the messaging application.");
      phone.turnOn();
      phone.goTo(MESSAGING_APPLICATION);
      phone.deleteAllMsg();
  Test :
      description("Create a SMS message.");
      SMS msg = phone.create(SMS_MESSAGE);
      msg.addContent("Test SMS message");
      msg.addDestination(MY_OWN_NUMBER)
      phone.setFields(msg);

      description("Send SMS message.");
      phone.send(msg);

      description("Verify the receiving of SMS message.");
      phone.openSMS(msg);
      phone.checkContent(msg);
  Cleanup :
      description("Delete the message and go back to the initial status.");
      phone.deleteAllMsg();
      phone.goTo(IDLE);
```

Fig. 4. An instance of a standard test script

```
TC_Send_SMS_Message =
 <setup, turnOn, goTo.MESSAGING_APP, delete.ALL_MESSAGES,
  test, create.SMS, send.SMS, verify.SMS,
  cleanup, delete.SMS, goTo.IDLE>
```

It is worth noting the similarity of the CSP event names with the elements in Fig. 4. For instance, the `Setup` method became the `setup` event. After the previous task is done in all test cases that form a given feature under test, we can build an overall model to capture all test cases in a single behavioural unit (CSP process). It will represent a specific feature of the phone that the test cases are supposed to cover. To give an idea of the previous effort, we present the generated CSP process from a set of formal test cases. Thus, initially we have three test cases: one for sending a SMS message

```
TC1 = <setup, turnOn, goTo.MESSAGING_APP,
       test, create.SMS, send.SMS, verify.SMS,
       cleanup, delete.SMS, goTo.IDLE>
```

another for a MMS message

```
TC2 = <setup, turnOn, goTo.MESSAGING_APP,
       test, create.MMS, send.MMS, verify.MMS,
       cleanup, delete.MMS, goTo.IDLE>
```

and the last one for an EMS message.

```
TC3 = <setup, turnOn, goTo.MESSAGING_APP,
       test, create.EMS, send.EMS, verify.EMS,
       cleanup, delete.EMS, goTo.IDLE>
```

The composition of the previous formal test cases (the test cases model) yields the following CSP process.

```
TEST_MODEL = setup -> turnOn -> goTo.MESSAGING_APP ->
             test ->
             (    create.SMS -> SENDING(SMS)
               [] create.EMS -> SENDING(EMS)
               [] create.MMS -> SENDING(MMS) )

SENDING(msg) = send.msg -> verify.msg ->
               cleanup -> delete.msg -> goTo.IDLE -> SKIP
```

The test cases model, or test model, is represented as a finite CSP process (see `TEST_MODEL`). This is always possible because a typical test case has not recursive calls, it only follows simple sequential execution flow (see the test cases `TC1`, `TC2`, and `TC3`) and always end in a `SKIP` process (or successful termination).

4.2 From Requirement to CSP Model

The requirements are described by use case descriptions, where each use case is divided in main and exception flows. Each flow has one or more steps described in natural language. Recall from Fig. 1, it shows a standard use case. Each use case must also be represented following the CSP notation. The task of modelling use cases as CSP processes can be found in [4]. It basically takes each step written in CNL and represents them as a CSP event (see [3, 4] for more details). The events are generated and organized following the flows contained in the use case. Finally, we have a CSP process that contains all generated events in their respective flows. In what follows we illustrate a use case written formally. The `UC_01` represents a formal use case generated from the use case of Fig. 2.

```
UC_01 = turnOn -> MAIN_FLOW
MAIN_FLOW = goTo.MESSAGING APP -> create.(SMS, NUMBER.5555555,
CONTENT.Test) ->
HANDLE((SMS, NUMBER.5555555, CONTENT.Test))
```

```
HANDLE(msg) = send.msg -> verify.msg ->
            ( EXCEPTION_FLOW_01(msg) [] EXCEPTION_FLOW_02(msg) )
EXCEPTION_FLOW_01(msg) =thereIsNot.msg ->checkOnMesg.NUMBER ->MAIN_FLOW
EXCEPTION_FLOW_02(msg) =thereIs.msg -> delete.msg -> goTo.IDLE -> UC_01
```

After each use case is translated to CSP, they must be composed together to form the use model, which is a unique behaviour unit (CSP process). The composition of use cases is out of the scope of this paper, so we assume that there is this model composed initially. A more detailed description about how to translate standard use cases to formal use cases and also how to compose formal use cases can be found in [4, 3]. The `REQUIREMENTS_MODEL` below illustrates a final (composed) requirements model generated from two use cases (similar to `UC_01`), where both are regarding to actions of sending messages (`SMS` and `EMS`).

```
REQUIREMENTS_MODEL = turnOn -> MAIN_FLOW
MAIN_FLOW = goTo.MESSAGING_APP ->
            ( create.SMS -> HANDLE(SMS) [] create.EMS -> HANDLE(EMS) )
HANDLE(msg) = send.msg -> verify.msg ->
              ( EXCEPTION_FLOW_01(msg) [] EXCEPTION_FLOW_02(msg) )
EXCEPTION_FLOW_01(msg) = thereIsNot.msg ->
                         checkOnMesg.PHONE NUMBER -> MAIN_FLOW
EXCEPTION_FLOW_02(msg) = thereIs.msg ->
                         delete.msg -> goTo.IDLE -> REQUIREMENTS_MODEL
```

In the previous requirements model (`REQUIREMENTS_MODEL`), note the generated choice between `create.SMS` and `create.EMS` in the external choice of the process `MAIN_FLOW`. Such choice well characterizes the unified use cases.

Similarly to the test model, the requirements model is also a CSP process, although it differs because the requirements model contains recursive calls. Due to recursive behaviour of CSP process the requirements model can generate infinite traces. The same does not apply to the test model as explained farther.

5 Defining the *merge* Operator

Our merge operator must behave similar to parallelism on common events and as external choice on distinct ones. Fig. 5 and Fig. 6 are illustrating our merging approach. Note that, the points A, D and E are common to both models (they are indeed our intersection points). Each one must be factorized as a single sequence in the final (resulting) model as represented in Fig. 6.

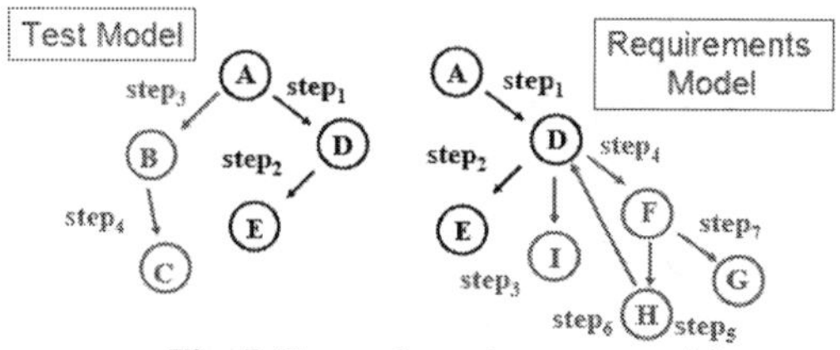

Fig. 5. Test and requirements models

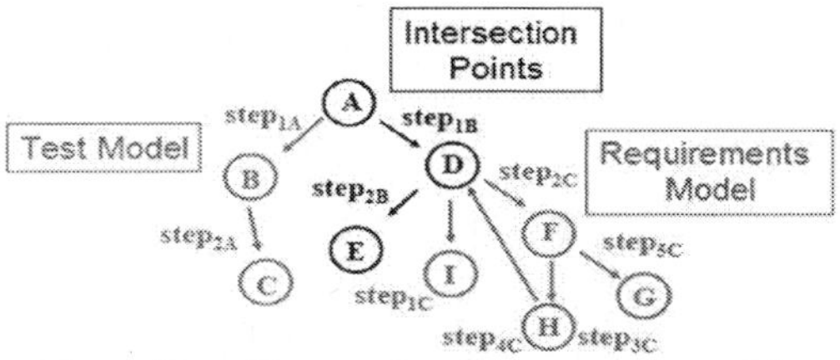

Fig. 6. Use of intersection points to unify models

According to Fig. 6 the unified model is composed by three distinct parts: the test model (nodes B and C), the intersection points (nodes A, D and E) and the requirements model (nodes F, G, H and I). The unified model of Fig. 6 is generated using the test model (left-side) and requirements model (right-side) of Fig. 5. It is important to note that, in real terms, in order to well define the intersection points the test and requirement models should describe the same set of functionalities (feature).

A requirements model, differently of the test case model, is based on recursive calls, that is, it has infinite behaviours. Thus, to compose both models into a single one we cannot use the functional features of CSP. Thus, we have two main ways of doing this: (i) by using a combination of CSP operators; (ii) by proposing a new CSP operator. In this paper we explore the latter alternative.

5.1 CSP *merge* Operator

As it was mentioned before, we define the merge operator using an approach based on operational semantics. This new CSP operator, ⊕ (the merge operator), is responsible for unifying CSP models. Fig. 7 shows the approach of updating the requirements model using the merge operator. Initially we have an out of date requirements model and an up to date test case model. The merge operator receives both models and performs the unification. The result of this unification effort is a new updated requirements model.

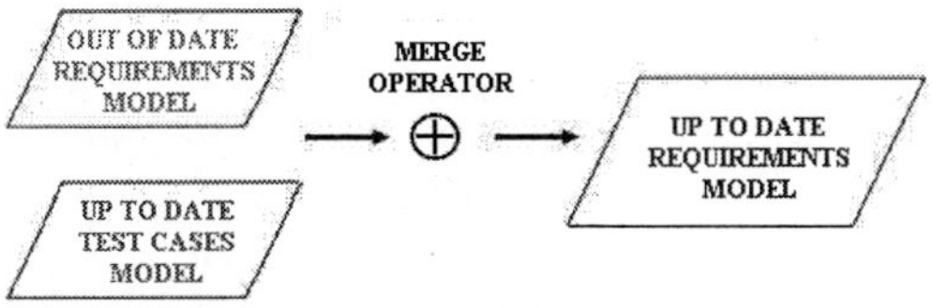

Fig. 7. Unifying CSP models: requirements and test cases

Our merge operator, as previously cited, must behave similar to parallelism on common events and as external choice on distinct ones. Thus, similar to Roscoe's [5] definition, we have rules to promote τ actions:

$$\frac{P \xrightarrow{\tau} P'}{P \oplus Q \xrightarrow{\tau} P' \oplus Q} \qquad \frac{Q \xrightarrow{\tau} Q'}{P \oplus Q \xrightarrow{\tau} P \oplus Q'} \tag{1}$$

The merge operator also needs to handle distributed termination (see rules (2)), similarly to the rules of parallelism.

$$\frac{P \xrightarrow{\checkmark} P'}{P \oplus Q \xrightarrow{\tau} \Omega \oplus Q} \qquad \frac{Q \xrightarrow{\checkmark} Q'}{P \oplus Q \xrightarrow{\tau} P \oplus \Omega} \quad \textbf{(2)}$$

Once all arguments have terminated and become Ω, we can finish the whole process using the following rule:

$$\frac{}{\Omega \oplus \Omega \xrightarrow{\checkmark} \Omega} \quad \textbf{(3)}$$

There are two rules for ordinary visible events: one for common events (a parallel behaviour):

$$\frac{P \xrightarrow{a} P', Q \xrightarrow{a} Q'}{P \oplus Q \xrightarrow{a} P' \oplus Q'} \ (a \neq \tau) \quad \textbf{(4)}$$

and another for distinguishing events (an external choice behaviour):

$$\frac{P \xrightarrow{a} P', Q \xrightarrow{b} Q'}{P \oplus Q \xrightarrow{a} P'} \ (a \neq b) \qquad \frac{P \xrightarrow{a} P', Q \xrightarrow{b} Q'}{P \oplus Q \xrightarrow{b} Q'} \ (a \neq b) \quad \textbf{(5)}$$

6 Unifying CSP Models

The strategy of unifying CSP models has the support of some tools: the *Use Model Generator* [4] (Requirements to CSP Models), the *TCRev* [9] (Test Cases to CSP Models and Unifying Models) and the *CSP2CNL* [10] (CSP Models to Requirements). These tools have been developed to be part of a major tool, called *TaRGeT*. They are not yet working attached to the TaRGeT, but the idea is that they will be accessed from the TaRGeT's menu, as illustrated in Fig. 8. Thus, all CSP formalism (models) will be hidden from the user. There is no need to have a CSP background, once the user will only deal with the Requirements and Test Cases documents written in English (controlled natural language).

The TaRGeT or Test and Requirements Generation Tool is also related to Motorola's context, and it is being developed by the Research Team. The TaRGeT tool as suggested, gives support to automatic generation of test cases and requirements. TaRGeT automates a systematic approach for dealing with requirements, design and test artefacts in an integrated way. Test cases can be automatically generated from both use cases written in natural language and UML sequence diagrams. Moreover, existing test cases can be used to automatically generate or indicate necessary updates to requirement documents.

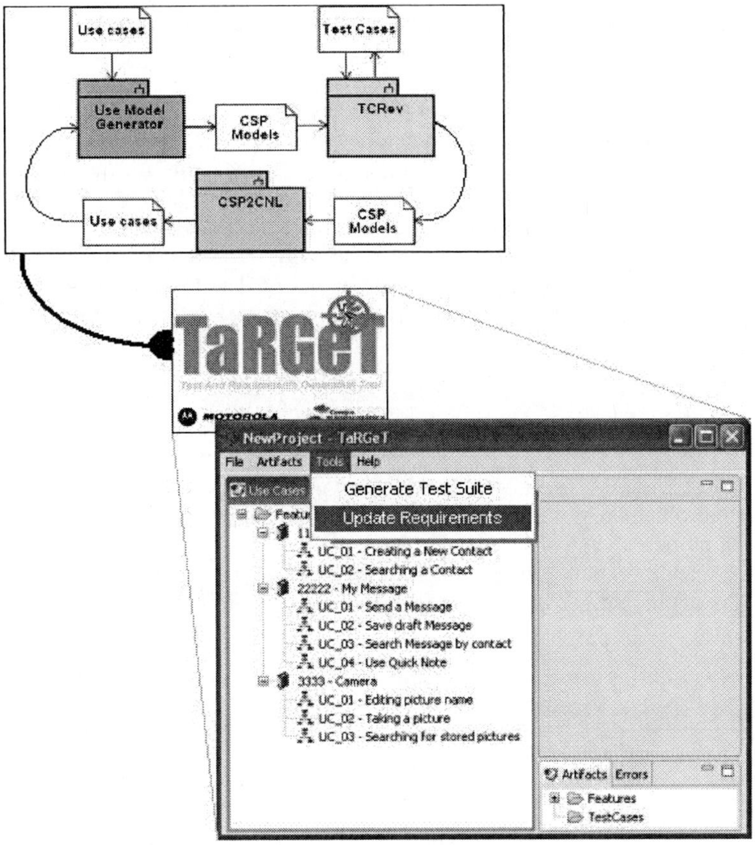

Fig. 8. Tools integration with TaRGeT

As the tools are not yet working attached to the TaRGeT, in this paper we use each tool separately. First, the *Use Model Generator* translates a requirements document into its CSP model and the *TCRev* translates the test cases documents related to those requirements into their CSP models. Then, the *TCRev* with both models, test and requirements models specified in CSP, can start the unifying step. It consists in updating the original requirements model using the test model. Thus, the result of this unification effort is a single CSP model, which contains information about the original requirements (out of date) as well as that provided by test cases (up to date). Then, with the resulting CSP model, it is now possible to translate it to an updated requirements document written in English. For this effort, we use the *CSP2CNL* tool.

In order to present our unifying strategy in the context of an industrial project, we are considering test cases and requirements that deal with a specific functionality of mobile phone. Thus, test cases as well as requirements which describe similar functionalities are grouped in specific features. For instance, a set of test cases related to sending and receiving messages are grouped in a same feature, whereas test cases related to multimedia (such as, playing audio and video files, and others) are grouped in another feature. Our case study deals only with messaging based features. In our context, the messaging feature deals with three possible types of messages: SMS, EMS, and MMS messages.

The first step is to model the set of test cases as a unique formal model. Thus, for simplification we consider the test model of Section 4.1. After modelling the test cases as a single behavioural model (TEST_MODEL), we can use the final model to update the requirements formal model. This is simply achieved by applying our proposed merge operator in the test and requirements models. As an example of an out of date requirements model we have the same requirements models shown in Section 4.2. The REQUIREMENTS_MODEL is out of date because it deals only with two kinds of messages (SMS and EMS), it does not characterize MMS messages. Thus, we define the process UPDATED_USE_MODEL in terms of the previous formal models and our proposed *merge* operator ⊕, as follows:

```
UPDATED_USE_MODEL = REQUIREMENTS_MODEL ⊕ (TEST_MODEL \ TEST_ALPHA)
```

where TEST_ALPHA = {|setup, test, cleanup|} is the set of specific test events, which are not found in the requirements model and are exclusively related to testing purposes.

By expanding the process UPDATED_USE_MODEL using the operational semantics of the merge operator, we can obtain the following explicit CSP process version.

```
UPDATED_USE_MODEL = turnOn -> MAIN_FLOW
MAIN_FLOW = goTo.MESSAGING_APP ->
            ( create.SMS -> HANDLE(SMS) [] create.EMS -> HANDLE(EMS) []
              create.MMS -> HANDLE(MMS) )
HANDLE(msg) = send.msg -> verify.msg ->
              ( EXCEPTION_FLOW_01(msg) [] EXCEPTION_FLOW_02(msg))
EXCEPTION_FLOW_01(msg) = thereIsNot.msg ->
                         checkOnMesg.PHONE_NUMBER -> MAIN_FLOW
EXCEPTION_FLOW_02(msg) = thereIs.msg -> delete.msg ->
                         goTo.IDLE -> UPDATED_USE_MODEL
```

In the previous specification we have the final updated model, which it was added a new branch to handle MMS messages ([] create.MMS -> HANDLE(MMS)). This information, not found in the original requirements model, is provided from the test model. Furthermore, the work reported in [11] translates back the previous CSP representation into a CNL use case description.

7 Conclusion

In this paper, we present an approach of unifying models using the process algebra CSP. Our models are originated from test cases and requirements, and the main goal is to update the original requirements formal model with the updated information provided from the test cases model.

We propose a new CSP operator, called *merge*, by using the CSP operational semantics. The merge operator, defined via firing rules, is responsible for updating the original specification of the system, which is, in general, incomplete and out of date. The effort in this direction was to propose a composition mechanism to deal with infinite traces. Finite traces are common to test cases because they do not have recursive calls. Requirements, on the other hand, are more general, and thus it is common to find recursive calls, which allows the generation of infinite traces.

As future work we intend to verify and prove some properties of the merge operator, such as, associativity, commutativity, and others. Another future work is to implement the merge operator using parallel composition and functional aspects of CSP [12]. This is an attempt to define the merge behaviour in syntactical terms instead of semantical ones, which was presented here. Both merge descriptions (syntactical and semantical) are possible solutions, but it is necessary to consider the benefit of each one. In syntactic terms we have more power for expressing the merge behaviour, while using a semantical approach we gain more abstraction on the unification.

We are also working toward the integration of the cited tools. The aim is to integrate the *Use Model Generator* [4], the *TCRev* [9] and the *CSP2CNL* [10] tools in the TaRGeT tool, so that the transformation of test cases and the unification with the use cases to generate an up to date final requirements documents could be executed automatically, without interruptions and users' interaction. An additional effort is to link the TaRGeT tool with FDR [7]. In order to establish this link we intend to reuse FDR features as much as possible. Thus, it will be possible to check system properties of the generated formal models (test and requirements models, and also the unified model) in a complementary and interactive way.

8 References

1. I. Sommerville. *Software Engineering*. Addison Wesley, 6th edition, 2000.
2. C. J. Fillmore. *Frame semantics and the nature of language*. In Annals of the New York Academy of Sciences: Conference on the Origin and Development of Language and Speech, Vol. 208: 20-32, 1976.
3. D. Leitão, D. Torres, and F. Barros. *NLForSpec: Translating natural language descriptions into formal test case specifications*. Technical report (TR-0606), Jun 2006.
4. G. Cabral and A. Sampaio. *Formal specification generation from requirement documents*. In Proceedings of III Brazilian Symposium on Formal Methods, pages 217–232, Natal, RN, Brazil, 2006.
5. A. W. Roscoe. *The Theory and Practice of Concurrency*. Prentice-Hall (Pearson), 1997.
6. B. Scattergood. *The Semantics and Implementation of Machine Readable CSP*. PhD thesis, University of Oxford, 1998.
7. Formal Methods (Europe) Ltd. *FDR User's Manual*, version 2.28 edition, 1997.
8. Formal Methods (Europe) Ltd. *PROBE Users Manual*, version 1.25 edition, 1998.
9. C. F. Sousa. *Modelling and Integrating Formal models: from Test Cases and Requirements Models*. Master's thesis, Universidade Federal de Pernambuco, Recife, PE, Brasil, 2006.
10. G. Peres. *Automatic English Requirements Generation from CSP Models*. Graduation work, Universidade Federal de Pernambuco, Recife, PE, Brasil, 2007.
11. G. Peres and A. Mota. *A Tool to Translate CSP Models into English Requirements*. II Encontro Brasileiro de Teste de Software, 2007 (http://ebts2007.cesar.org.br).
12. W. Mesquisa, A. Sampaio, and A. C. V. de Melo. *A strategy for the formal composition of frameworks*. SRFM, pages 404–413, 2005.

Grounding Software Domain Ontologies in the Unified Foundational Ontology (UFO): The case of the ODE Software Process Ontology

Giancarlo Guizzardi, Ricardo Falbo, Renata S.S.Guizzardi

Computer Science Department
Federal University of Espírito Santo (UFES), Vitória, Brazil
{gguizzardi,falbo,rguizzardi}@inf.ufes.br

Abstract. *Foundational Ontologies* are theoretically well-founded domain-independent systems of categories that have been successfully used to improve the quality of conceptual modeling languages and models. In this paper, we present the latest developments in the UFO ontology. Moreover, we elaborate on the relevance of these foundational ontologies in the development of domain ontologies by showing a case study in the software process domain.

Keywords: Foundational Ontology, Ontology in Software Engineering, Software Process

1 Introduction

Ontologies have been acknowledged as a useful conceptual tool in computer science since the late sixties, chiefly in the areas of data modeling and artificial intelligence [1]. In the past seven years, an explosion of works related to ontology has happened in several different fields of computer science, chiefly motivated by the growing interest on the Semantic Web, and by the key role played by them in that initiative. In the area of Software Engineering, domain ontologies have been used mainly as an enhanced representation for what is termed a domain model in the field of Domain Engineering. Ontologies for domains such as software process, software quality, software resource management, software project risks, among many others have been used for: (i) deriving reusable domain-specific frameworks [2]; (ii) integrating knowledge in semantic software environments [3].

An important point that should be emphasized is the difference in the senses of the term ontology when used by the data modeling community, on one side, and artificial intelligence, software engineering and semantic web communities on the other [1]. In data modeling and related areas (e.g., organizational engineering), the term has been used in ways that conform to its definitions in philosophy, namely, as a philosophically well-founded domain-independent system of formal categories that can be used to articulate domain-specific models of reality. In contrast, in the other areas aforementioned, the term ontology is, in general, used as: (i) a concrete engineering artifact designed for a specific purpose and without paying much attention for foundational issues; (ii) a representation of a singular domain (e.g., molecular biology, finance, logistics, ceramic materials) expressed in knowledge representation languages (e.g., RDF, OWL, F-Logic) or conceptual modeling grammars (e.g., UML, EER).

Ontologies, in the philosophical sense, have been developed in philosophy since Aristotle's theory of Substance and Accidents and, recently, a number of such theories have been proposed in the area of Applied Ontology in Computer Science under the name *Foundational Ontologies*. In this paper, we discuss a particular Foundational Ontology named *UFO (Unified Foundational Ontology)*.

UFO has been developed based on a number of theories from Formal Ontology, Philosophical Logics, Philosophy of Language, Linguistics and Cognitive Psychology. The core of this ontology (UFO-A) is presented in depth and formally characterized in [1]. Moreover, in a number of publications, UFO has been successfully employed to evaluate, re-design and integrate the models of conceptual modeling languages as well as to provide real-world semantics for their modeling constructs (e.g., [1,4-6]). In [1], a complete evaluation and re-design of the UML 2.0 metamodel using UFO is presented. In [5], we show how a modeling language based on this ontology can be used to address a number of semantic interoperability problems which cannot be handled by semantic web languages such as OWL and RDF. Finally, in [6], we evaluate, redesign and integrate two well-known modeling languages which are used in different phases of agent-oriented development processes, namely, TROPOS (for requirements engineering and early design) and AORML (for detailed design).

The purpose of this article is two fold. Firstly, we present a new version of two fragments of this foundational ontology, named UFO-B and UFO-C. UFO-B is an ontology of events; UFO-C builds on top of A and B to systematized social concepts such as plan, action, goal, agent, intentionality, commitment, appointment, among many others. Secondly, we elaborate on the relation between the two senses of ontologies aforementioned by illustrating the importance of foundational ontologies in the development of domain ontologies. In particular, we demonstrate how UFO has been used to evaluate, re-design and to give real-world semantics to an ontology in the software engineering domain, namely, the software process ontology which is the core of the ODE Ontology-Centered Software Development Environment [3].

The remaining of this article is organized as follows: in section 2, we present a small fragment of UFO-A discussing only those categories which are essential for the understanding of the sections to follow. In section 3 and 4 we introduce the new developed theories for UFO-B and C, respectively. Section 5 discusses the original ODE Software Process Ontology and demonstrates the evaluation and re-design of this ontology when mapped to (interpreted in terms of) UFO. Finally, section 6 elaborates on some final considerations of this article.

2 UFO-A: An Ontology of Endurants

A fundamental distinction in this ontology is between the categories of ***Particular (Individual)*** and ***Universal (Type)***. Particulars are entities that exist in reality possessing a unique identity. Universals, conversely, are pattern of features, which can be realized in a number of different particulars. ***Substances*** are existentially independent particulars. Examples include ordinary mesoscopic objects such as an individual person, a dog, a house, a hammer, a car, Alan Turing and The Rolling Stones. The word ***Moment,*** in contrast, denotes, what is sometimes named a trope, or an individualized (objectified) property or property in particular. Therefore, in the scope of this work, the word bears no relation to the notion of time instant in colloquial language. A moment is an individual that can only exist in other individuals. Typical examples of moments are a color, a connection, an electric charge, a symptom, a covalent bond. Moments have in common that they are all dependent of other individuals (their bearers). An important feature that characterizes all *moments* is that they can only exist in other individuals (in the way in which, for example, electrical charge can exist only in some conductor, or that a covalent bond can only exist if those connecting atoms exist). To put it more technically, we say that moments are *existentially dependent* on other individuals. Existential dependence can also be used to differentiate intrinsic and relational moments: ***intrinsic moments*** are dependent of one single individual (e.g., color, a headache, a temperature); ***relators*** depend on a plurality of individuals (e.g., an employment, a medical treatment, a marriage). Finally, we consider here the categories of ***substantial universal*** and ***moment universal***. Examples of the former include Apple, Planet and Person. Examples of the latter include Color, Electric Charge and Headache.

An attempt to model the relation between intrinsic moments and their representation in human cognitive structures is presented in the theory of *conceptual spaces* introduced in [7]. The theory is based on the notion of ***quality structure***. The idea is that for several perceivable or conceivable moment universals there is an associated quality structure in human cognition. For example, height and mass are associated with one-dimensional structures with a zero point isomorphic to the half-line of nonnegative numbers. Other properties such as color and taste are represented by multidimensional structures. In [7], the perception or conception of an intrinsic moment can be represented as a point in a quality structure. Following [8], this point is named here a ***quale***. Quality structures and qualia are together with sets, number and propositions examples of ***Abstract Particulars***.

Relations are entities that glue together other entities. In the philosophical literature, two broad categories of relations are typically considered, namely, *material* and *formal* relations [9]. Formal relations hold between two or more entities directly, without any further intervening individual. In principle, the category of formal relations includes those relations that form the mathematical superstructure of our framework including *existential dependence, part-of* (<), *subset-of, instantiation*, among many others not discussed here [1]. *Material relations*, conversely, have material structure of their own and include examples such as *working at*, *being enrolled at*, and *being connected to*. Whilst a formal relation such as the one between Paul and his knowledge x of Greek holds directly and as soon as Paul and x exist, for a material relation of *being treated in* between Paul and the medical unit MU_1 to exist, another entity must exist which *mediates* Paul and MU_1. We name these entities *relators*. Relators are individuals with the power of connecting entities. For example, a medical treatment connects a patient with a medical unit; an enrollment connects a student with an educational institution; a covalent bond connects two atoms. The notion of relator (relational moment) is supported by several works in the philosophical literature [1,9] and, the position advocated here is that they play an important role in answering questions of the sort: what does it mean to say that John is married to Mary? Why is it true to say that Bill works for Company X but not for Company Y?

Suppose that John *is married to* Mary. In this case, we can assume that there is an individual relator (relational moment) m_1 of type *marriage* that mediates John and Mary. In this case, there are many moments that John acquires by virtue of being married to Mary. For example, imagine all the legal responsibilities that John has in the context of this relation. These newly acquired properties are intrinsic moments of John which, therefore, are existentially dependent on him. However, these moments also depend on the existence of Mary. We name this type of moment ***externally dependent moment***, i.e., externally dependent moments are intrinsic moments that inhere in a single individual but are existentially dependent on (possibly multiple) other individuals. The relator marriage in this case is the sum of all externally dependent moments that John and Mary acquire by virtue of being married to each other.

Finally, we consider here the notion of ***Situations*** proposed, for example, in [9]. Situations are special types of endurants. These are complex entities that are constituted by possibly many endurants (including other situations). Situations are taken here to be synonymous to what is named *state of affairs* in the literature, i.e., a portion of reality that can be comprehended as a whole. Examples of situations include *"John being with fever and influenza", "John being in the same location as Paul while Mary is in the same location as David", "Mary being married to Paul who works for the University of Twente"*. Finally, we define a relation of *"being present at"* between endurants and the situations they constitue. For instance, we can state that both the substantial John, and the intrinsic moments m_1 (John's Fever) and m_2 (John's influenza) are present in situation s_1: *"Jonh being with fever and influenza"*. For a more detailed discussion on our view of situations and contexts, one should refer to [10].

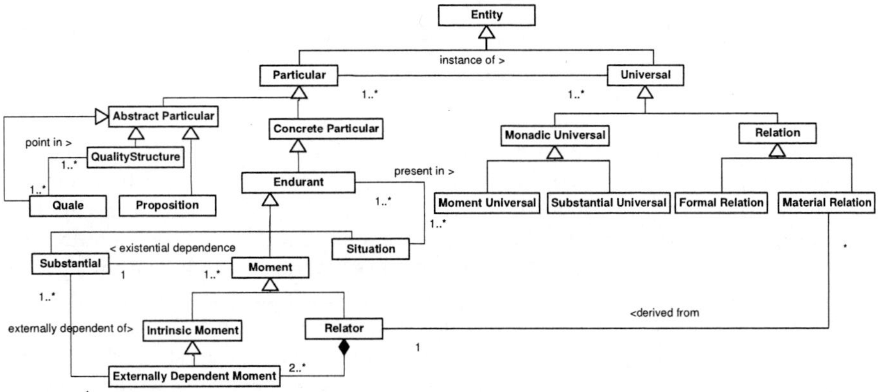

Fig.1. A Fragment of a Foundational Ontology of Endurants (UFO-A).

3 UFO-B: An Ontology of Perdurants

UFO-B makes a distinction between enduring and perduring individuals (henceforth named *endurants* and *perdurants*). Classically, this distinction can be understood in terms of their behavior w.r.t. time. Endurants are said to be wholly present whenever they are present, i.e., they *are in time*, in the sense that if we say that in circumstance c_1 an endurant *e* has a property P_1 and in circumstance c_2 the property P_2 (possibly incompatible with P_1), it is the very same endurant *e* that we refer to in each of these situations. Examples of endurants are a house, a person, the moon, a hole, an amount of sand. For instance, we can say that an individual John weights 80kg at c_1 but 68kg at c_2. Nonetheless, we are in these two cases referring to the same particular John.

Perdurants are individuals composed of temporal parts, they *happen in time* in the sense that they extend in time accumulating temporal parts. Examples of perdurants are a conversation, a football game, a symphony execution, a birthday party, the Second World War and a business process. Whenever a perdurant is present, it is not the case that all its temporal parts are present. For instance, if we consider a business process "buy product" at different time instants when it is present, at each of these time instants only some of its temporal proper parts are present. As a consequence, perdurants cannot exhibit change in time in a genuine sense since none of its temporal parts retain their identity through time.

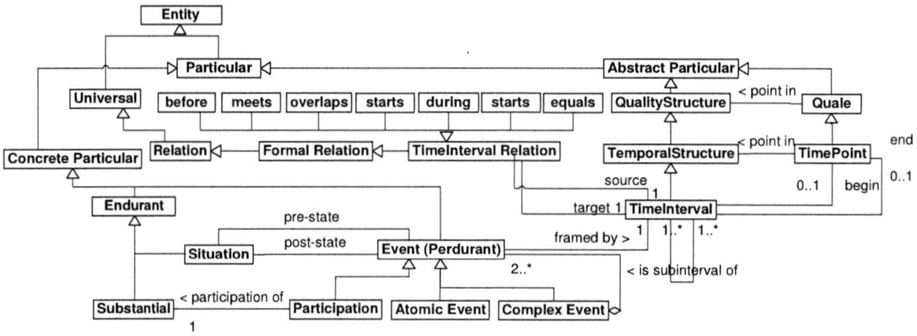

Fig.2. A Fragment of a Foundational Ontology of Perdurants (UFO-B).

Figure 2 depicts a fragment of our ontology of perdurants named UFO-B. The main category on this ontology is ***Event*** (Perdurant, Occurrent). Events can be Atomic or Complex, depending on their mereological structure, i.e., whilst atomic events have no improper parts, complex events are aggregations of at least two events (that can themselves be atomic or complex). Events are possible transformations from a portion of reality to another, i.e., they may change reality by changing the state of affairs from one (pre-state) situation to a (post-state) situation. Events are ontologically dependent entities in the sense that they existentially depend on their participants in order to exist. Take for instance the event *e*: *the stabbing of Caesar by Brutus*. In this event we have the participation of Caesar himself, of Brutus and of the knife. In this case, *e* is composed of the individual participation of each of these entities. Each of these participations is itself an event that can be complex or atomic but which existentially depends on a single substantial. It is important to emphasize that being atomic and being instantaneous are orthogonal notions in this framework, i.e., atomic participations can be time-extended as well as an instantaneous event can be composed of multiple (instantaneous) participations. In summary, the model of figure 2 depicts these two aspects on which events can be analyzed, namely, as time extended entities with certain (simple or complex) mereological structures, and as ontologically dependent entities which can comprise of a number of individual participations.

As in [8], we have that all spatial properties of events are defined in terms of the spatial properties of their participants. In contrast, all temporal properties of substantials are defined in terms of the events they participate. Analogous to what has been discussed for endurants, the temporal properties of events have their values taken (their qualia) by projecting these properties into a quality structure. We here take the time conceptual space to be a structure "composed of" Time Intervals. Time intervals themselves are "composed of" Time Points. Time points could be represented as real numbers and Time Intervals as sets of real numbers. However, they could also be interpreted as sui generis entities such as Chronoids and Time Boundaries in GFO [9]. In other words, we avoid making unnecessary ontological commitments at this point. Additionally, we admit: (i) intervals that are delimited by begin and end points as well as open intervals; (ii) continuous and non-continuous intervals; (iii) intervals with and without duration (instants). In particular, this model allows a diversity of temporal structures such as linear, branching, parallel and circular time. For the case of ordered structures we have considered the so-called *Allen Relations* [11] between intervals from which corresponding relations between events can be derived. It is important to emphasize that it is outside the focus of this article to further elaborate on the nature of these temporal structures. For this reason, we aim at characterizing only the properties which are germane to the objectives pursued here.

4 UFO-C: An Ontology of Social Entities

The third layer of the Unified Foundational Ontology is an ontology of social entities (both endurants and perdurants) built on top of UFO-A and UFO-B. A fragment of this ontology is shown in Figure 3. We start by making a distinction between Agentive and Non-agentive substantial particulars, termed here ***Agents*** and ***Objects***, respectively. Agents can be physical (e.g., a person) or social (e.g., an organization, a society). Objects can also be further categorized in physical and social objects. Physical objects include a book, a tree, a car; Social objects include money, language and ***Normative Descriptions.*** A normative description defines one or more rules/norms recognized by at least one social agent and that can define nominal universals such as social moment universals (e.g., social commitment types), social objects (the crown of the king of Spain) and social roles such as president, prime minister, PhD candidate or pedestrian. Examples of normative descriptions include the Italian Constitution, the University of Twente PhD program regulations, but also a set of directives on how to perform some actions within an organization (a description of a plan [12]).

Agents are substantials that can bear special kinds of moments named ***Intentional Moments***. As argued in [13], intentionality should be understood in a much broader context than the notion of "intending something", but as the capacity of some properties of certain individuals to refer to possible situations of reality. Every intentional moment has a type (e.g., ***Belief***, ***Desire***, ***Intention***) and a propositional content. The latter being an abstract representation of a class of situations referred by that intentional moment. Thus, "intending something" is a specific type of intentionality termed

Intention. The propositional content of an Intention is a ***Goal***. The precise relation between an intentional moment and a situation is the following: situation in reality can satisfy the propositional content of an intentional moment (i.e., satisfy - in the logical sense – the proposition representing that propositional content). Beliefs can be justified by situations in reality. Examples include my belief that Rome is the Capital of Italy, and the Belief that the Moon orbits the Earth; Desires and Intentions can be fulfilled or frustrated. Whilst a desire expresses a will of an agent towards a state of affairs in reality (e.g., a Desire that Brazil wins the Next World Cup), intentions are desired state of affairs for which the agent commits at pursuing (internal commitment) (e.g., the Intention of going to a beach resort for the next summer break) [13,14]. For this reason, intentions cause the agent to perform **Actions**.

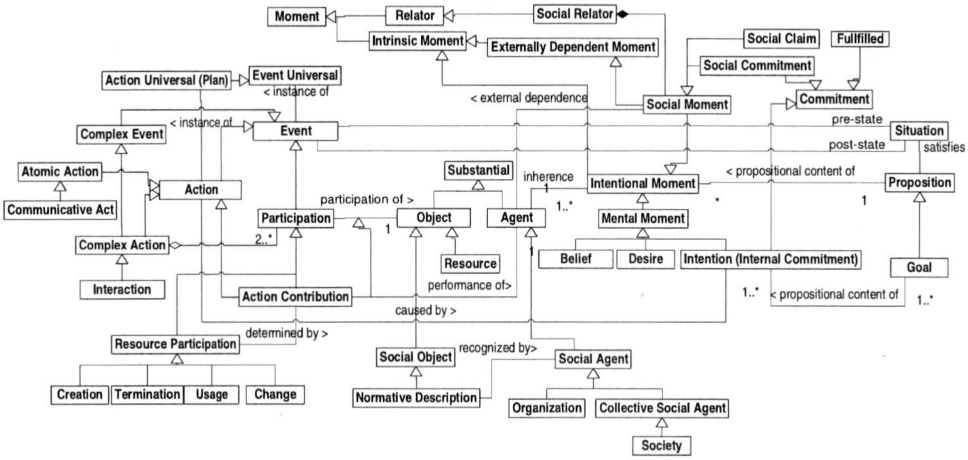

Fig.3. A Fragment of a Foundational Ontology of Social Entities (UFO-C).

Actions are intentional events, i.e., events which instantiate a ***Plan*** (Action Universal) with the specific purpose of satisfying (the propositional content of) some intention. Examples of actions include writing this paper, a business process, a communicative act. In particular, a ***Communicative Act*** (a speech act such inform, ask or promise) [13] is an example of an atomic action. As events, actions can be atomic or complex. A complex action is composed of two or more participations. These participations can themselves be intentional (i.e., be themselves actions) or unintentional events. For example, the stabbing of Caesar by Brutus includes the intentional participation of Brutus and the unintentional participation of the knife. In other words, following philosophical action theories [15], we take that it is not the case that any participation of an agent is considered an action, but only those intentional participations – termed here ***Action Contributions***. Only agents (entities capable of bearing intentional moments) can perform actions. An object participating in an action is termed a ***Resource***. A complex action composed of action contributions of different agents is termed an ***Interaction***. Two artists collaborating to create a sculpture is an example of an interaction, and so is a dialogue between two agents. In the former case, the sculpture as well as the tools and raw materials used to create it are examples of resources. Objects can participate in actions in different ways. In this article, we countenance four different modes of ***Resource Participation***, namely, ***Creation***, ***Termination***, ***Change*** or ***Usage***, which can be characterized as follows: Let *r* be a resource, *a* an action, and s_1, s_2 two situations such that they are the pre and post state of action *a*. Then we have that (i) creation: a resource participation of *r* in *ac* is a creation iff (*r is not present in* s_1) and (*r is present in* s_2) and (there is at least one action contribution *ac* that is also part of *a* and such that s_2 satisfies the propositional content of *ac*); (ii) termination: a resource participation of *r* in *a* is a termination iff (*r is present in* s_1) and (*r is not present in* s_2) and (there is at least one action contribution *ac* that is also part of *a* and such that s_2 satisfies the propositional content of *ac*); (iii) change: a resource participation of *r* in *a* is a change iff there is at least a moment *m* such that ((*m inheres in r in* s_1 and *m does not inhere in r in* s_2) OR (*m does not inhere in r in* s_1 and *m inheres in r in* s_2)) and (there is at least one action contribution *ac* that is also part of *a* and such that s_2 satisfies the propositional content of *ac*); (iv) a resource participation which is not any of the three aforementioned modes of participation is a usage participation.

As discussed in [6], a resource participation can be the cause of a *resource dependence* and the result of a *resource acquisition* between agents. In a resource acquisition from agent *B* to agent *A*, *A* gives permission of resource *r* to *B*. For this to happen, *A* must have the right to grant permission to agent *B* and, moreover, the right to grant the right mode of permission (e.g., to use, to modify). In other words, different modes of resource participations can be connected to different deontic consequences of the relation between agents. In summary, a resource participation in an action is the intended use, modification, termination or creation of an object in that action. Thus, for instance, we consider a resource change of resource *r* in action *a* when this change is the content of the intention of at least one of the agents in that action.

Communicative Acts can be used to create ***Social Moments***. In this view, language not only represents reality but also creates a part of reality [13]. Thus, social moments are types of intentional moments that are created by the exchange of communicative acts and the consequences of these exchanges (e.g., goal adoption, delegation [6]). For instance, suppose that I rent a car at a car rental service. When signing a business agreement, I perform a communicative act (a promise). This act creates a ***Social Commitment*** towards that organization: a commitment to *return the car in a certain state, etc* (the propositional content). Moreover, it also creates a ***Social Claim*** of that organization towards me w.r.t. that particular propositional content. Commitments/Claims always form a pair that refers to a unique propositional content. A ***Social Relator*** (or ***Social Bond***) is an example of a relator composed of two or more pairs of associated commitments/claims (social moments). Finally, a commitment (internal or social) is fulfilled by an agent *A* if this agent performs an action *x* such that the post-state of that action is a situation that satisfies that commitment.

4.1 The Distinction between Action Universals, Action Occurences and Scheduled Actions

In this section, we elaborate on some of the concepts discussed above with the intention of clarifying a distinction which is commonly blurred in several process models, namely, the distinction between Action Universals, Action Occurences and Scheduled

Actions. In figure 4 below, we present additional UFO-C ontological categories needed to discuss these distinctions.

We start by elaborating on the notions of commitments. Commitments (internal or social) can be ***Fulfilled*** or ***Unfulfilled***. Unfulfilled commitments can be ***Pending***, ***Dismissed*** or ***Broken***. A Social Commitment *C* is a commitment of an agent *A* towards another agent *B*, thus, as an externally dependent moment, we state that *C* inheres in *A* and is externally dependent on *B*. Differently from an internal commitment, in this case, *C* can only be dismissed by *B*. Internal commitments cause the agent to perform actions. Thus, following [14], we have that social commitments necessarily cause the creation of internal commitments, i.e., if I promise to bring you a specific book by tomorrow, asides from the commitment with you, I must also create the intention (internal commitment) of bringing the book by tomorrow.

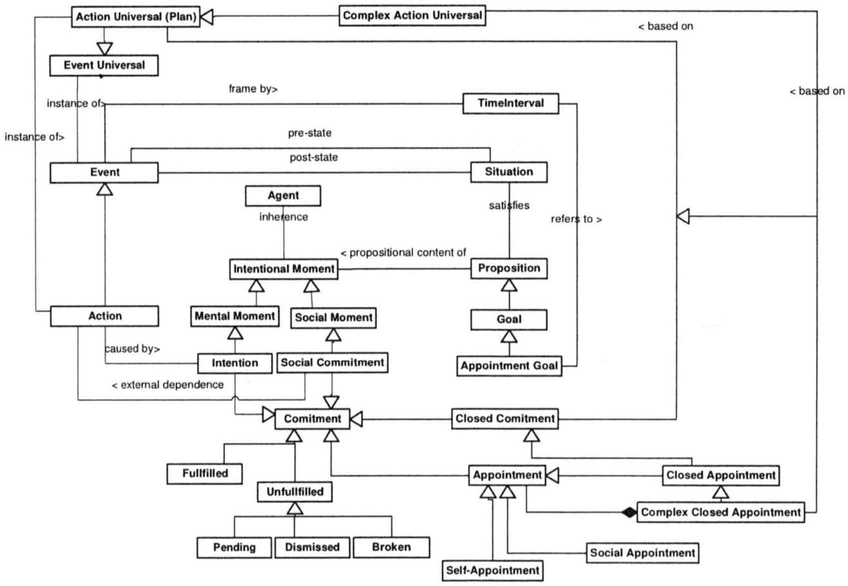

Fig.4. A Fragment of UFO-C dealing with Appointments.

As discussed in the previous section, a commitment (internal or social) is fulfilled by an agent *A* if this agent performs an action *a* such that the post-state of that action is a situation that satisfies the propositional content of that commitment. For many situations, there are a number of possible actions that can bring about that situation. We differentiate between ***Open*** and ***Closed commitments***, the difference being that, in the latter case, the agent must fulfil the commitment (i.e., bring about the desired situation) by executing a specific action. We state then that a closed commitment C is based on an Action Universal (Plan) *P* such that *C* is fulfilled by agent *A* iff *A* brings about a situation that satisfies the propositional content of *C* by executing an action *a* which is an instance of *P*. Open and Closed commitments can explain the notions of Open and Closed Delegation [14], respectively. These, in turn, can explain the difference between what is named *Goal* and *Plan Dependence* in requirements engineering languages such as TROPOS and i* [6].

A special type of Commitment is an ***Appointment***. An appointment is a commitment whose propositional content explicitly refers to a time interval. For instance, while "I will return the book to you" is a social commitment, "I will return the book between now and the end of this working week" is an appointment. An appointment can be either Internal (***Self-Appointment***) or a ***Social Appointment***. A ***Closed Appointment*** is a Closed Commitment whose propositional content explicitly refers to a time interval. A ***Complex Closed Appointment*** is based on a ***Complex Action Universal***. On one hand, a complex closed appointment *C* is composed of a number of commitments that should be achieved by executing a number of actions that are part of a complex action (instance of the complex action universal on which *C* is based). On the other hand, *C* stands for a number of commitments to enact a complex action universal by executing its specific sub-actions (i.e., by creating instances of these actions) that must occur in specific time intervals (referred by the propositional content of these constituting commitments).

Now, we can make clear that scheduled actions are neither action occurrences (i.e., particular events that occur in specific time intervals) nor action universals (patterns of features instantiated by multiple action occurrences). In fact, a scheduled action is not an action at all. Instead, it is a commitment to instantiate a specific action universal (plan) in a specific time interval, i.e., a closed appointment.

5 Analyzing and Improving a Software Process Ontology in terms of UFO

In [16], Falbo and Bertollo presented a Software Process Ontology that was developed for establishing a common conceptualization for software organizations to talk about software processes. This ontology is used as basis for the development of a process infrastructure for ODE [3], a Process-Centered Software Engineering Environment. Futhermore, in [16], this ontology is shown to be expressive enough to be used as a common ground for mapping the software process fragments of standards such as ISO/IEC 12207-ISO 9001:2000-ISO/IEC 15504, CMMI, RUP and SPEM. Figure 5 shows a fragment of this ontology.

As shown in figure 5, a *software process* can be decomposed into *activities* or other processes, called *sub-processes*. An *activity* is a piece of work that can produce *artifacts* (*outputs*). To be performed, an activity requires *resources*, adopts *procedures* and uses *artifacts* (*inputs*) produced by other activities. An activity can be decomposed into *sub-activities*, and can depend on the accomplishment of other activities, said *pre-activities*. Artifacts can be decomposed in *sub-artifacts*. *Resources* are used during, or to support, the execution of activities. These resources can be grouped into three main categories: (i) *human resource* are the roles that human agents is required to perform in an activity, such as requirement analyst, project manager, client and so on; (ii) *hardware resources* include any hardware equipment required to perform an activity, such as computers and printers; (iii) *software resources* concern any software product that is used in the accomplishment of an activity, such as a network management software or a data base management system. *Procedures* are adopted in the accomplishment of activities. There are several types of procedures. *Document Templates*, for instance, are models to be followed when preparing an artifact in an activity. A *method* is a systematic procedure that defines a *workflow* of activities (a set of steps) and heuristics to perform one or more activities. When a method can be adopted in the accomplishment of more than one activity, it has a workflow of activities for each one of them.

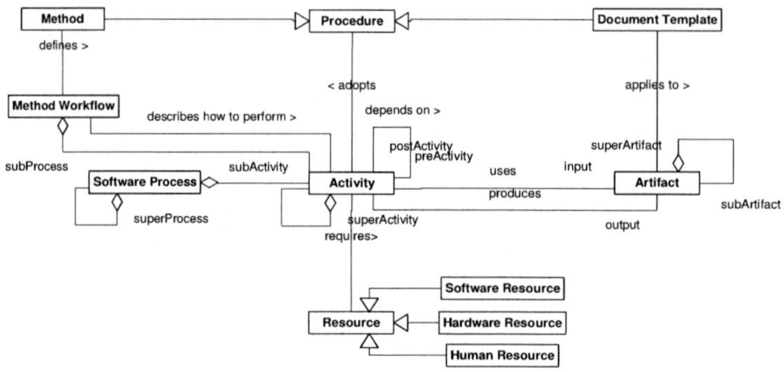

Fig.5. A Fragment of the ODE Software Process Ontology

Figure 6 represents a reengineered model of the Software Process Ontology by mappings its concepts to the fragments of the UFO-C ontology in figures 3 and 4. In figure 6, the concepts from UFO-C are shown in grey. By interpreting the ODE ontology in terms of UFO-C, it becomes clear that the former collapses the two notions of Action universal and Action Execution. We have performed this separation by introducing the terms Activity Occurrence (AO) and Software Process Occurrence (SPO) to denote particular actions that take place in specific time intervals. An activity occurrence can be atomic or complex. A SPO, in contrast, is necessarily a complex action. In fact, the distinction between a Software Sub-Process Occurrence (i.e., a SPO which is part of another SPO) and a Complex Activity Occurrence is not clear in the original ontology. Here, in order to eliminate this ambiguity, we assume that a SPO is the supreme of the composition lattice, i.e., a SPO is a complex action which is not part of any other complex event. A consequence of this definition is that there can be no subprocesses of a SPO and, thus, the reflexive parthood relation between SPO's has been removed from the model. In summary, a SPO is an instance of a Software Process which is in turn a subtype of a Complex Action Universal; an activity occurrence is an instance of an Activity which is a subtype of Action Universal (Plan).

In the software process ontology, an artifact is a type of Object (non-agentive substantial). The subArtifact/superArtifact relation between artifacts is thus governed by the mereological axioms defined for the (different types of) parthood relation between substantials defined in [1]. Although this cannot be elaborated here, we have that, generally, parthood between objects define an irreflexive, asymmetric and nontransitive relation; Parthood between processes is a strict partial order relation.

The notion of resource in the original ontology can also be mapped to the notion of Substantial in UFO-A, and the relation *requires* subsumes different modes of participating in an AO. We believe this issue should be elaborated in this domain ontology in order to make justice to the distinction between action contributions and (UFO-C) resource participations. In particular, a human resource (an Agent in UFO-C) cannot be *used, modified, created* or *terminated* by an AO. Instead, an action contribution of a human resource actually denotes a social commitment of that agent (with consequent permissions and obligations) of performing part of that AO. In terms of the formal relations we have put forth in [6], the *requires* relation for the case of human resources is a type of *dependence* relation between agents that will lead to a *delegation* relation when the process is instantiated or scheduled. In a nutshell, an agent *A* depends on an agent *B* iff *A* has a goal *G* that she cannot achieve by herself (either by lack of capacity or by the fact that *G* contrasts with one of her other goals), and *B* can achieve *G*. Agent *A* delegates goal *G* to *B* iff *A* depends on *B* for *G*; and *B* commits at achieving *G* for *A*. Software and Hardware resources are types of Objects and, thus, their modes of participations must be one of the types of (UFO-C) resource participation, namely, an usage participation. Notice, however, that whilst an output artifact is a (UFO-C) resource with a create participation in an AO, an input artifact is also a (UFO-C) resource with a usage participation. It is important to emphasize that a (UFO-C) resource is a *role* that an object plays in an event. As consequence, the same then must be the case for its subclasses: both artifact and resource must be roles played by objects in the scope of an AO. As a consequence, an object *O* that is an input artifact for an AO is an output artifact from another AO. Now, can an object *O* that is an output artifact for an AO be a software resource used by another AO? In other words, once human agents are not considered as resources, what characterizes the different roles output artifact and resource since both are played by objects with usage participations? The answer is the following: if an object plays the role of software resource in AO *ac* then there is no creating participation of this object in another AO *ac*' that is part of the same SPO.

A Procedure is a type of Normative Description. Two special types of Normative Descriptions in UFO-C are Object and Plan Descriptions. An Object Description is a description of an Object Universal (e.g., a blueprint of a house). In an analogous manner, a Plan Description is a description of a Plan (e.g., directives on how to assemble an IKEA chair). A method is a type of Plan Description; a Document Template is an Object Description.

Another issue in the original ontology is the relation of dependence between activities (now, activity occurrences). Dependence between activity occurrences is defined in terms of resources and, more specifically, of artifacts: an AO *a* depends on an AO *b* iff *a* uses as input a resource produced by *b*. However, the rolenames used for the relata of this relation are preActivity and posActivity indicating that there is an ordering relation hidden between these AO's. What temporal ordering relation(s) would this relation correspond to? It turns out it is not possible to extrapolate this answer from the data contained in the original ontology. In general, the only two temporal relations that can be eliminated from start are *finishes* and *equals*, i.e., if an AO *a* depends on something produced by an AO *b* then *a* cannot finish simultaneously or before *b*. Thus, considering ordering relations between instantaneous activity occurrences then dependence implies that *b* occurs *before a* (see UFO-B), since *starts* and *during* are not defined for instants and *meets* degenerates to *equals* in that case. However, for the case of time-extended AO, we are left with four possibilities: before, meets, starts and during. In any case, all these four relations are strict total orders (irreflexive, asymmetric and transitive) if we assume a linear model of time. In summary, since dependence between AOs is a total order plus a resource dependence, as a result we have that this relation must obey a partial order relation, i.e., an irreflexive, asymmetric and transitive but not necessarily totally defined relation between AOs.

The two relations between method workflow in the ontology of fig. 5 can be further clarified by making explicit the distinction between Action Universal and a description of that universal. A method workflow is an example of a description. Thus, it cannot be said to be composed of Activities. We take that, as a Plan description, a method workflow "describes how to perform" a complex action universal (a software process or a complex activity). This relation of "describe how to perform" is, hence, a specialization of the relation "describes" between Plan description and Plan. Moreover, as a description of a complex action universal, a method workflow describes how to perform the two or more actions that compose the instances of this universal.

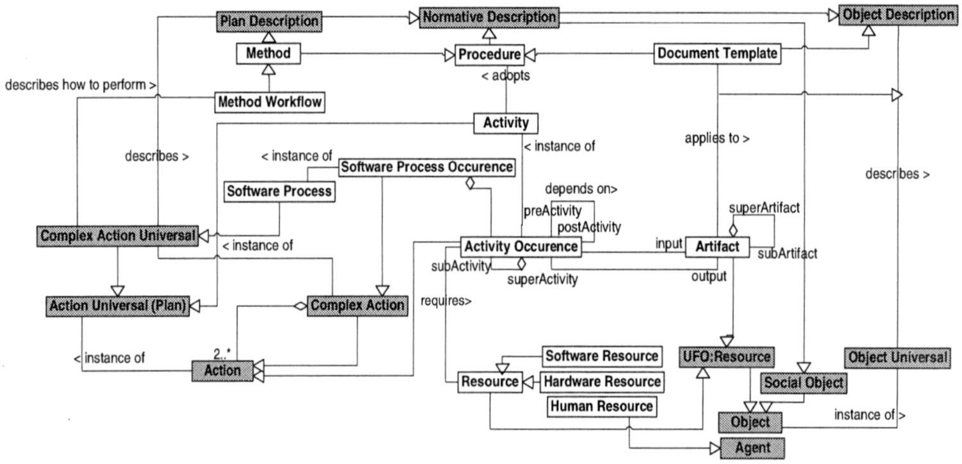

Fig.6. A Fragment of the Reengineered ODE Software Process Ontology

6 Final Considerations

In this paper, we presented the latest developments in the UFO foundational ontology. In particular, we discussed new versions of two fragments of UFO, namely UFO-B (concerned with *events*) and UFO-C (dealing with *social and intentional concepts*). In previous initiatives, UFO has been used to evaluate, re-design and integrate (meta) models of different conceptual modeling languages as well as to provide real-world semantics for their modeling constructs. In this paper, we illustrated the role played by philosophically grounded foundational ontology in the design of domain ontologies. In particular, we demonstrate how UFO can be used to evaluate, re-design and give real-world semantics to an ontology in the software engineering domain, namely, the software process ontology which is the core of the ODE Ontology-Centered Software Development Environment. By doing this, we have corrected a number of conceptual problems in this software engineering ontology by making it more truthful to the domain being represented and by making explicit its ontological commitments. Truthfulness to reality and conceptual clarity are fundamental quality attributes of conceptual models, in general, and of domain ontologies, in particular, and are directly responsible for the effectiveness of these models as reference frameworks for the tasks of reuse and semantic interoperability [1,5].

The foundational ontology as well as the domain ontologies discussed in this article are endowed with corresponding formal characterizations, which are not shown here, firstly, due to lack of space, but also since they are not essential to objectives of this paper. The Interested reader should refer to, for example, [1,16].

Acknowledgements This research has been partially supported by the TeleCardio Project (FAPES #31024866/2005), FAPES DCR Grant #37274554/2007 and INFRA-MODELA Project (FAPES/MCT/CNPq/CT-INFRA #019/2006).

References

1. Guizzardi, G. Ontological Foundations for Structural Conceptual Models, Universal Press, The Netherlands, 2005, ISBN 90-75176-81-3.
2. Falbo, R. A. et al., An Ontological Approach to Domain Engineering, Proceedings of the 14th SEKE, Ischia, Italy, ACM 2002.
3. Falbo, R.A., ODE: Ontology-based software Development Environment, IX Congreso Argentino de Ciencias de la Computación, La Plata, Argentina, Outubro 2003.
4. Guarino, N.; Guizzardi, G., In the Defense of Ontological Foundations for Conceptual Modeling, Scandinavian Journal of Inf. Systems, Vol.18, No. 1, ISSN 0905-0167, 2006.
5. Guizzardi, G., The Role of Foundational Ontology for Conceptual Modeling and Domain Ontology Representation, Proceedings of 7th DB&IS, Vilnius, IEEE Press 2006.
6. Guizzardi, R.S.S.; Guizzardi, G. Integrating Agent-Oriented Modeling Languages Using a Foundational Ontology, in Social Modeling for Requirements Engineering, P. Giorgini, N. Maiden, J. Mylopoulos, E. Yu (eds.), Cooperative Inf. Systems Series, MIT Press, 2008 (forthcoming).
7. Gärdenfors, P., Conceptual Spaces: the Geometry of Thought, USA, MIT Press 2000.
8. Masolo, C., Borgo, S., Gangemi, A., Guarino, N., Oltramari, A. 'Ontology Library', WonderWeb Deliverable D18, 2003.
9. Herre, H. et al, General Formal Ontology (GFO): A Foundational Ontology Integrating Objects and Processes. Technical Report Nr. 8. University of Leipzig, 2006.
10. Dockhorn, P., Guizzardi, G. et al., Situations in Conceptual Modeling of Context, Proceedings of the 2nd VORTE, Hong Kong, IEEE Digital Library 2006.
11. Allen, J.F., Maintaining Knowledge About Temporal Intervals, Communications of the ACM, Vol.26, no. 11, 1983.
12. Bottazzi, E.; Ferrario, E., Towards a DOLCE Ontology of Organizations, Journal of Business Process Integration and Management (IJBPIM), Inderscience Pub., 2008 (forth).
13. Searle, J., Mind, Language and Society, Basic Books, 2000.
14. Conte, R., Castelfranchi, C., Cognitive and Social Action, UCL Press, London, 1995.
15. Stanford Encyc. of Philosophy, Action, http://plato.stanford.edu/entries/action/, 2002.
16. Falbo, R.; Bertollo, G., Establishing a Common Vocabulary for Helping Organizations to Understand Software Processes, Proceedings of the 1st VORTE, Enschede, The Netherlands, ISSN 1574-0846, 2005.

Aplicando un Proceso de Ingeniería de Requisitos de Seguridad de Dominio para Líneas de Producto Software

Daniel Mellado[1], Eduardo Fernández-Medina[2] y Mario Piattini[2]

[1] Ministerio de Trabajo y Asuntos Sociales; Gerencia de Informática de la Seguridad Social; Centro de Desarrollo del Instituto Nacional de la Seguridad Social; Madrid, España.
Daniel.Mellado@alu.uclm.es
[2] Grupo Alarcos, Dpto. de Tecnologías y Sistemas de Información, Centro Mixto de Investigación y Desarrollo de Software UCLM-Indra; Universidad de Castilla-La Mancha.
Paseo de la Universidad 4, 13071 Ciudad Real, España.
(Eduardo.Fdez-Medina, Mario.Piattini)@uclm.es

Resumen. La gestión de los requisitos de seguridad es especialmente importante en las líneas de producto software, debido a que una brecha o vulnerabilidad de seguridad puede provocar problemas a todos los productos de la línea y afectar a todo el ciclo de vida. La principal contribución de este trabajo es ilustrar a través de un escenario de aplicación real, cómo de una forma guiada, sistemática e intuitiva se pueden tratar los requisitos de seguridad y facilitar su gestión desde las primeras fases del desarrollo basado en líneas de producto software, mediante la aplicación de SREPPLine. El cual es un proceso de ingeniería de requisitos de seguridad que hemos desarrollado y que está particularizado para el desarrollo de líneas de producto software seguras con el fin de facilitar la compleja gestión de la variabilidad y reutilización, así como las relaciones de trazabilidad de los requisitos de seguridad en éstas. Para lo cual se propone la utilización de las últimas técnicas de variabilidad de requisitos en líneas así como las técnicas de requisitos de seguridad, junto con la integración de los Criterios Comunes (ISO/IEC 15408). De esta forma se facilita que la línea y sus productos sean conformes con los estándares de seguridad más relevantes (ISO/IEC 27001, ISO/IEC 17799, ISO/IEC 15408 e ISO/IEC 21827) en lo relativo a la gestión de requisitos de seguridad.

Palabras clave: Ingeniería de Requisitos; Requisitos de Seguridad; Líneas de Producto Software; Criterios Comunes; ISO 27001.

1 Introducción

En la actualidad, está ampliamente defendido el principio que establece que la seguridad debería considerarse desde las primeras fases del desarrollo y que los requisitos de seguridad deberían definirse junto con los demás requisitos del SI, como se recoge en varios estudios recientes [11, 14, 19],ya que esto permite soluciones más eficientes y robustas así como ayuda a reducir los conflictos entre los requisitos de seguridad y los demás requisitos. Asimismo, en los últimos años se está observando un incremento en la demanda de software y en su complejidad requerida, lo cual aumenta la potencialidad de presentar brechas de seguridad [25]. Por esto, hoy, para poder alcanzar los niveles deseados de calidad y mejorar la productividad multitud de sistemas se están desarrollando basándose en el paradigma de ingeniería de Líneas de Producto Software (LPS), ya que las LPS ayudan a reducir significativamente el tiempo de puesta en producción y los costes de desarrollo, mediante la reutilización de todo tipo de artefactos [3, 4].

Debido a la complejidad y a la naturaleza extensiva de las LPS, la seguridad y la ingeniería de requisitos son mucho más importantes para la puesta en práctica del desarrollo basado en LPS, de lo que ya son para el desarrollo de un Sistema de Información (SI), ya que una brecha de seguridad o vulnerabilidad en la línea puede provocar importantes problemas a largo plazo a todos los productos de la misma [9]. Es por ello que la disciplina conocida como Ingeniería de Requisitos de Seguridad [12], sea una parte muy importante en el proceso de desarrollo software y especialmente dada su complejidad para conseguir LPS seguras, ya que facilitan técnicas, métodos y normas para abordar esta tarea desde las primeras fases del desarrollo e implica el uso de procedimientos repetibles y sistemáticos para asegurar que el conjunto de requisitos obtenidos es completo, consistente y fácilmente comprensible y analizable por parte de los diferentes actores implicados en el desarrollo de la LPS y sus sistemas.

Después de analizar en [17, 18] las propuestas más recientes y relevantes relativas a los requisitos de seguridad en SI como: [6, 7, 15, 21, 23, 24], etc.; junto con las propuestas más importantes sobre gestión de requisitos en LPS, como [4, 9, 10, 20, 22], así como las arquitecturas de seguridad de referencia para LPS, como [1, 5, 8], llegamos a la conclusión de que las propuestas existentes no eran lo suficientemente específicas para facilitar la gestión de requisitos de seguridad en LPS de una forma sistemática e intuitiva y estaban orientadas a la solución en lugar de a la ingeniería de requisitos de seguridad. Por ello, desarrollamos el proceso de ingeniería de requisitos de seguridad para LPS, SREPPLine (Security Requirements Engineering Process for software Product Lines) [16], cuyo objetivo es facilitar una integración concreta de las actividades relativas a la gestión de requisitos de seguridad en el resto de actividades del desarrollo basado en LPS y proporcionar un soporte metodológico específico para la gestión de requisitos de seguridad y del modelo de variabilidad de seguridad de la línea. Asimismo, ayuda a que las LPS y los sistemas que de ella se deriven sean conformes respecto a la gestión de requisitos de seguridad con los estándares de seguridad internacionales más importantes (como ISO/IEC 15408, ISO/IEC 17799, ISO/IEC 27001 o ISO/IEC 21827).

Por último y dada la actual escasez de literatura que describa casos de estudio reales donde se describa la gestión de los requisitos de seguridad en LPS, en este artículo se presenta un escenario real de aplicación SREPPLine [16], a fin de realizar una validación preeliminar de la aplicabilidad del mismo y verificar cómo nuestro proceso facilita la actual gestión de requisitos de seguridad en LPS y sus actividades correspondientes.

El resto del artículo está organizado de la siguiente forma: en la sección 2, se resumen los principales conceptos de la ingeniería de requisitos en las LPS. A continuación, en la sección 3, se describe de forma general el proceso SREPPLine. Seguidamente en la sección 4, se describirá la aplicación del proceso SREPPLine en un escenario real. Y por último, en la sección 5, presentamos nuestras conclusiones y trabajos futuros.

2 La Ingeniería de Requisitos en las Líneas de Producto Software

Una Línea de Producto Software es "un conjunto intensivo de sistemas software que comparten un conjunto común y gestionado de características (features, entendidas como una característica visible para el usuario final del sistema), dónde estas características están pensadas para satisfacer las necesidades especificas de una misión o de un segmento de mercado. Asimismo, los productos son desarrollados de una forma pre-establecida a partir de un conjunto común de componentes" [4].

El paradigma de ingeniería de Líneas de Producto Software se compone de dos procesos: ingeniería del dominio e ingeniería de la aplicación [20]. La ingeniería del dominio es el proceso de ingeniería de Líneas de Producto Software en el que se define la variabilidad y elementos comunes. La ingeniería de aplicación es el proceso de ingeniería de Líneas de Producto Software en el que se construyen las aplicaciones de la línea reutilizando los artefactos del dominio y aprovechándose de la variabilidad de la Línea de Producto Software.

Por lo tanto, los requisitos de una línea de productos definen los productos de dicha línea y sus características comunes y variables [4]. La gestión de requisitos para líneas de productos debe gestionar los requisitos de la línea de productos y los requisitos de los productos concretos de la línea. Se tiene que hablar por tanto de gestión de requisitos del dominio y gestión de requisitos de la aplicación, siguiendo a [20]. La gestión de requisitos para líneas de productos debe incorporar un mecanismo mediante el cual el conjunto de requisitos para un producto concreto sea producido de manera fácil y rápida a partir de los requisitos de la línea de productos.

3. Descripción General de SREPPLine: Proceso de Ingeniería de Requisitos de Seguridad para Líneas de Producto Software

El Proceso de Ingeniería de Requisitos de Seguridad para Líneas de Producto Software (SREPPLine) [16] es un add-in de actividades (que se descomponen en tareas, donde se generan artefactos de entrada y salida, y con la participación de distintos roles) que se integran sobre el proceso de desarrollo de LPS existente en una organización, proporcionándole un enfoque en ingeniería de requisitos de seguridad específico para LPS. Los sub-procesos y actividades descritos en este artículo se pueden combinar con los procesos de desarrollo como el Proceso Unificado u otros. En este artículo describiremos la integración de SREPPLine en el marco de trabajo de ingeniería de LPS propuesto por Pohl et al. en [20].

SREPPLine es un proceso basado en activos y dirigido por el riesgo para el establecimiento de requisitos de seguridad en el desarrollo de LPS seguras. Básicamente este proceso facilita la integración los Criterios Comunes (CC) y los controles de la ISO/IEC 27001 en el desarrollo de LPS junto con el uso de un repositorio de recursos de seguridad para facilitar la variabilidad y reutilización de requisitos, activos, amenazas, test y contramedidas en la LPS. Asimismo, facilita la gestión del modelo de variabilidad de la seguridad y los distintos tipos de trazabilidad implicados entre los artefactos de seguridad entre sí, así como entre los de las aplicaciones con los de la línea. Igualmente ayuda a que la LPS y las aplicaciones o sistemas de información de dicha LPS sean conformes a los estándares de seguridad actualmente más relevantes relativos a la gestión de requisitos de seguridad (como ISO/IEC 15408, ISO/IEC 27001, ISO/IEC 17799 o ISO/IEC 21827) y tratando de minimizar la participación de los expertos de seguridad en el desarrollo de los productos y el conocimiento de los estándares.

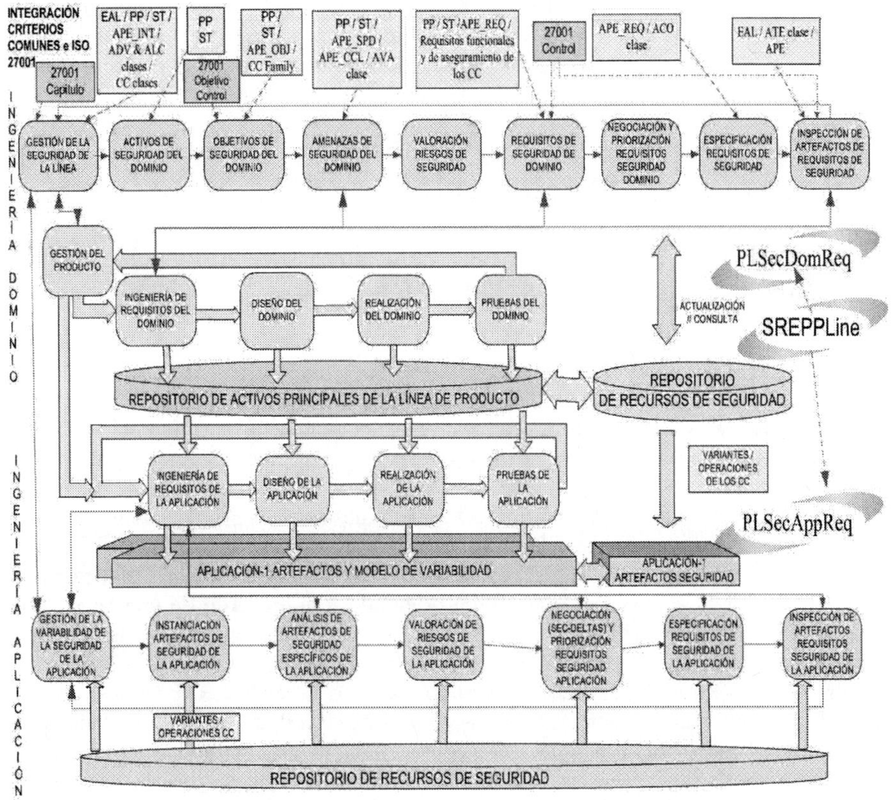

Fig. 1 Marco de Trabajo para la Ingeniería de Requisitos de Seguridad en Líneas de Producto

Como se puede observar en la Fig. 1, SREPPLine se compone de dos sub-procesos con sus respectivas actividades: PLSecDomReq (Product Line Security Domain Requirements Engineering sub-process) y PLSecAppReq (Product Line

Security Application Requirements Engineering sub-process). Estos sub-procesos cubren las cuatro fases básicas de la ingeniería de requisitos [12]: elicitación de requisitos; análisis y negociación de requisitos; documentación de requisitos; y validación y verificación de requisitos. Estos sub-procesos se ejecutarán al menos por cada iteración del proceso de ingeniería del dominio y/o de la aplicación de la LPS, respectivamente. Sin embargo, dadas las restricciones de espacio, en este artículo se describirán de forma general y sin iteraciones como se aplican en la práctica las actividades del sub-proceso PLSecDomReq en un escenario real con el objetivo de facilitar una comprensión clara y global de la aplicación de dicho proceso.

Asimismo, como se observa en la Fig. 1, el Repositorio de Recursos de Seguridad se debe de integrar en el repositorio de activos comunes de la LPS, para posibilitar las relaciones de trazabilidad entre el modelo de variabilidad de la LPS y los diferentes tipos de artefactos de seguridad y otros artefactos de desarrollo, así como la trazabilidad entre los artefactos de la línea y los productos. El modelo de variabilidad de seguridad implementado por SREPPLine se apoya en el concepto de modelo de variabilidad ortogonal [20], lo cual nos permite flexibilidad para aplicarlo, ya que permite que el proceso se integre con otros modelos de desarrollo software (como modelos de 'features', de casos de uso, de diseño, o modelos de componentes o de pruebas).

4. Aplicando SREPPLine en la Práctica

En esta sección se describe cómo el subproceso de SREPPLine, PLSecDomReq, puede aplicarse en la práctica en un escenario real.

4.1 Escenario de aplicación

Se utilizará nuestro proceso propuesto (PLSecDomReq) para obtener una especificación de los requisitos de seguridad junto con sus artefactos relacionados de una línea de producto de sistemas CRM (Customer Relationship Management) para la Seguridad Social española, cuya arquitectura se muestra en la Fig. 2. Dichos sistemas deberán tener configuraciones diferentes para cubrir las particularidades de tres instituciones públicas del sistema de seguridad social de España. Por tanto, el sistema, al que llamaremos SS-CRM, se desarrollará orientado a la creación de una LPS cuyos miembros/productos variarán por configuración para adaptarse a las necesidades particulares de cada institución aunque conservando un núcleo de funcionalidades comunes y una serie de servicios específicos propios de cada CRM de cada institución. Obviamente, dado el limitado alcance de la variabilidad de la LPS se trata de un caso a modo representativo, que sirve como ejercicio instructivo de aplicación de nuestro proceso en un escenario real, teniendo en cuenta el hecho de que este caso de estudio se ha simplificado y resumido para permitir ajustarse a las restricciones de espacio y así ilustrar fácilmente los puntos principales del subproceso PLSecDomReq en este artículo.

El departamento de tecnologías de información del Organismo será el responsable del desarrollo de la LPS denominada SS-CRM así como del desarrollo de los sistemas CRM derivados de la misma. Previamente, se cargará en el Repositorio de Recursos de Seguridad un perfil básico de seguridad de LPS genérico para el Organismo, con los artefactos de seguridad más habituales en los sistemas actuales del mismo, como los requisitos legales, normas internas, política de seguridad de la organización así como los requisitos de seguridad de los Criterios Comunes (CC) y los controles de la ISO/IEC 27001 tal y como describe SREPPLine para su aplicación.

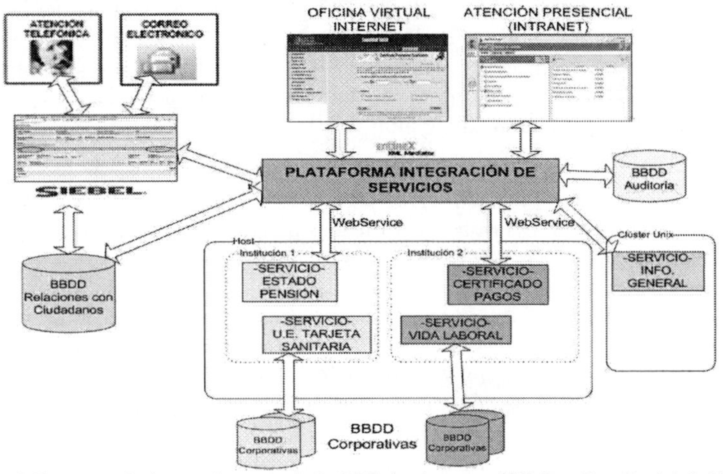

Fig. 2 Esquema de la arquitectura de la LPS de sistemas CRM en Seg-Social de España

4.2 Aplicación de SREPPLine

SP1 - Actividad A1.1: Gestión de las Características de Seguridad de la Línea. Como entrada de esta actividad se recibió el modelo de variabilidad en un árbol de características del SS-CRM en el que se describía la variabilidad de los componentes funcionales del dominio. A partir de este modelo de características identificamos las características de seguridad y sus dependencias y se desarrollo el modelo ortogonal de variabilidad de la seguridad, el cual se especificó usando XML. También se seleccionaron las clases de los CC y capítulos de la norma ISO 27001 relacionadas a dichas características de seguridad. En la Fig. 3 se muestra parte del modelo de variabilidad de seguridad, en el que se representa las características básicas de la LPS SS-CRM junto con sus activos relacionados así como la característica de seguridad de autenticación de usuario y sus relaciones con los diferentes activos según las variantes.

Se identificaron los siguientes objetivos o dimensiones de seguridad [13]: integridad (I), confidencialidad (C), disponibilidad (D), autenticidad del usuario del servicio (A_S), autenticidad del origen de los datos (A_D), trazabilidad del uso del servicio (T_S) y trazabilidad del acceso a los datos (T_D). Además, después de analizar la política de seguridad de la organización, sus procesos de negocio, los casos de uso de negocio del SS-CRM y entorno de la LPS, se identificaron los siguientes tipos o categorías de características que engloban a los activos, como se muestra en la primera columna de la Tabla 1: Servicios finales de negocio y datos de negocio, servicios internos y equipamiento (hardware, software y comunicaciones). Aunque no se tendrá en cuenta esta última categoría a fin de simplificar la aplicación y comprensión de SREPPLine.

También se llegó al acuerdo sobre varias definiciones de conceptos de seguridad así como el nivel de seguridad requerido para la LPS en base a los CC (estableciéndose el nivel de conformidad EAL 2 de los CC como mínimo para la LPS y por tanto para los sistemas que se deriven de la misma), al igual que se decidió dado el tipo de información que gestionarán los sistemas SS-CRM que se tendrá que cumplir con la legislación española de protección de de datos de carácter personal en lo referente a datos clasificados con nivel medio y alto.

SP1 - Actividad A1.2: Activos de Seguridad del Dominio de la LPS. En esta actividad se identificaron los activos de seguridad comunes y variables para cada una de las características de seguridad identificadas anteriormente, así como se establecen las dependencias entre ellos. En la primera columna de la Tabla 1 se listan parte de los activos de seguridad (identificados con '(A)' delante), categorizados por característica de seguridad. Además, en la Fig. 3 se representa en el modelo de variabilidad de seguridad sus dependencias. Asimismo, nos ayudamos del Repositorio para la realización de la identificación y categorización de los activos de seguridad, de manera que si la característica de seguridad identificada en la actividad anterior estaba ya previamente en el repositorio, éste te proponía los activos de seguridad relacionados con dicha característica. En las siguientes actividades el repositorio de recursos de seguridad se puede usar de la misma manera para la identificación del resto de artefactos de seguridad: objetivos de seguridad, amenazas y requisitos.

SP1 - Actividad A1.3: Objetivos de Seguridad del Dominio de la LPS. En esta actividad a partir de las dimensiones de seguridad identificadas en la actividad A1.1, se establecieron los objetivos de seguridad para cada uno de los activos de seguridad (junto con el análisis de variabilidad y elementos comunes, y a la vez que se determinaron los objetivos de control de la ISO 27001 y familias de los CC) así como se valoró cualitativamente cada activo de seguridad con cada uno de sus objetivos de seguridad relacionados. Para la realización de esta tarea, se realizaron entrevistas con los distintos interesados utilizando el método de evaluación Delphi y la escala de valoración propuesta en MAGERIT [13] (de 0 a 10), ya que iba a ser el método de análisis y gestión de riesgos que se utilizara a continuación. De esta forma y siguiendo el modelo cualitativo de MAGERIT únicamente los activos más altos en el árbol de dependencias entre activos obtenido en la actividad anterior son evaluados explícitamente, de manera que esta valoración se propaga automáticamente (matemáticamente) a través del árbol de dependencias del modelo de variabilidad de seguridad. Con lo que se obtuvo como resultado una tabla con los valores acumulados para cada uno de los activos identificados en la LPS. Parte de esta tabla de valores acumulados de los activos se muestra en Tabla 1. En dicha tabla, el primer valor de cada celda se corresponde con la valoración del activo y si dicho número se encuentra entre corchetes indica que se trata de una valoración propagada. Por último, se registró formalmente en XML los objetivos de seguridad y su valoración para cada uno de los activos.

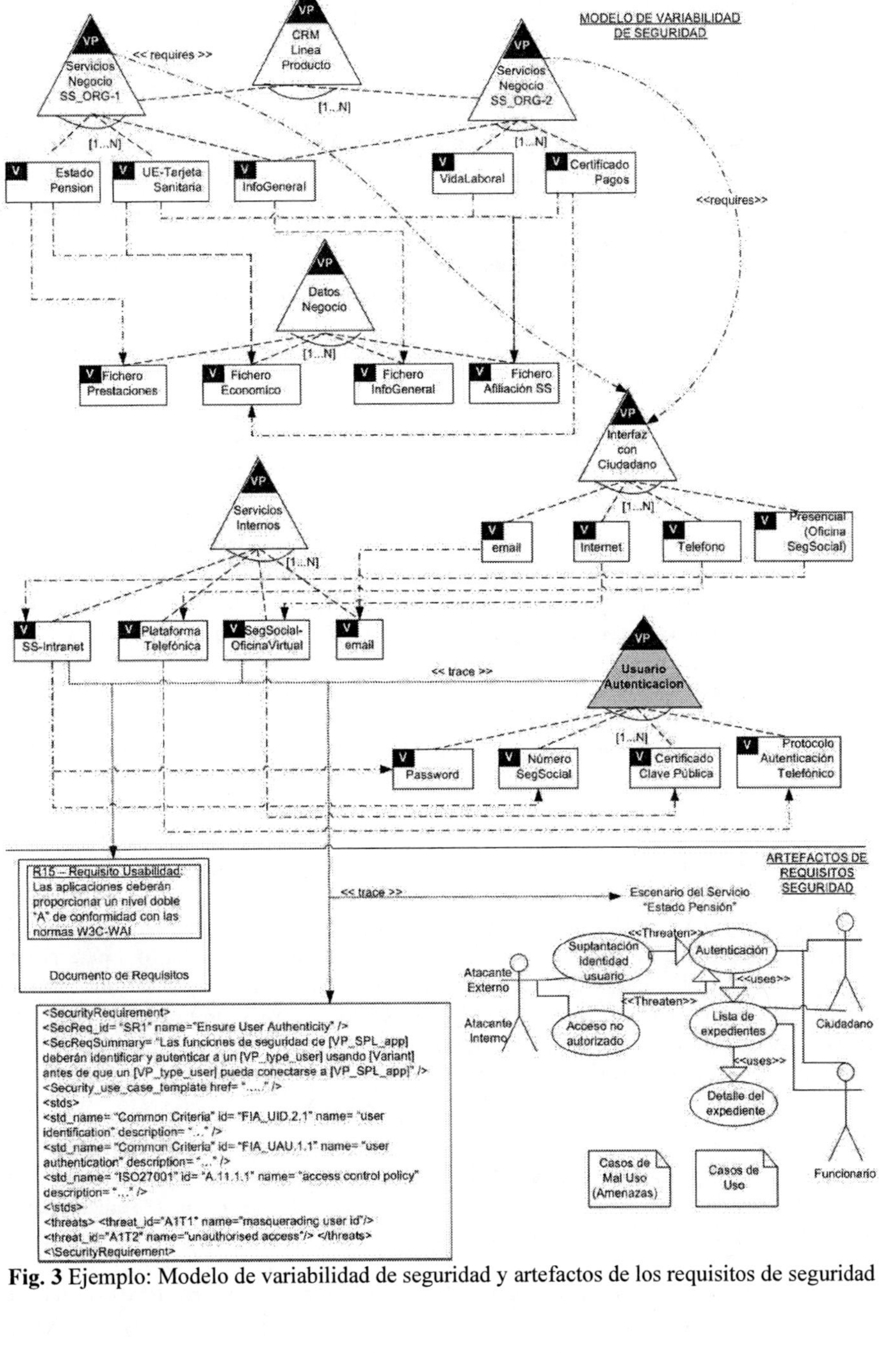

Fig. 3 Ejemplo: Modelo de variabilidad de seguridad y artefactos de los requisitos de seguridad

SP1 - Actividad A1.4: Amenazas de Seguridad del Dominio de la LPS. Como entrada de esta actividad se recibió la lista de las vulnerabilidades, amenazas y patrones de ataque más comunes en la Organización así como el catalogo de amenazas listado en la Organización. Con todos estos datos, junto con la ayuda del repositorio (que te propone posibles amenazas dados los activos que se tienen identificados) y después de analizar los casos de uso de negocio, se desarrollaron los casos de mal uso y se identificaron a la vez los atacantes potenciales con la participación del experto de seguridad. Seguidamente, se identificaron las amenazas comunes para cada activo de seguridad y utilizándose para su especificación las plantillas de casos de mal uso, y por último se incluyeron en el modelo de variabilidad de seguridad, estableciéndose las relaciones de trazabilidad correspondientes con los objetivos y activos de seguridad.

Algunas de estas amenazas se listan en la Tabla 1, donde se listan las amenazas intencionadas que amenazan al activo "Servicio de Negocio de Estado Pensión". Además, en la Fig. 3 se muestra en un ejemplo de un escenario con un caso de mal uso donde se muestran parte de los casos de mal uso del escenario del punto de variación "Autenticación" para el caso de la variante "Servicio de Negocio de Estado Pensión".

SP1 - Actividad A1.5: Valoración de Riesgos de Seguridad de la LPS. En esta actividad se realizó la estimación de riesgos utilizando MAGERIT [13]. Por lo tanto, en primer lugar se estimó la probabilidad de ocurrencia de las amenazas para cada uno de los activos relacionados (en términos de frecuencia de ocurrencia de 0 a 100: 100 para muy frecuentes, diarios; 10 para frecuentes, mensuales; 1 para normal, anual; 0'1 para poco frecuente, cada varios años). Así como se estimó el grado de degradación del activo sobre su valor expresado en porcentaje en caso de que se materializara la amenaza, para lo cual se contó con la ayuda del repositorio y con la información histórica de la Organización. A continuación, el impacto acumulado de los activos se estimó teniendo en cuenta el valor acumulado de los activos y el grado de degradación que causarían las amenazas. Con lo que seguidamente, el riesgo acumulado para los activos se estimó considerando tanto el impacto acumulado como la frecuencia de ocurrencia de cada amenaza. En la Tabla 1 se muestra parte de la estimación de impactos acumulados como parte del análisis de riesgos realizado (clasificándose el riesgo en un rango desde: 0, casi nulo; 1-2 para riesgo bajo; 3 para riesgo medio; 4 para riesgo alto; y 5 para riesgo muy alto). En dicha tabla el segundo número que aparece en cada una de las celdas se refiere al factor de degradación en los activos que causaría la amenaza correspondiente, el tercer valor se refiere al impacto acumulado en el activo y el último (cuarto) valor hace referencia al riesgo acumulado sobre el activo.

SP1 - Actividad A1.6: Requisitos de Seguridad de Dominio de la LPS. En esta actividad, como primer paso se analizaron los casos de mal uso y lo que suponía las amenazas relacionadas. Seguidamente y con la ayuda del repositorio se seleccionaron los requisitos de seguridad funcionales de los Criterios Comunes y los controles de seguridad de la ISO/IEC 27001 adecuados para mitigar las amenazas de la línea de producto software. Después, realizamos la identificación de los requisitos de seguridad comunes según los requisitos elicitados y con el análisis de riesgos realizado anteriormente, se determinaron los requisitos de seguridad variables y se definió su variabilidad interna así como sus relaciones de dependencia, al mismo tiempo que se establecen las operaciones permitidas sobre los requisitos funcionales de seguridad por los sistemas que se deriven de la LPS, en el caso de los CC las operaciones serán: iteración, asignación, selección o refinamiento. Finalmente se modelaron los requisitos de seguridad usando casos de uso de seguridad y se establecieron las relaciones de trazabilidad correspondientes entre ellos y sus artefactos asociados (test de seguridad y medida/métrica de seguridad, amenaza, etc.) según el modelo de variabilidad definido en SREPPLine [16]. En la Fig. 3 se muestra un ejemplo de un requisito de seguridad que usando la plantilla para casos de uso de seguridad y especificándose con XML para el escenario con la variante "Servicio de Negocio de Estado Pensión".

SP1 - Actividad A1.7: Priorización y Negociación de los Requisitos de Seguridad del Dominio de la LPS. En esta actividad priorizamos los requisitos en función al riesgo estimado de las amenazas relacionadas. Seguidamente, se identificaron y se especificaron en nuestro modelo de variabilidad de seguridad las interdependencias de los requisitos de seguridad con otros requisitos funcionales y no funcionales mediante el análisis de los casos de uso y del modelo de características (en la Fig. 3 se muestra un ejemplo de interdependencia entre un requisitos de seguridad y otro tipo de requisito). Además realizamos un somero análisis coste-beneficio valorando por un lado el coste que supondría implementar cada una de las contramedidas asociadas a los requisitos de seguridad y el riesgo que supondría su no implementación. De manera que llegamos al acuerdo con los interesados en que se tendrían en cuenta aquellos requisitos de seguridad que tuvieran asociados amenazas que supongan un riesgo calificado como alto o muy alto, sea cual sea el conflicto con otros requisitos o su coste (dentro de lo que se determinó como razonable o estratégico). Sin embargo, para los requisitos de seguridad con menos riesgo se tuvieron que llegar a acuerdos cuando entraban en conflicto con otros requisitos (como por ejemplo como se muestra en la Fig. 3, el requisito de usabilidad).

SP1 - Actividad A1.8: Especificación de Requisitos de Seguridad de Dominio de la LPS. Durante esta actividad se modelaron y especificaron los requisitos de seguridad formalmente. Para ello se uso la técnica de los casos de uso de seguridad y plantillas XML parametrizadas para permitir la variabilidad y los enlaces de trazabilidad requeridos por el modelo de variabilidad de seguridad. En la Fig. 3 se puede ver un ejemplo de parte de la especificación de requisitos de seguridad especificados usando la técnica de especificación requisitos en XML orientada a aspectos así como las correspondientes trazas al modelo de variabilidad de seguridad y a la plantilla del caso de uso de seguridad utilizado.

SP1 - Actividad A1.9: Inspección de Artefactos de Requisitos de Seguridad de Dominio de la LPS. En esta actividad verificamos el grado de conformidad de la LPS con los controles de la norma ISO/IEC 27001 y a los requisitos de aseguramiento de los CC (ISO/IEC 15408) correspondientes al EAL2, así como se valida que los requisitos sean conformes al estándar IEEE 830-1998. Además, se estima el riesgo residual de la LPS para evaluar la eficacia de los requisitos de seguridad y sus contramedidas asociadas (siguiéndose de esta manera el modelo Plan-Do-Check-Act).

Tabla 1 Parte del mapa de análisis de riesgos de SREPPLine

(A) Activos (T) Amenazas	Frecuencia	Objetivos / Dimensions de Seguridad [D]	[I]	[C]	[A_S]	[A_D]	[T_S]	[T_D]
[BS] Servicios Finales de Negocio								
(A) [BS_EstadoPension] Como Va Prestación Ciudadano		5; 70%; 5; 4			7; 100%; 7; 5		6; 100%; 6; 5	
(T) Manipulacion de configuracion	0,1	50%; 4; 2			100%; 7; 4		100%; 6; 3	
(T) Suplantacion identidad usuario	100				100%; 7; 5			
(T) Uso no previso o malintencionado	10	70%; 5; 4			10%; 4; 4		50%; 5; 4	
(T) Re-enrutamiento de mensajes	10				50%; 6; 5		50%; 5; 4	
(T) Acceso No Autorizado	100	10%; 2; 3			50%; 6; 5			
(T) Repudio	10						100%; 6; 5	
(T) Denegación de Servicio	10	50%; 4; 4						
(A) [BS_UE-TarjetaSanitaria] Tarjeta Sanitaria Europea		5; 70%; 5; 4			7; 100%; 7; 5		6; 100%; 6; 5	
(A) [BS_InfoGeneral] Informacion General SegSocial		5; 70%; 5; 4			1; 100%; 1; 3		1; 100%; 1; 2	
(A) [BS_VidaLaboral] Certificado Vida Laboral		5; 70%; 5; 4			7; 100%; 7; 5		6; 100%; 6; 5	
(A) [BS_CertificadoPagos] Estar al dia pagos SegSocial		5; 70%; 5; 4			7; 100%; 7; 5		6; 100%; 6; 5	
[BD] Datos de Negocio								
(A) [D_Pension] Fichero Prestaciones		[5]; 90%; 5; 5	5; 50%; 4; 4	7; 100%; 7; 5	[7]; 100%; 7; 5	7; 100%; 7; 4	[6]; 100%; 6; 3	5; 100%; 5; 3
(A) [D_SS_Economicos] Fichero		[5]; 90%; 5; 5	5; 50%; 4; 4	6; 100%; 6; 5	[7]; 100%; 7; 5	6; 100%; 6; 3	[6]; 100%; 6; 3	5; 100%; 5; 3
(A) [D_InfoGeneral] Informacion General SegSocial		[5]; 90%; 5; 5	3; 50%; 2; 3	0; 100%; 0; 1	[1]; 100%; 1; 2	2; 100%; 2; 1	[1]; 100%; 1; 1	1; 100%; 1; 1
(A) [D_Laborales] Fichero afiliacion SegSocial		[5]; 90%; 5; 5	5; 50%; 4; 4	6; 100%; 6; 5	[7]; 100%; 7; 5	6; 100%; 6; 4	[6]; 100%; 6; 3	5; 100%; 5; 3
[IS] Servicios Internos								
(A) [IS_email] email		[5]; 70%; 5; 4	[3]; 50%; 2; 3	[0]; 50%; 0; 0	[1]; 100%; 1; 3	[2]; 100%; 2; 3	[1]; 100%; 1; 2	[1]; 100%; 1; 1
(A) [IS_Telefono] Telefonía		[5]; 70%; 5; 4	[5]; 50%; 4; 5	[5]; 50%; 5; 5	[7]; 100%; 7; 5	[6]; 100%; 6; 5	[6]; 100%; 6; 5	[5]; 100%; 5; 4
(A) [IS_OficinaVirtual] Oficina Virtual SegSocial		[5]; 70%; 5; 4	[5]; 50%; 4; 5	[7]; 50%; 6; 5	[7]; 100%; 7; 5	[7]; 100%; 7; 5	[6]; 100%; 6; 5	[5]; 100%; 5; 4
(A) [IS_Intranet] Intranet funcionarios del CRM		[5]; 70%; 5; 4	[5]; 50%; 4; 5	[7]; 50%; 6; 5	[7]; 100%; 7; 5	[7]; 100%; 7; 5	[6]; 100%; 6; 5	[5]; 100%; 5; 4

5. Conclusiones y Trabajo Futuro

Hoy en día, debido a la creciente necesidad de obtener SI de alta calidad y con una productividad alta, el desarrollo basado en LPS se ha convertido en el enfoque de más éxito para asegurar la calidad, eficiencia económica y mantenibilidad de los SI [2]. Es por ello, y dada la complejidad y a la naturaleza extensiva de las LPS [9], que sea fundamental la incorporación de la ingeniería de requisitos de seguridad en las líneas de producto software, siendo mucho más importantes para la puesta en práctica del desarrollo basado en LPS, de lo que ya son para el desarrollo de un Sistema de Información (SI).

Debido a que los trabajos existentes que apuntan a especificar seguridad en líneas de producto, en los que se integre la perspectiva de la ingeniería de requisitos de seguridad, son escasos y no proporcionan soporte metodológico y sistemático para la gestión de la seguridad en LPS basada en la ingeniería de requisitos de seguridad y en los estándares de seguridad internacionales más importantes. En este artículo se presenta la aplicación en la práctica de un proceso sistemático que ayuda a desarrollar líneas de producto software seguras mediante la gestión integral de los requisitos de seguridad desde las primeras fases del ciclo de desarrollo y apoyándose en los estándares de seguridad internacionales más importantes (como ISO/IEC 15408 e ISO/IEC 21827; ISO/IEC 17799:2005, secciones: 0.3, 0.4, 0.6 y 12.1; ISO/IEC 27001, secciones: 4.2.1, 4.2.3, 4.3, 6.a y A.12.1.1), con el objeto de aportar una perspectiva que permita mejorar la calidad, tanto en las líneas de productos software como en los productos de dicha línea, los cuales serán conformes a dichos estándares.

Asimismo, a raíz de la realización de este caso de estudio presentado anteriormente podemos destacar las siguientes lecciones aprendidas más importantes:

- La aplicación de este caso de estudio nos ha permitido mejorar y refinar varias actividades de SREPPLine así como el modelo de variabilidad de seguridad y por tanto el repositorio de recursos de seguridad.
- El soporte de una herramienta es crucial para la aplicación práctica de este proceso en LPS de gran magnitud con mayor complejidad debido al número de artefactos manejados y las complejas relaciones de trazabilidad y gestión de la variabilidad de la línea que se tiene que realizar.
- Avanzar en el refinamiento del prototipo de herramienta CARE (Computer Aided Requierements Engineering) que estamos desarrollando, denominada SREPPLineTool, para avanzar en el nivel de automatización de SREPPLine.
- En lo relativo a los beneficios obtenidos por la Organización en la que se ha realizado el caso de estudio, se ha conseguido tener un proceso normalizado específico que sistematice la gestión de requisitos de seguridad en LPS y que facilite la conformidad de sus sistemas con la ISO/IEC 15408 e ISO/IEC 27001, así como la creación de un repositorio de recursos de seguridad cuyos artefactos serán reutilizables para el desarrollo de los sistemas que se deriven de la LPS o para el desarrollo futuro de otras LPS en la Organización.

Por último, hay una serie de aspectos planeados para el futuro, como es el refinamiento a partir de la realización de más casos de estudio del modelo teórico así como del prototipo de la herramienta (SREPPLineTool) que estamos desarrollando para automatizar la utilización de SREPPLine y nos permita incrementar el nivel de automatización de la aplicación de SREPPLine y mejorar así la eficiencia del proceso de ingeniería de requisitos de seguridad de LPS.

Agradecimientos

Este artículo es parte del proyecto ESFINGE (TIN2006-15175-C05-05) del Ministerio de Educación y Ciencia, y de los proyectos MISTICO (PBC-06-0082) y DIMENSIONS (PBC-05-012-2) de la Consejería de Ciencia y Tecnología de la Junta de Comunidades de Castilla- La Mancha y el FEDER.

Referencias Bibliográficas

1. Arciniegas, J.L., Dueñas, J.C., Ruiz, J.L., Cerón, R., Bermejo, J., and Oltra, M.A., *Architecture Reasoning for Supporting Product Line Evolution: An Example on Security*, in *Software Product Lines: Research Issues in Engineering and Management*, Käkölä, T. and Dueñas, J.C., Editors. 2006, Springer.
2. Birk, A., Heller, G., John, I., MaBen, T.v.d., Müller, K., and Schmid, K., *Product line engineering industrial nuts and bolts*. 2003, Fraunhofer IESE: Kaiserslautern.
3. Bosh, J., *Design & Use of Software Architectures*. 2000: Pearson Education Limited.
4. Clements, P. and Northrop, L., *Software Product Lines: Practices and Patterns*. SEI Series in Software Engineering. 2002: Addison-Wesley.
5. Faegri, T.E. and Hallsteinsen, S., *A Software Product Line Reference Architecture for Security*, in *Software Product Lines: Research Issues in Engineering and Management*, Käkölä, T. and Dueñas, J.C., Editors. 2006, Springer.
6. Firesmith, D.G., *Security Use Cases*. Journal of Object Technology, 2003: p. 53-64.
7. Giorgini, P., Massacci, F., Mylopoulos, J., and Zannone, N. *ST-Tool: A CASE Tool for Security Requirements Engineering*. in *IEEE International Conference on Requirements Engineering (RE'05)*. 2005.
8. Immonen, A., *A Method for Predicting Reliability and Availability at the Architecture Level*, in *Software Product Lines: Research Issues in Engineering and Management*, Käkölä, T. and Dueñas, J.C., Editors. 2006, Springer.
9. Käkölä, T. and Dueñas, J.C., *Software Product Lines: Research Issues in Engineering and Management*. 2006: Springer.
10. Kim, J., Kim, M., and Park, S., *Goal and scenario bases domain requirements analysis environment*. The Journal of Systems and Software, **79**(7) (2005). p. 926 - 938.
11. Kim., H.-K., *Automatic Translation Form Requirements Model into Use Cases Modeling on UML*. ICCSA 2005, LNCS, 2005: p. 769-777.
12. Kotonya, G. and Sommerville, I., *Requirements Engineering Process and Techniques*. Hardcover ed. 1998, UK: John Willey & Sons. 294.

13. López, F., Amutio, M.A., Candau, J., and Mañas, J.A., *Methodology for Information Systems Risk Analysis and Management*. 2005: Ministry of Public Administration.
14. McDermott, J. and Fox, C. *Using Abuse Case Models for Security Requirements Analysis*. in *Annual Computer Security Applications Conference*. 1999. Phoenix, Arizona.
15. Mead, N.R. and Stehney, T. *Security Quality Requirements Engineering (SQUARE) Methodology*. in *Software Engineering for Secure Systems (SESS05), ICSE 2005 International Workshop on Requirements for High Assurance Systems*. 2005. St. Louis.
16. Mellado, D., Fernandez-Medina, E., and Piattini, M., *SREPPLine: Towards a Security Requirements Engineering Process for Software Product Lines*. 9th International Conference on Enterprise Information Systems (ICEIS 2007). 5th International Workshop on Security In Information Systems (WOSIS-2007), 2007: p. 220-232.
17. Mellado, D., Fernández-Medina, E., and Piattini, M., *A Comparative Study of Proposals for Establishing Security Requirements for the Development of Secure Information Systems*. The 2006 International Conference on Computational Science and its Applications (ICCSA 2006), Springer LNCS 3982, 2006. **3**: p. 1044-1053.
18. Mellado, D., Fernández-Medina, E., and Piattini, M., *A Common Criteria Based Security Requirements Engineering Process for the Development of Secure Information Systems*. Computer Standards and Interfaces, 2007. **29**(2): p. 244 - 253.
19. Mouratidis, H. and Giorgini, P., *Integrating Security and Software Engineering: Advances and Future Visions*. 2007: Idea Group Publishing.
20. Pohl, K., Böckle, G., and Linden, F.v.d., *Software Product Line Engineering. Foundations, Principles and Techniques*. 2005, Berlin Heidelberg: Springer.
21. Popp, G., Jürjens, J., Wimmel, G., and Breu, R., *Security-Critical System Development with Extended Use Cases*. 2003: 10th Asia-Pacific Software Engineering Conference. p. 478-487.
22. Schmid, K., Krennrich, K., and Eisenbarth, M., *Requirements Management for Product Lines: A Prototype*. 2005, Fraunhofer IESE.
23. Sindre, G. and Opdahl, A.L., *Eliciting security requirements with misuse cases*. Requirements Engineering 10, 2005. **1**: p. 34-44.
24. Toval, A., Nicolás, J., Moros, B., and García, F., *Requirements Reuse for Improving Information Systems Security: A Practitioner's Approach*. Requirements Engineering, **6**(4) (2002). p. 205-219.
25. Walton, J.P., *Developing a Enterprise Information Security Policy*. 2002, ACM Press: Proceedings of the 30th annual ACM SIGUCCS conference on User services.

Custos associados à execução de um programa de medição em uma organização de desenvolvimento de software de médio porte

Carlos Augusto Lima Malbouisson[1,2], Manoel Gomes de Mendonça Neto[2]

[1] Fábrica de Software – ZCR Informática Ltda.
Rua Rubens Guelli, nº134, CEP 41.815-150 – Salvador – BA – Brasil

[2] NUPERC - Universidade Salvador (Unifacs)
Salvador – BA – Brasil
{caugusto@zcr.com.br, mgmn@unifacs.br}

Abstract. Measurement is a key software development process area. However, data collection has a cost associated with it. It is important that managers can quantify these costs to evaluate the cost-benefit trade-off of a software measurement program. This work introduces a simple methodology to determine the costs associated with the execution of a software measurement program. The methodology is applied to study the costs of a software organization that has just achieved a CMMI 2 maturity level. The case study, encompassing four projects ranging from 200 to 500 function points, shows that the measurement program of the studied organization ranges from 4.18 to 5.15% of the overall project costs.

Resumo. Medição é uma das áreas chaves do processo de desenvolvimento de software. Entretanto coletar dados tem um custo associado. É importante que gerentes possam quantificar estes custos para que possam avaliar a relação custo-benefício associada a um programa de medição. Este trabalho apresenta uma metodologia para determinar os custos de execução de um programa de medição e sua conseguinte aplicação numa organização que acabou de ser avaliada com o nível de maturidade 2 do CMMI. O estudo de caso, englobando quatro projetos com tamanho variando entre 200 e 500 pontos de função, mostra que programa de medição tem custos que variaram de 4,18 a 5,15% do custo total dos projetos

1 Introdução

A necessidade de se produzir softwares mais complexos, robustos e confiáveis, tem exigido uma melhora significativa nos processos de desenvolvimento e nas técnicas de controle e gestão de projetos de software. Em função desta necessidade, o segmento de desenvolvimento de software passou a buscar modelos de qualidade criados a partir de práticas bem sucedidas de desenvolvimento e gerência de software. Entre estes modelos pode-se citar o SW-CMM [1], CMMI [2], SPICE [3] e as normas ISO [4]. Como resultado da adoção destes modelos, técnicas de controle e gestão de projetos têm sido adotas e aprimoradas.

Para que estas técnicas sejam melhoradas, é desejável o aproveitamento da experiência obtida ao longo do desenvolvimento de cada produto. À medida que a organização vai compondo uma base de conhecimento, seus processos vão continuamente sendo ajustados, tornando-se progressivamente mais adequados, robustos, estáveis e previsíveis.

O grau com que as lições aprendidas podem contribuir para a maturidade de uma organização dependerá de sua capacidade de capturar e organizar estas informações [5,6]. E a uma das formas de obter tal conhecimento é através de medições. Medições permitem a obtenção de dados quantitativos relacionados ao esforço do desenvolvimento, tamanho e qualidade dos produtos. Ajudam também, durante o curso de um projeto, a avaliar o seu progresso, tomar as medidas corretivas baseadas nesse julgamento, e avaliar o impacto de tal ação.

Infelizmente, poucas referências lidam com o aspecto custo dos programas de medição [7,8]. Isto tem levado muitas organizações a assumir que estes custos não influenciam significativamente no orçamento de seus projetos. Embora os benefícios trazidos pela implantação de um programa de medição em uma organização sejam grandes [9], os custos de execução deste programa podem exceder os custos esperados pela própria organização [8]. Um programa de medição pode ser concebido com um número excessivo de métricas, se a dimensão custo não for considerada. Em contrapartida, se os gastos com as medições são periodicamente avaliados, o plano de medição da organização pode ser continuamente aprimorado, a fim de ser se adaptar as necessidades da organização.

O fato é que medição não é de graça, e ela deve ser trabalhada no seu escopo, e custo, para ajustar-se aos objetivos e orçamentos de uma organização [10]. Um programa de medição deve comprometer-se com as expectativas de que o seu retorno valerá o investimento. Infelizmente existem poucos trabalhos que lidam com o problema de quantificar o custo de um programa de medição em uma organização que desenvolve software.

Este trabalho propõe uma metodologia que oriente na determinação dos custos de execução de um programa de medição e em seguida a aplica esta metodologia a uma organização selecionada como objeto de estudo, a fim de se obter dados reais dos custos associados à execução de um plano de medição.

2 Custo de Medição

Para obter sucesso em um programa de qualidade, uma organização deve estabelecer um programa de medição e análise com o objetivo de avaliar quantitativamente a gestão de projetos e gerência da organização. Os benefícios deste programa de medição não são trazidos pela simples coleta de dados, mas pelas decisões e ações tomadas como resposta à análise dos dados coletados durante o andamento de todo processo de desenvolvimento de software e de qualidade da organização.

Infelizmente muitas organizações não enxergam que um programa de medição e análise pode exceder aos custos esperados, e que os custos deste programa não influenciam significativamente no orçamento dos projetos. Planejadores freqüentemente assumem que o custo de medição ocorre apenas durante o desenvolvimento e manutenção dos softwares. Esta parte das despesas, que incluem preenchimento de formulários, identificação das características do projeto e encontro com analistas, é atualmente o menos caro dos três elementos de custo de um programa de medição. Segundo o Laboratório de Engenharia de Software da NASA [8], três papéis distintos podem ser definidos como elementos de um programa de medição de sucesso:

- A Fonte dos Dados, que provê os dados das medidas ligados ao desenvolvimento e manutenção;
- Análise e Empacotamento, que examina dados das medidas e deriva os modelos de processos;
- Suporte Técnico, que coleta, valida e armazena as informações obtidas.

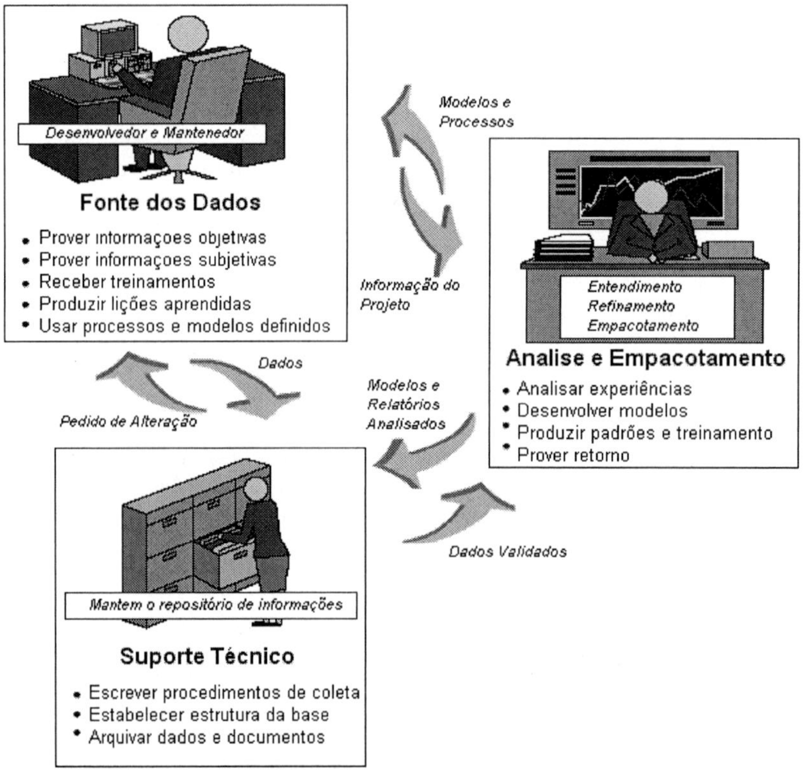

Fig. 1. Os três elementos de um programa de medição, adaptado de [8].

A Figura 1 mostra em mais detalhes os elementos que compõem um programa de medição. Este modelo da NASA mostra que existe um custo mínimo associado com o estabelecimento e operação de qualquer programa de medição. Segundo a mesma, o custo total irá variar dependendo do que a organização quer, ou dispõe.

Na experiência deles, o custo de medição para o desenvolvimento e manutenção do projeto não excede 2% do custo total do desenvolvimento do projeto. O suporte técnico, em média consome 5% do custo do projeto. E a análise e empacotamento requerem em média 7%.

3 Metodologia Proposta

Considerando os dados apresentados acima, não é difícil imaginar que uma organização possa desenvolver um programa de medição muito custoso. Esta situação ocorre com freqüência em organizações que enxergam apenas os possíveis benefícios de um programa de medição sem considerar o esforço e tempo requerido para sua execução. Este tipo de organização inicia um programa de medição tentando medir tudo o que for possível em seus projetos. Este cenário pode trazer frustrações dos gerentes e desenvolvedores com o programa de medição e ceticismo quanto ao uso de métricas de software. Um programa de medição deve ser concebido com o tamanho (e custo) adequado aos objetivos e orçamento de cada organização.

O problema é que não existem no mercado métodos práticos que determinem os custos associados à execução de um programa de medição. Este artigo propõe um método simples para determinar os custos associados à execução de um programa de medição, fornecendo à gerência sênior da organização subsídios para avaliar o custo-benefício de se estabelecer, expandir, ou enxugar tal programa.

A execução de um programa de medição compreende: (1) os processos de medição, que englobam o preenchimento de formulários e participação em entrevistas por parte dos analistas e programadores; (2) a coleta das medições, que engloba a validação das informações e seu arquivamento; (3) a manutenção, que envolve o gerenciamento da base de dados, a manutenção das bibliotecas e ferramentas de medição e análise; e (4) a confecção e preparação de relatórios, que engloba a análise dos dados coletados.

Propõe-se portanto uma divisão do custo total da execução do programa de medição em quatro componentes:

- **Custo Direto de Medição** = Custos de preenchimento de formulários e de participação de entrevistas por parte dos envolvidos;
- **Custo de Coleta das Medições** = Custos envolvidos com a coleta e consistência das medições e armazenamento das informações coletadas;
- **Custo de Preparação e Divulgação dos Resultados** = Custos envolvidos com a análise das coletas das medições realizadas, com a confecção e com a distribuição dos relatórios de medição e análise;
- **Custo Indireto** = Custo de gerenciamento da base de dados, manutenção das bibliotecas e execução das ferramentas de suporte ligadas à execução do programa de medição e análise.

A Figura 2 mostra a relação existente entre os elementos de um programa de medição descrito por SEL-NASA [8], e os quatro componentes propostos na nossa metodologia.

Fig. 2. Relação entre os quatro componentes da metodologia apresentada neste trabalho e os elementos descritos em [8].

Como resultado, o custo da execução de um programa de medição e análise é obtido a partir da soma dos custos dos quatro componentes listados anteriormente, gerando a fórmula 1.

$$\text{Custo de Execução} = \text{Custo Direto de Medição} + \text{Custo de Coleta das Medições} + \text{Custo de Preparação e Divulgação dos Resultados} + \text{Custo Indireto} \quad (1)$$

Para se obter os custos de cada componente, deve-se seguir os seguintes passos para cada métrica definida no plano de medição da organização:

1. Coletar o Tempo Gasto e Calcular o Tempo Médio de Medição - Indicar o tempo levado para realizar as medições / coletas / preparação / manutenção, escolhendo o período adequado para coleta das informações desejadas;
2. Indicar os Profissionais Envolvidos - Indicar os profissionais envolvidos no processo de medição / coleta / preparação / manutenção e seus respectivos custos por hora;
3. Determinar a Periodicidade de Preenchimento - Indicar com que periodicidade os funcionários irão medir / coletar / preparar os resultados / manter, considerado o tempo do projeto;
4. Observar Distorções e Particularidades da Medição - Devem ser observadas qualquer distorção ou particularidade nas medições / coletas / preparação / manutenção. A depender da distorção ou particularidade, o custo poderá ser desconsiderado ou revisado;
5. Calcular o Custo dos Recursos Utilizados - Calcular o custo de medição / coleta / preparação / manutenção para cada recurso. Total por recurso = Custo do Recurso (R$ por hora) * Tempo Médio * Total de medições / coletas / preparações / manutenções para o projeto (utilizando a periodicidade das coletas nos cálculos);

6. Calcular o Percentual do Custo - O percentual de custo da execução da métrica para um determinado projeto deve ser calculado dividindo-se o custo total pelo custo total dos recursos humanos envolvidos no projeto.

4 Estudo de Caso

Nesta seção, a metodologia proposta na seção anterior é aplicada a um estudo de caso. Neste estudo, a metodologia é usada em um ambiente de fábrica de software de uma empresa de médio porte que acabou de ser avaliada como CMMI Nível 2. Dados são coletados de quatro projetos típicos que usam as práticas ditadas por este nível de maturidade de processos. Eles refletem portanto o custo típico de um programa de medição de uma organização deste porte operando no contexto de desenvolvimento. Os resultados são expressos como um percentual do custo total do esforço (tempo de trabalho dos colaboradores) nos projetos.

4.1 Objeto de Estudo

Muitos programas de medição são concebidos no contexto da implantação e amadurecimento de programas do CMMI nível 2. Este é o cenário da organização em que o estudo de caso foi elaborado. O estudo foi executado na ZCR Informática, uma empresa com 14 anos de mercado que trabalha no desenvolvimento de soluções de software e integrações tecnológicas. A empresa possui atualmente 100 colaboradores, sendo cerca de 60 da área de desenvolvimento e manutenção de software.

O CMMI, proposto pelo Software Engineering Institute (SEI) da Carnegie Mellon University, representa um modelo de maturidade para empresas que pretendem incrementar a qualidade dos seus processos de desenvolvimento e manutenção de software e produtos relacionados [2], [11]. No seu modelo em estágios o CMMI é dividido em níveis, que vai do nível 1, caótico, ao nível 5, otimizado.

O CMMI trata do assunto medição como uma das áreas de processo para a obtenção da qualidade. Ela é exigida logo no nível 2 de maturidade e aplicada em todos os seus níveis seguintes. Segundo [11], a área de processo "Medição e Análise" tem como objetivo desenvolver e implantar a capacidade de avaliação das medidas (métricas) que servirão como importantes fontes de informação para a gestão de projetos e gerência da organização.

Para Medição e Análise (MA), a ZCR Informática possui um processo e um procedimento bem definidos e detalhados para garantir a execução destas atividades dentro da empresa. O processo ZCR de MA determina o que deve ser feito para que a Área de Processo de Medição e Análise, exigida pelo CMMI nível 2, seja totalmente cumprida. Pode-se pensar que o processo é uma tradução da Área de Processo nos moldes da empresa. O procedimento de Medição e Análise determina como, quando e por quem devem ser realizadas as atividades inerentes a MA.

Citado diversas vezes no procedimento, o Plano de MA da organização e conseqüentemente dos projetos, torna-se a base de todas as ações responsável pela MA na empresa. O plano descreve os objetivos organizacionais e na seqüência todas as métricas que darão suporte ao alcance dos objetivos almejados.

É de responsabilidade dos profissionais de MA a garantia do cumprimento do Plano de MA da organização e conseqüentemente da execução das métricas descritas nele e de suas coletas quando necessárias (descritas também no plano). Outra responsabilidade destes profissionais é a preparação e comunicação dos resultados obtidos. Na preparação dos resultados (geralmente através de relatórios), as informações de medições coletadas devem ser analisadas e reportadas aos interessados (geralmente a alta gerência da organização, SEPG - *Software Engineering Process Group* e gerente do projeto envolvido).

Outros profissionais envolvidos nas coletas das medições são: os gerentes dos projetos, que durante suas monitorações e controle do projeto utilizam-se das métricas para verificar o andamento do projeto e caso necessário tomar alguma ação corretiva naquele momento; e o PPQA, que mensalmente (conforme determinado no plano de MA), coletam as métricas ligadas à monitoração e controle dos processos. O plano de MA da organização é sumarizado a seguir.

4.2 Modelo GQM da Empresa – Plano de Medição e Análise da Organização

O plano de MA é a base do programa de medição e análise. Nele a organização apresenta seus objetivos e define métricas que trarão indicadores importantes e critérios de análises capazes de conduzir a organização aos objetivos almejados.

A organização define no seu plano de MA dois grandes grupos de objetivos:

- Organizacional
- Monitoração e Controle dos Processos

Para cada grupo de objetivos, seguindo o modelo GQM [12], foram definidas questões e métricas, definindo o processo de medição e análise da organização. Este plano GQM é apresentado nas Tabelas 1 e 2..

Tabela 1. Modelo GQM para o Grupo Organizacional.

Identificação	GQM – Objetivos/Questões/Métricas
G1	Melhorar estimativa de tempo, tamanho e esforço dos projetos
Q11	Qual a precisão das estimativas de tempo dos projetos?
M111	Precisão da Estimativa de Tempo do Projeto (PET)
Q12	Qual a precisão das estimativas de tamanho dos projetos?
M121	Precisão da Estimativa de Tamanho do Projeto (PETAM)
Q13	Qual a precisão das estimativas de esforço dos projetos?
M131	Precisão da Estimativa de Esforço do Projeto (PEE)
G2	Aumentar Produtividade da Equipe
Q21	Qual é a produtividade das equipes dos projetos?
M211	Produtividade
G3	Melhorar Estimativas de Custo dos Projetos
Q31	Qual a precisão das estimativas de custo dos projetos?
M311	Precisão das Estimativas de Custo (PEC)

Tabela 2. Modelo GQM para o grupo Monitoração e Controle dos Processos.

Identificação	GQM – Objetivos/Questões/Métricas
G1	Monitorar e Controlar os Processos
Q11	O processo de Gerência de Configuração está sendo monitorado e controlado?
M111	Número de Solicitações de Mudanças de Artefatos Abertas
M112	Número de Solicitações de Mudanças de Artefatos Fechadas
M113	Número de auditorias realizadas
Q12	O processo de Monitoração e Controle está sendo monitorado e controlado?
M121	Número de Desvios (Plano de ação do PMC)
M122	Número de ações corretivas abertas em função de ações corretivas anteriores não efetivas
Q13	O processo de Planejamento do Projeto está sendo monitorado e controlado?
M131	Número de avaliações necessárias para aprovar a 1ª versão do Plano do Projeto
Q14	O processo de PPQA está sendo monitorado e controlado?
M141	% de avaliações devidas e efetivamente realizadas
M142	Número de desvios encontrados na execução do processo
M143	Número de desvios encontrados em produtos
M144	IAP – Índice de Aderência aos Processos
Q15	O processo de REQM está sendo monitorado e controlado?
M151	Número de Solicitações de Mudanças de Requisitos
M152	Número de avaliações necessárias para aprovar a 1ª versão da Especificação de Requisitos
M153	ISMR – Índice de Solicitações de Mudanças de Requisitos (F e NF)
Q16	O processo de MA está sendo monitorado e controlado?
M161	Número de ações corretivas geradas por causa de critérios de análise da métrica.

Conforme o processo de medição e análise da organização, no plano de medição da organização, deve constar ainda para cada métrica citada acima: a descrição completa da métrica, o procedimento de coleta, forma de armazenamento e o procedimento de análise. As métricas que compõem o plano não foram apresentadas em detalhes neste trabalho, no intuito de preservar o trabalho realizado pela empresa durante todo processo de implantação do programa de medição.

Da mesma forma que o grupo de objetivos organizacionais, que estão ligados diretamente aos objetivos almejados pela alta gerência da organização, a ZCR Informática definiu também questões e métricas ligadas à monitoração e controle dos processos. Métricas que apenas indicam o andamento (aderência) dos processos ligados a cada área de processo definidas no modelo CMMI nível 2.

Para melhor visualização das métricas descritas no plano GQM da empresa, a Tabela 3 apresenta um quadro de resumo que identifica unicamente a métrica, seu tipo e o grupo de origem, além de decompor todas as métricas que não são obtidas de forma direta. Este quadro é posteriormente referenciado na apresentação dos resultados do estudo de caso.

As métricas apresentadas na Tabela 3 são divididas em dois grandes grupos (Objetivos Organizacionais e Objetivos de Monitoração e Controle dos Processos). As métricas também são divididas em diretas e indiretas. As medidas diretas, ou básicas, são aquelas mensuradas a partir de observação direta dos atributos envolvidos. As indiretas, ou derivadas, são aquelas que não podem ser mensuradas diretamente e são calculadas a partir de combinações de outras medidas.

Table 3. Quadro de Resumo das Métricas.

ID	Métricas	Tipo	Grupo[1,2]
M1	Precisão da Estimativa de Tempo do Projeto (PET)	Indireta	Org
M2	TR – Tempo Real do Projeto	Direta	Org
M3	TE – Tempo Estimado para o Projeto	Direta	Org
M4	TMR - Tempo de Mudança de Requisitos	Direta	Org
M5	Precisão da Estimativa de Tamanho do Projeto (PETAM)	Indireta	Org
M6	TAMR - Tamanho Real do Projeto	Direta	Org
M7	TAME - Tamanho Estimado do Projeto	Direta	Org
M8	TAMMR - Tamanho da Mudança de Requisitos do Projeto	Direta	Org
M9	Precisão da Estimativa de Esforço do Projeto (PEE)	Indireta	Org
M10	ER - Esforço Real do Projeto	Direta	Org
M11	EE - Esforço Estimado para o Projeto	Direta	Org
M12	EMR - Esforço de Mudança de Requisitos	Direta	Org
M13	Produtividade	Indireta	Org
M14	Precisão das Estimativas de Custo (PEC)	Indireta	Org
M15	CR - Custo Real do Projeto	Direta	Org
M16	Orçamento do Projeto	Direta	Org
M17	CMR - Custo por Mudança de Requisitos	Direta	Org
M18	Número de Solicitações de Mudanças de Artefatos Abertas	Direta	Proc
M19	Número de Solicitações de Mudanças de Artefatos Fechadas	Direta	Proc
M20	Número de auditorias realizadas	Direta	Proc
M21	Número de Desvios (Plano de ação do PMC)	Direta	Proc
M22	Número de ações corretivas abertas em função de ações corretivas anteriores não efetivas	Direta	Proc
M23	Número de avaliações necessárias para aprovar a 1ª versão do Plano do Projeto	Direta	Proc
M24	% de avaliações devidas e efetivamente realizadas	Indireta	Proc
M25	Número de desvios encontrados na execução do processo	Direta	Proc
M26	Número de desvios encontrados em produtos	Direta	Proc
M27	IAP – Índice de Aderência aos Processos	Indireta	Proc
M28	Número de Solicitações de Mudanças de Requisitos	Direta	Proc
M29	Número de avaliações necessárias para aprovar a 1ª versão da Especificação de Requisitos	Direta	Proc
M30	ISMR – Índice de Solicitações de Mudanças de Requisitos (F e NF)	Indireta	Proc
M31	Número de ações corretivas geradas por causa de critérios de análise da métrica.	Direta	Proc

4.3 Projetos Selecionados

Para o estudo de caso, foram selecionados quatro projetos com características de desenvolvimento semelhantes no que se refere ao ciclo de vida do projeto, e que possuem recursos humanos – gerentes de projetos, líderes de projetos, analistas de sistemas, programadores, testadores e projetistas – distintos. Estes projetos estão resumidos na Tabela 4.

Table 4. Projetos utilizados no estudo de caso.

Projeto	Dt. Inicial	Dt. Final	Qtd Recursos	FPA	Custo (R$)
SAHUEC	10/03/05	03/08/05	5	500	15.250,00
EXPSINTEGRA	18/03/05	03/08/05	3	289	12.000,00
GACS	18/01/05	05/01/06	4	350	47.000,00
SHOT	10/02/05	02/09/05	3	300	14.000,00

Todos os projetos foram desenvolvidos em cascata. O SAHUEC e o EXPSINTEGRA são aplicativos cliente-servidor para *desktops*, que rodam em rede local. Eles foram desenvolvidos em Delphi 6.0. Os projetos GACS e SHOT são aplicativos desenvolvidos para ambiente WEB, utilizando como linguagem de programação o ASP e PHP respectivamente.

Estes projetos foram selecionados por possuírem seus ciclos de vida de desenvolvimento completos e seguirem completamente as práticas definidas no CMMI Nível 2 da organização. Todos eles iniciaram na definição do escopo do produto e passaram pelas atividades de planejamento do projeto, análise de requisitos, projeto técnico, codificação, testes, implantação, treinamento e encerramento do projeto. Desta forma, pode-se obter todos os custos de desenvolvimento dos mesmos.

4.4 Coleta dos Dados

A metodologia proposta foi aplicada aos quatro projetos selecionados. Para cada componente proposto na metodologia foram cuidadosamente seguidos todos os passos indicados para a obtenção dos custos para cada uma das 31 métricas do programa de medição da ZCR. Este é um processo trabalhoso pois os seis passos da metodologia envolvem não só a identificação das métricas, mas a identificação do custo de cada coleta, a determinação da freqüência de coleta de cada métrica, a determinação das análises feitas com estas métricas, a identificação das pessoas responsáveis por estas atividades, e a identificação do custo destas pessoas, para então calcular os custos associados com a métrica. Somente após a realização desta análise para cada uma das métricas é que se pode gerar um perfil detalhado do custo do programa de medição. Os detalhes da aplicação da metodologia às 31 métricas nos quatro projetos encontram-se descritos em [13].

A Tabela 5 apresenta os resultados dos custos de execução do programa de medição para o projeto SAHUEC. Nela observam-se os custos agrupados por cada componente definido na metodologia e ainda, mais detalhadamente, por cada métrica concebida no plano de medição da organização. Nesta tabela, vê-se que, para o projeto SAHUEC, o custo total ligado ao processo de medição foi de R$ 822,13, e representou 5,391% do valor total dos custos com recursos humanos empregados no projeto, que foi de R$ 15.250,00. Este custo é calculado com a soma do custo direto de medição, custo de coleta das medições, custo de preparação de análises e custos indiretos.

É importante notar que os custos indiretos são determinados como um percentual dos custos operacionais da organização (considerando os custos de manutenção da base de dados e o número de projetos em andamento) multiplicado pela duração do projeto.

Table 5. Resumo do Custo de MA para o Projeto SAHUEC.

Custo Direto de Medição			
Métrica	Duração	Custo (R$)	Custo (%)
TE – Tempo Estimado para o Projeto	3:30 h	131,25	0,860%
TAMR - Tamanho Real do Projeto, TAME - Tamanho Estimado do Projeto e TAMMR - Tamanho da Mudança de Requisitos do Projeto	4:50 h	146,16	0,958%
ER - Esforço Real do Projeto	4:04 h	93,04	0,610%
EE - Esforço Estimado para o Projeto	0:30 h	18,75	0,122%
Orçamento do Projeto	0:25 h	15,62	0,102%
TMR - Tempo de Mudança de Requisitos, EMR - Esforço de MR e CMR - Custo por MR	1:00 h	27,00	0,177%
Total Custo Direto de Medição	**14:19 h**	**R$ 431,82**	**2,829 %**
Custo de Coletas das Medições			
Métrica	Duração	Custo	% do Custo
TR – Tempo Real do Projeto e TE – Tempo Estimado para o Projeto	16,25 m	10,15	0,066%
TAMR - Tamanho Real do Projeto e TAME - Tamanho Estimado do Projeto	1 m	0,62	0,004%
ER - Esforço Real do Projeto	0:26 h	16,25	0,106%
EE - Esforço Estimado para o Projeto	6,5 m	4,06	0,026%
CR - Custo Real e Orçamento do Projeto	19,5m	12,18	0,079%
TMR - Tempo de Mudança de Requisito, TAMMR - Tamanho da MR, EMR - Esforço de MR e CMR - Custo por MR	6 min	3,75	0,024%
Custo com as coletas das medições ligadas a monitoração e controle dos processos	1:32 h	33,75	0,221%
Total Custo de Coletas das Medições	**2:47 h**	**R$ 80,76**	**0,529%**
Custo de Preparação e Divulgação dos Resultados			
Total de Medições Previstas	Duração	Custo da Métrica	% do Custo
1	4:00 h	150,00	0,983%
Total do Custo de Preparação	**4:00 h**	**150,00**	**0,983%**
Custo Indireto de Medição			
Valor Individual	Meses de Projeto	Custo da Métrica	% do Custo
32,04	5	159,55	1,046%
Total Custo Direto de Medição	**5**	**159,55**	**1,046%**
Custo do Projeto: R$ 15.250,00	**Custo de MA: 822,13**	**% Custo: 5,391%**	

Table 6. Resumo do Custo de Medição por Componentes para todos os Projetos.

Custo/Projeto	SAHUEC		EXPSintegra		GACS		SHOT	
	R$	%	R$	%	R$	%	R$	%
Custo Direto de Medição	431,82	2,829	358,25	2,985	1.039,73	2,212	379,87	2,711
Custo de Coletas das Medições	80,76	0,529	74,19	0,618	243,17	0,517	130,12	0,929
Custo de Preparação e Divulgação dos Resultados	150,00	0,983	112,50	0,937	300,00	0,638	150,00	1,071
Custo Indireto de Medição	159,55	1,046	144,18	1,201	384,48	0,818	159,55	1,139
Total	**822,1**	**5,39**	**689,1**	**5,74**	**1.967,4**	**4,18**	**819,5**	**5,85**

Os resultados detalhados para todos os projetos selecionados para pesquisa podem ser encontrados em [13]. Um resumo dos resultados do estudo para os quatro projetos agrupados pelos componentes sugeridos na metodologia se encontra na Tabela 6.

4.5 Discussão dos Resultados

Como resultado da aplicação da metodologia sobre o objeto de estudo descrito, uma organização que desenvolve software e possui o modelo CMMI como referência de desenvolvimento, pôde-se observar que os custos obtidos representaram entre 4,18% e 5,85% do orçamento total do projeto.

Segundo o SEL [8], os custos de medição com o preenchimento dos formulários e entrevistas (destacado no elemento Fonte de Dados), não devem exceder 2% do custo total do projeto, embora os custos iniciais citados devam ser altos, em média 5%.

Os resultados obtidos no estudo de caso para o *custo direto de medição* (respectivamente 2,829%, 2,985%, 2,212 e 2,711 para os projetos SAHUEC, EXPSINTEGRA, GACS e SHOT), excederam um pouco os percentuais citados em [8]. O que se pode observar é que os processos e ferramentas ligados à medição ainda podem ser amadurecidos e reduzidos num futuro próximo. Isto deverá diminuir os custos associados a algumas atividades de coleta de dados. Observe todavia que, a não ser que se desenvolvam abordagens completamente não intrusivas de coleta de dados, estes custos têm uma margem limitada para redução.

Observe que há uma diferença percentual do custo de medição existente entre os projetos de menor porte SAHUEC (R$15.250,00), EXPSINTEGRA (R$12.000,00) e SHOT (R$14.000,00), e o projeto GACS (R$47.000,00). O custo de execução para o projeto GACS foi o menor de todos, 4,185% do custo total do projeto, enquanto que os do projeto SAHUEC, EXPSINTEGRA e SHOT, representaram respectivamente 5,391%, 5,742% e 5,853%. Esta diferença é provavelmente motivada pelas métricas que são executadas pontualmente durante a execução dos projetos. Considere por exemplo a métrica TAM (Tamanho do Projeto), que é medida em apenas dois momentos do projeto, na fase de planejamento e no seu encerramento. O cálculo do tamanho do projeto (em pontos de função) para projetos maiores, como é o caso do GACS, leva um pouco mais de tempo e conseqüentemente é um pouco mais custoso. Todavia este custo é significantemente diluído no valor total do projeto. Diferentemente, as métricas que são medidas durante todo o andamento do projeto têm seus custos acrescidos em direta proporção ao tamanho do projeto. Conseqüentemente seu impacto percentual tende a ser constante sobre o custo total. Este é o caso, por exemplo, da métrica ER – Esforço Real do Projeto, que é medida por todos os recursos do projeto durante todo o seu ciclo de vida. Para este tipo de métrica, diferenças percentuais não são observadas entre projetos de portes diferentes.

5 Conclusão

O custo é um dos atributos críticos para o sucesso de um programa de medição de software. Algumas empresas assumem que um programa de medição não gera custos adicionais ou que estes custos não irão gerar impacto significativo nos custos globais dos projetos. Isto é um erro grave, especialmente em organizações que operam com uma pequena margem de lucro. Ao implementar seus programas de medição estas organizações tendem a coletar tudo o que podem. Seu plano GQM, tem poucas metas e muitas métricas. Com pouco tempo de operação estas organizações observam que o custo de medição é excessivo e que os benefícios obtidos (objetivos de medição) não justificam o estabelecimento de um programa para tal finalidade. Não é desta forma que um programa de medição e análise deve ser concebido. Um programa deve ser enxuto, coletando um conjunto de métricas que atendam a um grande número de metas de medição.

Este trabalho foi desenvolvido no intuito de apoiar a avaliação dos custos ligados à execução de um programa de medição em organizações que desenvolvem software. Desta forma, organizações podem avaliar seus respectivos custos de medição e adequá-los às suas expectativas financeiras e operacionais. A metodologia desenvolvida facilita a sistematização da obtenção dos custos ligados à execução de planos de medições em organizações que desenvolvem software, mas sua aplicação exige esforço. Ela deve ser aplicada periodicamente para se avaliar o programa de medição. Isto é, a aplicação da metodologia possui um custo associado, mas o risco de operar um plano de medição mal elaborado e custoso durante muito tempo certamente torna válida a aplicação da mesma pelo menos uma vez para cada grande classe de projeto de uma organização.

Um dos pontos importantes observados com o estudo é que a aplicação da metodologia pode ser repetida periodicamente no intuito de se acompanhar como os custos de execução do plano de medição de uma empresa estão evoluindo. Mesmo que não seja aplicada periodicamente, sugere-se que a metodologia seja ser aplicada quando houver uma alteração significativa no plano de medição da empresa.

Os custos levantados pelo estudo de caso podem ser considerados como um ponto de referência para uma organização de porte e perfil similar a ZCR, todavia é fundamental que cada organização determine os custos de seu próprio programa de medição. Na análise de resultados vimos que os custos variam com o tipo de métrica e tamanho de projeto. É de se esperar que estes custos variem também com domínio e estrutura organizacional da empresa. Os resultados apresentados aqui podem ser utilizados como referência, mas não devem ser generalizados. É importante que cada instituição use a metodologia proposta para determinar seus próprios custos.

Neste contexto deve-se observar que a metodologia apresentada aqui é simples na determinação dos seus quatro tipos componentes de custo e nos seus passos listados no começo deste artigo. Todavia, não se deve confundir simplicidade com facilidade de execução, o levantamento de todos componentes de um programa de medição é bastante trabalhoso. Cabe aos profissionais responsáveis pelo programa de medição da empresa assumir a responsabilidade de aplicá-la sempre que uma avaliação do seu programa for necessária.

Observe que o custo do programa é somente uma das duas dimensões de uma análise custo-benefício. É importante que se possua uma boa metodologia para se avaliar o quanto as medições estão sendo efetivamente utilizadas na organização. Este é um excelente tema para trabalhos futuros. Sugere-se, por exemplo, relacionar-se o número de metas GQM efetivamente alcançadas por um programa de medição e o grau de utilização dos seus resultados pela gerência sênior, como métricas para se avaliar o benefício efetivo deste programa.

Referências

1. Paulk, Mark C.; Garcia, Suzanne M.; Chrissis, Mary Beth; Weber, Charles V., Bush, Marilyn. (1993) Key Practices of the Capability Maturity Model SM , Version 1.1. (CMU/SEI-93-TR-025). Pittsburgh, PA: Software Engineering Institute, Carnegie Mellon University.
2. CMMI Product Team. (2002) CMMI for Software Engineering, Version 1.1, Staged Representation (CMMI-SW, V1.1, Staged). Pittsburgh, PA: Software Engineering Institute, Carnegie Mellon University.
3. Emam, Khaled El (Editor), Jean-Normand Drouin (Editor), Walcélio Melo (Editor), Alec Dorling (Foreword by). (1997) SPICE: The Theory and Practice of Software Process Improvement and Capability Determination. Wiley-IEEE Computer Society Press. 496p.
4. ISO. (2001) The International Organization for Standardization. ISO/IEC 15939; Software Engineering – Software Measurement Process.
5. Falbo, Ricardo de A. (1998) "Integração de Conhecimento em um Ambiente de Desenvolvimento de Software". Rio de Janeiro. Tese de Doutorado, COPPE/ UFRJ.
6. Villela, K. (2004) "Definição e Construção de Ambientes de Desenvolvimento de Software Orientados a Organização". Tese (Doutorado) – Universidade Federal do Rio de Janeiro UFRJ.
7. Fuggetta, Alfonso, Luigi Lavazza, Sandro Morasca, Stefano Cinti, Giandomenico Oldano, and Elena Orazi. (1998) Applying GQM in an Industrial Software Factory. ACM Transactions on Software Engineering and Methodology, 7(4):411-448.
8. SEL, (1995) Nasa Software Engineering Laboratory, Greenbelt. Software Measurement Guidebook, revision 1 (SEL-94-102). Greenbelt: NASA Goddard Space Flight Center.
9. Fenton, Norman E. (1991) Software Metrics: A Rigorous Approach. Chapman Hall.
10. Solingbn, Rini, Berghout, Egon. (1999) The Goal/Question/Metric Method; a practical guide for quality improvement of software development. London: McGraw-Hill.
11. Chrissis, Mary Beth; Konrad, Mike; Shrum, Sandy. (2003) CMMI – Guidelines for Process Integration and Product Improvement. Addison Wesley.
12. Basili, Victor; Caldiera, G. and H.D. Rombach, The Goal Question Metric Approach, Encyclopedia of Software Engineering, pp. 528-532, John Wiley & Sons, Inc., 1994.
13. Malbouisson, Carlos Augusto Lima. (2006) Metodologia para Obtenção dos Custos Associados à Execução do Programa de Medição de uma Organização. Dissertação de Mestrado. Universidade Salvador - BA.

Diseño Multidimensional guiado por Ontología

Sebastián Giménez, Regina Motz, Fernando Carpani, Diego Gayoso, Cecilia Colombatto

Instituto de Computación, Universidad de la República, Julio Herrera y Reissig 565, 11300 Montevideo, Uruguay
{carpani, rmotz }@fing.edu.uy

Resumen. Este trabajo presenta guías de diseño conceptual multidimensional para data warehouses basadas en el análisis de requerimientos y en la ontología del dominio. Se ejemplifica con un caso de estudio real y se compara la propuesta con otras existentes.

Keywords: Modelo Conceptual Multidimensional, Data Warehouse, Ontología.

1 Introducción

El diseño multidimensional es ampliamente utilizado como representación conceptual de un Data Warehouse. Un Data Warehouse (DW) es una base de datos que almacena información para la toma de decisiones, que no es un sistema transaccional sino fuertemente caracterizado por ser un sistema OLAP, acrónimo en inglés de procesamiento analítico en línea (On-Line Analytical Processing). El modelo multidimensional, o la metáfora del cubo, sirven para organizar los datos en torno a un eje de datos a ser analizados (*hechos*), un eje de las descripciones más importantes de esos datos (*medidas*) y otro eje que describe las *dimensiones* en que los datos pueden ser analizados. Si bien no existe un consenso de estándar en el modelo multidimensional a usar, sí existe acuerdo en la importancia de distinguir entre un diseño conceptual, un diseño lógico y un diseño físico [1, 2, 3]. El diseño conceptual apunta a la construcción de un esquema conceptual en concordancia con el modelo conceptual elegido que sea independiente de la implementación y que sea expresivo en la representación de los requerimientos del usuario. El diseño lógico toma el esquema conceptual y crea el correspondiente esquema lógico en la plataforma elegida considerando restricciones operacionales. El diseño físico se enfoca en el desarrollo específico referente a una implementación. Como señalado en [4], existen varias propuestas de metodologías para diseños en estos tres niveles, pero no existen aún metodologías sencillas, prácticas, para que desde el punto de vista industrial sirvan para mejorar el diseño conceptual de un DW.

En este trabajo presentamos una propuesta para realizar el diseño conceptual multidimensional con el desafío de obtener un diseño fácil de reutilizar, de extender y de administrar. Nuestra propuesta es trabajar desde una fase de captura de requerimientos del usuario con correspondencias tanto desde una ontología de dominio como desde el modelo conceptual utilizado. Mostramos como estas correspondencias permiten el diseño conceptual del DW de manera ordenada y documentada y permiten además desarrollar una clara trazabilidad de los conceptos presentes en la realidad hasta su representación en el modelo multidimensional, favoreciendo de esta forma, la administración de los cambios en los requerimientos. Generalmente ocurre que una vez que se implanta un DW, los requerimientos que originaron al mismo van cambiando, además de adicionarse nuevos. Por esto es importante que el Data Warehouse sea flexible a nuevos cambios, y que su mantenimiento sea lo menos costoso posible.

Una ontología se puede definir como *la especificación explícita de una conceptualización* [5]. Cuando el conocimiento de un dominio es representado en un formalismo declarativo, el conjunto de objetos que pueden ser representados es llamado el universo de discurso. Este conjunto de objetos, y las relaciones descriptibles entre ellos, es reflejado en el vocabulario con el cual se representa conocimiento. En una ontología se asocian mediante definiciones los nombres de las entidades en el universo de discurso (por ejemplo clases, relaciones, funciones u otros objetos) con cierto texto expresado en lenguaje natural que las describe y con axiomas que restringen la interpretación y otorgan la característica de "bien formados" a dichos términos. Uno de los principales objetivos que tiene la utilización de ontologías es la de realizar inferencias sobre los conceptos. Mediante el uso de herramientas tales como razonadores es posible detectar inconsistencias, con el beneficio de obtener puntos de retrocesos menores y por lo tanto con menor costo asociado al mantenimiento del diseño guiado por ontología.

El resto del artículo está organizado de la siguiente forma. La Sección 2 presenta las características particulares del modelo multidimensional utilizado, CMDM. La Sección 3 presenta las fases de nuestro enfoque mientras que la Sección 4 presenta la derivación del modelo conceptual desde la ontología de dominio. Para una mejor comprensión, la Sección 5 presenta una aplicación práctica de nuestra propuesta, experimentada en un ambiente real de diseño de DW. Finalmente la Sección 6 presenta algunas conclusiones y líneas de trabajo futuro.

2 El Modelo Multidimensional CMDM

El objetivo fundamental de CMDM [6, 7] es permitir la especificación de una determinada realidad en términos multidimensionales.

En una base de datos multidimensional, la información se representa como matrices multidimensionales, cuadros de múltiples entradas o funciones de varias variables sobre conjuntos finitos. Cada una de estas matrices se denomina Cubo. El esquema de un cubo queda determinado dando a conocer sus ejes con sus respectivas estructuras y la estructura de los datos que se presentan en cada celda de la matriz. Se asume que los datos en todas las celdas son uniformes, es decir, todas las posiciones de la matriz tienen datos con igual estructura. A los ejes se les llama Dimensiones y al dato que se presenta en la matriz, se le llama Medida. Generalmente, las dimensiones se estructuran en jerarquías de agregación. A cada nivel de una jerarquía se le llama Nivel de Agregación o simplemente Nivel. De esta forma, se puede considerar que toda dimensión siempre tiene por lo menos una jerarquía con un único nivel. Pero una dimensión puede tener más de una jerarquía. Un ejemplo típico, es una dimensión que representa tiempo. En este caso, los niveles bimestre y trimestre no están relacionados entre sí, a pesar de que ambos están relacionados con mes y año. Para lograr representar esta realidad, CMDM presenta tres estructuras básicas: Niveles, Dimensiones y Relaciones Dimensionales.

Niveles: Un nivel representa un conjunto de objetos que son de un mismo tipo. Cada nivel debe tener un nombre y un tipo. Conceptualmente, no tiene diferencia con cualquier elemento del Modelo Entidad Relación que pueda ser considerado un conjunto de Entidades.

Dimensiones: Una dimensión está determinada por una jerarquía de niveles.

Las dimensiones deben poder estructurarse en niveles, donde cada nivel debe tener una declaración en el conjunto de declaraciones del esquema. De esta forma, una dimensión es una tupla formada por un conjunto de niveles previamente declarados y un orden parcial con mínimo definido sobre los niveles. Toda dimensión, además, tendrá un identificador.

Relaciones Dimensionales: Una relación dimensional representa el conjunto de todos los cubos que se pueden construir a partir de los niveles de un conjunto dado de dimensiones. Se asume que en cada uno de los cubos que pertenecen a la instancia de la relación dimensional, debe aparecer al menos un nivel de cada una de las dimensiones que participan en la relación. En CMDM, un cubo es una función que va del producto cartesiano de las instancias de los niveles en los booleanos. De esta forma, cualquier nivel puede cumplir el rol de medida. Por lo tanto, el esquema de una relación dimensional está dado por un grafo en forma de estrella.

En las siguientes secciones mostramos el proceso a seguir para poder derivar qué conceptos de la realidad deben modelarse como dimensiones, cuáles como niveles, y cuál es la jerarquía que modela varios niveles. Más detalles sobre el modelo CMDM pueden consultarse en [6,7].

3 Fases en el Diseño Multidimensional

En el presente trabajo se propone una metodología que abarca desde la etapa inicial de "Business modeling" [8] hasta el diseño conceptual del DW. La metodología propuesta está soportada por una serie de fases apoyadas por el uso de una ontología de dominio. Esto permite lograr una visión global de los conceptos, realizar inferencias, verificar la consistencia del modelo y obtener la trazabilidad de los conceptos a lo largo del proceso. El ciclo de vida de la metodología propuesta consiste en tres fases secuenciales, diagramadas en la Figura 1, donde cada uno de los óvalos identifica una fase y las flechas marcadas en negro indican las dependencias más importantes y frecuentes entre las mismas.

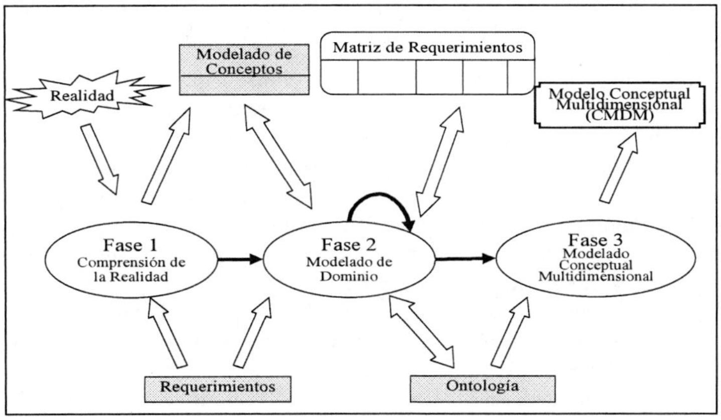

Fig. 1: Fases del Diseño Multidimensional guiado por Ontología.

Fase I – Análisis de la Realidad. El objetivo de esta fase es identificar todos los conceptos que componen el dominio del problema, junto con las relaciones existentes entre los mismos y las restricciones identificada para cada uno. Esta fase pretende transformar el conocimiento tácito que se encuentra en los expertos conocedores de la realidad en conocimiento explícito, de forma que el mismo se encuentre documentado y almacenado para que cualquier otro interesado en comprender la realidad pueda hacer uso de dicho conocimiento cuando lo considere necesario. Como entrada de esta fase se requiere el conjunto de requerimientos iniciales y la realidad planteada. Como resultado de la fase se cuenta con el documento *Metadata de Conceptos*, el cual contiene la información de contexto y datos importantes identificados para cada concepto. En este documento se incluye una descripción del dominio relevado, sobre el cual se deberá resolver los requerimientos, siendo la base para la realización del modelo de la realidad que se realizará en la Fase II (Modelado del Dominio). Los participantes de esta fase son los expertos conocedores de la realidad y analistas del equipo de desarrollo. Como condiciones para la finalización de la fase es necesario considerar que todo concepto que forme parte de la resolución de un requerimiento esté definido en el documento *Metadata de Conceptos*.

Fase II – Modelado del Dominio. El objetivo de esta fase es construir un modelo que represente, utilizando un modelo formal, los conceptos de la Fase I, detallados en el documento *Metadata de Conceptos*. El modelo incluirá la información y características más importantes, relaciones definidas y las restricciones consideradas en el análisis de la realidad, abstrayendo la realidad presentada y eliminando posibles inconsistencias y/o conflictos que no se hubieran identificado en la Fase I. Como entrada de la fase se requiere el documento *Metadata de Conceptos* obtenido en la fase I y el conjunto de requerimientos. Como resultado de la fase se obtiene la ontología que es el modelo semántico de dominio que representa la realidad relevada, modelando la información de contexto y datos importantes identificados para cada concepto, las relaciones entre estos y las restricciones identificadas. Adicionalmente, al finalizar la fase se cuenta con la *Matriz de Requerimientos* que refleja la interacción entre los conceptos y relaciones del modelo de dominio, y los requerimientos

analizados. Los participantes de esta fase son los analistas del equipo de desarrollo, diseñadores que formen parte del equipo de desarrollo y expertos conocedores de la realidad para consultas puntuales. Como condiciones para la finalización de la fase es necesario considerar que todo concepto que forme parte de la resolución de un requerimiento esté definido en la ontología de dominio. En los casos que se realicen cambios en la realidad será necesario validar que estas modificaciones se encuentren reflejadas en el documento *Metadata de Conceptos* y el modelo de dominio.
Fase III – Construcción del Modelo Multidimensional. El objetivo de esta fase es construir el modelo multidimensional CMDM a partir de la ontología de dominio guiado por los requerimientos. Como entrada de la fase se requiere el documento *Metadata de Conceptos* resultante de la Fase I del proceso, la Ontología del Dominio y la Matriz de Requerimientos obtenidos en la Fase II y el conjunto de Requerimientos iniciales. Para realizar el proceso de transformación de los conceptos y relaciones definidos en la ontología del dominio al modelo conceptual multidimensional es necesario contar con reglas que dirijan dicha transformación (estas reglas se muestran en la siguiente sección). Como resultado de la fase se cuenta con el modelo conceptual multidimensional. Como condición para finalizar la fase es necesario considerar que todos los requerimientos estén resueltos mediante el modelo conceptual.

4 Propuesta de Derivación del Modelo Multidimensional

Para realizar la transformación del modelo de dominio, representado mediante una ontología, al modelo multidimensional CMDM, se propone un conjunto de once reglas, a partir de los cuales se podrán inducir pautas o condiciones que permitan tomar decisiones de diseño al momento de construir el modelo multidimensional CMDM.

Regla 1 – Definición de clases candidatas a niveles del modelo multidimensional. Para aplicar esta regla es necesario contar con la matriz de requerimientos y la Ontología de dominio. Para cada clase del conjunto *C* se identifican sus restricciones propias (no heredadas). Se agrega al conjunto *C* las clases correspondientes al rango de cada una de las propiedades participantes en las restricciones antes identificadas. Para cada una de las clases del conjunto *C* se identifica si la misma pertenece a una categorización en la ontología. En caso que se cumpla esta condición todas sus superclases se agregan al conjunto *C*. Las clases del conjunto *C* que en la ontología tengan al menos una propiedad que no sea heredada, son consideradas como correspondientes a niveles en CMDM.
Regla 2 – Definición de niveles del modelo multidimensional. Para aplicar esta regla es necesario contar con el conjunto de clases candidatas a niveles (Regla 1) y la ontología de dominio. Para cada una de las clases del conjunto de clases consideradas como correspondientes a niveles del modelo multidimensional, se identifica en la ontología su nombre y las propiedades definidas como datos simples (Data Properties). Cada uno de los niveles se nombrará según el nombre que la clase tenga

definido en la ontología. Los atributos de los niveles quedarán determinados por las propiedades definidas como propias, considerando solo los datos simples.

Regla 3 – Definición de Cardinalidades. Esta regla sirve para identificar las relaciones existentes entre las clases del conjunto de clases a mapearse como niveles. Para aplicar esta regla es necesario contar con el conjunto de clases a corresponderse como niveles y la Ontología de dominio. A continuación se detallan las consideraciones realizadas para obtener la cardinalidad.

1. En las relaciones para las cuales no se haya definido una restricción de cardinalidad se considera que la cardinalidad asociada desde la clase dominio a la clase rango es N. Esto se define así porque al no existir restricción de cardinalidad definida se establece que un individuo del dominio puede relacionarse con N entidades de la clase rango.
2. Si una relación tiene definida una relación inversa, la cardinalidad definida en la dirección rango-dominio está dada por las restricciones de cardinalidad para la relación inversa definida.
3. Si una relación no tiene definida una relación inversa, la cardinalidad definida para esta relación inversa se asume como cardinalidad N, en dirección rango-dominio. Con esto se denota que un individuo de la clase rango puede relacionarse con N individuos de la clase dominio.

En las relaciones para las cuales no se haya definido una restricción de cardinalidad se considera que la cardinalidad asociada desde la clase dominio a la clase rango es N. Si una relación no tiene definida una relación inversa, la cardinalidad definida para esta relación inversa se asume como cardinalidad N, en dirección rango-dominio. La cardinalidad entre dos clases queda definida por la cardinalidad de la relación entre estas dos clases y la cardinalidad de su relación inversa.

Regla 4 – Identificación de orden entre niveles a partir de cardinalidad N:1. Esta cardinalidad establece que las entidades pertenecientes a la clase dominio pueden relacionarse con una única entidad del rango y que a la vez una entidad del rango puede asociarse "a muchos" (denotando esto como N) individuos del dominio. Esto puede interpretarse como una posible relación de agrupación de datos desde la clase dominio hacia la clase rango. Para aplicar esta regla es necesario contar con la ontología de dominio, el conjunto de relaciones identificadas con cardinalidad N:1 y el conjunto de niveles. Para cada relación del conjunto de relaciones identificadas con cardinalidad N:1 se define un orden entre dos niveles donde la clase que participa con cardinalidad N se corresponde como nivel inferior y la clase que participa con cardinalidad 1 se corresponde como nivel superior. De esta manera se obtiene un orden entre los niveles en CMDM.

Regla 5 – Identificación de orden entre niveles a partir de cardinalidad 1:N. Para aplicar esta regla es necesario contar con la ontología de dominio, el conjunto de relaciones identificadas con cardinalidad 1:N y el conjunto de niveles. Para cada relación del conjunto de relaciones identificadas con cardinalidad 1:N, se define un orden entre dos niveles donde la clase con cardinalidad 1 se corresponde como nivel superior y la clase que participa con cardinalidad N se corresponde como nivel inferior. De esta manera se obtiene un orden entre los niveles en CMDM.

Regla 6 – Identificación de orden entre niveles a partir de cardinalidad N:N. Esta cardinalidad establece que cualquier elemento de una de las clases que interviene en la cardinalidad, puede asociarse con una cantidad no definida de elementos de la otra clase participante. Para aplicar esta regla es necesario contar con la ontología de dominio, el conjunto de relaciones identificadas con cardinalidad N:N, y el conjunto de niveles. Esta regla define cuando dos niveles no pueden ser parte de una misma jerarquía. Las clases que definen estas relaciones son independientes entre sí, no existiendo características por la cual sea posible agruparlas. Es posible considerar dos posibles casos.(Figura 2): (i) las clases se corresponden como niveles de jerarquías diferentes en una misma dimensión, y (ii) las clases se corresponden como niveles de diferentes dimensiones. La decisión entre (i) y (ii) depende del caso en particular que se esté resolviendo pero las clases nunca podrán corresponderse como niveles de una misma jerarquía.

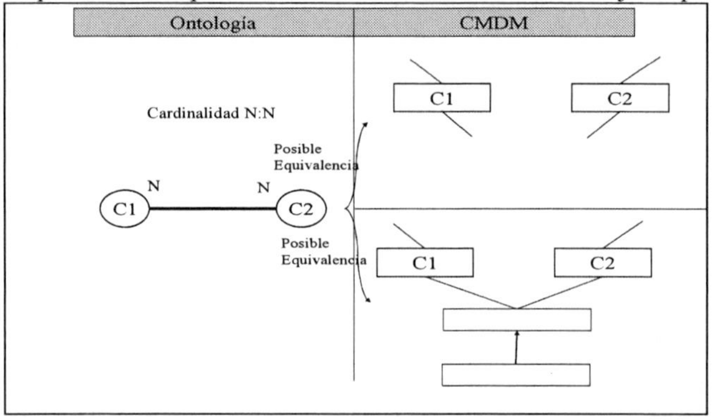

Fig. 2 : Correspondencias de cardinalidad N:N

Regla 7 – Identificación de orden entre niveles a partir de relaciones 1:1 con totalidad. Dada la relación que cumple con cardinalidad 1:1 y cuenta con la propiedad de totalidad, ya sea para la clase dominio o para la clase rango, se construye la jerarquía haciendo corresponder la clase para la cual se cumple la totalidad como nivel superior y la clase restante conforma el nivel inferior. De este modo, al realizar las operaciones entre niveles, es posible obtener elementos que cumplan las características dadas, descartando aquellos que no lo hagan. Para aplicar esta regla es necesario contar con la ontología de dominio, el conjunto de niveles identificados que participan en una relación con cardinalidad 1:1 con totalidad.

Regla 8 – Identificación de orden entre niveles a partir de cardinalidad 1:1. Cualquiera de las clases participantes en la cardinalidad puede ser considerada como nivel superior o inferior, quedando a criterio del diseñador definir el orden entre los niveles. Esta decisión depende del caso en particular que se esté resolviendo

Regla 9 – Categorización de las subclases. Cuando una clase tiene un conjunto de subclases y a su vez estas clases tienen la propiedad de ser disjuntas entre sí, se cumple que cada subclase es una categorización o clasificación de los elementos de la superclase, según alguna característica. (Por ejemplo las clases Auto, Camioneta y Camión son disjuntas entre sí y son subclases de la clase Vehículo). Dado que las subclases son una especialización de la superclase, es posible considerar un nuevo nivel que permita representar la característica común de las subclases (en el ejemplo todas son un tipo de vehículo). Según lo definido es posible conformar un nuevo orden entre niveles, donde la superclase sé corresponde como el nivel inferior y el nuevo nivel como superior. El nuevo nivel tiene miembros que representan las distintas categorizaciones, para esto se define un atributo que permite identificar cada uno de los elementos que conforman el nivel. Por lo tanto, en este regla, para cada clase del conjunto de clases a corresponderse como niveles, se debe identificar aquellas que son superclases y cuyas subclases sean disjuntas. Dada una superclase del conjunto, pueden obtenerse un nuevo orden entre niveles donde la superclase se corresponda como nivel inferior y como nivel superior se crea un nivel que agrupe todas las subclases. Al nivel superior se le asigna un nombre que identifique la agrupación, por ejemplo TipoCategoría. (Figura 3). Para este nivel se define un atributo que permita identificar cada uno de los elementos que lo conforman. Para aplicar esta regla es necesario contar con la ontología de dominio y el conjunto de clases a corresponderse como niveles.

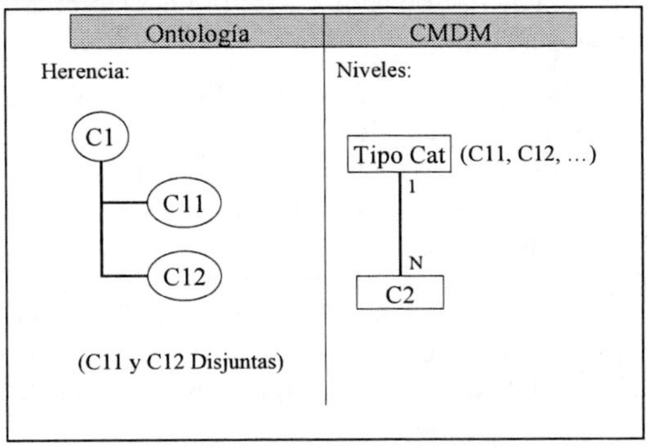

Fig. 3: Correspondencia de herencia

Regla 10 – Identificación de dimensiones en CMDM. En esta regla se busca identificar las tuplas de niveles ordenados las cuales tengan algún nivel en común. Una dimensión queda formada por el subconjunto de tuplas de niveles previamente ordenados que tengan algún nivel en común, manteniendo el orden parcial definido entre ellos. Las dimensiones deben tener un nivel mínimo donde exista un identificador para cada elemento de la misma. Gráficamente la dimensión se forma uniendo las tuplas ordenadas según el nivel en común, manteniendo el orden definido. Todos los niveles deben formar parte de alguna dimensión. Puede ocurrir que exista una dimensión con un único nivel. Para aplicar esta regla es necesario contar con el conjunto de niveles y el conjunto de niveles parcialmente ordenados.

Regla 11 – Identificación de relaciones dimensionales en CMDM. En el caso de contar con una dimensión donde a partir de su nivel inferior I se desprendan varias jerarquías, y a su vez la cardinalidad entre I con los niveles superiores sea N:1 en todos los casos, es posible definir una relación dimensional donde I sea el eje central de la relación. Las dimensiones que definen dicha relación dimensional quedan formadas por el conjunto de niveles superiores a partir del eje central. En el caso de contar con un conjunto de dimensiones donde su nivel inferior I es común a todas, y a su vez la cardinalidad entre I y los niveles superiores sea N:1 en todos los casos, es posible definir una relación dimensional donde I sea el eje central de la relación. Las dimensiones que definen dicha relación dimensional quedan formadas por el conjunto de niveles superiores a partir del eje central. Esta consideración queda en manos del diseñador, ya que debe ser él quien defina el eje central de la discusión.

5 Ejemplo Práctico

Como caso practico, para poder aplicar la metodología desarrollada en el proyecto y poder comparar los resultados, se realizó el re-diseño de un conjunto de indicadores existentes. El DW que alberga dichos indicadores se encuentra desarrollado sobre el sistema OPEN SIC (Sistema de Información Clínica) de la empresa Soluziona. OPENSIC es un Sistema de Información Clínico Integrado orientado a organizaciones prestadoras de servicios de salud.

Fase I. En primera instancia se presentaron los siguientes 4 requerimientos que forman el conjunto de requerimientos iniciales: *(R1)* Porcentaje de egresos quirúrgicos, *(R2)* Promedio de estancia, *(R3)* Tasa de mortalidad infantil y *(R4)* Tasa de mortalidad infantil post neo-natal. Lo primero es realizar un análisis conceptual de cada uno de los requerimientos. Para esto, en el caso presentado se desglosó cada uno en los conceptos que lo conforman, como por ejemplo egreso quirúrgico, estancia, mortalidad infantil y mortalidad infantil post neo-natal. Se define entonces, junto a personal de la empresa, una descripción para cada requerimiento de manera de dejar explícito el objetivo de cada uno. Las descripciones definidas para cada requerimiento son las siguientes:

1. Porcentaje de egresos quirúrgicos: porcentaje de egresos quirúrgicos sobre la cantidad de egresos totales en un período determinado
2. Promedio de estancia: promedio de tiempo de internación (días) de los pacientes en un período determinado
3. Tasa de mortalidad infantil: cantidad de defunciones de pacientes menores de 1 año en relación con el número de nacidos vivos durante el mismo período
4. Tasa de mortalidad infantil post neo-natal: cantidad de defunciones de pacientes entre 28 y 364 días de edad en relación con el número de nacidos vivos durante el mismo período.

Analizando el requerimiento 1.se deriva que para este requerimiento existen tres conceptos identificados *egreso quirúrgico, egreso hospitalario y tiempo*. Como resultado de esta fase se tiene el documento *Metadata de Conceptos* en el cual se establece el sentido y la semántica de cada uno de los conceptos identificados en la realidad guiada por los requerimientos. La propuesta que planteamos presenta una plantilla diseñada con el fin de brindar ayuda al momento de definir la información de contexto y datos importantes identificados para cada concepto, sin embargo, por motivos de espacio omitimos el desarrollo de esta fase pero la misma se puede encontrar en [9].

Fase II. En esta fase se trabaja sobre la Ontología del Dominio definiendo el conjunto de conceptos, las relaciones existentes entre estos y las restricciones de cada uno. Esta ontología permitió, mediante el uso del razonador Racer [10], realizar el chequeo de consistencia del modelo. Como observación particular del caso propuesto, ocurre que al momento de crear la ontología además de modelar las relaciones definidas en el documento *Metadata de Conceptos* surgieron nuevas relaciones, inferidas del modelo que no se habían identificado hasta el momento pero que efectivamente se cumplen entre los elementos del modelo. La Figura 4 ilustra gráficamente las relaciones encontradas para el requerimiento 1.

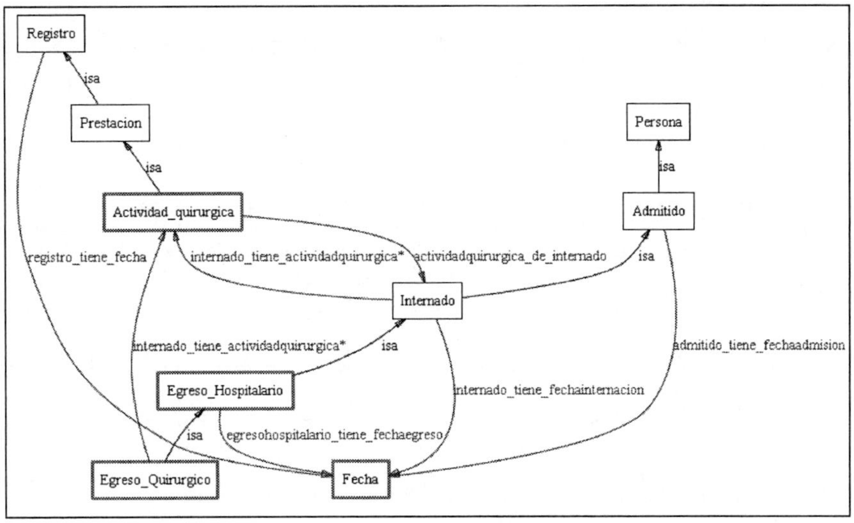

Fig. 4 : Gráfica de la ontología de dominio correspondiente al requerimiento 1.

Una vez identificados los conceptos y relaciones participantes en la resolución del requerimiento analizado, éstos se agregan a la *Matriz de Requerimientos*. De esta manera resulta sencillo verificar si un cambio afecta o no la resolución de un requerimiento simplemente identificando si el concepto o relación modificada participa o no en la resolución del requerimiento en cuestión. En [9] se utiliza una tabla que define, para cada requerimiento, el conjunto de dimensiones y medidas necesarias para su resolución. La matriz propuesta en esta etapa, a diferencia de la matriz utilizada en [9], vincula cada requerimiento con los conceptos y relaciones que participan en su resolución, es decir vincula cada requerimiento con un concepto semántico y no con una estructura del modelo conceptual.. En la Figura 5 se presenta la matriz de requerimientos con los conceptos identificados para el requerimiento R1.

Fase III. Aplicando la Regla 1 se obtiene que las clases candidatas a corresponderse como niveles en el modelo multidimensional son: Egreso_Hospitalario y Actividad_Quirurgica. Aplicando la Regla 2 de forma iterativa se identifican las clases Prestación, Internado, Admitido, Persona y Registro que son agregadas al conjunto de candidatas a niveles del modelo. La Regla 3, a partir de las nuevas clases participantes de la resolución del requerimiento, actualiza la matriz de requerimientos de manera de incluir las clases y las *is-a*. De esta manera, ante cambios en el requerimiento se puede seguir la traza de las clases y relaciones que se ven afectadas (Figura 6).

Concepto	R1	R2	R3	R4
Clases				
Egreso_Quirurgico	✓			
Egreso_Hospitalario	✓			
Actividad_Quirurgica	✓			
Fecha	✓			
Relaciones				
internado_tiene_actividadquirurgica	✓			
egresohospitalario_tiene_fechaegreso	✓			
Herencia				
Egreso_Quirurgico "is a" Egreso_Hospitalario	✓			

Fig. 5 - Matriz de Requerimientos luego de la Fase II.

Concepto	R1	R2	R3	R4
Clases				
Egreso_Quirurgico	✓			
Egreso_Hospitalario	✓			
Actividad_Quirurgica	✓			
Prestación	✓			
Internado	✓			
Admitido	✓			
Persona	✓			
Registro	✓			
Relaciones				
internado_tiene_actividadquirurgica	✓			
actividadquirurgica de_internado	✓			
Herencia				
Egreso_Quirurgico "is a" Egreso_Hospitalario	✓			
Egreso_Hospitalario "is a" Internado	✓			
Internado "is a" Admitido	✓			
Admitido "is a" Persona	✓			
ActividadQuirurgica "is a" Prestacion	✓			
Prestacion "is a" Registro	✓		1	

Fig. 6 - Matriz de Requerimientos Fase III, luego de la Regla 3.

Las jerarquías del modelo multidimensional se obtendrán mediante la ejecución de las Reglas 4 a la 9, donde las Reglas 4 a la 7 se basan totalmente en la cardinalidad de las relaciones identificadas. Las Reglas 8 y 9 consideran, además, la condición de totalidad de las relaciones. La cardinalidad definida para las relaciones de interés son lasque muestra la Figura 7. Es importante aclarar que la relación internado_tiene_actividadquirurgica no es de interés dado que depende de la clase Egreso_Quirurgico que no es candidata a nivel en el modelo CMDM. Aplicando la Regla 4 a la relación actividadquirurgica de_internado se obtiene Internado como nivel superior a Actividad_quirurgica, y aplicando la Regla 5 al resto de las relaciones se obtiene que Egreso_Hospitalario, Internado y Admitido corresponde a niveles superiores respectivamente de Internado, Admitido y Persona. Aplicando luego la Regla 10 se obtienen las dimensiones ilustradas en la Figura 8.

Relación	Clase Origen (Co)	Clase Destino (Cd)	Cardinalidad desde Co a Cd
actividadquirurgica de_internado	Actividad_quirurgica	Internado	N:1
Egreso_Quirurgico "is a" Egreso_Hospitalario	Egreso_Quirurgico	Egreso_Hospitalario	N:1
Egreso_Hospitalario "is a" Internado	Egreso_Hospitalario	Internado	1:N
Internado "is a" Admitido	Internado	Admitido	1:N
Admitido "is a" Persona	Admitido	Persona	1:N
ActividadQuirurgica "is a" Prestacion	Actividad_quirurgica	Prestacion	1:N
Prestacion "is a" Registro	Prestacion	Registro	1:N

Fig. 7: Cardinalidad de la Relaciones de interés.

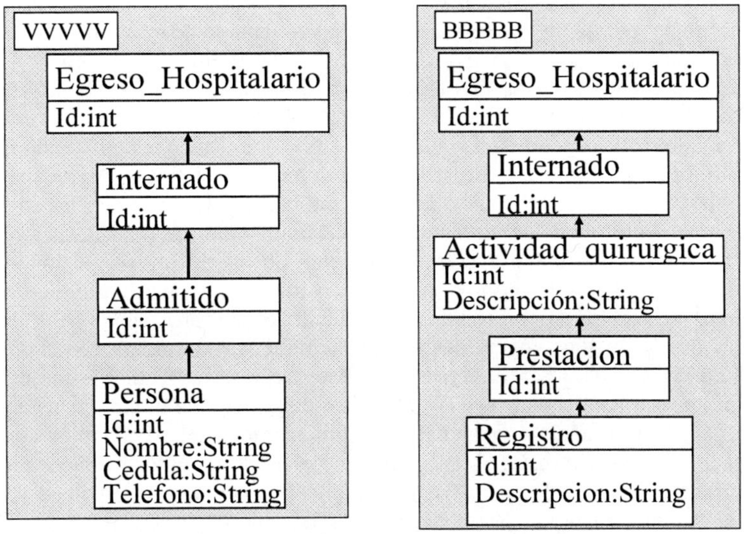

Fig. 8: Dimensiones resultado de la aplicación de la Regla 10.

Para la identificación de las relaciones dimensionales no se puede aplicar la Regla 11 ya que no se está en el caso de tener un conjunto de dimensiones donde su nivel mínimo forme parte de más de una dimensión o a partir de su nivel mínimo se desprendan varias jerarquías, resultando entonces las relaciones dimensionales de la Figura 9.

Fig. 9: Relaciones Dimensionales.

6 Conclusiones y Trabajos Futuros

En este trabajo presentamos una propuesta metodológica para el diseño conceptual multidimensional guiado por ontología del dominio. Existen diversos trabajos sobre como realizar el diseño multidimensional. En [11] se presenta una metodología guiada por los requerimientos para el diseño conceptual, sin embargo no cuenta con un relevamiento del significado de los conceptos del dominio como lo proponemos a través de la ontología, ni prevé mecanismos para ayudar a la evolución de los requerimientos como la Matriz de Requerimientos que presentamos. En [12] se propone una adaptación de una arquitectura estándar para el desarrollo de software, llamada MDA (Model Driven Architecture) que guía el ciclo de vida completo del diseño, desarrollo, integración y administración de aplicaciones utilizando modelos en desarrollo de software. Se describe como crear los distintos artefactos (modelos) MDA por medio de extensiones de UML, también se describen las transformaciones necesarias entre modelos utilizando la aproximación Query/View/Transformatcin (QVT). Aunque se explicita la transformación de los distintos modelos, no es claro como se construye el modelo multidimensional, del cual parte la arquitectura. Creemos que las pautas presentadas para las tres Fases del diseño Multidimensional acompañadas con las Reglas de derivación desde la Ontología son un mecanismo práctico, viable para ser ensayado en casos reales. La Tabla 1 compara nuestra propuesta, que llamamos MD4DW [13], con otras. Los parámetros considerados son: si se genera un modelo conceptual multidimensional, si hay ejemplos complejos de aplicación de la propuesta, si se justifican los pasos seguidos en la obtención de la propuesta, si se consideran los requerimientos en la etapa de Análisis y Diseño, si existe trazabilidad desde los conceptos de la realidad hasta el modelo conceptual multidimensional, si la propuesta brinda soporte para la realización del análisis de impacto frente a cambios en los requerimientos, la última columna indica si la propuesta propone la elaboración de un modelo semántico que contenga el significado de los conceptos del dominio.

En estos momentos estamos a la búsqueda de diseñadores de DW que quieran experimentar nuestra propuesta, creemos que es necesario que sea aplicada por terceras partes externas al proyecto para poder evaluar objetivamente sus impactos.

Como trabajo futuro es importante estudiar la viabilidad de automatizar el proceso generando un software integral que permita asistir la construcción de un DW, basándose en MD4DW, desde el análisis de la realidad hasta el diseño físico.

Tabla 1. Comparación de Metodologías para diseño de DW.

PROPUESTA	**M.Concep.**	**Ej**	**Justif.**	**Req.**	**Traza**	**Imp.**	**M. Semántico**
Golf98 [1]	X	X	--	--	--	--	--
Gio05 [11]	X	X	--	X	--	--	--
Maz05 [12]	X	--	--	X	X	--	--
Kim98 [14]	--	X	--	--	--	--	--
MD4DW [13]	X	X	X	X	X	X	X

Referencias

[1] Golfarelli, M.; Rizzi S.: A methodological framework for data warehouse design. In Proc. DOLAP, pages 3-9 (1998).

[2] Huesemann B., Lechtenboerger J., Vossen G.: Conceptual data warehouse design. In Proc. DMDW, pages 3-9 (2000).

[3] Luján-Mora S., Trujillo J.: A comprehensive method for data warehouse design. In Proc. DMDW (2003).

[4] Rizzi, S., Abelló A., Lechtenboerger J., Trujillo J.: Research in DataWarehouse Modeling and Design: Dead or Alive? DOLAP, USA (2006).

[5] Gruber T. R: A Translation Approach to Portable Ontology Specifications. Knowledge Acquisition, **5**(2), 1993, pp. 199-220 (1993).

[6] Carpani .F.: CMDM: Un Modelo Conceptual para la Especificación de Bases Multidimensionales,Tesis de Maestría, Facultad de Ingeniería, UdelaR, (2000).

[7] Carpani, F. , Ruggia R.: An Integrity Constraints Language for a Conceptual Multidimensional Data Model XIII International Conference on Software Engineering & Knowledge Engineering (SEKE'01), Buenos Aires, Argentina, (2001).

[8] IBM Rup: Rational Unified Process, 2001.

[9] Ballard, C. , Herreman D., Schau D. Bell D. Kim R., Valncic E.: Data Modeling Techniques for Data Warehousing SG24-2238-00. IBM Red Book.ISBN 0738402452 (1998).

[10] Racer - http://www.racer-systems.com/products/racerpro/

[11] Giorgini P., Rizzi S., Garzetti M.: Goal-Orientes Requierement Analysis for Data Warehouse Design. Engineering Applications of Artificial Intelligence, Elsvier (2005).

[12] Mazon J., Trujillo J.,.Serrano M., Piattini M., Applying MDA to the Development of Data Warehouse, DOLAP´05 (2005).

[13] Gimenez S. , Godoy D. Colombatto C. Carpani F, Motz R.: Proyecto MD4DW: Metadata for Data Warehouse. Universidad de la República (Uruguay) http://www.fing.edu.uy/~pgmetadw/Website/website.html

[14] Kimball, R. Reeves, L. Ross, M. Thornthwaite, W.: The Datawarehouse Lifecycle Toolkit. John Wiley & Son, Inc.(1998).

Requisitos Arquiteturais como Base para a Qualidade de Ambientes de Engenharia de Software

Elisa Yumi Nakagawa and José Carlos Maldonado

Instituto de Ciências Matemáticas e de Computação
Universidade de São Paulo – Campus de São Carlos
Av. Trabalhador São Carlense, 400,
Cx. Postal 668, 13560-970, São Carlos, SP
{elisa,jcmaldon}@icmc.usp.br

Resumo. Nos últimos anos, uma proliferação de ferramentas e Ambientes de Engenharia de Software (AESs) tem sido observada, com impactos positivos na produção de software. Apesar do reúso ser foco de muitas pesquisas em desenvolvimento de software, ferramentas e ambientes têm sido, muitas vezes, construídos individualmente, sem atenção ao reúso dos esforços de desenvolvimento desses sistemas. Além disso, as arquiteturas desses sistemas, bem como as arquiteturas de referência, não têm sido largamente investigadas, o que pode estar influenciando nas dificuldades de evolução e integração que esses sistemas têm sofrido. Dessa forma, este trabalho tem o objetivo de apresentar uma investigação que resultou em um conjunto de requisitos arquiteturais de AESs e que deu origem ao estabelecimento de uma arquitetura de referência para esses ambientes. Resultados parciais têm mostrado a viabilidade dessa arquitetura como base para o desenvolvimento incremental e evolutivo de AESs, evidenciando que os requisitos estabelecidos têm sido atendidos.

Palavras-chave: requisito arquitetural, arquitetura de referência, ambiente de engenharia de software

1 Introdução

Nas últimas décadas, sistemas de software têm conquistado papel essencial e crítico na sociedade. Esses sistemas passaram a ser produtos grandes e complexos e, conseqüentemente, difíceis de desenvolver e testar. Aliado a isso, a satisfação do cliente tem sido a atual preocupação de muitas organizações que desenvolvem software. Diante desse quadro, pesquisadores têm focado as atenções no entendimento e na melhoria da qualidade dos softwares desenvolvidos. Nesse contexto, atividades de Engenharia de Software têm-se tornado essenciais para o desenvolvimento de sistemas de software, o que tem resultado em um forte investimento e conseqüente proliferação de ferramentas de apoio a essas atividades. Essas ferramentas, bem como os AESs (Ambientes de Engenharia de Software) — coleção integrada de ferramentas de Engenharia de Software — têm contribuído para melhorar a qualidade do processo de desenvolvimento de software, e conseqüentemente, a qualidade dos produtos resultantes desse processo, impactando positivamente na produção de software.

Apesar da proliferação de ferramentas e AESs, bem como o reúso ser foco atual de muitas das pesquisas em Engenharia de Software, a grande maioria dessas ferramentas e ambientes é construída de forma individual, sem a preocupação com o reúso dos esforços de desenvolvimento. Quando à disponibilização de ferramentas e AESs, apesar da Web estar sendo adotada como plataforma de sistemas de software dos mais diversos domínios de aplicação, são poucas ainda as ferramentas e ambientes disponibilizados sobre essa plataforma, havendo também a necessidade de mais pesquisas nessa área. Há também uma carência de trabalhos atuais que abordam o estabelecimento de arquiteturas de software calcadas em novas tecnologias e que sejam adequadas a essas ferramentas e ambientes, dando continuidade aos trabalhos que se iniciaram nos anos 80 e início de 90, tais como o apresentado em [1]. É de conhecimento que a utilização de arquiteturas de software adequadas pode ter um impacto positivo em diversos aspectos do desenvolvimento de software, tais como no entendimento, na reutilização, na evolução, na análise e no gerenciamento do sistema [2], constituindo-se um fator de suma importância na qualidade dos sistemas de software.

Além disso, um tema bastante evidente nas pesquisas envolvendo AESs é a evolução e a integração desses ambientes [3]. A capacidade de evolução desses ambientes é crucial, uma vez que eles precisam dar apoio à própria evolução que a área de Engenharia de Software sofre com o advento de novos métodos, técnicas, processos, entre outros. Quanto à integração em AESs, diversos mecanismos têm sido investigados e propostos, a exemplo dos apresentados em [4,3,5,6]. Contudo, não existe ainda um consenso sobre qual o melhor mecanismo de integração, bem como a melhor estrutura arquitetural que promova a evolução contínua desses ambientes.

Observa-se que, comumente, as pesquisas na área de Engenharia de Requisitos têm focado atenção nos processos, métodos, técnicas e ferramentas para o levantamento e gerenciamento de requisitos de software. Contudo, considerando-se arquiteturas de software como parte essencial dos sistemas de software, o estabelecimento de requisitos arquiteturais é certamente indispensável para a qualidade dos sistemas de softwares resultantes dessas arquiteturas. Nesse contexto, o objetivo deste trabalho é apresentar o resultado de uma investigação por requisitos arquiteturais de AESs, bem como apresentar uma arquitetura de referência, chamada RefASSET (*Reference Architecture for Software Engineering Tools*), construída com base nesses requisitos. Vale salientar que este trabalho faz parte de um trabalho maior que envolve o estabelecimento de um mecanismo de apoio ao desenvolvimento incremental e evolutivo de ferramentas e AESs.

Este artigo está organizado da seguinte forma. Na Seção 2 é discutida brevemente arquiteturas de software, arquiteturas de referência e sua relevância como mecanismo de apoio ao desenvolvimento de software. Na Seção 3 é apresentada uma visão geral sobre os AESs e discutidas suas limitações e desafios com relação ao desenvolvimento desses ambientes. Na Seção 4 são apresentados os requisitos arquiteturais de arquitetura de AESs. Na Seção 5 é mostrada a arquitetura proposta com base nos requisitos arquiteturais estabelecidos. Por fim, na Seção 6, encontram-se as conclusões.

2 Arquitetura de Software: Visão Geral

À medida que a complexidade e o tamanho dos sistemas de software têm aumentado, engenheiros de software têm lançado mão de princípios de projeto, tais como a modularização e o ocultamento da informação, de modo a obter sistemas com maior qualidade e a um baixo custo. Para isso, o projeto da estrutura global do software, ou seja, a arquitetura do software, é uma questão que vem sendo largamente considerada.

A arquitetura de software é dita como tendo principal papel na determinação da qualidade e da manutenibilidade do software [7], na mesma linha da SEI[1] que afirma que os atributos de qualidade dos sistemas de software são estreitamente relacionados às suas arquiteturas. De acordo com Garlan [8] e a SEI[2], a arquitetura de software é uma estrutura de componentes de um programa/sistema, os relacionamentos entre esses componentes, os princípios e diretrizes que governam os projetos e a evolução dos softwares. Para um determinado sistema de software, pode-se descrever sua arquitetura; essa arquitetura é referenciada como instância arquitetural. Mais abrangentes são os estilos arquiteturais que definem as restrições sobre a forma e a estrutura de uma família de instâncias arquiteturais [2]. Como exemplos de estilos arquiteturais mais conhecidos, pode-se citar o Pipes e Filtros, Camadas, Cliente-Servidor, entre outros, bem como estilos resultantes da combinação desses e outros estilos. Já uma arquitetura de referência, na mesma linha do adotado por Metalla [9], pode ser vista como uma estrutura que provê uma caracterização das funcionalidades dos sistemas de software de um dado domínio de aplicação, promovendo assim o reúso do projeto arquitetural e o entendimento de uma área específica. Nesse contexto, arquiteturas de referência para os mais diversos domínios têm sido propostos, inclusive para o domínio de Engenharia de Software, por exemplo, para ferramentas de teste de software [10], para o desenvolvimento baseado em componentes [11], entre outros. A proposição de arquiteturas de referência não é uma tarefa trivial, envolvendo profundo conhecimento sobre o domínio para o qual a arquitetura está sendo criada [10].

Vale ressaltar que a investigação de arquiteturas de sistemas interativos, em especial, de sistemas Web, é bastante relevante, visto que essa classe de sistemas tem-se despontado recentemente para os mais diversos domínios de aplicação. Além disso, frente às características de sistemas Web, em especial a evolução contínua e a necessidade de disponibilização rápida, arquiteturas desses sistemas devem ser flexíveis facilitando a evolução. Dentre as arquiteturas de sistemas interativos, um dos mais conhecidos é o padrão arquitetural MVC (*Model-View-Controller*) [12]. O MVC divide a aplicação em três componentes: o Modelo

[1] http://www.sei.cmu.edu/architecture/definitions.html
[2] http://www.sei.cmu.edu

(*Model*) que contém as funcionalidades básicas e principais e gerencia os dados; a Visão (*View*) que gerencia informações a serem mostradas para o usuário; e o Controlador (*Controller*) que processa as entradas (eventos) do usuário. Uma outra arquitetura sendo experimentada é a arquitetura 3-camadas (do inglês, *3-tiers architecture*)[3]. Basicamente, essa arquitetura é composta da camada do cliente que contém a interface do usuário no qual residem os serviços do usuário, da camada de aplicação que contém a lógica de negócio e da camada de persistência cujo papel é gerenciar os objetos/elementos persistentes da aplicação. Observa-se que aplicações baseadas nessa arquitetura são mais flexíveis, além de poderem ser fisicamente implantadas em diferentes servidores, p. ex., a camada de negócios e a de persistência em dois servidores distintos. Dessa forma, a escalabilidade do sistema e a capacidade de processar requisições de diversos clientes podem ser promovidas [13].

Segundo Zhao [14], a arquitetura 3-camadas não se adequava bem a aplicações Web. Dessa forma, com base nessa arquitetura, Zhao propõe uma arquitetura cuja camada do cliente é dividida em [14]: camada do cliente propriamente dita (no qual se encontra o navegador Web no lado do cliente) e a camada de interação com o usuário e de controle da aplicação (camada de apresentação que reside no lado do servidor). Na mesma linha, mais recentemente, o trabalho de Anderson [13] propõe a junção do padrão arquitetural MVC e a arquitetura 3-camadas, na qual a camada de apresentação contém o Controlador e a Visão, e a camada de aplicação contém o Modelo. Particularmente, essa arquitetura tem sido utilizada tanto em projetos acadêmicos quanto na indústria com resultados bastante positivos no desenvolvimento de sistemas Web. Além dessas arquiteturas, outras vêm sendo investigadas, propostas e experimentadas para sistemas Web, buscando adequar a facilidade de desenvolvimento e manutenção com o desempenho que esses sistemas devem apresentar.

3 Ambientes de Engenharia de Software: Visão Geral

Ferramentas e AESs têm-se tornado cada vez mais cruciais para o desenvolvimento de software, dado que a demanda, a diversidade e a complexidade de sistemas de software têm aumentado, enquanto que o tempo necessário para o software estar no mercado tem diminuído [3]. Além disso, tem também aumentado a diversidade de processos, métodos e técnicas que esses ambientes e ferramentas precisam dar apoio. Dessa forma, observa-se, atualmente, que uma vasta coleção de ferramentas (protótipos ou comerciais) têm sido propostas e/ou construídas, a exemplo têm-se [15,16,17,18,19,20,5,21], automatizando diversas atividades de Engenharia de Software, desde atividades fundamentais (p. ex., análise, projeto e teste) a atividades de apoio (p. ex., gerência de configuração e documentação) e organizacionais (p. ex., gerência e planejamento). Algumas dessas ferramentas têm sido desenvolvidas no contexto de ambientes integrados, outras possibilitam alguma integração, no entanto, muitas delas são autônomas.

[3] http://www.sei.cmu.edu/str/descriptions/threetier.html

Buscando explorar as vantagens que sistemas Web têm apresentado, tais como o acesso remoto e a capacidade de "servir" simultaneamente diversos usuários, na literatura disponível sobre AESs, pode-se identificar iniciativas de ferramentas e ambientes sendo disponibilizados sobre a Web; a exemplo, pode-se citar a MILOS [20], HyperDev [19] e Proteum/CPN [22]. Um trabalho recente que discute desafios para a construção de ferramentas dessa categoria para a Web é o apresentado em [16] que mostra uma ferramenta de diagramação para ambiente Web. Outras iniciativas, tais como a Merlin [17] e a Orion [18], apresentam mecanismos que possibilitam serem utilizados remotamente, contudo sem ser por meio da Web. É importante ressaltar que existe a preocupação da comunidade científica em investigar e propor ferramentas que possibilitem uso remoto, inclusive por meio da Web, contudo, há a carência de AESs completos e integrados disponibilizados sobre essa plataforma.

Além disso, a evolução, a adaptação e a integração dos AESs atuais são custosos e difíceis se forem necessários serem realizados [3]. O maior desafio para a comunidade que investiga ferramentas e AESs é então encontrar meios para construir e integrar ferramentas de forma que eles possam ser facilmente adaptadas para serem usadas em novos contextos, p. ex., para outras linguagens de programação ou outras plataformas de software e hardware. Além disso, novos domínios, tais como computação pervasiva e comércio eletrônico, irão requerer métodos, ferramentas e AESs diferentes dos tradicionais. Observa-se que há uma diversidade de trabalhos que focam no problema da integração, evidenciando a relevância dada pela comunidade científica ao tema, o que motiva para que se investiguem mecanismos de integração mais novos, eficazes e eficientes. Recentemente, as pesquisas envolvendo integração têm explorado o uso do XML como base para a integração de dados [3,4,6].

Apesar da diversidade de ferramentas e AESs, não existem ainda um consenso sobre qual seria a melhor maneira de estruturar, organizar e disponibilizar essas ferramentas e ambientes. Muitos dos trabalhos dessa área não dão atenção à arquitetura de software, o que poderia estar impactando nas dificuldades e desafios que essa área vem enfrentando, principalmente no que tange à integração e à evolução das ferramentas e ambientes existentes.

4 Requisitos Arquiteturais de Ambientes de Engenharia de Software

Frente a relevância do estabelecimento de uma arquitetura de referência de AESs, nesta seção são apresentadas uma experiência de identificação de requisitos arquiteturais e a construção de uma arquitetura de referência de AESs. Essa experiência é descrita em um processo ilustrado na Fig. 1. Apesar de ser um processo preliminar e diferente de outros trabalhos que abordam o estabelecimento de requisitos arquiteturais e arquiteturas de referência, tais como [23] ou aqueles relacionados à linhas de produto e engenharia de domínio, vale ressaltar que os resultados alcançados têm sido positivos. De modo geral, esse processo é composto dos seguintes passos: identificação das fontes de informação (Passo 1), estabelecimento dos requisitos arquiteturais (Passo 2) e projeto da arquitetura de referência (Passo 3), descritos em mais detalhes a seguir.

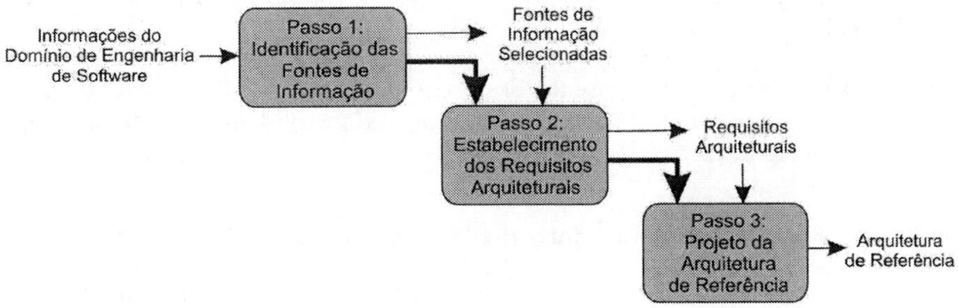

Fig. 1. Processo de Estabelecimento de Arquiteturas de Referência com Base em Requisitos Arquiteturais

4.1 Passo 1: Identificação das Fontes de Informação

Diferentemente do desenvolvimento de um determinado sistema de software, no qual se pode contar com elementos típicos do domínio, tais como clientes, documentos, entre outros, para a atividade de extração dos requisitos, quando se trata da extração dos requisitos para o desenvolvimento de arquiteturas de referência, outras fontes de informação são requeridas, inclusive fontes mais abrangentes, uma vez que a arquitetura de referência é base para o desenvolvimento de um conjunto de sistemas de software de um determinado domínio. Para a elaboração dos requisitos arquiteturais, foram investigadas diversas fontes de informação e selecionadas as mais relevantes e que contribuíssem de fato para a atividade de identificação dos requisitos arquiteturais, sendo elas:

- pesquisadores e desenvolvedores de ferramentas e AES: foram levantadas informações por meio da investigação junto aos pesquisadores envolvidos no projeto e desenvolvimento de ferramentas e de AESs. Embora considerando-se uma parcela pequena de pesquisadores e desenvolvedores se comparado com a comunidade existente, foi relevante no sentido de identificar a problemática da área, as limitações e necessidades;
- ferramentas e AESs: foi investigada uma diversidade de ferramentas e AESs, muitas delas, por meio da literatura disponível, dentre eles, pode-se citar ferramentas e ambientes bastante distintos, tais como o Field [5], o HyperDev [19], o Orion [18] e o Odyssey [15]. Foram também investigadas as instâncias arquiteturais dessas ferramentas e ambientes, quando disponíveis, procurando observar a capacidade de evolução e adaptação que essas arquiteturas possibilitam; e

– publicações da área: além das publicações relacionadas às ferramentas e AESs, foram consideradas outras publicações da área [3,24], bem como aquelas disponíveis sobre arquitetura de software, dentre elas [2,8], e que devem ser consideradas em se tratando do estabelecimento de arquiteturas de referência.

Vale salientar que, no contexto deste trabalho, as fontes de informação descritas acima foram suficientes para a condução da atividade de extração de requisitos arquiteturais.

4.2 Passo 2: Estabelecimento dos Requisitos Arquiteturais

Com base na investigação das fontes de informação, norteado principalmente pelos desafios e limitações das ferramentas e AES atuais, foi consolidado um conjunto de requisitos arquiteturais de AESs, listados resumidamente a seguir:

Requisito 1 : A arquitetura deve possibilitar o desenvolvimento de AESs que devem dar apoio a qualquer atividade de Engenharia de Software, sejam elas, fundamentais, de apoio ou organizacionais;

Requisito 2 : A arquitetura deve possibilitar o desenvolvimento de AESs que possam ser utilizados em modelos distintos de processos de desenvolvimento de software, tais como nos processos de desenvolvimento clássico e nos processos ágeis;

Requisito 3 : A arquitetura deve possibilitar o desenvolvimento de AESs que devem ser capazes de evoluir de maneira incremental por meio da integração de novas ferramentas ou módulos que automatizam atividades — tanto fundamentais quanto de apoio e organizacionais — de Engenharia de Software;

Requisito 4 : A arquitetura deve possibilitar o desenvolvimento de AESs *standalone* ou disponibilizados por meio da plataforma Web;

Requisito 5 : A arquitetura deve possibilitar o desenvolvimento de AESs que permitam que ferramentas de Engenharia de Software desenvolvidas independentemente dessa arquitetura possam ser integradas a esse ambiente; e

Requisito 6 : A arquitetura deve possibilitar o desenvolvimento de AESs que devem apresentar facilidade de integração. Cinco tipos de integração, conforme estabelecidos por [24], devem ser satisfeitos:
(i) Integração de plataforma: As ferramentas do AES deve contar com uma mesma plataforma de software e de hardware que fornece serviços e dão apoio a sua execução;
(ii) Integração de apresentação: As ferramentas que compõem o AES devem apresentar uma mesma interface, ou seja, um "*look and feel*" comum do ponto de vista do usuário; (iii) Integração de dados: O AES deve possibilitar o compartilhamento de dados entre as ferramentas que o compõem;
(iv) Integração de processo: O AES deve possibilitar o gerenciamento de processos de software; e (v) Integração de controle: O AES deve dar apoio à notificação de eventos entre ferramentas que o compõem e deve também ter a capacidade de ativar outras ferramentas.

Um ponto relevante deste trabalho é a comprovação de que os requisitos arquiteturais possuem características distintas dos requisitos funcionais de um determinado sistema de software, sendo inclusive mais abrangentes e relacionados com requisitos de qualidade ou requisitos não funcionais, como o já abordado pela comunidade de arquitetura de software [7].

4.3 Passo 3: Projeto da Arquitetura de Referência

Para o projeto da arquitetura de referência, foi realizada a análise dos requisitos estabelecidos visando à identificação de estilos arquiteturais adequados, conceitos, normas, padrões arquiteturais, tecnologias e abordagens de desenvolvimento de software que atendessem a esses requisitos. Isso dá evidências de que o estabelecimento de arquiteturas de referência é uma atividade complexa que requer conhecimento sobre diversos temas no que tange o desenvolvimento de software. A arquitetura proposta é apresentada a seguir.

5 Arquitetura de Referência Proposta

Como resultado do passo de projeto da arquitetura de referência, foi estabelecida a RefASSET[4] [25], mostrada na Fig. 2, sendo essa a primeira iniciativa recente de estabelecimento de uma arquitetura de referência de AESs. A apresentação em detalhes da RefASSET não é foco deste trabalho, contudo, uma descrição sucinta é dada, de modo a facilitar o entendimento do restante do artigo.

De modo geral, a RefASSET agrega diversos princípios, conceitos, padrões e tecnologias para atender aos requisitos estabelecidos, a saber a separação de interesses (do inglês, *separation of concerns*), a ISO/IEC 12207 [26], os aspectos (da Programação Orientada a Aspectos (POA) [27]) e os *frameworks*, em especial, os *frameworks* transversais. Entende-se por *framework* uma aplicação semi-completa contendo componentes estáticos e dinâmicos (classes abstratas e concretas) que podem ser adaptados para produzir aplicações específicas [28]. Já um *framework* transversal é uma aplicação composta de classes e aspectos concretos e abstratos e que implementa um determinado interesse transversal [29]. Um interesse transversal (do inglês, *crosscutting concerns*) refere-se a um interesse/funcionalidade que está entrelaçado com outros interesses dentro do sistema, como por exemplo a persistência [30]. Além disso, a RefASSET tem como base arquitetura de sistemas interativos, no caso o MVC e a arquitetura em 3-camadas, como pode ser observado na Fig. 2.

Assim, a adequada separação de interesses é um elemento chave da RefASSET e que foi realizada com base na ISO/IEC 12207 [31]. Além disso, buscando explorar a característica de *obliviousness* da POA na qual módulos que implementam interesses/funcionalidades distintas são desenvolvidos de forma independente, cada atividade de apoio ou organizacional estabelecida pela ISO/IEC

[4] Por questões de espaço, é apresentada somente a estrutura geral da RefASSET. A descrição arquitetural completa pode ser encontrada em [25].

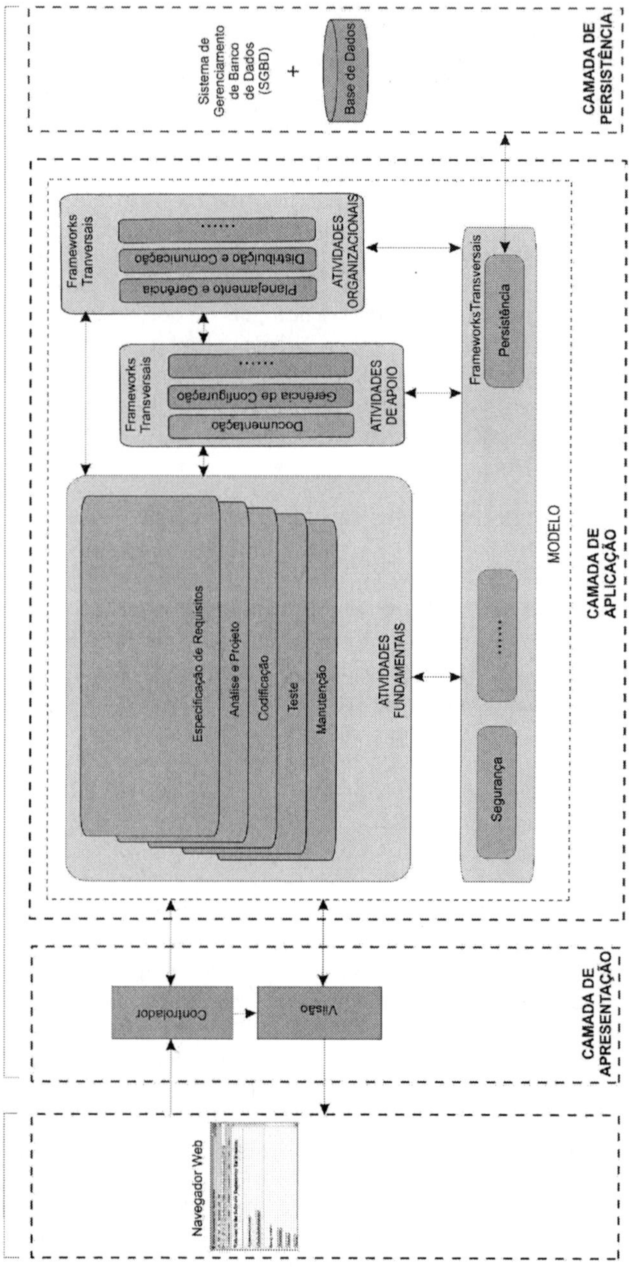

Fig. 2. Visão Geral da Arquitetura de Referência de Ambientes de Engenharia de Software

12207 foi considerada como um interesse transversal, sendo que cada um desses interesses é implementado por meio de um *framework* transversal. Vale ressaltar que estudos preliminares conduzidos em [25] mostram a viabilidade da separação de interesses conduzida dessa maneira e implementada por meio de *frameworks* transversais. Além disso, um outro elemento chave da RefASSET é o uso de aspectos como mecanismo para integração e evolução do AES. Apesar do uso de aspectos para esse fim ser inovador no contexto das pesquisas em AESs, em [25,32] foram conduzidos estudos que mostram a viabilidade e as vantagens do uso de aspectos nesse contexto.

Na Tabela 1 são listadas de maneira resumida as características da RefASSET considerando-se cada requisito arquitetural estabelecido. Como mecanismo de validação da RefASSET e, conseqüentemente, dos requisitos estabelecidos, a RefASSET foi especializada para o domínio de teste de software [32] e tem sido utilizada para migrar a JaBUTi [33], uma ferramenta de teste implementada inicialmente para ser *stand-alone*, para a plataforma Web. Além disso, para investigar a viabilidade de utilização de *frameworks* transversais na implementação de módulos que automatizam atividades de apoio e organizacionais, um *framework* transversal de documentação tem sido projetado e instanciado para o domínio de teste de software, dando origem a um módulo de documentação de teste que está sendo acoplado à ferramenta de teste por meio do uso de aspectos. Observa-se que a RefASSET tem sido utilizada primeiramente no domínio de teste, entretanto, outros domínios, tais como a gerenciamento de requisitos, estão em fase de investigação. Além disso, nossa experiência tem mostrado também a viabilidade de ferramentas de Engenharia de Software disponibilizados na plataforma Web. Quanto às ferramentas que necessitam de funcionalidades de diagramação, tais como as ferramentas de análise e projeto, pretende-se utilizar novas tecnologias, tais como o AJAX (*Asynchronous Javascript And XML*)[5] que possibilita o desenvolvimento de sistemas mais interativos. Resultados parciais já alcançados têm mostrado a viabilidade da arquitetura de referência proposta como base para o desenvolvimento incremental e evolutivo de AESs para a Web, ou seja, há evidências de que os requisitos estabelecidos são atendidos.

6 Conclusão

Uma das principais contribuições deste trabalho está no fato de ser um dos primeiros trabalhos que focam especificamente requisitos de arquiteturas de referência de AESs. Vale ressaltar que a atividade de extração de requisitos arquiteturais tem impactado positivamente na elaboração da arquitetura de referência proposta, sendo, portanto, um mecanismo essencial de apoio à elaboração de arquiteturas de software. De modo geral, a constatação sobre os desafios e limitações das ferramentas e AESs atuais nortearam o estabelecimento dos requisitos arquiteturais. Observa-se que requisitos arquiteturais são mais abrangentes e relacionam-se a requisitos não funcionais ou de qualidade dos sistemas de

[5] http://www.adaptivepath.com/ideas/essays/archives/000385.php

Tabela 1. Requisitos Arquiteturais x Características da Arquitetura de Referência de Ambientes de Engenharia de Software

Requisito	**Característica**
1	A RefASSET é construída com base na ISO/IEC 12207 que prevê atividades fundamentais, de apoio e organizacionais para o desenvolvimento de software.
2	A RefASSET prevê um módulo de gerência e planejamento resultante de um *framework* transversal de gerência e planejamento, cuja principal função é o gerenciamento de *workflows* que possibilitam que diferentes processos de desenvolvimento de software sejam modelados e informados ao ambiente.
3	A RefASSET é baseada na separação de interesses segundo a ISO/IEC 12207 e também faz uso de *frameworks* transversais para a implementação de módulos que implementam interesses transversais (no caso, aqueles relacionados às atividades de apoio e organizacionais). Assim, esses módulos são acrescentados incrementalmente ao AES por meio do uso de aspectos.
4	A RefASSET é baseada nas arquiteturas de sistemas interativos e sistemas Web bastante consolidadas, no caso, o MVC e a arquitetura 3-camadas. A modularização resultante dessas arquiteturas possibilita o desenvolvimento tanto de sistemas *stand-alone* quanto de sistemas Web.
5	Em virtude da modularização da RefASSET, há evidências de que a integração de ferramentas legadas é facilitada. Há a necessidade de se desenvolver *wrappers* que viabilizem a integração. Contudo, mais estudos devem ser conduzidos nessa linha.
6	Integração de plataforma: Buscando investigar a plataforma Web para a disponibilização de AESs, a exemplo do que vem ocorrendo com diversos outros sistemas de diferentes domínios, a RefASSET foi proposta de maneira a produzir AESs para essa plataforma. Integração de apresentação: Interfaces Web podem ser consideradas como uma das mais novas classes de interfaces para sistemas de software e, buscando disponibilizar AESs com essa classe de interface, a concepção da RefASSET dá respaldo para a construção de ambientes com essa interface. Integração de dados: A RefASSET prevê então o armazenamento de dados por meio do emprego de SGBDs (Sistemas de Gerenciamento de Banco de Dados), o que pode colaborar na integração de dados, uma vez que ter-se-á um repositório por meio do qual todas as ferramentas poderão acessar os dados. Integração de processo: Para apoiar a integração de processo, pode-se utilizar *workflows* para representar e gerenciar os processos de software. Um módulo responsável por gerenciar *workflows* – resultante de um *framework* transversal de gerência e planejamento — é prevista na RefASSET. Integração de controle: Entre os módulos base (que implementam atividades fundamentais) e os módulos resultantes dos *frameworks* transversais, a integração de controle ocorre por meio da utilização de aspectos. Aspectos são capazes de "acompanhar" o funcionamento do módulo base e atuar conforme sua necessidade, ou seja, o módulo base não requer mais o envio de eventos para os módulos que implementam atividade de apoio e organizacionais. Já a ativação dos módulos base ocorre por meio do *workflows*.

software. Portanto, concentrar atenção nos requisitos arquiteturais e no estabelecimento de arquiteturas de referência, certamente contribuem para a qualidade dos sistemas de software resultantes dessas arquiteturas. Vale salientar que os requisitos arquiteturais estabelecidos neste trabalho são relevantes para o estabelecimento de outras arquiteturas para AESs, tendo como base outras arquiteturas bases, tais como a arquitetura Cliente-Servidor-Distribuído e a arquitetura de *Web services*[6].

Buscando atender aos requisitos arquiteturais, foi proposta uma arquitetura de referência para AESs — a RefASSET — baseada em interesses (aspectos) e construída com base no padrão internacional ISO/IEC 12207, nas arquiteturas de sistemas interativos e sistemas Web bastante consolidadas, bem como no uso de *frameworks* transversais para a implementação de módulos que implementam interesses transversais. Pela própria concepção da RefASSET, AESs construídos com base nessa arquitetura possuem como característica chave a capacidade de evolução contínua, bem como o crescimento incremental por meio da inserção de novas funcionalidades/módulos.

Agradecimentos. Os autores gostariam de agradecer à FAPESP, Capes e CNPq pelo apoio financeiro.

Referências

1. ECMA, NIST: Reference model for frameworks of software engineering environments (1991) Special Publication Report No. ECMA TR/55, 2nd Ed.
2. Garlan, D., Perry, D.: Introduction to the special issue on software architecture. IEEE Transactions on Software Engineering **21** (1995)
3. Harrison, W., Ossher, H., Tarr, P.: Software engineering tools and environments: a roadmap. In: ICSE '00: Proc. of the Conference on The Future of Software Engineering, New York, NY, USA, ACM Press (2000) 261–277
4. Feng, L., Chang, E., Dillon, T.: A semantic network-based design methodology for XML documents. ACM Transactions on Information Systems **20** (2002) 390–421
5. Reiss, S.P.: FIELD: A Friendly Integrated Environment for Learning and Development. Kluwer Press (1994)
6. Spinola, R.O.: Uma infra-estrutura para integração de ferramentas CASE baseada em XML, esquemas e ontologias. Dissertação de mestrado, COOPE/Universidade Federal do Rio de Janeiro, Rio de Janeiro, RJ (2004)
7. Wasserman, A.I.: Towards a discipline of software engineering. IEEE Software **13** (1996) 23–31
8. Garlan, D.: Software architecture: a roadmap. In: ICSE '00: Proc. of the Conference on The Future of Software Engineering, New York, NY, USA, ACM Press (2000) 91–101
9. Mettala, E., Graham, M.H.: The domain-specific software architecture program. Special Report, CMU/SEI-92-SR-009, Software Engineering Institute, Carnegie Mellon University (1992)

[6] http://www.w3.org/2002/ws/arch/

10. Eickelmann, N.S., Richardson, D.J.: An evaluation of software test environment architectures. In: Proc. of the 18th International Conference on Software Engineering, Berlin, Germany, IEEE Computer Society Press (1996) 353–364
11. Collins-Cope, M., Matthews, H.: A reference architecture for component based development. In: OOIS'00: Proceedings of the 6th International Conference on Object Oriented Information Systems, London, UK, Springer-Verlag (2000) 225–237
12. Buschmann, F., Meunier, R., Rohnert, H., Sommerlad, P., Stal, M.: Pattern-oriented Software Architecture: A System of Patterns. Volume 1. John Wiley & Sons (1996)
13. Anderson, D.J.: Using MVC pattern in web interactions. [*On-line*], *World Wide Web* (2004) Disponível em: http://www.uidesign.net/Articles/Papers/UsingMVCPatterninWebInter.html 3.ed, revisado em maio de 2004 (Acesso em 29/09/2007).
14. Zhao, W., Kearney, D.: Deriving architectures of web-based applications. In: Proc. on 5th Asia-Pacific Web Conference, APWeb 2003, Xian, China (2003) LNCS 2642.
15. Braga, R., Werner, C., Mattoso, M.: Odyssey: A reuse environment based on domain models. In: Proc. of IEEE Symposium on Application-Specific Systems and Software Engineering Technology (ASSET'99), Richardson, Texas (1999) 49–57
16. Cao, S., Grundy, J.C., Hosking, J.G., Stoeckle, H., Tempero, E.D.: An architecture for generating web-based, thin-client diagramming tools. In: 19th IEEE International Conference on Automated Software Engineering (ASE 2004), Linz, Austria (2004) 270–273
17. Junkermann, G., Peuschel, B., Schäfer, W., Wolf, S.: Merlin: Supporting cooperation in software development through a knowledge-based environment. In Nuseibeh, B., Finkelstein, A., Kramer, J., eds.: Software Process Modelling and Technology, John Wiley & Sons (1994) 103–129
18. Lucrédio, D., Bianchini, C.P., Prado, A.F., Trevelin, L.C., Almeida, E.S.: Orion – a component-based software engineering environment. Journal of Object Technology (JOT) **4** (2004) 51–74 Special issue: TOOLS USA 2003.
19. Maidantchik, C.L.L.: Gerência de Processos de Software para Equipes Geograficamente Dispersas. Tese de doutorado, COOPE/Universidade Federal do Rio de Janeiro, Rio de Janeiro - RJ (1999)
20. Maurer, F., Succi, G., Holz, H., Kötting, B., Goldmann, S., Dellen, B.: Software process support over the internet. In: Proc. of the 1999 International Conference on Software Engineering, Los Angeles, California, USA, IEEE Computer Society Press (1999) 642–645
21. Rocha, A.R.C., Aguiar, T.C., Souza, J.M.: TABA: a heuristic workstation for software development. In: Proc. of the 1990 IEEE International Conference on Computer Systems and Software Engineering (COMPEURO'90), Tel Aviv, Israel (1990) 126–129
22. Simão, A.S.: Aplicação da Análise de Mutantes no Contexto do Teste e Validação de Redes de Petri Coloridas. Tese de doutorado, Instituto de Ciências Matemáticas e de Computação – ICMC/USP, São Carlos, SP (2004)
23. Bragança, A., Machado, R.J.: Adopting computational independent models for derivation of architectural requirements of software product lines. In: Proc. of the 4th Int. Workshop on Model-Based Methodologies for Pervasive and Embedded Software - MOMPES'07, Braga, Portugal (2007) 91–101

24. Wasserman, A.I.: Tool integration in software engineering environments. In: Proc. of the International Workshop on Software Engineering Environments, New York, NY, USA, Springer-Verlag New York, Inc. (1990) 137–149
25. Nakagawa, E.Y.: Uma Contribuição ao Projeto Arquitetural de Ambientes de Engenharia de Software. Tese de doutorado, Instituto de Ciências Matemáticas e de Computação – ICMC/USP, São Carlos, SP (2006)
26. International Organization for Standardization: ISO/IEC 12207. Information technology – software life-cycle processes (1995)
27. Kiczales, G., Irwin, J., Lamping, J., Loingtier, J., Lopes, C., Maeda, C., Menhdhekar, A.: Aspect-oriented programming. In Akşit, M., Matsuoka, S., eds.: Proc. of the European Conference on Object-Oriented Programming. Volume 1241., Springer-Verlag (1997) 220–242
28. Fayad, M.E., E.Johnson, R., Schmidt, D.C.: Building Application Frameworks: Object-Oriented Foundations of Framework Design. John Wiley & Sons, New York – NY, USA (1999)
29. Camargo, V.V., Masiero, P.C.: Frameworks orientados a aspectos. In: SBES'2005 – Simpósio Brasileiro de Engenharia de Software, Uberlândia, MG (2005)
30. Rashid, A., Chitchyan, R.: Persistence as an aspect. In: AOSD'03: Proc. of the 2nd International Conference on Aspect-oriented Software Development, New York, NY, USA, ACM Press (2003) 120–129
31. Nakagawa, E.Y., Simão, A.S., Maldonado, J.C.: Addressing separation of concerns in software engineering environments. In: IASTED Int. Conf. on Software Engineering, Innsbruck, Austria (2007)
32. Nakagawa, E.Y., Simão, A.S., Ferrari, F., Maldonado, J.C.: Towards a reference architecture for software testing tools. In: 19th SEKE - Int. Conf. on Software Engineering and Knowledge Engineering, Boston, USA (2007)
33. Vincenzi, A.M.R.: Orientação a objeto: definição, implementação e análise de recursos de teste e validação. Tese de doutorado, Instituto de Ciências Matemáticas e de Computação – ICMC/USP, São Carlos, SP (2004)

Em Busca de Agilidade na Análise de Impacto: O Artefato FIR

Antonio Oliveira Filho[1], Manoel Mendonça[1], Christina Chavez[2]

[1] NÚCLEO INTERDEPARTAMENTAL DE PESQUISA EM REDES DE COMPUTADORES (NUPERC)
UNIVERSIDADE SALVADOR (UNIFACS)
SALVADOR - BA - BRASIL
aoliveiraf@gmail.com, mgmn@unifacs.br

[2] DEPARTAMENTO DE CIÊNCIA DA COMPUTAÇÃO (DCC)
UNIVERSIDADE FEDERAL DA BAHIA (UFBA)
SALVADOR, BA - BRASIL
flach@ufba.br

Resumo A Gerência de Requisitos (GR) utiliza as informações de rastreabilidade para manter a consistência entre requisitos e entre requisitos e artefatos do projeto de software. Ao mesmo tempo, a Análise de Impacto depende de informações de rastreabilidade para estimar com agilidade as conseqüências de mudanças nos requisitos. A necessidade em ser ágil impõe demandas específicas sobre a rastreabilidade que podem trazer dificuldades para a GR. Este artigo apresenta o artefato FIR (Funcionalidade-Informação-Regra), que através de elos mais especializados, dá suporte à rastreabilidade de modo a contemplar essas demandas.

Palavras-chave: Análise de impacto, gerência de requisitos, rastreabilidade, regras de negócio.

1 Introdução

Todo software está sujeito a mudanças que, naturalmente, podem levar a modificações em seus requisitos e artefatos relacionados, bem como à incorporação de novos requisitos. A Gerência de Requisitos (GR) é o processo geral de compreender e controlar mudanças nos requisitos de um sistema [1], buscando manter a consistência entre eles e demais artefatos de software. O processo de GR inclui atividades de rastreamento de requisitos e de análise de impacto, dentre outras. O rastreamento de requisitos permite a identificação de relacionamentos entre requisitos, suas fontes e componentes que os implementam [2]. A análise de impacto permite identificar consequências e prover estimativas em termos de custos e prazos de uma solicitação de mudança antes que a mesma seja implementada [3]. A rastreabilidade de requisitos é a base para uma análise de impacto eficiente. Idealmente, ela deve ser realizada a cada nova sugestão de mudança nos requisitos de um software [4].

Em geral, a rastreabilidade é mantida por elos que relacionam os requisitos a outros requisitos (elos de dependência), a artefatos que os atendem (elos de satisfação) e às suas fontes [2]. Sob o ponto de vista da GR, esta rastreabilidade convencional pode impor dificuldades para a realização da análise de impacto de requisitos. Estas dificuldades se revelam, quando se deseja responder, com agilidade, à seguinte pergunta: "quais são os requisitos funcionais que sofrem o impacto de uma mudança em outro requisito funcional"? Esta mudança pode ocorrer no nível da regra de negócio [5] ou das informações geradas pelas funcionalidades, quer seja porque altera ou remove alguma regra ou informação já existente, ou porque adiciona alguma nova regra ou informação em algum requisito funcional. Diante desta situação, a GR tem que (1) considerar cada requisito dependente (parte funcionalidade) presente na matriz de rastreabilidade; (2) para cada requisito dependente, procurar por suas regras de negócio (parte regra) através dos elos de satisfação que indicam cada artefato que o atende; e (3) para cada regra encontrada, procurar descobrir se a mudança provoca algum impacto. Para cada requisito dependente que sofrer impacto, deve-se repetir o processo a partir de (1) até que não haja mais impactos ou requisitos dependentes. Este processo deve ser executado sempre, mesmo que uma nova sugestão de mudança ocorra para um requisito já modificado.

Nestas condições, dois importantes problemas relacionados à análise de impacto podem ser observados. Em primeiro lugar, o esforço para a identificação dos requisitos impactados pode ser grande, envolvendo vários elos e artefatos, comprometendo a agilidade normalmente necessária para uma tomada de decisão relativa a uma mudança. Além disso, a demanda por agilidade pode favorecer a ocorrência de erros nas estimativas e inconsistências nos artefatos, por falta de tempo ou devido a erros durante a realização da atividade em si. Em segundo lugar, a forte dependência desta atividade em relação a artefatos utilizados no projeto, dificulta a criação de um processo geral para a análise de impacto, que seja independente de paradigmas de desenvolvimento.

Este artigo apresenta o artefato FIR (Funcionalidade-Informação-Regra) que representa requisitos funcionais através do relacionamento entre suas partes. No FIR, a parte funcionalidade é chamada simplesmente de funcionalidade (F) e a parte regra de negócio é decomposta em dois elementos (ou abstrações): informação (I) e regra (R). A rastreabilidade é conseguida a partir de elos especializados que relacionam essas abstrações, de modo a permitir que a GR possa identificar de modo ágil os impactos nos requisitos devido a uma mudança. Os benefícios esperados com o uso do FIR para a GR são: agilidade na análise de impacto, potencial redução na ocorrência de erros em estimativas (em geral, decorrentes da demanda por agilidade da análise de impacto) e a perspectiva de se ter um processo geral, independente de paradigmas, para a análise de impacto.

Este trabalho está organizado como se segue. A seção 2 apresenta a motivação do trabalho e um exemplo para ilustrar as dificuldades relacionadas à análise de impacto sobre a rastreabilidade convencional. A seção 3 apresenta o artefato FIR e ilustra sua aplicabilidade em termos do exemplo apresentado na seção 2.

A seção 4 discute trabalhos relacionados. A seção 5 apresenta as conclusões e trabalhos futuros.

2 Motivação

Esta seção apresenta alguns conceitos relacionados à atividade de análise de impacto (seção 2.1) e utiliza um exemplo para ilustrar problemas que emergem em face à demanda por agilidade na mudança de requisitos (seção 2.2) e levantar questões para discussão (seção 2.3).

2.1 Uma Visão Convencional da Análise de Impacto

Atualmente, a análise de impacto é realizada sobre uma rastreabilidade mantida por elos que relacionam os requisitos a outros requisitos (elos de dependência), a artefatos que os atendem (elos de satisfação) e às suas fontes [6,7]. A análise de impacto pode identificar, através dos elos de satisfação, os artefatos afetados por uma mudança de requisito, auxiliando a equipe de projeto a manter a qualidade do projeto de software [4]. Adicionalmente, a análise de impacto precisa identificar os requisitos que sofreram impactos. Os elos de dependência facilitam a identificação de requisitos interdependentes, que são candidatos naturais a sofrer algum impacto pela mudança. Uma das técnicas mais usadas pelas organizações para manter elos de dependência é a referência cruzada, utilizando matrizes de rastreabilidade.

Figura 1. Elos de dependência e elos de satisfação.

A Figura 1 representa a rastreabilidade através dos elos de dependência entre os requisitos funcionais RF1, RF2 e RF3, em uma matriz de rastreabilidade, e elos de satisfação, que indicam que os requisitos são atendidos em artefatos do projeto (casos de uso, diagramas de classe, etc.). A Figura 1 mostra que um requisito funcional pode ser constituído de duas partes complementares. A parte funcionalidade (PF), que compreende a funcionalidade propriamente dita (representada na matriz de rastreabilidade) e a parte regra de negócio (PRN), formada pelas regras de negócio [5] (presentes em artefatos de projeto). Em geral, a PF pode ser facilmente identificada na matriz de rastreabilidade, porém a PRN pode estar espalhada em diversos artefatos do projeto, o que dificulta sua identificação.

Diante de uma sugestão de mudança em um requisito funcional, a GR precisa, através da rastreabilidade apresentada, obter resposta para a pergunta: "quais são os requisitos que sofrerão impactos por causa de uma mudança"? Para cada requisito dependente que sofrer impacto, deve-se repetir as atividades 1, 2 e 3 do processo descrito na seção 1 até que não haja mais impactos ou requisitos dependentes. A execução de todas as atividades deste processo, sobre uma rastreabilidade rigorosamente mantida, garante para a GR que todos os impactos serão descobertos.

2.2 Um Exemplo Ilustrativo

Como motivação, apresentamos um exemplo simples, com três requisitos funcionais, que ilustra os passos utilizados pela GR para manter a rastreabilidade. Em seguida, diante de uma sugestão de mudança, discutimos os passos necessários e dificuldades para realizar a análise de impacto.

Os requisitos funcionais apresentados fazem parte da especificação de um sistema para administração de parques de diversões, que inclui emissão de ingressos, controle de acesso para cada brinquedo e distribuição de brindes, entre outras funcionalidades.

- RF1 - O sistema deve emitir ingressos para todos os brinquedos do parque (PF). Em cada ingresso emitido devem ser impressos a idade do cliente, o brinquedo e o código de controle do ingresso. A idade, o brinquedo e o código são obrigatórios (PRN);
- RF2 - O sistema libera o acesso para cada brinquedo a partir do destravamento de suas respectivas catracas (PF). A catraca só deve destravar, se a idade presente no ingresso for maior ou igual à idade mínima permitida para o brinquedo. Por exemplo, a montanha-russa tem a idade mínima fixada em 8 anos (PRN);
- RF3 - O sistema deve permitir promoções com entrega de brindes (PF). O brinde deve ser entregue apenas a portadores de ingressos cuja idade esteja entre 8 e 10 anos (PRN).

Nos requisitos apresentados, destacamos as partes que os compõem (PF e PRN), com o propósito de facilitar o entendimento dos elementos representados na Figura 1. É importante observar que a PRN de cada requisito pode ter surgido em algum momento após o surgimento da PF, embora elas apareçam juntas na descrição anterior. Além disso, assume-se que cada um dos requisitos pode ter sido adicionado à especificação em momentos distintos. À medida em que os requisitos são elicitados, total ou parcialmente, a GR provê recursos para que a rastreabilidade seja atualizada.

Atualização da Rastreabilidade Como a PRN de um requisito funcional pode surgir em um momento seguinte ao da PF deste mesmo requisito, a GR tem que conseguir atualizar a rastreabilidade para qualquer uma das partes em qualquer momento que elas surjam. No nosso exemplo, a GR providencia a adição da PF de cada requisito na matriz de rastreabilidade, enquanto a PRN é devidamente representada nos inúmeros artefatos suportados pelo projeto através da criação de elos de satisfação.

Ao considerar os requisitos RF2 e RF3, sob a ótica de suas respectivas PRNs, percebe-se que ambos dependem de RF1, pois compartilham em suas PRNs informações contidas no ingresso. O requisito RF2 utiliza *idade* e *brinquedo*, enquanto RF3 utiliza apenas *idade*. A matriz de rastreabilidade deve tornar explícita esta dependência, relacionando estes requisitos. Para que a GR descubra esta relação de dependência de RF2 e RF3 sobre RF1 (assumindo-se que RF1 surgiu antes dos outros dois requisitos), é necessária a realização de uma investigação sobre a rastreabilidade mantida, que já inclui RF1. Para isto, é necessária a execução de uma análise sobre os artefatos em busca das PRNs. Este tipo de análise é semelhante à investigação realizada para a análise de impacto. Neste caso, se as partes funcionalidade e de regras de negócio de RF1 já se encontram representadas na rastreabilidade, a GR precisa encontrar as regras de negócio de RF1 a partir dos elos de satisfação (que indicam os artefatos que atendem RF1).

Primeiro Cenário de Mudança Considere a seguinte solicitação de mudança relacionada ao requisito RF1: *Além da idade mínima de 8 anos, o sistema deverá considerar a idade máxima para acesso a alguns brinquedos, inclusive a montanha-russa. A idade máxima requerida deve ser de 80 anos.* A GR precisa descobrir os requisitos impactados por esta solicitação de mudança. Para realizar esta análise, seguindo o processo de investigação apresentado na seção 2.1, os requisitos RF2 e RF3 precisam ser considerados, pois eles dependem de RF1. Uma vez que cada requisito dependente é facilmente encontrado na matriz de rastreabilidade, cada um deles deve ser investigado segundo suas PRNs. Para isto, precisamos investigar os demais artefatos que atendem cada requisito.

De acordo com o processo delineado na seção 1, as atividades 1, 2 e 3 devem ser repetidas até que não haja mais impactos ou requisitos dependentes. A partir da análise, pode-se concluir que o requisito RF2 será impactado, uma vez que a *idade máxima* precisa ser considerada durante a liberação do acesso, enquanto que RF3 não sofrerá impacto algum, tendo em vista que sua PRN já considera o limite máximo de 10 anos e este está consistentemente dentro do limite máximo de 80 anos imposto pela restrição da emissão do ingresso.

Segundo Cenário de Mudança Considere que outra mudança foi solicitada para o mesmo requisito RF1, uma semana após a primeira mudança ter sido investigada. O brinquedo *montanha-russa* precisa ter sua *idade mínima* alterada para 11 anos. Assim como na primeira mudança, a GR deve seguir o processo de investigação para descobrir se há impacto em algum requisito. Desta vez, RF3 será impactado, pois como o *limite máximo* para entrega do brinde é de 10 anos e o novo *limite mínimo* para a *montanha-russa* é de 11 anos, pessoas que comprarem ingressos para este brinquedo não receberão brindes. Por outro lado, RF2 não sofre impacto algum, pois este novo *limite mínimo* não inviabiliza o acesso ao brinquedo.

2.3 Discussão

Nesta seção, foram mostrados os passos para se chegar a rastreabilidade de requisitos funcionais, bem como os passos para se chegar a uma análise de impacto de mudança, sob a ótica da GR. Neste contexto, alguns problemas relacionados à rastreabilidade podem ser observados. Tais problemas comprometem a agilidade da análise de impacto de requisitos funcionais e dificultam a detecção de certas inconsistências nestes requisitos.

Dificuldade em detectar inconsistências. Se, durante o processo de atualização da rastreabilidade, apenas as informações trocadas entre os requisitos funcionais forem consideradas, importantes inconsistências podem ficar encobertas. No exemplo apresentado, quando se observa a PRN de RF2 com atenção, percebe-se que o acesso ao brinquedo está restrito por uma regra que condiciona o *brinquedo* à *idade*, mas este condicionamento não aparece em RF1. Isto poderia fazer com que, pessoas comprassem ingressos e não pudessem ter acesso ao respectivo brinquedo.

Ausência de um artefato apropriado. As observações que levaram à descoberta das relações de dependência entre os requisitos não são aproveitadas na rastreabilidade, de modo a possibilitar sua reutilização mais ágil no futuro. Apesar de uma investigação nas dependências de RF1 já ter sido realizada durante a atualização da rastreabilidade, foi necessária a realização de uma nova investigação que explorou os mesmos artefatos usados na primeira investigação.

Ausência de uma rastreabilidade de granularidade mais fina. Quando se observa a realização da análise de impacto em requisitos, percebe-se que ela ocorre mesmo em situações onde os requisitos dependentes não são afetados pela mudança. Isto ocorre no primeiro cenário de mudança – quando o requisito RF3 teve que ser investigado – e no segundo cenário, quando RF2 teve que ser investigado.

As causas dos problemas relatados são as mesmas: (1) todos os artefatos que participam na rastreabilidade precisam estar consistentes, juntamente com os requisitos que são atendidos por eles; (2) a rastreabilidade não tem um meio de possibilitar a análise que procura por impactos apenas nos requisitos funcionais, sem que seja necessária a realização de uma trabalhosa investigação nos artefatos do projeto.

Neste contexto, define-se o tipo de agilidade que este trabalho pretende prover para a análise de impacto de requisitos:

> Ser ágil é *realizar o que se propõe, sem ter que realizar uma ou mais atividades consideradas preparatórias reiteradamente.*

Na seção 3, apresentamos uma proposta de artefato que tem como principal motivação contornar os problemas discutidos e dar suporte a uma análise de impacto ágil e menos suscetível a erros.

3 O Artefato FIR

O FIR (Funcionalidade-Informação-Regra) tem como objetivo principal dar suporte à rastreabilidade de requisitos funcionais e promover uma análise de impacto mais ágil, sem a necessidade recorrente de um extenso processo de investigação nos artefatos, em busca das regras de negócio.

O FIR organiza cada requisito funcional analisado em três elementos básicos: funcionalidade, informação e regra. O uso do FIR requer uma adaptação nos elos de dependência que consideram esses elementos, de modo a prover uma rastreabilidade de requisitos com granularidade mais fina.

Nesta seção, o artefato FIR é apresentado em termos de suas abstrações (seção 3.1) e elos de dependência (seção 3.2). O exemplo da seção 2 é utilizado para ilustrar as características do FIR (seção 3.3) e discutir seus benefícios e limitações (seção 3.4).

3.1 Abstrações do FIR

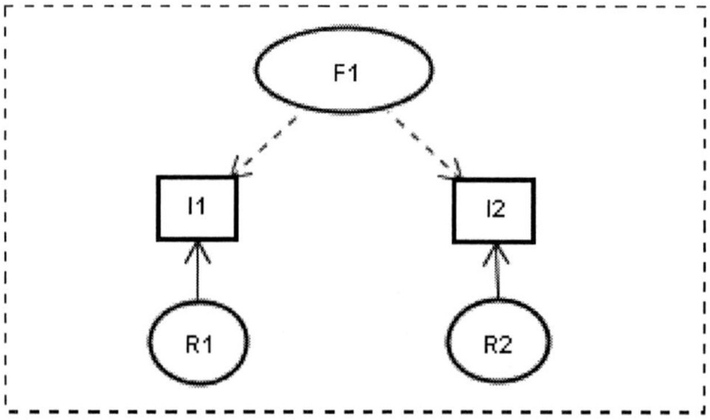

Figura 2. Abstrações do FIR

O artefato FIR estrutura um requisito funcional em três partes: funcionalidade, informação e regra. *Funcionalidade* é a abstração que denota um requisito funcional propriamente dito. Ela representa, portanto, a PF de um requisito funcional. *Regra* é uma afirmação que define ou restringe algum aspecto do negócio [5]. As regras guiam o negócio em suas atividades, podendo representar validações ou computações que são aplicadas sobre os dados para produzir as informações. *Informação* é todo dado ou conjunto de dados resultante de alguma funcionalidade após a execução de alguma regra. Uma funcionalidade produz uma ou mais informações. A combinação de regra e informação (IR) corresponde a PRN do requisito funcional.

A Figura 2 ilustra as abstrações do FIR e algumas de suas relações. Funcionalidades são representadas por elipses, informações por retângulos e regras por círculos. A produção da informação I1 a partir da funcionalidade F1 é representada por uma linha tracejada que parte de F1 e chega em I1, e a indicação de que esta mesma informação (I1) resulta de uma regra R1 é representada por uma linha cheia que parte de R1 e chega em I1. Linhas cheias representam outras relações entre funcionalidade, regra e informação que serão detalhadas na seção 3.2.

3.2 Elos do FIR

A seção 2.3 explicita algumas demandas específicas, que não são atendidas pela rastreabilidade convencional – por exemplo, a necessidade de se conhecer em um nível maior de detalhes a relação de dependência entre os requisitos funcionais. Por este motivo, a rastreabilidade no FIR é conseguida através de duas classes distintas de elos: *elos IR-I* (informação-regra-informação) e *elos IR-F* (informação-regra-funcionalidade). Estes elos são os responsáveis por comunicar de modo ágil à GR sobre os requisitos impactados por uma sugestão de mudança em uma regra de negócio.

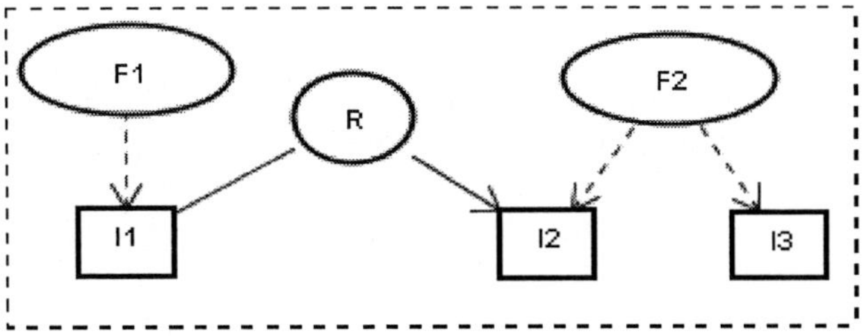

Figura 3. Elos Informação-Regra-Informação (IR-I)

Elos IR-I. Para que o FIR possa atender às demandas da rastreabilidade, ele dispõe do elo IR-I que relaciona informações (I1) de uma funcionalidade (F1) a informações (I2) de uma outra funcionalidade (F2) dependente, utilizando para isto a regra (R). Isto pode ser observado na Figura 3, que mostra um elo IR-I – representado por uma linha cheia que sai de uma ou mais informações e chega em outra informação. A seta denota qual é o lado dependente. A interpretação deste elo para a GR é: primeiro, o requisito funcional denotado pelas abstrações F2, I2 e I3 (RFj) é dependente do requisito funcional denotado pelas outras abstrações F1 e I1 (RFi); segundo, RFj utiliza a informação I1, após a execução da regra de negócio R por RFi, epecificamente para produzir I2; terceiro, o impacto de uma solicitação de mudança no requisito RFi, mesmo que ocorra na regra R, pode ser agilmente percebido.

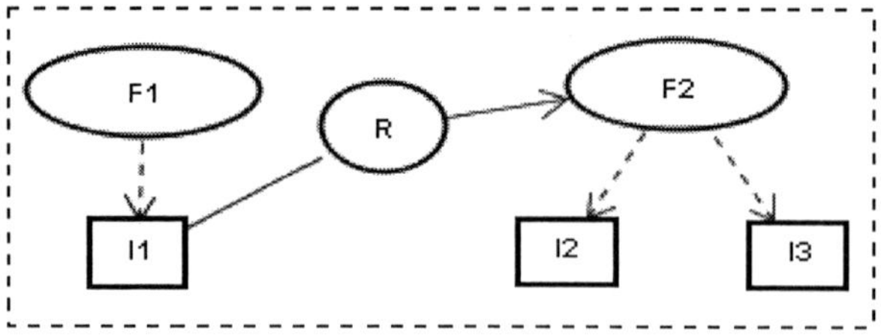

Figura 4. Elos Informação-Regra-Funcionalidade (IR-F)

Elos IR-F. Outro elo utilizado no FIR para atender às demandas da rastreabilidade é o IR-F. Este elo, relaciona informações (I1) de uma funcionalidade (F1) a uma outra funcionalidade (F2) dependente, utilizando para isto a regra (R). Isto pode ser observado na Figura 4, que mostra um elo IR-I – representado por uma linha cheia que sai de uma ou mais informações e chega a uma funcionalidade. A seta denota qual é o lado dependente. A interpretação deste elo para a GR é: primeiro, o requisito funcional denotado pelas abstrações F2, I2 e I3 (RFj) é dependente do requisito funcional denotado pelas outras abstrações F1 e I1 (RFi); segundo, RFj utiliza a informação I1, após a execução da regra de negócio R por RFi, para produzir todas as suas informações (no caso, I2 e I3); terceiro, o impacto de uma solicitação de mudança no requisito RFi, mesmo que ocorra na regra R, pode ser agilmente percebido.

Os elos IR-Fs são utilizados para simplificar o artefato FIR. Eles são necessários, sempre quando a informação (no caso, I1) que participa do elo, após a execução de sua regra (no caso, R) é utilizada pela funcionalidade (no caso, F2) do requisito dependente de modo a afetar igualmente todas as informações (no caso, I2 e I3) produzidas por esta funcionalidade (no caso, F2). Observe que, em todos as situações onde um elo IR-F é utilizado, um elo IR-I também poderia ser, mas isto implicaria em uma excessiva quantidade de linhas chegando às informações da funcionalidade do requisito dependente, uma vez que IR-I teria que ligar todas as informações do requisito dependente.

3.3 Exemplo de Uso

Esta seção ilustra, através da descrição dos requisitos RF1 e RF2, como o FIR pode auxiliar a GR a perceber de modo mais direto, a inconsistência entre a emissão de ingressos e a liberação de acesso.

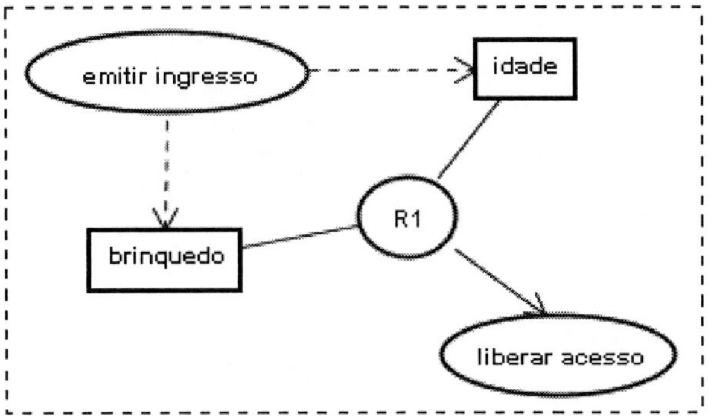

Figura 5. FIR - RF1 e RF2

Os requisitos RF1 e RF2 A Figura 5 mostra a solução da rastreabilidade com o FIR para os requisitos RF1 e RF2. Um elo IR-F foi definido entre as informações *brinquedo* e *idade* pela regra R1 (*a catraca só deve destravar, se a idade presente no ingresso for maior ou igual à idade mínima permitida para o brinquedo*). A presença de R1 expõe de forma clara a necessidade da validação da idade pelo brinquedo também no ato da emissão do ingresso. Como ambas as funcionalidades executam uma mesma regra, a regra R1 que aparece no elo, pode ser considerada em ambas as funcionalidades.

O requisito RF3 A Figura 6 representa o requisito funcional FR3:

– RF3 - O sistema deve permitir promoções com entrega de brindes a portadores de ingressos por faixa de idade.

Neste exemplo, a regra R5 (*idade menor que a idade máxima permitida*) afeta tanto a *data entrega* quanto o *brinde*; se a *idade* não estiver de acordo com a regra, o *brinde* não é entregue e a *data* não é gerada.

Um novo requisito: RF4 A Figura 7 modela a funcionalidade *invalidar ingresso*, uma nova funcionalidade do sistema de parque de diversões.

– RF4 - O sistema deve invalidar os ingressos após a liberação do acesso ao brinquedo (PF), exceto se a data de acesso não for uma data especial, por exemplo, dia das crianças(PRN).

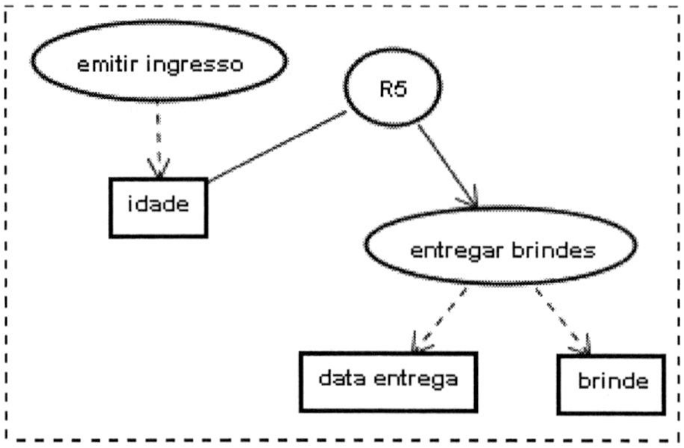

Figura 6. Elos IR-F e a funcionalidade *entregar brindes*

Neste requisito, a regra R6 (*se a data não for especial*) afeta o código do ingresso que será invalidado e a data da invalidação; isto está registrado através do elo IR-F. Com este elo, percebe-se de forma ágil que qualquer modificação em R6 tem impacto na funcionalidade *invalidar ingresso*.

3.4 Discussão

Nesta seção, os elementos do FIR e benefícios esperados são confrontados com algumas dificuldades enfrentadas pela GR durante a análise de impacto (seção 1 e seção 2.3).

- *Dificuldade em prover uma análise de impacto independente de paradigmas e processos de desenvolvimento* - O FIR representa os relacionamentos entre as partes (PF e PRN) dos requisitos funcionais. Isto permite que a análise de impacto de mudanças possa ser realizada utilizando apenas esse artefato. Desse modo, através do uso do FIR, pode-se definir um processo geral para a análise de impacto que seja independente de paradigma e de processos de desenvolvimento de software.
- *Dificuldade em prover uma análise de impacto ágil* - A condição agnóstica da análise de impacto realizada sobre o FIR, somada ao relacionamento claro e direto entre as partes dos requisitos funcionais, permite que a análise de impacto possa ser realizada a partir de elos especializados, que orientam a sua realização. Assim, não é necessária uma exploração trabalhosa e dependente de vários tipos distintos de artefatos.

Se a GR passar a considerar o FIR, poderá dispor de duas rastreabilidades orientadas à análise de impacto. A rastreabilidade do FIR provê uma análise nos requisitos impactados de forma ágil, através de elos que relacionam as partes dos requisitos funcionais. A rastreabilidade convencional, por outro lado, provê uma análise dos artefatos impactados. A primeira análise tem uma relação direta

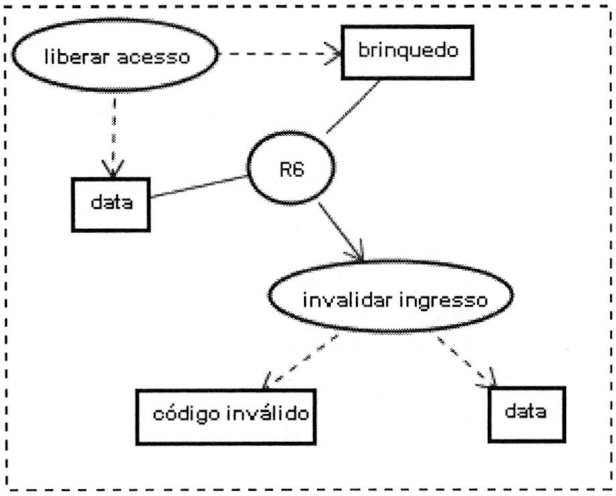

Figura 7. Elos IR-F e a funcionalidade *invalidar ingresso*

com a consistência do sistema em si, enquanto a segunda, está voltada para a consistência do processo de desenvolvimento.

4 Trabalhos Relacionados

Este trabalho tem como principal interesse a rastreabilidade de requisitos, por ela apoiar fortemente a GR durante a análise de impacto de requisitos. Gotel e Finkelstein [8] publicaram os resultados de um estudo empírico sobre a rastreabilidade, onde sugeriram importantes recomendações, como a divisão da rastreabilidade em pré-especificação e pós-especificação. Esse trabalho serve de referência para outros trabalhos, como os de Ramesh e Jarke [6] e de Toranzo [7]. Em seu trabalho, Ramesh e Jarke criaram um meta-modelo que compreende elos de rastreabilidade (satisfação, dependência, evolução e rationale) relacionados ao produto e ao processo. Toranzo, dedicou-se a responder questões sobre a classificação de informações dentro da pré e da pós-especificação. Tais trabalhos são importantes representantes do caráter geral que foi dado à rastreabilidade. Neles, os relacionamentos entre as partes que compõem os requisitos funcionais não estão evidentes, o que implica em algumas dificuldades apontadas na seção 1. O nosso trabalho resolve esta questão através da representação explícita das relações existentes entre as partes dos requisitos.

Na comunidade de Early Aspects, alguns trabalhos propõem frameworks para a separação de interesses nas etapas iniciais do ciclo de vida do software [9,10]. Kassab e Ormandjieva [11] consideram a rastreabilidade para a resolução de conflitos entre requisitos funcionais e requisitos não-funcionais. Berg e colegas [12] propuseram a identificação de relacionamentos entre as fontes e os seus respectivos alvos, estendendo a matriz de rastreabilidade.

Nos trabalhos pesquisados, não identificamos esforços em resolver as dificuldades da Gerência de Requisitos apontadas neste artigo.

5 Conclusões

Este artigo apresentou o artefato FIR (Funcionalidade-Informação-Regra), proposto com o objetivo de tornar a análise de impacto mais ágil. A principal idéia subjacente ao uso do FIR é que, para alcançar maior agilidade na análise de impacto, é preciso organizar a rastreabilidade de requisitos funcionais em termos de sua parte funcionalidade (PF) e suas regras de negócio (PRN). Além disso, o FIR torna explícita a necessidade de rastrear as *informações* provenientes das funcionalidades, através das regras que as determinam, de modo a melhorar a capacidade de avaliar de modo ágil os impactos resultantes de uma mudança.

O FIR evidenciou a existência das partes que compõem os requisitos funcionais e, com isto, a grande fragmentação necessária para se chegar a uma análise de impacto ágil. Neste cenário, uma questão que se coloca é se os custos de construção e evolução do FIR superam muito os custos da rastreabilidade convencional. Se considerarmos que os esforços para construção e evolução da rastreabilidade convencional incluem necessariamente operações de decomposição que resultam na identificação das partes explicitadas e mantidas pelo FIR, temos um indício de que o esforço e os custos de construção não são muito diferentes.

O uso do artefato FIR foi ilustrado através de um exemplo que, embora simples, consegue expressar algumas dificuldades enfrentadas pela GR para realizar uma análise de impacto dos requisitos. Entretanto, para avaliar a eficácia da análise de impacto realizada sobre o FIR em relação à realizada sobre a rastreabilidade convencional, é necessário realizar estudos de caso de maior porte, de preferência envolvendo um conjunto mais rico de requisitos, proveniente de um cenário real de desenvolvimento.

A granularidade mais fina dos elos, proposta pelo FIR, requer investigações mais aprofundadas acerca do armazenamento, apresentação e manipulação de suas abstrações. Encontra-se em estágio inicial de desenvolvimento uma ferramenta para desenhar e armazenar diagramas FIR, usando o *Graphical Modeling Framework* (GMF) [13] e XML [14], respectivamente.

Certamente, o uso do FIR requer um processo para sua construção e evolução, a partir de documentos de requisitos e outros artefatos. Ainda que algumas atividades de tal processo estejam implícitas ao longo do artigo (a decomposição de requisitos funcionais em suas abstrações), sua definição ainda precisa ser trabalhada. No estágio atual, a construção do artefato FIR depende de análise textual detalhada dos requisitos, feita por analistas. A atividade de construção pode ser facilitada através do uso de ontologias [15] e da representação de regras de negócio em notação formal [5].

Referências

1. Sommerville, I.: Software engineering (7th ed.). Addison Wesley Longman Publishing Co., Inc. (2006)

2. Sayão, M., do Prado Leite, J.C.S.: Rastreabilidade de requisitos. RITA **13**(1) (2006) 57–86
3. Arnold, R.S.: Software Change Impact Analysis. IEEE Computer Society Press (1996)
4. Kasse, T.: Practical Insight Into CMMI. Artech House, Boston, USA (2004)
5. Halle, B.V.: Business Rules Applied: Building Better Systems Using the Business Rules Approach. John Wiley & Sons, Inc., New York, NY, USA (2001)
6. Ramesh, B., Jarke, M.: Toward reference models of requirements traceability. Software Engineering **27**(1) (2001) 58–93
7. Toranzo, M., Castro, J., Mello, E.: Uma proposta para melhorar o rastreamento de requisitos. In: WER. (2002) 194–209
8. Gotel, O.C.Z., Finkelstein, A.C.W.: An analysis of the requirements traceability problem. In: First International Conference on Requirements Engineering (ICRE), IEEE Computer Society Press (april 1994) 94–101
9. van der Linden, J., Laney, R., Thomas, P.: Traceability and AOSD - from requirements to aspects. In: Workshop on Early Aspects, na 5th Intl Conf. on Aspect-Oriented Software Development, Bonn, Germany (March 2006)
10. Tabares, M., Moreira, A.: Towards a meta aspect for traceability. Workshop on Early Aspects, na 5th Intl Conf. on Aspect-Oriented Software Development (March 2006)
11. Kassab, M., Ormandjieva, O.: Towards an aspect-oriented software development model with tractability mechanism. Workshop on Early Aspects, na 5th Intl Conf. on Aspect-Oriented Software Development (March 2006)
12. van den Berg, K.G., Conejero, J.M., Hernandez, J.: Analysis of crosscutting across software development phases based on traceability. In: Early Aspects at ICSE2006: Workshop in Aspect-Oriented Requirements Engineering and Architecture Design, Shanghai, China, New York, NY, USA, ACM Press (May 2006) 43–50
13. Eclipse: Graphical modeling framework (GMF) - http://www.eclipse.org/gmf
14. W3C: Extensible markup language (XML) - http://www.w3c.org/xml
15. Rêgo, E., Pacheco, G., Salvador, L., Chavez, C., Santos, W.: Extração de visões centradas em stakeholders a partir de ontologias: Uma abordagem MDA. In: Second Workshop on Ontologies and Metamodeling in Software and Data Engineering (WOMSDE 2007). (October 2007)

Proceso de Valoración para la Mejora de Procesos Software en Pequeñas Organizaciones

Francisco J. Pino[1,2], Félix García[2] y Mario Piattini[2]

[1] Grupo IDIS
Facultad de Ingeniería Electrónica y Telecomunicaciones
Universidad del Cauca
Calle 5 No. 4 – 70. Popayán, Cauca, Colombia.
fjpino@unicauca.edu.co. Web: http://www.unicauca.edu.co/idis/
[2] Grupo Alarcos
Escuela Superior de Informática
Universidad Castilla-La Mancha
Paseo de la Universidad 4, Ciudad Real, España.
{Felix.Garcia, Mario.Piattini}@uclm.es. Web: http://alarcos.inf-cr.uclm.es/

Resumen. Un área que desde finales de los años noventa ha tomado gran fuerza es la Mejora de Procesos Software –SPI– en pequeñas organizaciones. Para conducir SPI en pequeñas organizaciones es importante realizar evaluaciones internas que consuman poco tiempo, pocos recursos y que tengan poca rigurosidad, las cuales se conocen como valoraciones de procesos. El objetivo de estas valoraciones es obtener información relevante sobre la ejecución de los procesos que luego es usada en el control y mejora de los mismos. Con el fin de ayudar a obtener tal información, en este artículo se presenta un proceso para la valoración de procesos software el cual guía paso a paso la actividad de *diagnóstico de procesos* software en pequeñas organizaciones. Este trabajo ha sido desarrollado en el contexto del Proyecto COMPETISOFT, y también muestra la experiencia de la aplicación del proceso descrito en varias pequeñas organizaciones software participantes en dicho proyecto.

Palabras clave: Proceso de valoración, Valoración de procesos, Mejora de procesos software, Pequeñas organizaciones, SPI, Proyecto COMPETISOFT.

1 Introducción

Las pequeñas organizaciones software (con menos de 50 empleados) son fundamentales para el crecimiento de muchas economías nacionales y representan la mayoría de las organizaciones software. En Europa el 85% de las compañías del sector de las tecnologías de la información son muy pequeñas, entre 1 y 10 empleados [4]. En Iberoamérica el 75% de las empresas software tienen menos de 50 empleados [7]. Además según [5] aproximadamente el 94% de empresas que desarrollan software son pequeñas organizaciones y desarrollan productos significativos que, para su construcción, necesitan prácticas eficientes de Ingeniería del Software adaptadas a su tamaño y tipo de negocio. Una práctica que a partir de finales de los años noventa ha tomado gran fuerza en la comunidad de Ingeniería del Software (industria e investigadores) es la Mejora de Procesos Software (conocida por las siglas inglesas SPI, Software Process Improvement) en pequeñas organizaciones software.

En este sentido, actualmente organizaciones internacionales como el Software Engineering Institute –SEI– o el International Organization for Standardization –ISO– trabajan con el objetivo de que sus estándares de mejora de procesos software (o adaptaciones de éstos) puedan ser aplicados a pequeñas organizaciones software, un buen ejemplo de ello es el International Process Research Consortium –IPRC– [21] del SEI y el grupo de trabajo SC7-WG24 [6] del ISO. Una razón de la aparición de éstos y otros trabajos sobre mejora de procesos para pequeñas organizaciones es el hecho que muchos autores están de acuerdo en que las características especiales de estas organizaciones hacen que los programas de mejora de procesos deban aplicarse de un modo particular y diferente a como se hace en las grandes organizaciones. No es tan sencillo como el hecho de considerar dichos programas de mejora versiones a escala de las grandes compañías [18]. Además las propuestas de mejora del SEI e ISO (como CMMI, IDEAL, SCAMPI, ISO 12207, ISO 15504) han sido creadas y están estructuradas para ser utilizados por organizaciones grandes y difícilmente pueden ser aplicadas a organizaciones pequeñas. Esto se debe a que un proyecto de mejora supone gran inversión en dinero, tiempo y recursos, así como a la alta complejidad de estas recomendaciones y el retorno a la inversión se produce a largo plazo [12, 19].

Actualmente en el ámbito Iberoamericano también se esta trabajando en esta área. En este momento se está desarrollando el Proyecto COMPETISOFT [11], el cual busca incrementar el nivel de competitividad de las pequeñas organizaciones software de la región mediante la creación y difusión de un marco metodológico común que, ajustado a sus necesidades específicas, pueda llegar a ser la base sobre la cual establecer un mecanismo de evaluación y certificación de la industria del software. El marco metodológico está formado por un modelo de referencia de procesos, un método de evaluación de procesos y un modelo que guía la implementación mejoras. El modelo que guía la mejora de COMPETISOFT define un componente que es un proceso para dirigir la mejora continua de procesos denominado PmCOMPETISOFT [17], el cual define 5 actividades: *instalación del ciclo*, *diagnóstico de procesos*, *formulación de mejoras*, *ejecución de mejoras* y *revisión del ciclo*.

Para poder realizar esta mejora de procesos es fundamental la actividad de *diagnóstico de procesos*, ya que permite obtener información relevante acerca del estado general de los procesos de la organización y analizar los resultados con el objetivo de establecer las oportunidades de mejora de un proceso. Para el diagnóstico de procesos las pequeñas organizaciones pueden llevar a cabo evaluaciones de procesos internas que consumen poco tiempo, pocos recursos y que tienen poca rigurosidad, conocidas como valoraciones rápidas de procesos software [3]. Las valoraciones rápidas son un factor de éxito en la mejora de procesos llevados a cabo en una organización, ya que pueden ser aplicadas frecuentemente, en poco tiempo y con pocos recursos.

Así pues en este artículo se presenta un proceso para la valoración de procesos software, denominado PvalCOMPETISOFT, el cual guía paso a paso la actividad de *diagnóstico de procesos* software en pequeñas organizaciones con el fin de generar información de alta calidad que identifiquen los problemas de los procesos software y que esta información sirva como base para tomar decisiones al interior de la organización. Este artículo también muestra la experiencia de la aplicación del éste proceso en tres pequeñas organizaciones partícipes en el Proyecto COMPETISOFT. Para la construcción de PvalCOMPETISOFT se tuvo en cuenta que las pequeñas organizaciones generalmente son extremadamente reactivas y flexibles, tienen típicamente una estructura plana, un estilo de gestión de libre flujo que potencia el espíritu emprendedor y la innovación, poseen disponibilidad económica limitada, procesos livianos, además no tienen suficiente personal para desarrollar funciones especializadas que permitirían realizar tareas complejas y secundarias a sus productos.

Además de esta introducción el artículo presenta en la sección 2 una panorámica de los trabajos relacionados. En la sección 3 se introduce el proceso para la valoración de procesos software. La sección 4 describe la aplicación y utilización del proceso en un proyecto SPI. La sección 5 muestra las conclusiones y trabajos futuros.

2 Trabajos relacionados

Actualmente, la mejora de procesos software es una estrategia de creciente interés para las pequeñas organizaciones con el objetivo de asegurar la calidad de sus productos. Con respecto a este tema (mejora de procesos en pequeñas organizaciones) en los últimos años han aparecido diferentes propuestas relacionadas con los modelos de referencia, las guías de mejora y los métodos de evaluación, como por ejemplo:

- MoProSoft [10], MR-MPS [22] (relacionadas con el modelo de referencia de procesos). Además, existen numerosas propuestas de adaptación de estándares como CMM, CMMI, SPICE, ISO 9001, ISO 12207.
- MESOPyME [2], IMPACT [20] (relacionadas con el modelo para guiar la mejora).
- RAPID [3], MARES [1], EvalProsoft [9], ADEPT [8], MA-MPS [22] (relacionadas con el método de evaluación de procesos).

La Tabla 1 presenta una comparación de algunas propuestas relacionados con el método de evaluación de procesos desde la perspectiva de las tareas que describen.

A excepción de ADEPT, todas las propuestas se basan y están en conformidad con ISO/IEC 15504-2. MA-MPS y EvalProSoft describen un método y un proceso para llevar a cabo una evaluación formal de los procesos de desarrollo de software y poder otorgar (a través de una organización certificadora) un nivel de capacidad a los procesos y un nivel de madurez a la organización.

El aporte de la propuesta presentada en este artículo es la definición de un proceso de valoración de procesos (evaluación interna no formal) integrado en un modelo que guía la implementación de mejoras, el cual a su vez pertenece a un marco metodológico desarrollado específicamente para la mejora de procesos software en pequeñas organizaciones. Este proceso describe explícitamente: actividades, roles, productos de trabajo, entre otros aspectos, con el objetivo de guiar paso a paso el diagnóstico de los procesos cuando se lleva a cabo la implementación de mejoras de procesos software en pequeñas organizaciones. El proceso propone las actividades de *priorización de procesos* y *planificación preliminar de mejoras*, la primera es esencial en un proyecto de mejora ya que ésta permite establecer una estrategia sobre el orden de las prácticas a realizar en las pequeñas organizaciones cuando emprendan un ciclo de mejora, y la segunda permite aprovechar la sinergia de la valoración con el fin de continuar con la formulación y ejecución de las oportunidades de mejora encontradas.

Tabla 1. Propuestas de valoración de procesos software para pequeñas organizaciones

Nombre/Características	Tareas del proceso de evaluación
RAPID (Evaluación interna no formal, Conformidad con ISO 15504)	1. Preparar y enviar cuestionario de demografía de la organización; 2. Completar cuestionario demográfico de la organización; 3 Preparar el plan de valoración; 4. Realizar la valoración RAPID; 5. Preparar reporte de la valoración.
MARES (Evaluación interna no formal, Conformidad con ISO 15504)	1. Planificación; 2. Contextualización; 3. Ejecución; 4. Monitoreo y control; 5.Revisión postmortem.
EvalProSoft (Evaluación formal, conformidad con ISO 15504)	1. Preparación; 2. Planificación; 3. Ejecución; 4. Generación de resultados; 5. Entrega de resultados; 6. Cierre de evaluación.
ADEPT (Evaluación interna no formal)	1. Desarrollar el programa de la valoración; 2. Presentar una visión general de la valoración; 3. Analizar la documentación software; 4. Realizar las entrevistas de las áreas de proceso; 5. Generar resultados de la valoración y crear el reporte de hallazgos; 6. Liberar el reporte de hallazgos; 7. Desarrollar un camino para la mejora de procesos con la compañía; 8. Revisar el camino para la mejora y generar el reporte final.
MA-MPS (Evaluación formal, conformidad con ISO 15504)	1. Contratar la evaluación; 2. Preparar la realización de la evaluación; 3. Realizar la evaluación; 4. Documentar los resultados de la evaluación.

3 Proceso de valoración – PvalCOMPETISOFT

Esta sección presenta el proceso de valoración propuesto mediante la descripción de su contexto, las consideraciones para su creación y algunos de sus elementos constitutivos. El objetivo es describir con detalle el proceso PvalCOMPETISOFT.

3.1 Contexto del proceso de valoración

El proceso para la valoración de procesos –PvalCOMPETISOFT– es un componente del modelo que guía la implementación de mejoras del Proyecto COMPETISOFT. Este modelo forma parte junto con el método de evaluación y el modelo de referencia, del marco metodológico desarrollado por el Proyecto COMPETISOFT. Para la definición, refinamiento y aplicación de los componentes del marco metodológico se ha empleado el método de investigación I-A (Investigación - Acción), el cual divide los participantes del proyecto en dos grupos: el primero constituido por investigadores de distintas universidades y el segundo, denominado grupo crítico de referencia, engloba a los profesionales informáticos de las pequeñas organizaciones.

En este momento el modelo de implementación de mejoras esta compuesto además por: un proceso para guiar la mejora continua de procesos denominado PmCOMPETISOFT [17], el modelo ligero de valoración de procesos Light MECPDS [15], un conjunto de medidas para estimar el rendimiento y la capacidad de los procesos [16], una herramienta Web de soporte a la valoración de procesos [13] y una estrategia para la selección y priorización de procesos [14] (ver Fig. 1).

Fig. 1. Componentes del modelo de implementación de mejoras.

3.2 Consideraciones generales del proceso de valoración

El proceso PvalCOMPETISOFT pretende dar soporte a la actividad de *diagnóstico de procesos* de PmCOMPETISOFT. PvalCOMPETISOFT apoya el principio de diagnóstico continuo y rápido de procesos propuesto por el modelo que guía la implementación de mejoras de COMPETISOFT.

El proceso PvalCOMPETISOFT ha sido desarrollado con el fin de:

- Establecer los elementos necesarios para conducir la valoración de procesos enmarcada dentro de la mejora de procesos en una pequeña organización software.
- Facilitar su aplicación en las pequeñas organizaciones software de forma económica, con pocos recursos y en poco tiempo.
- Diagnosticar continuamente los procesos de la pequeña organización con el fin de verificar si el ciclo de mejora está cumpliendo con el objetivo de incrementar el nivel de capacidad de sus procesos.

3.3 Descripción del proceso de valoración

PvalCOMPETISOFT sigue el patrón de procesos establecido por el Proyecto COMPETISOFT, con el objetivo de que sea más intuitivo y fácil de usar. A continuación se describe el proceso PvalCOMPETISOFT presentando su propósito, objetivos, diagrama de actividades, descripción, productos de trabajo y roles.

Propósito. El proceso de valoración de procesos tiene como propósito generar información confiable con la cual identificar de manera general las fortalezas, debilidades y riesgos de los procesos software de la organización, esta información debe ser la base para tomar decisiones relacionadas con el ciclo de mejora.

Objetivos. PvalCOMPETISOFT define los siguientes objetivos.

– Realizar el diagnóstico de procesos mediante la valoración de procesos de manera disciplinada mediante el cumplimiento y realización sistemática de las actividades y productos de trabajo propuestas.
– Definir objetivos y metas para la valoración de procesos con base en los objetivos de mejora descritos en la *Propuesta de Mejora* de la organización.
– Apoyar la evaluación de los resultados de cada ciclo de mejora con respecto a las mejoras introducidas en los procesos, así como el monitorear y supervisar el ciclo de mejora evaluando frecuentemente su eficiencia en la organización.

Roles. Los roles involucrados en PvalCOMPETISOFT se muestran en la Tabla 2.

Tabla 2. Descripción de los roles de PvalCOMPETISOFT

Nombre	Rol	Competencias
EV	*Evaluador*	Conocimiento en la metodología y aplicación de evaluación de procesos, así como del análisis de los datos recolectados.
RMP	Responsable de mejora de procesos (*Facilitador*)	Capacidad de liderazgo y de gestión. Conocimientos en mejora de procesos. Capaz de diseñar procesos, guiar la implantación y entrenar al personal en los nuevos procesos definidos en el ciclo de mejora.
RP	Responsable del proceso (Particip.)	Conocimiento del proceso el cual es responsable. Es un administrador de conocimientos asociados al proceso, a su diagnóstico y mejora.

Diagrama de actividades. Las actividades de PvalCOMPETISOFT se presentan en la Fig. 2, en la cual se incluyen las actividades, los roles y los productos de trabajo. Dada la importancia del *diagnóstico de procesos* es importante proporcionar un proceso que brinde soporte a esta actividad. La Fig. 2 muestra como a través de las actividades presentadas por el Proceso de valoración PvalCOMPETISOFT se puede abordar el *diagnóstico de procesos* de PmCOMPETISOFT. Esta figura también presenta la relación que tiene la actividad de *diagnóstico de procesos* con las de *instalación del ciclo* de mejora y *formulación de mejoras* de PmCOMPETISOFT.

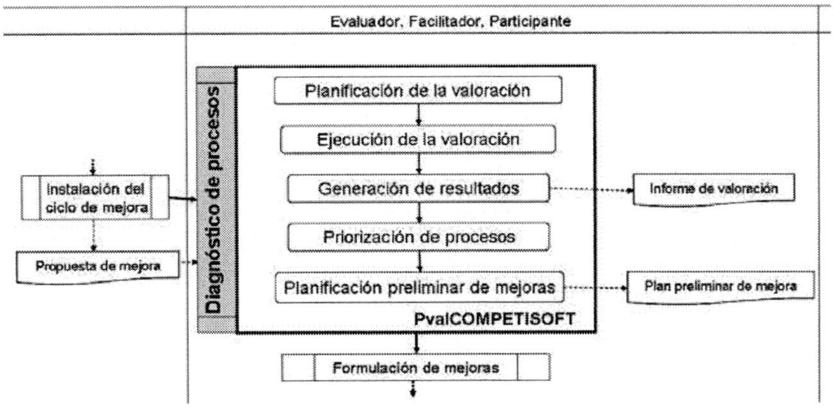

Fig. 2. Flujo de trabajo de PvalCOMPETISOFT

Descripción. El proceso de valoración de procesos software consta de 5 actividades: *Planificación de la valoración, Ejecución de la valoración, Generación de resultados, Priorización de procesos* y *Planificación preliminar de mejoras*. A continuación se presentan estas actividades:

- Actividad 1, *Planificación de la valoración*. A partir de la *Propuesta de Mejora* que contiene: el objetivo general de mejora, el proceso de mejora continua, el alcance, las metas globales y los recursos del ciclo de mejora actual, se desarrolla y documenta un plan de valoración. El *Evaluador* y el *Facilitador* describen los objetivos y el alcance de la valoración, el instrumento de recolección de información a aplicar en la organización, el método de evaluación utilizado para determinar la capacidad de los procesos, el proyecto a evaluar y un cronograma de la valoración (involucrando fecha, actividades, tiempo estimado para realizar cada actividad y roles involucrados, entre otros).
- Actividad 2, *Ejecución de la valoración*. Teniendo en cuenta el alcance definido en la actividad anterior el *Evaluador* recolecta y valida sistemáticamente los datos necesarios para la valoración de procesos mediante la aplicación de técnicas de recolección de evidencias como la entrevista y la encuesta, siguiendo los instrumentos de recolección de información definidos ó creados para tal fin. Para validar la información el *Evaluador* aplicar la técnica de recolección de información de manera separada al *Responsable del proceso* a evaluar (con el cual se revisa la documentación de los procesos de la organización) y a una persona involucrada en la ejecución de este proceso.
- Actividad 3, *Generación de resultados*. El *Evaluador* analiza y sintetiza los datos obtenidos con los instrumentos de recolección de información para determinar el estado actual de los procesos mediante el hallazgo de sus debilidades, riesgos y fortalezas. Por cada proceso valorado se presenta información relacionada con su diagrama de actividades, los hallazgos, los productos de trabajo, así como las oportunidades de mejora. Finalmente el *Evaluador* asigna un valor a los atributos de procesos para establecer un perfil del nivel de capacidad de los procesos valorados en la organización. El *Evaluador* entrega al *Facilitador* el producto de trabajo *Informe de valoración* (PT02_1_IV) con los resultados de la valoración de los procesos de la organización para su validación y refinamiento.
- Actividad 4, *Priorización de procesos*. El *Facilitador* con la información presentada en el *Informe de valoración* prioriza los procesos a mejorar en la organización. La priorización se puede hacer teniendo en cuenta diferentes enfoques, como por ejemplo: (i) basado en mejorar los procesos básicos y fundamentales para el adecuado funcionamiento de un pequeña organización como son los procesos de desarrollo de software y administración de proyectos, (ii) basado en mejorar procesos que den soporte a los objetivos del plan estratégico de la organización, (iii) basado en establecer la mejora continua de procesos siguiendo el enfoque de la gestión de procesos, como el presentado en [14].
- Actividad 5, *Planificación preliminar de mejoras*. El *Facilitador* registra y planea las estrategias a seguir para abordar las oportunidades de mejora presentadas en el *Informe de valoración* con las cuales se guía las diferentes iteraciones de mejora que se llevará a cabo dentro de la organización. El *Facilitador* describe el número de iteraciones del actual ciclo de mejora y la planificación general de éstas, además define el plan de medición de procesos, el plan de capacitación y el de manejo de riesgos del ciclo de mejora. El *Facilitador* genera con los entregables de las tareas realizadas el producto de trabajo *Plan preliminar de mejora* (PT02_2_PPM).

Productos de trabajo. Para cada uno de los productos de trabajo de PvalCOMPETISOFT se ha desarrollado una plantilla auto-contenida, con el objetivo de facilitar su construcción. Asimismo, en cada uno de los productos de trabajo se registra el esfuerzo de realizar las tareas asociadas con cada actividad y relacionadas con estos productos. Los productos de trabajo de salida de PvalCOMPETISOFT son:

- (PT02_1_IV) *Informe de valoración*. Recopila el estado de los procesos con respecto a la capacidad al iniciar un ciclo de mejora, así como las oportunidades de mejora de los procesos valorados. Es un documento que describe los responsables y participantes en la valoración, la *planificación y ejecución de la valoración*, los hallazgos y el nivel de capacidad de los procesos.
- (PT02_2_PPM) *Plan preliminar de mejora*. Recopila las directrices de mejora para el trabajo a realizar en las fases siguientes al *diagnóstico de procesos*. Es un documento que describe el número de iteraciones del ciclo de mejora, la planificación general, el plan de mediciones, el plan de capacitación, el plan de manejo de riesgos y cronograma de las diferentes iteraciones del ciclo de mejora.

4 Aplicación del proceso de valoración PvalCOMPETISOFT

El proceso de valoración ha sido aplicado para dar soporte a la actividad de *diagnóstico de procesos* al interior de la implantación de un ciclo SPI en distintas pequeñas organizaciones software de Colombia y España. En España concretamente se esta trabajando con dos pequeñas organizaciones y una mediana organización, las cuales forman parte grupo crítico de referencia del Proyecto COMPETISOFT. Con el objetivo de preservar su anonimato estas organizaciones se denominan en este artículo *PeqEmpUno*, *PeqOrgDos* y *MedOrgTres*.

La *PeqEmpUno* es una pequeña empresa desarrolladora de software con 4 años de trayectoria en el ámbito nacional. Actualmente la empresa cuenta con siete empleados, de los cuales seis se dedican a la parte de desarrollo, operación y mantenimiento de los productos software. La *PeqOrgDos* es una pequeña organización académica (de una universidad española) que desarrolla software a través de contratos y convenios con 12 años de trayectoria en el ámbito nacional. Actualmente la organización cuenta con 21 personas, 15 de las cuales están dedicadas a la parte de desarrollo, operación y mantenimiento de los productos software. La *MedOrgTres* es una mediana organización del estado que se concentra en el diseño y desarrollo de nuevas soluciones basadas en sistemas abiertos y software libre de sistemas integrales de gestión de servicios especializados basados en el uso de las tecnologías de la información online. En este momento la organización cuenta con aproximadamente 60 personas dedicadas a la parte de desarrollo, operación y mantenimiento de los productos software, y cuenta con 17 años de trayectoria en el ámbito nacional e internacional.

La alta dirección de las dos pequeñas empresas ha decidido apostar por la mejora de procesos para dar soporte a su propia organización, consolidación y crecimiento de manera sistemática, estas empresas pretenden incrementar el nivel de capacidad de sus procesos con el fin de poder tener claridad, seguimiento y organización de los procesos que realizan para el desarrollo de sus productos software. El departamento de calidad de la mediana empresa ve en la mejora de procesos software una estrategia para lograr la mejora continua de procesos. De las tres organizaciones las dos pequeñas organizaciones no tienen experiencia en mejora de procesos software. La mediana organización tiene experiencia en gestión y calidad de procesos, y esta certificada con un sistema de gestión de calidad ISO 9001:2000.

En el presente año se ha comenzado un ciclo de mejora de procesos en cada una de estas organizaciones con el soporte de un asesor en mejora de procesos que es parte del grupo de investigadores del Proyecto COMPETISOFT. En las iniciativas de mejora se están involucrando diferentes componentes creados este proyecto. El modelo que guía la mejora y el modelo de referencia de procesos escogido es el desarrollado en el Proyecto COMPETISOFT, el método de evaluación utilizado para determinar la capacidad de los procesos es Light MECPDS el cual se basa en el estándar internacional ISO/IEC 15504. Para llevar a cabo la actividad de *diagnóstico de procesos* del ciclo de mejora se siguió el proceso de valoración presentado en este artículo. En las siguientes líneas se presenta el trabajo realizado en las tres organizaciones relacionado con la actividad de *diagnóstico de procesos*.

4.1 *Diagnóstico de procesos* en las organizaciones

Para poder llevar a cabo el *diagnóstico de procesos* en las tres organizaciones se realizó primero un trabajo previo que consistió en la *instalación del ciclo* de mejora en cada una de ellas, para lo cual se realizaron las siguientes tareas:

- Despegue del ciclo de mejora, con la cual se recopiló información de las empresas y se firmó por parte de su alta gerencia y el asesor de COMPETISOFT un compromiso de las partes para la ejecución del ciclo de mejora.
- Creación de la *Propuesta de Mejora*. Para las tres organizaciones se estableció como alcance del ciclo de mejora los *Procesos de Administración de un Proyecto Específico –APE– y Desarrollo de Software –DS–* del modelo de referencia de procesos de COMPETISOFT, y se estableció como meta cuantitativa incrementar en uno el nivel de capacidad de estos procesos. Se asignaron los recursos necesarios y la planificación para llevar a cabo el ciclo de mejora, definiendo para cada una de las organizaciones el proyecto piloto con el cual se va a trabajar.
- Socialización del ciclo de mejora, con el cual el asesor compartió el trabajo que se va a realizar y se realimentó con las expectativas que tienen los empleados.
- La Tabla 3 muestra la medición del esfuerzo implicado para realizar esta actividad.

Tabla 3. Esfuerzo de llevar a cabo la *instalación del ciclo* de mejora

	PeqEmpUno	***PeqOrgDos***	***MedOrgTres***	***Total***
COMPETISOFT	1 Ps. por 245 min	1 Ps. por 525 min	1 Ps. por 410 min	*1Ps. por 1180 min*
Organización	1 Ps. por 240 min	1 Ps. por 240 min	1 Ps. por 330 min	*1Ps. por 810 min*
Total	*1 Ps. por 485 min*	*1 Ps. por 765 min*	*1 Ps. por 740 min*	

Para conducir el *diagnóstico de procesos* en cada organización se utilizó el proceso de valoración PvalCOMPETISOFT, cuya aplicación se describe a continuación:

Planificación de la valoración. Para realizar la planificación se tuvo en cuenta como producto de trabajo de entrada la *Propuesta de mejora* creada y aprobada por las organizaciones en la *instalación del ciclo* de mejora. Se asignó el responsable de cada uno de los roles involucrados en la valoración. El objetivo fue determinar de manera general el estado actual de los procesos de la organización con respecto al nivel de 2 de capacidades del modelo Light MECPDS. El alcance de la valoración para el primer ciclo de mejora fue conocer el estado de los procesos DS y APE de un proyecto específico de la organización. El asesor de COMPETISOFT creó un instrumento para la recolección de información basado en las practicas base de los procesos a valorar (DS y APE) y en los atributos de proceso de los niveles de capacidad 1 y 2 del modelo Light MECPDS. Se describió y planeó cada una de las 5 actividades a realizar asignando el rol responsable y los roles participantes, así como los recursos y el tiempo estimado para llevar a cabo esta actividad. Dentro de la asignación de roles, el rol de *Evaluador* es desempeñado por el asesor del Proyecto COMPETISOFT.

Ejecución de la valoración. Cada una de las organizaciones se visitó por un periodo de dos días para realizar la valoración inicial de los procesos escogidos. Para valorar estos procesos se aplicaron las técnicas de recolección de evidencias: entrevista y encuesta, siguiendo el instrumento de recolección de información creado para tal fin.

Debido que la *PeqEmpUno* y en la *PeqOrgDos* no tenían documentación sobre sus procesos se realizó una reunión con una persona responsable de los procesos a valorar para levantar el diagrama de actividades de estos procesos. También se realizó una reunión en cada una de estas organizaciones con una persona participante del *Proceso de DS* con el fin de aplicar el instrumento de valoración. No se hizo una reunión con el responsable del *Proceso de APE* porque ambas organizaciones expresaron que no hacían ninguna actividad visible y formal relacionada con este proceso.

En la *MedOrgTres* la revisión de la documentación y la aplicación de los instrumentos de valoración de los *Proceso de DS y de APE* se realizó primero a dos personas responsables de calidad de la organización y luego se hizo la aplicación del instrumento de valoración del *Proceso de DS* a la persona responsable del departamento de desarrollo de la organización.

Generación de resultados. La información generada a partir de los datos obtenidos puede ser de diferente tipo con el fin de determinar el estado de los procesos de la organización. Por ejemplo, la Fig. 3 muestra el diagrama de actividades del *Proceso de DS* levantado de la *PeqEmpUno* a través de su valoración.

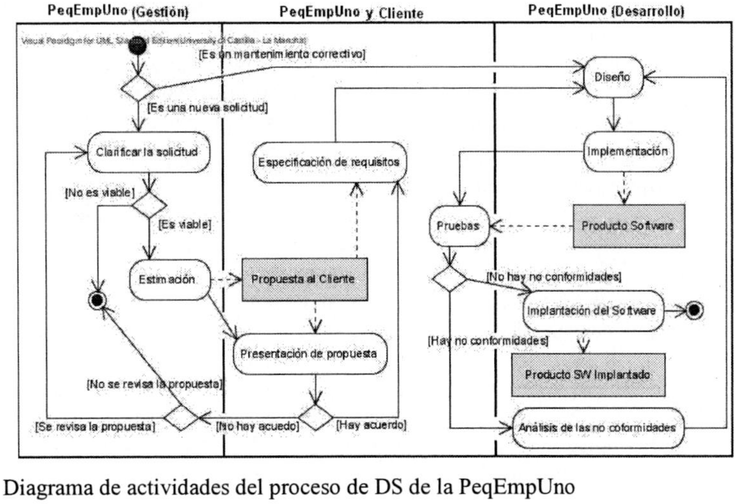

Fig. 3. Diagrama de actividades del proceso de DS de la PeqEmpUno

También se presenta información relacionada con las fortalezas de los procesos. Ejemplos de fortalezas encontradas en la *MedOrgTres* son entre otros: (i) Procesos claramente descritos por la documentación que tiene la organización debido a contar con un sistema de gestión de calidad ISO 9001, y (ii) Estabilidad del personal del área de desarrollo de software de la organización.

La información relacionada con la capacidad de los procesos se obtuvo después de analizar y sintetizar los datos de los *Procesos de DS y APE* con respecto a los atributos de procesos: AP1.1 Realización del proceso, AP2.1 Gestión de la realización y AP2.2 Gestión de productos de trabajo, definidos en Light MECPDS (ver Tabla 4).

Tabla 4. Capacidad de procesos de las organizaciones participantes en la valoración

Organización	**Proceso**	**Atributos de Proceso**			**Nivel de Capacidad**
		AP 1.1	**AP 2.1**	**AP 2.2**	
PeqEmpUno	*DS*	0.18 (**PI**)	0.04 (**NI**)	0.0 (**NI**)	**0 (Proceso Incompleto)**
	APE	0 (**NI**)	0 (**NI**)	0 (**NI**)	**0 (Proceso Incompleto)**
PeqOrgDos	*DS*	0.21 (**PI**)	0.10 (**NI**)	0.10 (**NI**)	**0 (Proceso Incompleto)**
	APE	0 (**NI**)	0 (**NI**)	0 (**NI**)	**0 (Proceso Incompleto)**
MedOrgTres	*DS*	0,87 (**CI**)	0,70 (**AI**)	0,72 (**AI**)	**2 (Proceso Gestionado)**
	APE	0,72 (**AI**)	0,80 (**AI**)	0,75 (**AI**)	**1 (Proceso Realizado)**

Analizando toda la información recogida se presentó las oportunidades de mejora de las organizaciones. Por ejemplo, para el *Proceso de DS* de la *MedOrgTres* se encontraron entre otras: (i) Establecer un repositorio de componentes (conjunto de unidades de código relacionadas que realizan una función), (ii) Realizar un registro de rastreo para garantizar la relación (trazabilidad) entre los requisitos, elementos de análisis y diseño, componentes y los planes de pruebas, y (iii) Describir un conjunto de elementos que faciliten la compresión y la realización de las modificaciones futuras (especificación de requisitos, manual de mantenimiento).

Priorización de procesos. Para este ciclo de mejora el Proyecto COMPETISOFT ha definido que los procesos a mejorar son los de su perfil 1, es decir los procesos DS y APE, por esta razón en las tres organizaciones sólo se ha valorado estos procesos. Sin embargo en relación con estos dos procesos las dos pequeñas organizaciones primero decidieron mejorar el *Proceso de DS*, y una vez lograron el nivel 1 de este proceso entonces pasaron a mejorar el proceso APE. La *MedOrgTres* en cambio se interesó primero por mejorar el proceso APE, con el fin de complementar las prácticas que le permita cumplir la meta de ejecutar un proyecto en el tiempo y con el costo previsto.

Planificación preliminar de mejoras. El asesor de COMPETISOFT y el *Responsable de mejora de procesos* crearon el *Plan preliminar de mejora* para aprovechar la sinergia de la valoración con el fin de iniciar la formulación y ejecución de las oportunidades de mejora de procesos encontradas. Se definió para cada una de las organizaciones el *Plan preliminar de mejora* en el cual se registró el número de iteraciones que conforman el ciclo de mejora, su orden de ejecución y la planificación general de las mismas. Se realizó la gestión proactiva de los riesgos críticos para la realización del ciclo de mejora, y se registró su manejo correspondiente. Se planeó la capacitación de las personas involucradas en el ciclo de mejora. Se definió que la medición básica de procesos se realizaría para dos entidades: (i) Los procesos a mejorar en la organización (basado en obtener su nivel de capacidad) y (ii) El proceso de mejora utilizado (midiendo el esfuerzo de realizar este proceso).

La Tabla 5 muestra la medición del esfuerzo implicado para realizar esta actividad.

Tabla 5. Esfuerzo de llevar a cabo el diagnostico de procesos a través de PvalCOMPETISOFT

	PeqEmpUno	*PeqOrgDos*	*MedOrgTres*	*Total*
COMPETISOFT	1 Ps. por 370 min	1 Ps. por 1140 m.	1 Ps. por 780 min	*1Ps. por 2290 min*
Organización	1 Ps. por 260 min	1 Ps. por 260 min	1 Ps. por 860 min	*1Ps. por 1380 min*
Total	*1 Ps. por 630 min*	*1 Ps. por 1400 m.*	*1 Ps. por 1640 m.*	

4.2 Discusión

En esta sección se resaltan los aspectos más relevantes en la aplicación del proceso de valoración PvalCOMPETISOFT en las tres organizaciones.

- De este primer ejercicio de aplicación del proceso de valoración PvalCOMPETISOFT se puede expresar que aunque fue desarrollado pensando en las pequeñas organizaciones, su aplicación satisfactoria en la *MedOrgTres* indica que también puede ser adecuado para medianas organizaciones.
- Para conducir las valoraciones de procesos en los primeros ciclos de mejora hay un acompañamiento del asesor de COMPETISOFT, el cual trabaja en estrecha relación con los *Responsables de mejora de procesos* (RMP) de cada una de las organizaciones con el fin de que estos adquieran la capacitación y experiencia necesaria y suficiente en valoración de procesos. Se pretende en los primeros ciclos de mejora que con PvalCOMPETISOFT se establezca la infraestructura básica de valoración de procesos que apoye la mejora y gestión de procesos software, con el fin de que funcionando permanentemente estos procesos en la organización soportados por su propio personal y que no dependan de un asesor externo.
- De las Tablas 3 y 5 se puede analizar que el esfuerzo del asesor de COMPETISOFT es mayor en la *PeqOrgDos*. Este esfuerzo mayor se debe a que en la *PeqOrgDos* fue donde primero se realizó la valoración. Es decir el análisis y síntesis de los datos para generar los resultados de la valoración se hizo primero para esta organización y luego para las otras dos, razón por la cual este esfuerzo adicional está relacionado con el aprendizaje y la experiencia adquirida por parte del asesor de las tareas y productos de trabajo que deben ser ejecutadas para la realización de estas actividades del proceso de valoración. En la Tabla 5 se observa que el esfuerzo de realizar el diagnóstico es superior en la *MedOrgTres* debido a que su mayor tamaño hizo más dispendiosa la *ejecución de la valoración* (la revisión de la documentación de sus procesos conllevo más tiempo y además habían más personas involucradas en la valoración).
- Las actividades se han desarrollado con un esfuerzo promedio para las pequeñas organizaciones de 17 horas, de las cuales 13 horas corresponden al asesor y 4 horas a la empresa, y para la mediana organización con un esfuerzo de 27 horas, de las cuales 13 horas corresponden al asesor y 14 horas a la empresa. Consideramos que el esfuerzo es apropiado para las características de cada una de las organizaciones involucradas en la valoración.
- La capacidad de los procesos reflejada por la valoración debe ser interpretada por las empresas para: (i) sensibilizarse de la forma como realizan el software y (ii) capturar oportunidades que les permita mejorar la forma como realizan software. Como se puede apreciar de la Tabla 4 el nivel de capacidad de los procesos

valorados en las dos organizaciones pequeñas es 0. Esto evidencia que no hay visibilidad de los procesos en este tipo de empresas, lo que hace que el desarrollo de software tenga una dependencia fuerte de las personas más que de los procesos.

– Las prácticas base implantadas mediante la aplicación de PvalCOMPETISOFT en las organizaciones están conforme con el 88% de las descritas por el proceso de valoración del estándar ISO/IEC 15504-5:2006 (PIM.2 Process Assessment). Los productos de trabajo de entrada y salida del proceso de valoración propuesto son los indicadores donde existe la evidencia de la realización de estas prácticas base.

5 Conclusiones y trabajo futuro

En este artículo se ha presentado un proceso para la valoración de procesos, el cual está integrado en un modelo para la implementación de mejora de procesos, que a su vez hace parte de un marco metodológico desarrollado específicamente para mejorar procesos en pequeñas organizaciones software. También se ha presentado su aplicación en tres organizaciones que actualmente llevan a cabo un proyecto SPI.

El proceso de valoración propuesto establece los elementos necesarios para guiar paso a paso la valoración de procesos enfocado en pequeñas organizaciones, y busca facilitar su aplicación de forma económica, con pocos recursos y en poco tiempo. De la aplicación inicial y teniendo en cuenta el esfuerzo involucrado en las tres organizaciones se observa que el proceso de valoración propuesto es adecuado para diagnosticar procesos en pequeñas y medianas empresas. Con la información generada por el proceso de valoración y a partir del *Plan preliminar de mejora* se condujo en las dos pequeñas organizaciones la formulación y ejecución de las oportunidades de mejora encontradas. Al final del ciclo de mejora se ejecutó de nuevo el proceso de valoración y se encontró que estas dos pequeñas organizaciones habían incrementado en uno el nivel de capacidad de sus *Procesos de DS y APE*.

Como trabajo futuro se hará el seguimiento a la utilización del proceso de valoración propuesto en los proyectos SPI llevados a cabo por parte de las empresas involucradas en COMPETISOFT. El objetivo es que a partir de un conjunto representativo de casos de estudio se obtenga la realimentación necesaria para proceder a la evaluación, refinamiento, mejora y validación del proceso propuesto.

Agradecimientos. Este trabajo ha sido parcialmente financiado por los proyectos: MECENAS (JCCM, Consejería de Educación y Ciencia, PBI06-0024) y COMPETISOFT (CYTED – 506PI0287).

Referencias

1. Anacleto, A., C.G.v. Wangenheim, C.F. Salviano, and R. Savi. *A Method for Process Assessment in Small Software Companies.* 2004. 4th International SPICE Conference on Process Assessment and Improvement (SPICE 04). Portugal. pp. 69-76.
2. Calvo-Manzano, J.A., G. Cuevas, T. San Feliu, A. De Amescua, and M. Pérez, *Experiences in the Application of Software Process Improvement in SMES.* Software Quality Journal, 2002. Vol. 10(3) November pp. 261-273.

3. Cater-Steel, A.P. *Low-rigour, Rapid Software Process Assessments for Small Software Development Firms.* 2004. Australian Software Engineering Conference (ASWEC'04). pp. 368-377.
4. ESI. *Europe Software Institute.* 2007. www.esi.es/en/main/iitmark.html
5. Fayad, M.E., M. Laitinen, and R.P. Ward, *Software Engineering in the Small.* Communications of the ACM, 2000. Vol. 43(3) March pp. 115-118.
6. ISO_WG_24. *ISO/IEC JTC1/SC7 Working Group 24.* 2006. http://iso-iec-sc7wg24.gelog.etsmtl.ca/Webpage/iso-iec-sc7wg24_english.html
7. Mayer&Bunge. *Panorama de la Industria del Software en Latinoamérica.* Mayer & Bunge Informática LTDA. Brasil. 2004
8. McCaffery, F., I. Richardson, and G. Coleman. *Adept – A Software Process Appraisal Method for Small to Medium-sized Irish Software Development Organisations.* 2006. European Systems & Software Process Improvement and Innovation (EuroSPI 2006). Joensuu, Finland. pp. 7.12-7.21.
9. Oktaba, H. *Método de Evaluación de procesos para la industria de software - EvalProSoft - Versión 1.1, Marzo de 2004. NMX-I-006/(01 al 04)-NYCE-2004.* Organismo nacional de normalización y evaluación de la conformidad - NYCE. Ciudad de México. 2004
10. Oktaba, H. *Modelo de Procesos para la Industria de Software - MoproSoft - Versión 1.3, Agosto de 2005. NMX-059/01-NYCE-2005.* Organismo nacional de normalización y evaluación de la conformidad - NYCE. Ciudad de México. 2005
11. Oktaba, H., F. Garcia, M. Piattini, F. Pino, C. Alquicira, and F. Ruiz, *Software Process Improvement: The COMPETISOFT Project.* IEEE Computer, 2007. Vol. 40(10) October pp. 21-28.
12. Paulk, M.C. *Using the Software CMM in Small Organizations.* 1998. Proc. Joint 16th Pacific Northwest Software Quality Conf. and 8th Int'l Conf. Software Quality. 350-360.
13. Pino, F., F. Garcia, and M. Piattini, *Herramienta de soporte a la valoración rápida de procesos software.* IEEE Latin America Transactions, 2007. Vol. 5(4) Julio pp. 218-223.
14. Pino, F., F. Garcia, and M. Piattini. *Priorización de procesos como apoyo a la mejora de procesos en pequeñas organizaciones software.* 2007. XXXIII Conferencia Latinoamericana de Informática, CLEI 2007. pp. 77.
15. Pino, F., F. Garcia, F. Ruiz, and M. Piattini. *A Lightweight Model for the Assessment of Software Processes.* 2006. European Systems & Software Process Improvement and Innovation (EuroSPI 2006). Joensuu, Finland. pp. 7.1-7.12.
16. Pino, F., F. Garcia, M. Serrano, and M. Piattini. *Estimating the Performance and Capacity of Software Processes according to ISO/IEC 15504.* 2006. Proceedings of the International Conference on Software Process and Product Masurement - Mensura 2006. Cádiz, Spain. pp. 171-180.
17. Pino, F., J. Vidal, F. Garcia, and M. Piattini. *Modelo para la Implementación de Mejora de Procesos en Pequeñas Organizaciones Software.* 2007. XII Jornadas de Ingeniería del Software y Bases de Datos, JISBD'2007. pp. 326-335.
18. Richardson, I., *Software process matrix: a small company SPI model.* Software Process: Improvement and Practice, 2001. Vol. 6(3) September pp. 157-165.
19. Saiedian, H. and N. Carr *Characterizing a software process maturity model for small organizations.* ACM SIGICE Bulletin, 1997. Vol. 23(1) July pp. 2-11.
20. Scott, L., R. Jeffery, L. Carvalho, J. D'Ambra, and P. Rutherford. *Practical Software Process Improvement -The IMPACT Project.* 2001. Proceedings of the Australian Software Engineering Conference. pp. 182-189.
21. SEI. *Improving Processes in Small Settings (IPSS Project).* 2006. http://www.sei.cmu.edu/iprc/ipssbackground.html
22. Weber, K., E. Araújo, A. Rocha, Machado, D. Scalet, and C. Salviano, *Brazilian Software Process Reference Model and Assessment Method*, in *Computer and Information Sciences.* 2005, Springer Berlin / Heidelberg. p. 402-411.

ASREF: An Adaptive Service Requirements Elicitation Framework Based on Goal-Oriented Modelling

Wei Qiao Lin Liu Jian Xiang

Knowware Group, School of Software, Tsinghua University, Beijing, China 100084
{qiaow05, xiangj05}@mails.tsinghua.edu.cn, linliu@tsinghua.edu.cn

Abstract: This paper formulates the service-oriented requirements analysis process as a feedback control system, in which the classical "once for all" philosophy is replaced with a continuous negotiation and adaptation process. Based on existing requirements model and new service request, the proposed service requirements elicitation framework ASREF aims to achieve an optimal service supply and demand relationship. Current control variable is the similarity of the service requirements model and the service capability model. Major contributions include: a dynamic questionnaires system for service requirements elicitation, the construction process of goal-oriented service models based on user's answers to the elicitation questions and the dual feedback control mechanism to service requestor and provider. A virtual travel agency example is used to illustrate the proposed ideas.

Keywords: Services, Requirement Engineering, Dynamic Questionnaire, Feedback

1 Introduction

Service orientation is becoming a leading form of web-based software applications, a common feature of which is the need to understand and characterize what the customer wants and to compose services to meet those requirements effectively. While many techniques of conventional requirements elicitation could potentially be applied to services, the open dynamic nature of service orientation introduces new challenges. Comparing with the conventional requirements engineering, in which the elicitation process usually takes a "face-to-face" mode, the case of services has to take a "back-to-back" mode. In the former case, requirements engineers obtain original requirements information from the targeted customers directly using methods such as interviews and task analyses. In opposite, the later means that services requestors and services providers have to conduct a double blind search during the requirements elicitation process due to the fact that they have seldom chance to interact face to face in advance of the development of services or the formation of business agreements.

Developing a new methodology to assure the quality of requirements elicitation in the "back-to-back" mode is a critical task of requirements engineers in the services era. The success of services as a business and computational paradigm depends on how well the two sides understand requirements and constraints of each other. Ill-defined and misrepresented requirements of services may lead to unbalanced service-level agreement, or no agreement can be formed in the worst case. Thus, Requirements engineering for services plays a definitive role in service engineering. In order to achieve efficient service design, publication, discovery, binding and evolution, requirements facilities to handle these service requirements issues automatically and systematically is needed. It is even more preferable if the service manipulation framework can be adaptive to the evolving requirements of users, and incrementally obtain new service capabilities according to the changing needs.

Thus, the essential questions regarding the elicitation process should include: How a prospective service provider can map its core competence into a maximum set of users requirements? Where and how can we acquire and accumulate valuable service requirements knowledge? Is it from existing published service profiles, from Service-Level Agreements, or from logs of user queries? Unfortunately, there is no systematic approach in requirements engineering or service engineering that can address these issues yet. We need a mechanism to guide the service providers through the process of transforming legacy systems into easily reusable and adaptable services according to user's real needs, which should lead into a win-win situation in the service-oriented world.

Based on our previous work on a service modelling ontology [7] and service requirements elicitation mechanism, *SREM* [21], this paper further elaborates and enhances the ideas by formulating the service-oriented requirements analysis process as a feedback control framework *ASREF*. Thus, the classical "once for all" elicitation philosophy is replaced with a continuous negotiation and adaptation process. Based on the existing goal-oriented service requirements model and new service requests, the proposed service requirements elicitation framework *ASREF* dynamically issues elicitation questions to help form an optimal service supply and demand relationship. Current control variable is the similarity of the service requirements model and the service capability model.

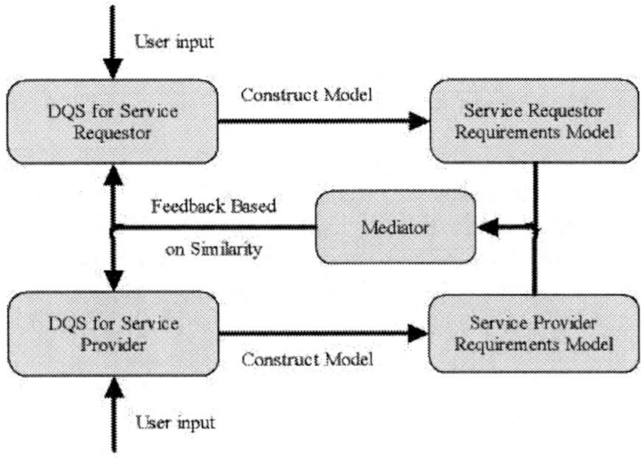

Fig. 1. ASREF Architecture

As shown in **Fig. 1**, *ASREF* is an iterative process. First, rough requirements statements are extracted by a Dynamic Questionnaire System (*DQS*) residing on either service requestors or service providers' site. Then the requirements models, which are based on the Service Requirements

Ontology (*SRMO*), are constructed using a "Natural Language Processing (NLP) based approach. Naturally, there are gaps between the two models constructed separately from the two sides due to their different intentions and starting points. From service providers' view, they have to meet users' needs by adjusting their own model and capability. On the other hand, the requestors' model should be refined to remove the inconsistency, misrepresentation, incompleteness and especially over or under constraints. As a result, a dual adjustment is conducted to bridge the gap between the two models. It is necessary to have a quantitative measurement to evaluate how well the two sides match with each other. When the similarity value reaches a preset threshold, the iteration could be terminated. Otherwise the feedback is provided to the *DQS*, which generates new questions based on it.

DQS includes a set of questions which can be organized into a dynamic questionnaire. The questionnaire based technique is adopted because the face-to-face communication between the requirement engineers and the users is impossible. From answers to this questionnaire, a graphical requirements model describing key elements and structure of each service requirements can be built. This model is based on the Service Requirements Ontology (*SRMO*), which inherits some basic concepts from the agent-oriented requirements modeling framework *i**. Besides requirements modeling, *ASREF* includes a mechanism for improving the quality of models iteratively based on a set of heuristic rules.

The structure of the paper is arranged as the following: Section 2 introduces the goal-oriented ontology for service requirements elicitation *SRMO*, the dynamic questionnaire system *DQS* and how requirements models are built from *DQS* using NLP techniques. Section 3 describes in detail the elicitation mechanism, including the satisfaction measurement of two models, and the feedback system. Section 4 introduces experiments and an example application of *SREM*. Section 5 discusses related work. Section 6 concludes the paper.

2 Services Requirements Model Construction

2.1 Service Requirements Modeling Ontology (SRMO)

Ontology-based approach is widely used to solve problems that require common knowledge and understanding. Concepts, relationships and their categorizations in an ontology can be used as a source of shared knowledge in a specific application domain. Using ontology based approaches, many existing semantic processing techniques can be employed in requirements analysis without getting into rigorous NLP techniques. *SRMO* defines the ontology for service requirements modeling based on concepts of goals and actors, which inherits its key modeling concepts from *i**, and extend it with the concepts of provider actor, requestor actor and services. Providers have capable services, while requestors have required services. Every actor in the service network is motivated to get their required service served [7].

Figure 2 shows the concepts in the proposed service requirements ontology. It models services at a higher level of abstraction than current service ontology such as, *OWL-S*, which focuses more on service design details not accessible to general end-users. The level of abstraction adopted by the proposed mechanism aims to achieve more precise profiling of service requirements. At the same time, *SRMO* are designed to be easily mapped to *OWL-S* description when necessary. Individual service requests can be easily collected and crystallized as requirements knowledge.

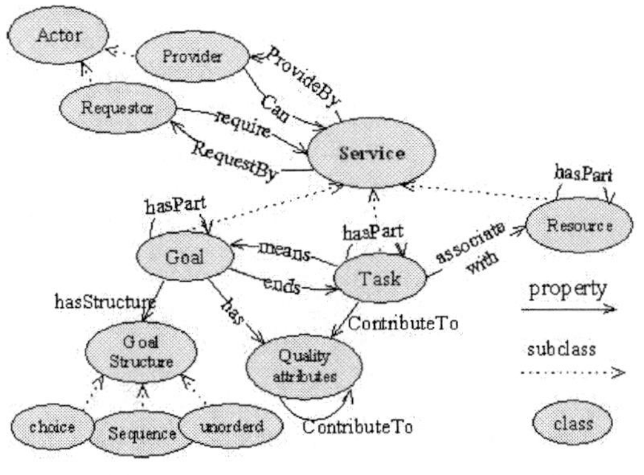

Fig. 2. Service Requirements Modeling Ontology

2.2 Dynamic Questionnaire System

A series of questions and answer schemas are presented to formulate the rough sketch of requirements model. The questions can be organized to 5W2H style [22], that is Who, What, Why, When, Where, How and How well. According their functions, the 5W2H questions can be categorized into 5 series as in table 1:

Table 1. Questions Catalog

Series	Type	Purpose	Sample Questions
S1	Who	Identify actors	Who is involved in the service?
S2	What	Identify goals	What is your goal?
		Identify tasks	What task do you want to perform?
S3	Why	Refine goals upstream	Why is this goal needed?
	How	Refine goals downstream	How can this goal be broken down? How can this goal be achieved?
S4	Why	Refine tasks upstream	Why is this task needed?
	How	Refine tasks downstream	How can this task be decomposed?
S5	How well, When, Where	Identify and refine Quality Attributes	How well do you need this quality attribute to be? Which task influence this quality? Is this quality influence another quality? When and Where do you want the task to be performed?

Series1: This series includes all questions regarding actors. E.g., "Who is involved in the service?" is used to identify actors. "Who is the best one to satisfy your needs?" is used to pick up the user preferred service provider. Answers to these questions can be modeled as *Actors*: 

Series2: This series includes all questions to identify model elements. Answer to "What is your primary goal?" could be a *goal* (

), which state a condition to be satisfied with the help of the service; answer to "What action do you want to perform?" could be a *task* (

), which specify a procedure of actions to be performed during the service execution; answer to "What resource do you need?" could be a *resource* (

), which is made available by the service.
Series3: Questions in this series are used to refine *goals*. The WHY questions, e.g. "why is this goal needed?" can be used to explore the goal tree upstream, finding out the fundamental intentions of the requestor. On the other hand, the HOW questions can be used to explore goal tree downstream. The question "How can the goal be broken down" decomposes the goal into sub-goals, which is modeled as the following:

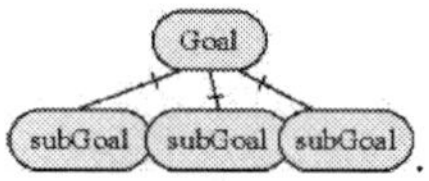

Answers to "How can the state of the *Goal* are achieved?" identify the task achieving a goal. It adds a means-ends link between *Goal* and *task*, *task* is a means for achieving *Goal*, while *Goal* being the end of performing the *task*. We may have various *tasks* for one *Goal*; each *task* stands for one alternative way of achieving this *Goal*. The answers can be modeled as:

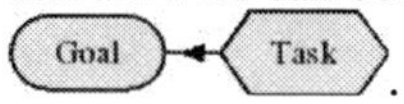

Series4: Similar to series3, series4 also includes WHY and HOW questions, but they are used to refine tasks. WHY questions, such as "Why is this task needed?" are used to find high-level tasks or goals, while the HOW questions, for example "How can this task be decomposed?", decompose task into sub-tasks, which can be modeled as following:

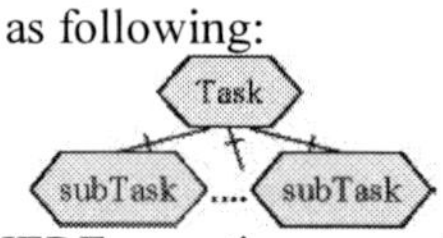

Series5: HOW WELL, WHEN, WHERE questions are all fallen into series5. They can elicit requirements on *Quality Attributes,* which are the decision-making rules for evaluating its quality. Answers to HOW WELL questions can be modeled as:

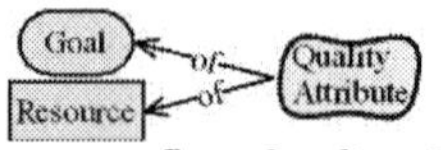

This series also includes other questions to refine *Quality*. For example, how does a specific *task* influence quality of service? How does one quality attribute influence another quality attribute? Answers to these questions can be modeled as follows:

In addition, WHEN/ WHERE questions also contribute to enrich the *Quality Attributes* we extract.

These questions help us collect requirement fragments from requestors and providers. Figure 2 shows an example integrated view for a requirement model constructed from all question answers.

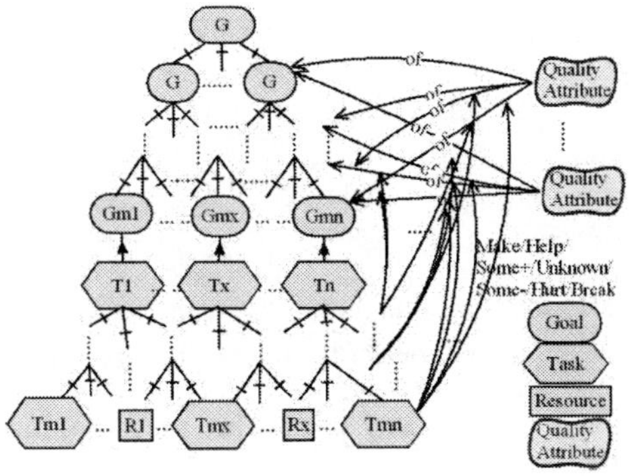

Figure.3. A Hierarchical Requirement Model in SRMO

3 Iteration of Service Requirements Elicitation

This section introduces the iteration process to make the requirements we gathered evolved. As a mediator, *ASREF* supports following functions: first, it extracts requirements fragments iteratively from either requestors. Second, it accumulates these requirements to a knowledge repository of graphical goal-oriented models for service providers about the needs and preference of service requestors with regard to the their capable services. Third, it serves as a matchmaker for the two sides. Using knowledge provided by the repository, *ASREF* makes it possible for requestors to find out the services matching their needs as well as for providers to connect to their potential customers. Finally, *ASREF* improves the requirements quality iteratively using feedbacks of matching results. For example, it can elicit hidden requirements which requestors are not aware of, or suggests service providers to adapt their function or quality to fit into popular user needs.

3.1 Satisfaction Measurement

Being a match maker for the two sides, *ASREF* needs a satisfaction measurement. Because the requirements models are based on ontologies, the matching process is an ontology similarity calculation process in nature [25].

In order to get the overall similarity, it is necessary to calculate each element's *MatchScore* separately, including goals, tasks and resources. The *MatchScore* has major two considerations: functional similarity and non-functional similarity. The non-functional similarity *simSG* is captured by following formula,

$$simSG(s,t) = \frac{1}{m}\sum_{i=1}^{m}\frac{Min[Q_i(s),Q_i(t)]}{Max[Q_i(s),Q_i(t)]} \,. \tag{1}$$

Where s and t are elements being compared; $Q_i(s)$ means value of the *ith* quality attribute of s; m is the maximal number of attributes the two elements have. *MatchScore* is calculated as follow:

$$MatchScore(s,t) = k^n * sim(s,t) * simSG(s,t) \,. \tag{2}$$

sim(s,t)=1 if existing *t* in service provider which is the same with *s* in service requestor, otherwise set the value to 0. k^n is a penalty factor which reflect the structure distance. k can be set to a fix number such as 0.9, and n is the level distance of s and t. Combination of $k^n * sim(s,t)$ captures the functional similarity of the two elements. Finally, the overall satisfaction degree can be calculated as follow:

$$satisfaction(S,T) = \frac{\sum_{i=1}^{\#Nodes(S)} MatchScore(S_i, T_i)}{\# Nodes(S)} \quad (3)$$

Where S and T are models of requestor and provider; *#Nodes(S)* returns the number of nodes in S. The calculate process will be explained in more detail with an example in section 4.

3.2 Reaction rules based on feedbacks

If the satisfaction degree cannot reach the threshold, the iteration will continue. Feedbacks are provided to the DQS, which generate new elicitation questions. In general, there are eight rules including the feedbacks and respective actions taken by DQS. The formal presentation of these rules is given by SWRL language in the OWL file [28].

Rule1: Provider model needs refinement.

Feedback: Certain goals or tasks of service provider are so general that the requestor's model is difficult to match them. Suppose there are model fragments as follows:

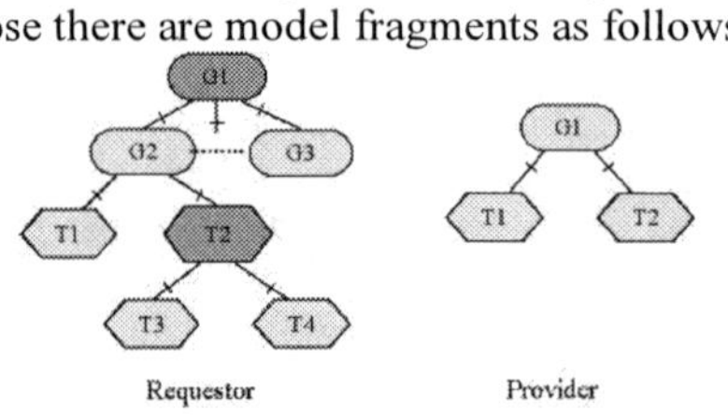

Fig. 4. A provider model needs refinement

It is obvious that the G1 and T2 of provider have not been decomposed enough, so we provide this information to DQS of providers.

Action: With this feedback, DQS should raise more HOW questions for service provider to break down the coarse goals and tasks so that the requestor's model is matched better.

Rule2: Requestor model needs refinement.

Feedback: Contrary to previous class, it is the requestor instead of provider who includes high-level goals or tasks. As shown in the following figure Fig. 5, G1 and T2 of requestor have not been decomposed completely.

Action: DQS should raise more HOW questions for service requestor to break down the particular goals and tasks.

Rule3: Laddering Provider's model.

Feedback: In certain situation, service providers didn't realize that their functional capability can achieve a higher level goal. As shown in following figure, the provider considers that it can only satisfy the goal G2 in the beginning. But after the requestor shows a fact that satisfaction of G2 can lead to the satisfaction of G1, the provider knows he can raise the level of goal G2 to G1. Such information can be provided to DQS of service providers.

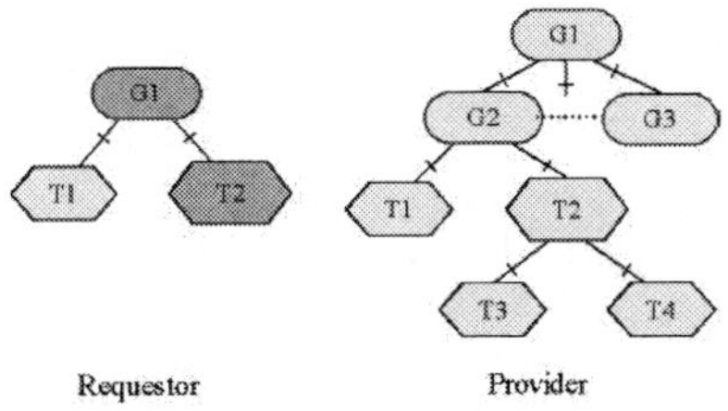

Fig.5. A requestor model needs refinement

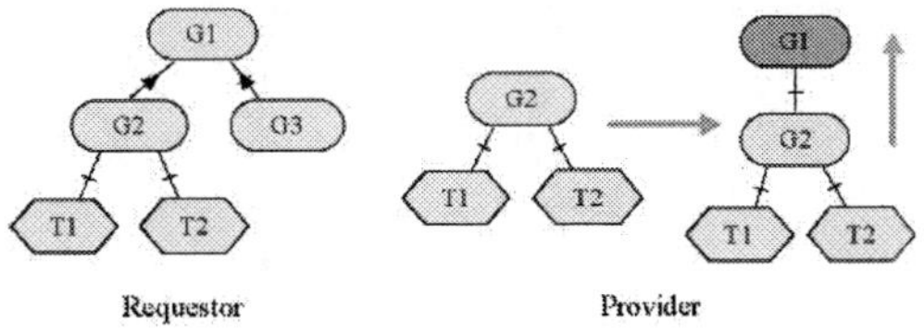

Fig. 6. Low Level of Provider's Goal

Action: More WHY questions should be asked to provider so that exploring the provider's goal tree upstream. By doing this, a service provider can map its core competence into a maximum set of users requirements that can be satisfied by it.

Rule4: Seeking Alternatives.

Feedback: When some functional requirements, modeled as task sub-trees, are not satisfied by provider, it is reasonable to find an alternative option. If a goal of provider is linked by some tasks through means-end relationship, these tasks are replaceable. We can offer this information to improve the satisfaction degree.

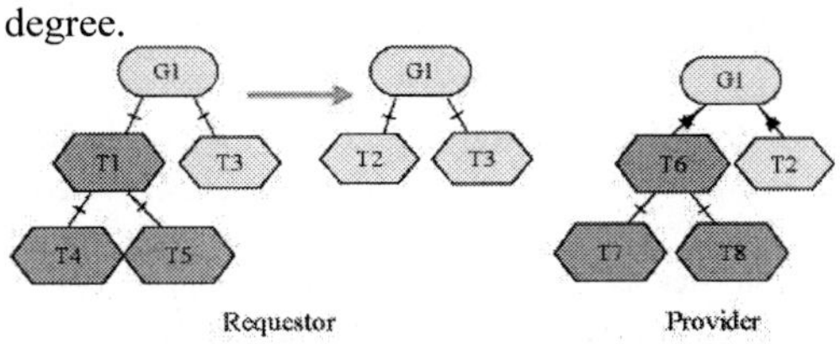

Fig. 7. Alternative Option

Action: DQS asks the requestor whether or not he want to replace the task with another equivalent one. This action increases opportunities of matching the two sides.

Rule5: Adding New Services.

Feedback: If there is no alterative option to choose, and the actions introduced in class 1-4 does not work, we should inform DQS the result.

Action: Suggest the provider to add new services to meet user's requirements, if it is needed. We can measure the worthiness of implementing that service by utilizing the knowledge accumulated, which indicates how often that function is requested.

Rule6: Outsourcing Services.

Feedback: Same as above.

Action: Within a service network, it is possible to use abundant outside services. DQS can advise the provider to extend its competence by using outsourced services while keeping transparent to end users. This would extremely improve the matching ratio.

Rule7: Quality Conflict Resolution

Feedback: *Quality Attributes* have extremely important impact on matching results. It is common that one task has different types of contribution to the same quality attribute in diverse perspective. As illustrated in following figure, task T1 *helps* the quality attribute of G1 in requestor's view as well as *hurts* it in provider's view. This conflict of quality attributes will be reported to DQS.

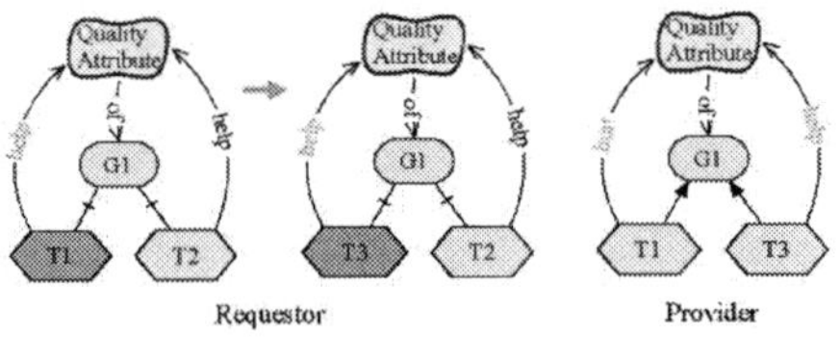

Fig.8. Quality Conflict

Action: Similar with rule 4, DQS suggests that the requestor replace the task with an alternative that helps the quality attribute, say, T3 in this example.

Rule8: Quality negotiation and tradeoff

Feedback: If the quality attributes requested are too difficult to fulfill by provided services, we should take actions to make a trade-off.

Action: DQS should either suggest the requestors to reduce the unnecessary quality requirements, or advise the providers to increase the quality degree they offered.

4 Example Case Study

The proposed approach is applied to a widely referenced example in the domain of e-Tourism, which was originally built as a use case of the *WSMO* project [26]. There is an online travel agency, WorldStar, providing various e-Tourism services to customers, such as booking of flights, hotels, rental cars, etc. Mr. Joe, a customer living in Beijing, wants to enjoy his 10 days vacation in Paris. In order to save time, he decides to employ an online travel agency to deal with travel issues for him. But Joe has not taken an international travel before, so he doesn't know how to express his requirements to travel agencies and which agent meets his needs the best. In this situation, our approach, *ASREF*, is applied to elicit Joe's requirements and build model based on it.

In order to elicit Joe's initial requirements, a set of basic questions are generated by the *DQS*. Due to limitation of space, we skip the step of raising questions, but starts building an initial requirements model from the answers to these questions as in Fig. 9.

Where the meanings of labels are:

G1: One-stop travel services are provided.
G2: Ticket to Paris is booked.
G3: Paris hotel is booked.
G4: Car is rented in Paris.
T1: Book flight ticket from Beijing to Paris.
T2: Book train ticket from Beijing to Paris.
T3: Search possible train connections.
T4: Select one train connection.

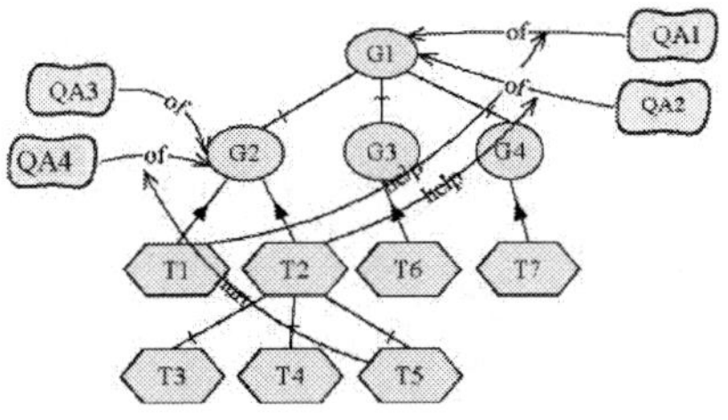

Fig. 9. Initial Model of Joe

T5: Get the ticket.
T6: Book hotel room online.
T7: Rent a Benz car.
QA1: Convenience; **QA2:** Cost;
QA3: Security; **QA4:** Response time

On the other hand, models of travel agencies have been constructed using the same approach when they registered in. Take WorldStar as an example, the Constructed model is shown as follow:

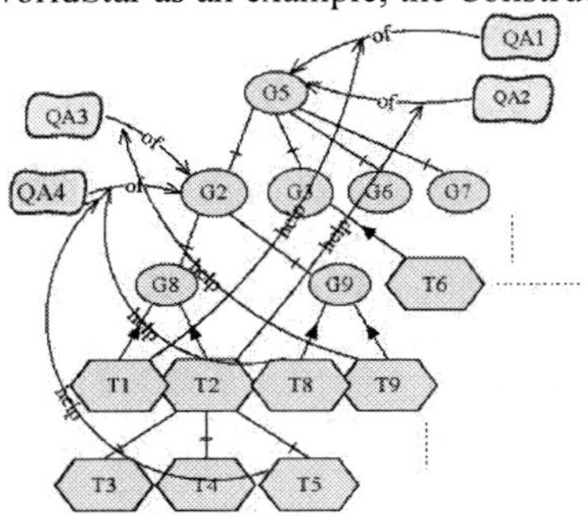

Fig. 10. Initial Model of WorldStar

Beside labels defined above, these labels are added:
G5: Benefits earned by providing travel services.
G6: Travel guide is provided.
G7: Meal plan is provided.
G8: Ticket is booked.
G9: Ticket is delivered.
T8: Deliver electronic ticket.
T9: Deliver physical ticket by express.
T10: Deliver physical ticket by priority express.

ASREF then compares Joe's initial model with all models of current registered travel agencies, and returns a ranking of agency with best matching ratio. To illustrate how to get the satisfaction degree, we calculate it between models of Joe and WorldStar. Suppose all *Quality Attributes* can be expressed by a number, for example, the security level Joe desired can be set to 0.8 as well as the value of WorldStar provided can be set to 1. In addition, the response time Joe desired is 15 minutes, but the WorldStar can only offer it in 30 minutes. Using formula 1 we can get: simSG(G2,G2')=1/2*(0.8/1 + 15/30)=0.65. The functional similarity of G2 can be get by $k^n sim$, where sim(G2,G2')=1 because matched goal G2' exists in WorldStar's model. The penalty factor k

is set to 0.9 and n is 0 because G2 and G2' is in the same level. *MatchScore* values of all the nodes in Joe's model are calculated as the following table.

Table 2. Matching Ratio Calculate Process

Nodes	***Match Score***	***simSG***	***$k^n sim$***
G1	0	N/A	0
G2	0.65	0.65	1
G3	1	1	1
G4	0	N/A	0
T1	0.9	1	0.9
T2	0.9	1	0.9
T3	1	1	1
T4	1	1	1
T5	1	1	1
T6	1	1	1
T7	0	N/A	0

According to formula 3, the overall satisfaction degree is (0.65+1+0.9+0.9+1+1+1+1)/11=0.677. If we set the threshold to 0.92, the iteration continues.

We can find the node with low *MatchScore* in Table 2 to locate the problem. Then the heuristic rules mentioned in section 3.2 could be applied to adjust the two models step by step.

Iteration 1: We noticed that *MatchScores* of nodes T1 and T2 in Joe's model are all 0.9 because the value of n is 1 in $k^n sim$. It can be easily understood: T1 and T2 are direct children of G2 in Joe's model, but they are grandchildren of G2 in WorldStar's model. So there is 1 level distance between them. The level distance is caused by G8, which isn't in Joe's model, which means G2 has not been decomposed completely. In this situation, we apply Rule2 to refine the service requestor's goal. After received this feedback, *DQS* raises more *HOW*-type questions to break down G2, such as: "In order to get the ticket, what other goals should be achieved?", "Shouldn't the ticket be delivered?" etc. By answering such questions, Joe realizes that he ignored the delivery step. Then our *ASREF* help append G8 and G9 in his model. Due to limitation of space, we skip the process of calculating satisfaction degree at the end of this iteration, and give the value, 0.72, directly. Although the satisfaction degree is improved, it still doesn't reach the threshold. So the next iteration begins.

Iteration2: Because the new goal G9 is added, it's necessary to apply Rule2 again to elicit its means. Suppose question "In which way do you prefer to receive your ticket?" is asked, and the answer is "By priority express". Thus T10 is attached as a means of G9. After such an adjustment, the satisfaction degree is still lower than expected, so the iteration continues.

Iteration3: In the process of re-calculating satisfaction degree, we find that *MatchScore* of T10 just added is zero because there is no corresponding task provided by WorldStar. Joe wants to get the ticket by priority express, but WorldStar only provides delivery services either by normal express or by sending electronic tickets in an email. In order to conduct agreement, Rule4 is applied to recommend Joe to pick up another choice. *DQS* asks "For your requested delivery method is not available, why not try to use an electronic ticket?" If Joe answers "yes", then the T10 in his requirements model is replaced by T8. Again, the process continues.

Iteration4: Improvement of models takes place on both the customer side and the service provider side. In this step, we find *MatchScore* of G4 is zero. It is also because there is no corresponding node in WorldStar's model. Joe wants to rent a car when he arrives at Paris, but WorldStar has not realized this customer's requirement. Thus both Rule5 and Rule6 can be applied. That means *DQS* can either suggest WorldStar to develop a new car renting service, or outsource this service to a third-party partner. Once such actions are executed, G4 can be attached as a child node of G5 in WorldStar's model. Again, the process continues.

Iteration5: Another node with zero valued *MatchScore* is G1, which can't find any matched goal in WorldStar's model. Joe desires a one-stop travel services, including ticket service, hotel booking service, car renting service, etc. At the beginning, WorldStar didn't offer the car renting service, so it can't be called as "one stop travel services". Thus, G1 is not contained in WorldStar's model. After G4 was added in iteration 4, WorldStar has the capability to provide so called "one stop travel services", so G1 is achievable. The raising of goal level to G1 is based on the Rule4.

Iteration6: According to Table2, G2 got a low *MatchScore* because of the mismatch of its *Quality Attributes*, especially the QA4, response time. Joe requests the ticket should be booked in 15 minutes, but WorldStar only promises to response in 30 minutes. Here Rule8 should be applied to have a negotiation. Depending on different cases, *DQS* either recommends Joe to increase the response time or suggests WorldStar to reduce it. Suppose Joe re-sets this value to 20 and WorldStar changes it to 25, then the result would be quite impressive. The overall satisfaction degree reaches 0.973, which has reached the threshold, so the iteration can be terminated.

Above example demonstrated an example execution scenario for the proposed service requirements elicitation process, including how to generate questionnaire, how to construct requirement models and how to improve these models based on rules step by step.

5 Related Work

Requirements elicitation has focused primarily on developing, implementing, and evaluating various techniques, methods, and tools. Many of these were adopted from other research areas such as the social sciences [2, 4] and knowledge engineering [9, 11]. These approaches reduced the complexity of the elicitation process and improved the quality of the requirements. In fact, there are more than one hundred approaches used for requirements elicitation. [5] has examined a few number of the traditional techniques such as interviewing, observation, and task analysis at a relatively high level. In a more recent survey on the theory and practice of requirements elicitation [4], more approaches were examined including those based on goals [3], scenarios [10], viewpoints [11], and domain knowledge [12].

Our approach can be considered as a natural migration of the goal-oriented requirements elicitation approach into services-oriented computing. In the service-oriented requirements engineering, the elicitation process has to be conducted within the service life-cycle, with assistance of web-based tools. Due to specific requirements of the services context, a questionnaire technique [18] is employed. Satisfaction measurement actually is the semantic similarity of ontologies [20]. Finally, we presented a set of adjust rules to improve the quality of models. Service requirement negotiation [14] servers the same purpose.

There is an early day homonymous requirement methodology *SREM*[1] for large embedded computer systems, descriptions of real world objects, data requirements and message processing. There are also other slightly related works such as [2] which targets at similar problems on collecting users' preferences in order to guide service composition. It suggests user to present a service request with an external e-Service schema of a finite state machine. We consider such work as targeting as similar problem using different conceptual mindsets and treatments.

6 Conclusion

In summary, this paper propose a service-oriented requirements analysis framework ASREF, which turns the classical "once for all" philosophy into a continuous negotiation and adaptation process. Based on existing requirements model and new service request, ASREF aims to achieve an optimal service supply and demand relationship based on dual feedback loop. Current control variable is the similarity of the service requirements model and the service capability model. Major technical contributions include: a dynamic questionnaires system for service requirements elicitation, the construction process of goal-oriented service models based on user's answers to the elicitation questions and the dual feedback control mechanism to service requestor and provider. A virtual travel agency example is used to illustrate the proposed ideas.

In the future, the ASREF service requirements elicitation framework will be integrated with an actual service execution platform SAFARY[27], so that the proposed techniques can be evaluated and improved. The goal-oriented service modelling ontology SRMO will be used in combination with existing service ontologies such OWL and WSMO, so we need to look deeper into extension and integration mechanism of service ontologies.

Acknowledgement

Partial financial support from NSF China (no.60503030), National High Tech. 863 Program (no.2006AA01Z155), National Basic Research and Development 973 Program (no.2002CB312004), and Basic Research Foundation of Tsinghua National Laboratory for Information Science and Technology (TNList) is gratefully acknowledged.

Reference:

1. Alford M.W., Software Requirements Engineering Methodology (SREM) at the Age of Two, COMPSAC78. Proceedings: 332-339, 1978.
2. Berardi D., Calvanese D. etc, Automatic composition of e-services that export their behavior, Proc. Of 1st International Conference on Service Oriented Computing, 2003, pp. 43-58.
3. Dardeene A., van Lamsweerde A., Fickas S., Goal-Directed Requirements Acquisition. Science of Computer Programming 20(1-2): 3-50, 1993
4. Zowghi D., Coulin C., Requirements Elicitation: A Survey of Techniques, Approaches, and Tools. In Engineering and Managing Software Requirements, Springer: US, 2005.
5. Goguen J.A., Linde C., Techniques for Requirements Elicitation. International Symposium on Requirements Engineering, 152-164, January 4-6, San Diego, CA, 1993.
6. Hudlicka E., Requirements Elicitation with Indirect Knowledge Elicitation Techniques: Comparison of Three Methods. International Conference on Requirements Engineering, 4-11, April 15-18, Colorado Springs, CO. 1996.
7. Liu L., Chi C., Jin Z., Yu E., Strategic Capability Modelling of Services. The second Workshop of Service-Oriented Computing Consequences and Experience of Requirements, SOCCER 2006, Paris, France.
8. Maiden N.A.M., Rugg G., Knowledge Acquisition Techniques for Requirements Engineering.

Requirements Elicitation for Systems Specification, July 12-14, Keele, UK, 1994.
9. Munindar P. Singh, Michael N. Huhns. Service-Oriented Computing: Semantics, Processes, Agents. Wiley, London, UK, 2005
10. Potts C., Takahashi K. etc, Inquiry-Based Requirements Analysis. IEEE Software: 21-32, 1994
11. Sommerville I., Sawyer P., Viller S., Viewpoints for Requirements Elicitation: A Practical Approach. International Conference on Requirements Engineering, 74-81, April 6-10, Colorado Springs, CO, 1998.
12. Sutcliffe A, Maiden N., The Domain Theory for Requirements Engineering. IEEE Transactions on Software Engineering 24(3): 174-196, 1998.
13. Breitman, K. K. and J. C. S. do Prado Leite., Ontology as a requirements engineering product. Requirements Engineering Conference, 2003. Proceedings. 11th IEEE International: 309-319.
14. Briggs, R. O. and P. Gruenbacher., EasyWinWin: managing complexity in requirements negotiation with GSS. Proceedings of the 35th Annual Hawaii International Conference on System Sciences: 10, 2002.
15. In, H. P., D. Olson, et al., Multi-criteria preference analysis for systematic requirements negotiation. COMPSAC 2002: 887-892, 2002
16. Kaiya, H. and M. Saeki., Using Domain Ontology as Domain Knowledge for Requirements Elicitation, IEEE Computer Society Washington, DC, USA: 186-195, 2006.
17. Kof, L., Natural Language Processing: Mature Enough for Requirements Documents Analysis?, 10th Intl. Conf. on Applications of Natural Language to Information Systems: 15-17, 2005.
18. Moore, J. M. and F. M. Shipman Iii., A comparison of questionnaire-based and GUI-based requirementsgathering, The Fifteenth IEEE International Conference on Automated Software Engineering: 35-43, 2000.
19. van der Raadt, B., J. Gordijn, et al., Exploring Web Services from a Business Value Perspective, Requirements Engineering: 114-134, 2005.
20. Zhang, R., I. B. Arpinar, et al., Automatic Composition of Semantic Web Services. International Conference on Web Services, 2003.
21. Jian X, Lin L, Wei, Q, JingWei, Y., SREM: A Service Requirements Elicitation Mechanism based on Ontology. COMPSAC 2007, to appear.
22. Julio Cesar Sampaio do Prado Leite, Yijun Yu, Lin Liu, Eric S. K. Yu, John Mylopoulos: Quality-Based Software Reuse. CAiSE 2005: 535-550.
23. FernÃ¡ndez-LÃ³pez, etc: "Methontology: from ontological art towards ontological engineering". "Proc. Symposium on Ontological Engineering of AAAI". 1997.
24. Leite, J.C.S.P., Franco, A.P.M.v. A Strategy for Conceptual Model Acquisition. Proceedings of the First International Symposium on Requirements Engineering, IEEE Computer Society Press, pp. 243-246, (1993).
25. B. Aleman-Meza, C. Halaschek-Wiener, S. S. Sahoo, A. Sheth, I. Budak Arpinar. Template Based Semantic Similarity for Security. Applications Technical Report, LSDIS Lab, Computer Science Department, University of Gerogia, January 2005.
26. WSMO's use case (VTA): http://www.wsmo.org/2004/d3/d3.3/v0.1/.
27. J. Xiang, W. Qiao, Z.. Xiong, T. Jiang, L. Liu. SAFARY: A semantic web service implementation platform. In: Proceedings of APSEC-SOPOSE'06. Bangalore, India, December 9, 2006
28. ASREF OWL file: http://learn.tsinghua.edu.cn:8080/2005212713/ASREF.ow

Early Aspects Refactoring

Ricardo A. Ramos[1], Jaelson Castro[1], João Araújo[2], Ana Moreira[2], Fernanda Alencar[1] and Rosangela Penteado[3]

1 Centro de Informática - Universidade Federal de Pernambuco (UFPE)
{rar2, jbc}@cin.ufpe.br, frma@ufpe.br

2 Departamento de Informática, FCT, Universidade Nova de Lisboa (UNL)
{amm, ja}@di.fct.unl.pt

3 Universidade Federal de São Carlos (UFSCAR)
rosangel@dc.ufscar.br

Abstract. Typical problems of a requirements document, regarding its contents and organization, involve deficient modularization where requirements artifacts may deal with too much information, duplication of requirements, scattering requirements, tangled problems, among other problems. In this paper we describe how to improve requirements documents by removing duplication of information using aspect-oriented refactoring.

Keywords: Refactorings and Early Aspects.

1 Introduction

Several approaches are used to express the requirements of a software system and are extensively used in both academia and industry. These approaches describe the functionalities to be provided and the interactions between the users and the system. Requirements are structured and described using, for example, use cases, viewpoints, textual descriptions, activity diagrams or sequence diagrams [2].

Over the past years, we have observed that a set of typical issues seems to plague the requirements specifications, such as requirements that are abandoned and no longer relevant, descriptions that are unnecessarily long and complex, and information that is duplicated. Inspired in the code refactoring literature [9], we set off to identify a bad smell related to duplicated requirements that could indicate potential refactoring opportunities.

These bad smells decrease reuse, not only during implementation, but throughout the development process [1] and can be minimized by the identification of their symptoms and the removal of their causes. These symptoms may indicate potential problems with the software [2] and can be removed using appropriate refactoring transformations. The removal of these bad smells in the early stages of a software development process reduces the costs associated with software changes. This cost reductions could be three to six times bigger in later stages than during requirements activities [10].

Opdyke, in [9], initially coined the term refactoring as the process of improving the design of existing software using transformations, without changing its observable behaviour. The term is also used to refer to program restructuring operations aiming to support the design, evolution and reuse of object-oriented software. Refactorings express ideas of good style, which can have a significant impact on the maintainability and evolvability of code bases.

There are some tools for refactoring requirements documents [21] , [22], [16] but they focus on specific techniques, such as use case models and do not directly address textual descriptions or other mechanisms used to detail requirements. Moreover, these approaches do not provide any guidelines about how to identify the problems. As such, they say nothing about which refactoring can be used to address those issues.

In this paper we describe a generic approach to identify duplicated, tangled and scattered requirements as a refactoring opportunity in requirements descriptions, together with an associated early aspect refactoring. The approach can be instantiated with any of the existing requirements description techniques (e.g., use cases, viewpoints, goals). In this paper we will demonstrate our ideas using Multi-Dimensional Separation of Concerns [8] and use cases approaches. In summary, the main contributions of this paper are twofold:

i) The definition of the refactoring opportunity that helps to find duplicated, tangled and scattered requirements in requirements document. We describe (a) how to identify occurrences of these problems and (b) indicate how to use the refactoring that can to minimize the effects of the problem.

ii) The definition of the Extract Early Aspect refactoring. This refactoring contains the context that suggests the application of the refactoring, the type of solution provided by the refactoring, a motivation for the transformations, its mechanics (a set of well defined steps) and an example of a refactored description.

We are using early aspects for having had demonstrated a good alternative to deal with duplicated, tangled and scattered requirements. The Early Aspects [3] focuses on managing crosscutting properties at the early development stages of requirements engineering and architecture design using the aspect oriented paradigm [15].

This paper is structured as follows: Section 2 introduces the concept of refactoring opportunity. Section 3 presents the extract early aspect refactoring to manipulate requirement descriptions. Section 4 discusses related work. In Section 5, conclusions are discussed.

2. The Refactoring Opportunity

Fowler in [4] introduces bad smells as indications of deficiencies that can appear in existing software artifacts. The use of refactoring techniques might address the causes of these deficiencies. In this paper, we use the term refactoring opportunity to refer to the types of bad smells that can appear in requirements artifacts.

Refactoring opportunities should not be seen as exact rules to the automatic application of refactorings. The requirements engineer needs to decide about the interest in changing the requirements and needs to choose which refactoring is more adequate for each opportunity.

In this section, we describe the duplicated, tangled and scattered requirements refactoring opportunity as well as associated refactoring. A brief textual description and an explanation of "when" to use the refactoring that could help in the solution of the identified problem are provided. The Extract Early Aspect refactoring is described in more detail in section 3.

2.1. Duplicated Requirements

A duplicated requirement is a situation that occurs when (i) the same requirement is duplicated in different places in a requirements document or (ii) the same requirements or the same pre-post conditions appear in several requirements structures.

A requirement that appears in more than one place offers an opportunity for refactoring. In the simplest case, the requirement is duplicated in one requirements structure. A possible solution is to use the Extract Early Aspect refactoring (Section 3.1), to remove the duplication and to create a new Early Aspect expressing this specific set of requirements.

Another common duplication problem occurs when an individual requirement appears in several requirements structures. This duplication could be removed using Extract Early Aspect refactoring as mentioned above. If the requirements are similar but not exactly the same, we may need to separate the duplicated piece from the rest of the requirement.

2.2. Tangled Requirements

A tangled requirement is a situation that occurs when a requirements unit contains descriptions of several properties or different functionalities [15].

A requirement unit that contains several different properties could be hard to understand. Thus it offers an opportunity for refactoring. A possible solution is to use the Extract Early Aspect refactoring (Section 3.1), to create a new Early Aspect that expresses specific and separated set of requirements. This solution needs to be analyzed with caution, because it may increase the number of the units.

Another possible solution is to use the Move Activity [14] (see more details in Section 4). With this solution requirement units are not created, they are just grouped in existing units that already express the same requirements. Thus, this second solution could be an alternative when the first, with aspects, were so expansive.

An example of Move Activity refactoring is showed in Figure 1. In the Order Processing System [19] described with use case, consider a Login use case that is concerned with user authentication and also with the functionalities selected by the user (two properties in the same unit). The shaded lines show the activities that could be moved to another use case, responsible for the functionality selection flow.

Main flow of events:	...
1. The use case starts when the user starts the application. 2. The system will display the Login Screen. 3. The user enters a username and password. ... 6. The system will display the Main Screen 7. The user will select a function ...	8. While the user does not select Exit loop 9. If the user selects Place Order then Use Place Order. 10. else if the user selects Cancel Order then Use Cancel Order. 11. ... end if. 16. The user will select a function. end loop. 17. The use case ends.

Fig. 1. Login use case.

2.3. Scattered Requirements

A scattered requirement is a situation that occurs when the specification of one property is not encapsulated in a single requirements unit [15].

When the requirements that treat of the same goal are disperse by the requirement document the general localization is more difficult harder and in consequence difficult they reuse and maintenance, this situation could be solved with the Refactoring application. A possible solution is to use the Extract Early Aspect refactoring (Section 3.1) to create a new requirement unit that encapsulates a specific requirement that is scattered and then use the *Move Activity* (see more details in Section 4) refactoring [14] to put all scattered pieces in this new requirement unit.

3. Refactoring Requirements

In this section we define and describe the requirements refactoring Extract Early Aspect. This refactoring was mentioned in the previous section to provide solutions to: i) scattered requirements, ii) duplicated requirements and iii) tangled requirements.

For the refactoring we provide a context, a solution, the motivation for the application of the refactoring, a set of mechanics to apply the refactoring and an example illustrating the application of the refactoring. We use the format recommended by Fowler in [4] and we add some figures and a description of the solution for each mechanism steps.

The solutions described in this section are abstract, therefore we have the intention of being able uses them in any situation that occurs "bad smells". Thus, to a requirement engineer to uses them, first he already must have chosen the early aspect oriented technique to later applying the solutions.

The example used is described using the Multi-Dimensional Separation of Concerns approach [8]. The requirements are represented in XML format.

3.1 Extract Early Aspect

Context. A set of duplicated information is used in several places. This could be better modularized in an early aspect. This refactoring is also used when a requirement is too large or contains information related to a feature that is scattered across several requirements and is tangled with other requirements.
Solution. Extract that information to a new requirement and name it according to the context.
Motivation. This refactoring should be applied when there is duplicated information that can be split into two or more new requirements. The duplicated information could increase the costs of the requirements document maintenance and the potential for errors insertion. Every time that a change is needed, it is necessary to modify all the places where the duplicated requirements appear. [20].

The use of aspect-oriented requirements engineering [15] provides a good mechanism to modularize these requirements that are scattered among several places in a requirements document. The use of aspectual requirements [15], [5] promotes better modularization of the requirements artifacts.
Mechanics. The following steps should be performed:
1. Create a new early aspect and name it.

Figure 2 shows in detail how to create a new early aspect. Also it is considered when does not have to create a new early aspect.

```
Verify IF exist a <Early Aspect> that encapsulate the
same segment of information that will be encapsulate in
the structure that desire to create.
 IF Yes then
   Verify IF exist the possibility of to use the
   <Early Aspect> existent to encapsulate the new
   information.
     IF Yes then
       The new structure <Early Aspect> isn't created;
     END_IF;
     ELSE
       The new structure <Early Aspect> is created;
     END_ELSE;
 END_IF;
 ELSE
   The new structure <Early Aspect> is created;
 END_ELSE;
```

Fig. 2. The detailing mechanism to create a new structure <Early Aspect>.

2. Select in the original requirement the information you want to extract. An Early Aspect Mining Tool like the EA-Miner [17], [18] may be used in this step. Figure 3 illustrate an example with 10 requirements structures that only in 3 had been found the information desired.

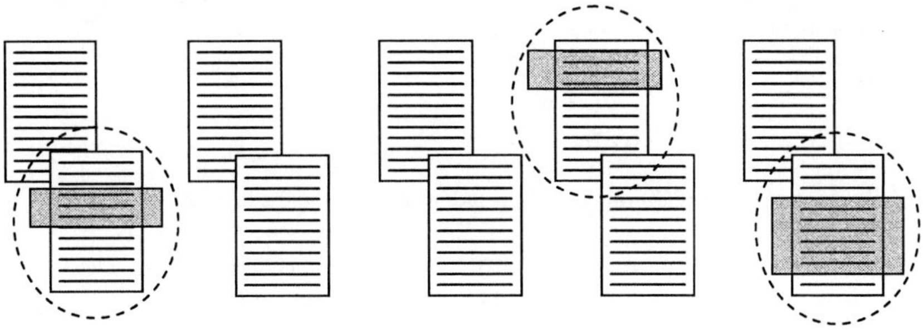

Fig. 3. Illustration of the requirements document and the selected segments.

Figure 4 shows in detail how to select in the original requirement the information you want to extract.

```
WHILE not be the end of the requirements document do
  To each structure of the requirement document:
    Verify IF exist the information you want to
    extract
    IF Yes then
      To select the segments that corresponds to the
      information desired;
      Go to the next structure;
    END_IF
    ELSE
      Go to the next structure;
    END_ELSE
END_WHILE.
```

Fig. 4. The detailing mechanism to select the information you want to extract.

3. Add the selected information to the new early aspect. Figure 5 illustrate the situation of the 3 selected information (in the previous step) to being added to the new early aspect.

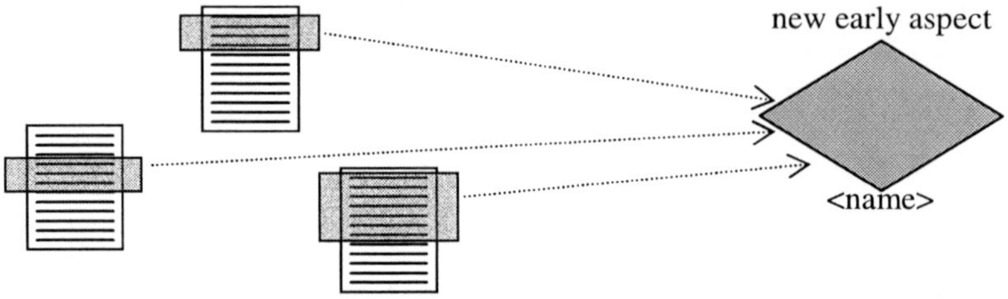

Fig. 5. Illustration of the addition of the selected information in the new early aspect.

To add the information in the new structure it is important to analyze the existence of a priority between the selected information. Figure 6 shows how to add the selected information in the new early aspect.

```
To all structures of the requirement document that
exists the information selected do:
  Verify IF exist a priority order:
  IF Yes then
    Order the selected information and do:
      To each structure of the requirement document
      that exists the information selected do:
        Verify IF the selected information already
        exists in the <new early aspect>
        IF Yes then
          Go to the next selected information;
        END_IF;
        ELSE
          Add (copy) the selected information to the
          new early aspect;
          Go to the next selected information;
        END_ELSE;
  END_IF;
  ELSE
    To each structure of the requirement document that
    exists the information selected do:
      Verify IF the selected information already
      exists in the <new early aspect>
        IF Yes then
          Go to the next selected information;
        END_IF
        ELSE
          Add (copy) the selected information to the
          new early aspect;
          Go to the next selected information;
        END_ELSE;
  END_ELSE;
```

Fig. 6. The detailing mechanism to add the selected information to the new early aspect.

4. Remove the selected information from the original requirement and collect information about the future composition. Figure 7 illustrate the selected information being removed of the original requirement and the collect of composition informations.

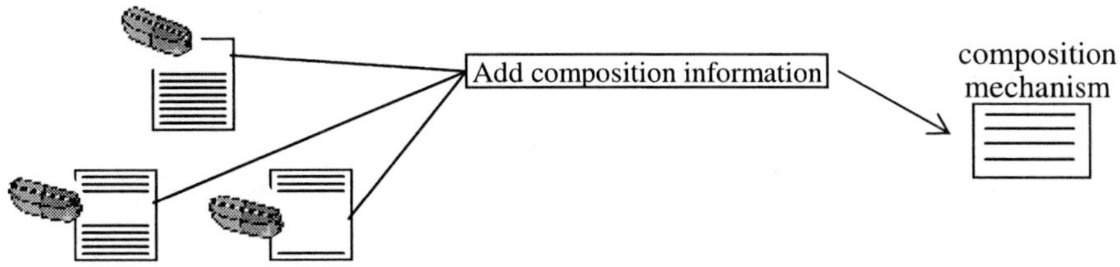

Fig. 7. Illustration of the removal of the selected information and the collects of composition guides.

All the information that need be collected is showed detailed in the Figure 8.

```
To each structures of the requirement document that
have information that was added to the new early aspect
do:
   To each selected information that was added to the
   new early aspect do:
      To make note of:
         - The name and/or the identification of the
         source structure (original requirement);
         - The localization inside of the structure (what
         it comes before and after);
         - The name of the destination structure (Early
         Aspect);
      Remove the select information;
```

Fig. 8. The detailing mechanism to removal the selected information of the original requirement.

5. Create the composition mechanism from the new early aspect to the original requirement(s). Using the collected information in the previous step is the composition mechanism is create. Figure 9 illustrate a situation in that the new early aspect has relationships with others 3 requirements structures.

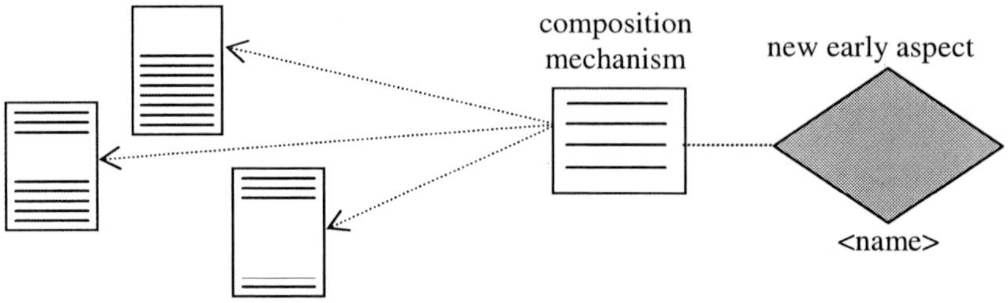

Fig. 9. Illustration of the creation of the composition mechanism.

```
In the composition mechanisms do:
  Provide pointers and/or rule with the following
  information:
    - The name and/or the identification of the source
    structure (original requirement);
    - Where the information will be introduced in the
    original requirement?
    - When the information will be introduced in the
    original requirement (before or after)?
```

Fig. 10. The detailing mechanism to create the composition mechanism.

6. Check if the original requirement is acceptable[1] without the removed information.
7. Update the references in dependent requirements to original requirements.
Example. The two excerpt requirements, shown in Figures 11 and 12, deal with the registration of a new employee and a new product, but we can see that the two initial requirements (1.1, 1.2 and 2.1, 2.2) in both figures are duplicated.

```
...
<Requirement id="1.1"> The employee provides the login
 and password. </Requirement>
<Requirement id="1.2"> The system validates the typed
 password. </Requirement>
<Requirement id="1.3"> The employee provides the
 following information about the new employee: Name,
 Login Password </Requirement>
<Requirement id="1.4"> The employee confirms the new
 employee register. </Requirement>
...
```

Fig. 11. Register new employee.

[1] Adequate for the original purpose.

```
...
<Requirement id="2.1"> The employee provides the login
 and password. </Requirement>
<Requirement id="2.2"> The system validates the typed
 password. </Requirement>
<Requirement id="2.3"> The employee provides the
 following information about the new product:
 Description, Size, Color, Location and Price.
 </Requirement>
<Requirement id="2.4"> The employee confirms the new
 product register. </Requirement>
...
```

Fig. 12. Register new product.

Applying the Extract Early Requirement to solve this duplicated requirements problem, we have the new Early Aspect shown in Figure 13 and the composition rules partially showed in the Figure 14.

```
...
<Requirement id="3.1"> The employee provides the login
 and password. </Requirement>
<Requirement id="3.2"> The system validates the typed
 password. </Requirement>
...
```

Fig. 13. Login early aspect.

Applying the step 4 (described in the refactoring mechanics) the duplicated information showed in the Figures 11 and 12 need to be removed. The composition Mechanism was created in agreement with the used approach MDSOC (Multi-Dimensional Separation Of Concerns [8]). Figure 14 shows the composition rules that maintain the original functionality to the Register New Employee and to Register New Product.

```
...
<Req.= "Register_New_Employee" id="1" children="include">
      <Constraint action="provide" operator="on">
           <Requirement concern="Login" id="3" children="include"/>
      </Constraint>
         <Outcome action="fulfilled"/>
   </Requirement>
...
<Req.= "Register_New_Product" id="2" children="include">
      <Constraint action="provide" operator="on">
           <Requirement concern="Login" id="3" children="include"/>
      </Constraint>
         <Outcome action="fulfilled"/>
   </Requirement>
...
```

Fig. 14. Composition rules (partial).

4. Related Work

Rui, Ren and Butler in [16] describe a meta-model for use case modelling and categorize a list of use case refactorings. Instead of simply listing the refactorings, we present a refactoring opportunity and a requirements refactoring definition, providing the context for the application of a given refactoring, a possible solution, motivation to perform the transformations and an example of the practical use of the described refactoring.

Yu, Li and Butler in [22] explain how refactoring can be applied in order to improve the organization of use case models. They focus on the decomposition of a use case and the reorganization of relationships between use cases. They also describe ten refactorings that could be used to improve the overall organization of use case models, such as inclusion or extension mechanisms introduction, use case deletion or refactorings that manipulate the inheritance tree. While Yu et al. focus on refactoring the use case models, we focus on refactoring requirements descriptions. As a consequence, our refactorings are finer grained than theirs. We also discuss in details the mechanics of the refactoring and possible refactoring opportunities in the context of requirements descriptions.

Xu, Yu, Rui and Butler in [21] present a tool that helps in refactoring of use case models and use it to conduct a case study using an ATM application. While they focus on the automation side of the use case refactoring process, we concentrate on providing definitions for deficiencies in requirements descriptions and refactorings in this context. Further research is needed to attain automatic identification of problems as proposed in this paper.

Ramos et al in [14] describes a collection of refactoring opportunities that might occur in requirements and provides a collection of refactorings that can be used to improve the quality of requirements where these opportunities appear. A collection of examples for practical use for both refactorings and the identification of refactoring opportunities are described. In this work we are describing a refactoring in the early aspects context. Below (Figure 15) we are showing the Move Activity refactoring that it is cited in this article. Is important to note that the example of the application to this refactoring appears in the section 2.2, Figure 1.

Move Activity

Context. A set of activities is better accommodated in another requirement description.

Solution. Move the activity to the desired requirement. If the requirement does not exist yet, create a new requirement with the selected activities using the Extract Requirement refactoring.

Motivation. This refactoring is done to improve modularity and to ameliorate the balance of activities among the requirements. Activities are moved from one requirement to another also when a new requirement is created, either manually or by an Extract Requirement refactoring. This improvement in modularity could lead to a better understanding of the system in the long term [20].

Mechanics. The following activities should be performed:

1. Select the activities you want to move.
2. Move them to the desired requirement.
3. Update references to these activities if needed.

Fig. 15. The move activity refactoring [14].

5. Conclusions

This paper describes the refactoring opportunities that might occur in requirements and provides an Extract Early Aspect refactoring that can be used to improve the requirements where these opportunities appear. We describe an example for practical use for both refactoring and the identification of refactoring opportunity.

It is important to note that refactorings are usually described as two-way transformations and depending on a given situation one direction is more convenient than the other.

This work is part of a project whose objective is to evaluate the requirements document quality, finding pieces that can be improved with the application of requirements patterns and refactorings [11], [12], [13] and [14].

The refactoring opportunities that we have identified have the goal of making the requirements more understandable and to improve overall organization of the project. But depending on the system quality attributes considered (for example: reusability, maintainability, etc) the requirements engineer might take actions that slightly differ from the guidelines proposed here. Also, the expected granularity of the requirements descriptions might influence the use of the refactoring opportunity. The requirements engineer should take these issues into consideration.

References

1. Boehm, B.W., Sullivan, K.J.: Software economics: a roadmap. In: ICSE - Future of SE Track. 319-343 (2000)
2. Elssamadisy, A., Schalliol, G.: Recognizing and responding to bad smells in extreme programming. In: Proceedings of the 24th International conference on Software Engineering (2002)
3. Early-Aspects.net. Early Aspects: Aspect-Oriented Requirements Engineering and Architecture Design. http://www.early-aspects.net/
4. Fowler, M., Beck, K., Brant, J., Opdyke, W., Roberts, D.: Refactoring: improving the design of existing code. Object Technology Series. Addison-Wesley (2000)
5. Jacobson, I.: Use cases and aspects-Working seamlessly together. Journal of Object Technology 2(4) (2003)
6. Jacobson, I., Ng, P.W.: Aspect-Oriented Software Development with Use Cases. Addison-Wesley (2005)
7. Li, L.: A semi-automatic approach to translating use cases to sequence diagrams. In: TOOLS '99: Proceedings of the Technology of Object-Oriented Languages and Systems, Washington, DC, USA, IEEE Computer Society, 184 pg (1999)
8. Moreira, A., Araújo, J., Rashid., A.. A Model for Multi-Dimensional Separation of Concerns in Requirements Engineering. The 17th Conference on Advanced Information Systems Engineering (CAiSE'05), 13-17 June 2005, Porto, Portugal. Lecture Notes in Computer Science, Volume 3520 (2005)
9. Opdyke, W.F.: Refactoring object-oriented frameworks. PhD thesis, University of Illinois at Urbana-Champaign (1992)
10. Pressman, R.: Software Engineering: A Practitioner's Approach. McGraw-Hill (2005)
11. Ramos, R.A., Araújo, J., Castro, J., Moreira, A., Alencar, F., Silva, C.: "Uma abordagem de instanciação de métricas para medir documentos de requisitos orientados a aspectos", in: 3° Brazilian Workshop on Aspect Oriented Software Development - WASP2006. Florianopolis, Brazil (2006)
12. Ramos, R. A.; Araújo, J. ; Moreira, A. ; Castro, J. ; Alencar, F. and Penteado, R.: "Um Padrão para Requisitos Duplicados", in: 6th Latin American Conference on Pattern Languages of Programming (SugarLoafPlop'2007), Porto de Galinhas, Recife, Pernambuco , Brazil (2007a)
13. Ramos, R. A. ; Alencar, F. ; Araújo, J. ; Moreira, A. ; Castro, J. and Penteado, R.: "i* with Aspects: Evaluating Understandability", in: Workshop on Requirements Engineering, 2007, Toronto, Canada (2007b)
14. Ramos, R., Piveta, E., Castro, J., Araújo, J., Moreira, A., Guerreiro, P., Pimenta, M., and Tom Price, R.. Improving the Quality of Requirements with Refactoring. In: VI Simpósio Brasileiro de Qualidade de Software – SBQS2007, Porto de Galinhas, Recife, Pernambuco, Brasil, Junho 27 – 30 (2007c)
15. Rashid, A., Moreira, A., Araújo, J.: Modularisation and composition of aspectual requirements. In Aksit, M., ed.: Proc. 2nd Int' Conf. on Aspect-Oriented Software Development (AOSD-2003), ACM Press 11-20 (2003)
16. Rui, K., Ren, S., Butler, G.: Refactoring use case models: A case study. In: International Conference on Enterprise Information Systems (ICEIS) (2003)
17. Sampaio, A., Loughran, N., Rashid, A., Rayson, P.: Mining Aspects in Requirements. In: Workshop on Early Aspects. Held with the 4th International Conf. on Aspect-Oriented Software Development AOSD 2005 (2005)

18. Sampaio, A., Rashid, A., Chitchyan, R., and Rayson, P. EA-Miner: Towards Automation in Aspect-Oriented Requirements Engineering. Transactions on Aspect-Oriented Software Development: Special Issue on Early Aspects (Accepted to Appear). Editor(s): J. Araujo, E. Baniasaad. Springer (2007)
19. Schneider, G., Winters, J.P.: "Applying Use Cases: A Practical Guide", in: Addison Wesley - Object Technology Series (1998)
20. Sommerville, I.: Software Engineering, 7th edition. Pearson Education (2004)
21. Xu, J., Yu, W., Rui, K., Butler, G.: Use case refactoring: a tool and a case study. In: Software Engineering Conference, 2004. 11th Asia-Pacific. 484-491 (2004)
22. Yu, W., Li, J., Butler, G.: Refactoring use case models on episodes. In: Automated Software Engineering, 2004. Proceedings. 19th International Conference on. 328-335 (2004)

Análisis Comparativo de Métodos de Elicitación de Requisitos para Sistemas Basados en Agentes

Lorena Rodriguez[1], Alethia Hume[1], Luca Cernuzzi[1], Emilio Insfrán[2]

[1] Universidad Católica "Nuestra Señora de la Asunción", Paraguay
Campus Universitario – C.C. 1683 Asunción, Paraguay, Tel: +595-21-334650
lcernuzz@uca.edu.py, alethia_hume@uca.edu.py, lorerod@gmail.com
[2] DSIC – Universidad Politécnica de Valencia, España
einsfran@dsic.upv.es

Resumen. En los últimos años han sido presentadas varias propuestas para la captura de requisitos haciendo uso de enfoques de diferentes tipos. Por otro lado, en la ingeniería de software basada en agentes, varias metodologías no contemplan la etapa de elicitación de requisitos. El presente estudio se centra en un análisis de algunos métodos que podrían resultar interesantes para cubrir este déficit. En este trabajo se presentan los resultados de una comparación entre métodos, en particular identificando un conjunto de abstracciones más comunes de los sistemas basados en agentes y algunas cualidades deseables durante la elicitación de requisitos. En particular, se consideran los enfoques propuestos por Agentis, GBRAM y RETO. Además, este tipo de análisis podría ser de utilidad para dar soporte a la elección de un método o la adopción e integración del mismo por las metodologías de agentes que no cuentan con una fase de requisitos.

Palabras claves: Modelado de Agentes, Metodologías basadas en agentes, Ingeniería de requisitos.

1 Introducción

En los últimos años, la tecnología basada en agentes es una de las áreas de mayor desarrollo de la ingeniería de software. Sin duda alguna, existen numerosas razones, pero probablemente una de las principales es que el concepto de agente, como un ente autónomo capaz de interactuar con otros persiguiendo el logro de sus objetivos, resulta una metáfora natural para diseñadores y desarrolladores.

De hecho, es creciente la demanda de sistemas abiertos con componentes complejos, interactivos, donde cada uno tiene su propio flujo de control y que pueden ser adecuadamente modelados a través del paradigma de agentes. Para alcanzar una solución adecuada para estos sistemas y explorar todos sus beneficios y características especiales es necesario contar con metodologías y técnicas que ayuden al análisis, diseño y desarrollo de software garantizando la consecución del propósito para el cual fue construido. Como consecuencia se ve una creciente atención por parte de los investigadores, en proponer nuevas metodologías y herramientas [15].

Por otra parte, sabemos que la ingeniería de requisitos es la encargada de cubrir el vacío entre el mundo informal del cliente y el mundo formal de la ingeniería de software. La captura y modelado de requisitos, puede constituirse en un desafío importante en el área de agentes, donde las partes participantes en el sistema pueden ser numerosas y estar distribuidas. Asimismo sus metas pueden ser diversas y entrar en conflicto, dependiendo de su entorno de trabajo y las tareas que pretenden cumplir [8, 10].

Cabe señalar que no todas las metodologías de agentes propuestas en los últimos años cubren la fase de requisitos [10]. Entre las metodologías que la cubren, varias lo hacen a través de la identificación y modelado de casos de usos. Lo cual es apropiado para la captura de requisitos funcionales, mientras que presenta ciertas limitaciones para algunas de las principales abstracciones de los agentes y los MAS (Multi Agent Systems), en particular con relación a la interacción con el ambiente, los aspectos organizacionales y las interacciones entre agentes.

Debido a la importancia de la fase de requisitos, resulta interesante analizar métodos y técnicas de ingeniería de requisitos que nos permitan la captura de las principales abstracciones en las tempranas fases del proceso de desarrollo de sistemas basados en agentes y ofrezcan otras características generales deseables. En particular en el presente estudio se analizan Agentis [11], RETO [7] y GBRAM [2].

En la sección 2 se define brevemente los conceptos necesarios para el análisis de los requisitos de sistemas basados en agentes y se especifican algunos puntos que se tendrán en cuenta para la comparación de metodogías, en la sección 3 se introducen las metodologías analizadas en el trabajo, mientras que en la sección 4 se realiza una comparación entre las mismas; finalmente, en la sección 5 se presentan algunas conclusiones y trabajos futuros.

2 Análisis de Requisitos para Sistemas Basados en Agentes

Los MAS, por su naturaleza están típicamente diseñados para operar en ambientes dinámicos y son sistemas abiertos donde los agentes pueden interactuar y evolucionar. En particular, es ampliamente reconocido que la interacción es probablemente la característica más importante de dichos sistemas complejos. En los últimos años han surgido varias propuestas de metodologías para el análisis, diseño y desarrollo de dichos sistemas. Sin embargo, un problema abierto del área es la etapa de análisis de requisitos.

Para hablar del análisis de requisitos para sistemas basados en agentes es necesario considerar las abstracciones que los caracterizan. En este sentido, tomando en cuenta varias propuestas metodológicas en el área de ingeniería de software de sistemas basados en agentes (entre las cuales cabe destacar a [5, 6, 16, 4, 12]), las abstracciones más comunes identificadas, independientes de la aplicación, y que hemos seleccionado para este estudio comparativo son:

- Agentes: Son entidades de software autónomas y proactivas (constituyen los componentes implementativos del sistema), que logran sus objetivos interactuando entre ellas y se encuentran en un ambiente particular.

- Actores: Es una entidad de comportamiento autónomo, interna o externa al sistema, que tiene algún interés sobre el mismo y contribuye a la definición de los roles. Un actor podría constituirse en agente del sistema, pero no necesariamente.
- Roles: Definen el comportamiento del agente, y tienen asociados las metas y las tareas especificas que deben llevar a cabo en el contexto de la organización.
- Metas: Definen los objetivos tanto del sistema en general como de cada actor. Cada meta puede referirse a aspectos funcionales (asociados con los servicios) o no funcionales (asociados con la calidad del servicio).
- Tareas: Un conjunto estructurado de actividades para alcanzar una meta.
- Aspectos organizacionales: Definen una sociedad organizada de individuos (agentes). La sociedad puede estar dividida en sub-organizaciones (estructura), cada una siguiendo patrones y reglas que gobiernan su comportamiento (control).
- Restricciones (reglas y normas): Definen el comportamiento deseado tanto para la organización como para cada agente.
- Interacción entre agentes: Normalmente, los agentes operan dentro de un contexto en el que necesitan cooperar, competir o simplemente comunicarse entre ellos para poder alcanzar sus propias metas.
- Interacciones con el ambiente: Los agentes típicamente interactúan (perciben y afectan) con un ambiente dependiendo de sus roles, y sus estados actuales.
- Recursos: Constituyen los componentes concretos de interacción con el ambiente.

Como es posible observar no todas las abstracciones definidas se traducirán en componentes concretos del MAS, por ejemplo únicamente los agentes serán componentes concretos del sistema mientras que los roles y actores solo contribuyen a la identificación de agentes. De toda forma, el nivel de cobertura que ofrece una metodología para la captura de dichas abstracciones, puede ser una buena métrica para la calificación de su fase de requisitos.

También existen otros aspectos que hacen a una metodología mas adecuada que otra en lo que se refiere a la captura de requisitos. Estos no corresponden solamente a MAS, sino que influyen en el proceso de desarrollo de cualquier sistema complejo y por ende es importante tenerlos en cuenta en el marco comparativo. A continuación se presentan aquellos que consideramos particularmente relevantes para facilitar la elicitación y la especificación de requisitos además de ofrecer un mejor seguimiento de los mismos en etapas sucesivas.

- Guías metodológicas para la identificación de elementos y abstracciones cubiertas por la metodología a partir de las necesidades de los actores externos.
- Claridad en el proceso: Es importante que la metodología no favorezca ambigüedades en el proceso de elicitación y modelado de requisitos.
- Modelos contemplados: Cada metodologías hace uso de diversos modelos. Es importante evaluar la utilidad de estos modelos en cuanto a su aporte efectivo (claridad, facilidad de uso, estándar, nivel de formalidad, etc.) en el proceso de captura de requisitos.
- Notaciones por cada modelo previsto: El nivel de formalidad y claridad de las diversas notaciones, podría resultar clave para la estandarización de su uso.
- Validación/Verificación: Consiste en el proceso de evaluar si los requisitos y modelos obtenidos reflejan efectivamente las necesidades de los actores.

- Trazabilidad: Se trata dc un conjunto de medidas, acciones y procedimientos que permiten dar seguimiento en la vida del requisito. Este aspecto es de gran importancia en el proceso de verificación y adaptación del MAS.
- Herramientas de Soporte: Para integrar la captura de requisitos al proceso de desarrollo de software sería deseable contar con herramientas automatizadas que sirvan de guía al ingeniero.

Resulta claro que una metodología que cubra las diversas abstracciones y contemple las cualidades arriba señaladas consituirá una base solida para la ingeniería de requisitos de los sistemas basados en agentes.

3 Análisis de métodos para RE

Para el modelado de requisitos, existen diferentes enfoques que ofrecen varias formas de análisis y razonamiento, dependiendo de su aplicación. Los más significativos para el diseño y desarrollo de los MAS son: modelado organizacional, modelado de comportamiento, modelado de dominio y modelado de metas. Las dos tendencias principales consideran la perspectiva de los actores o bien la perspectiva de las metas que se pretenden alcanzar para el modelado de los distintos aspectos de un sistema.

En el primer grupo (perspectiva de actores o escenarios) podemos mencionar CREWS [9] y AUML [12, 1], mientras que en la perspectiva orientada a metas se encuentran GBRAM, RETO, KAOS [14], i* [15]. Entre los métodos basados en metas citados todos cubren el modelado de metas y de comportamiento, mientras que ninguno cubre el modelado de dominio; GBRAM e i* cubren también el modelado organizacional, mientras RETO lo hace parcialmente. Por otro lado, las metodologías CREWS y AUML se limitan al modelado de comportamiento, si bien AUML ha sido a veces utilizado para modelar ciertos aspectos de la perspectiva organizacional.

Un enfoque particularmente relevante orientado a metas es aquello propuesto por Tropos [5]. Tropos adopta el framework ofrecido por i* y resulta muy bueno para la elicitación de entorno de los actores, es decir sus metas, tareas, interacciones, dependencias, recursos que necesitan, etc. Sin embargo, no permite la representación completa de restricciones y no propone un modelado para el ambiente. Siendo que estimamos particularmente interesante la orientación a metas para la captura de requisitos para los MAS, creemos necesario en este enfoque analizar otros métodos complementarios.

Por otro lado, en la perspectiva orientada a actores, considerando que la extensión de UML para Agentes (AUML) [12, 1] tiende a afirmarse como un estándar notacional en varias metodologías, una de las propuestas más comunes para la etapa de requisitos es la adopción de los diagramas de Casos de Uso. Dicho formalismo ha demostrado buenos resultados para la representación de requisitos funcionales y también es una buena herramienta de comunicación con los actores debido a que no es necesario un alto nivel de abstracción para entenderlos. Sin embargo, la notación presenta limitaciones para la representación de características no funcionales, requisitos que no impliquen interacción, y el modelado de restricciones. Además, se requiere de cierta habilidad para diseñar los Casos de Uso, ya que la claridad no está garantizada por el diagrama sino se encuentra en manos del especialista. También cabe señalar que los Casos de Uso tienen limitaciones en la captura de aspectos cualitativos y del ambiente así como las interacciones con el mismo [13].

En la literatura especializada tanto de ingeniería de requisitos como de las metodologías de agentes se encuentran diferentes propuestas que incorporan el modelo de Casos de Uso integrándolo en un conjunto de pasos metodológicos que podrían superar algunas de las limitaciones identificadas. En particular en el presente estudio se analizan Agentis [11] y RETO [7]. Ambas propuestas utilizan los Casos de Uso y los Diagramas de Secuencia, Agentis está orientado a actores mientras RETO está orientado a metas (funcionales u organizacionales). Además, ambos complementan los modelos propuestos por UML con otras técnicas y guías metodológicas.

Otra propuesta relevante de la ingeniería de requisitos tradicional orientada a metas y que se analiza en este estudio es GBRAM [2]. GBRAM provee una guía procedural para la identificación y elaboración de metas e introduce técnicas que ayudan al análisis metódico, y sistemático de las mismas.

Para el análisis utilizamos como caso de estudio el diseño de un Conference Management System (CMS), que soporta la organización de una conferencia que se realizará como un proceso de múltiples fases, involucrando a varios individuos y grupos. Durante la fase de postulación (*submission*), los autores envían sus trabajos, y son informados de su correcta recepción y del identificador que se le asignó al mismo. En la fase de revisión (*reviewing*), el presidente del comité de programa debe coordinar la revisión de los trabajos contactando potenciales evaluadores y solicitando a los mismos la revisión de un número de trabajos. Las evaluaciones son enviadas al presidente del comité de programa y son utilizadas para decidir acerca de la aceptación o rechazo del trabajo. En la fase final, los autores necesitan ser notificados de esta decisión y, en caso de aceptación, se solicita la elaboración de una versión revisada del trabajo. El editor colecta las versiones finales y las publica.

3.1 Agentis

La metodología Agentis propone un ciclo de vida para el proceso de desarrollo de sistemas, este proceso cuenta con un conjunto de actividades con fuerte restricción en el orden en el que son realizadas: 1) Requisitos; 2) Análisis; 3) Diseño; 4) Implementación; y 5) Ensamblaje y Entrega.

En el proceso de requisitos se pone énfasis en la captura y el modelado de las funcionalidades necesarias y las restricciones con las que tiene que cumplir el sistema. La fase de requisitos se descompone a su vez en las etapas de *preparación*, *análisis de alto nivel*, *especificación inicial del diseño general*, *determinación de áreas de análisis* y *validación*. Para el desarrollo de estas etapas se cuenta con una descripción de la secuencia de pasos a seguir, para llevar adelante el modelado siguiendo la metodología.

Durante la ***preparación*** para la captura de requisitos se busca obtener toda la información disponible con relación al sistema deseado. Se elabora una breve descripción del contexto del sistema (lista informal de servicios que serán soportados).

A continuación, se realiza el ***análisis de alto nivel*** que apunta a la obtención de un modelo global del sistema que provea las bases para el diseño del mismo usando el diagrama de casos de uso de UML.

Primeramente, se identifican actores externos (stakeholders), en término de roles que interactúan con el sistema, y para cada stakeholder se identifican sus metas. En este paso, la metodología propone además la identificación de metas organizacionales. Todas las metas identificadas se descomponen en sub-metas hasta llegar a metas funcionales.

En el proceso de identificación de metas queda poco claro el nivel de abstracción a utilizar para la separación de las metas y para su descripción. Además, los actores externos pueden contar con metas que exceden el alcance de las funcionalidades del sistema mientras la metodología no diferencia entre tipos de metas. Tampoco se proponen notaciones o técnicas para establecer una jerarquía entre las metas lo cual sería de gran utilidad para comprender qué relación existe entre ellas.

En el siguiente paso se identifican las metas funcionales y se clasifican en grupos de metas relacionadas. Para cada grupo funcional se define un servicio que lo identifique y los mismos son considerados casos de usos. En esta actividad nos encontramos con un parámetro subjetivo (metas relacionadas) donde se demuestra una falta de claridad en el nivel de abstracción esperado.

Una vez que se cuenta con los casos de uso es necesario definir como los stakeholders interactuarían con ellos por lo que se vuelve necesaria la identificación de las interfaces y luego la identificación de agentes internos quienes serían proveedores de esos casos de uso.

Esta distinción entre agentes internos y externos en el momento de aplicación de la metodología con el caso de estudio resultó en cierta confusión, ya que no queda claro el objetivo de dicha separación y tampoco como llevarla adelante.

El último paso realizado está dado por la especificación de los escenarios para cada caso de uso, seguido del modelado del comportamiento de los mismos (diagramas de actividad).

En la especificación del ***diseño general inicial*** se busca obtener una vista interna de los requisitos de implementación con propósitos de planificación y estimación. Para ello se revisa la infraestructura de hardware y software disponible buscando poder identificar requisitos arquitecturalmente significativos, y posteriormente definir como sería implementada cada área, a fin de poder dividir el sistema en piezas de implementación más manejables.

Para seguir adelante y realizar el análisis en la siguiente etapa a partir de la especificación de requisitos es necesario ***determinar áreas de análisis e interacción*** que consiste en dividir el sistema en unidades de trabajo, la identificación de las mismas puede estar guiada por diferentes criterios

Para este trabajo se tuvieron en cuenta como criterios: las metas, actores y roles, cohesión y acoplamiento. Por otra parte como la metodología no define una notación formal, solo se refiere a una lista de áreas: Authors, Program Committe, Reviewers.

Posterior a la identificación de áreas es necesario establecer una relación entre las mismas para indicar como interactúan y definir cualquier relación de precedencia que exista entre ellas.

Por último se lleva a cabo la ***revisión*** del alcance de los resultados obtenidos y la planificación para la actividad de análisis.

3.1 GBRAM

GBRAM (Goal-Based Requirement Analysis Method) tiene como objetivo identificar y refinar las metas que un sistema debe alcanzar para posteriormente convertirlas en requerimientos operacionales. Especialmente, este método provee una guía procedural para la identificación y elaboración de metas en la especificación de sistemas, así también como introduce técnicas que ayudan al análisis profundizado, metódico, y sistemático para aclarar las metas deseadas [2].

El método asume que las metas del sistema no han sido previamente documentadas o explícitamente identificadas por los usuarios y que el analista deberá trabajar a partir de varias fuentes de información para determinarlas. El resultado del método es un documento de requisitos de software, que incluye los requisitos funcionales y no funcionales.

El documento producido por GBRAM trata el problema de la ambigüedad pero sin basarse en notaciones formales. Permite expresar los requisitos en lenguaje natural, motivando así la participación de los usuarios a través del proceso.

GBRAM consta de dos fases con actividades bien definidas que el analista deberá llevar a cabo al aplicar el método.

- Goal analysis:

Se comienza por la exploración ***(Explore)***, el análisis y examinación de los inputs, documentaciones existentes de diferentes fuentes. Donde se asume contar solo con una descripción en lenguaje natural del sistema.

A continuación se identifican ***(Identify)*** y extraen de las fuentes previamente analizadas las metas y toda la información posible acerca de las mismas. Se identifican también los stakeholders, que determinan quién o qué demanda un interés sobre cada meta por lo que esto contribuye al entendimiento del comportamiento del sistema, desde diferentes puntos de vista. Luego se identifican los agentes y se relacionan con las metas de las que serán responsables. El método describe de manera clara las diferencias entre stakeholders y agentes, para su fácil identificación. Varios agentes pueden ser responsables de una misma meta en diferentes momentos, pueden ser agentes humanos o agentes del sistema. Los resultados del caso de estudio CMS se resumen en la tabla 1 que cita los campos identificados.

Tabla 1. Modelado en GBRAM del CMS

Goal	Stakeholders	Agente
G1: Recibir Trabajo	Autor - PC Chair	PC Chair
G2: Notificar recepcion	Autor - PC Chair	PC Chair
G3: Asignacion de id	Autor - PC Chair	PC Chair
G4: Distribuir trabajos	PC Chair - PC Member - Revisor	PC Chair - PC Member
G5: Revisar trabajo	Revisor - PC Member - PC Chair	PC Member - Revisor
G6: Notificar decision	Autor - PC Chair	PC Chair
G7: Solicitar version corregida	PC Chair - Autor	PC Chair
G8: Publicar	Editor	Editor

La siguiente actividad ***(Organize)*** tiene como principales objetivos clasificar y organizar las metas. La clasificación se realiza entre metas de mantenimiento o de logro y la organización de acuerdo a sus dependencias.

En el desarrollo del CMS todas las metas encontradas son clasificadas como metas de logro dado que las metas de mantenimiento sugieren la continuidad de un estado en el sistema y por lo tanto suelen ser mapeadas con requisitos no funcionales.

Una relación de dependencia existe entre pares de metas, e implican que una meta dada depende de otra meta para poder completarse. Existen tres tipos de dependencias: dependencias de precedencia, de agentes y de restricciones.

Por último se construye una jerarquía de metas, y menciona dos maneras de representarlas (topografías) outline y jerárquica. Y se prosigue con la siguiente fase.

- Goal Refinement

Se inicia con el refinamiento ***(Refinement)*** del conjunto de metas, eliminando metas redundantes o sinónimas. En la siguiente actividad ***(Elaborate)*** se identifican obstáculos y restricciones de las metas y se construyen los escenarios para identificar metas y requisitos escondidos. Para todo lo mencionado anteriormente, GBRAM como en todas las etapas ofrece técnicas para facilitar la identificación de cada elemento, y para la representación sólo propone el uso del lenguaje natural, utilizando tablas para ordenar cada campo identificado.

Para converger todos los pasos anteriores y tener un conjunto más claro y ordenado de las metas se construye un esquema para cada una ***(Operationalize)***. Las metas, agentes responsables, stakeholders, restricciones, obstáculos y escenarios son mapeados en acciones.

3.3 RETO

El enfoque presentado en [7, 8] propone la integración de técnicas de la ingeniería de requisitos y diseños de sistemas con métodos orientados a objetos para el modelado conceptual con el fin de lograr la generación de un esquema conceptual a partir de la especificación de un modelo de requisitos.

El proceso se divide en dos fases principales:

- Fase de Modelado de Requisitos: Tiene como objetivo capturar las necesidades del cliente con una notación clara, precisa y simple con el fin de que un usuario sin un entrenamiento riguroso las pueda entender y corregir.
- Proceso de Análisis de Requisitos: Cuyo objeto es proveer guías metodológicas para traducir el modelo resultante de la etapa anterior y obtener un esquema conceptual donde dicha transición se realiza de forma automatizable.

Para los fines de esta investigación principalmente nos interesa la fase de creación del Modelo de Requisitos (MR) y por consiguiente será analizada en este documento.

Si bien la metodología no define un orden de pasos a seguir, encontramos un orden implícito, y no muy estricto, definido por la herramienta RETO (Requirements Engineering Tool) que soporta el modelado de sistemas siguiendo la metodología. Con el objetivo de evaluar también la utilidad y el aporte de la herramienta se hace uso de la misma para el presente trabajo comparativo y en adelante haremos referencia a los pasos previstos por la herramienta como si estos fuesen implícitamente propuestos por la metodología.

En particular el Modelo de Requisitos captura tanto aspectos funcionales como de uso y utiliza tres técnicas que se complementan mutuamente:
Se parte de la elaboración de la misión del sistema ***(Mission Statement)***, que constituye una forma de especificar el objetivo general del sistema y disponer de una visión global del sistema a construir.
A partir de allí se construye el árbol de refinamiento de funciones ***(Function Refinement Tree - FRT)*** que la metodología plantea como una sub-división de la función principal en tipos de actividades, áreas de negocios o grupos de funciones elementales. Esta sub-división continúa hasta llegar a funciones elementales que constituyen las hojas del árbol, una función es elemental si es disparada por un evento enviado por un usuario del sistema o por la ocurrencia de un evento temporal.
Cada hoja del FRT corresponde a un caso de uso del sistema y juntas conforman la base del modelo de casos de uso. Se completa el modelo de casos de uso ***(Use Case Model)*** identificando los actores, las relaciones de comunicación entre actores y casos de uso y las relaciones entre casos de uso (inclusión y extensión). El comportamiento es especificado con escenarios y tiene por objetivo la descripción del flujo de eventos que modifican el sistema y a través de los cuales se interactúa con los actores. Este flujo de eventos es representado por la definición de pasos (steps) en la especificación del caso de uso.

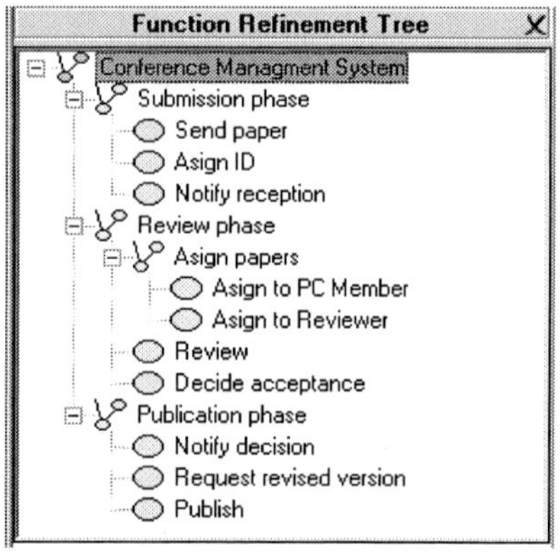

Fig. 1. Árbol de refinamiento de funciones del CMS en RETO

La metodología propone el uso de una plantilla estándar siguiendo la estructura convencional de tres secciones: summary, basic course and alternative section, sin embargo esto no marca un orden en la elaboración del modelo.

Si un caso de uso incluye a otro caso de uso, en la especificación de pasos se indica con una llamada explicita al cada caso de uso incluido. Por otra parte, un aporte del método consiste en la tipificación de pasos, teniendo en cuenta su naturaleza, con el fin de cubrir el contexto dentro del cual se desarrolla el caso de uso. Así tenemos que se clasifican en:

- General: representan acciones o actividades que se realizan fuera del alcance de los requisitos del sistema. Proporcionan información acerca del contexto en el cual ocurre el caso de uso, por ejemplo: "el revisor decide revisar un nuevo trabajo".
- Actor/System communication: acciones de los actores para interactuar con el sistema, por ejemplo: "el revisor introduce el identificador del trabajo a revisar"

- System response: representan la reacción del sistema y cambios de estado que se dan como consecuencia de la ocurrencia del caso de uso, por ejemplo: "el sistema verifica si el revisor está autorizado"

El uso del FRT en conjunto con el mission statement apuntan a solucionar el problema de encontrar el nivel de abstracción adecuado para la construcción del Modelo de Casos de Uso, ya que los casos de uso se obtienen directamente a partir del FRT (son las hojas del árbol) proporcionando una noción clara y uniforme del concepto de caso de uso y de la noción de meta a la que responde cada caso de uso.

4 Un análisis comparativo

En base a la aplicación de cada metodología analizada en el caso de estudio del CMS, en esta sección se resume la comparación llevada a cabo en función a los atributos (abstracciones y cualidades de los métodos de elicitación de requisitos) presentados en la sección 2. Se utiliza una métrica del 0 al 4, con la siguiente interpretación: 0, el atributo no se encuentra presente; 1, el atributo no está presente directamente pero podría inferirse; 2, el atributo está parcialmente presente; 3, el atributo está bastante soportado y 4, el atributo está muy bien soportado. Estas métricas permiten expresar los niveles de cobertura observados al realizar la comparación.

Tabla 2. Comparación de Métodos vs. Abstracciones

Métodos	**Abstracciones**								**Total**
	Actor/Agente	**Meta**	**Tarea**	**Organización**	**Reglas/Normas**	**Interacción**	**Entorno**	**Recurso**	
Agentis	3	3	2	1	2	2	1	0	14
GBRAM	3	4	3	1	3	3	3	4	24
RETO	3	4	4	2	2	2	2	1	20

La tabla 2 presenta los resultados con relación a las abstracciones. La calificación asignada indica el nivel de cobertura de los métodos para dar soporte a las abstracciones independientemente a la utilidad de las representaciones que proponen, ya que esto será presentado a través del criterio correspondiente en la tabla 3.

En líneas generales las tres metodologías encaran de manera similar a los actores/agentes, se permite su identificación y representación, pero el análisis se centra principalmente en las abstracciones que los caracterizan. Otro punto de amplia coincidencia entre las metodologías es que ninguna propone explícitamente el modelado del enfoque organizacional, mientras que se podría resaltar que existe cierta noción implícita de la organización, en RETO más que en las otras dos. Todas mencionan la posibilidad de una jerarquización de las metas pero RETO lo hace de una manera más sistematizada y completa. En efecto, propone un modelo, ofrece pautas para la subdivisión de las funciones del sistema en grupos funcionales y además orienta a que los grupos funcionales sean posibles áreas de negocios los cuales podrían reflejarse en sub-organizaciones.

Agentis, abarca la identificación, el modelado y representación de las metas. Sin embargo no se realiza un análisis muy profundo para la identificación de las mismas y se puede observar falta de claridad en el proceso de identificación. A diferencia de GBRAM no ofrece pautas y heurísticas para facilitar la identificación de metas, y tampoco propone un modelo específico para representarlas, como hace RETO. Las Tareas tanto como las reglas y normas son encaradas a través de la especificación de escenarios estándar, que tiene sus limitaciones en cuanto a expresividad. Por otra parte la existencia de interacciones entre actores/agentes se puede percibir durante el modelado del comportamiento de los casos de uso pero la metodología no apunta a identificarlas explícitamente en la fase de requisitos, sino más adelante. El concepto de entorno tanto como el de recursos de Agentis es bastante pobre en comparación a los demás métodos analizados, debido a que no se encara la identificación de ninguna de las dos abstracciones.

GBRAM, como se mencionó anteriormente está orientado a la identificación de metas por lo tanto el soporte que provee para esta abstracción merece la calificación más alta. El método encara el modelado de las tareas por medio de los esquemas de acción que se desprenden de las metas contando con buenas especificaciones y se cuenta con una buena guía para la identificación; sin embargo no se representa la secuencia en que se deben realizar las acciones para el cumplimiento de la meta, siendo esa secuencia importante para fases posteriores. GBRAM enfrenta las reglas y normas a nivel de metas donde se hace explicita la identificación de los obstáculos y las restricciones para las mismas pero la falta de formalidad en la notación influye levemente en su calificación. Por otra parte este método es el que mejor soporte ofrece para la identificación de las interacciones entre agentes ya que se realizan a través de tres tipos de relaciones de dependencia. El concepto de entorno como abstracción no se maneja completamente sin embargo sí se identifican los recursos que forman parte del ambiente por lo que un concepto general de mismo existe.

RETO, incorporando el modelo de casos de uso orientado a las metas e integrándolo al FRT logra un buen nivel de cobertura en cuanto a la identificación de metas. Las tareas al igual que en Agentis se cubren por medio de la especificación de escenarios, con la diferencia de que RETO propone un enriquecimiento en esta especificación que aporta mayor expresividad. Con relación a las reglas y normas este método se limita a condicionar el comportamiento, de vuelta, a través de los escenarios sin permitir la captura de restricciones generales. Las interacciones entre agentes están implícitas al igual que la existencia de un entorno y no se capturan los recursos que son parte de este último. Sin embargo la metodología insiste en la importancia de la especificación del contexto.

El segundo grupo de elementos que se tuvo en cuenta tiene como fin complementar la información que se obtiene de la primera tabla, ya que, como se explico en la sección 2 constituyen características deseables de las metodologías

Tabla 3. Comparación de Métodos vs. Características deseables

Métodos	Otros aspectos							Total
	Guías	Claridad	Modelos	Notación	Validación	Trazabilidad	Herramienta	
Agentis	3	0	3	3	4	0	3	16
GBRAM	4	4	0	0	3	3	0	14
RETO	2	3	4	3	4	4	4	24

Agentis, cuenta con una guía de pasos detallada lo cual sin embargo no garantiza la claridad de la misma. La falta de claridad se observa principalmente en la separación entre actores internos y externos, donde no queda claro el objetivo de la separación ni como realizarla, y el nivel de abstracción a utilizar para la identificación de las metas y para la agrupación de las mismas en grupos funcionales, ya que la indicación es "agrupar metas relacionadas" lo cual es un parámetro subjetivo. Esta falta de claridad influye negativamente en la utilidad de su guía metodológica. Al hacer uso de los modelos de AUML se puede explotar la estandarización de los mismos al igual que las notaciones pero aquí se ven limitaciones en cuanto a la expresividad de los modelos más que en las notaciones.

Por otra parte Agentis apunta e insiste en la validación de los requisitos capturados y esto es una ventaja que ayuda a sobrellevar la falta de trazabilidad en el proceso de desarrollo ya que resulta difícil observar las derivaciones de la modificación o extensión de los requisitos. Esto se debe a que el proceso de identificación de algunas abstracciones no se define como un flujo de pasos claros. Por ejemplo el proceso de identificación de metas requiere la agrupación de metas relacionadas y el mapeamiento de estos grupos a casos de uso, para luego construir el escenario y por ende especificar el logro de todas las metas que están cubiertas por dicho escenario. En el momento de identificar nuevas metas es difícil ver qué repercusiones tendría sobre el conjunto de casos de uso y escenarios. Si bien Agentis no cuenta con una herramienta propia, se pueden hacer uso de numerosas herramientas para el modelado de diagramas UML.

GBRAM, sufre de una gran carencia en cuanto a formalidad, esto abarca la falta de modelos, notaciones formales y herramientas que soporten el modelado siguiendo el método. Por otra parte las guías que ofrece y el nivel de claridad son muy buenos, también pone énfasis en la verificación de los requisitos a través de su etapa de refinamiento donde se marcan ciertas pautas a seguir haciendo este proceso más confiable. Es posible realizar un seguimiento sobre los requisitos capturados, reflejándose este hecho en la trazabilidad ofrecida.

RETO, cuenta con una herramienta propia que sirve de forma implícita como guía en el proceso, esto sumado a la integración de los casos de uso con el FRT aporta claridad. Contribuyendo este último también a la trazabilidad ya que hace visible las consecuencias que acompañarían a la modificación de los requisitos. RETO propone la utilización de modelos estándares de UML, con pequeñas extensiones que superan ciertas limitaciones de los mismos. Las notaciones utilizadas son semi-formales y se pone énfasis en la verificación de la completitud y coherencia de los requisitos capturados.

Como se puede notar, cada método ofrece de diferentes formas la cobertura de las abstracciones propias de los MAS. No obstante existen algunas ventajas comparativas de GBRAM con respecto a los demás. Un aspecto común que también puede ser revelado es la escasa consideración de la perspectiva organizacional que sin embargo está siendo particularmente utilizada por las metodologías basadas en agentes.

En cuanto las características deseables de los métodos, RETO ofrece ventajas con respecto a los demás y tal vez sería razonable pensar en su incorporación a una metodología basada en agentes.

Otros análisis tanto globales como puntuales pueden ser efectuados a partir de los resultados obtenidos. Sin embargo, por motivos de espacio, nos limitamos a aquellos expuestos anteriormente.

5 Conclusiones y Trabajos futuros

En este trabajo se ha presentado el análisis de métodos y técnicas de ingeniería de requisitos que nos permitan la captura de las principales abstracciones en las tempranas fases del proceso de diseño y desarrollo de sistemas basados en agentes.

En particular, se presenta un análisis comparativo de métodos considerando enfoques complementarios basados en metas y en casos de uso.

Para contar con un marco comparativo se han identificados las abstracciones que caracterizan a los MAS y se han definidos otras características generales deseables en los métodos que soportan el proceso de diseño de cualquier sistema. Además, se han definidos métricas para facilitar la evaluación comparativa. Para la comparación se ha utilizado el caso de estudio de un sistema de Conference Management System. De la evaluación se desprende que GBRAM ofrece una mejor cobertura de las abstracciones de agentes y RETO ofrece mejores características desde la perspectiva de las cualidades deseables de un método. Por ende, se podría sugerir una integración de ambos para obtener un proceso más consolidado en la fase de requisitos de las metodologías para sistemas basados en agentes.

Considerando el mayor desarrollo y soporte que ofrece RETO, se considera un interesante trabajo futuro la extensión y adaptación específica del método a nivel metodológico y también de la herramienta CASE correspondiente. Por otra parte, en los proyectos industriales, algunas abstracciones y características pueden tener mayor relevancia que otras y por lo tanto como trabajo futuro se podría asignar diferentes pesos a las mismas para ofrecer la posibilidad de elección en función de las necesidades particulares de cada proyecto.

Referencias

1. Agent UML. http://www.auml.org
2. Anton, A.: "Goal-based requirements analysis". ICRE 96, pp.136–144, Colorado Springs, Colorado USA, (1996).
3. Cernuzzi, L., Cossentino, M., Zambonelli, F.: "Process Models for Agent-based Development". Journal of Engineering Applications of Artificial Intelligence, Vol. 18, No. 2, Elsevier, pp. 205-222, (2005).
4. DeLoach, S., Wood, M., and Sparkman C.: Multiagent systems engineering. International Journal of Software Engineering and Knowledge Engineering, 11(3):231-258, (2001).
5. Giorgini, P., Kolp, M., Mylopoulos, J. and Castro, J.: "Tropos: A Requirements-Driven Methodology for Agent-Oriented Software". In Agent-Oriented Methodologies (B. Henderson-Sellers and P. Giorgini, Eds.), Idea Group, 20–45, (2005).
6. Gómez-Sanz, J. and Pavón, J.: Agent Oriented Software Engineering with INGENIAS. Proceedings of the 3rd Central and Eastern Europe Conference on Multiagent Systems, Springer Verlag, LNCS 2691, pp. 394-403, (2003).
7. Insfrán, E.: A Requirements Engineering Approach for Object-Oriented Conceptual Modeling. PhD Thesis, Universidad Politécnica de Valencia, España, (2003).
8. Insfrán, E., Pastor, O., Wieringa, R.: Requirements Engineering-Based Conceptual Modeling. Accepted for the Requirements Engineering Journal, (2002).
9. Maiden, N.: CREWS-SAVRE: Scenarios for Acquiring and Validating Requirements. Automated Software Engineering, 5(4): 419-446, (1998).
10. Nuseibeh, B. and Easterbrook, S.: "Requirements Engineering: A Roadmap". In Proceedings of the 22nd International Conference on Software Engineering, ICSE'00.
11. Odell, J.: "The Agentis Development Approach Methodology: Core Development". Agentis Software Inc., (2005).
12. Odell, J., Parunak, H. V. D. and Bauer, B.: Extending UML for agents. In G. Wagner, Y. Lesperance, and E. Yu, editors, Proceedings of the Agent-Oriented Information Systems Workshop at the 17th National conference on Artificial Intelligence, Austin, Texas, July (2000). ICue Publishing.
13. Richard Hill, S., Beer, M.: Managing Community Healthcare Information in a Multi-Agent System Environment. Proceedings of the Fourth International Joint Conference on Autonomous Agents and Multiagent Systems (AAMAS): BIOMED Workshop, Utrecht University, Netherlands, (2005).
14. Van Lamsweerde, A., Darimont, R. and Letier, E.: Managing conflicts in goal-driven requirements engineering. IEEE Transactions on Software Engineering, 24(11): 908-926, (1998).
15. Yu, E.: "Towards Modelling and Reasoning Support for Early-Phase Requirements Engineering". Proceedings of the 3rd IEEE Int. Symp. on Requirements Engineering (RE'97), Washington D.C., USA. pp. 226-235, (1997).
16. Zambonelli, F., Jennings, N. R., Wooldridge, M.: Developing Multiagent Systems: the Gaia Methodology. ACM Transactions on Software Engineering and Methodology, Vol. 12, No. 3, pp. 417-470, (2003).
17. Zambonelli, F. and Omicini, A.: Challenges and Research Directions in Agent-Oriented Software Engineering. Journal of Autonomous Agents and Multiagent Systems, vol. 9, No. 3, Kluwer Academic Publishers, pp 253-283, (2004).

A Modeling Language for Advanced Separation of Concerns in Multi-Agent Systems

Carla Silva[1,*], João Araújo[2], Jaelson Castro[1], Ana Moreira[2], Márcia Lucena[1] and Leonardo Sarmento[1]

[1] Centro de Informática, Universidade Federal de Pernambuco, 50732-970, Recife, Brazil
{ctlls, jbc, mjnrl, lcms}@cin.ufpe.br
[2] Dept. Informática, FCT, Universidade Nova de Lisboa, 2829-516 Caparica, Portugal
{ja, amm}@di.fct.unl.pt

Abstract. The development of complex systems in open and dynamic environments benefits from the use of autonomous software architectures provided by multi-agent systems (MAS). Agent orientation offers a higher level of abstraction when thinking about software systems features and behavior, but this paradigm does not support the modularization of some properties that affect several system components. These properties are called crosscutting concerns. To proper describe the detailed design of MAS, it is required to model crosscutting abstractions. This paper proposes a metamodel to describe and modularize crosscutting concerns in detailed design of multi-agent systems. To illustrate the use of the proposed modeling language, we use an e-commerce example.

Keywords. Software Design, Modeling Language, Multi-agent Systems, Aspect-oriented Software Development

1 Introduction

Multi-agent based software engineering is appropriate to develop complex systems as autonomous entities that take the initiative to achieve system goals and represent software users. Several methodologies, specification languages and support tools have been proposed to support the development of such systems. In particular, this work aims at improving Tropos [10], a requirements-driven framework aimed at building multi-agent systems.

Multi-agent systems (MAS) are not free of *crosscutting concerns*, i.e., concerns that cut across the boundaries of other concerns. For example, it is recognized that the current use of design patterns can lead to the tangling and scattering of design patterns concerns with the functional modules concerns of the application [17] [11] [19] [2] [21]. Moreover, other systemic crosscutting concerns, such as exception handling, fault tolerance and context awareness, have been detected in MAS [9]. To handle

* Currently in post-doc position at Universidade Nova de Lisboa

these issues, we can use aspect orientation [12] which proposes means for modularization and composition of crosscutting concerns. In Aspect Oriented Software Development (AOSD), crosscutting concerns are encapsulated into separated units, called *aspects*. This improved separation of concerns increases software modularity and, consequently, software reusability, maintainability and understandability, as well as it reduces development costs. Several design modeling languages have been proposed to support the development of aspect oriented systems [4][5][24], but none of them is tailored for multi-agent systems using agent abstractions as first-order elements.

In this paper, we extend the agency metamodel, introduced in [20], with aspectual abstractions to modularize crosscutting concerns in multi-agent systems design. The proposed metamodel, called aspectual metamodel, is initially described as a UML profile [18] to benefit from the available tool support. A modeling language, based on the aspectual metamodel, is illustrated by a classical case study for multi-agent systems: the Medi@ System [3].

This paper is organized as follows. Section 2 reviews Tropos, social patterns, the agent-oriented notation, based on the agency metamodel, and the AOSD. Section 3 introduces the aspectual metamodel as well as the aspectual notation to describe MAS detailed design. Section 4 presents the Medi@ case study. Section 5 discusses related works. Last but not least, section 7 summarizes our work and points out future work.

2 Background

The purpose of this work is to propose a metamodel to support aspect oriented abstractions in MAS detailed design. Based on this metamodel, a modeling language is defined to separate and modularize crosscutting concerns in detailed design phase of Tropos framework, such as social patterns concerns. The proposed modeling language is based on the agent-oriented notation introduced in [20]. Thus, this section overviews Tropos framework and Social Patterns (section 2.1), the agent-oriented notation (section 2.2) and the aspect oriented software development (section 2.3).

2.1 Tropos and Social Patterns

Tropos supports five phases of software development: early requirements, late requirements, architectural design, detailed design and implementation [3].

This paper focuses on the detailed design, which is intended to introduce additional detail for each architectural component of a system. In this phase, designers can be guided by a catalogue of multi-agent patterns which offer a set of standard solutions. Tropos has defined a set of design patterns, called social patterns [14], focusing on social and intentional aspects that are recurrent in multi-agent and cooperative systems. Examples of social patterns include booking, subscription, monitor, broker, mediator, wrapper and matchmaker. However, it has been recognized that the use of design patterns can make application core dependent on patterns, decreasing the possibilities of reuse [17].

For example consider the Matchmaker pattern, which involves an intermediary agent (Yellow Pages Server) that receives requests from service Providers to subscribe/unsubscribe its services into the Yellow Pages maintained by it. A Client may need a specific service provided by an unknown Provider. The Yellow Pages Server also receives requests from Clients to locate some Providers which offer a specific service. If there is some Provider for the requested service, the Yellow Pages Server informs that Provider's identification to the Client which, in turn, can directly interact with it [21].

JADE is a suitable agent platform to support the implementation of MAS. In JADE, a behavior represents a task that an agent can carry out. For example in the case of the Matchmaker pattern, the implementation of each pattern participant concern (i.e., Client, Yellow Pages Server and Provider concerns) will be provided by the JADE's API (Application Programming Interface) [1]. In particular, the behavior of the main participant of the Matchmaker pattern [14], i.e., the Yellow Pages Server agent, is encapsulated into the DF (Directory Facilitator) agent. Hence, it provides a service by means of which a client agent can find other agents providing the services it requires in order to achieve its goals. A provider agent willing to publish one or more services must inform the DF a description including its Agent Id (AID) and the list of available services. The services provided by the DF agent (Yellow Pages Server) are usually used by the MAS agents implemented in JADE. Thus, all agents who need to register or unregister its services in the Yellow Pages of the DF agent will implement the Provider's concern. Similarly, all agents who need to find a specific provider agent in the Yellow Pages will implement the Client's concern. Note that the Yellow Pages Server concern is implemented within the DF agent and its implementation is hidden in the JADE's API. In this case, the Yellow Pages Server participant concern will not crosscut the application functional modules.

However, both the Provider and Client concerns of the Matchmaker pattern are going to be implemented by several agents in a multi-agent system. Consequently, these concerns become tangled with the concerns of these agents (i.e., application core functionality) and scattered in the system, compromising reusability, maintainability and understandability. To address these issues, we advocate the use of aspect oriented abstractions and mechanisms in the detailed design of MAS.

2.2 Agent Oriented Notation

To support the detailed design phase of Tropos, in [20] we have proposed a metamodel wherein an extended version of UML 2.0 [18] is used as a notation to describe MAS design. The agency metamodel defines the constructs required to specify structural and dynamic features of MAS detailed design. Due to lack of space, in this paper we only review the structural diagram (for an example see Fig. 1). According to Tropos, multi-agent systems are designed in terms of AgentRoles. A Dependum defines an "agreement" of service providing between two AgentRoles. An AgentRole is an abstract characterization of the behavior of a social actor within some specialized context, domain or endeavor. It pursues a Goal, which is a condition or state of affairs in the world. A MacroPlan encapsulates a partial recipe for achieving a goal and is composed of ComplexActions which, in turn, determines abstract steps to perform a MacroPlan. Some ComplexActions can be directly involved with the accomplishment of a Dependum, so that they are placed in the operation compartment of this Dependum. The AgentRole responsible for providing the service possesses a SocialPort playing the role of dependee and is related to the Dependum through a Dependee relationship. The AgentRole which requests the service possesses a SocialPort playing the role of depender and is related to the Dependum through a Depender relationship. A dependum can be of four types: goals, softgoals, tasks and resources [25], defined as the enumeration class DependumKind. A SocialPort is a property of a classifier that specifies a distinct interaction point between that AgentRole and its environment. To accomplish some Dependum an AgentRole exchange messages through SocialPorts connected by a SocialConnector. SocialConnector specifies a link that enables communication between two AgentRoles. Since a SocialConnector connector is an extension of *assembly* connector [18], we can use a dependency as a notation for SocialConnector.

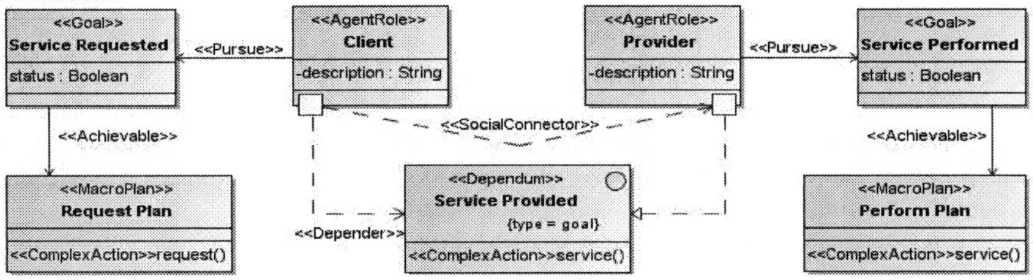

Fig. 1. Structural Diagram

To illustrate the use of the modeling language based on the agency metamodel, let's consider the situation where a client requests some services to a provider. The model in Fig. 1 shows the Provider agentRole, responsible for performing the service defined in the Dependum. This AgentRole aims at achieving the ServicePerformed goal by executing the PerformPlan MacroPlan, which, in turn, consists of performing the service() ComplexAction. The Client agentRole aims at achieving the ServiceRequest goal by executing the RequestPlan MacroPlan, which, in turn, consists of performing the request() ComplexAction. Therefore, the Client agentRole is responsible for requesting the service defined in the Dependum. Both the message for requesting the service execution and the message for confirming whether the service was successfully concluded are sent through the SocialConnector.

2.3 Aspect Oriented Software Development

Crosscutting concerns can be found in most systems; many of them are related to software global constraints and system properties, such as security, reliability, persistence, exception handling, logging and distribution [12].

In Aspect Oriented Software Development (AOSD), crosscutting concerns are encapsulated into separated units, called *aspects*, to improve the modularization of these concerns [12]. Composition mechanisms are then responsible for weaving an aspect with the base units it affects. To do so, it is necessary to have a:

- Join point: indicating the point where the crosscutting concern should join the behavior of the base unit(s) (e.g. a class or even an aspect) it cuts across [13];
- Composition rule: expressing the sequential order into which each aspect must be composed with the base unit(s) it cuts across. It specifies if the aspect behavior is going to be applied *before*, *after* or *around* the join point [13]:
  - Before: the composition happens whenever a join point is reached and before the actual computation proceeds;
  - After: the composition happens after the computation "under the join point" finishes, i.e. after the method body has run, and just before control is returned to the caller;
  - Around: the composition happens whenever a join point is reached, and has explicit control whether the computation under the join point is allowed to run at all.

Aspect oriented design modeling requires higher-level models that addresses the aspect oriented programming concepts but avoiding language specific details. It should allow the designer to work at a more abstract level during software construction and evolution. In fact, design models must conform to design principles, such as low coupling and high cohesion, as well as promote understandability of software solution [4]. Taking this premise into account, we propose the aspectual metamodel to provide an aspectual modeling language for MAS detailed design.

3 A Metamodel to Support Aspect Orientation in MAS Design

The mechanisms provided by agent-orientation are not sufficient to modularize properly the crosscutting concerns. In fact, some system properties such as context-awareness, fault-tolerance [9], security, as well as design patterns [21] cannot be located in separated modules using only agent-oriented abstractions. This issue can be solved by using abstractions and practices provided by the aspect orientation for separating system crosscutting concerns [12]. In doing so, we present an Aspectual Metamodel able to specify aspectual modules and how they must be composed with the base unit(s) it cut across. To describe aspect oriented abstractions we need to define: (i) a unit to encapsulate the crosscutting concern – the Aspect class; (ii) each behavior a crosscutting concerns comprises – the Advice operation; (iii) the definition of the distinct ways a crosscutting concern may affect a base unit – the Enhancement interface; (iv) the point where the crosscutting concern should join the behavior of the base unit it cuts across – the BaseOperation operation; (v) the specification of how and in which sequence the crosscutting behavior must be applied to the base units – the PointCut expression; (vi) the definition of a distinct interaction point between the crosscutting concern and the base unit – the AspectualPort port; and (vii) the explicit relationship between them – the Crosscut connector.

To make easier the understanding of the Aspectual Metamodel, in the following we present first the modeling language based on this metamodel. Thus, let us consider the situation presented in Fig. 1, where a Client requests a Provider to perform a service. In particular, we intend to keep track of the Provider's behavior. To do so, we can use the logging concern [16], which is a classical example of a crosscutting concern. Logging is an intrusive concern that watches what the base application does by sending messages to a *logfile* with information from the base application. In this case, we can create an aspect to encapsulate the logging concern and separate it from the other components. Observe in Fig. 2 that a stereotyped class is used to represent the Logging Aspect in the MAS detailed design.

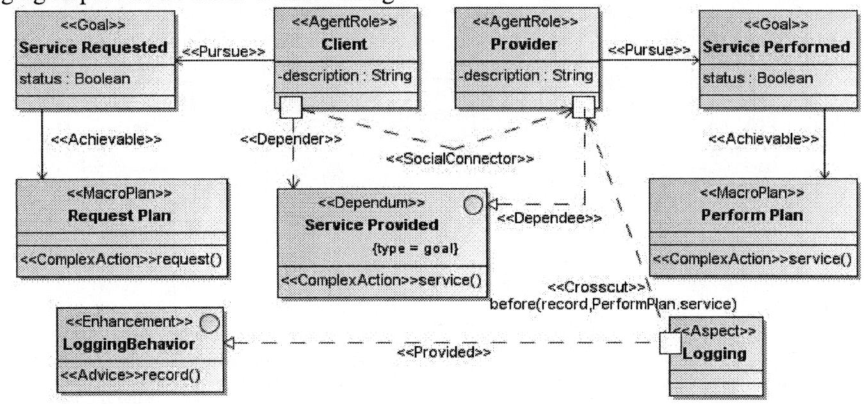

Fig. 2. Aspectual Model

Fig. 2 shows the Provider AgentRole being affected by the Logging Aspect. It means that every execution of service ComplexOperation is going to be logged through record Advice. Observe that the Crosscut connector contains expressions responsible for composing the Aspect to the AgentRole. As specified in UML metamodel [18], an expression can be placed in the form *symbol (operand1, operand2).* In our approach, we have defined the PointCut element as an expression in which the symbol is a CompositionRule, the operand1 is an Advice and the operand2 is a ComplexOperation. It means that the operand1 will affect the operand2 in the situation stated by the symbol.

The presented notation is based on the Aspectual Metamodel depicted in Fig. 3. In particular, this metamodel is an extension of the agency metamodel [20] in which we added constructs required to specify aspectual modules, base modules and the relationship between them. For the sake of space, Fig. 3 presents only some of the concepts already defined in the agency metamodel (highlighted in gray color).

In the Aspectual Metamodel (Fig. 3) an Aspect encapsulates a crosscutting concern and each of its distinct behaviors is defined in an Enhancement interface provided by the Aspect. Each Aspect possesses at least one AspectualPort which specifies a distinct interaction point between that Aspect and the base modules. Thus, an Aspect will affect a base module through a Crosscut connector which is attached to its AspectualPort by a CrosscutEnd and to the base module's port by a BaseConnectorEnd. Observe that the base module affected by the Aspect can be either an AgentRole (Fig. 1) or an Aspect, since the BaseConnectorEnd can be specialized in SocialConnectorEnd or CrosscutEnd. Considering the base module as an AgentRole, the other extreme of the Crosscutt connector is attached to a SocialPort through a SocialConnectorEnd. If the base module is an Aspect, the other extreme of the Crosscutt connector is also attached to an AspectualPort through a CrosscutEnd.

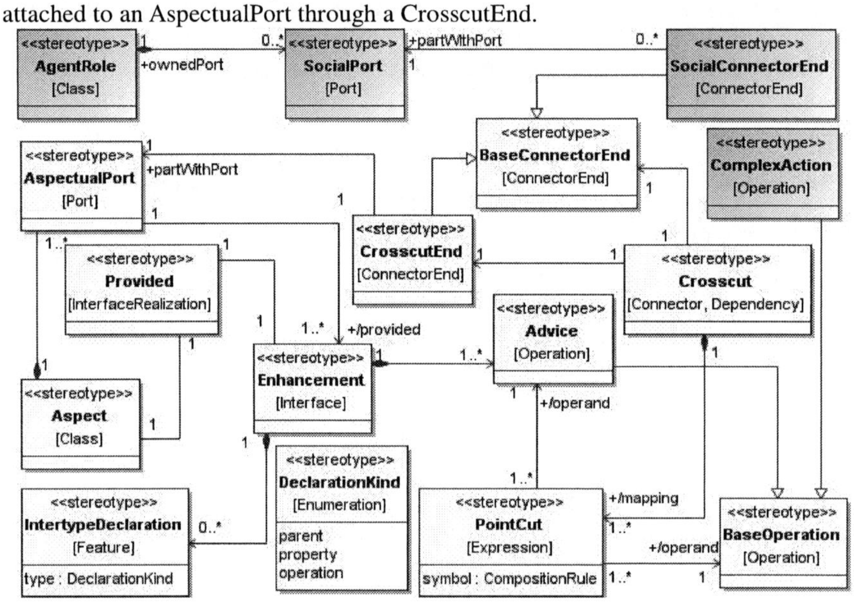

Fig. 3. Aspectual Metamodel

A Crosscut connector is an extension of the Assembly Connector (a kind of connector) [18], but it overwrites the constraint of the Assembly Connector, i.e., instead of being defined from a required port to a provided port, a crosscut connector is defined from a provided port to another provided port (in the case of an Aspect affecting another Aspect) or from a provided port to a dependee port (in the case of an Aspect affecting a AgentRole).

Observe that the Enhancement interface realized by the Aspect is composed of at least one advice which comprises a crosscutting behavior to be added to the base modules. Other feature that can compose an Enhancement interface is the IntertypeDeclaration. This declaration specifies a new member (property or operation) to the classes to which the aspect is attached, or changes the inheritance relationship between classes [8]. Thus, IntertypeDeclarations can be of three types: parent, property and operation. A *parent* IntertypeDeclaration changes the inheritance hierarchy of a base module by changing or adding a supertype to it. A *property* IntertypeDeclaration changes the static structure of a base module by adding a new property, while an *operation* IntertypeDeclaration changes it by adding a new operation.

An important feature of the Crosscut connector is that it possesses the information related to the binding between the Aspect and the base module. This information is a PointCut expression which maps an Advice operation (provided by the Aspect) to an Operation (performed by the base module) by using a CompositionRule (after, around or before). This expression informs the point and the situation in which the Aspect will affect the base module.

In the next section we present a case study based on an e-commerce multi-agent system to illustrate the use of our design modeling language to modularize both systemic crosscutting concerns, such as security, and patterns crosscutting concerns, such as the matchmaker social pattern.

4 Medi@ System Aspectual Detailed Design

Media Shop [3] sells and ships different kinds of media items such as books, newspapers, magazines, audio CDs, videotapes, and the like. To increase market share, Media Shop has decided to open up a B2C retail sales front on the Internet. The basic objective for the new system is to allow an on-line customer to examine the items in its catalogue and place orders. Fig. 4 shows one view of the Medi@ detailed design by using the aspectual notation.

Medi@ system is structured into three AgentRoles: Front Store, Back Store and Billing Processor. *Front Store* is responsible for supplying a customer with a web shopping cart to keep track of items the customer is buying when visiting *Medi@*. *Back Store* keeps track of all web information about customers and other data of strategic importance to Media Shop. *Billing Processor* is in charge of the management of orders, bills and other financial data [3].

As expected to an e-commerce system, security is an essential non-functional requirement to be achieved in this system. In fact, clients exposed to the internet are, like servers, at risk in web applications. It is possible for web browsers and application servers to download or upload content and programs that could represent a certain degree of risk to the system and the information it manages. Thus, a security requirement might be operationalized by requesting client authorization, encrypting personal data or checking data consistency for each business transaction.

4.1 The Security Concern

The security concern is tangled and scattered with all Medi@ agentRoles. For example, when the customer places an order for the first time in the Medi@ system, he has to fulfill a profile form. It contains the Customer's personal data such as address, credit card number, phone number, etc. Thus, all the customer data might be encrypted by the Front Store agentRole before sending it to the Back Store agentRole.

To finish the order of items added to custormer's shopping cart, the Front Store agentRole must request specific customer's information for authorization. Moreover, to process the billing information, it is needed to access customer's information such as the credit card number and delivery address. This data must be also encrypted by the Back Store agentRole before sending it to the Billing Processor agentRole.

In order to avoid that scattering and tangling of the security with base modules of MAS, a proper notation to locate crosscutting concerns in separate modules is required. Thus, we can use the aspectual notation to proper describe the Medi@ detailed design. In the model depicted in Fig. 4, the Security concern is modularized into an aspect which encapsulates two crosscutting behaviors: the Encryption and Authorization behaviors. They are defined in each Enhancement interface provided by the Aspect, namely the Encryption enhancement and Authorization enhancement, which will affect differently each module of the Medi@ system.

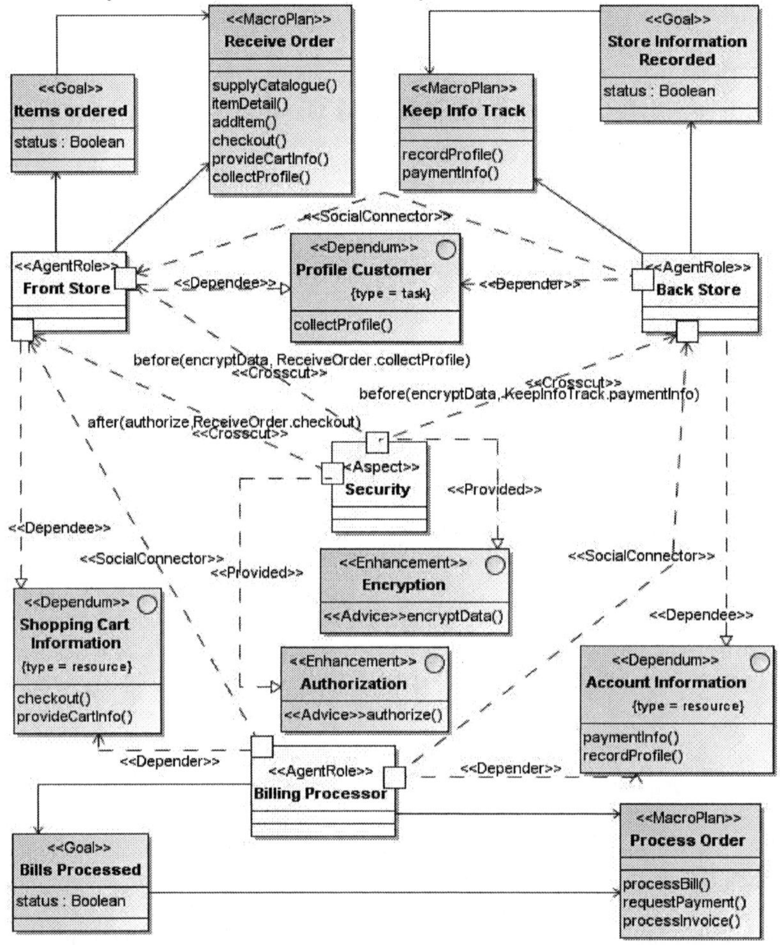

Fig. 4. First view of the Aspectual Model for Medi@

For example, the Security aspect crosscuts the Front Store agentRole with both the Encryption and Authorization enhancements, as well as the Back Store agentRole with the Encryption enhancement. The Encryption enhancement adds to the Front Store agentRole the ability to encrypt data before collecting the customer's profile. It also adds to the Back Store agentRole the ability to encrypt data before sending payment information to the Billing Processor agentRole. The Authorization enhancement, in turn, adds to the Front Store agentRole the ability to authorize the customer after performing checkout of the shopping cart. This improved separation of concerns in MAS produces software artifacts that are easier to maintain and reuse, since each concern in located into separate components.

For the sake of simplicity, some of the dependencies between the AgentRoles composing Medi@, as well as the «ComplexAcion» stereotypes were omitted. Observe that each ComplexAction defined in a MacroPlan must be available in some Dependum implemented by an AgentRole. An interested reader can find the complete specification of the Medi@ design in [22].

Some systemic properties are recognized as being crosscutting concerns, such as error handling, fault tolerance [9] and security, as illustrated in this section. In addition, other concerns present crosscutting characteristics such as design patterns concerns [11] [19] [2] [21]. Next section we use the proposed aspectual notation to modularize the Matchmaker pattern concern in the Medi@ detailed design.

4.2. The Matchmaker Pattern Concern

The Medi@ system has the Availability requirement, i.e., the system has to ensure easier recovery of the system if some agent in the system stops running. This requirement could not be shown in the case study because we did not present the requirements models of the Medi@ system. However, the interested reader can find it in [3].

Analyzing the description of several patterns [14], we have concluded that the most suitable pattern to address the Availability requirement is the Matchmaker, since it enables the search for another agent to replace the one that has stopped. Thus, the focus of the aspectual model depicted in Fig. 5 is to present the Matchmaker Aspect and its composition with the agentRoles of Medi@ system. For this reason, in this view of the aspectual model, we have omitted the Security Aspect for the sake of simplicity. The Matchmaker Aspect encapsulates two crosscutting behaviors: the Client and the Provider behaviors. They are defined in each Enhancement interface provided by the Aspect, namely the Client enhancement and Provider enhancement. Each of these behaviors is going to affect the agentRoles in the system in a distinct way. For example, the Client enhancement will affect an agentRole by adding the ability to request the identification of a specific service provider to the Yellow Pages Server agentRole. The Provider enhancement, in turn, will affect an agentRole by adding the ability to subscribe or unsubscribe in the yellow pages of the Yellow Pages Server agentRole.

Since we have chosen JADE as the target agent implementation environment, we are going to consider the JADE's Directory Facilitator (DF) agent as the implementation of the pattern's Yellow Pages Server participant. For this reason, the Matchmaker Aspect does not present a third enhancement, called Yellow Pages Server enhancement. Thus, we do not need to worry about the separation of the Yellow Pages Server participant concern since it is already implemented in the JADE's API.

According to the Fig. 5, the Matchmaker Aspect crosscuts the Front Store agentRole with the Provider enhancement, as well as the Back Store agentRole with the Client enhancement. The Provider enhancement adds to the Front Store agentRole the ability to request its subscription in DF's yellow page before collecting the customer's profile. It also adds to the Front Store agentRole the ability to request its unsubscription in DF's yellow page after performing checkout of the shopping cart. The Client enhancement, in turn, adds to the Back Store agentRole the ability to request the information of a specific provider to the DF while it is recording a profile. For the sake of simplicity we have omitted some of the crosscut relationships. For example, the Matchmaker aspect also crosscut the Billing Processor agentRole with Client enhancement since it needs to locate the Back Store to request the Customer's payment information. Therefore, the Back Store agentRole is also affected by the Matchmaker aspect with Provider enhancement.

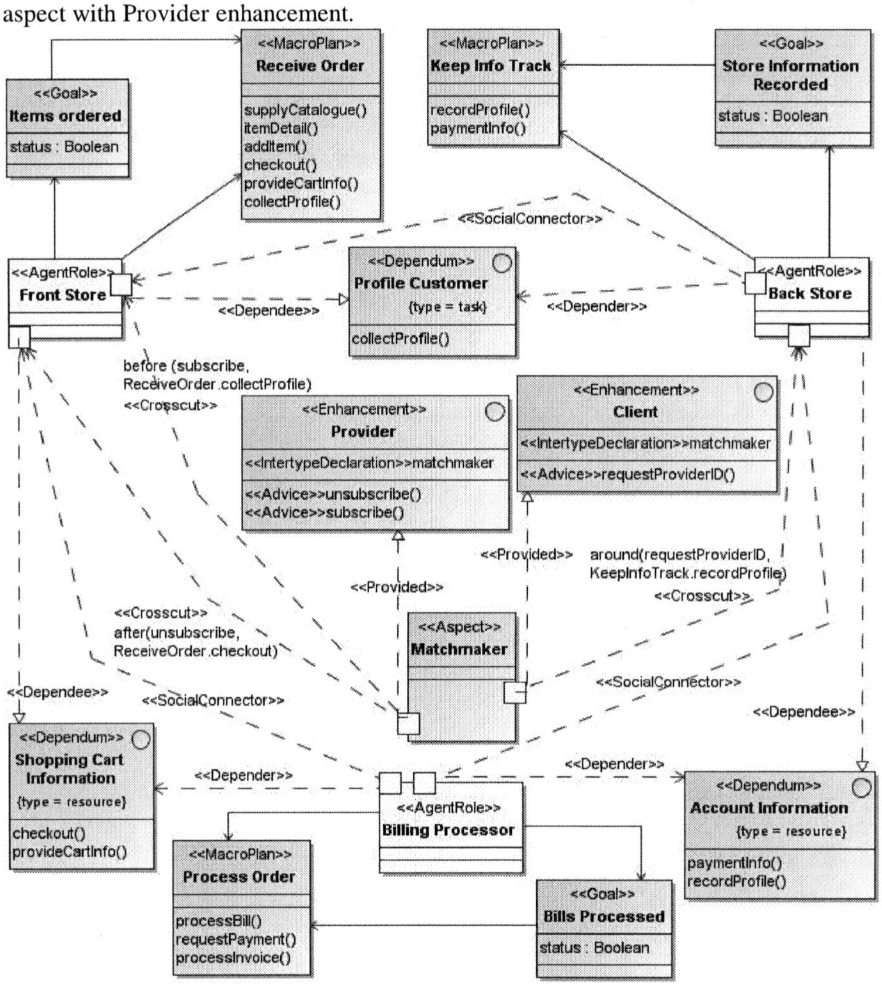

Fig. 5. Second view of the Aspectual Model for Medi@

The Matchmaker pattern ensures the decoupling among modules contributing to the achievement of the system's availability. For example, if a Front Store agentRole contacted by a Back Store agentRole stops running, the Back Store may replace it by requesting to the Directory Facilitator to locate another one in its yellow pages.

5 Related Work

Aspect oriented design requires models that facilitate the specification of systems in the presence of multiple aspects and crosscutting, as well as reduce the gap between system design and implementation [4]. In this light, several modeling languages have been proposed to support the design of aspect oriented systems. For example, Aspect Oriented Design Model (AODM) [24] enhances the existing UML specification with aspect oriented concepts that reproduces the crosscutting characteristics of the AspectJ language. The aSideML [4] is an aspect oriented modeling language based on the UML that provides notation, semantics and rules for specifying aspects and crosscutting at the design level of OO systems. Theme/UML [5] is an approach that handles crosscutting concerns at design level by means of themes. In this proposal, each model contains its own theme, i.e., the design of an individual requirement. A composition relationship specifies how thematic design models are to be composed by identifying overlapping concepts in different models and specifying how models should be integrated. These proposals do not support MAS development.

A particular approach, proposed by Garcia [8], promotes separation of specific agent concerns by using aspect oriented abstractions and methods. These specific agent concerns include interaction, adaptation, autonomy, knowledge, collaboration, roles, learning, and mobility. In particular, we consider these concerns as agent abilities. In [8], aspects were used to capture these agent abilities that are hard to modularize with existing abstractions of object-oriented software engineering. This proposal uses the aSideML notation [4]. We are also interested in multi-agent systems development. However, we are not concerned with the separation of agent abilities since we consider them as internal, i.e., already built-in and supported by some agent implementation platform. We use aspect oriented abstractions to support the separation and modularization of agent-oriented design patterns concerns instead of agent abilities.

In Silva et al. [21], we have proposed a technique to describe social patterns by promoting the separation and modularization of its concerns and the latter systematic composition with the MAS base modules. This technique is called Agent Pattern Specification (APS) and was developed by specializing the agency metamodel [20] with the use of model roles [7]. In contrast to our current work, the APS technique does not consider the aspectual abstractions as first-order elements. Moreover, the APS technique was used only to modularize social patterns concerns and other crosscutting concerns, such as security, were not taken into account until that moment. However, the authors intend to investigate if the APS technique can be used to modularize systemic crosscutting concerns and compare the results to our current proposal.

6 Conclusions

Aspect orientation complements current paradigms aiming at improving the separation of crosscutting concerns in software development and, therefore, providing better understandability, maintainability and reusability to the artifacts generated during software development lifecycle.

This paper has focused on a detailed design modeling language for complex software systems developed with agent technology. We have introduced a metamodel to describe the detailed design of multi-agent systems by separating and modularizing crosscutting concerns in aspectual abstractions. Modeling MAS behavior has already been proposed in [20] as an extension of the UML's sequence diagram. However, modeling the dynamic composition between the aspect and the base modules in MAS is required. This is theme for future work.

A problem that needs to be handled when developing MAS is related to models' scalability. In fact, modeling even simple agent-oriented systems tends to produce complex models, since there is much information to capture. This issue can be handled by using views of the models to the extent that the models' complexity increases (such as we did in Fig. 4 and Fig. 5).

Besides supporting detailed design phase of Tropos with proper modeling language, our purpose in defining the Aspectual Metamodel also includes using the principles of Model Driven Engineering [23] to generate models through model transformations rules.

In this work we have chosen to define the Aspectual Metamodel as an extension of the UML metamodel, in doing so we can benefit from the available CASE tool support. However, we intend to create our own concrete syntax (graphical representation) for the modeling language defined by the Aspectual Metamodel, rather than using the UML concrete syntax. To achieve this, we can describe the proposed metamodel using the eCore metametamodel [6] and use other features provided by the Eclipse to support automatized checking of completeness and consistency of models.

Acknowledgements

This work was supported by the CAPES-GRICES (Project 129/05) and PICDT-CAPES research grants.

References

1. Bellifemine, F., Caire, G., Poggi, A., Rimassa, G.: JADE - A White Paper. In: Special issue on JADE of the TILAB Journal EXP (2003)
2. Cacho, N., Sant'Anna, C., Figueiredo, E., Garcia, A., Batista, T., Lucena, C.: Composing Design Patterns: A Scalability Study of Aspect-Oriented Programming. In: 5th Aspect-Oriented Software Development (AOSD'06). Bonn, Germany (2006)
3. Castro, J., Kolp, M., and Mylopoulos, J.: Towards Requirements-Driven Information Systems Engineering: The Tropos Project. In: Information Systems Journal, Vol. 27. Elsevier, (2002) 365–89
4. Chavez, C., Garcia, A., Kulesza, U., Sant'Anna, C., Lucena, C.: Taming Heterogeneous Aspects with Crosscutting Interfaces. J. of the Brazilian Computer Society. SBC (2006)
5. Clarke, S., Baniassad, E.: Aspect-Oriented Analysis and Design. Addison-Wesley (2005)
6. The Eclipse Foundation. Eclipse Modeling Framework, http://www.eclipse.org/modeling/emf/, last access in 09/2007.

7. France, R., Kim, D., Ghosh, S., Song, E.: A UML-Based Pattern Specification Technique. In: IEEE Transactions on Software Engineering, Vol. 30 (2004) 193–2006
8. Garcia, A.: From Objects to Agents: An Aspect-Oriented Approach. PhD Thesis, Computer Science Department, PUC-Rio, Rio de Janeiro, Brazil (2004)
9. Garcia, A., Kulesza, U., Sant'Anna, C., Chavez, C., Lucena, C.: Aspects in Agent-Oriented Software Engineering: Lessons Learned. In: Agent-Oriented Software Engineering at AAMAS 05. Utrecht, The Netherlands (2005)
10. Giorgini, P., Kolp, M., Mylopoulos, J., Castro, J.: Tropos: A Requirements-Driven Methodology for Agent-Oriented Software. In: Henderson-Sellers, B., Giorgini, P. (eds.): Agent-Oriented Methodologies. Idea Group (2005) 20–45
11. Hannemann, J., Kiczales, G.: Design Pattern Implementation in Java and AspectJ. In: 17th Annual ACM Conference on Object-Oriented Programming, Systems, Languages, and Applications (OOPSLA'02). Seattle, WA (2002) 161–173
12. Kiczales, G., Lamping, J., Mendhekar, A., Maeda, C., Lopes, C., Loingtier, J., Irwin, J.: Aspect-Oriented Programming. In: 11th European Conference on Object-Oriented Programming (ECOOP'97). Finland, Springer-Verlag (1997)
13. Kiczales, G., Hilsdale, E., Hugunin, J., Kersten, M., Palm, J., Griswold, W.G.: An Overview of AspectJ. In: Knudsen, J.L. (eds.): 15th European Conference on Object-Oriented Programming (ECOOP'01). LNCS, Vol. 2072. Springer Verlag (2001) 327–353
14. Kolp, M., Do, T.T., Faulkner, S. and Hoang, H.T.T.: Introspecting Agent Oriented Design Patterns. In: Chang, S. (eds.): Advances Software Engineering and Knowledge Engineering, Vol. 3. World Publishing (2005)
15. Kulesza, U., Garcia, A. and Lucena, C.: Towards a Method for the Development of Aspect-Oriented Generative Approaches. In: Workshop on Early Aspects: Aspect-Oriented Requirements Engineering and Architecture Design at OOPSLA'04. Vancouver, CA (2004)
16. Lieberherr, K.: Controlling the Complexity of Software Designs. In: International Conference on Software Engineering (ICSE'04) (2004) 2–11
17. Noda, N. and Kishi, T.: Implementing Design Patterns Using Advanced Separation of Concerns. In: Workshop on Advanced Separation of Concerns in Object-Oriented Systems (OOPSLA'01), Tampa Bay, FL (2001)
18. Object Management Group (OMG). Unified Modeling Language (UML) Superstructure, Version 2.0. http://www.omg.org/docs/formal/05-07-04.pdf (2005) last access in 09/2007
19. Sant'Anna, C., Garcia, A., Kulesza, U., Lucena, C. and von Staa, A.: Design Patterns as Aspects: A Quantitative Assessment. In: J. of the Brazilian Computer Society. SBC (2004)
20. Silva, C. et al.: Improving Multi-Agent Architectural Design. In: Choren, R., Garcia, A., Giese, H., Leung, H., Lucena, C., Romanovsky, A. (eds.): Software Engineering for Multi-Agent Systems V: Research Issues and Practical Applications. LNCS, Vol. 4408. Springer-Verlag (2007) 165–184
21. Silva, C., Araújo, J., Moreira, A., Castro, J.: Designing Social Patterns using Advanced Separation of Concerns. In: Krogstie, J., Opdahl, A., Sindre, G. (eds.): 19th International Conference on Advanced Information Systems Engineering (CAiSE'07). LNCS, Vol. 4495. Springer-Verlag (2007) 309–323
22. Silva, C. et al.: A Modeling Language to Support Separation of Crosscutting Concerns in MAS. http://www.cin.ufpe.br/~ctlls/DLASoC.pdf (2007) last access 24/09/2007.
23. Stahl, T., Volter, M.: Model-Driven Software Development. 1st edition. John Wiley, Glasgow, UK (2006)
24. Stein, D.: An Aspect-Oriented Design Model Based on AspectJ and UML. Master Thesis, University of Duisburg-Essen, Germany (2002)
25. Yu, E.: Modelling Strategic Relationships for Process Reengineering. Ph.D. Thesis, Department of Computer Science, University of Toronto, Canada (1995)

Modelado de Requisitos de Seguridad para Almacenes de Datos

Emilio Soler[1], Veronika Stefanov[2], Jose-Norberto Mazón[3], Juan Trujillo[3], Eduardo Fernández-Medina[4], Mario Piattini[4]

[1] Departamento de Informática
Universidad de Matanzas, Cuba
emilio.soler@umcc.cu

[2] Women's Postgraduate College for Internet Technologies
Institute of Software Technology and Interactive Systems
Vienna University of Technology, Austria
stefanov@wit.tuwien.ac.at

[3] Departamento de Lenguajes y Sistemas Informáticos
Universidad of Alicante, Spain
{jnmazon,jtrujillo}@dlsi.ua.es

[4] Departamento de Tecnologías y Sistemas de Información
Universidad de Castilla-La Mancha, Spain
{Eduardo.FdezMedina,Mario.Piattini}@uclm.es

Abstract. Las propuestas de análisis de requisitos para almacenes de datos (AD) se centran únicamente en las necesidades de información de los usuarios, sin tener en cuenta otro tipo de requisitos como la seguridad o el rendimiento. Sin embargo, el modelado de estos aspectos en etapas tempranas del desarrollo es fundamental para obtener un AD que satisfaga las expectativas del usuario. En este artículo, se definen dos tipos de requisitos a considerar en el diseño del AD: requisitos de *información* y de *calidad de servicio*. Estos requisitos se definen dentro del marco de MDA (*Model Driven Architecture*), lo que permite su trazabilidad hacia etapas posteriores de diseño conceptual y lógico. Cabe destacar que este artículo se centra en proponer un modelo de requisitos de seguridad (como un tipo concreto de requisitos de calidad de servicio), así como un proceso en tres fases para su modelado conjuntamente con los requisitos de información.

Key words: Almacén de datos, seguridad, requisitos

1 Introducción

El objetivo de un almacén de datos (AD) es facilitar el análisis del estado y el desarrollo de una organización con el fin de mejorar el proceso de toma de decisiones [5]. Para ello, el AD integra, en un modelo multidimensional (MD), enormes cantidades de datos procedentes de fuentes de datos heterogéneas. Este tipo de modelo permite obtener fácilmente información como el número de transacciones por cliente o el incremento de ventas durante una promoción. Esta información se usa para descubrir tendencias o decidir sobre futuras inversiones.

Los modelos MDs permiten el acceso a los datos de forma más natural para los analistas. Los datos se localizan en un espacio n-dimensional, con las dimensiones representando las diferentes maneras de ver y clasificar los datos (p.e. según fecha, tienda, cliente, producto, etc.). Los diseñadores de modelos MD especifican un modelo conceptual estructurando la información en hechos y dimensiones. Los hechos son medidas de un proceso de negocio (p.e. cantidad de producto vendida, número de pacientes tratados, etc.), mientras que las dimensiones representan el contexto de análisis de esas medidas.

Hoy en día el análisis de requisitos en AD se centra en el modelo de datos [13]. Como entrada para definir el modelo conceptual MD, se usa el esquema de las fuentes de datos disponibles junto con los requisitos de información del usuario con el fin de obtener un modelo conceptual MD que sea compatible con ambos [4, 9, 18]. El problema es que el producto final que se debe obtener en un proceso de diseño para ADs no es únicamente un modelo de datos sino un sistema de AD completo, donde los usuarios necesitan que la información obtenida cumpla con algunas características (seguridad, rendimiento, visualización, etc.). Estas características son restricciones que el AD debe cumplir al suministrar la información requerida para satisfacer las expectativas de los usuarios, por lo que las hemos denominado requisitos de calidad de servicio (QoS). Estos requisitos son, por tanto, características adicionales que el AD debe cumplir para añadir calidad al uso de la información suministrada por el AD. Informalmente, los requisitos de información se relacionan con *qué* información se espera que el AD suministre, mientras que los requisitos de QoS se relacionan con *cómo* la información debe ser suministrada para su correcto uso.

Los requisitos de QoS influyen en el modelo de datos y también entre ellos, por lo que deben considerarse de manera conjunta en etapas tempranas del diseño. Incluso siendo externos a los requisitos de información, los requisitos de QoS están íntimamente ligados a aquellos. Por lo tanto, existe una necesidad de tener una aproximación tal y como se muestra en la figura 1, donde se consideren los requisitos de QoS

- junto con los requisitos de información, y
- desde etapas tempranas del desarrollo.

En este artículo, se presenta una aproximación global para el análisis de requisitos en ADs. Se describe la integración de requisitos de QoS en nuestra aproximación para el análisis de requisitos de información en ADs [7]. La inclusión de nuestra propuesta en esta aproximación, basada en MDA (*Model-Driven Architecture*), permite al diseñador [8] (i) derivar no sólo el esquema de la base de datos, sino otras partes del AD como la configuración del control de acceso y (ii) analizar de manera independiente requisitos de información y requisitos de QoS sin perder la conexión entre ambos, mediante el modelado en un CIM (*Computation Independent Model*).

Los requisitos de QoS abarcan muchos aspectos: cómo se deben presentar los datos para una correcta visualización, cómo se debe acceder a los datos de

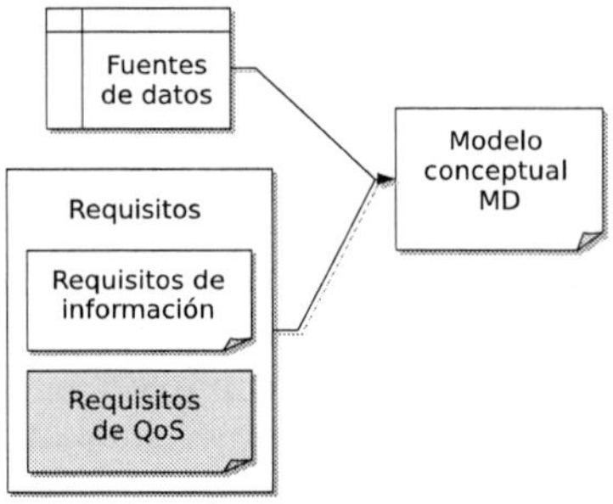

Fig. 1. Los requisitos de QoS son necesarios en el diseño de ADs.

una manera segura, cómo se debe realizar la implementación para suministrar los datos con un adecuado rendimiento, etc. Debido a esta amplia variedad de requisitos de QoS y la limitada longitud del artículo, nos centramos en un único aspecto: la *seguridad*. La sección 4 describe en detalle cómo se definen los requisitos de seguridad y cómo se integran con los requisitos de información. Se presenta un modelo para requisitos de seguridad en ADs y un proceso en tres etapas para su especificación en un CIM mediante una aproximación basada en objetivos. Todo ello se ilustra con un ejemplo procedente del dominio farmacéutico. El trabajo relacionado se trata en la sección 2, seguido de nuestra propuesta para modelar requisitos de información y de QoS (sección 3). Finalmente, la sección 5 presenta las conclusiones y el trabajo futuro.

2 Trabajo Relacionado

Hasta ahora, sólo unas pocas propuestas han considerado el análisis de requisitos como una tarea crucial a realizar en las etapas tempranas del desarrollo del AD. En [18], se propone un método para determinar los requisitos de información de los usuarios del AD y emparejar dichos requisitos con las fuentes de datos disponibles. La propuesta de [12] presenta un proceso de obtención de requisitos específico para ADs en el cual se identifican los objetivos del usuario y la información que se necesita para llevarlos a cabo. Finalmente, en [4] los autores presentan una aproximación en la que definen los requisitos del AD mediante el modelado de objetivos.

Sin embargo, estas propuestas sólo consideran requisitos de información (medidas de interés y su contexto de análisis) relacionados con el proceso de toma de decisiones. Solamente la propuesta llamada *data warehouse requirements definition* (DWARF) [10, 11] adapta el proceso tradicional de ingeniería de requisitos para la definición y gestión de requisitos para el AD, teniendo en cuenta la especificación de otros requisitos además de los de información, tales como seguridad o rendimiento (de manera similar a los requisitos de QoS). Los autores describen una clasificación de estos requisitos (llamados no-funcionales) con el fin de facilitar su especificación mediante el uso de *softgoals*. Desafortunadamente, el modelado de estos requisitos se considera como un aspecto aislado, sin tener en cuenta los requisitos de información relacionados. No obstante, con el fin de obtener un modelo MD conceptual que guíe el desarrollo del AD, satisfaciendo necesidades de información y expectativas de QoS, ambos tipos de requisitos deben modelarse juntos. Además en este trabajo, los autores se centran únicamente en la operacionalización de las *softgoals*. Por lo tanto, en el presente trabajo proponemos un análisis de requisitos para ADs como una etapa fundamental de una aproximación global basada en MDA, en la cual se defina cómo modelar de manera conjunta tanto los requisitos de información como los requisitos de QoS.

QoS es un concepto relacionado con el *uso* del AD, tal y como se describe en [17]. Los modelos de uso describen cómo se utiliza un AD, p.e. los grupos de usuarios, la flexibilidad de los requisitos, la disponibilidad de ciertos servicios que suministra el AD, etc. Los modelos de uso pueden (i) derivarse de un AD existente con el fin de encontrar mejoras potenciales o (ii) crearse a la vez que se diseña el nuevo AD. Los diferentes aspectos del uso pueden reflejarse en los requisitos de QoS, ya que ambos conceptos intentan capturar no solamente *qué* información suministra el AD sino también *cómo* se utiliza el AD.

3 Análisis de Requisitos en Almacenes de Datos

El desarrollo de un AD se centra en el diseño de un modelo MD conceptual. Tal y como se muestra en la figura 1, la especificación de este modelo debe estar dirigida por un análisis de (i) las fuentes de datos operacionales, (ii) los requisitos de información y (iii) los requisitos de QoS. De esta manera, el modelo MD conceptual satisfará las expectativas de los usuarios a la vez que será fiel a las fuentes operacionales que poblarán el AD. En este artículo, nos centramos en describir una aproximación global para el análisis de requisitos en ADs que consta de dos partes[5]:

1. **Análisis de requisitos de información,** cuyo objetivo es obtener los requisitos de información que tienen los usuarios para el apoyo a la toma de decisiones, i.e. medidas interesantes y el contexto para su análisis. Estos requisitos deben especificarse en un modelo de requisitos de información.
2. **Análisis de requisitos de QoS,** los cuales enriquecen el modelo de requisitos de información con el fin de reflejar bajo qué restricciones se suministra la información. La razón de este análisis es que el modelo de requisitos de información sólo refleja requisitos para un modelo MD "simple", es decir, que sólo suministra la información adecuada a los usuarios e ignora cómo se debe suministrar esa información para usarse de manera correcta.

Esta propuesta se ha alineado con nuestra aproximación basada en MDA para el desarrollo de ADs [8]. En MDA, los requisitos se especifican en un CIM

[5] En [9] se puede encontrar más información acerca del análisis de las fuentes de datos operacionales.

(*Computation Independent Model*). Una vez se obtiene este CIM, se deriva un modelo MD conceptual, llamado *Platform Independent Model* (PIM), el cual guía la implementación del AD. En el presente trabajo, nos centramos en definir una propuesta para modelar el CIM, sin embargo se puede encontrar más información (p.e. transformaciones entre modelos) acerca de nuestra aproximación basada en MDA para el desarrollo de ADs en [7–9].

3.1 Análisis de Requisitos de Información

Los usuarios del AD con frecuencia ignoran como describir de manera apropiada los requisitos de información, ya que son más conscientes de los objetivos que el AD les ayudará a cumplir. Por lo tanto, una fase de análisis de requisitos para ADs debe comenzar por el descubrimiento de estos objetivos. Los requisitos de información pueden descubrirse a partir de estos objetivos de manera más sencilla.

Los objetivos relacionados con el AD pueden especificarse a tres niveles [6]: *objetivos estratégicos*, los cuales son objetivos principales del proceso de negocio: "incrementar ventas", "incrementar el número de clientes", "decrementar costes", etc. *Objetivos de decisión*, cuya finalidad es realizar las acciones apropiadas para cumplir un objetivo estratégico, por ejemplo "definir algún tipo de promoción" o "abrir nuevas tiendas". Finalmente, los *objetivos de información* se relacionan con la información necesaria para cumplir con los objetivos de decisión; ejemplos de este tipo de objetivos serían "analizar las compras de los clientes" o "examinar existencias". Una vez que se definen estos objetivos, los requisitos de información se obtienen directamente de los objetivos de información. Los diferentes elementos MD, tales como *hechos* o *dimensiones*, se pueden descubrir a partir de estos requisitos de información con el fin de derivar el correspondiente modelo MD conceptual del AD.

Para modelar todos estos elementos en un CIM, se ha definido un *profile* de UML (*Unified Modeling Language*) para *i** [19] (ver figura 3), pudiendo representar así los diferentes actores del AD, sus dependencias y objetivos. En i* se definen dos modelos: el modelo SD (*strategic dependency*) que describe las relaciones de dependencias entre diferentes actores en el contexto organizacional y el modelo SR (*strategic rationale*), usado para describir los intereses de los actores y cómo deben ser alcanzados.

Los requisitos de información de cada actor se describen en modelos SR. El modelo SR (definido con el estereotipo *SR* y representado como ◌) permite el modelado de elementos intencionales y sus relaciones de cada actor (*IActor*, ○). Para definir modelos SR para ADs, los objetivos (*Goal*, ⬭), tareas (*Task*, ⬡) y recursos (*Resource*, ▭) se representan como elementos intencionales de cada actor del AD, tal y como se puede ver en la figura 2. Entre estos elementos intencionales puede haber dos tipos de relaciones: medio-fin (*MeansEnd*, —▷) o tarea-descomposición (*Decomposition*, —+).

Además, nuestro *profile* para *i** se ha extendido con el fin de poder modelar características propias de requisitos para ADs. En concreto, los objetivos

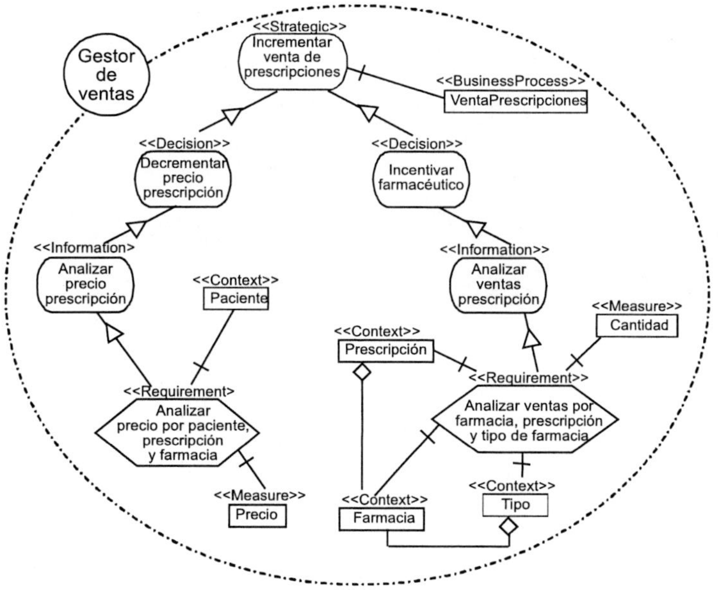

Fig. 2. Modelo de requisitos de información.

para el AD pueden definirse usando los estereotipos *Strategic*, *Decision* y *Information*, los cuales especializan el anteriormente definido estereotipo *Goal*. A partir de los objetivos de información, se pueden derivar los requisitos de información (*Requirement*) como tareas. Por otro lado, el análisis de requisitos para ADs necesita de la definición de algunos conceptos MD [4], los cuales se añaden como recursos estereotipados en el CIM: procesos de negocio relacionados con los objetivos de los usuarios del AD (estereotipo *BusinessProcess*), medidas relevantes relacionadas con los requisitos de información de los usuarios del AD (*Measure*) y el contexto de análisis para analizar dichas medidas (*Context*). El uso de estos elementos se muestra en la figura 2. Además, se pueden modelar relaciones entre contextos de análisis. Por ejemplo, el contexto *farmacia* y el contexto *tipo* están relacionados porque las farmacias pueden agruparse según su tipo. Para modelar estas relaciones se añade a la notación de i^* la agregación de UML (metaclase *Association*, representada como —◇). Todos los elementos descritos se han especificado en un *profile* UML para i^* extendido para ADs [7] (ver figura 3).

Los diferentes tipos de objetivos y los requisitos de información para el AD se modelan y se relacionan con elementos MD en un CIM mediante diferentes pasos: (i) descubrir los diferentes actores (usuarios del AD), definiendo modelos

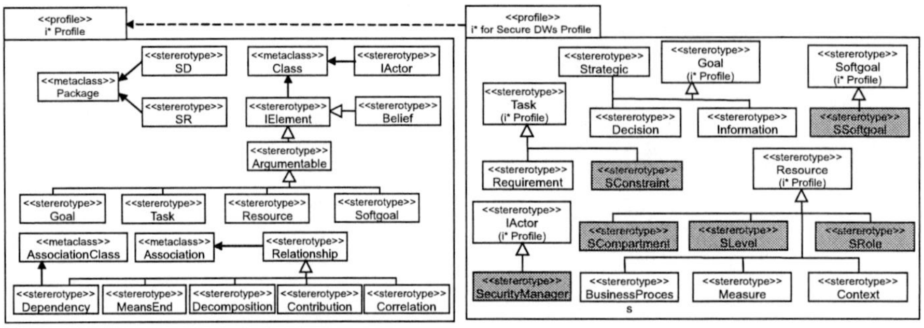

Fig. 3. *Profiles* de i* para definir requisitos de seguridad en ADs.

SR para cada uno, (ii) descubrir los diferentes tipos de objetivos, (iii) derivar los requisitos de información de los objetivos de información y (iv) obtener los conceptos MDs relacionados con los requisitos de información.

3.2 Análisis de Requisitos de QoS

Una vez que los requisitos de información han sido especificados en el CIM, el modelo debe enriquecerse mediante la adición de requisitos de QoS. Estos requisitos son múltiples, por lo que para no pasar por alto ningún aspecto importante, es necesario definir una clasificación de requisitos de QoS para ADs. La figura 4 muestra una clasificación para capturar los diferentes aspectos que deben considerarse cuando se diseña un AD. Esta clasificación está basada en un catálogo de requisitos no-funcionales para el diseño del AD presentada en [10]:

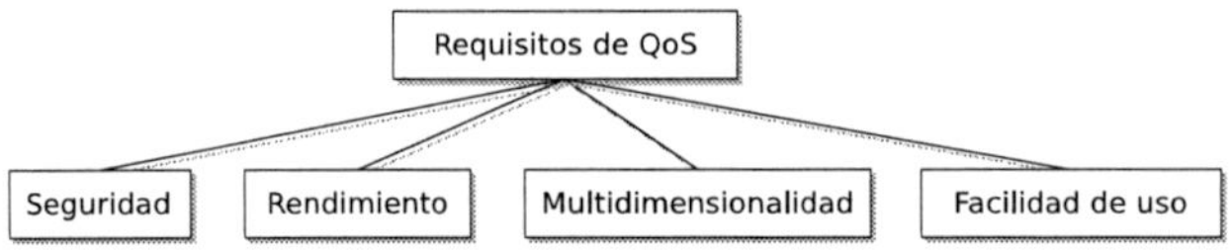

Fig. 4. Aspectos a tener en cuenta durante el diseño del AD.

Seguridad, incluye requisitos relacionados con la protección de recursos valiosos en el AD. Los requisitos de seguridad describen cómo se gestiona el acceso, a qué información se puede acceder y por quién y bajo qué condiciones se puede acceder a esa información

Rendimiento, puede dividirse en rendimiento relacionado con el tiempo (tiempo de proceso o tiempo de respuesta) y con el espacio (cantidad de memoria usada, memoria principal o secundaria).

Multidimensionalidad, cubre aspectos relacionados con el acceso a datos multidimensionales como interpretación o integración.
Facilidad de uso, que requiere flexibilidad y facilidad de aprendizaje.

Cabe destacar que esta lista de requisitos de QoS no es exhaustiva, sino que pretende ser una lista representativa cuyo propósito es mostrar la necesidad de modelar requisitos de QoS junto con los requisitos de información en una aproximación global para el desarrollo del AD. Cada concepto en esta clasificación debe analizarse a nivel de requisitos. Deben desarrollarse nuevas técnicas para especificar tales requisitos de QoS en el CIM junto con los requisitos de información. En este artículo, nos centramos en uno de los requisitos de QoS más importantes para ADs: la *seguridad*.

4 Requisitos de Seguridad para Almacenes de Datos

Cada tipo de requisito de QoS necesita un tipo especial de técnica para poder ser especificado en un CIM. En este artículo, nos centramos en los requisitos de seguridad. Los requisitos de seguridad son requisitos de QoS asociados con la protección de recursos valiosos del sistema. Estos requisitos de seguridad describen cómo se gestiona el acceso, a qué información se puede acceder y por quién y bajo qué condiciones se puede acceder a la información. Por ello, son denominados con frecuencia políticas de control de acceso (*Access Control Policies*, ACP).

Nuestra aproximación ACP para ADs se describe en [2, 3], donde se define un modelo de control de acceso y auditoría (*Access Control and Audit*, ACA) con el fin de especificar los aspectos de seguridad para ADs. Sin embargo, esta aproximación está aislada de la fase de análisis de requisitos para el AD y puede causar incongruencias entre las políticas de seguridad y la implementación del AD. Muchos investigadores han reconocido la necesidad de integrar el análisis de requisitos y la definición del control de acceso mediante la especificación de requisitos de seguridad en el desarrollo de sistemas de información [1]. A continuación, nos centramos en describir cómo alinear el modelo ACA con el análisis de requisitos de QoS.

4.1 Modelo de Auditoría y Control de Acceso (ACA)

El modelo ACA [2, 3] describe un mecanismo de control de acceso, permitiendo representar confidencialidad y auditar medidas del AD mediante la clasificación de sujetos y objetos del sistema. En concreto, se usan clases de acceso basadas en tres maneras diferentes pero compatibles de clasificar usuarios: por su *nivel* de seguridad, por su *rol* y por su *categoría*. Una clase de acceso es un elemento de un conjunto de clases parcialmente ordenado, donde una clase de acceso c1 domina una clase de acceso c2 *si y sólo si* el nivel de seguridad de c1 es mayor o igual que el nivel de seguridad de c2, las categorías de c1 incluyen a las de c2 y, al menos, uno de los roles de usuario de c1 se define para c2. Para poder especificar un modelo ACA, se deben definir las siguientes clases:

Roles de seguridad de usuario, usados para organizar usuarios según una estructura jerárquica, dependiendo de sus responsabilidades. Cada usuario puede tener más de un rol.

Niveles de seguridad, indican el nivel de acreditación del usuario. Usualmente, corresponde a un elemento de un conjunto ordenado jerárquicamente, tal como *Top Secret* (TS), *Secret* (S), *Confidential* (C) y *Unclassified* (U), donde $TS > S > C > U$.

Categorías de seguridad de usuario, indican una clasificación horizontal de usuarios atendiendo a ciertos criterios como localización geográfica o área de trabajo. Cada usuario puede pertenecer a una o más categorías.

4.2 Modelado de Requisitos de Seguridad

Para poder especificar requisitos de seguridad en un CIM, se necesita extender el profile de $i*$ para ADs definido en la sección 3.1. Nuestra nueva extensión (ver elementos sombreados de la figura 3) ofrece mecanismos para representar un actor especial llamado gestor de seguridad (*SecurityManager*,), el cual representa a un encargado de la seguridad de la organización. Los requisitos de seguridad son requisitos de QoS y deben modelarse usando *softgoals* (*SSoftgoal*,). Estas *softgoals* representan y refinan la política de seguridad de la organización. Los elementos del modelo ACA se consideran como recursos etiquetados como <<SCompartment>> (categorías), <<SLevel>> (niveles) y <<SRole>> (roles). Además, con el fin de especificar restricciones a los recursos, se introduce una tarea especial etiquetada como <<SConstraint>>, la cual contribuye a cumplir con las *softgoals* a través de asociaciones de contribución (*Contribution*, —>—). El proceso de refinamiento de *softgoals* se realiza mediante asociaciones medio-fin (*MeansEnd*). Finalmente, cada *softgoal* se asocia con procesos de negocio (*BusinessProcess*), medidas (*Measure*) o contexto de análisis de las medidas (*Context*).

Para poder definir un modelo de requisitos de seguridad compatible con el modelo ACA, se proponen los siguientes dos pasos, a realizar una vez se ha obtenido el modelo de requisitos de información (ver sección 3.1):

Análisis de requisitos de seguridad. Durante esta fase se especifica un modelo de requisitos de seguridad que consiste en tres pasos:

1. Detectar vulnerabilidades y necesidades del sistema según las políticas de la organización, leyes y regulaciones.
2. Obtener los requisitos de seguridad del gestor de seguridad mediante técnicas de obtención de requisitos como entrevistas. Estos requisitos se modelan mediante *softgoals* y se refinan en *softgoals* de más bajo nivel. Durante este refinamiento, se descubren diferentes responsabilidades y tareas (i.e. roles y categorías) y los niveles que podrán usarse.
3. Asociar las *softgoals* con los correspondientes recursos (i.e. *SCompartment*, *SRole* y *SLevel*).

Análisis conjunto de información y seguridad. Hasta ahora hemos obtenido un modelo de requisitos de información y un modelo de requisitos de seguridad. El próximo paso consiste en relacionar ambos modelos:

1. Cada *softgoal* refinada se asocia con los correspondientes elementos del modelo de requisitos de información (i.e. *BusinessProcess*, *Measure* y *Context*).
2. Considerar otros posibles aspectos de seguridad para los requisitos de información, adicionales a los establecidos con anterioridad. En concreto, se definen tareas *SConstraint* asociadas a *softgoals* para indicar que contribuyen positivamente a su cumplimiento.

4.3 Caso de Estudio

En esta sección se describe un ejemplo de aplicación de nuestra propuesta. Un consorcio farmacéutico gestiona varias farmacias. Este consorcio desea analizar las ventas de medicinas por medio de prescripciones médicas. Por tanto, nos centramos en el proceso de negocio relacionado con las ventas. Dentro del consorcio existen varios grupos: (i) un grupo de vigilancia de fármacos que comprueba el correcto uso de ciertas medicinas, (ii) un comité que vela por la salud de los clientes y (iii) un grupo comercial que gestiona la venta de medicamentos.

Análisis de Requisitos de Información La primera fase se desarrolla mediante la aproximación para el modelado de requisitos de información descrita en la sección 3.1. El modelo $i*$ definido se muestra en la figura 2. El proceso de negocio *venta de prescripciones* se relaciona con el actor principal, *gestor de ventas*, mediante el objetivo estratégico *"incrementar ventas de prescripciones"*. A partir de este objetivo estratégico, se obtienen dos objetivos de decisión: *"decrementar el precio de la prescripción"* e *"incentivar al farmacéutico"*. A partir de estos objetivos de decisión, se obtienen los siguientes objetivos de información: *"analizar el precio de las prescripciones"* y *"analizar las ventas de las prescripciones"*. Los requisitos de información que se derivan son los siguientes (mostrados como tareas en la figura 2): *"analizar el precio por paciente, prescripción y farmacia"* y *"analizar ventas por farmacia, prescripción y tipo de farmacia"*. Además, se deben asociar varios recursos a los requisitos de información (medidas y contexto de análisis). Las medidas son *cantidad vendida* y *precio*. Los elementos que representan el contexto de análisis son *paciente, prescripción* y *farmacia*. El *tipo de farmacia* también pertenece al contexto de análisis y representa una manera de agregar los datos de las farmacias.

Análisis de Requisitos de Seguridad Esta fase se lleva a cabo según la propuesta descrita en la sección 4.2. El modelo resultante se muestra en la figura 5. Nos centramos en la política de seguridad del proceso de negocio de las ventas de prescripciones, la cual es llevada a cabo por el actor *gestor de seguridad* mediante la *softgoal* *"garantizar la seguridad en las ventas con prescripciones"*. Mediante un refinamiento se obtienen tres nuevas *softgoals*: *"proteger el uso de ciertos medicamentos y el derecho de los consumidores"*, *"mantener la privacidad de las ventas, el precio y los datos del paciente"* e *"imponer niveles de autorización al proceso de prescripción"*. Durante este proceso se descubren varias responsabilidades y se asocian a sus *softgoals* correspondientes (ver figura 5):

1. Se obtienen relaciones jerárquicas: *empleado*, que se especializa en dos roles: *farmacéutico* y *administrativo.*
2. Se detectan las categorías (grupos horizontales): *departamento de vigilancia de fármacos* y *departamento comercial.*
3. Se establecen los niveles de restricción: *TopSecret* y *Secret.*

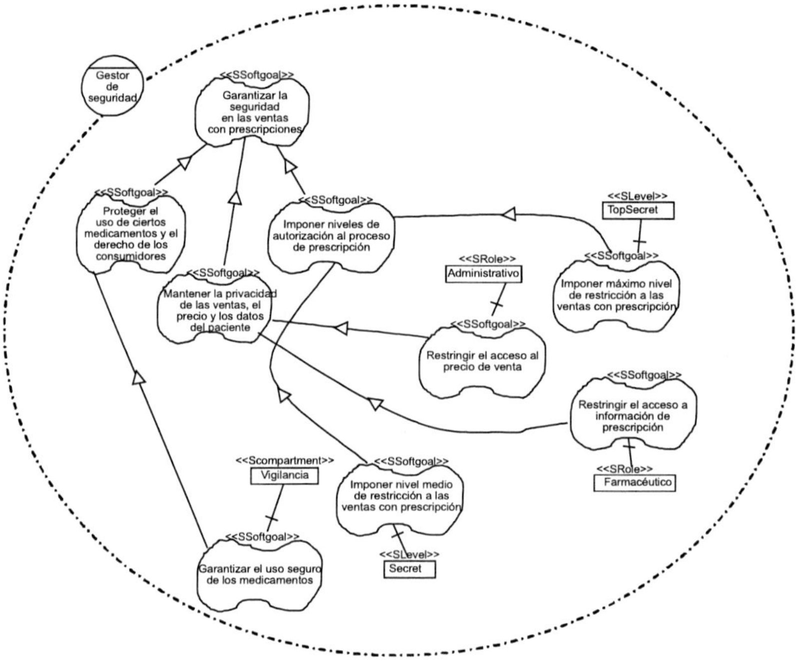

Fig. 5. Modelo de requisitos de seguridad

Análisis Conjunto de Información y Seguridad Una vez obtenidos los modelos de requisitos de información y de seguridad, se necesita relacionar los recursos asociados a los requisitos de información (i.e. *venta de prescripciones, cantidad vendida, precio, paciente, prescripción, farmacia* y *tipo de farmacia*) con las *softgoals* definidas en el modelo de requisitos de seguridad (p.e. *"garantizar el uso seguro de los medicamentos"* o *"imponer máximo nivel de restricción a las ventas con prescripciones"*). El *gestor de seguridad* depende del *gestor de ventas* para poder alcanzar dichas *softgoals* (ver figura 6). *Ventas de prescripciones* se asocia con la *softgoal "imponer máximo nivel de restricción a las ventas con prescripciones"*, la cual tiene *TopSecret* como *SLevel*. Análogamente, el contexto *prescripción* se asocia con la *softgoal "garantizar el uso seguro de los medicamentos"*, por lo que tiene *Vigilancia* como *SCompartment*. Debido a que *ventas* y *prescripción* permiten un futuro refinamiento del modelo, se necesitan restricciones adicionales: la figura 6 muestra cómo la *SConstraint SRule* contribuye a cumplir con las tres *softgoals* obtenidas anteriormente, por lo que se asocia con el proceso de negocio *ventas de prescripciones*. El mismo razonamiento asegura que el contexto *prescripción* se relacione con la *SConstraint Audit*.

El beneficio de aplicar nuestra propuesta es que los niveles, roles y categorías de seguridad para cada usuario del AD se modelan fácilmente en un CIM. Concretamente, en nuestro ejemplo se puede concluir que un usuario tiene acceso a las *ventas* si su clase de acceso domina la clase de acceso de *ventas*, i.e. su nivel de seguridad es *TopSecret*. Este CIM puede usarse para derivar un PIM [7] que refleje cada requisito de seguridad a nivel conceptual [2, 3], asegurando que la implementación del AD satisfará las expectativas de los usuarios.

5 Conclusiones y Trabajo Futuro

En este artículo proponemos el modelado conjunto de requisitos de información y de QoS en una etapa explícita del desarrollo de ADs, como paso previo a la derivación de un modelo MD conceptual del AD que satisfaga las expectativas del usuario. Concretamente, este artículo se centra en los requisitos de seguridad. Hasta ahora, hemos propuesto un marco de trabajo general [15, 16] basado en MDA en el cual se usan nuestras propuestas para el diseño de un AD seguro a nivel conceptual [2, 3] y lógico [14]. En este artículo, se amplía este marco de trabajo para considerar una etapa de análisis de requisitos de seguridad a nivel CIM. Los elementos de seguridad definidos a este nivel deben reflejarse en un PIM que sirva de base a la implementación final. Por ejemplo, los elementos *SConstraint*, deben definirse a nivel PIM siguiendo los patrones definidos en el modelo ACA (*AuditRule*, *SecurityRule* o *AuthorizationRule*).

Por otro lado, la seguridad es únicamente un aspecto de los requisitos de QoS, por lo que nuestro trabajo futuro se centra en definir mecanismos para modelar otros tipos de requisitos de QoS, así como estudiar las relaciones y dependencias entre estos requisitos.

6 Agradecimientos

Este trabajo ha sido financiado por los proyectos METASIGN (TIN2004-00779) del Ministerio de Educación y Ciencia y DADS(PBC-05-012-2) de la Consejería de Educación y Ciencia de Castilla-La Mancha. Veronika Stefanov dispone de una beca (31.963/46-VII/9/2002) del Ministerio de Educación, Ciencia y Cultura de Austria y del Fondo Social Europeo (ESF). Jose-Norberto Mazón dispone de una beca FPU (AP2005-1360) del Ministerio de Educación y Ciencia de España.

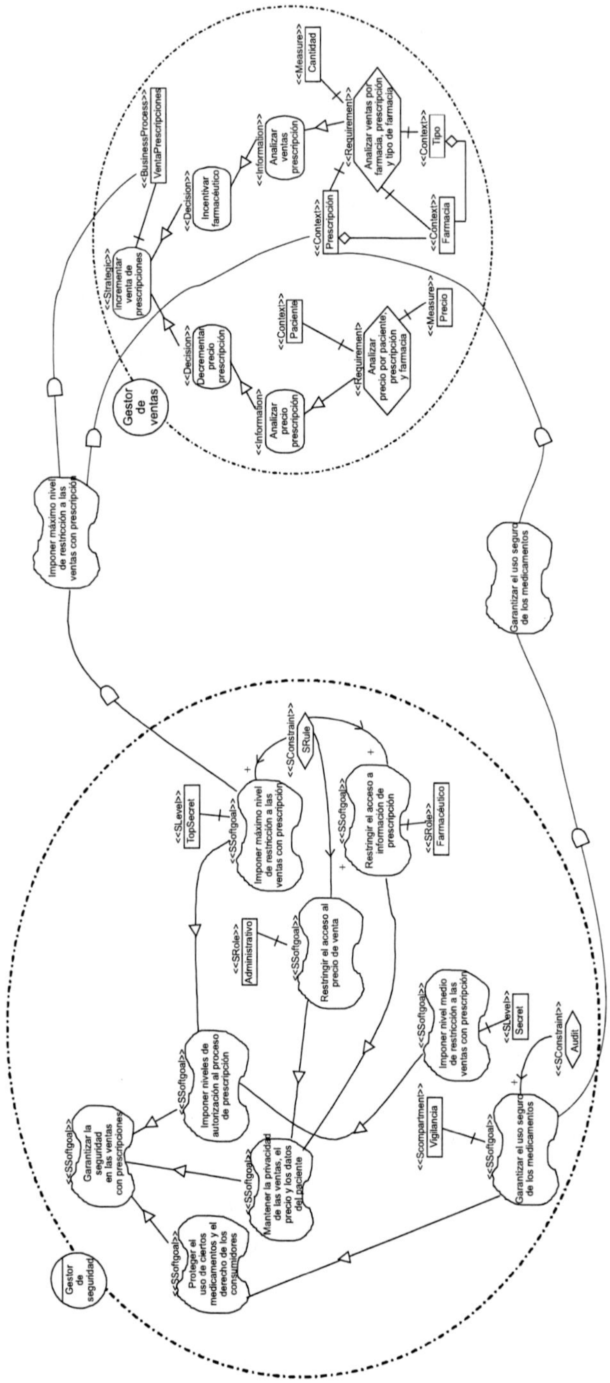

Fig. 6. Modelo integrado de requisitos de información y seguridad.

References

1. Antón, A.I., Earp, J.B., Carter, R.A.: Precluding incongruous behavior by aligning software requirements with security and privacy policies. Information and Software Technology **45**(14) 2003 967–977
2. Fernández-Medina, E., Trujillo, J., Villarroel, R., Piattini, M.: Access control and audit model for the multidimensional modeling of data warehouses. Decision Support Systems **42**(3) 2006 1270–1289
3. Fernández-Medina E., Trujillo J., Villarroel R., Piattini M.: Developing secure data warehouses with a UML extension. Inf. Syst. 32(6): 826-856 (2007)
4. Giorgini, P., Rizzi, S., Garzetti, M.: Goal-oriented requirement analysis for data warehouse design. In: DOLAP 2005, 47–56
5. Kimball, R., Ross, M.: The Data Warehouse Toolkit. Wiley & Sons (2002)
6. Mazón, J.N., Trujillo, J., Serrano, M., Piattini, M.: Designing data warehouses: from business requirement analysis to multidimensional modeling. REBNITA 2005
7. Mazón, J.N., Pardillo J., Trujillo, J.: A Model-Driven Goal-Oriented Engineering Approach for Data Warehouses. Workshop on Requirements, Intentions and Goals in Conceptual Modeling (RIGiM). ER Workshops 2007. Lecture Notes in Computer Science 4802, pp. 255-264. Springer 2007.
8. Mazón, J.N., Trujillo, J.: An MDA approach for the development of data warehouses. Decision Support Systems. **doi:10.1016/j.dss.2006.12.003**
9. Mazón, J.N., Trujillo, J., Lechtenbörger, J.: Reconciling requirement-driven data warehouses with data sources via multidimensional normal forms. Data and Knowledge Engineering 63(3): 725-751 (2007)
10. Paim, F.R.S., Castro, J.: Enhancing Data Warehouse Design with the NFR Framework. In WER 2002, 40–57
11. Paim, F.R.S., Castro, J.: DWARF: An approach for requirements definition and management of data warehouse systems. In RE 2003, 75–84
12. Prakash, N., Singh, Y., Gosain, A.: Informational scenarios for data warehouse requirements elicitation. ER 2004, Vol. 3288 of Lecture Notes in Computer Science, 205–216
13. Rizzi, S., Abelló, A., Lechtenbörger, J., Trujillo, J.: Research in data warehouse modeling and design: dead or alive? In: DOLAP 2006, 3–10
14. Soler E., Villarroel R., Trujillo J., Fernández-Medina E., Piattini M.: Representing Security and Audit Rules for DWs at the Logical Level by Using the Common Warehouse Metamodel. ARES 2006: 914-921
15. Soler E., Trujillo J., Fernández-Medina E., Piattini M.: A Framework for the Development of Secure DWs based on MDA and QVT. ARES 2007, pp. 294-300
16. Soler E., Trujillo J., Fernández-Medina E., Piattini M.: Aplicación de QVT al Desarrollo de Almacenes de Datos Seguros: Un Caso de Estudio. IDEAS 2007. Isla Margarita (Venezuela).
17. Stefanov, V, List, B.: A UML Profile for Modeling Data Warehouse Usage. In: 3rd International Workshop on Foundations and Practices of UML (FP-UML 2007). ER Workshops 2007. Lecture Notes in Computer Science 4802, pp. 137-147. Springer 2007.
18. Winter, R., Strauch, B.: A method for demand-driven information requirements analysis in data warehousing projects. HICSS 2003.
19. Yu, E.: Towards modeling and reasoning support for early-phase requirements engineering. RE 1997, 226-235.

Especificação dos Requisitos de um Sistema de Gerenciamento de Alarmes baseado na Recomendação de Ações

Heider Quintão, Rosário Girardi

DEINF/GESEC– Universidade Federal do Maranhão (UFMA) Avenida dos Portugueses s/n, Campus do Bacanga – 65.085-580 – São Luís – MA Brasil
heider_quintao@yahoo.com.br, rgirardi@deinf.ufma.br

Resumo. Quando ocorrem falhas de equipamento em plantas industriais complexas, o sistema de automação e controle gera uma grande quantidade de eventos e alarmes que podem confundir os operadores e induzi-los a tomar decisões erradas – o tempo para tomada de decisão é muito curto e a quantidade de informação gerada é muito grande, sendo impossível que o operador consiga ler todas antes de tomar a decisão correta. Neste artigo é apresentada uma análise dos principais conceitos, técnicas e ferramentas existentes para a construção de Sistemas Informatizados de Gerenciamento de Alarmes (SIGA). Realiza-se também uma análise preliminar dos requisitos de um SIGA baseado na recomendação de ações, com o desenvolvimento dos modelos de conceitos e de objetivos, conforme metodologia MAAEM. Através desses modelos é especificado o conhecimento necessário para o desenvolvimento de um SIGA baseado na recomendação de ações.

Palavras Chaves: Gerenciamento de alarmes, Gerenciamento de condições críticas, Engenharia de Requisitos, Sistemas de recomendações.

1 Introdução

Estima-se que os sistemas de automação de processos em operação em todo o mundo atinjam o valor de 65 bilhões de dólares. A maioria está com 15 anos ou mais e ràpidamente se aproximam do fim de sua vida útil [1]. Alguns destes sistemas não têm a funcionalidade atual de PAS ("*Process Automation Systems*") e, atualmente, uma parte deles está buscando se adequar às novas normas de segurança e proteção.

Enquanto a tecnologia de Automação avança em complexidade e sofisticação, os operadores encontram uma complexidade crescente para lidar com os processos de tomada de decisões que gerenciam condições críticas [2]. O objetivo desse avanço é levar as plantas automatizadas para uma utilização máxima dos seus recursos, enquanto o impacto para a sociedade aumenta em níveis inaceitáveis: com a redução da quantidade e da qualidade da mão-de-obra experiente através da substituição por recém-formados. Deve-se então fornecer informações mais precisas e no momento adequado às equipes de operação e manutenção, de modo que auxiliem suas tarefas.

O mercado de software de gerenciamento de alarmes está em ascensão, apresentando desenvolvimento realizado por fabricantes de equipamentos e soluções customizadas, institutos de pesquisa e universidades. Porém, não existe ainda um padrão na área de gerenciamento de alarmes aceito pelo mercado.

O objetivo deste trabalho é realizar uma análise preliminar dos requisitos dos Sistemas Informatizados de Gerenciamento de Alarmes (SIGA) e, em particular, dos Sistemas Informatizados de Gerenciamento de Alarmes baseados na Recomendação de Ações (SIGARA) a partir das informações pesquisadas e apresentadas neste trabalho sobre sistemas informatizados de automação industrial, avaliando também a capacidade de representatividade das ferramentas utilizadas para essa aplicação.

No próximo capítulo é apresentado e analisado o estado da arte no desenvolvimento de sistemas informatizados de gerenciamento de alarmes presentes em plantas industriais. No capítulo 3 os principais requisitos desses sistemas são modelados, utilizando-se uma metodologia para o desenvolvimento de sistemas multiagentes: a metodologia MAAEM (*"Multi-Agent Application Engineering Methodology"*) [3] [4] [5]. No capítulo 4 é avaliada a análise realizada e os modelos construídos, sendo também apresentados novos trabalhos relacionados em andamento.

2 Análise e Classificação dos Principais Padrões e Técnicas existentes para criação de SIGA

A ISA (*"The Instrumentation, Systems, and Automation Society"*) oferece o documento "ISA TR91.00.02 - *Criticality Classification Guideline*" [6] que é um guia que define características mínimas para equipamentos críticos de instrumentação industrial, utilizados na operação e também para sinalizarem emergências e alarmes; e também, o "ANSI/ISA S18.1 1992 – *Annunciator Sequences and Specifications*" [7]. Esse documento teve a primeira versão em 1979, quando os sistemas eram discretos. Estabelece um padrão para a terminologia de anunciadores, define e apresenta seqüências, especificando e documentando os anunciadores. Além desses padrões, ISA publicou também "ISA-SP18 *Instrument Signals and Alarms"* [8] definindo padrões para interfaces do usuário e, também, sinalização e alarmes de instrumentos em sistemas industriais.

O IEC (*"International Electrotechnical Commission"*) tem os documentos *"IEC 61508 - Functional Safety of Electrical/Electronic/Programmable Electronic Safety-Related Systems*" [9] e o *"IEC 61511 - Functional Safety: Safety Instrumented Systems for the Process Industry Sector*" [10], que relacionam segurança e sistemas de instrumentação, para aplicações que gerenciam os alarmes durante eventos críticos.

A HSE (*"The British Health & Safety Executive"*) possui também um guia que fornece alguma assistência, em "*Better Alarm Handling*" [11].

Um dos padrões para criação de SIGA mais conhecidos é o da EEMUA (*"The British Engineering Equipment and Materials Users Association"*) [12], exemplificado na Figura 1. Esse guia possui métricas para o bom desempenho do sistema de alarmes.

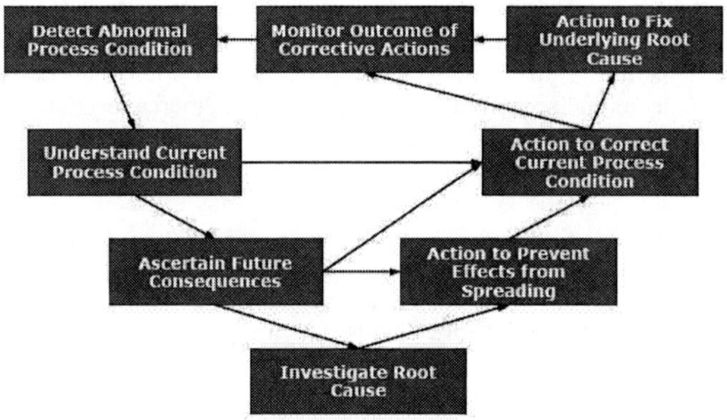

Fig. 1. EEMUA – Mapa de recomendações de ações para o operador quando da ocorrência de eventos pendentes ou anormais [12]

A EEMUA define que um operador de DCS (“*Discrete Control System*”) pode efetivamente gerenciar até 150 alarmes em um dia, o que na média significa um alarme a cada dez minutos. Um alarme a cada cinco minutos ou 300 alarmes por dia ainda é considerado gerenciável, como mostra a Figura 2. Naturalmente, a realidade é muito diferente. Os alarmes típicos para uma grande refinaria podem atingir 14 mil ocorrências por dia [13].

Long Term Average Alarm Rate in Steady Operation	Acceptability
More than 1 per minute	Very likely to be unacceptable
One per 2 minutes	Likely to be over-demanding
One per 5 minutes	Manageable
Less than one per 10 minutes	Very likely to be acceptable

Fig. 2. EEMUA –Critério de ocorrência de alarmes para condições normais de operação [12]

O EEMUA define que os alarmes devem ser ajustados no ponto onde o operador deve tomar alguma ação. Se os alarmes forem ajustados de forma conservadora, serão acionados durante operação normal. Agora, se os alarmes forem ajustados fora da faixa de operação normal da planta, será tarde para o operador tomar a ação, conforme a Figura 3.

O ASM (“*The Abnormal Situation Management*”) [2] [14], consórcio criado em 1992 com objetivo de definir melhorias e padrões no sistema de alarmes existentes, formado por grandes empresas e universidades tem realizado considerável esforço no desenvolvimento de sistemas para gerenciamento de situações anormais/críticas e gerado também um grande número de publicações.

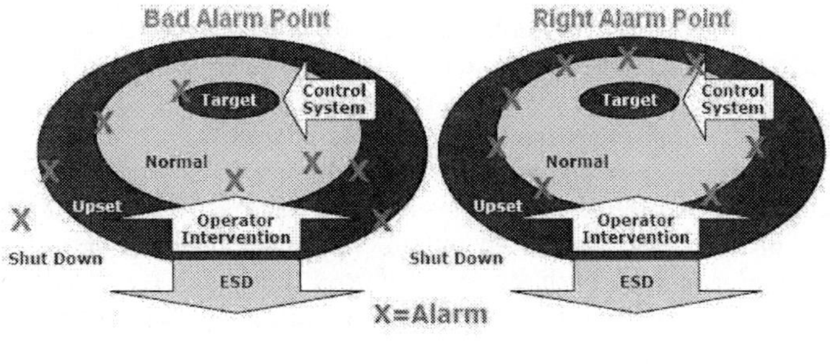

Fig. 3. EEMUA – Definição de alarme efetivo [12]

O "*ARC Advisory Group*" fundado em 1986 tem como objetivo melhorar o desempenho operacional obtendo maior retorno dos ativos existentes, reduzindo os custos de propriedade. Em outras palavras, o grupo visa buscar o nível correto de automação nos ativos existentes, de modo a produzir mais, obter maior ganho e lucro, com o menor custo possível.

Algumas das empresas que fornecem sistemas de gerenciamento de alarmes e produtos de racionalização dos alarmes [2] são Chemtech, Process Systems Consultants, Control Arts, PAS ("*Process Automation Services*"), Exida, Honeywell, Matrikon, TiPS, Rockwell, Wonderware, GE Fanuc, Yokogawa e ABB.

Para melhor compreensão dos requisitos dos SIGA, realizou-se uma pesquisa detalhada das ferramentas e métodos existentes, cujo resultado será apresentado resumidamente a seguir.

2.1 Sistemas Industriais de Gerenciamento de Alarmes

Os sistemas de automação industriais atualmente concentram toda a supervisão e controle da planta industrial nas salas de controle, onde os operadores recebem uma quantidade muito grande de informação relacionada com alarmes e eventos da planta. Além de serem geradas em grande número e com grande rapidez, estas informações muitas vezes não são claras e a ação imediata não é óbvia, pois não há uma correlação entre os vários alarmes acionados quando um problema ocorre.

Por definição, temos que os alarmes são um sinal ao operador, indicando que eles devem intervir na operação do processo para corrigir uma condição indesejada na planta, retornando o processo a um estado normal ou para impedir que o processo entre em condição anormal/insegura [16].

Os operadores devem ver alarmes no contexto da operação da planta como um todo. Não faz nenhum sentido, por exemplo, que um operador tenha que responder a um alarme para o fluxo baixo quando a bomba que controla o fluxo é desligada para a manutenção. Alarmes que funcionam corretamente devem alertar o operador da ocorrência de uma mudança, informar o operador da natureza dessa mudança, e guiar o operador para realização de uma ação corretiva [13]. Os SIGA devem tratar de forma inteligente as informações de alarme das plantas, organizando as mesmas para uma melhor compreensão do problema e para uma resposta mais rápida pelo lado dos operadores [15].

As melhores práticas para o gerenciamento de alarmes requerem distinções entre alarmes e alertas. Os alertas fornecem um mecanismo de advertência, mas não requerem necessariamente a ação imediata. Os alarmes nunca devem ser usados como um aviso, e devem sempre requerer a ação do operador [13].

Um alarme é efetivo quando este marca o ponto onde o operador deve agir (Figura 3). A eficiência de um sistema de alarmes não está na quantidade de alarmes e sim na qualidade da informação que eles transmitem e na capacidade dos mesmos de orientar a ação do operador. Quando um alarme espúrio é removido, o operador fica focado apenas naqueles que têm importância, e para os quais se espera uma ação.

2.2 Sistemas de Gerenciamento de Condições Críticas

Asish Ghosh define "Condição Critica" [16] como um estado do processo de manufatura, o qual está além do estado normal, mas por pouco ainda não atingiu a situação de emergência. Define ainda que a função de gerenciamento da condição crítica – CCM ("*Critical Condition Management*") deve estar sempre ativa sendo executada em background, para reduzir a possibilidade da transição do um estado normal para o estado critico, no caso de ocorrer uma emergência, minimizando o seu efeito [16].

Condições críticas são usualmente causadas por uma combinação de eventos que normalmente não se espera que ocorram simultaneamente. No acidente de Bhopal, por exemplo, a quantidade de Methyl Isocyanate armazenado estava abaixo do limite, o sensor do limite de temperatura estava desligado, a leitura do medidor de pressão estava incorreto e sendo ignorado, e os operadores tinham pouca experiência e nenhum guia para lidar com condições críticas que ocorressem de maneira inesperada [2]. Todos esses itens levaram à ocorrência do acidente.

A boa notícia é que as condições mais criticas não levam a situações de catástrofes, explosões, incêndios. Elas, entretanto, levam a outros sérios impactos negativos no desempenho e rentabilidade da planta, causando [2] produtos fora da especificação, paralisações não planejadas da planta, danos aos equipamentos, atrasos em cronogramas, baixa utilização dos recursos e problemas ambientais e de segurança. Esses eventos mais críticos usualmente fazem parte da categoria referenciada como "incidentes levam a perdas" [16]. Nas indústrias de processo, paradas não programadas comprometem em média de dois a cinco por cento da produção. Analisando somente as indústrias químicas, a média de perdas por falhas é de aproximadamente 19 milhões de dólares por ano [16].

As funções necessárias para o gerenciamento das condições críticas são apresentadas na Figura 4, e descritas a seguir [11]:

- "*Deductive alarm notification*" - A notificação dedutiva do alarme gera um diagnóstico e uma análise da falha para o alarme de um equipamento individualmente, e também monitora e filtra alarmes de toda planta;
- "*Predictive decision support*" – Sistema preditivo de suporte às decisões que auxilia a equipe operacional a identificar a causa raiz do alarme, auxiliando também na tomado de ações corretivas;

- "*Guidance to operating personnel*" – Fornecem orientação à equipe operacional notificando condições de perigo potencial, ações requeridas para evitar condições de perigo e também para minimizar os efeitos de um desastre;

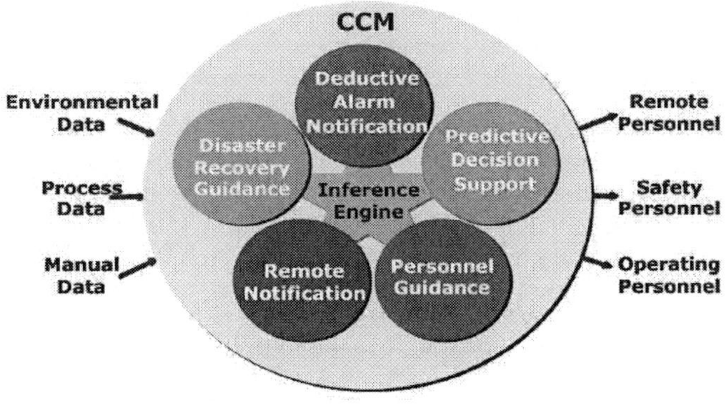

Fig. 4. Funções necessárias para o gerenciamento de condições criticas - CCM [11]

- "*Guidance to maintenance personnel*" – Fornecem orientação à equipe de manutenção quanto à expectativa do ciclo de vida dos equipamentos da planta, identifica os problemas potenciais dos equipamentos, de forma individual, e orienta ações de reparo/troca dos equipamentos da planta;
- "*Guidance to safety personnel*" – Fornecem orientação à equipe de segurança notificando condições de perigo potencial, indicam ações requeridas para evitar condições do perigo e/ou minimizar efeitos de um desastre;
- "*Remote notifications*" - Fornecem notificações a áreas remotas, como médicos, policiais e autoridades civis;
- "*Disaster recovery*" – Suporta a recuperação da planta após um desastre, orientando as equipes para a recuperação do desastre, e orienta ações de reparo/troca dos equipamentos da planta.

CCM prove benefícios econômicos significantes para indústrias. Um ganho típico de otimização de processo em uma grande planta industrial, como uma refinaria ou uma planta petroquímica, é em torno de três por cento, enquanto uma aplicação de CCM pode adicionar cinco por cento ou mais de rendimento detectando e evitando condições criticas antes que elas ocorram, reduzindo a necessidade de paradas de produção em emergência. Asish Ghosh [16] recomenda então que CCM deva ser considerado em processos importantes de plantas industriais, onde há riscos consideráveis para a saúde humana e também de grandes perdas monetárias.

2.3 Sistema Colaborativo de Suporte a Decisão para Pessoal Operacional

Honeywell, empresa participante do consórcio ASM desenvolveu o AEGIS ("*Abnormal Event Guidance and Information System*") [14], desenvolvido através do programa ATP (*"Advanced Technology Program"*) da NIST (*"U.S. National Institute of Standards and Technology"*), voltado para indústrias petroquímicas.

A Figura 5 apresenta um modelo adotado pela ASM, que prove a descrição de como a equipe operacional de uma planta industrial responde intervindo em uma situação anormal [14]. O lado esquerdo representa a ocorrência de uma situação anormal externa, e a equipe representada pela caixa pontilhada, então intervêm para estabilizar o processo. Essa intervenção é dividida em três partes:

- Orientação – um distúrbio no processo é detectado;
- Avaliação – a equipe operacional desenvolve uma hipótese para a causa da condição anormal detectada, que pode ser pulada, para causas conhecidas;
- Ação – a equipe operacional realiza uma ação corretiva ou compensatória, incluindo ações que determinam se a hipótese está correta.

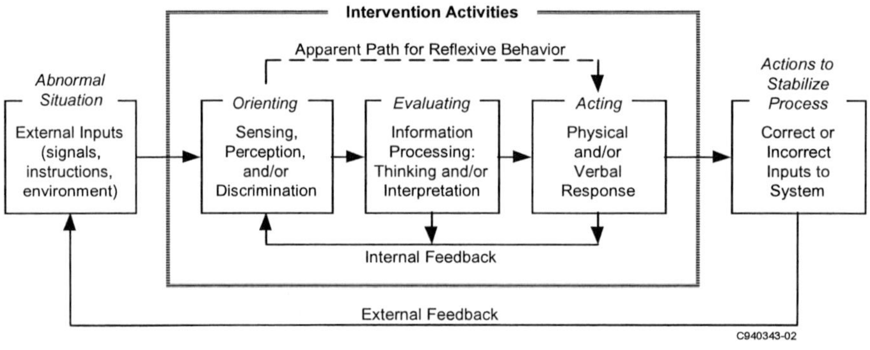

Fig. 5. Modelo de um sistema de suporte a decisões [14]

O propósito do AEGIS é suportar a equipe operacional da planta, de modo a atingir os quatro objetivos definidos pelo ASM [14]:

- Manter o processo em operação normal;
- Falhando isso, restaurar o processo para operação normal;
- Falhando isso, trazer o processo para um estado ou condição segura;
- Falhando isso, minimizar a severidade de algum acidente ou perda de produção.

O AEGIS trabalha com seis papéis funcionais, conforme apresentado na visão da Figura 6. Detalhando a função desses papéis, teremos:

- Estimador do Estado (*"state estimator"*) - fornece uma estimativa dinâmica e concisa do que esta acontecendo realmente na planta, incluindo informações de tendências que podem ser utilizadas para predizer os estados futuros;
- Apontador do objetivo (*"goal setter"*) - examina o resultado e propõe ações priorizadas em função de objetivos que necessita perseguir;
- Planejador (*"planner"*) - cria um plano para conseguir atingir os objetivos, a partir do estado atual da planta;

- Executor ("*executor*") – realiza o plano, assegurando-se de que cada etapa esteja sendo corretamente executada;
- Comunicador ("*communicator*") - controla a relação entre os outros papéis e o pessoal de planta;
- Monitor ("*monitor*") - examina a operação dos outros papéis e regula suas atividades.

O AEGIS foi desenvolvido e testado em quatro etapas distintas, usando uma arquitetura aberta de modo que suas principais funções, como estimador de estados, interface com usuário, modelos, gerenciamento de dados, podem ser facilmente incorporadas e\ou interagir com sistemas existentes. O atual protótipo está em uso em plantas da Exxon, Mobil e Union Carbide Corporation.

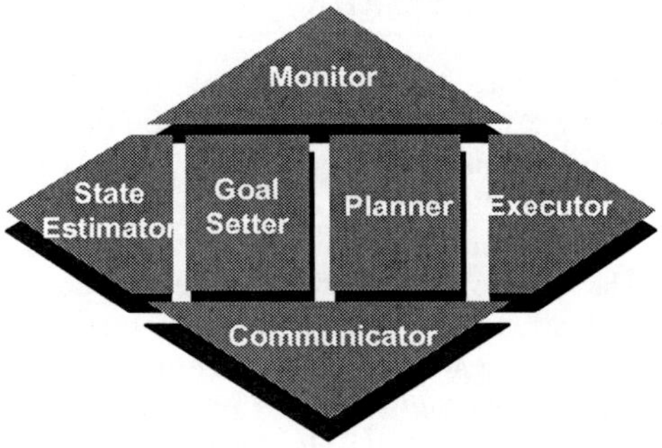

Fig. 6. Papéis funcionais do AEGIS [14]

3 Um Modelo de Requisitos para Construção de uma SIGA baseado na Recomendação de Ações

Nesta seção é apresentado parte de um modelo de requisitos que busca representar as necessidades de informação dos diferentes tipos de usuários que trabalham com um SIGA baseado na Recomendação de Ações (SIGARA), segundo os conceitos analisados nas seções anteriores. Para essa modelagem foi utilizada a metodologia MAAEM [3] [4] [5].

MAAEM é uma metodologia para a construção de sistemas multiagentes que fornece um conjunto de técnicas integradas para a análise dos requisitos, projeto e implementação da aplicação. A análise dos requisitos é realizada através das seguintes tarefas de modelagem: modelagem de conceitos de domínio, modelagem de objetivos, modelagem de papéis, modelagem de interações entre papéis e prototipagem da interface com o usuário.

Os sistemas de recomendação [17] são uma das principais aplicações das técnicas de filtragem de informação. Estes sistemas buscam atender às necessidades e o comportamento heterogêneos dos usuários através da captura, representação e atualização de seus perfis e o fornecimento de itens de informação (por exemplo, ações a serem realizadas por um operador após a ocorrência de um alarme) que satisfazem esses perfis, na forma de recomendações.

A técnica de filtragem utilizada no SIGARA é a filtragem baseada em conteúdo [17] [18], onde um item é recomendado se esse item é similar a outros itens que o usuário avaliou como relevantes no passado. Nestas técnicas são feitas comparações e cálculo de similaridade entre as representações dos itens de informação e os perfis de usuário. Os perfis dos usuários podem ser atualizados com base nas avaliações que o usuário fez de itens de informação no passado. A hipótese nesta abordagem é que, se um usuário manifestou interesse por um item de informação no passado, ele tendera a preferir itens com conteúdo similar no futuro.

3.1 Modelagem de Conceitos do SIGARA

A tarefa de Modelagem de Conceitos tem como produto o Modelo de Conceitos, que é uma rede semântica com os conceitos-chaves do domínio da aplicação, conceitos esses que serão abordados a seguir, referenciando os estudos apresentados nas seções anteriores.

Definem-se primeiro os requisitos mínimos necessários para o sistema de Gerenciamento de Alarmes, o qual deve apresentar ao usuário alarmes com significado claro e relevante, e todo alarme deve ter uma resposta definida [13]. È necessário inicialmente um sistema de detecção de condições anormais no sistema, conforme conceito "*Detect Abnormal Process Condition*" apresentado pela EEMUA na Figura 1 [12]. Para garantir que todo alarme a ser apresentado tenha relevância, deve-se aplicar várias técnicas apresentadas na seção 2, como a definição de alarme efetivo da EEMUA, presente na Figura 3 [12], que define que os alarmes sejam ajustados no ponto onde o operador deve tomar alguma ação. O SIGARA deve avaliar também a condição operacional do sistema, através do conceito "*Understand Current Process Condition*" da Figura 1. Outros conceitos interessantes que não podem faltar em nenhum SIGARA são "*Action to Correct Current Process Condition*" e "*Action to Fix Underlying Root Causes*", que apresentam ações aos usuários, suportando-os na tomadas das decisões necessárias para corrigira a condição atual do sistema de alarme ou de condição crítica, baseando-se para isso no conceito "*Investigate Root Cause*" que busca a identificação da causa da condição anormal, e somente após identificar a real causa, realiza a recomendação.

Na Figura 4 [2], temos as funções necessárias para o gerenciamento de condições críticas definidas pela ARC, principalmente as funções "*Deductive alarm notification*" e "*Predictive decision support*", que somados aos conceitos "*Detect Abnormal Process Condition*" e "*Investigate Root Cause*" se completam gerando um diagnóstico e uma análise da origem da falha mais completa para o alarme, e serão representados no nosso modelo apresentado na Figura 7 pelos conceitos "*Alarm Evaluation*" e "*Alarm Cause Identification*".

As funções "*Guidance to operating personnel*" e "*Guidance to maintenance personnel*" apresentadas pela ARC na Figura 4 somadas aos conceitos "*Action to Correct Current Process Condition*" e "*Action to Fix Underlying Root Causes*" também se completam, garantindo uma orientação mais completa aos usuários das ações necessárias para evitar condições de perigo, problemas potenciais dos equipamentos, e também para minimizar os efeitos de um desastre, e serão representados no nosso modelo da Figura 7 pelo conceito, "*Action Recommender System*".

Além desses conceitos acima, é necessário também ao SIGARA ajudar os usuários do sistema a cumprirem seus objetivos [2] [13] (conceito "*Action Recommender System*" da Figura 7). O SIGARA não deve inibir o usuário de tomar ações necessárias [2]; não esconder informações ou condições necessárias [2] [13]; não apresentar ou bloquear informações ou condições desnecessárias, como alarmes ativos por longo período ou avisos [2] [12] [19]; inibir que pequenas flutuações de variáveis gerem um número significativo de alarmes [13]; identificar alarmes espúrios, falsos e repetitivos [12] [19] e em pequenas paradas e interrupções gerar pequeno número de alarmes [12] (conceito "*Alarm Evaluation*" da Figura 7). Finalmente, deve priorizar a importância de alarmes através da avaliação de riscos e suprimir alarmes que sejam conseqüências diretas de outros alarmes [13]; guiar o operador às possíveis causas do alarme [2] [6] [19], suportando tanto o operador quanto a equipe de manutenção na solução do problema através de procedimentos em tempo-real [13] (conceitos "*Alarm Cause Identification*" e "*Action Recommender System*" da Figura 7).

A seguir, são detalhados os conceitos e relacionamentos apresentados no modelo de conceitos do SIGARA (Figura 7):

- Sistema informatizado de recomendação de ações ("*Action Recommender System*"), que recomenda ações aos usuários ("*Users*"), através da filtragem baseada em conteúdo ("*Content Based Alarm Filtering*"). Para isso é necessário realizar a identificação da causa dos alarmes ("*Alarm Cause Identification*") e uma avaliação da criticidade dos alarmes ("*Alarm Evaluation*");
- Os Usuários ("*Users*" – operadores, equipe de manutenção e engenharia) pertencem a uma área de responsabilidade ("*Responsability Area*"), definida em função da sua atividade e nível de responsabilidade dentro da planta industrial, a qual ajuda a definir o perfil do usuário ("*User profile*") que cada usuário possui;
- Modelo do usuário ("*User Model*") representa o perfil do usuário ("*User profile*"), que é classificado dentro do conceito de grupo de itens relevantes para um perfil de usuário ("*Groups of items relevant to a user profile*"). Com a definição dos usuários e do modelo dos usuários, garante-se que somente serão recomendadas ações necessárias para esses usuários cumprirem suas obrigações;
- Os dados obtidos da filtragem baseada em conteúdo ("*Content Based Alarm Filtering*"), realizada baseando-se no modelo do usuário (que define quais alarmes e ações irão interessar a esses usuários), utilizam os itens de informação obtidos do sistema de automação industrial, que são os registros de eventos ("*Events Log*"), registro de estado operacional da planta ("*Operational Status Log*") e registro de alarmes ("*Alarm Log*");
- "*Alarm Evaluation*" avalia os alarmes realizando a classificação e análise de relevância, baseado nos interesses dos usuários ("*Groups of items relevant to a user profile*"), a partir do banco de dados de alarmes críticos ("*Repository of Critical Alarms*") que serve para priorizar de maneira efetiva os alarmes [12], utilizando para isso os dados dos alarmes filtrados ("*Content Based Alarm Filtering*"), que estão incluídos nesse repositório de dados de alarmes críticos.

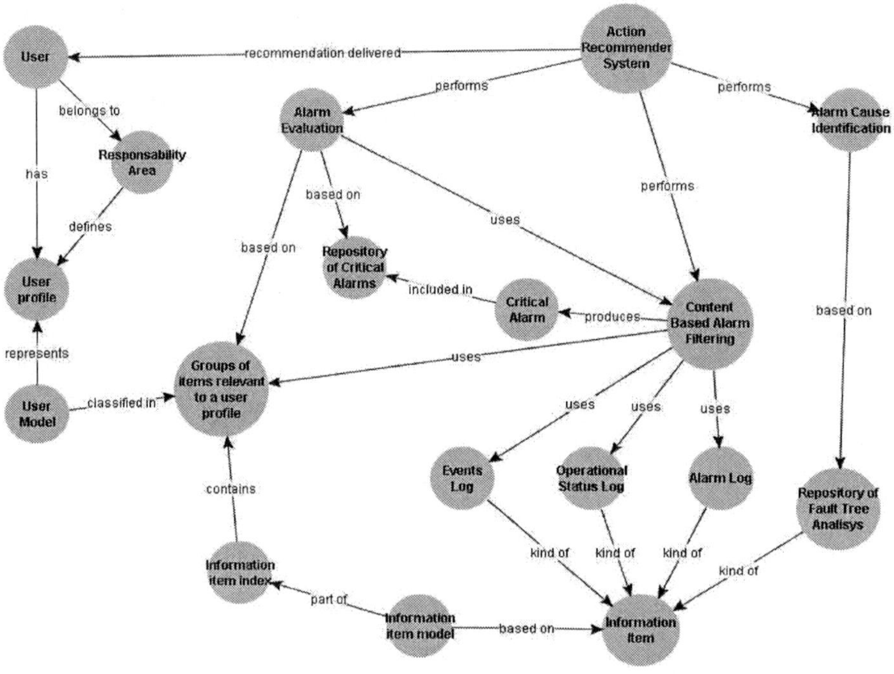

Fig. 7. Modelo de Conceitos do SIGARA

3.2 Modelagem de Objetivos do SIGARA

A próxima tarefa da MAAEM [3] [4] [5] a ser desenvolvida é a Modelagem de Objetivos, realizada a partir do conhecimento adquirido com a construção do modelo de conceitos. A seguir, é descrito o Modelo de Objetivos do SIGARA, apresentado Figura 8:

- O objetivo geral "*Provide personalized action recommendation*" provê recomendação de ações personalizadas através da realização das responsabilidades dos objetivos específicos, tendo como referencia o conhecimento adquirido das funções "*Guidance to operating personnel*" e "*Guidance to maintenance personnel*" apresentadas pela ARC na Figura 4 e dos conceitos "*Action to Correct Current Process Condition*" e "*Action to Fix Underlying Root Causes*" definidos pela EEMUA na Figura 1, "*Goal Setter*" que examina o resultado da avaliação do estimador de estados "*State Estimator*" e propõe ações priorizadas em função de objetivos que necessita perseguir, conforme Figura 6, e finalmente do modelo de suporte a decisões apresentado na Figura 5;

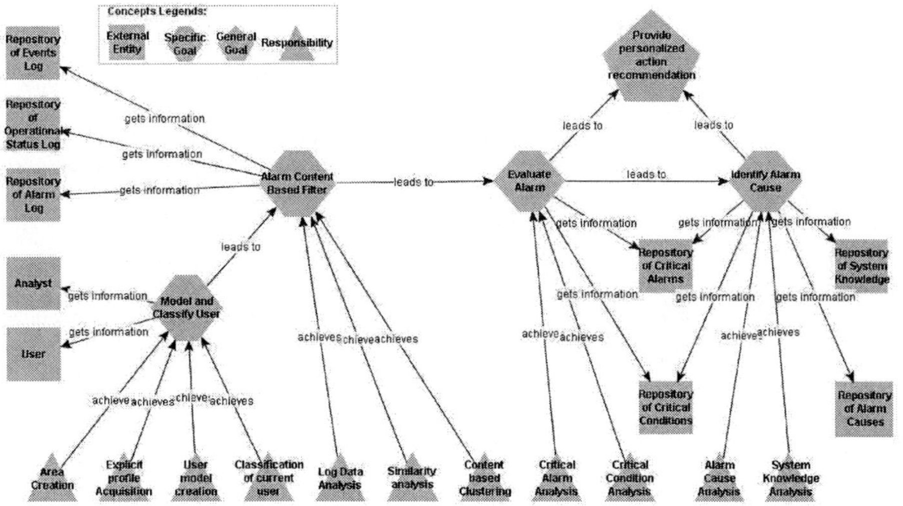

Fig. 8. Modelo de Objetivos do SIGARA

- Os objetivos específicos "Model and Classify User", "Alarm Content Based Filter", "Evaluate Alarm" e "Identify Alarm Cause" suportam o sistema a atingir o objetivo geral "Provide personalized action recommendation".
- Para atingir o objetivo específico "Model and Classify User" é preciso executar as seguintes responsabilidades: "Area Creation", para criar explicitamente as áreas de responsabilidades; "Explicit Profile Acquisition" para capturar explicitamente o perfil do usuário; "User model creation" para criar o modelo do usuário, a partir das informações das entidades externas "Users" e "Analyst", e das responsabilidades anteriores. A responsabilidade "Classification of current user", é obtida a partir das informações obtidas das entidades externas e das responsabilidades anteriores, classificando o usuário atual conforme os modelos de usuários criados.
- Para atingir o objetivo específico "Alarm Content Based Filter" é preciso executar as seguintes responsabilidades: "Log Data Analysis" que analisa os dados de alarmes gerados pelas entidades externas "Repository of Events Log", "Repository of Operational Log" e "Repository of Alarm Log" detectando a condição anormal do processo, conforme conceito "Detect Abnormal Process Conditions" da Figura 1; "Similarity Analysis" realiza a análise de similaridade baseada em conteúdo; "Content Based Clustering" cria clusters dos log de dados que já foram analisados pela responsabilidade "Log Data Analysis", realizando clusterização a partir da análise de similaridade gerada pela responsabilidade "Similarity Analysis". Atingindo a meta desse objetivo específico, que é a filtragem baseada em conteúdo, contribuímos para realização do objetivo específico "Evaluate Alarm".
- Para atingir o objetivo específico "*Evaluate Alarm*" é preciso executar as seguintes responsabilidades: "*Critical Alarm Analysis*" e "*Critical Condition Analysis*" que analisam se os alarmes gerados e já filtrados, são alarmes críticos conforme os

dados da entidade externa "*Repository of Critical Alarms*" ou se são condições críticas, conforme os dados da entidade externa "*Repository of Critical Conditions*". Para avaliar a condição crítica, essa responsabilidade necessita buscar entender a condição atual do processo conforme "*Understand Current Process Condition*" da Figura 1 ou estimar o estado operacional da planta industrial, conforme conceito "*State Estimator*" apresentado na Figura 6. Atingindo este objetivo específico, que é a avaliação dos alarmes gerados, contribuímos para o alcance do objetivo específico "*Identify Alarm Cause*".

- Para atingir o objetivo específico "*Identify Alarm Cause*" é preciso executar as seguintes responsabilidades: "*Alarm Cause Analysis*" e "*System Knowledge Analysis*", que analisa as possíveis causas dos alarmes já avaliados e filtrados pelos objetivos anteriores, a partir dos bancos de dados "*Repository of System Knowledge*" e "*Repository of Alarm Causes*", conforme conceito "*Investigate Root Cause*" da Figura 1.

4 Conclusão

A partir da pesquisa realizada sobre os sistemas de gerenciamento de alarmes existentes no mercado e da análise dos seus requisitos utilizando-se a Metodologia MAAEM, apresentou-se o Modelo Conceitual e o Modelo de Objetivos, que são os primeiros produtos da fase de análise da aplicação do SIGARA.

A abordagem do SIGARA apresentada possui dois grandes diferenciais frente às existentes hoje no mercado, sendo que o primeiro diferencial é o uso de técnicas de filtragem de informação, que irão filtrar os alarmes e as ações que o sistema irá recomendar aos usuários de maneira diferenciada, de modo que operadores receberão alarmes e ações que dizem respeito à sua responsabilidade, diferenciando usuários da manutenção, engenharia e segurança, por exemplo. Alguns sistemas existentes apresentam ações em função do estado operacional da planta industrial, porém, o SIGARA através das técnicas de filtragem, executará essa função de maneira mais diferenciada ainda, pois filtrará os estados e alarmes antes de recomendar as ações, apresentando novamente, somente o que diz respeito a certo grupo de usuários. Reduz-se assim drasticamente a sobrecarga dos usuários por estarem recebendo alarmes e ações que não lhes dizem respeito, agilizando o processo de tomada de decisões e garantindo um retorno mais rápido à condição normal de operação.

O segundo diferencial presente nesse estudo diz respeito à aplicação de técnicas da Engenharia de Software Multiagente nesse domínio, como o uso da metodologia MAAEM, que apresenta grande capacidade de expressar um domínio de conhecimento, neste caso, o gerenciamento de alarmes de sistemas industriais. Obteve-se assim, uma representação para um SIGARA, cobrindo a lacuna existente no mercado que não possui modelos de SIGA e SIGARA aceitos por todos, permitindo inclusive que esses modelos possam servir de base para desenvolvimentos futuros sendo reutilizados por outros estudiosos da área, recebendo novos conceitos ou sendo adequados para outros domínios de conhecimento.

Como proposta de trabalho futuro, tem-se a continuação da aplicação da metodologia MAAEM para a modelagem e prototipação do SIGARA.

Referências

1. **Hill, Dick.** Time To Re-Think Alarm Management Strategies. *ARC INSIGHT 049MH&MP.* 2001.
2. **ARC Advisory Group.** Use Critical Condition Management to Improve You Bottom Line. *ARC Strategies.* April 2002.
3. **Lindoso, Alisson N. e Girardi, Rosário.** The SRAMO Technique for Analysis and Reuse of Requirements in Multi-agent Application Engineering. *IX Workshop on Requirements Engineering, Cadernos do IME, UERJ Press, 20.* Rio de Janeiro 2006, pp. 41-50.
4. **Lindoso, Alisson Neres.** Uma metodologia baseado em ontologias para a Engenharia de Aplicações Multiagente. *Dissertação de Mestrado em Engenharia Elétrica – Área de Ciência da Computação. UFMA.* 2006.
5. **Lindoso, Alisson and Girardi, Rosário.** Uma Técnica baseada em Ontologias para o Reuso de Padrões de Software e de Frameworks no Projeto de Aplicações Multiagente. *First Workshop on Software Engineering for Agent-oriented Systems (SEAS 2005), 19º Simpósio Brasileiro de Engenharia de Software (XIX SBES). Uberlândia, Minas Gerais, Brasil.* October 3, 2005.
6. **ISA.** Technical Report ISA – TR91.00.02–2003 - Criticality Classification Guideline for Instrumentation. *ISA - The Instrumentation,Systems, and Automation Society. International Standard.* January 2003.
7. **ISA —.** Standard ISA—18.1—1979 (R2004) - Annunciator Sequences and Specifications. *ISA - The Instrumentation,Systems, and Automation Society. International Standard presented at ISA EXPO.* 2005.
8. **Dunn, D. G. and others.** ISA SP-18 – Alarm Systems Management and Design Guide. *ISA EXPO 2005. Illinois USA.* October 25-27, 2005.
9. **IEC.** IEC 61508 - Functional Safety of Electrical/Electronic/Programmable Electronic Safety-Related Systems. *International Standard IEC 61.508-1, First Edition.* December 1998.
10. **IEC.** IEC 61511 - Functional Safety: Safety Instrumented Systems for the Process Industry Sector. *International Standard IEC 61.511-1, First Edition.* January 2003.
11. **HSE.** Better Alarm Handling. *HSE Chemical Sheet number 6.*
12. **EEMUA.** Alarm systems, a guide to design, management and procurement. *No. 191 Engineering Equipment and Materials Users Association.* 1999.
13. **O'Brien, Larry and Woll, Dave.** Alarm Management Strategies. *ARC Strategies.* November 2004.
14. **Bullemer, P. T., et al.** Collaborative Decision Support for Operations Personnel. *INTERKAMMA 99 - ISA Technical Conference.*
15. **CHEMTECH e Guimarães, Flávio.** *www.chemtech.com.br.* 2007. [Acessado em: 04 de 06 de 2007.] http://www.chemtech.com.br/templates/chemtech/publicacao/publicacao_sol.asp?cod_Canal=2&cod_Publicacao=539&cod_menu=2.
16. **Ghosh, Asish e Woll, Dave.** Best Practices in Critical Condition Management. *ARC Insights - 13MPH.* 2004.
17. **Adomavacius, G. e Tuzhilin, A.** Toward the Next Generation of Recommender Systems: A Survey of the State-of-the-Art and Possible Extensions. *IEEE Transactions on Knowledge and Data Engineering, v. 17, n. 6.* June de 2005.
18. **Balabanovic, M. and Shoham, Y.** Combining Content-Based and Collaborative Recommendation. *Communications of the ACM.* March 1997.
19. **Liu, J., et al.** Intelligent Alarm Management Through Suppressing Nuisance Alarms and Providing Operator Advice. *Chemical & Process Engineering Center, National University of Singapore.*

Estudio Comparativo de Técnicas de Modelado de Negocio

Juan José Cadavid[1], Carlos Andrés Ospina[1], Juan Bernardo Quintero[2]

[1] Avansoft S.A. Medellín, Colombia
{jjcadavid, caospina}@avansoft.com
[2] ABC-Flex Ltda. – Universidad EAFIT. Medellín, Colombia
jquinte1@eafit.edu.co

Resumen. La acelerada evolución de los sistemas de información y las telecomunicaciones, ha desencadenado drásticos cambios en los esquemas de negocio; este fenómeno ha motivado el auge de técnicas de modelado de negocio que le permiten a las empresas la representación de sus estrategias, para alinear sus sistemas de información con sus objetivos de negocio.

Palabras claves: Modelos de Negocio, Procesos de Negocio, Ingeniería de Modelos, BPMN, UML.

1 Introducción

El modelado de procesos de negocio es la actividad de representar el estado actual (*as is*, como es) y el estado futuro (*to be*, como será) de los procesos de una empresa para su comparación y contraste, de tal forma que permitan el análisis y mejoramiento para llegar a la situación deseada. Los modelos son construidos por analistas de negocio y administradores [1].

Históricamente, el aporte académico a la ingeniería de software se ha caracterizado por realizar un gran énfasis en las disciplinas de ingeniería de requisitos, análisis y diseño, pero pocas propuestas se han construido alrededor de actividades más tempranas como el modelado de negocio.

Este estudio define un referente para que las industrias de software adopten la técnica de modelado de negocio que más se ajuste a sus necesidades; asignando un peso diferente a cada uno de los criterios evaluados en este estudio comparativo, para complementar un procedimiento de toma de decisiones como el propuesto en el área de proceso DAR (*Decision Analysis and Resolution*) de CMMI (*Capability Maturity Model Integration*) [2].

2 Técnicas de Modelado de Negocio Evaluadas

Las técnicas de modelado de negocio que por su relevancia y popularidad fueron consideradas para este trabajo evaluativo son:

- **Extensiones de Ericsson y Penker para UML (*Unified Modeling Language*)**, aunque UML fue creado para especificar la arquitectura y el diseño de un sistema, éste presenta la característica de la extensibilidad para crear aditamentos para cubrir otras necesidades de modelado. La propuesta de [3] sugiere el uso del diagrama de actividades, pues de acuerdo a la definición dada en [4], un proceso de negocio es esencialmente una secuencia de actividades. Para este diagrama, se propone un conjunto de extensiones para el modelado de negocio.
- **Modelado de Negocio con BPMN (*Business Process Modeling Notation*)**, el organismo BPMI (*Business Process Management Initiative*) propuso el estándar BPMN [5], una notación gráfica altamente intuitiva que le permite a los individuos con mayor conocimiento sobre el negocio construir modelos sin requerir conocimiento alguno de estándares o mecanismos formales involucrados en las soluciones tecnológicas para soportar la gestión de procesos de negocio.
- **Modelado de Negocio con RADs (*Role Activity Diagrams*)**, los diagramas de actividades de roles toman como su elemento de modelado principal los individuos o grupos en una organización, y el rol que asumen dentro de un proceso, sus actividades de componentes y sus interacciones, junto con eventos externos y la lógica que determina cuales actividades se ejecutan y cuando [6].
- **Modelado de Negocio con IDEF3: Captura de Descripción de Procesos**, el estándar IDEF3 fue creado por la Fuerza Aérea de EEUU. IDEF3 describe procesos como secuencias ordenadas de eventos o actividades. Su objetivo es formular el *como*, mientras que IDEF0 se encargaba de mostrar el *qué* de las actividades de negocio [7].
- **Modelado de Negocio con UML: Propuesta Universidad de Murcia**, en [8] se hace un análisis de las actividades de modelado en las etapas tempranas del proceso de desarrollo de software, y señala algunos problemas con los enfoques metodológicos actuales. Este estudio indica que utilizar el modelado de casos de uso como punto de partida, como suele hacerse comúnmente, sin tener antes una representación del dominio, puede conllevar a la identificación, especificación e implementación de funcionalidades no adecuadas para el dominio en el cual se construye la solución.

3 Criterios de Comparación

Los criterios de comparación son definidos en tres categorías que constituyen los pilares de MDA (*Model Driven Architecture*) propuestos en el Manifiesto MDA [9] planteado por IBM: (a) *representación directa* para enfocarse en el dominio del problema, (b) *automatización* de tareas mecánicas y (c) *estándares abiertos* que posibiliten la interoperabilidad de las herramientas y plataformas.

3.1 Representación Directa

Se refiere a reducir la distancia semántica entre el dominio del problema y su representación en un modelo, de manera que se permita un acoplamiento directo de las soluciones hacia los problemas para las cuales fueron construidas.

- **R1. Adopción de CIM (*Computation Independent Model*)**: modelado desde un punto de vista independiente de la computación según lo definido en [10], un CIM es un modelo de un sistema que muestra el sistema en el entorno en el cual operará, y como tal ayuda a presentar lo que se espera que el sistema realizará.
- **R2. Estructura y Comportamiento:** capacidad para representar las vistas estructural y de comportamiento de la organización a través de procesos de negocios.
- **R3. Reglas de Negocio:** Soporte para el modelado de reglas de negocio, debido a que estos son elementos altamente cambiantes en el devenir de los procesos de negocio, y los usuarios de los modelos deberían poder visualizarlos y manipularlos claramente [11].
- **R4. Roles:** Capacidad para representar los diferentes roles que ejecutan las diferentes funciones en los procesos de negocio.
- **R5. Objetivos y E/S:** Capacidad para representar objetivos de negocio, entradas y salidas de información en las actividades del proceso, ya sea en la forma de documentos (información estructurada) o mensajes (información sin estructurar).
- **R6. B2B (*business to business*):** Capacidad para representar interacciones negocio a negocio (B2B) a través de la cadena de abastecimiento, de manera que las organizaciones externas con las que se colabora asumen un rol externo dentro del proceso.
- **R7. Usabilidad:** Usabilidad por parte de stakeholders no técnicos, tales como analistas de negocio, administradores o diseñadores de procesos. Estas personas son quienes mas conocen el negocio, y a menudo hace parte de los mismos procesos.

3.2 Automatización

En esta categoría se mide la capacidad de las técnicas de modelado de negocio para permitir la automatización de las tareas de desarrollo de software, de manera que se incremente la productividad y se reduzca el esfuerzo requerido. Este es uno de los propósitos fundamentales de la naciente disciplina de Ingeniería de Modelos [12].

- **A1. Respaldo Metodológico:** Existencia de un respaldo metodológico para el modelado de negocio y la ejecución de procesos que proporcione una guía clara y concisa acerca de como construir un modelo que represente al negocio en todos sus aspectos relevantes.
- **A2. Brecha modelado-ejecución:** Brecha entre la técnica de modelado y la ejecución de procesos de negocio. Los modelos de negocio deben convertirse en activos que posibiliten la automatización de los procesos de negocio.
- **A3. Motor de ejecución:** Existencia de un ambiente de infraestructura (motor de ejecución) o estándar de ejecución de los procesos de negocio modelados. Los

modelos de procesos deberían contar con un mapeo directo al entorno de producción en donde darán soporte a los procesos.

- **A4. SOA (*Service Oriented Architecture*):** Compatibilidad con estrategias actuales para arquitecturas de aplicaciones empresariales compuestas, como SOA, que se caracterizan por ser distribuidas, de bajo acoplamiento y apoyo directo a los procesos de negocio.

3.3 Estándares Abiertos

En esta categoría se evalúa cada técnica de modelado en la medida en que esté definida alrededor de un estándar, que fomentan el desarrollo de un ecosistema de proveedores de herramientas interoperables para diversos propósitos.

- **E1. Respaldo Consorcio Industrial:** Respaldo por parte de algún consorcio de estándares abiertos reconocido por la industria, debido a que éstos representan un consenso entre las compañías con más experiencia en el tema.
- **E2. Metamodelo disponible:** Existencia y disponibilidad del metamodelo para posibilitar la transformación de modelos, que proporciona la ingeniería de modelos. Un ejemplo característico de dicho metamodelo se puede evidenciar en [13].
- **E3. Framework de Modelado:** Implementación del metamodelo en un framework de modelado como el propuesto en [14], con el propósito de usarlo en herramientas de transformación de manera que se facilite el mapeo hacia otros tipos de modelos en otros niveles de abstracción.
- **E4. Herramientas open source:** Existencia de herramientas open source que soporten la técnica, ya que de ésta forma se obtendrá el beneficio de la comunidad que provee el desarrollo de software libre.

4 Escala de Comparación

En la Tabla 1 se presenta la escala de valores usada en el análisis comparativo. La escala se basa en el nivel de soporte que tienen las técnicas para cada uno de los criterios de comparación.

Tabla 1. Escala de comparación

Valor	Nombre	Nivel de Soporte
1	Nulo	No soportado, no documentado.
2	Pobre	Soportado con artificios, poca o ninguna documentación.
3	Regular	Soportado y documentado, pero difícilmente aplicable.
4	Bueno	Soportado, documentado y fácilmente aplicable.
5	Nativo	Soportado, documentado y fácilmente aplicable desde la definición inicial de la técnica.

5 Análisis Comparativo

La calificación dada al estudio comparativo esta basada en la aplicación de un caso de estudio que fue desarrollado en cada una de las técnicas descritas en la sección 2.

El escenario esta dado por una empresa de servicios que tiene un proceso de Quejas y Reclamos que hace parte fundamental de su cadena de valor, cuyo objetivo de negocio es asegurar la satisfacción de sus clientes. Los principales actores identificados en el proceso de negocio son: cliente inconforme, usuario interno, gerente comercial y el encargado de la solución.

En la Tabla 2 se presentan las calificaciones dadas a cada ítem propuesto en los criterios de comparación descritos en la sección 3.

Tabla 2. Análisis comparativo

Cód.	Criterio	EyP	BPMN	RAD	IDEF3	UMurcia	Prom.
R1	Adopción de CIM	4	5	5	5	5	4.8
R2	Estructura y Comportamiento	4	4	4	3	5	4
R3	Reglas de Negocio	3	3	1	1	3	2.2
R4	Roles	2	5	5	1	5	3.6
R5	Objetivos y E/S	5	4	2	1	5	3.4
R6	B2B	3	5	3	1	4	3.2
R7	Usabilidad	3	5	3	3	3	3.4
Promedios Representación Directa		3.4	4.4	3.3	2.1	4.3	**3.5**
A1	Respaldo Metodológico	4	3	3	4	5	3.8
A2	Brecha modelado-ejecución	3	5	1	1	5	3
A3	Motor de ejecución	2	5	1	2	3	2.6
A4	SOA	1	5	1	2	3	2.4
Promedios Automatización		2.5	4.5	1.5	2.3	4.0	**3.0**
E1	Respaldo Consorcio Industrial	3	5	4	4	2	3.6
E2	Metamodelo disponible	3	5	1	3	5	3.4
E3	Framework de Modelado	2	5	1	1	5	2.8
E4	Herramientas open source	1	5	1	1	5	2.6
Promedios Estándares Abiertos		2.3	5.0	1.8	2.3	4.3	**3.1**
Totales		**43**	**69**	**36**	**33**	**63**	**48.8**

En la tabla 2 el ranking de los totales de las columnas ilustra el orden de cumplimiento de los criterios por parte de las técnicas evaluadas, mientras que el promedio de las filas ilustra el nivel de adopción de cada criterio en una escala de uno a cinco. Los promedios por categoría ilustran la forma como las técnicas de modelado de negocio están evaluadas en los frentes de la representación directa, automatización y estándares abiertos.

Los modelos del caso de estudio en cada una de las técnicas y el soporte de los valores de la tabla 2 se encuentran en los reportes técnicos disponibles en: http://docencia.udea.edu.co/ingenieria/ArquitecturaSoftware/BPM.

6 Conclusiones y trabajos futuros

La principal fortaleza de la propuesta de la Universidad de Murcia es la robustez y completitud para representar el negocio y la utilización purista de diagramas UML de actividades. La fortaleza de BPMN es su acercamiento al entorno de negocio, convirtiéndose en una técnica simple y usable para personas sin conocimientos técnicos.

Este estudio no pretende brindar un resultado concluyente sobre la técnica de modelado a usar en todos los casos; la decisión de qué técnica es la adecuada, es potestad de quienes usen este trabajo comparativo como herramienta para la toma decisiones; según las necesidades especificas de un proyecto o equipo de desarrollo se asignan pesos a los criterios de evaluación propuestos en este estudio comparativo.

El trabajo brinda una perspectiva de las diferentes posibilidades para construir modelos independientes de la computación (CIM). Con los resultados obtenidos, se proyectan trabajos futuros en el campo de la ingeniería de modelos, con el propósito de incorporar los modelos de negocio como artefactos de entrada para procesos de transformación de modelos y automatización de actividades de desarrollo de software.

Referencias

1. Business Modeling Forum. http://www.businessmodelingforum.com. (Citada Jun. 2, 2007)
2. Chrissis, Mary. Konrad, Mike. Shrum, Sandy. "CMMI Guidelines for Process, Integration and Product, Improvement". Wiley (2003)
3. HE Eriksson, M Penker. "Business Modeling with UML" (2000)
4. Davenport, Thomas H. Process Innovation: Reengineering Work through Information Technology. Harvard Business School Press (1993)
5. Object Management Group. "Business Process Modeling Notation Specification". Especificación Final Adoptada (Febrero 2006)
6. Sprint Toolkit: "A Guide to Role Activity Diagrams" http://www.sprint.gov.uk/pages.asp?id=77 (Citada Jun. 2, 2007)
7. Mayer, Richard et al. "IDEF3 Process Description Capture Method Report". Knowledge Based Systems, Inc. (Septiembre 1995)
8. MJ Ortín, J García, B Moros, J Nicolás. "El Modelo de Negocio como Base del Modelo de Requisitos". Grupo de Investigación de Ingeniería del Software, Universidad de Murcia, España (2000)
9. Booch, G., Brown, A. y Rumbaugh, J. An MDA Manifesto. IBM Rational Software, 2004.
10. Object Management Group: Model Driven Architecture (MDA) Guide Version 1.0.1. OMG, 2003. http://www.omg.org/docs/omg/03-06-01.pdf (Citada Sept. 29, 2007)
11. Debevoise, Tom. Business Process Management with a Business Rule Approach. Business Knowledge Architects (2005)
12. Stahl, Thomas. Voelter, Markus. "Model-Driven Software Development: Technology, Engineering, Management". Wiley (Mayo, 2006)
13. Object Management Group. A review of OMG MOF 2.0 Query / Views / Transformations Submissions and Recommendations towards the final Standard. OMG, 2003. http://www.omg.org/docs/ad/03-08-02.pdf (Citada Jun. 8, 2006)
14. Merks, Ed et al. "Eclipse Modeling Framework". The Eclipse Series (http://www.eclipse.org/emf) (Agosto, 2004)

Uma Experiência com Engenharia de Requisitos baseada em Modelos de Processos*

Evellin Cardoso[1], João Paulo A. Almeida[1,2], Giancarlo Guizzardi[1]

[1]Computer Science Department, Federal University of Espírito Santo (UFES), Av. Fernando Ferrari, s/n, Vitória, ES, Brazil
[2]Centre for Telematics and Information Technology, University of Twente, PO Box 217, 7500 AE Enschede, the Netherlands
evellinc@gmail.com, jpalmeida@ieee.org, gguizzardi@inf.ufes.br

Sumário. Este artigo estabelece uma comparação entre uma abordagem convencional de engenharia de requisitos e uma abordagem de engenharia de requisitos baseada em modelos de processos de negócio obtida em estudo realizado em uma empresa de grande porte. O estudo mostra a viabilidade da modelagem de processos de negócio como ferramenta útil na engenharia de requisitos de sistema.

Palavras-chave: engenharia de requisitos, processos de negócio, modelagem de processos de negócio.

1 Introdução

A engenharia de requisitos consiste em "um processo sistemático de desenvolvimento de requisitos através de um processo iterativo de análise do problema, documentação das observações resultantes e verificação acerca da precisão de entendimento" [1]. É uma atividade cujo sucesso depende diretamente da realização de uma comunicação eficaz. Diante disto, consideramos a modelagem de processos de negócio como técnica para facilitar a comunicação entre clientes e analistas.

Este artigo relata uma experiência que demonstra a possibilidade de derivação de requisitos e regras de negócio a partir de modelos de processos e que estes embasarão a geração de requisitos de sistema. Como objeto de estudo, consideramos o desenvolvimento de um sistema responsável por realizar a gestão de certos processos do setor de Recursos Humanos (RH) de uma empresa nacional no setor de energia. A especificação de requisitos foi derivada previamente através da técnica convencional de engenharia de requisitos (por uma equipe independente), e depois contrastada com a especificação de requisitos derivada através da abordagem de engenharia de requisitos baseada em modelos de processos de negócio.

O artigo é estruturado da seguinte forma: a seção 2 caracteriza o que consideramos a abordagem de engenharia de requisitos "convencional"; a seção 3 apresenta a abordagem de engenharia de requisitos baseada em modelos de processos de negócio;

* Este trabalho foi parcialmente desenvolvido com fomento do projeto INFRA-MODELA (Edital FAPES / MCT/ CNPq / CT-INFRA, Nº 019/2006).

a seção 4 constrasta os resultados obtidos pela aplicação das duas abordagens e a seção 5 discute trabalhos relacionados. Finalmente, as conclusões gerais são apresentadas na seção 6, assim como recomendações para trabalhos futuros.

2 Abordagem Convencional de Engenharia de Requisitos

A primeira técnica empregada na elicitação de requisitos é denominada *abordagem convencional* neste artigo, pois não emprega a modelagem de processos como ferramenta. Esta técnica descrita a seguir é embasada por referências pertencentes à documentos privados da companhia na qual a experiência desenvolveu-se.

A tabela 1 mostra as fases deste processo, assim como os produtos gerados ao término de cada uma.

Tabela 1. Fases do Processo de Engenharia de Requisitos e os produtos gerados em cada uma das etapas

Fase	Produto	Tipo de Requisito	Domínio
Etapa preliminar de identificação do problema	Documento de Visão	Negócio (macro-requisitos)	Problema
Etapa detalhada de descrição do problema	Documento de Solução (de Negócio)	Negócio (funcionais, não-funcionais e inversos)	
	Regras de Negócio	Negócio	
	Descrição de Documento de Glossário		
Etapa da solução (sistema)	Especificação de Casos de Uso	Sistema (funcional)	Solução (Sistema)
	Especificação Suplementar	Sistema (não-funcionais)	

3 Abordagem Orientada a Modelos de Processos de Negócio

3.1 Modelagem de Processos de Negócio

A abordagem de engenharia de requisitos orientada a modelos de processos de negócio se diferencia da abordagem denominada convencional pela inclusão de uma etapa de formalização explícita dos processos de negócios que serão apoiados ou geridos pelo sistema em desenvolvimento. Esta etapa visa facilitar a compreensão do ambiente organizacional no qual o sistema será usado e fornece subsídios para a adequação dos requisitos com os objetivos organizacionais.

A técnica de modelagem de processos empregada inicia-se pelo mapeamento da cadeia de valor organizacional que representa todos os macro-processos realizados para a concretização das estratégias organizacionais. O refinamento de macro-processos leva a cadeias de processos que representam os procedimentos coorporativos. Quando os processos atingem seu maior nível de refinamento, é possível a construção do modelo de atividades. No modelo de atividades, é possível então atribuir recursos próprios à execução destas ações atômicas.

3.2 Engenharia de Requisitos Orientada a Modelos de Processos de Negócio

Após a etapa de formalização dos processos de negócio, a etapa de engenharia de requisitos utiliza os modelos para a geração de seus respectivos requisitos de sistema.

Na análise do processo podem ser identificados três conjuntos de atividades. O primeiro conjunto consiste nas atividades não passíveis de automatização, tais como certas atividades operacionais exclusivamente realizadas por atores humanos. O segundo conjunto consiste nas atividades que podem ser apoiadas por sistemas, enquanto o terceiro conjunto refere-se àquelas totalmente automatizáveis, ou seja, que podem ser realizadas por sistemas sem intervenção humana.

A distribuição das atividades nos três grupos acima citados é realizada conjuntamente entre o cliente e o analista de sistemas [2] e deve levar em consideração uma série de fatores dentre os quais podemos citar políticas da organização, leis, restrições de segurança, dentre outros. Dessa forma, deste ponto de vista, a utilidade do modelo de processos do negócio reside no fato de que ele é fonte de subsídios para descoberta dos serviços a serem prestados pelo sistema.

A figura 1 representa esquematicamente a relação entre um modelo de processos e uma gama de conjuntos de requisitos para sistemas que podem suportar este processo, cada conjunto de requisitos correspondendo um diferente conjunto de escolhas de nível de automatização das atividades deste processo. Nesta figura o modelo de processos é considerado o ponto de partida para o esforço de engenharia de requisitos, que envolve os *stakeholders* do sistema. A partir do mesmo modelo de processos é possível obter um conjunto de requisitos R_1 para um sistema S_1 que irá apoiá-lo, ou ainda obter um conjunto de requisitos R_2 para um sistema S_2 que possui um nível maior de automatização. Caminhando-se na escala de soluções, no limite da automatização, a escolha do conjunto de requisitos R_N referente ao sistema S_N também é viável e consiste no maior nível de automatização para o processo.

Cabe ressaltar que a menção do termo nível de automatização, no texto, refere-se às atividades que podem ter sua execução suportada por certos sistemas que lhes provêem mecanismos de acompanhamento ou podem ser atividades cuja automatização é totalmente realizada por sistemas.

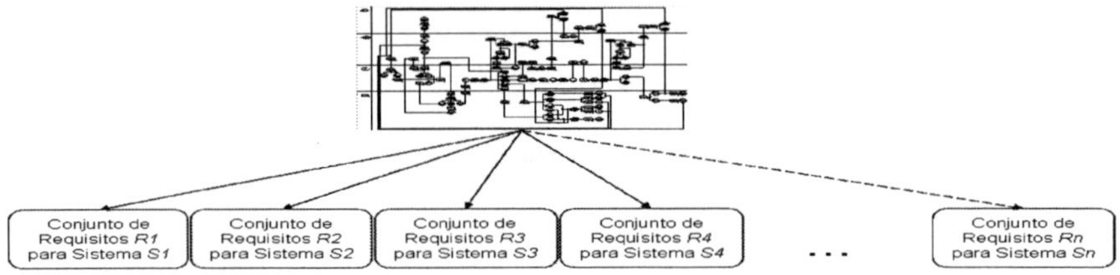

Fig.1. Geração de conjuntos de requisitos a partir de um modelo de processos

Neste momento, após a escolha mais adequada do sistema no suporte do processo e a divisão das atividades nas três categorias acima mencionadas, os requisitos podem ser elicitados a partir das atividades previamente escolhidas. Todo o procedimento acima descrito corresponde à fase de análise de requisitos e de regras relacionados ao processo e pode ser executado a partir da metodologia acima descrita. Neste momento, ocorre a transição dos modelos conceituais (relacionados com os processos em alto nível) para os modelos lógicos (relacionados com o projeto do sistema).

As funcionalidades providas pelos sistemas às atividades são consideradas requisitos funcionais destes sistemas e são mapeadas nos casos de uso correspondentes. Os requisitos não funcionais que estão relacionados à qualidade dos serviços providos pelo sistema tais como desempenho, segurança e disponibilidade, são geralmente propriedades ou características de vários casos de uso [2].

4 Comparação dos Resultados Obtidos pela Aplicação das Diferentes Abordagens

As duas abordagens foram aplicadas na etapa de elicitação de requisitos para um sistema responsável por realizar a gestão de alguns processos do setor de Recursos Humanos (RH) de uma empresa nacional no setor de energia. Consideramos aqui: (i) uma especificação de requisitos derivada previamente (por uma equipe independente) através da técnica convencional de engenharia de requisitos (descrita na seção 2), e (ii) uma especificação de requisitos baseada na abordagem de modelagem de processos apresentada na seção 3. As especificações de requisitos são omitidas por limitações de espaço e relatamos nesta seção as conclusões da comparação entre a aplicação das duas abordagens. São usados critérios apresentados em [6] entre outros.

Completude. Na abordagem convencional, o conjunto de requisitos gerados não contemplava as ações de todos os atores presentes no processo. Durante a modelagem de processos, verificou-se a ausência de tais requisitos e a necessidade da inserção das decisões da Assistência Médica (um ator) no sistema. A inserção das mesmas é considerada aspecto indispensável ao negócio visto que resguarda certas decisões do empregado. Por isso, a elicitação de requisitos concentra-se na interação pontual entre sistema e ator, apresentando deficiências na identificação de situações excepcionais e que envolvam outros atores que influenciam indiretamente a interação com o sistema.

Correção. Após o INSS analisar um pedido de licença de perícia médica, ele deveria emitir algum resultado e o empregado poderia tomar certas decisões baseado no resultado do INSS. Na elicitação de requisitos convencional, o analista situou a decisão de pedido de prorrogação (PP) como uma decisão possível a ser escolhida pelo funcionário, caso o INSS lhe concedesse o resultado de não incapacidade para o trabalho. No entanto, por meio da modelagem do processo, vislumbrou-se que não havia possibilidade do empregado tomar tal decisão, visto que não era possível realizar pedido de prorrogação para licença que não havia sido concedida.

Consistência. No decorrer da modelagem de processos, a reunião dos executores do processo permitiu que fosse estabelecida uma visão abrangente de todo o contexto do sistema, possibilitando a identificação das divergências recíprocas nas descrições dos trechos do processo que são compartilhados por muitos executores. Tais inconsistências não são percebidas porque não existe reflexão conjunta como durante a modelagem, mas sim, um relato da interação de cada um em particular.

Contextualização ao Cliente e ao Analista. Na aplicação da abordagem convencional no estudo, a contextualização do problema e as necessidades que o sistema deve satisfazer não são adequadamente formalizadas. Isso dificulta a validação porque estas informações não foram documentadas. Na abordagem que considera a modelagem de processos, a contextualização do processo é parte do método, isto é, os propósitos de construção do sistema e as atividades que serão automatizadas são adequadamente formalizadas nas etapas preliminares, o que permite posterior validação. Esse é principal melhoria que pode ser observada no escopo do estudo: o contexto no qual o sistema está inserido foi considerado como parte integral na aplicação da abordagem orientada a modelos de processos.

Rastreabilidade. A partir da modelagem de processos, os modelos são mais significativos ao usuário uma vez que apresentam linguagem gráfica e permitem a identificação de erros e pontos de melhoria no domínio do problema. Posteriormente, após a elicitação dos requisitos de negócio e a geração dos seus respectivos requisitos de sistema, o analista consegue verificar a existência das funcionalidades pretendidas pelo usuário. Portanto, é possível se conseguir rastreabilidade dos requisitos identificados pelo método, ou seja, a relação entre cada necessidade de negócio e cada funcionalidade ou restrição identificada para o sistema pode ser mantida [3].

5 Trabalhos Relacionados

Existem na literatura trabalhos que exploram a modelagem de processos de negócio como subsídios para engenharia de requisitos.

Dentre estes, o trabalho apresentado em [4] procura estabelecer uma ligação entre os modelos de processo, representados através do diagrama de atividades da UML, e os requisitos representados através dos diagramas de casos de uso. Com relação ao grau de automatização, ainda que no modelo de negócios existam atividades realizadas por pessoas, por máquinas especializadas ou por sistemas de informação considera-se nos casos de uso que todas atividades serão apoiadas por sistemas.

Outra proposta que considera a modelagem dos processos de negócio na trajetória que leva à engenharia de requisitos é apresentada em [5]. No entanto, o modelo de processos não é utilizado diretamente como fonte de subsídios à atividade de elicitação de requisitos de sistema (sendo usado apenas para melhorar o entendimento sobre o sistema).

Diferentemente das propostas anteriores, no trabalho apresentado em [2], sempre que existir a necessidade da construção de um sistema na organização, o cliente decide o escopo do sistema e o solicita aos engenheiros de software. Estes, por sua vez, baseado no escopo delimitado *a priori* pelo cliente, buscam no modelo de processos subsídios para entendimento do contexto organizacional.

Com relação às abordagens anteriores, o presente trabalho relata uma experiência de engenharia de requisitos de sistema por meio da utilização de modelos de processos de negócio, na qual o conjunto de requisitos gerado depende do nível de automatização pretendido para o processo. Dado um modelo de processos, existe a possibilidade de geração de vários conjuntos de requisitos de sistema diferentes, dependendo dos objetivos pelos quais a inserção do sistema se justifica. Isso difere das abordagens anteriores (e da convencional) porque permite a criação de diversos conjuntos de requisitos que, por sua vez, poderão gerar diversos sistemas tão alinhados aos processos quanto desejável.

6 Conclusão

A experiência relatada neste artigo fornece indícios de que a engenharia de requisitos pode ser beneficiada pela adoção dos modelos de processos. A modelagem de processos complementa as práticas convencionais de engenharia de requisitos, auxiliando o cliente a adquirir maturidade acerca da complexidade do seu próprio negócio e revelando o grau de adequação dos requisitos elicitados com os processos (e objetivos) da organização. Na comparação conduzida, a abordagem baseada em modelos de processos levou a um conjunto requisitos mais completo, correto, rastreável e que reflete consistentemente a visão dos vários *stakeholders*.

Ressaltamos que a modelagem de processos de negócios independe do desenvolvimento de sistemas e pode ser conduzida independentemente para a construção de uma arquitetura organizacional de referência. Quando necessária a construção de um sistema que dê apoio a partes dos processos modelados nesta arquitetura, é necessário apenas o retorno ao cliente somente para a elicitação dos detalhes referentes ao projeto lógico do sistema (requisitos de sistema), e não àqueles referentes ao modelo conceitual do negócio (desde que o processo não sofra alterações conceituais).

Enquanto a abordagem convencional conduz à geração de um determinado conjunto de requisitos que suporta um conjunto arbitrário de atividades de um processo, a formalização dos processos permite a geração de vários conjuntos de requisitos de sistema com níveis de automatização variados. A escolha de qual conjunto será utilizado é um passo explícito do processo e depende dos propósitos dos sistemas que automatizam os processos considerados, levando consideração uma série de fatores dentre os quais podemos citar políticas organizacionais, restrições legais e tecnológicas.

Esse passo explícito permite ainda o equacionamento entre o nível de automatização do processo e a volatilidade dos requisitos. Como regra geral, quanto maior a volatilidade, menor deve ser o nível de automatização do processo, visto que constantes alterações nos requisitos e regras de negócio levariam a alterações nos sistemas. Pretendemos investigar tal equacionamento em trabalhos futuros assim como investigar o grau de alinhamento de processos com sistemas *off-the-shelf*, como sistemas de gestão corporativa e sistemas de *workflow* customizáveis.

Referências

1. Kang, K.C., Christel, M.G.: Issues in requirements elicitation (Tech. Rep. No. SEI-92-TR-012). Carnegie Mellon University, Pittsburgh, EUA. (1992)
2. Knight, D. M.: Elicitação de Requisitos de Software a partir do Modelo de Negócio, Dissertação de Mestrado em Informática, UFRJ/NCE, Rio de Janeiro, (2004).
3. Gotel, O., Finkelstein, A.: "An Analysis of the Requirements Traceability Problem,". In: Proc. First Int'l Conf. Requirements Eng., (1994) pp. 94-101.
4. Cruz, P.O.S.: Heurísticas para Identificação de Requisitos de Sistemas de Informações a partir de Modelos de Processos, Tese de Mestrado, NCE, UFRJ, Rio de Janeiro (2004).
5. Sharp, A., McDermott, P.: Workflow Modeling: Tools for Process Improvement and Application Development, Artech House Computing (2001).
6. Institute of Electrical and Electronics Engineers: IEEE recommended practice for software requirements specifications, IEEE Standard 830-1998 (1998).

Modelagem Intencional de Requisitos de Segurança

Herbet de Souza Cunha, Julio Cesar Sampaio do Prado Leite

Departamento de Informática, Pontifícia Universidade Católica - Rio de Janeiro (PUC-Rio)

{herbet,julio}@inf.puc-rio.br

Abstract. *Adding security requirements to software architectures after they are built is hard and error prone. Security concepts must be an issue on the entire software development process, from requirement engineering to deployment, passing by design, coding and test. This work presents a process to security requirements modeling based on i*.*

Resumo. *Adicionar requisitos de segurança às arquiteturas de software após elas terem sido construídas é uma tarefa bastante difícil. Conceitos de segurança devem permear todo o ciclo de desenvolvimento do software, desde a engenharia de requisitos, passando por desenho (design), implementação, testes e distribuição. Este trabalho apresenta um processo para modelagem de requisitos de segurança baseado em i*.*

Key words: *Requirement, Security*

1 Introdução

Existe um consenso, tanto na comunidade acadêmica quanto nas empresas, que a segurança dos sistemas de software é importante. A sociedade moderna depende criticamente de uma variedade destes sistemas de software. Apresentamos a seguir um processo - evolução do trabalho de Liu, Yu e Mylopoulos [4] - para definição (elicitação, modelagem e análise) de requisitos de segurança específicos de aplicação, através do qual são construídos modelos intencionais para os requisitos do domínio e para os requisitos de segurança. O escopo do trabalho está delimitado em requisitos de segurança (*security*) - não é objetivo deste trabalho abordar fidedignidade (*dependability*) nem seguridade (*safety*).

2 O Framework i*

i* [1] é um *framewok* usado para obter um melhor entendimento dos relacionamentos entre os vários atores organizacionais e das razões internas destes atores, uma vez que as mesmas são expressas explicitamente. Optamos pelo i* para modelagem de requisitos de segurança por ser um *framework* intencional e por haver um mapeamento direto entre as metas flexíveis de i* e os requisitos não-funcionais, o que permite que os mesmos sejam integrados aos requisitos funcionais através do refinamento das metas flexíveis e com a contribuição, seja ela positiva ou negativa, deste refinamento para os demais requisitos. Com isto, é possível fazer uma análise mais rica das alternativas de operacionalização dos requisitos não-funcionais e, ao mesmo tempo, tornar explícito o *rationale* da escolha destas alternativas.

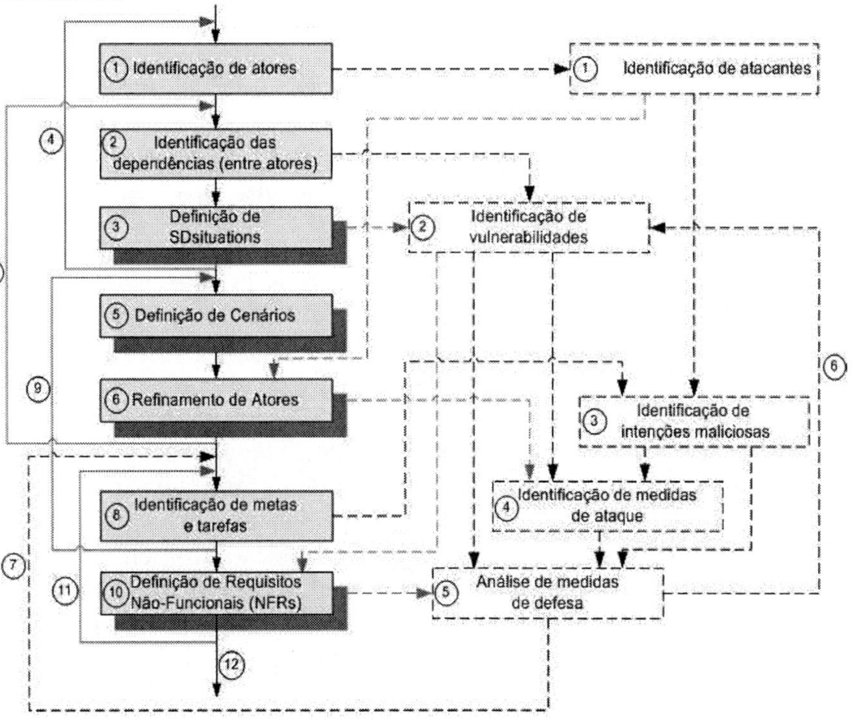

Fig. 1 - Fluxograma do processo evoluído a partir de [4]

Ao *framework* i* original nós acrescentamos duas extensões: (i) *SDSituations* - forma de representação estruturada de uma situação de dependência estratégica, proposta por Oliveira e Cysneiros em [3]; e (ii) modelo Strategic Actor (SA) [13] - usado especificamente para modelar atores em i*, auxiliando o entendimento dos mesmos e seus relacionamentos, do ponto de vista estrutural.

3 Processo para definição de requisitos de segurança

A Fig. 1 apresenta o fluxograma do processo evoluído composto por duas partes interrelacionadas: (i) um processo básico de definição de requisitos gerais - caixas com linhas sólidas, à esquerda; e (ii) um processo para definição de requisitos específicos de segurança - caixas com linhas tracejadas, à direta. Os passos 3 - Definição de *SDsituations*, 5 - Definição de Cenários, 6 - Refinamento de Atores e 10 - Definição de Requisitos Não-Funcionais (representados pelas caixas sombreadas na Fig. 1) são contribuições nossas ao processo original [4], e têm o objetivo de ajudar a lidar com a complexidade (para análise) dos modelos produzidos pelo *framework* i*; melhorar o entendimento dos atores e suas relações; tornar explícito o processo de definição dos requisitos não-funcionais, em especial, os de segurança; e, auxiliar a validação dos requisitos pelos usuários e demais interessados. O detalhamento dos passos do processo pode ser consultado em [11].

Durante a execução do processo os requisitos não-funcionais são definidos (elicitados, modelados e analisados) e, em seguida, operacionalizados através de requisitos funcionais. Mais adiante no processo, os requisitos não-funcionais de segurança, devidamente refinados, são acrescentados aos modelos SR representando a intenção de proteger as vulnerabilidades identificadas previamente (a operacionalização é derivada das medidas de defesa que são escolhidas para neutralizar as vulnerabilidades). Ao final, os cenários terão então incorporado os requisitos não-funcionais (descritos em forma de *constraints*) e a alternativa de operacionalização (medida de defesa) escolhida, como no exemplo do cenário *Article Review* do estudo de caso do *Expert Committee*[1] apresentado na Fig. 2 - o estudo completo pode ser consultado em [11].

---

[1] O *Expert Committee* (EC) [6] é um sistema para suporte ao gerenciamento de submissões e revisões de artigos submetidos a uma conferência ou workshop.

4 Conclusões

A abordagem proposta em nosso trabalho propicia uma maior transparência do software [2], na medida em que auxilia a documentar o *rationale* da escolha da alternativa para operacionalização de um requisito e possibilita o rastro dos requisitos de segurança de alto nível até sua operacionalização (como são refinados em requisitos de nível de abstração menor, como são operacionalizados).

Scenario definition	
Title: **Articles Review**	Precondition: Proposal Acceptance.
Goal: ArticlesBeReviewed	Resource: Computer, Internet, Articles
Context: Geographical Location: WEB; Temporal: Before deadline to send reviews	Actors: Chair, Reviewers
Episodes:	
1 Chair prepares standards to review 2 Chair selects an article to sends to review 3 Chair selects an article to sends to review 4 Chair selects reviewers that have accepted the proposal of review for the selected article **5 Constraint External Confidentiality [Article]** **5.1 Encrypt Article** **5.2 Use a 128bits Key (to encrypt article)** 6 Reviewer receives the article sent by Chair **7 Constraint External Confidentiality [Article]** **7.1 Decrypt Article** **7.2 Use a 128bits Key (to decrypt article)** 8 Reviewer makes the article review **9 Constraint Internal Confidentiality [Reviewed Article]** **9.1 Authorize Access** **9.2 Reviewer uses an Identification Key** **9.3 Authenticate Reviewer with Password** **9.4Reviewer uses Single Passoword** **9.5 Uses Access Validation Rules to check if Reviewer can make the review to this article** **10 Constraint Consistency [Reviewed Article]** **10.1 Check Consistency of Reviewed Article** **10.2 Use hash function to generate a 'fingerprint'** 11 Reviewer sends reviewed article to Chair	**12 Constraint External Confidentiality [Reviewed Article]** **12.1 Encrypt Reviewed Article** **12.2 Use a 128bits Key (to encrypt article)** 13 Chair receives the reviewed articles **14 Constraint Internal Confidentiality [Reviewed Article]** **14.1 Authorize Access** **14.2 Chair uses an Identification Key** **14.3 Authenticate Chair with Password** **14.4 Chair uses Single Passoword** **14.5 Uses Access Validation Rules to check if Chair can access this article** **15 Constraint External Confidentiality [Reviewed Article]** **15.1 Decrypt Article** **15.2 Use a 128bits Key (to decrypt article)** **16 Constraint Consistency [Reviewed Article]** **16.1 Check Consistency of Article** **16.2 Use DVD midia to make an Article's copy** 17 Chair checks if there is conflict (incompatible evaluations) in reviews of each article
Exceptions: If an article has a conflict: (scenario: Conflict Resolution)	

Fig. 2 – Exemplo de cenário com a incorporação de requisito de segurança detalhado

A documentação do *rationale* da escolha da alternativa para operacionalização dos requisitos de segurança é alcançado através dos modelos elaborados durante a execução do Passo 5 – Análise de medidas de defesa. Apresentamos também os requisitos através de cenários, que evoluem ao longo do processo desde a versão inicial (elaborada na primeira execução do passo 5, onde os requisitos de segurança tipicamente aparecem como restrições) para cenários que apresentam os requisitos de segurança integrados aos demais requisitos com as respectivas escolhas de operacionalização. Estes cenários podem ser usados na validação dos requisitos através da leitura dos mesmos pelos clientes e demais interessados. O uso de cenários, a elicitação de requisitos não-funcionais de alto nível a partir de vulnerabilidades identificadas nas *SDsituations* e o refinamento explícito destes requisitos de alto nível até sua operacionalização são contribuições nossas ao processo original.

Alguns trabalhos recentes têm abordado a modelagem de requisitos de segurança, dentre os quais podemos destacar o trabalho de van Lamsweerde [10] que tem uma abordagem intencional, semelhante a nossa, e o trabalho de Firesmith [9], com uma abordagem descritiva não intencional. Há também trabalhos voltados para verificação de requisitos como o *Common Criteria* [5] que podem servir de base também para a elicitação de requisitos. Uma análise resumida destes trabalhos é apresentada na Tabela 1.

Trabalho Analisado	Ponto de partida	Idéia chave	Diferencial
Elaborating security requirements by construction of intentional anti-models [10]	Anti-metas geradas através da negação das metas originais	Construção de anti-modelos para os anti-requisitos a partir da negação do modelo de requisitos	A geração de obstáculos para a construção do anti-modelo pode ser feita formalmente.
Security Use Cases [9]	"Casos de mau uso" (misuse cases)	Casos de uso de segurança são derivados a partir dos "casos de mau uso"	Expressos de forma descritiva, semelhante aos casos de uso
Requirement Elicitation Based on Goals with Security and Privacy Policies in Electronic Commerce [14]	Elicitação das metas dos atores	As metas são elicitadas e refinadas até sua operacionalização, avaliando-se a conformidade com as políticas de segurança existentes ou criando-se novas políticas	Atribuição de valor às metas, tratamento de riscos mais apurado e uso de políticas de segurança
Security Design Based on Social Modelling [12]	Elicitação das metas dos atacantes (intenções maliciosas)	Construção de modelos intencionais, incluindo atacantes e suas metas	Estabelecimento de um par de fronteiras de confiança para restringir o espaço de busca por atacantes
Information technology - Security techniques - Evaluation criteria for IT security - Part 2: Security functional requirements [5]	Critérios estabelecidos na própria norma	Conjunto de boas práticas e critérios para aferição de segurança	Foco na atividade de verificação
Modelagem Intencional de Requisitos de Segurança	Elicitação das metas dos atacantes (intenções maliciosas)	Construção de modelos intencionais, incluindo atacantes e suas metas	Uso de SDsituations para lidar com a complexidade dos modelos e cenários para apresentação dos requisitos de segurança

Tabela 1 – Resumo de características dos trabalhos analisados

Como trabalhos futuros, esperamos aplicar o processo proposto para elaboração de requisitos de segurança em casos reais com o objetivo de validá-lo e modelar os requisitos de segurança com o objetivo de transformá-los em aspectos. O desenvolvimento de uma ferramenta de modelagem integrada também é necessário para viabilizar o uso eficiente do processo proposto.

5 Referências

1. Yu, E. Modelling Strategic Relationships for Process Reengineering, PhD Thesis, Graduate Department of Computer Science, University of Toronto. (1995)
2. Leite, J. C. S. P. Sistemas de Software Transparentes. In: Simpósio Brasileiro de Engenharia de Software. Anais do XX Simpósio Brasileiro de Engenharia de Software. Florianópolis (2006) 319-319
3. Oliveira, A.; Cysneiros, L. Defining Strategic Dependency Situations in Requirements Elicitation. In: Proceedings of WER'2006). Rio de Janeiro, Brasil (2006) 12-23
4. Liu, L.; Yu. E.; Mylopoulos, J. Security and Privacy Requirements Analysis within a Social Setting. In: Proceedings of the International Conference on Requirements Engineering (RE'03). Monterey, California (2003) 151-161.
5. ISO/IEC 15408-2:2005(E): Information technology - Security techniques - Evaluation criteria for IT security - Part 2: Security functional requirements. Genebra (2005)
6. DESCRIÇÃO do Expert Committee. Disciplina Engenharia de Software de Sistemas Multi-Agentes, Curso de mestrado em Informática, Departamento de Informática, PUC-Rio. 1º Semestre de 2005. Acesso em: http://web.teccomm.les.inf.puc-rio.br/uploads/7/74/ExpertCommittee3.doc
7. Chung, L.; Nixon, B.; Yu, E.; Mylopoulos, J. Non-Functional Requirements in Software Engineering. Kluwer Academic Publishers. Boston/Dordrecht/London (2000)
8. Giogini, P.; Massacci, F.; Zannone, N. Security and Trust Requirements Engineering. In: FOSAD 2005 - Foundations of Security Analysis and Design III. (2005) 237-272
9. Firesmith, D. Security Use Cases. Journal of Object Technology, vol. 2, no.3, May-June (2003) 53-64
10. van Lamsweerde, A. Elaborating security requirements by construction of intentional anti-models. Proceedings. 26th International Conference on Software Engineering, 2004. ICSE (2004) 148-157.
11. Cunha, H Dissertação de Mestrado: Uso de estratégias orientadas a metas para modelagem de requisitos de segurança. Departmento de Informática, Pontifícia Universidade Católica. Rio de Janeiro, Brasil (2007)
12. Liu, L.; Yu, E.; Mylopoulos, J. Security Design Based on Social Modelling. In: 30th Annual International Computer Software and Applications Conference – (2006) 71-78
13. Leite, J.C.S.P; Werneck, V.; Oliveira, A.; Cappelli, C.; Cerqueira, A.; Cunha, H.; Gonzalez-Baixauli, B. Understanding the Strategic Actor Diagram: An Exercise of Meta Modeling. 10th Workshop on Requirements Engineering. Toronto (2007)
14. Rocha, S.; Abdelouahab, Z.; Freire, E. Requirement Elicitation Based on Goals with Security and Privacy Policies in Electronic Commerce. Anais do WER05 - Workshop em Engenharia de Requisitos, Porto, Portugal. (2005) 63-74

Uma Abordagem para Tratamento de Regras de Negócio nas Fases Iniciais do Desenvolvimento

Marco Antonio De Grandi, Valter Vieira de Camargo, Edmundo Sérgio Spoto

Centro Universitário Eurípides de Marília (Univem)
Caixa Postal 2041 – 17.525-901 – Marília – SP – Brazil
marcodgrandi@gmail.com, {valter, dino}@univem.edu.br

Resumo. Neste artigo é mostrada uma abordagem para apoiar a identificação e classificação de regras de negócio. As diretrizes mostradas fornecem apoio para que os próximos passos do desenvolvimento possam tratar as regras de negócio de forma separada do núcleo do software.

Palavras-Chave: Regras de Negócio.

1 Introdução

Regras de negócio (RNs) são declarações cujo objetivo é influenciar, ou guiar, o comportamento de um negócio [8]. Elas têm por objetivo definir as características do negócio que norteiam a execução dos requisitos funcionais de um software.

Pesquisadores argumentam que a sensibilidade das RNs às mudanças de requisitos faz com que elas devam ser tratadas de forma mais adequada e sistemática durante o desenvolvimento de um sistema [1,8,9]. Uma maneira de prover esse tratamento é fornecer mecanismos para que as RNs sejam identificadas, classificadas, registradas e implementadas separadamente do núcleo do software, facilitando a manutenção, a modularização e conseqüentemente fornecendo melhores níveis de reúso.

O objetivo principal desse artigo é fornecer diretrizes para a identificação e classificação das RNs, fornecendo apoio para que as próximas etapas do desenvolvimento possam tratá-las de forma separada do núcleo do software, facilitando sua manipulação e resultando em sistemas mais manuteníveis e reusáveis. Para isso são definidos critérios para a identificação e classificação das RNs, fornecendo assim a base inicial para que os próximos passos do desenvolvimento possam tratar as regras de negócio de forma separada do núcleo do software.

O artigo está organizado da seguinte forma: Na Seção 2 são apresentados os conceitos relevantes às RNs. Na Seção 3 é apresentada a abordagem. Na seção 4 encontram-se os trabalhos relacionados a esse, e na Seção 5 as considerações finais.

2 Regras de Negócio

As RNs podem ser classificadas em diversas formas [2,6,8,9]. Nesse trabalho é utilizada a classificação proposta por [9], por ser uma síntese de outros tipos de classificação e possuir foco nos tipos de RNs que normalmente são utilizados em sistemas de informação. Nesse esquema, as RNs são separadas em três grupos (Informações Restritivas, Habilitadoras e Derivações) que originam os cinco tipos de RNs: Restrições, Diretrizes, Habilitadoras de Ações, Derivação por Computação e por Inferência.

A implementação das RNs em um sistema de informação deve respeitar alguns princípios básicos [8,9] que visam viabilizar a manutenção das RNs, devido à sua natureza volátil. Esses princípios são:

1. **Separação** (*Separate*): As RNs devem ser implementadas de forma separada dos requisitos e do próprio sistema. Esse princípio busca incentivar o reúso das regras e possibilitar que elas possam ser alteradas independentemente de outras características do sistema;
2. **Rastreamento** (*Trace*): As RNs devem possuir uma rastreabilidade que permita identificar os artefatos de software utilizados para sua implementação, com isso, o impacto sobre a alteração de uma regra pode ser mensurado;
3. **Externalização** (*Externalize*): Toda a regra deve ser expressa num formato compreensível para que seja possível a realização de auditorias de negócio, por pessoas não-técnicas;
4. **Posicionamento** (*Position*): As RNs devem estar preparadas para mudanças, uma vez que por meio das regras pode-se mudar o curso regular do negócio.

Para o cumprimento desses princípios, é necessário que o desenvolvimento das RNs possa ser acompanhado durante as fases iniciais do ciclo de vida de um sistema. Esse acompanhamento pode ser feito mediante mecanismos que permitam identificar, classificar, modelar e mapear as regras de uma fase para a outra do desenvolvimento.

3 A Abordagem Proposta

A abordagem proposta neste artigo envolve duas etapas: a elaboração de casos de uso com gabarito e a identificação/classificação das RNs. Na Figura 1 são mostradas algumas etapas genéricas do desenvolvimento clássico de um sistema e também os pontos que sofrem influência da abordagem proposta neste artigo, sendo que, os quadros pontilhados representam os novos artefatos utilizados, e o quadro adicionado na fase de Análise representa uma nova atividade, necessária à proposta desse trabalho e que é discutida nas próximas subseções.

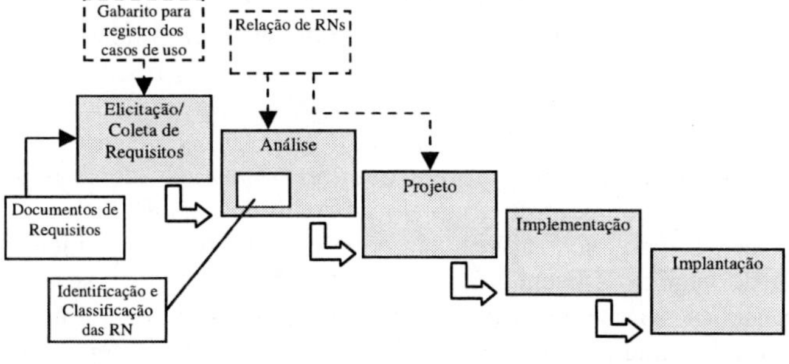

Figura 1. Adaptação do ciclo de vida de desenvolvimento de software à proposta.

3.1 Elaboração de Casos de Uso com Gabarito

A identificação de RNs durante o levantamento de requisitos deve ser auxiliada por meio do uso de um gabarito (*template*) para a documentação e registro dos casos de uso. O gabarito utilizado nesse trabalho (Figura 2) é uma adaptação do gabarito proposto por [4]. A extensão foi feita para apoiar de forma mais adequada a identificação das RNs. Isso ocorre por meio do registro de informações específicas, oriundas do documento de requisitos que posteriormente irão se tornar RNs.

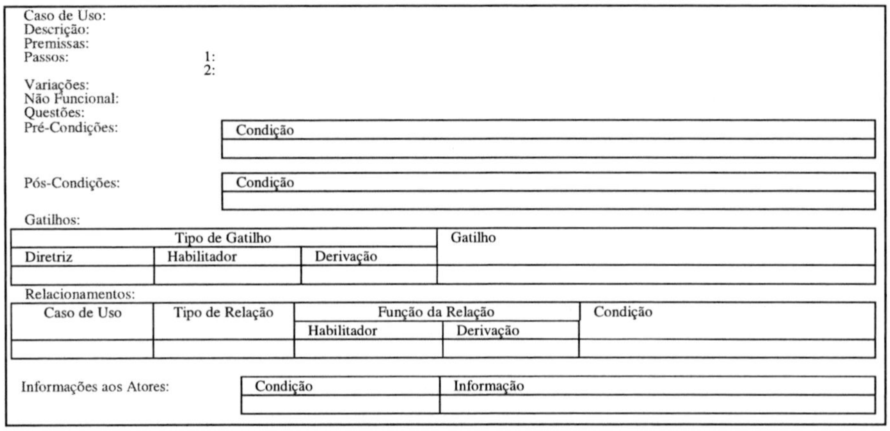

Figura 2. Gabarito para Documentação de Caso de Uso

Para o preenchimento das novas seções do gabarito proposto, deve-se utilizar informações obtidas no documento de requisitos do sistema com o apoio de diretrizes que devem ser aplicadas aos documentos de requisitos. São elas:

1. **Pré-Condições:** Indicam as condições, tais como restrições de negócio, que devem ser satisfeitas na ocorrência do caso de uso;
2. **Pós-Condições**: Indicam condições de negócio que devem ser satisfeitas para que o caso de uso seja concluído;
3. **Gatilhos**: São procedimentos que devem ser disparados, independente do cluxo de execução do caso de uso, após a execução, com sucesso, de um caso de uso, sempre que a condição estabelecida for satisfeita;
4. **Relacionamentos**: São todos os relacionamentos que o caso de uso possua com os demais, desde que exerçam uma função de negócio. O tipo de relação pode ser: Associação, Extensão ou Inclusão. A função da relação pode ser derivação ou habilitadora de ações;
5. **Informações aos Atores:** São informações fornecidas aos atores relacionados ao caso de uso, podendo ocorrer em qualquer ponto de um caso de uso.

Essas diretrizes devem ser aplicadas com o objetivo de identificar os comportamentos de negócio presentes nos requisitos. Portanto deve-se atentar para que essas informações sejam políticas da companhia, padrões de indústria, leis e regulamentações governamentais, ou ter outro tipo de origem que esteja vinculado ao comportamento que o software deve ter para refletir um comportamento específico da companhia. As demais pré e pós-condições, gatilhos, relacionamentos e informações aos atores, devem ser implementadas no software da forma convencional, sem necessariamente serem tratadas como RNs, e sem, portanto, estarem informadas nas novas seções do gabarito proposto.

Portanto, antes da inserção das informações em cada uma das novas seções do gabarito é necessário fazer uma crítica no intuito de certificar que realmente trata-se de uma informação que reflete um comportamento de negócio.

3.2 Identificação e Classificação de Regras de Negócio

Uma vez que os casos de uso estejam documentados com o gabarito proposto, é possível a identificação das RNs mediante aplicação de alguns critérios. Na Tabela 1 são apresentados os critérios de identificação e subseqüiente classificação das RNs. Esses critérios que foram elaborados com o objetivo de extrair as RNs dos casos de uso e classificá-las, tomando como base sua localização nas seções do gabarito mostrado na Figura 2.

Tabela 1. Critérios para Identificação e Classificação das Regras de Negócio

Tipo de RN	Critério de Identificação
Restrições	-Itens informados na seção Pré-Condições ou Pós-Condições.
Diretrizes	-Itens informados na seção Informações aos Atores. -Itens informados na seção Gatilhos, que sejam do tipo Diretrizes.
Habilitadoras de Ações	-Itens informados na seção Gatilhos e que tenha a função Habilitador. -Itens informados na seção Associações e que a função Habilitador.
Derivação	-Itens informados na seção Gatilhos e que tenham a função Derivação. -Itens informados na seção Associações e que tenham a função Derivação.

Com a aplicação desses critérios em todos os casos de uso, obtêm-se o conjunto total de RNs existentes no sistema. Em seguida sugere-se a elaboração de um artefato para registrar as regras que foram identificadas no passo anterior. Esse artefato é mostrado na Tabela 2. Na primeira coluna desse artefato deve ser informado a RN em si, em seguida seu tipo, e o caso de uso que deu origem a ela. Na quarta coluna deve ser informada a seção do caso de uso que gerou a regra e na quinta a identificação da RN. Note-se que esse registro propicia um mapeamento entre as RNs e cada caso de uso que deram origem a elas, auxiliando na rastreabilidade dessas RNs nessas fases iniciais do desenvolvimento.

Tabela 2. Relação de Regras de Negócio (por caso de uso)

Regra	Tipo	Caso de Uso	Seção	Id. RN
No preenchimento da data de chegada e da data de saída, o número de dias da reserva não deve exceder a 7	Restrição	Realizar Reserva	Pré-Condição 1	Duração Reserva
Caso o hóspede possua faturas vencidas e não pagas o sistema deverá gerar uma advertência por débitos, na efetivação da reserva.	Diretriz	Realizar Reserva	Gatilho 1	Inadimplência

Sugere-se também que as RNs identificadas sejam representadas graficamente como casos de uso. Dessa forma, pode-se ter uma visão mais ampla do sistema e dos relacionamentos que essas RNs mantêm com os demais casos de uso funcionais. Para que os casos de uso referentes às RNs sejam diferenciados dos demais, sugere-se também a utilização do estereótipo <<business rule>> e a criação de visões individuais para as RNs, com o intuito de não poluir o diagrama de casos de uso.

Os casos de uso que representam RNs devem ser relacionados aos seus casos de uso base por meio de relacionamentos do tipo Extensão (*Extend*), uma vez que geralmente as RNs dependem de uma condição para serem acionadas, ou seja, elas representam um comportamento adicional ao caso de uso base.

Um exemplo da modelagem de RNs no diagrama de casos de uso é mostrado na Figura 3, no qual o caso de uso base "RealizarReserva" possui duas RNs nomeadas "Inadimplência" e "DuraçãoReserva". Essa modelagem deve representar a influência de RNs sobre o comportamento de um caso de uso. Pode-se observar que essas RNs foram obtidas a partir do artefato Relação de Regras de Negócio mostrado na Tabela2 e modeladas de acordo com as diretrizes apresentadas anteriormente.

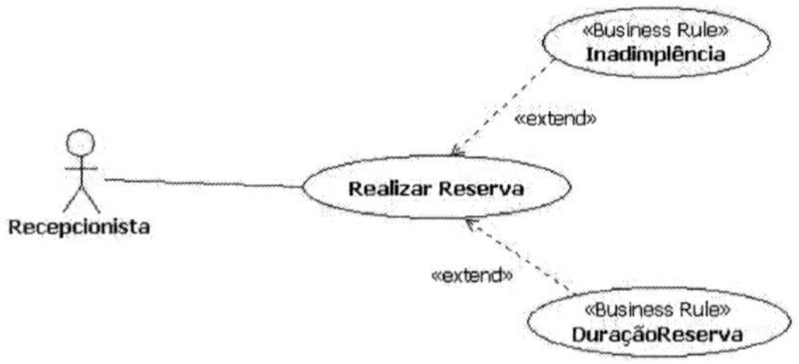

Figura 3. Exemplo da modelagem de RNs no diagrama de casos de uso.

4 Trabalhos Relacionados

Nos últimos anos a utilização das RNs na engenharia de software gerou diversas linhas distintas de pesquisa, entre elas estão as pesquisas que focam a captura e representação sistemática das RNs bem como sua posterior tradução para códigos de linguagens de programação [7], as que visam a implementação das RNs com a tecnologia *Adaptive Object Models* [10], as que focam a implementação das RNs por meio de tecnologias específicas, como por exemplo, as linguagens baseadas em regras [8,9]. Existem ainda as pesquisas que sugerem a implementação das RNs com POA [3,5], contudo, focando apenas a implementação do software sem abordar as fases de projeto. E por fim as pesquisas que focam o rastreamento das RNs nos artefatos do software no ambiente OO, como em [1,11].

5 Considerações Finais e Trabalhos Futuros

Nesse trabalho foi apresentada uma abordagem para apoiar a identificação e a classificação das RNs no início do desenvolvimento. Essa abordagem é composta um modelo de gabarito para a documentação dos casos de uso, e pelas diretrizes para a identificação e classificação das RNs, fornecendo apoio para que as próximas etapas do desenvolvimento possam tratá-las de forma separada do núcleo do software.

Com a aplicação da abordagem foi observado que as RNs podem ser tratadas de forma separada e independente do núcleo do software. Esse resultado é o inicio de um processo cujo objetivo é apoiar o desenvolvimento das RNs ao longo das fases de projeto do sistema, obtendo-se assim a implementação das RNs de forma separada do núcleo do software, o que resulta em sistemas mais legíveis e manuteníveis

Acredita-se que a contribuição principal desse artigo seja a proposta de identificação e classificação das RNs. Fornecendo assim, uma diretriz para o tratamento de RNs nas atividades de análise e projeto, permitindo sua modelagem de forma desvinculada e independente. Como contribuição secundária está a obtenção de uma rastreabilidade entre as RNs identificadas e o caso de uso no qual elas foram identificadas.

Referências

1. Bajec, M.; Krisper, M.: A methodology and tool support for managing business rules in organizations, In: Information Systems (2004)
2. Business Rules Group: Defining Business Rules: What Are They Really? Disponível em: http://www.businessrulesgroup.org
3. Camargo, V. V.; Masiero, P. C.: Frameworks Orientados a Aspectos, In XIX Simpósio Brasileiro de Engenharia de Software, Uberlândia, Brasil (2005)
4. Coleman, D.: A Use Case Template: draft for discussion, Disponível em: http:// citeseer.ist.psu.edu/476167.html
5. Cibrán, M. A.; Suvée, D.; D'Hondt, M.; Vanderperren, W.; Jonckers, V.: Integrating Rules with Object-Oriented Software Applications using Aspect-Oriented Programming. In: Proceedings of the International Conference of the Argentine Society for Computer Science and Operational Research, Córdoba, Argentina (2004)
6. Date, C. J.: What Not How – The Business Rules Approach to Application Development. Boston: Addison-Wesley (2000),
7. Morgado, G. P.: Regula – Uma Ferramenta para o Gerenciamento de Regras de Negócio. Monografia (Projeto Final de Curso), Universidade Federal do Rio de Janeiro – Departamento de Ciência da Computação, Rio de Janeiro, Brasil (2005)
8. Ross, R. G.: Principles of the Business Rule Approach. Boston: Addison-Wesley (2003)
9. Von Halle, B.: Business rules applied: building better systems using the business rules approach. New York: John Wiley & Sons, Inc (2002)
10. Yoder, J.; Balaguer, Federico; Johnson, Ralph: Adaptive Object-Models for Implementing Business Rules. In: Third Workshop on Best-Practices for Business Rules: Design and Implementation OOPSLA 2001, Tampa Bay (2001)
11. Wan-Kadir, W.M.N.; Loucopolos, P.: Relating evolving business rules to software design. In: Journal of Systems Architecture (2004)

Melhorando o Processo de Engenharia de Requisitos em Empresas de Produtos de Software – Um Estudo de Caso

Virgínia Heimann[1], Carina Alves[2]

[1] PROCENGE, Av. Marquês de Olinda, 50030-970, Recife, Brasil
vheimann@procenge.com.br
[2] Centro de Informática, Universidade Federal de Pernambuco, 50732-970, Recife, Brasil
cfa@cin.ufpe.br

Resumo. O desenvolvimento de produtos de software para um amplo mercado consumidor é uma tendência mundial. Atualmente, um número crescente de empresas de software desenvolve produtos visando atender a necessidade de inúmeros clientes, distribuídos geograficamente. Esta forma de desenvolvimento afeta profundamente o processo de engenharia de requisitos. Neste artigo apresentamos uma experiência de transferência tecnológica em engenharia de requisitos com empresas de produtos de software. O estudo de caso na PROCENGE, empresa desenvolvedora de produtos *Enterprise Resource Planning* é apresentado para discutir as lições aprendidas durante o programa de melhoria em engenharia de requisitos.

Palavras-chave: engenharia de requisitos, melhoria do processo de software, transferência tecnológica.

1 Introdução

O desenvolvimento de produtos de software representa um importante e crescente segmento da indústria de software. O objetivo principal de empresas desenvolvedoras de produtos de software é desenvolver e vender software para um amplo mercado consumidor, onde o produto de software não é desenvolvido visando um cliente específico, mas vários clientes distribuídos geograficamente [6].

Diversos estudos mostram que o processo de engenharia de requisitos é um fator crítico para o sucesso de projetos de software [4][8]. Um dos principais objetivos do processo de engenharia de requisitos envolve o entendimento das reais necessidades e metas de clientes e usuários [8]. Empresas que desenvolvem produtos de software visando um amplo mercado consumidor, geralmente com clientes distribuídos em várias localidades, sofrem dificuldades ainda maiores para atender satisfatoriamente clientes com diferentes realidades organizacionais e necessidades particulares.

Vários autores têm enfatizado a importância de realizar efetiva transferência tecnológica do estado da arte em engenharia de requisitos para a indústria a fim de garantir que avanços na área sejam adotados na prática [3]. A partir das motivações apresentadas acima, decidimos conduzir um programa de melhoria em engenharia de requisitos (ER) junto a quatro empresas desenvolvedoras de produtos de software. Este artigo apresenta um estudo de caso realizado junto a uma das empresas participantes do programa, a PROCENGE.

Este artigo está estruturado da seguinte forma: na Seção 2, apresentamos a metodologia utilizada para a condução do programa de melhoria em ER; na Seção 3, apresentamos uma visão geral da PROCENGE; na Seção 4, discutimos a experiência e lições aprendidas; e na Seção 5, apresentamos conclusões e trabalhos futuros.

2 Programa de Melhoria do Processo de Engenharia de Requisitos

Em pesquisa anterior, realizamos um estudo empírico junto a treze empresas de produtos de software baseadas em Recife – PE – Brasil [1]. O objetivo do estudo foi obter um melhor entendimento sobre o processo de ER e levantar os principais desafios e problemas enfrentados por empresas desenvolvedores de produtos de software para um amplo mercado consumidor. Observamos que dentre os principais problemas e desafios enfrentados pelas empresas participantes do estudo incluem: dificuldades em entender os reais requisitos de clientes distribuídos, marketing deficiente, falta de um processo de ER bem definido. A partir dos resultados obtidos neste estudo empírico podemos concluir que, de um modo geral, as empresas compreendem a importância de conduzir um processo bem definido de requisitos para melhorar a qualidade final do software e melhor satisfazer seus clientes. Acreditamos que iniciativas para introduzir e disseminar boas práticas em ER pode representar um importante passo para melhorar a qualidade dos processos de empresas de produtos de software. O programa de melhoria em ER foi concebido como continuidade desse estudo empírico. O programa foi realizado com quatro empresas pré-selecionadas do grupo de treze inicialmente estudadas. O programa de melhoria em ER foi conduzido durante o período de Maio até setembro de 2007. O programa envolveu a colaboração direta entre academia e empresas, caracterizando-se como uma ação de intervenção. Cada empresa selecionou um ou mais colaboradores para interagir com os pesquisadores. Este processo envolveu a condução de um projeto piloto para acompanhar a evolução do aprendizado e utilizar os novos conhecimentos em um projeto real da empresa [5]. O programa foi dividido em nove iterações, cada iteração cobriu uma área especifica da ER. A concepção do programa foi baseada em pesquisas já consolidadas, tais como trabalhos de Sommerville [8] e Robertson [4], assim como artigos relevantes da área.

O modelo de transferência tecnológica adotado foi inspirado em [2]. A Figura 1 apresenta as etapas do programa. O modelo inicia com a identificação das áreas de melhoria através de observação direta nas empresas e negociação com os participantes. Foram escolhidas as seguintes áreas: elicitação de requisitos, priorização de requisitos para plano de versão e especificação de requisitos. A etapa seguinte foi o estudo da literatura disponível sobre as áreas a serem investigadas.

Neste momento também foi realizada troca de conhecimento entre as empresas para garantir que as áreas correspondem às suas reais necessidades de melhoria. Em seguida, as possíveis soluções foram apresentadas durante reuniões individuais com cada empresa. Estes encontros eram chamados *reunião da iteração*. Durante as reuniões, era apresentado o pacote da iteração, que consiste na descrição da iteração, incluindo os objetivos da iteração e áreas cobertas, além de *templates* para a empresa preencher durante a execução do projeto piloto e artigos relevantes sobre os tópicos estudados. Após cada reunião, os colaboradores recebiam a "tarefa de casa" que era estudar o assunto coberto naquela iteração e preencher os *templates* a fim de preparar os artefatos de requisitos do projeto piloto. Além dos encontros individuais com cada empresa, foram organizados três grupos focais com todas as empresas. O objetivo dos grupos focais era estimular a troca de conhecimento entre as empresas. Os grupos focais foram especialmente bem aceitos pelas empresas que viam naqueles encontros, a oportunidade de aprender com outras empresas e dividir aprendizados.

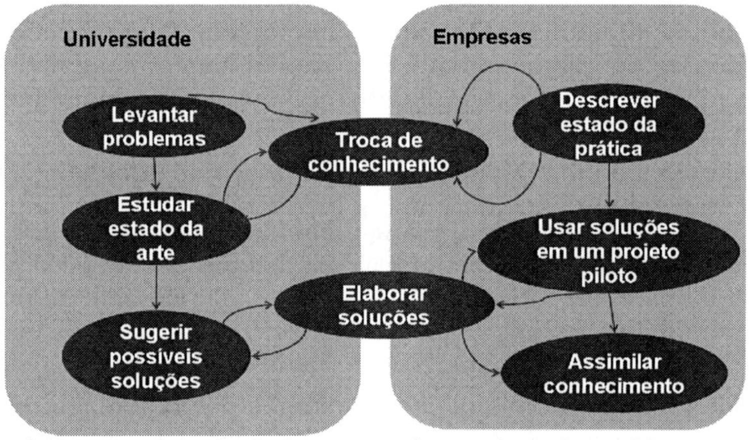

Fig. 1. Programa de melhoria do processo de engenharia de requisitos

3 Estudo de Caso – PROCENGE

Nesta seção apresentamos a experiência da PROCENGE durante a participação no programa de melhoria do processo de ER. O nosso objetivo é discutir os objetivos, desafios e lições aprendidas sob a perspectiva da empresa durante uma iniciativa de transferência tecnológica.

A PROCENGE é uma empresa com larga experiência na área de Tecnologia da Informação (TI) [7]. Um dos maiores projetos da PROCENGE é o **Pirâmide**, um ERP (*Enterprise Resources Plannig* ou Solução de Gestão Empresarial), utilizado hoje por mais de 400 empresas e com mais de quatro mil usuários no Brasil.

A estrutura do produto Pirâmide conta com uma fábrica de software, uma operação comercial de marketing e vendas e um grupo de consultoria de negócios e implantação de sistemas distribuídos em várias localidades do País. Esse ambiente tem certificação ISO 9001 e MPS.BR nível G, e está em processo de certificação do MPS.BR nível F e o CMMI-nível 2. O produto ERP-Pirâmide é um software em constante evolução, para o qual periodicamente são liberadas novas versões com manutenções evolutivas e corretivas que agregam novas funcionalidades e melhorias ao sistema. Estas manutenções são provenientes de solicitações de mudanças, feitas por clientes externos ou internos e que são implementadas através de projetos de desenvolvimento das novas versões. Embora as versões sejam liberadas a cada dois meses, a duração do projeto de uma versão é maior, sempre começa, aproximadamente, 15 dias antes da liberação da versão anterior. Este é um ciclo extremamente curto e os requisitos devem ser cuidadosamente especificados, levando em consideração a sua prioridade e contribuição para agregar valor ao produto em cada nova versão. Esta é uma das áreas desafiadoras que empresas desenvolvedoras de produtos de software precisam enfrentar.

4 Melhorando o Processo de ER na Empresa

A transferência de tecnologia foi realizada gradualmente a cada iteração do programa. Através do estudo da literatura e dos artigos entregues em cada iteração, foi possível adquirir uma visão melhor dos processos da empresa e realizar um diagnóstico dos problemas, identificando pontos de melhorias nos processos de ER.

O projeto escolhido como piloto para o Programa de Melhoria do Processo de ER foi o Projeto de Adequação a NF-e (Nota Fiscal Eletrônica). Esse projeto tem como principal objetivo aderir ao requisito legal das Secretarias da Fazenda dos Estados (SEFAZ) de emissão da NF-e por parte dos clientes do Pirâmide.

4.1 Resultados Obtidos

A presença do pesquisador na empresa foi fundamental para a transferência de conhecimento e a identificação das necessidades de melhorias nos processos já existentes. O conhecimento adquirido no estudo realizado proporcionou a formação da base teórica necessária para a realização do diagnóstico das necessidades de melhorias nos processos de requisitos do projeto de versão. Cada iteração contribuiu para consolidar os conhecimentos, quebrar paradigmas e identificar ausência de algumas práticas importantes que não eram realizadas. No momento do preenchimento dos *templates* já era realizada uma comparação dos artefatos e processos utilizados pela empresa e as informações propostas no *template*, identificando os pontos de melhoria.

4.2 Lições Aprendidas

As principais dificuldades da PROCENGE em relação ao processo de ER são: ter um processo definido para elicitação de requisitos para novos módulos que exige um levantamento maior de informações; obter validação do cliente na fase inicial do projeto; documentação insuficiente, gerando necessidade de ter muita comunicação entre as áreas. Muitas foram as lições aprendidas durante o Programa de Melhoria em ER, que muito ajudaram no processo de resolução dessas dificuldades, seguem as principais lições identificadas em cada iteração :

- **Iteração 1** : Identificação do nível de importância de cada *stakeholder* e utilização de diagramas de contexto para definição do escopo. Nessa iteração foram apresentados vários modelos de diagrama de contexto, cada um com a sua finalidade especifica.
- **Iteração 2** : Realizar análise dos riscos durante o levantamento de requisitos e incorporá-los ao projeto de versão. A análise de riscos era realizada apenas na fase do planejamento da versão, nessa iteração foi identificada a necessidade de acrescentar ao plano de projeto de versão os riscos inerentes aos requisitos que só são identificados na fase de especificação.
- **Iteração 3** : Proporcionou uma quebra de paradigma da empresa e definiu claramente a diferença entre casos de negócios, funcionalidades, casos de uso e requisitos. Mostrou a importância de compreender a essência do problema sem se preocupar em como implementar a solução tecnicamente.
- **Iteração 4** : Todas as iterações foram importantes, porém, particularmente para a PROCENGE a iteração 4, foi a que mais agregou conhecimento e foi fundamental para a identificação da importância da descrição textual dos casos de uso mais relevantes e da necessidade de pensar nos vários cenários de uso do produto. A descrição textual do caso de uso fornece o fluxo de eventos que deve ser a base para a criação dos casos de testes, minimizando o problema de transferência de informações entre as áreas de desenvolvimento e testes. Já a identificação dos vários cenários, é uma boa prática para ter a certeza da corretude do levantamento de requisitos.
- **Iteração 5** : Utilizar os critérios de aceitação, o grau de satisfação e de insatisfação no processo de requisitos, com o objetivo de ajudar na priorização dos requisitos.
- **Iteração 6** : Destacou-se pelo conteúdo de temas importantes como rastreabilidade, reuso e prototipação. Para um sistema do tamanho do Pirâmide é muito difícil ter e manter uma matriz de rastreabilidade.
- **Iteração 7** : A priorização de requisitos deve refletir a importância de cada requisito dentro da versão e o valor que o requisito trará ao produto e foram os estudos realizados nesta iteração que ajudou na implantação de melhorias da fase de planejamento do projeto, além de consolidar a importância da inspeções de requisitos para minimizar as falhas na documentação e diminuir a necessidade de comunicação desnecessária entre as áreas.
- **Iteração 8** : A consolidação de todas as informações levantadas para o preenchimento dos *templates* e o destaque para a importância da revisão de todos os requisitos realizada na fase de validar requisitos do projeto.
- **Iteração 9** : Realização do último grupo focal. Observou-se que cada empresa tem o seu ritmo para absorver a transferência de tecnologia e o apoio institucional é fundamental para que esse ritmo seja mais acelerado.

5 Conclusões e Trabalhos Futuros

Este artigo apresentou uma experiência de transferência tecnológica em ER para empresas desenvolvedoras de produtos de software. Nossa experiência sugere que tais empresas enfrentam dificuldades adicionais para conduzir um processo de ER adequado e garantir a satisfação de diversos clientes. Nossa meta foi garantir que a dinâmica das iterações do programa de melhoria em ER respeitasse as particularidades de cada empresa nas reuniões individuais, proporcionando a transferência do conhecimento na medida exata para a realidade de cada empresa, respeitando suas limitações e principalmente a necessidade de resultados rápidos e eficientes. O intercâmbio de experiências entre as empresas participantes foi um fator crítico de sucesso, acreditamos que grupo focal é um excelente método para apoiar programas de transferência tecnológica.

A visão da PROCENGE é que o programa foi bem sucedido, apesar do curto período em que ele foi realizado. Os trabalhos para melhoria nos processos da fase de especificação de requisitos serão revisados pelo SEPG (Grupo de Processos de Engenharia de Software) da PROCENGE responsável por monitorar e avaliar os processos, identificando e implementando as melhorias. Para a realização da mudança nos processos é necessária a avaliação do processo e o planejamento da melhoria que consiste na elaboração de um plano de projeto, com atividades, recursos e cronograma. Na definição dos novos processos serão selecionados os indicadores para a realização do monitoramento do processo.

Referências

1. Alves, C. Pereira, S. Valença, G. Pimentel, J. Andrade, R.: Preliminary Results from an Empirical Study in Market-Driven Software Companies. 10th Workshop of Requirements Engineering, Toronto, Canada.(2007)
2. Gorschek, T. Wohlin, C. Garre, P. Larsson, S. : A Model for Technology Transfer in Practice. IEEE Software. (2006)
3. Kaindl, H. Brinkkemper, S. Bunenko, J. A. Farbey, B. Greenspan, S. J. Heitmeyer, C. L. do Prado Leite, J. C. Sampaio. Mead, N. R. Mylopoulos, J. Sidddiqi, J. : Requirements Engineering and Technology Transfer: Obstacles, Incentives and an Improvement Agenda. Requirements Eng. J., vol. 7, pp. 113-123. (2002)
4. Robertson, S. Robertson, J. : Mastering the Requirements Process, Addison Wesley, 2 edition. (2006)
5. Rombach, D. : Engine for Applied Research and Technology Transfer in Software Engineering. Proceedings of the 24th Annual Software Engineering Workshop of the SEL, Greenbelt, USA, December 1-2. (1999)
6. Sawyer, S. : A Market-Based Perspective on Information Systems Development. Communications of the ACM, volume 44, issue 11, pp97-102. (2001)
7. Site PROCENGE, www.procenge.com.br (acessado em 10/09/2007)
8. Sommerville, I. Sawyer, P. : Requirements Engineering: A Good Practice Guide. Wiley, 3 edition. (2000)

Sistema multi-agente para medir la confiabilidad en las dimensiones de disponibilidad y fiabilidad de un sistema crítico envolviendo al sistema ERP, base de datos y sistema operativo

Angel Hermoza[1], Luis Rivera[2], David Mauricio[1],

[1] Universidad Nacional Mayor de San Marcos, Facultad de Ingeniería de Sistemas e Informática, Lima, Perú
{angelhermozasalas, dms_research}@yahoo.es
2 Universidade Estadual do Norte Fluminense, LCMAT-CCT, Rio de Janeiro, Brasil
rivera@uenf.br

Abstract. This paper plans to develop a model for the "Multi-agent system to measure the trustworthiness in the dimensions of availability and reliability of a critical system surrounding the ERP system, the data base and the operating system". These systems are used by several organizations to integrate all data and processes into a unified system. We used the Zeus methodology for constructing agents, the performance indicators are weighed and its identification for the ERP system is described, the modeling of the software agents using the Ingenias methodology is used and detailed in this work which are used in the development of the "CODA System".

Keywords: Critical systems, Indicators, Software Agents, Enterprise Resource Planning Systems.

1 Introducción

El monitoreo de los sistemas es una tarea muy antigua. Consiste en estar atento a los errores, alertas de problemas reportados por los sistemas de Planeamiento de Recursos Empresariales (ERP - *Enterprise Resource Planning*) y sus entornos, como bases de datos y sistema operativo. Para continuar operando, esos problemas deben tener solución inmediata: los especialistas identifican la causa del problema, dependiendo de éste, realizan determinadas acciones para resolverlos. Mientras tanto, las operaciones se interrumpen y/o el sistema queda inoperante por el tiempo que demande su atención. Ese lapso de tiempo podría disminuir con la ayuda de sistemas inteligentes de alertas de posibles fallas, determinando e indicando las posibles alternativas a ser ejecutadas.

Tradicionalmente, los problemas de los sistemas se resuelven reactivamente (a partir del problema sucedido), el especialista busca una solución recurriendo a experiencias en anteriores problemas similares. En contraste, las organizaciones modernas requieren que los sistemas críticos (*core systems*), estén operativos a tiempo integral, que existan sistemas de monitoreo, de medición y de exhibición de indicadores para las respectivas interpretaciones, a fin de que se tomen acciones oportunas.

Los sistemas de software requieren un monitoreo continuo de sus actividades, debido a que realizan operaciones importantes dentro de la empresa. Las interpretaciones de las fallas, a partir de las informaciones registradas en logs, pueden ser clasificadas en indicadores de confiabilidad, disponibilidad y fiabilidad del sistema. En este trabajo se formula un modelo de sistema llamado CODA, basado en multi-agente de software, que captura e interpreta los indicadores de confiabilidad en las dimensiones de disponibilidad y fiabilidad del sistema ERP, y sus entornos banco de datos y sistema operativo, y muestra esos indicadores a través de diagramas y tablas.

2 Antecedentes

Existen procedimientos manuales de detección y resolución de problemas de fallas de sistemas de software [1] [2] [3], los que requieren buscar soluciones a problemas similares; como también las tendencias de automatización de algunos aspectos de esos procedimientos de forma que mejore el tiempo y performance de atención. Se han identificado productos software de apoyo en detección y resolución de fallas de los sistemas de software en estudio, como BMC [4], Quest Software [5], Symantec [6] e IBM [3]. La BMC-SAP NetWeaver y Symantec i3 for SAP consideran el monitoreo de ERP, base de datos y sistema operativo, mientras los otros sólo consideran la base de datos y sistema operativo.

En cuanto a trabajo de investigación en monitoreo y mantenimiento de ERP, Kwon [7] presenta un modelo inteligente para detección y mantenimiento de fallas de ERP. Su modelo se basa en agentes que interactúan, obedeciendo un control de sincronismo de redes de Petri, para interpretar y analizar los errores de un sistema ERP; en algunos casos, dependiendo de la política, un agente trata el error del sistema. El modelo es eficiente para sistema ERP, pero no considera que los errores podrían ser relacionados en la interacción de ERP con el sistema operativo o la base de datos. Chandrashekhar et al. [8] enfocan el análisis completo del entorno de negocios con la ayuda de la tecnología de información, toma en cuenta varias interacciones entre diferentes procesos de negocio mientras se maneja un sistema ERP, también provee un marco de referencia basado en diagramas de eventos para registrar los flujos lógicos y otros detalles relevantes. Los diagramas de evento son útiles para el diseño del sistema de información inteligente. El uso de multi-agentes en problemas de monitoreo es común en diversas líneas de computación, como gestión de negocios electrónicos, en detección de fallas y problemas de funcionamiento usados en auditoría, abordados por Ling-yu et al. [9] en el modelo de auditoría ABCAM.

3 Indicadores de confiabilidad

Los sistemas críticos por razones desconocidas, algunas veces colapsan y dejan de suministrar los servicios deseados [10]. Por tanto, son sistemas no confiables, inclusive con sus efectos de caídas pueden dar perjuicios a la empresa.

Existen cuatro dimensiones de la confiabilidad: disponibilidad, fiabilidad, seguridad y protección. La disponibilidad es la probabilidad de que esté activo en cualquier momento. La fiabilidad es la probabilidad de que en un período el sistema suministre los servicios correctamente. La seguridad es una valoración de que tan probable es que el sistema provoque un daño a su entorno. La protección es una valoración de que tan probable es que el sistema resista a una intrusión accidental o provocada.

4 Arquitectura del Sistema CODA

Una representación formal del modelo de confiabilidad considerando la fiabilidad y disponibilidad se esquematiza mediante una estructura de árbol, ilustrada por la Fig.1., en la que el nodo de nivel superior representa a la confiabilidad (CODA) y los nodos hijos: ERP (CODA_ERP), base de datos (CODA_BD) y sistema operativo (CODA_SO); a su vez cada nodo tendrá sus respectivos hijos definiendo aspectos de confiabilidad (CODA_ERP01), disponibilidad (CODA_ERP02) y fiabilidad (CODA_ERP03).

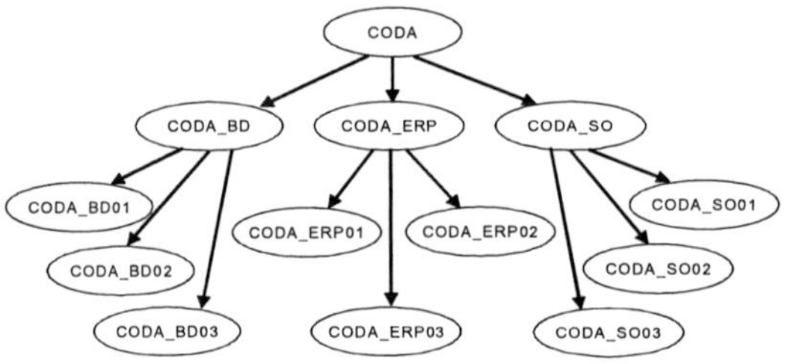

Fig. 1. Arquitectura del sistema CODA

4.1 Indicadores CODA

Los valores de los indicadores CODA se muestran en la Tabla 1, y son el valor real que se genera a partir de los datos extraídos por el sistema, el valor normal o promedio de los valores históricos al igual que el valor mínimo y máximo. El indicador de CODA es la media ponderada de los indicadores de confiabilidad de los tres sistemas (ERP, BD, SO), dado por (1):

$$CODA = \frac{1}{W1 + W2 + W3} \sum_{i=1,\ldots,999} \left(W1 * ERP_i + W2 * BD_i + W3 * SO_i\right) \quad (1)$$

Donde W1, W2 y W3 son los pesos asignados a cada componente.

Table 1. Indicadores del sistema CODA

Fecha	Indicador	Año	Periodo	Real	Normal	Minimo	Maximo
01/01/2006	BD0020001	2006	1	10	9	8	10
01/01/2006	BD0020002	2006	1	9	9	7	10
01/01/2006	BD0020003	2006	1	10	9	8	9
01/01/2006	BD0020004	2006	1	8	9	8	10
01/01/2006	SO0020001	2006	1	9	9	8	10
01/01/2006	SO0020002	2006	1	9	9	8	9
01/01/2006	SO0020003	2006	1	9	9	8	10
01/01/2006	ERP0010001	2006	1	7	8	5	9
01/01/2006	ERP0010002	2006	1	8	8	7	10
01/01/2006	ERP001	2006	1	93	90	78	98
01/01/2006	SO001	2006	1	90	90	90	97
01/01/2006	BD001	2006	1	65	80	80	95
01/01/2006	CODA	2006	1	83	87	73	96

Por lo que se afirma que este indicador es el resultado del procesamiento de los demás indicadores de Nivel 1 que a su vez son resultado de los del Nivel 2, además, cada indicador de tiene un valor real, normal o promedio, mínimo y máximo, se define que la media de los indicadores mínimos será el indicador mínimo de CODA; de la misma forma el indicador máximo de CODA es la media de los indicadores máximos de CODA.

Generalizando, para nivel 2, el indicador del sistema SIS_i (ERP_i, BD_i, SO_i) es (2):

$$SIS_i = \frac{10}{N} \sum_{j=1,\dots,999} SIS_{ij} \quad (2)$$

Aquí, como en el nivel superior, el N es total de indicadores a procesar diferente de cero; los valores de los indicadores, representan los indicadores respectivos del sistema en nivel 2. El valor permite expresar el resultado en porcentajes.

Indicadores de disponibilidad: identificación de eventos, alertas, mensajes por servidor debido a caídas del sistema, entre otros. Dentro de la base de datos se miden: tablespaces, extends, users, freespace, locks, shutdown, system, cursors, license, procedures, sessions, dumps, SGA, jobs, logs, etc. Dentro del sistema operativo se miden: memoria, discos duros, CPU, usuarios, logs,etc.

Indicadores de fiabilidad: existen muchos indicadores de fiabilidad del sistema ERP, como los módulos: finanzas, distribución, manufactura, proyectos, servicios, transportes, recursos humanos, desarrollo, mantenimiento, etc.

5 Modelo de multi-agentes colaborativos para el sistema CODA

El sistema CODA se implementa con varios agentes colaborativos, constituido por agentes especializados que interactúan con ERP, BD y SO. Existe un agente general (recopilador) que interactúa con los tres agentes especializados. El meta-modelo de organización incluye los grupos y agentes los que componen la organización y las aplicaciones, también muestra los flujos de la organización de modo que satisfaga sus objetivos. El sistema CODA está relacionado con esos componentes. La administración, compuesto por la plataforma de desarrollo, a la que se le agregará una base de datos local para almacenar la información recuperada de los servidores del sistema ERP. La comunidad a la que pertenecen los agentes del Sistema CODA. Sus actividades están organizadas en muchos flujos. El grupo de administración está relacionado con las tareas globales del sistema; esto es, aquellas compartidas entre los diferentes tipos y recursos de información.

Los agentes colaborativos conversan entre ellos para resolver un determinado problema [11]. Para eso requieren no sólo un protocolo de comunicación, sino también un lenguaje de comunicación común interagentes y una ontología compartida que represente los conceptos del dominio a ser comunicados. En este trabajo, los agentes especialistas (ERP, BD y SO) son sincronizados por el agente recopilador. También se describe la funcionalidad que el agente BD provee, algunos de ellos relacionados a la interacción. Los casos de uso ilustran la funcionalidad relevante en la gestión del agente de base de datos, refleja las acciones que toma cuando se desea ver si hay información relevante a recuperar. De manera análoga se han diseñado los modelos de organización y modelo de agente de sistema ERP y SO.

6 Análisis de resultados

Para efectos de análisis, se ha considerado los siguientes días de proceso: 01, 02 y 03 de enero de 2006 en la empresa Editora Peru, porque existen procesos anuales que sólo se ejecutan estos días. Se usaron Servidor IBM X Series Modelo H71, SAN Storage HP, Windows 2000 para el servidor (incluido IIS -Internet Information Services), Explorador de Internet, Manejador de base de datos MSSQL 2000, ASP (Active Server Pages), Sistema ERP, Sistema Operativo AIX v 4.3, Manejador de Base de Datos Oracle v 8.0, Sistema ERP BAAN IV C2. Se ha considerado los pesos siguientes W1=2 para el sistema ERP, W2=3 para la base de datos y W3=1 para el sistema operativo. Los resultados se ilustran en la Fig.2., para CODA que depende de fiabilidad y disponibilidad de los sistemas ERP, BD y SO.

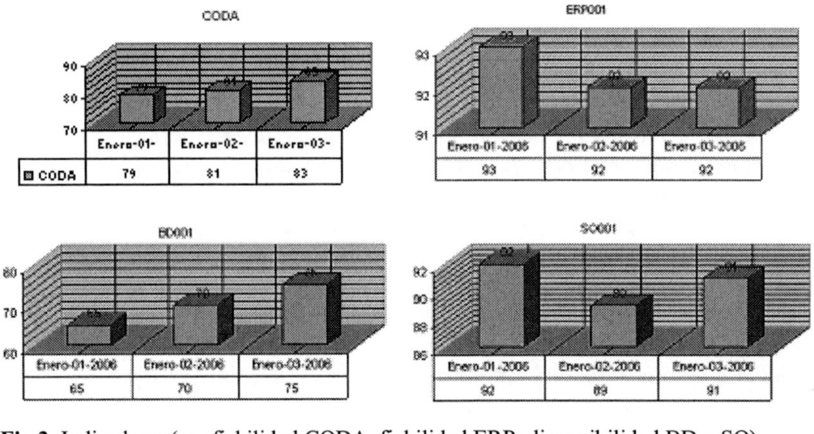

Fig.2. Indicadores (confiabilidad CODA, fiabilidad ERP; disponibilidad BD y SO).

Con la información procesada CODA muestra 79% de confiabilidad el día 01 de enero, el día 02 es de 81% y el 03 de enero del 2006 el valor es 83%, los valores se encuentran dentro del intervalo del valor normal y el valor mínimo considerado (87% y 73%) encontrando que el día 01 por tener el menor valor es por donde iniciaremos la revisión, luego se revisa los indicadores de disponibilidad y fiabilidad de los días 02 y 03 de enero de 2006. Analizando ERP (ERP001), se observa que en esos días se tiene 93% y 92% de fiabilidad, respectivamente, cuando el mínimo es 90% y máximo de 98%, que indica que el problema no está en el sistema ERP. Así se procede ha analizar la base de datos y el sistema operativo. El problema encontrado, tal como muestra la figura respectiva, está en la disponibilidad de base de datos (BD001), cuando el primer día está con 65%, y el tercer día con 75%. Ambos por debajo del mínimo que es 80%. En sistema operativo, se observa que el primer día arroja 92% de disponibilidad, el segundo día 89%, que es menor que el mínimo de 90%. Entonces, estos valores, en esos días, con esos indicadores considerados, afectaron la confiabilidad del sistema CODA.

7 Conclusiones y trabajos futuros

Se ha modelado un sistema multi-agente denominado sistema CODA que permite generar los indicadores de confiabilidad en las dimensiones de disponibilidad y fiabilidad en los componentes del sistema ERP Baan, base de datos y sistema operativo y mostrar estos indicadores a través de diagramas y tablas. También, el sistema CODA desarrollado permite al usuario final monitorear la actividad del sistema ERP mediante los indicadores, gráficos, alertas y mails. Se ha analizado los valores resultantes de confiabilidad, disponibilidad y fiabilidad del sistema ERP Baan IV, base de datos Oracle 8.0 y sistema operativo AIX de IBM. Los valores mínimos, normales y máximos, como mostrados en las tablas respectivas, indican las variaciones de los indicadores antes mencionados. Es conveniente mencionar que al calcular el indicador de confiabilidad utilizando la media ponderada se muestra un resultado mejor que utilizando la media simple como se hizo en el trabajo anterior.

Referencias

1. Baan, Base de datos de conocimiento, http://www.support.baan.com
2. Oracle, Base de datos de conocimiento, https://metalink.oracle.com
3. IBM, Soporte on line, http://www.ibm.com/support/us
4. BMC, http://www.bmc.com
5. Quest Software, http://www.quest.com/sap
6. Symantec, http://www.symantec.com/enterprise/products
7. Kwon, O. B. and Leeb, J. J. A multi-agent intelligent system for efficient ERP maintenance, pp. 191--202. (2001)
8. Chandrashekhar Ch., Deshmukh, S. G. and Chattopadhyay, R. Application of principles of event related open systems to business process reengineering, pp. 347--374. (2003)
9. Ling-yu, Ch. Ch., Dua, T and Lai, V. S. Continuous auditing with a multi-agent system, pp. 2274—2292. (2007)
10. Sommerville I.; Ingeniería de Software, Pearson Education, pp. 400, México (2002)
11. Zeus Agent Builder Toolkit, http://labs.bt.com/projects/agents/zeus

WGWSOA: Apoiando a Interoperabilidade entre as Atividades de Coordenação em Groupware

Rita Suzana P. Maciel, José Maria N. David

Faculdade Ruy Barbosa – Salvador – BA – Brasil
{rsuzana, josemaria}@frb.br

Resumo. Grupos distribuídos freqüentemente necessitam de aplicações distintas de suporte ao trabalho colaborativo, construídas em plataformas heterogêneas. Tal fato se deve à amplitude de requisitos que precisam ser atendidos. Dentre esses requisitos a interoperabilidade é um elemento essencial para apoiar o desenvolvimento de serviços de coordenação em *groupware*. Neste contexto, a ausência da interoperabilidade se caracteriza como um problema na medida em que impede a utilização de ferramentas diversas para apoiar uma mesma atividade. O objetivo deste artigo é apresentar uma solução de interoperabilidade para serviços de coordenação em *groupware* distribuído.

Palavras-Chaves. Coordenação, *Groupware*, SOA, Orientação a Serviços, *Middleware*.

1. Introdução

Mecanismos para apoiar a coordenação são essenciais em diferentes contextos para que se possam atingir os objetivos pré-estabelecidos para atividades colaborativas. A complexidade das interações e dos processos nos quais elas ocorrem freqüentemente impõe políticas e regras suficientemente flexíveis. Por exemplo, em um processo de autoria colaborativa, a partir do momento em que um documento evolui, papéis são modificados, bem como novas atividades definidas. Não é uma tarefa relativamente fácil para ser apoiada por aplicações de *groupware*.

Considerando *groupware* distribuído, tais atividades se tornam mais complexas e necessitam de requisitos difíceis de serem atendidos por uma única aplicação [2]. Essa dificuldade está relacionada tanto à quantidade de requisitos funcionais como à diversidade de requisitos não-funcionais que *groupware* distribuídos demandam. Dentre esses requisitos podemos mencionar a interoperabilidade entre plataformas heterogêneas. Tal interoperabilidade pode ser definida como a capacidade de aplicações distintas compartilharem dados e procedimentos entre equipamentos e plataformas [1].

Aplicações distribuídas de *groupware* são comumente construídas em plataformas de *middleware* [7]. Apesar de manipularem objetos (documentos, reuniões, agenda, listas de discussões, etc.) com a mesma semântica, não é possível para estas aplicações acessarem objetos e dados de uma outra aplicação, mesmo que elas sejam construídas sob uma mesma plataforma de *middleware*. A complexidade deste cenário se torna mais intensa quando necessitamos interoperar aplicações colaborativas construídas sob *middlewares* distintos, por exemplo, J2EE, CORBA e .NET. Conseqüentemente, *groupware* distintos não são comumente interoperáveis. A ausência de interoperabilidade é um problema tanto para os usuários como para os projetistas de mecanismos de coordenação em *groupware*.

Para apoiar atividades colaborativas, usuários devem escolher entre a utilização de um único ambiente de suporte ou a utilização de ferramentas diversas. A escolha de um único ambiente para apoiar as atividades de todos os membros de um grupo implica que além dos participantes precisarem aprender a trabalhar juntos, também necessitam de um relativo aprendizado em relação à utilização de tecnologias de apoio ao processo. Este aspecto é um fator limitante, pois além de ter que se adequar aos aspectos da colaboração (políticas, culturas, etc.), os usuários ainda devem utilizar ferramentas distintas com as quais não estão usualmente habituados [5].

A existência de uma grande diversidade de soluções faz com que a implementação do requisito de interoperabilidade seja uma tarefa de alto custo, devido tanto à heterogeneidade de plataformas de *hardware* e *software* que as hospedam, quanto ao número de soluções específicas (protocolos, APIs, componentes, etc.) que alguns ambientes disponibilizam, tais como: SAGA [3] , Groove [4] e Dyce [9]. Na prática, para cada novo ambiente inserido no projeto colaborativo, pode ser necessário um novo processo de desenvolvimento e implementação para prover a interoperabilidade entre estes ambientes. A quantidade de soluções específicas para satisfazer esse requisito é um problema para os desenvolvedores devido ao esforço de implementação envolvido.

Aplicações de *groupware* freqüentemente utilizam plataformas de *middleware*, mas elas lançam mão apenas dos seus serviços de distribuição [7]. Elas não se beneficiam das oportunidades de composição e reutilização de funcionalidades já implementadas para outras finalidades. A WGWSOA (*Web-based Groupware Service-Oriented Architecture*) é uma arquitetura orientada a serviços de *middleware* cujo objetivo é apoiar a reutilização e a interoperabilidade entre sistemas colaborativos [6]. É uma arquitetura na qual os serviços utilizados são "serviços de *middleware*" de acordo com Schantz e Schmidt [8]. Adicionalmente, pode ser mapeada para diferentes ambientes de *middleware*.

Na primeira etapa deste projeto o interesse maior está em apoiar atividades de coordenação em aplicações distribuídas de *groupware*. A coordenação é um elemento que necessita ser prontamente tratado para viabilizar o trabalho de um grupo que utiliza aplicações heterogêneas. O objetivo deste artigo é apresentar uma solução de interoperabilidade para serviços de coordenação através da utilização da WGWSOA.

Na próxima seção a solução proposta é discutida, bem como um exemplo de um serviço de coordenação para uma arquitetura orientada a serviços é apresentado. A seção 3 conclui este trabalho e apresenta algumas pesquisas futuras.

2. A Solução Proposta

Diferentes abordagens de desenvolvimento de *software* têm sido propostas a fim de capturar a semântica, a informação e os procedimentos mais comuns em um domínio particular e para reutilizar tais características em desenvolvimentos posteriores. Algumas limitações relacionadas ao projeto de *software* distribuído, ao seu projeto e à sua implementação e evolução podem ser superadas se suas funcionalidades forem definidas como serviços de *middleware* [10].

Um *middleware* oferece um conjunto de serviços (comuns e específicos) que são descritos – e disponibilizados – através de linguagens específicas de definição de interfaces [8]. Tais serviços permitem a comunicação e a distribuição transparentemente, apoiando assim o desenvolvimento de aplicações distribuídas.

A WGWSOA é uma infra-estrutura projetada para prover a interoperabilidade entre sistemas colaborativos construídos sob a mesma plataforma, ou sob plataformas distintas de *middleware*, por exemplo: .NET e J2EE. Ao mesmo tempo, ela busca oferecer serviços de colaboração capazes de evoluir de acordo com os requisitos de *groupware*. No contexto deste trabalho serão detalhados aspectos associados às atividades de coordenação.

Como uma arquitetura de *middleware*, WGWSOA possui três camadas: aplicação, *middleware* e persistência. Na primeira camada encontram-se as aplicações de *groupware* que utilizam serviços da WGWSOA. A camada de *middleware* é composta por serviços comuns e específicos. Estes últimos estão relacionados aos elementos de colaboração (comunicação, cooperação, coordenação e percepção). Descrições de serviços são armazenadas em repositórios na camada de persistência, permitindo a sua localização e assim, apoiar a implementação de requisitos de SOA. Uma descrição mais detalhada da WGWSOA pode ser encontrada em [6].

2.1. Um Exemplo de Serviços de Coordenação

Inicialmente, com o objetivo de avaliar os serviços disponíveis na WGWSOA (por exemplo, notificação de eventos, comunicação, registro de aplicações e registro de usuários), um serviço de coordenação foi implementado. A plataforma de *middleware* J2EE foi utilizada para que fosse possível uma portabilidade mais abrangente dos serviços. Embora CORBA 2.0, seja independente de plataforma e de linguagem, e CORBA 3.0 implemente os conceitos de componentes explicitamente, J2EE é freqüentemente utilizada como uma plataforma de *groupware* [11].

Funcionalidades da WGWSOA são agrupadas em serviços de coordenação, comunicação, cooperação e percepção, os quais podem ser estendidos e compostos para atender aos requisitos de *groupware*. Neste artigo apenas os serviços de coordenação são considerados.

Para iniciar uma colaboração na WGWSOA é necessário registrar um projeto. Um projeto possui um repositório de arquivos associados e pertence a um determinado grupo de usuários. Estes usuários podem desempenhar papéis diferentes em diferentes projetos. Por exemplo, um usuário pode ser líder em um determinado projeto e revisor em outro. Os papéis possuem, associados a eles, determinadas ações.

Ações geram resultados que serão registrados no repositório do projeto. Em um projeto atividades são delegadas e, quando finalizadas, tornam-se atividades realizadas. Por exemplo, após a atividade de revisar um documento, um usuário pode salvar no repositório uma nova versão do mesmo.

A Figura 1 apresenta um exemplo de um serviço de coordenação (`Coordination Service`) implementado para apoiar a gerência de projetos de autoria colaborativa assíncrona de documentos. Nesse contexto, autores interagem na revisão, comentário e anotações do texto em momentos diferentes.

Este serviço é composto por outros serviços relacionados ao projeto (`Project Management`), atividade (`Activity Management`), gerenciamento de documentos (`Document Management`) e gerência de grupos (`AuthorGroup Management`). Serviços de um projeto de autoria oferecem funcionalidades para a definição do grupo, dos autores e seus papéis, bem como para a configuração do espaço de trabalho. Serviços de atividades estão relacionados com a delegação de atividades, o seu registro e acompanhamento da sua realização. Serviços de documentos, por sua vez, podem ser compostos por outros serviços, tais como *upload/download* de documentos e controle de concorrência. Serviços de gerência de grupos estão relacionados às definições das informações dos autores e da composição do grupo.

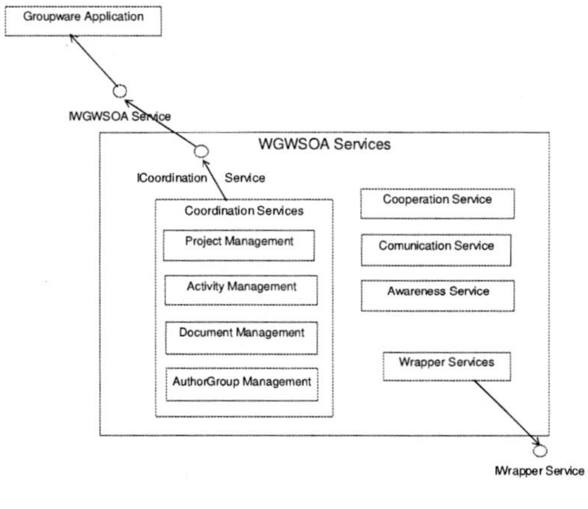

Fig. 1. Diagrama de Composição de um Serviço de Coordenação da WGWSOA.

A interface `ICoordinationService` abstrai informações relacionadas ao serviço de coordenação bem como reúne as interfaces dos outros serviços que o compõem. Já a interface `IWGWSOA Service` serve como contrato entre a WGWSOA e as aplicações de *groupware*. Ambas foram implementadas usando o padrão de projeto "façade". Enquanto a primeira é descrita em IDL, a segunda utiliza WSDL para tratar questões de heterogeneidade entre uma aplicação e a WGWSOA que foram implementadas em diferentes plataformas de *middleware*. A interface `IWrapperService` é descrita em WSDL para acessar os serviços para tratar a interoperabilidade entre instâncias de WGWSOA distintas na *web*.

Os serviços de percepção (`Awareness Service`), comunicação (`Comunication Service`) e cooperação (`Cooperation Service`) que compõem a WGWSOA não fazem parte do escopo deste trabalho.

Como um exemplo da utilização deste serviço consideramos um cenário composto por três aplicações de *groupware*: um editor colaborativo de documentos, um editor gráfico e uma aplicação para gerenciar o projeto de autoria. Cada uma possui funcionalidades específicas e implementa a coordenação através da composição de serviços da WGWSOA. Estas aplicações fazem chamadas ao serviço de coordenação para gerenciar um mesmo projeto de autoria. Todas elas podem definir e alterar características do grupo, delegar e registrar atividades. O serviço de coordenação permite assim que diferentes aplicações de *groupware* sejam utilizadas em um único projeto e interoperem através da WGWSOA. Além deste serviço o editor de texto cooperativo e o editor gráfico utilizam o serviço de gerência de documentos.

4. Conclusões

A interoperabilidade total de dados e procedimentos entre *groupware* distintos não é uma tarefa simples, pois tal fato demanda a adoção de aspectos comuns no projeto da aplicação (modelo de dados, controles, componentes, sincronização de eventos e políticas de replicação de dados, por exemplo). Como resultado, tais aplicações são freqüentemente construídas fortemente acopladas. Quando tais aspectos não são compartilhados, conversões de dados e mudanças no código são necessárias e dispendiosas.

Este trabalho apresentou uma solução para a interoperabilidade entre serviços de coordenação para *groupware*, através de uma arquitetura orientada a serviços: a WGWSOA. Este serviço foi selecionado considerando-se sobretudo que a coordenação se caracteriza como uma base para o desenvolvimento de outros serviços de *groupware* distribuídos. Assim, é possível permitir a utilização de aplicações de *groupware* em plataformas heterogêneas.

Nesta fase do projeto da arquitetura foi possível perceber a complexidade no desenvolvimento de *groupware* distribuídos interoperáveis. Tal fato se deve ao tratamento da heterogeneidade de plataformas, que demanda um esforço para a seleção da tecnologia mais adequada e da programação envolvida. Mais ainda: a identificação dos serviços que promovam a interoperabilidade das aplicações no que se refere aos requisitos funcionais.

Comumente, as aplicações de *groupware* são desenvolvidas com suas próprias especificidades. A partir do momento em que desejamos torná-las interoperáveis é necessário um processo de desenvolvimento específico para cada par de aplicações. Sendo assim a ausência de interoperabilidade é um problema não apenas para os usuários, mas sobretudo para os desenvolvedores, devido ao esforço envolvido na implementação das soluções freqüentemente propostas na literatura.

Como trabalhos futuros é essencial que sejam realizadas outras implementações e avaliações de mecanismos de coordenação, tanto em contextos diferentes da autoria colaborativa, bem como utilizando-se aplicações legadas.

Além disso, está sendo implementada uma outra instância da WGWSOA, na plataforma CORBA 3.0, reutilizando as interfaces previamente definidas. Com isso, buscam-se novas avaliações para o requisito interoperabilidade entre plataformas de *middleware* SOA heterogêneas.

Referências

1. Bernstein, P. A.: Middleware: A Model for Distributed System Services, Communication of the ACM, New York, v.39, n.2, Feb., pp. 86-98 (1996)
2. David, J. M. N., Borges, M. R. S.: COPSE-Web: An Infrastructure for Developing Web-Based Groupware Applications, In: Groupware: Design, Implementation and Use. Proc. of 8th International Workshop on Groupware (CRIWG'02), J. M. Haake and J. A. Pino (Eds.), pp. 275-284, La Serena, Chile (2002)
3. Fonseca, B., Carrapatoso, E.: SAGA: A Web Services Architecture for Groupware Applications, In: Groupware: Design, Implementation and Use. Proc. of 12th International Workshop on Groupware (CRIWG'06), pp. 246-261, Medina del Campo, Spain, Sept. (2006)
4. Groove Networks: The Groove Platform, White Paper. Available at: http://www.groove.net. (2001) Access in: Augst 2003
5. Li, D. et al.: Using Familiar Single-Users Editors for Collaborative Editing. In: Hawaii International Conference on System Sciences (HICSS'03), 36th, Hawaii. Proceedings. January, 10 p. (2003)
6. Maciel, R. S. P., David, J. M. N.: WGWSOA: A Service-Oriented Middleware Architecture to Support Groupware Interoperability. In: Proc. of the 11th International Conference on CSCW in Design, pp. 556-561, Melbourne, Austrália, Apr. (2007)
7. Maciel, R. S. P., Ferraz, C. G., Rosa, N. S.: InterDoc: Reference Architecture for Interoperable Services in Collaborative Writing Environments, In: Proc. of 9th International Conference on Computer Supported Cooperative Work in Design (CSCWD 2005), Coventry (2005)
8. Schantz, R., Schmidt, D.: Middleware for Distributed Systems: Evolving the Common structure for Network-centric Applications, Encyclopedia of Software Engineering,Wiley & Sons (2001)
9. Tietze, D.: A Framework for Developing Component-based Co-operative Applications, Ph. D. Dissertation (Computer Science), Technischen Universität Darmstadt, Germany, 178 p (2001)
10. Turner, M., Budgen, D., Bereton, P.: Turning Software into a Service, IEEE Computer, pp. 38-44 (2003)
11. WEBGVO: WebGVO Architecture – J2EE Groove Integration, Atlantic Shack. Available at: http://mrquintron.gla.mysterian.com/WebGVO/execute/architectureSetup. (2005) Access in: June 2005.

Ontology for a Case-based Organizational Memory

María de los A. Martín, Luis Olsina

GIDIS_Web, Department of Informatics,
Engineering School at Universidad Nacional de La Pampa, Argentina.
{olsinal,martinma}@ing.unlpam.edu.ar

Abstract. In this paper we introduce a case-based organizational memory ontology, which aims at contributing to the design of an organizational memory based on cases, so that it can be used to learn, solve problems, and as support in decision making as well. The objective of our ontology is to serve as base for the organizational knowledge exchange with semantic power, which in turn can facilitate the interoperability and automatic processing by agents. In addition, the ontology aims to be at a high level from which other more specific representations for specific domain applications can be formulated.

1 Introduction

The main aim of knowledge management systems (KMS) is to manage and store the organizational knowledge, so it can be used later to learn, solve problems, and ultimately to support decision making [4]. Most of the recent KMS capture and store the knowledge in repositories of documents like manuals, memos, and text files systems, and the knowledge transfer is made by means of meetings, courses or by documented manuals and guides. This traditional form of storing and transferring knowledge causes loss of time and high investment in human resources, since it does not consider mechanisms of semantic and automatic processing of knowledge.

A way of solving this problem is to store the knowledge in a structured way. We have followed this approach using the case-based organizational memory strategy. It combines organizational knowledge storage technology with case-based reasoning (CBR) in order to represent each item of informal knowledge. In general, organizational memories (OM) can store the whole formal and informal knowledge [4] present in an organization with automatic processing capabilities. In particular, by structuring an organizational memory in cases can also facilitate the automatic capture, recovery, transfer and reuse of knowledge.

Although the benefits of applying the KMS are well known, and the idea of applying CBR methods to lessons learned and best practices are not new in the KM area [15], there is almost no consensus yet on many of the concepts and terminology used in both KM and CBR areas. Despite the efforts made during the last decade in new research developments and international standardization, knowledge management is currently in the phase in which terminology are still being defined, consolidated, and agreed on. In particular, as we know, there is no ontology on case-based organizational memory (CBOM). In order to reach this aim we started to construct a common conceptualization for CBOM [11], where concepts, attributes and their relationships should be explicitly specified; such explicit specification of a conceptualization is one of the core steps for building an ontology. The sources of knowledge for the proposed CBOM ontology come from an australian related standard [2], from recognized research articles in the area [1, 8, 9], and from meetings among members of our research group in order to reach a consensus for this terminology. In addition, some concepts were taken from the WordNet [16] ontology. It is worthy mentioning that so far it does not exist any international standard (like ISO) in the knowledge management area [6]. The rest of this article proceeds as follows. Section 2 presents the CBOM ontology focusing on the conceptualization step. In Section 3, concluding remarks and future directions are drawn.

2 Case-based Organizational Memory Ontology

Our ontology specification's goal is to contribute in the integration of the OM and CBR-related concepts that can be useful as conceptual base for any organizational KMS. Specifically, we will integrate the knowledge acquired and stored in a case knowledge base from lessons learnt in measurement and evaluation projects [13] with a recommendation system to support decision making.

The OM ontology aims to be at a generic level from which other representations for specific domain applications can be formulated (Figure 1). On one hand, the CBOM ontology is defined at a generic OM level, and, on the other hand, to characterize the cases according to the specific knowledge domain and its context [12], a domain and context ontologies should also be provided.

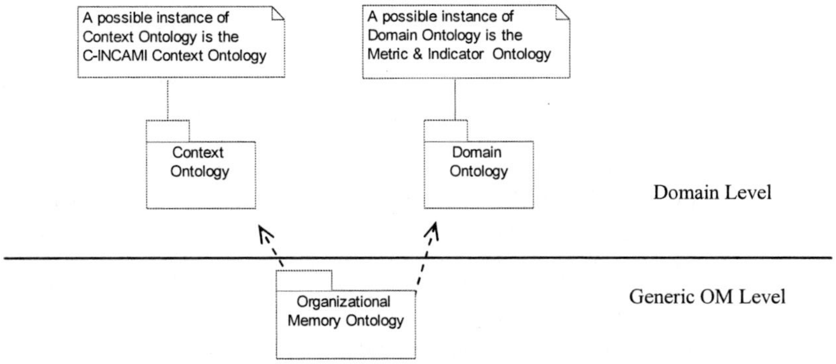

Fig. 1 The relationship between ontologies at the domain specific and generic OM level

For the CBOM ontology's conceptualization step we have employed a mixture of tables as suggested by the *Methontology* strategy [7] as well as the well-known UML language, which was previously used for this end [14, 10]. Next, we describe the main concepts of the ontology which are illustrated in the UML diagram of the Fig. 2. Notice that in the following text in *italic* the main concepts are highlighted (and defined also in Table 1).

An *organizational memory* is a repository that stores the whole formal and informal knowledge present in an organization and, then, it can have one o more *knowledge bases*. A type of knowledge base is a *case knowledge base* which stores the acquired knowledge in past experiences, good practices, lessons learnt, heuristics, etc. to different domains; that is, it stores cases. A *case* is a contextualized *knowledge item* representing an experience by means of a *problem* and its *solution*. Looking at the previous description for an organizational memory is of paramount importance keeping the *context* information [12] where each case happens. The representation of the knowledge through cases facilitates the reuse of the knowledge acquired in past problems to be applied to a new problem in similar situations [1].

Traditionally, there are several types of methods for representing cases that range from non-structured to completely structured and automatically processable representations [3]. We have chosen the latter strategy, where the meaning of concepts can formally be specified and processed by computers. A case can be seen as an ordered pair $< P, S >$, where P is the *problem* space, and S is the *solution* space. Because a problem can have several solutions not all with the same result, for a better selection and recommendation of a solution in decision making, it can also be relevant to store the *result* achieved in the application of a solution to a problem. Notice that any result can be yielded following the underlying INCAMI methodology [13].

There exists a general description of problems as P(x1, x2,..., xn), where each individual problem is an instance P(a1, a2,..., an); also a general description of solutions as S(y1, y2,..., yn), and every individual solution S(b1, b2,..., bn) is an instance of that general description. The xi are variables that characterize the problem (*problem feature*), and the yi are variables that characterize the solution (*solution feature*), where both are *features*. Since the stored cases refer to a specific knowledge domain, the features that characterize the problems and solutions are defined by a *domain concept* term; e.g., the concepts coming from the metric and indicator domain ontology [10] that intervene in actual measurement and evaluation projects.

The CBR process consists in assigning values to problem variables and finding the adequate instances for solution variables. To find the appropriate values for the instances of a solution, the similarity assessment of cases should be performed, so that for each case knowledge base a *similarity assessment model* should be specified. Most of the CBR applications have been focused on problems of specific domains [9]. However, in order to be useful to an organization, a CBR system should be fitted in with the main knowledge sources that can stem from diverse domains, and so the similarity functions appropriate to each case knowledge base. As we see in Fig. 2, each case knowledge base has a *similarity assessment model* that specifies it, which in turn combines several *similarity model elements*, one for each case feature. Usually, the similarity between a recovered case R and a new case C is defined as the sum of the similarities among its constituent feature values multiplied by their weights:

$$\textit{Similarity}\,(\mathrm{R}, \mathrm{C}) = \sum_{\mathrm{f}} \mathrm{w_f} * \textit{sim}_{\mathrm{f}}\,(f_{\mathrm{R}}, f_{\mathrm{C}}) \qquad (1)$$

where w_f is the weight of the feature *f*, and sim_f is the similarity measurement function to the feature. Therefore, in order to provide an appropriate representation of the similarity model, it is necessary to represent the weights that model the relative relevance, and the similarity function type for each specific feature.

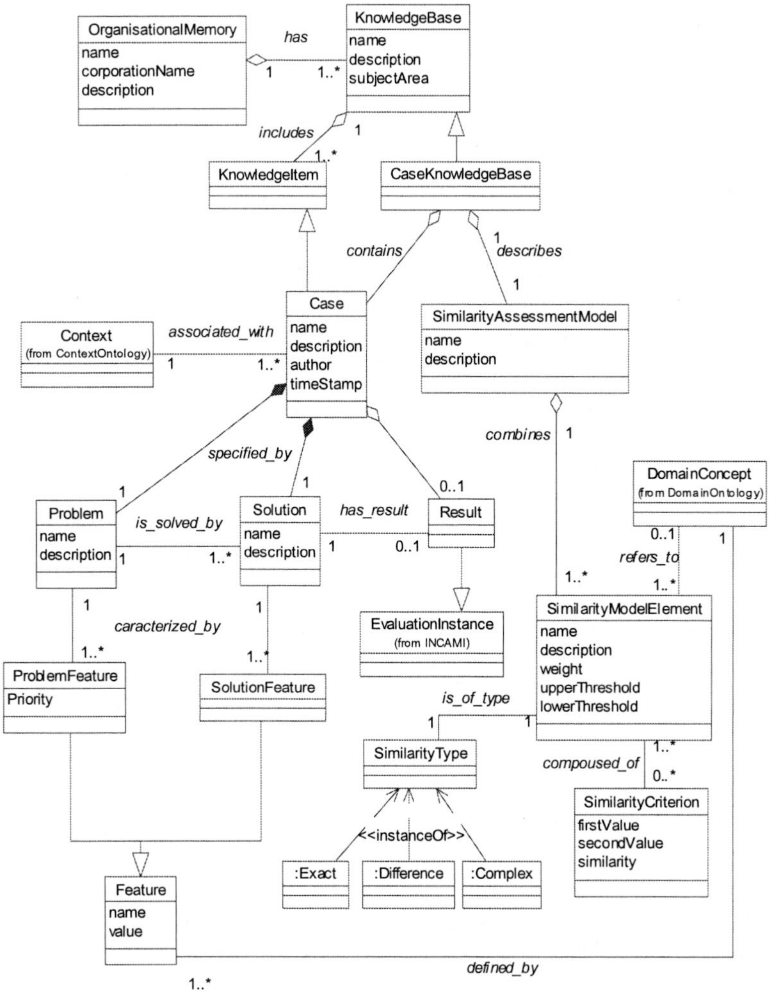

Fig. 2. UML diagram for the Case-based Organizational Memory Ontology

The weights are represented as an attribute inside each similarity element (see Fig. 2), and the *similarity type* is restricted to be one out of three general types, namely: *Exact*, *Difference* and *Complex*. The inclusion of these types of functions is based on the analysis of numerous investigations in the CBR area [1, 5]. Particularly:

- The *Exact* similarity function returns 1 if two feature values are the same and 0 otherwise.
- The *Difference* similarity function is inversely proportional to the difference between a feature values. It can only be applied when it is possible to define the

value difference; for instance, between numerical values the difference is the mathematical difference (i.e. the Euclidian distance).

- The *Complex* similarity function solves the similarity for all those situations where the two previous functions are not applicable; for example, the semantic difference between two synonymous terms that is neither completely the same nor completely different. If the number of a feature values is finite, it is feasible to have beforehand the similarity measure values for all possible values' pairs. In our model, these parameters are represented in the *Similarity Criterion* class.

Table 1. Case-based Organizational Memory Ontology: Glossary of Concepts.

Concept Name	Description
Case	A case is a contextualised knowledge item representing an experience by means of a problem and its solution.
Case Knowledge Base	A specific knowledge base where each knowledge item is represented through a case.
Complex	A similarity function type that keeps the similarity measure to each pair of possible values of a feature.
Difference	A similarity function type that is inversely proportional to the difference between a feature values.
Exact	A similarity function type that returns 1 if two feature values are the same and 0 otherwise.
Feature	A measurable physical or abstract property of an entity (synonym for the attribute term defined in ISO 14598-1).
Knowledge Base	An organized body of related knowledge. [2].
Knowledge Item	An atomic piece of knowledge. Comment: Knowledge is a body of understanding and/or lessons learnt from skills and experiences that is constructed by people.
Organisational Memory	The way an organization stores and keeps track of what it knows.
Problem	A state of difficulty that needs to be resolved [16].
Problem Feature	Feature that characterizes a problem.
Result	Satisfaction level achieved by the application of a solution to a problem.
Similarity Assessment Model	Algorithm or function with associated similarity elements that models the similarity assessment of cases.
Similarity Criterion	Assessment pattern used to determine the semantic similarities between two feature values.
Similarity Model Element	Algorithm or function with associated similarity criterion that models the similarity assessment of a feature.
Similarity Type	Specifies the similarity function type, which can be exact, difference or complex.
Solution	A statement that solves a problem or explains how to solve a problem
Solution Feature	Feature that characterizes a solution

3 Conclusions

In this work we have specified a CBOM ontology –that for space reasons will be thoroughly discussed in a forthcoming book chapter. The knowledge representation through cases facilitates the reuse of knowledge acquired in past problems to be applied to a new problem in similar situations, in addition facilitates the automatic knowledge processing as well. The utility of a CBOM based on ontologies resides in that the stored knowledge can be easily shared among heterogeneous and distributed systems at intra and cross organization levels. In order to enable the interoperability and flexibility our OM is based on three ontologies, that is: the *Domain Ontology* which provides the formal definition of the underlying domain concepts that are the basis for composing the cases (experiences) to be stored in the memory; the *Context Ontology* that provides the formal definition to specify contextual information to cases; and the *Case-based Organizational Memory Ontology* itself, which provides a common conceptual ground to share the knowledge in an interoperable way.

A future work is the implementation of the measurement and evaluation organizational memory system based on the proposed ontology and its integration with the C-INCAMI framework and tool [12]. The knowledge acquired and stored in a case knowledge base from lessons learnt in measurement and evaluation projects will serve as the basis to a recommendation system to support better decision making.

References

1. Aamodt, A. Plaza E. (1994) "Case-Based Reasoning: Foundational Issues, Methodological Variations, and System Approaches". *AI Communication. IOS Press*, V.7:1, pp.39-59.
2. Australian Standard (2005) "Knowledge Management - A guide".
3. Chen, H.; Wu, Z. (2003) "On Case-Based Knowledge Sharing in Semantic Web", *15th IEEE Int'l Conference on Tools with Artificial Intelligence (ICTAI'03)*, pp. 200-207.
4. Conklin, J. (1996) "Designing Organizational Memory: Preserving Intellectual Assets in a Knowledge Economy". *Group Decision Support Systems.*
5. Coyle, L.; Doyle, D.; Cunningham, P. (2004) "Similarity for CBR", *Technical Report TCD-CS-2004-25*, Trinity College: Dublin.
6. Ferguson, S., (2006) "AS 5037-2005: knowledge management blueprint for Australian organisations?", *Australian Library Journal*, V. 55:3, pp.196-209.
7. Fernández López, M., Gómez-Pérez, A. and Juristo, N., (1997) "METHONTOLOGY: From Ontological Art Towards Ontological Engineering". *AAAI Symposium.* University of Stanford; P.A., California, US, pp. 33-40.
8. Kemp, J.; Weber, F.; Pudlatz, M.; Wunram, M.; Bredehorst, B. (2001) "Knowledge Management 'Standardisation'", *European KM Forum.* IST Project No. 2000-26393
9. Kolodner J. (1993) *Case-based Reasoning*, Ed. Morgan Kaufmann
10. Martín M., Olsina L. (2003) "Towards an Ontology for Software Metrics and Indicators as the Foundation for a Cataloging Web System", *IEEE Computer Science Press, 1st Latin American Web Congress, LA-Web'03*, Santiago, Chile, pp103-113
11. Martín M.; Olsina L. (2006) "Memoria Organizacional Basada en Casos para dar Soporte al Proceso de Aseguramiento de Calidad", *XII CACIC 2006, Workshop WISBD*, San Luis
12. Molina H.; Olsina L. (2007) "Towards the Support of Contextual Information to a Measurement and Evaluation Framework", *In IEEE Computer Society, 6th Int'l Conference on the Quality of Information and Comm. Technology (QUATIC'07)*, Portugal, pp.154-163.
13. Olsina, L; Papa, F.; Molina, H. (2007) "How to Measure and Evaluate Web Applications in a Consistent Way", Ch. 13th In Springer Book titled *Web Engineering: Modeling and Implementing Web Applications*, Rossi, Pastor, Schwabe, and Olsina (Eds).
14. Wang, X. and Chan, C.W. (2001) "Ontology Modeling Using UML" *7th Int'l Conference on Object Oriented Information Systems Conference (OOIS'2001)*, pp. 59-68
15. Weber R., Aha, D., Becerra-Fernandez I. (2001) "Intelligent Lessons Learned Systems". *Int'l Journal of Expert Systems Research & Applications.* V. 20:1, pp. 17-34
16. WordNet, Retrieved: November 22, 2007, from http://www.cogsci.princeton.edu/~wn/

Una herramienta industrial para la medición del tamaño funcional de aplicaciones desarrolladas en entornos MDA[1]

Beatriz Marín[1], Giovanni Giachetti[1], Oscar Pastor[1]

[1] Departamento de Sistemas Informáticos y Computación
Universidad Politécnica de Valencia
Camino de Vera s/n
46022 Valencia, España
{bmarin, ggiachetti, opastor}@dsic.upv.es

Resumen. La aplicación industrial de OO-Method ha provocado que sus modelos conceptuales evolucionen para adaptarse a las necesidades de los usuarios. Este trabajo muestra la actualización del procedimiento de medición OOmFP, que permite medir el tamaño funcional de modelos conceptuales OO-Method, considerando las nuevas funcionalidades de los modelos conceptuales y los diferentes desafíos tecnológicos que implica el desarrollo de una herramienta industrial para medir aplicaciones generadas en entornos MDA. Finalmente, un análisis comparativo que evalúa cinco modelos asociados sistemas reales, muestra el impacto de las actualizaciones y mejoras propuestas.

Palabras claves: MDA, Medición de puntos de función, IFPUG FPA, Herramienta.

1 Introducción

La generación automática o semi-automática de los productos de software se ha posicionado fuertemente en la industria [10]. Este es el caso de MDA (Model Driven Architecture) [15], que tiene como recurso fundamental a los modelos conceptuales debido a que son la entrada para el proceso de generación de código. Por este motivo han surgido nuevos desafíos, entre los cuales destaca la capacidad de cuantificar el tamaño funcional de las aplicaciones generadas.

Varios procedimientos de medición de tamaño funcional de modelos conceptuales han sido definidos de acuerdo al estándar IFPUG Function Point Analisys (FPA) [5] [6]. Una de las limitaciones más importantes que presentan estos procedimientos es su incapacidad de medir de manera exacta los sistemas software, ya que los modelos utilizados carecen de la formalización semántica necesaria para hacer una descripción completa y sin ambigüedad de los sistemas.

[1] Este trabajo ha sido desarrollado con el soporte del MEC bajo el proyecto SESAMO TIN2007-62894.

OO-Method [9] [12] provee un modelo conceptual con la formalización semántica necesaria que permite la generación de un producto de software completo [14], haciendo posible obtener de forma completamente automática el tamaño funcional de la aplicación modelada. El procedimiento que realiza la medición del tamaño funcional asociado a un modelo conceptual OO-Method se denomina: OO-Method Function Points (OOmFP) [11] [2] [1] y la herramienta que lo implementa se llama Function Point Counter (FPC).

Debido a la evolución de los modelos conceptuales OO-Method es necesario actualizar OOmFP para conseguir una medición completa y correcta de los modelos especificados. Por otra parte, la herramienta FPC requiere un proceso de reingeniería para dar soporte a modelos de aplicaciones reales de manera eficiente.

El objetivo de este trabajo es mostrar las actualizaciones realizadas a OOmFP para cuantificar el tamaño funcional de los modelos conceptuales OO-Method de manera completa y correcta, e identificar los criterios que deben ser considerados en el desarrollo de una herramienta que permita medir de manera automática el tamaño funcional de aplicaciones generadas en entornos MDA según el estándar IFPUG FPA.

El resto del artículo está organizado como sigue: la sección 2 presenta un resumen de la actualización del proceso de medición OOmFP y la sección 3 presenta las consideraciones técnicas asociadas a la implementación de la herramienta FPC. La sección 4 presenta un análisis comparativo entre la antigua y la nueva herramienta FPC, y en último lugar, la sección 5 presenta las conclusiones y trabajos futuros.

2 Actualización de OOmFP

El trabajo realizado tiene como base el proceso estándar de medición de tamaño funcional: IFPUG Function Point Análisis (IFPUG FPA) [7], el enfoque OO-Method [13] y su proceso de medición OO-Method Function Points (OOmFP) [1]. Por razones de espacio no es posible entrar en detalles asociados a sus características, pero el lector puede encontrar información relevante en las referencias señaladas.

El proceso de medición asociado a OOmFP consiste en aplicar sus reglas de medición para clasificar y pesar funciones de datos y de transacciones presentes en el modelo conceptual OO-Method, que a su vez se compone de cuatro modelos: objetos, dinámico, funcional y de presentación. OOmFP se enfoca en el modelo de presentación [8] para identificar la vista que se quiere medir y la funcionalidad especificada en los otros modelos que está asociada a esa vista. Una vez que se ha identificado y medido la funcionalidad de la vista, los resultados son evaluados mediante las tablas definidas en el estándar IFPUG FPA para obtener el tamaño funcional de la aplicación. Las reglas de medición de OOmFP fueron definidas en [1].

La actualización de OOmFP en el *modelo de objetos* del modelo conceptual modificó una de las reglas definida para corregir el conteo de los atributos dato-valuados. También, se agregaron seis reglas asociadas a nuevas funcionalidades de los servicios de las clases, debido a que se han incorporado fórmulas para especificar formalmente el comportamiento de los argumentos del servicio.

La actualización de OOmFP en el *modelo dinámico* agregó treinta y dos nuevas reglas asociadas a un nuevo elemento funcional: los servicios globales. Los servicios globales tienen visibilidad sobre todas las clases del modelo de objetos y permiten ejecutar los servicios de cada una de ellas. Al igual que los servicios locales, los servicios globales pueden tener precondiciones, argumentos de entrada, argumentos de salida, valor por defecto de los argumentos y una fórmula que especifica formalmente lo que realiza el servicio.

La actualización de OOmFP en el *modelo funcional* no presentó cambios, por lo que no se agregaron, quitaron o modificaron las reglas de medición definidas.

La actualización de OOmFP en el *modelo de presentación* eliminó una regla asociada a las unidades de interacción de instancia, ya que contaba erróneamente el elemento de interacción que permite seleccionar un valor para los argumentos objeto-valuados de un servicio. Esta regla fue incorporada para las unidades de interacción de servicio. Además, se agregaron cuatro reglas en las unidades de interacción de instancia debido a que se asociaron fórmulas a las navegaciones y a los atributos derivados que pueden participar en una instancia. Finalmente, se agregaron siete reglas para las unidades de interacción de población asociadas a fórmulas en las navegaciones, en los atributos derivados y en las variables de filtro objeto-valudas.

El detalle de las reglas agregadas, modificadas y eliminadas en la nueva versión de OOmFP fueron presentadas en un trabajo anterior, que está referenciado en [4].

3 Proceso de reingeniería de la herramienta FPC

El uso industrial de la herramienta Function Point Counter (FPC) ha generado la necesidad de medir de manera completa y correcta los modelos conceptuales OO-Method, de tener una arquitectura flexible que permita adaptarse a la evolución de los modelos conceptuales, y de tener mayor agilidad en el proceso de conteo de las aplicaciones generadas. Para satisfacer estas necesidades se ha propuesto un proceso de reingeniería de la herramienta FPC original, desarrollada en Visual Basic 6, que ha dado como resultado el desarrollo de una nueva herramienta FPC, implementada en Visual Studio .Net 2003 con el lenguaje C#. Esta nueva herramienta incluye todas las reglas de medición definidas en OOmFP, permitiendo medir de manera completa el tamaño funcional de las aplicaciones generadas.

Para satisfacer la *arquitectura flexible*, a diferencia de la antigua herramienta, la arquitectura de la nueva herramienta FPC está separada en diferentes capas para facilitar la incorporación de nuevas reglas de medición o modificaciones a las reglas existentes.

La primera capa consiste en la precarga del modelo conceptual OO-Method, que se genera por la herramienta OlivaNova [3] en un archivo XML. Durante la precarga del modelo se organizan los elementos funcionales de manera jerárquica según las unidades de interacción contenidas en la vista que se quiere medir.

La segunda capa consiste en la identificación de los elementos a funcionales y su medición mediante las reglas actualizadas, que están organizadas de acuerdo a la figura 1. Para disminuir el acoplamiento de la medición de los elementos funcionales, cada regla está agrupada por elemento funcional y está implementada de forma independiente. El resultado del análisis de cada elemento funcional es almacenado en un arreglo que se pasa como parámetro a la tercera capa de implementación.

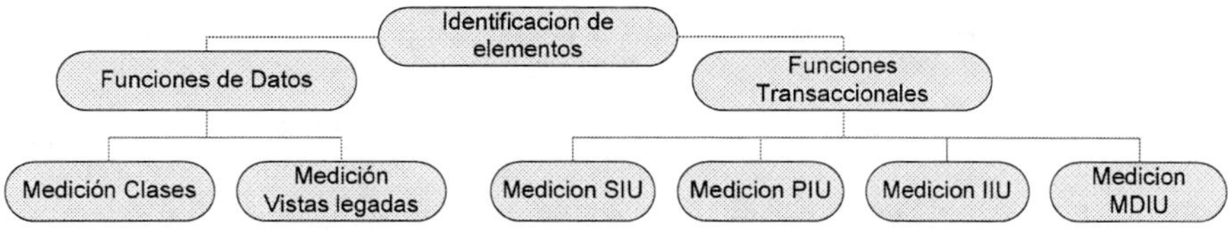

Fig. 1. Clasificación de reglas de medición.

La tercera capa de implementación consiste en la evaluación de los valores de cada unidad de interacción de acuerdo a las tablas de evaluación propuestas por el estándar IFPUG FPA para obtener el tamaño funcional y luego, sumando el resultado de cada elemento funcional, se obtiene el tamaño total de la aplicación.

Finalmente, la cuarta capa de implementación consiste en la generación de un reporte final, que se genera en un archivo XML que puede transformarse mediante XSLT en HTML o en el formato que requiera el cliente.

En cuanto a la *agilidad en el conteo*, se ha detectado que la mayor carga de procesamiento y tiempo de ejecución ocurre en la capa de identificación y medición de elementos funcionales. Para optimizar esta capa se ha implementado un mecanismo de caché, que se centra en reducir la gran cantidad de procesamiento invertido en analizar elementos que han sido analizados previamente. Un ejemplo de esta situación es el análisis de transacciones, ya que las transacciones en pueden invocar a otras transacciones o invocarse a sí mismas recursivamente. El mecanismo de caché almacena los resultados obtenidos en el análisis de cada elemento funcional con un identificador único. De esta manera, al analizar un nuevo elemento funcional primero se verifica si dicho elemento ya existe en el caché, y en ese caso el valor se recupera directamente del caché, evitando volver a analizar el elemento.

También se deben *evitar los desbordamientos de pila* al momento de ejecutar la medición. Debido a la naturaleza iterativa del análisis de puntos de función basados en el estándar IFPUG FPA, se ha detectado que en modelos de gran tamaño se puede producir desbordamientos durante la ejecución. Estos desbordamientos se producen por falta de memoria para el manejo de las iteraciones. Particularmente, en caso del framework .Net versión 1.1, la pila para el almacenamiento posee un tamaño de 512KB, que se ve sobrepasada en el análisis de modelos de más de 80 clases.

Para evitar el desbordamiento de pila, se almacenan en un arreglo auxiliar los elementos relacionados. De esta manera, una vez acabado el análisis del primer elemento, se continúa con un análisis secuencial sobre los elementos almacenados en el arreglo auxiliar. Si los elementos relacionados a su vez referencian a otros elementos, éstos se van agregando al final arreglo, eliminando el anidamiento de iteraciones y evitando el desbordamiento de pila (Fig. 2).

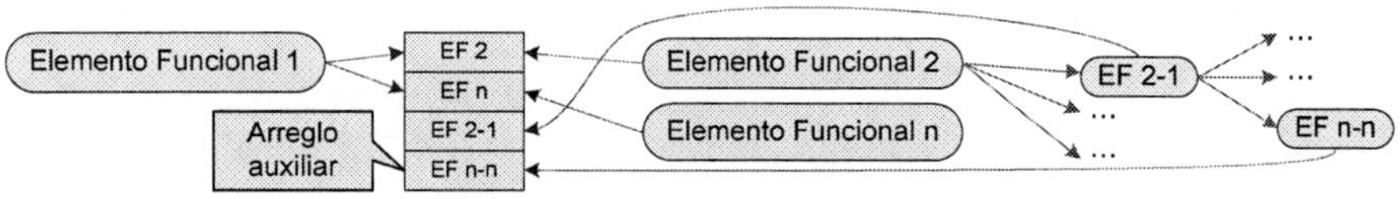

Fig. 2. Esquema de solución para el desbordamiento de pila.

4 Análisis comparativo

Se ha realizado un análisis comparativo del tamaño funcional de cinco modelos conceptuales asociados a sistemas reales. Todos esos modelos conceptuales pertenecen al dominio de aplicación de Sistemas de Información de Gestión.

El análisis compara las mediciones funcionales obtenidas por la versión original del contador de puntos de función y las mediciones funcionales obtenidas usando la nueva versión del contador de puntos de función, que implementa las reglas y mejoras tecnológicas propuestas en este trabajo. Antes de realizar el análisis, dos hipótesis fueron formuladas en relación a los resultados esperados del análisis comparativo:

- H1: Existirá una mayor número de elementos detectados por la nueva versión de OOmFP.
- H2: El tiempo de conteo de un modelo será menor con el Nuevo FPC.

La tabla 1 presenta los resultados obtenidos en la medición funcional de los modelos conceptuales.

Tabla 1. Elementos identificados, tamaño funcional y tiempo de medición con el antiguo FPC y el nuevo FPC.

Modelo	Clases	Antiguo FPC					Nuevo FPC				
		EIs	EQs	EOs	PF	Tiempo	EIs	EQs	EOs	PF	Tiempo
M1	8	18	6	4	171	2,12	20	6	4	182	1,20
M2	17	67	24	0	430	4,21	74	11	4	458	1,35
M3	32	128	30	17	951	17,34	132	13	27	985	3,87
M4	84	314	49	92	2.711	93,28	328	49	89	2.811	22,90
M5	193	720	368	36	5.990	373,88	727	280	59	6.267	44,37

De acuerdo a los resultados expuestos en la tabla 1, se puede afirmar que la hipótesis H1 es verdadera, ya que se obtiene un mayor número de elementos identificados en EIs y EOs. Para el caso de los EQs, se obtiene un menor número de elementos identificados debido a que la versión anterior no estaba teniendo en cuenta los atributos derivados para contar correctamente los EQs.

La hipótesis H2 también es verdadera. En la tabla 1 se puede apreciar el impacto que han tenido las consideraciones técnicas en los tiempos de medición con la nueva herramienta FPC. Por ejemplo, en el modelo M5 se alcanza una mejora en el tiempo de medición de un 842% con respecto al tiempo alcanzado por la antigua herramienta FPC.

5 Conclusiones y trabajo futuro

Este trabajo presenta una serie de consideraciones técnicas que deben tenerse en cuenta al momento de desarrollar de una herramienta que permita medir el tamaño funcional de aplicaciones generadas en entornos MDA según el estándar IFPUG FPA. Estas consideraciones están enfocadas a medir correctamente los elementos funcionales de los modelos conceptuales, para lo que es necesario tener un procedimiento con reglas que comprendan todas las primitivas del modelo conceptual. Además, las consideraciones están enfocadas a medir de manera eficiente los modelos conceptuales.

Las consideraciones identificadas han sido aplicadas a una herramienta que permite medir modelos conceptuales OO-Method, y un análisis comparativo ha sido realizado para mostrar las mejoras que se tienen al incluir estas consideraciones en el desarrollo de dicha herramienta. Basándonos en los resultados obtenidos en el análisis comparativo de sistemas de información reales, hemos identificado que a pesar de que el tamaño funcional y la complejidad sean mayores en algunos modelos, esto no se ve reflejado en el tamaño funcional de las aplicaciones generadas debido a las cotas superiores de las tablas de evaluación definidas en el estándar IFPUG FPA. Por este motivo se plantea como trabajo futuro la creación de un nuevo procedimiento de medición que supere las limitaciones de OOmFP.

Referencias

1. Abrahão, S., *On the Functional Size Measurement of Object-Oriented Conceptual Schemas: Desing and Evaluation Issues*, Doctoral thesis, Universidad Politécnica de Valencia, Valencia, España, 2004.
2. Abrahão, S. and Pastor, O., *Estimating the Applications Functional Size from Object-Oriented Conceptual Models* In: International Function Point User Group Annual Conference (IFPUG'01), Las Vegas, USA, 2001.
3. CARE Technologies Web Site, www.care-t.com
4. Giachetti, G.; Marín, B.; Condori-Fernández, N. and Molina, J.C., *Updating OO-Method Function Points* In: 6th International Conference on the Quality of Information and Communications Technology (QUATIC 2007), Lisboa, Portugal, 2007, pp. 55-64.
5. IFPUG: International Function Point Users Group Web Site, www.ifpug.org
6. IFPUG, *Function Point Counting Practices Manual Release 4.1*, International Function Point Users Group, Westerville, Ohio, USA, 1999.
7. IFPUG, *Function Point Counting Practices Manual Release 4.2*, International Function Point Users Group, Princeton Junction, New Jersey, USA, 2004.
8. Molina, P., *Especificación de interfaz de usuario: De los requisitos a la generación automática*, Doctoral thesis, Universidad Politécnica de Valencia, Valencia, España, 2003.
9. OO-Method Group Web Site, http://oomethod.dsic.upv.es
10. OMG: Web page of OMG with companies with products MDA, http://www.omg.org/mda/committed-products.htm
11. Pastor, O.; Abrahão, S. M.; Molina, J.C. and Torres, I., *A FPA-like Measure for Object-Oriented Systems from Conceptual Models* In: 11th International Workshop of Software Measurement (IWSM'01), Montreal, Canada, 2001.
12. Pastor, O.,;Gómez, J.; Insfrán E. and Pelechano, V., *The OO-Method Approach for Information Systems Modelling: From Object-Oriented Conceptual Modeling to Automated Programming*, Information Systems, vol.26, 2001.
13. Pastor, O. and Molina, J. C., *Model-Driven Architecture in Practice*, Springer, 2007.
14. Pastor, O.; Ramos, I.; Cuevas, J.; Devesa, J., *OASIS versión 2.0, An Object Definition Language for Object Oriented Databases*, 1994.
15. Sitio web MDA, http://www.omg.org/mda/

An Ontology for the WSRP Standard

Mª Ángeles Moraga[1], Ignacio García-Rodríguez de Guzmán[1], Coral Calero[1], and Mario Piattini[1]

[1] Alarcos Research Group. UCLM-INDRA Research and Development Institute. University of Castilla-La Mancha. Paseo de la Universidad 4 –13071 –Ciudad Real –Spain
{MariaAngeles.Moraga,Ignacio.GRodriguez,Coral.Calero,Mario.Piattini}@uclm.es

Abstract. The use of Web portals continues to rise, showing their importance in the current information society. Specifically, this work focuses on portlet-based portals. Recently, the WSRP (Web Services for Remote Portlets) standard has come into existence. Its aim is to provide a common interface in order to allow the communication between portal and portlets. Bearing all in mind, in this work we propose an ontology for this standard. The ontology leads both portlet and portal developers to focus their effort on developing the portlet domain logic instead of implementing its communication.

Keywords: portlets, web portals, WSRP standard, ontology

1 Introduction

Today, the emergence of portlets is leading to develop web portals as an aggregation of portlets. Portlets are used by portals as pluggable user interface components that is, they are displayed in the portal and provide content for it [4].

When portlets came into existence, their main problem was the lack of interoperability. Portlets had to be custom-developed for each portal server because the API was different for each server [5]. However, this problem was eliminated when the WSRP (Web Services for Remote Portlets) standard appeared.

In spite of the existence of the WSRP standard, there are different companies which offer portlets that do not adhere to this standard (see http://www.jahia.net/jahia/571). These portlets present several problems between them such as non-existence of interoperability between portlets and portal; and impossibility of offering these portlets to different portal developers.

Currently it is possible to find portlet repositories where portal developers can acquire a portlet which satisfies their's needs [6]. Indeed, the Open Source Portlet Repository Project has been recently launched [1] to foster the free and open exchange of portlets. Other similar portlet-sharing sites include Portlet Swap (jboss.org) and Portlet Exchange (portletexchange.com). The majority of portlets, which are offered in repositories, adhere to the WSRP standard. However, its specification is not easily understood.

On the other hand, ontologies allow us to share knowledge and facilitate the communication between people and/or systems [10]. Thereby, using an ontology both portlet and portal developers can focus their effort on developing the portlet domain logic instead of understanding the standard. In addition, it makes easier the creation of new portlets as well as the adaptation of portlets that do not adhere to the WSRP. For all these reasons, we have created a specific ontology (WSRP-O) for WSRP.

This paper is structured as follows. Section 2, the ontology for the WSRP is shown whereas in section 3 conclusions and future work are drawn.

2 An ontology for the WSRP standard: WSRP-O

The main objective of this work is to develop an ontology for the WSRP standard. For this reason, first of all, general information about WSRP should be given.

The goal of the WSRP standard is to enable an application designer or administrator to pick from a rich choice of compliant remote content and application providers (portlets), and integrate them with just a few mouse clicks and no programming effort [8]. The standard defines different interfaces and operations for carrying out the specified functionality. It may be worth emphasizing that the WSRP standard is independent of the programming language.

However, the use of a standard is not a trivial task, the vocabulary is complex and generally is hard to understand on your own. In view of this situation, a tool which simplifies the standard, such as an ontology, would be necessary.

On the other hand, we should provide a definition of ontology: "Defines the basic terms and relations comprising the vocabulary of a topic area as well as the rules for combining terms and relations to define extensions to the vocabulary [7]".

Nonetheless, different definitions about ontologies can be found in the literature. The majority of them provide a set of common elements. According to [3], these elements are: *Classes, Relations, Formal axiom* and *Instances*.

According to [2] the ontology representation language should have rich and formal abstractions. UML-based ontologies have the obvious advantage of being more widely understandable [9]. For this reason, in order to describe the ontology proposed in this work, UML class diagrams are used. In addition, the proposed ontology (figure 1) gives support to develop new portlets as well as to adapt existents portlets to the standard. The UML diagrams are accompanied by some constraint defined using OCL.

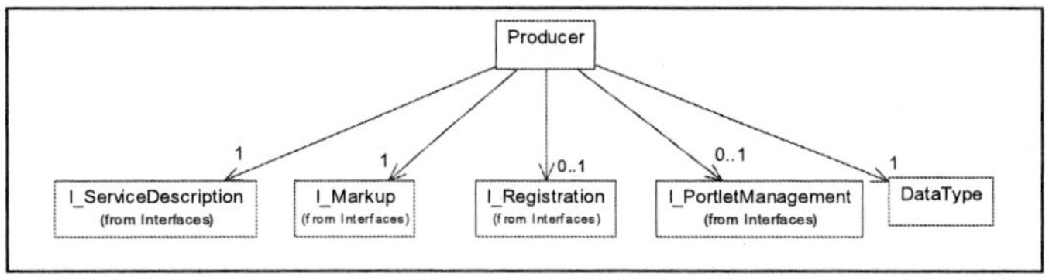

Fig. 1. A global overview of the ontology

As we can see, the ServiceDescription and Markup interfaces are compulsory whereas Registration and PortletManagement interfaces are optional. All these interfaces contain different operations. These operations have two common concepts:

fault and *result*. For this reason we have created a base class (named Operation) representing these common concepts (figure 2 (a)).

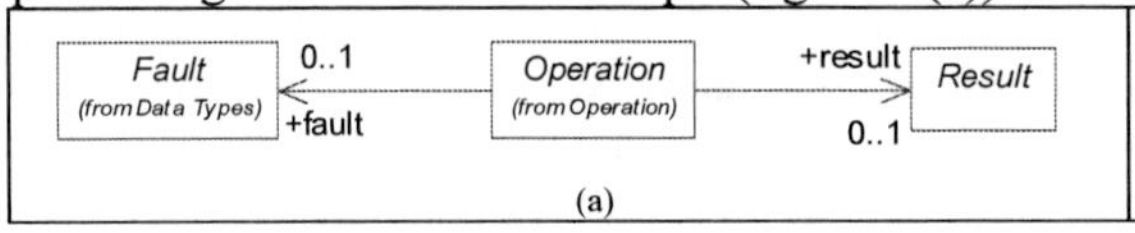


```
context Operation
 inv:
   ((result <> null) xor
(fault <> null))
```

(b)

Fig. 2. (a)"basicPortletOperation" as a base class for all the operations of the ontology; (b) constraint for the abstract *Operation* class

The *Fault* class represents the possible error message that can arise as a result of the operation, whereas the response represents the result of the operation when any error has happened. The error messages as well as the data type of the response depend on the operation. For this reason, a constraint for each operation will be created to specify the possible faults and results of an operation. The constraint indicates the kind of allowed error messages along with the allowed data type of the response for each operation. Finally, it may be worth emphasizing that an operation has to return a fault or a response but it is not possible to return both of them. In order to represent this restriction, the constraint of the figure 2 (b) has been defined.

The ontology is broken down according to interfaces decomposition into subontologies. In each subontology the different operations, which are allowed, are represented. Thus, in order to represent the allowed data types another subontology for data types has been included. Next, the different subontologies are presented.

Firstly, we are going to present the ServiceDescription subontology, this subontology represents the ServiceDescription interface. This interface defines an operation for acquiring the Producer's metadata. (figure 3)

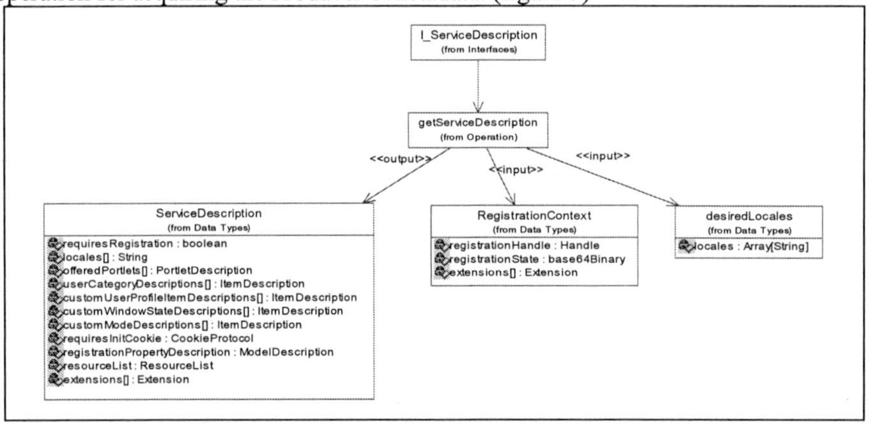

Fig. 3. ServiceDescription subontology

The well-formedness rules that complement the *ServiceDescription* subontology are the following:

```
context getServiceDescription
   inv allowedFaults:
(self.fault.name="InvalidRegistration"
or self.fault.name="OperationFailed))
```

```
context getServiceDescription
        inv resultKind:
self.result.isKindOf(ServiceDescription)
```

Secondly, the markup subontology is presented (Figure 4). The Markup interface has operations to generate markup and process interactions with that markup.

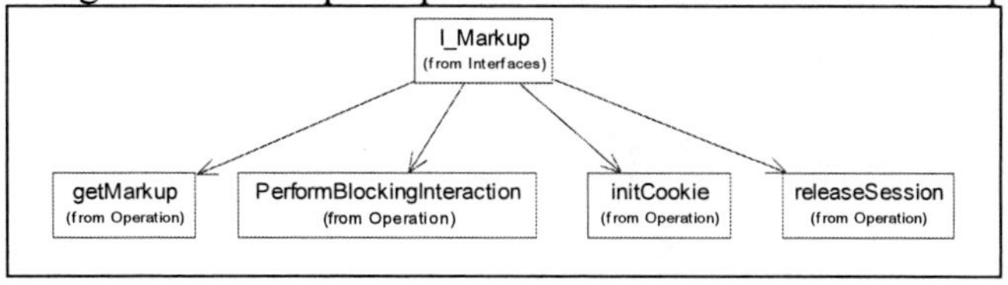

Fig. 4. Markup subontology

This subontology is composed of four different operations: a) *getMarkup*: renders the current state of a portlet (figure 5); b)*performBlockingInteraction*: sends user interactions to the producer; c) *initCookie*: provides assistance to initialize the cookies; d) *releaseSession*: informs the producer that it will no longer be using a set of sessions. The figures for the last three operations are not shown in this paper.

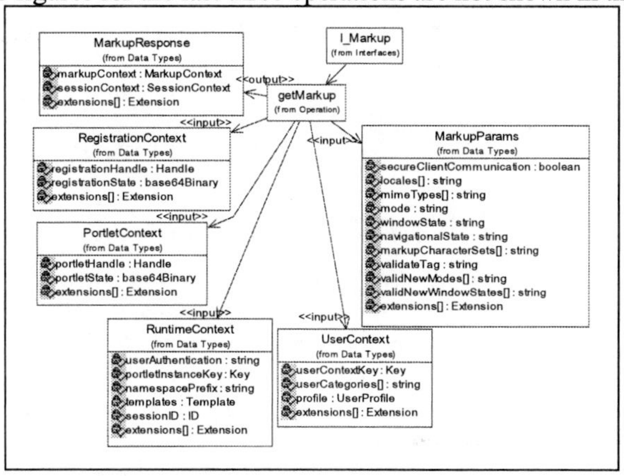

Fig. 5. getMarkup operation (it is part of Markup subontology)

The well-formedness rules for the initCookie operation are (it is similar for the rest of operations):

```
context getMarkup
inv allowedFauls:
 (self.fault.name="AccessDenied) or
self.fault.name="InconsistentParameters
)) or
 self.fault.name="InvalidRegistration"
or
 self.fault.name="MissingParameters" or
 self.fault.name="OperationFailed" or
 self.fault.name="InvalidUserCategory"
or
self.fault.name="InvalidHandle" or
 self.fault.name="InvalidCookie" or
 self.fault.name="InvalidSession" or
 self.fault.name="UnsupportedMode" or
self.fault.name="UnsupportedWindowState
" or
 self.fault.name="UnsupportedLocale" or
self.fault.name="UnsupportedMimeType")
context getMarkup
inv resultKind
 self.result.isKindOf(MarkupResponse)
```

Thirdly, the registration subontology is shown. The registration interface provides the necessary operations to allow a consumer to register with a producer [8].

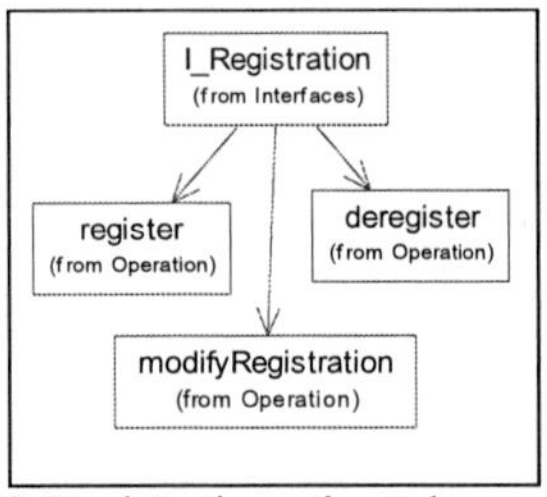

Fig. 9. Registration subontology

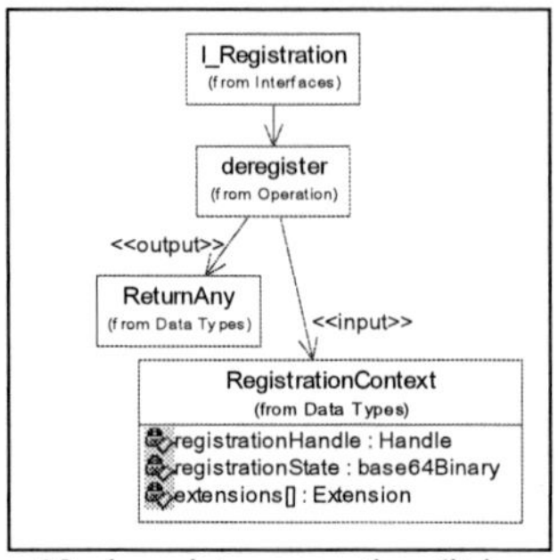

Fig. 10. deregister operation (it is part of Registration subontology)

As we can see in the subontology (figure 9), the operations for the Registration interface are: a) r*egister*: lets a consumer register with a producer, b)*modifyregister*: lets a consumer modify an existing relationship with a producer; c) *deregister*: lets a consumer terminate a registration (figure10). The register and modifyregister operations are not presented here.

The well-formedness rules for the deregister operation are (the rules for the rest of operations are built in a similar way):

```
context deRegister
  inv allowedFauls:
  (self.fault.name="InvalidRegistration"
 or
    self.fault.name="OperationFailed")
```

```
context deregister
  inv resultKind:
    self.result.isKindOf(ReturnAny)
```

In addition, the PortletManagement subontology has been built. The purpose of the PortletManagement interface is to let consumers manage the persistent state and lifecycle of portlets explicitly [8].

Finally, a DataType subontology focused on the allowed data types has been included into the ontology for WSRP. The objective of this subontology is to provide and constrain the different data types which can be used and specify their structure. Due to the lack of space, the last two subontologies are not presented in this paper.

4 Conclusions and future work

In this paper an ontology for WSRP standard, namely WSRP-O, has been proposed. Its objective is to help portlet developers to create or adapt a portlet according to WSRP. Thus, the portlet developer can easily establish the specific elements for portlets which have to be included. Moreover, the portlet developer can concentrate on the logic domain instead of the portlet characteristics.

It must be emphasized that the WSRP standard is generic, it is not specific of any programming language. All portlets must be conformed to the WSRP standard (independently of its programming language), therefore the WSRP-O ontology (which is independent of the programming language) can be used to ensure this fact. For this reason, different ontologies are under development. Each one of these ontologies will be specific for a given programming language.

As a result, we will have the ontology of the WSRP standard which will be generic. Using this ontology the portlet developer can establish the necessary generic elements. Next, taking into account the programming language in which the portlet has to be developed, the ontology specific to this programming language has to be used.

Acknowledgments. This work is part of the DIMENSIONS (PBC-05-012-1), ENIGMAS (PBI-05-058), FAMOSO (2007: FIT-340000-2007-71) and ESFINGE (TIM2006-15175-C05-05) projects and CALIPSO network (TIN2005-24055-E).

References

1. Blattman, J., N. Krishnan, D. Polla, and M. Sum. Open-Source Portal Initiative at Sun, Part 2: Portlet Repository. http://developers.sun.com/prodtech/portalserver/reference/techart/portlet-repository.html#2 (2006)
2. Calero, C., F. Ruiz, A. Baroni, F. Brito e Abreu, and M. Piattini, An Ontological Approach To Describe the SQL:2003 Object-Relational Features. Accepted in "Computer Standards and Interfaces", vol. 28(6): pp. 695-713. (2006)
3. Corcho, O., M. Fernández-López, and A. Gómez-Pérez, Chapter 1: Ontological Engineering: Principles, Methods, Tools and Languages., in Ontologies for Software Engineering and Software Technology, C. Calero, Ruiz, F., Piattini, M., (Ed)., Springer-Verlag: New York (2006)
4. Java Community Process. JSR 168 portlet specification. http://www.jcp.org/en/jsr/detail?id=168 (2003)
5. Linwood, J. and D. Minter, Building Portals with the Java Portlet API. New York: Apress.(2004)
6. Montejava. Los Portales Empresariales sacan el máximo partido a las aplicaciones de negocio. http://www.montejava.es/articulo3.asp, (2006)
7. Neches, R., R.E. Fikes, T. Finin, T.R. Gruber, R. Senator, and W.R. Swartout, Enabling technology for knowledge sharing. AI Magazine, vol.12(3): pp. 87-127 (1991)
8. OASIS. Web Service for Remote Portlets (WSRP). Version 1.0. http://www.oasis-open.org/commitees/wsrp/ (2003)
9. PlanetMDE. MDE (Model Driven Engineering). Community portal. http://www.planetmde.org (2005)
10. Ruiz, F. and J.R. Hilera, Chapter 2. Using Ontologies in Software Engineering and Technology, in Ontologies for Software Engineering and Software Technology, C. Calero, F. Ruiz, and M. Piattini, (Eds), Springer Verlag: New York (2006)

Un perfil UML para el análisis de series temporales con modelos conceptuales sobre almacenes de datos*

Jesús Pardillo[1], Jose Zubcoff[2] y Juan Trujillo[1]

[1] Dpto. de Lenguajes y Sistemas Informáticos,
Universidad de Alicante, España
{jesuspv,jtrujillo}@dlsi.ua.es
[2] Dpto. de Ciencias del Mar y Biología Aplicada,
Universidad de Alicante, España
Jose.Zubcoff@ua.es

Abstract. El *análisis de series temporales* (AST) es una potente herramienta para el descubrimiento de patrones y tendencias. Pero todavía no existen modelos conceptuales para esta técnica de minería, que podrían ayudar a solventar los problemas en el preprocesado de los grandes volúmenes de datos manejados. Dado que los *almacenes de datos* (AD) constituyen una fuente de datos idónea para la minería, proponemos extender UML (*Unified Modeling Language*) con un *perfil* para el modelado conceptual del AST sobre AD y emplear MDA (*Model Driven Architecture*) para la generación automática de código, facilitando notaciones y modelos intuitivos, independientes de herramientas y algoritmos.

Key words: Modelado conceptual, modelado multidimensional, UML, MDA, KDD, almacenes de datos, minería de datos, series temporales

1 Introducción

Hoy en día, los sistemas de información de todo tipo recogen grandes volúmenes de datos con referencias temporales, pudiéndose descubrir información valiosa acerca de comportamientos periódicos, patrones repetitivos o tendencias, de analizarse estas *series temporales* (ST) con la técnica adecuada.

El KDD (*Knowledge Discovery in Databases*) [1], proceso de extracción de información en grandes volúmenes de datos, se divide en tres fases: la integración y preprocesado, la minería de datos y el descubrimiento de conocimiento. El resultado de la integración es un *almacén de datos* (AD): "una colección que varía en el tiempo de datos orientados a un tema, integrados y no volátiles para el apoyo a la toma de decisiones" [2]. La ventaja del AD como repositorio es que los datos (i) se encuentran integrados y preparados para el análisis, (ii) están identificados con cierto momento temporal que habilita concretamente el AST y

* Financiación de proyectos METASIGN (TIN2004-00779) y DADS (PBC-05-012-2). La beca FPU (AP2006-00332) financió el trabajo de Jesús Pardillo. (España)

(iii) su organización *multidimensional* (MD) de los datos está próxima a la forma de pensar de los analistas. Sin embargo, la minería continúa realizándose más como un arte que como una ciencia, debido a la falta de un método y modelos que trabajen a nivel conceptual con datos bien estructurados.

Actualmente, sólo tres aproximaciones tratan, aunque sea tangencialmente, el modelado de técnicas de minería de datos. Éstas son: CWM (*Common Warehouse Metamodel*) [3], para la definición de los metadatos de aplicaciones de inteligencia empresariales; PMML (*Predictive Model Markup Language*) [4], para la descripción de modelos de aprendizaje automático; y PBMS (*Pattern Base Management System*) [5, 6], para la gestión y almacenamiento de patrones. Sin embargo, ninguna de las aproximaciones constituye una técnica fácilmente usable para la especificación de las técnicas de minería de datos.

En la línea de trabajos previos para el modelado de minería de datos con reglas de asociación [7] o *clustering* [8], presentamos aquí una extensión de UML (*Unified Modeling Language*) [3] mediante el mecanismo de *perfiles* para modelar la minería de datos con AST apoyado por el modelo MD del AD. Además, proponemos el uso de MDA (*Model Driven Architecture*) [3] para la generación automática de código a partir de los modelos de minería de datos. Por un lado, el modelado MD, que se expresa en términos de *hechos* y *dimensiones* de análisis, facilitará la comprensión de los datos bajo análisis. Por otro, el modelado conceptual abstrae los detalles de plataformas concretas de minería de datos. Esto permitirá al analista centrarse únicamente en el proceso de minería de datos, relegando implementaciones concretas a las herramientas de transformación.

2 Fundamentos del AST

El descubrimiento de patrones y tendencias en los datos es de gran relevancia en la actualidad. Las empresas necesitan anticipar o predecir los valores futuros de variables así como identificar la naturaleza del fenómeno bajo estudio. De esta manera, el AST se da como técnica natural para la minería de los datos. En una ST, el tiempo es un atributo presente en cada modelo de análisis (agregado incluso a diferentes escalas, e.g., días, semanas, meses); y la tendencia y periodicidad, los conceptos básicos en que se describe la ST.

Varios son los algoritmos que pueden utilizarse para revelar patrones temporales ocultos [9]: ARIMA (*AutoRegressive Integrated Moving Average*), ART (*AutoRegressive Tree*), *exponential smoothing* o VAR (*Vector AutoRegression*). Estos algoritmos requieren que se especifiquen *ajustes* para descubrir los patrones en los datos: el *período* (especificado por el analista o a descubrir *automáticamente* por los algoritmos), el *número total de períodos* bajo análisis, el rango total de tiempo (la *ventana*) o el umbral *mínimo de soporte* (por ejemplo, en el modelo de regresión). Respecto a las variables de estudio, algunas se utilizan como *entrada* del algoritmo (para propósitos de aprendizaje), mientras que otras agrupan los datos (como *casos*). Además, los analistas pueden *filtrar* variables bajo algún criterio dado. Para la eficiencia de los algoritmos también es importante especificar el tratamiento de los *valores ausentes* en la ST.

3 Modelado MD de AD en UML

Pese a que UML [3] es un lenguaje de modelado de propósito general, proporciona un mecanismo de *perfilado* para implementar lenguajes específicos como son el modelado MD o los AST. Un perfil UML contiene estereotipos de los elementos de modelado de UML como medio fundamental de extensión. Además, estos disponen de: atributos (definiciones etiquetadas), restricciones de dominio e iconos, con las que poder enriquecer la semántica original de UML.

El perfil para el modelado MD de AD. En un modelo MD, los datos son organizados en hechos y dimensiones. Mientras que un hecho conforma el foco de análisis, modelando colecciones de medidas; las dimensiones asociadas proporcionan un contexto para el análisis, formando jerarquías a través de las cuales las medidas pueden agregarse. Como prerequisito para el modelado de AST, hemos tomado nuestro perfil UML previo para el modelado MD de AD [10], que describe los conceptos MD extendiendo UML en términos de estereotipos, definiciones etiquetadas, restricciones y notaciones (iconos). Por motivos de espacio, omitimos la especificación de este perfil UML, que puede consultarse en [10].

4 Un perfil para el AST sobre AD

Hemos extendido UML mediante perfiles para modelar el AST sobre modelos MD. Por cada concepto expuesto en la Sec. 2, se han diseñado los estereotipos, definiciones etiquetadas y restricciones oportunas para contemplar su modelado. En la Fig. 1, se muestra el perfil resultante con la notación estándar de UML.

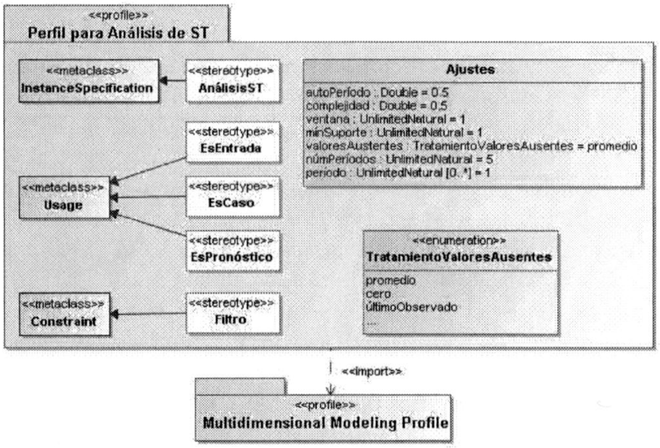

Fig. 1. El perfil UML para el análisis de ST

Por cada parámetro para los *Ajustes* del AST (e.g., *autoPeríodo*, *valores-Ausentes* o *período*), en el perfil se modela el valor por defecto, así como su dominio (e.g., el valor por defecto de la *ventana* es de 1, pudiendo ser cualquier entero no negativo). Para el parámetro *valoresAusentes*, el dominio se ha definido mediante la enumeración *TratamientoValoresAusentes* de los posibles valores.

Adicionalmente, cada estereotipo conlleva ciertas restricciones en el modelado en función de la semántica del dominio representado. Para su especificación se suelen utilizan lenguajes formales, siendo OCL (*Object Constraint Language*) [3] el más empleado. Por motivos de espacio, suprimimos aquí el listado de las restricciones identificadas en el dominio de AST para los estereotipos presentados.

5 Análisis en un proyecto real: la pesca en Alicante

Con nuestra aproximación, hemos modelado el AST de las capturas comerciales de peces en Alicante. Los datos analizados provienen de la lonja del pescado en esta región. Los valores observados y pronosticados de las capturas, se utilizarán para el soporte de la administración de pesquerías.

Tras la obtención de requisitos, diseñamos el AD integrando datos censales, datos ambientales y datos provenientes de bases de datos transaccionales. De esta forma, el AD contiene datos preprocesados preparados para el análisis con técnicas de minería de datos. En las siguientes líneas, mostraremos cómo se puede utilizar nuestra aproximación para descubrir el conocimiento requerido.

Modelado de datos MD. La Fig. 2 muestra las capturas de peces modeladas con el perfil UML para el modelado MD de AD [10]. El modelo se estructura con un hecho central de análisis (*Capturas*) alrededor del que se articulan las dimensiones sobre las que analizar (*Tiempo*, *Ubicación*, *Pez* y *Embarcación*). Nótese que, en el AD, la variable temporal del AST se modela como la dimensión etiquetada con $\{isTime\}$. En aras de la sencillez, hemos omitido la representación explícita de los atributos de las dimensiones no utilizadas en el AST.

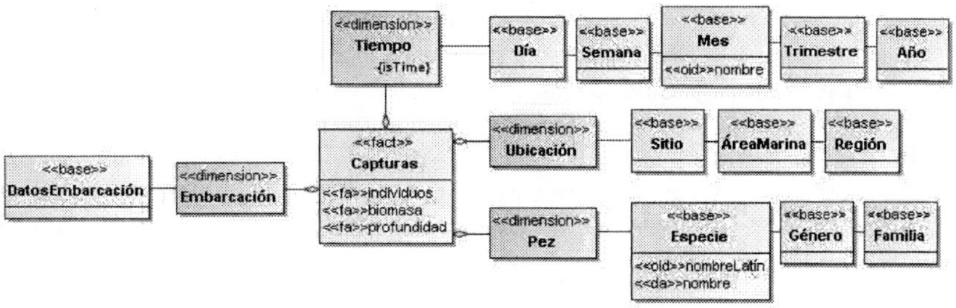

Fig. 2. Modelo MD de las capturas de peces

Modelado del AST sobre datos MD. Como ejemplo sencillo de AST, queremos analizar la ST del total de carpas capturadas mensualmente (Fig. 3). Hemos especificado una instancia (*InstanceSpecification* de UML) de los *Ajustes* estereotipada como *AnálisisST*, dados ciertos valores de los parámetros para configurar el algoritmo subyacente (la discusión acerca de su obtención queda fuera del ámbito de este trabajo). Los atributos de minería (las variables MD del AST), se modelan como un conjunto de dependencias de uso (*Usage*) desde el AST hacia los correspondientes atributos de los elementos MD (hechos y niveles de agregación). Además, dado que el AST está restringido a las carpas, modelamos además una restricción de filtro (representada como {*'carpa'*}), representando así, que el atributo *nombre* es filtrado en el AST.

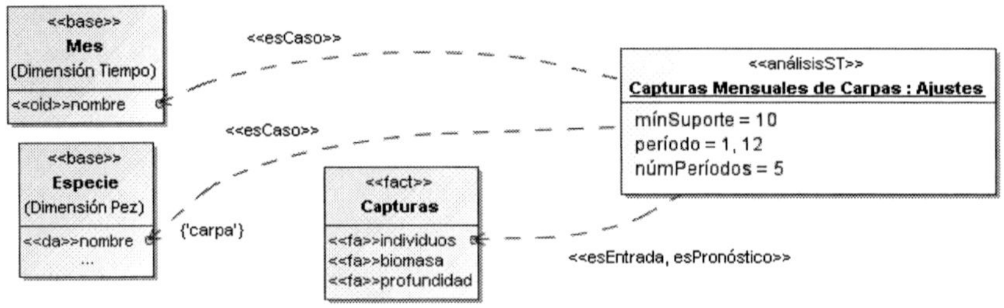

Fig. 3. Modelo conceptual para el AST de las capturas de peces en Alicante

6 Transformación a código

Dado un modelo conceptual como el AST diseñado, el código que lo implementa en distintas plataformas de minería de datos puede ser generado automáticamente siguiendo una propuesta del tipo de MDA [3]. Con estas aproximaciones, la generación de código se articula como una secuencia de transformaciones entre modelos a diferentes niveles de abstracción, siendo el propio código un modelo más (el más concreto), objeto final de transformación.

En este trabajo, hemos estudiado la transformación de nuestro perfil UML para el modelado de AST hacia el código que lo implementa en la plataforma *Microsoft SQL Server 2005 Analysis Services*. Concretamente al lenguaje DMX (*Data Mining eXtensions*), que permite especificar las tareas de minería de datos en esta plataforma. MDA propone el lenguaje Mof2Text (MOF *Models to Text Transformation Language*) [3] para especificar este tipo de transformaciones de modelos (representaciones visuales) a código (codificaciones textuales). Su descripción se realiza mediante plantillas de texto parametrizadas por los elementos de modelado a transformar. Estas plantillas serán luego tomadas por un motor de transformaciones Mof2Text para generar el código de la plataforma.

Las transformaciones se han realizado sobre el entorno Eclipse, con los proyectos MDT (*Model Development Tools*) para el modelado con UML y GMT (*Generative Modeling Technologies*) para la ingeniería dirigida por modelos. En particular, hemos utilizado MOFScript (subproyecto de GMT) para la especificación de las transformaciones modelo a código conforme a Mof2Text. De esta manera, hemos podido confirmar nuestra propuesta como una alternativa viable para el diseño e implementación de técnicas de minería de datos como los AST.

7 Conclusión

Este trabajo propone un perfil UML para el AST con modelos conceptuales sobre AD. Como grandes ventajas, nuestra aproximación utiliza (i) el modelo MD del AD, semánticamente rico y estructurado intuitivamente; (ii) los procesos de carga del AD para disponer de datos preprocesados listos para la minería y (iii) artefactos para minería de datos entendibles fácilmente por los analistas. Además, nuestros modelos conceptuales son codificados en distintas herramientas de minería mediante MDA. Para mostrar la viabilidad de esta aproximación, la aplicamos a un proyecto real y generamos automáticamente el código asociado para un sistema comercial mediante transformaciones Mof2Text.

Como trabajo futuro, estudiaremos el uso de CWM como punto intermedio de transformación, así como la implementación en más plataformas. Otros trabajos incluyen el enriquecimiento y validación del modelo conceptual presentado.

References

1. Fayyad, U., Piatetsky-Shapiro, G., Smyth, P., Uthurusamy, R.: Advances in knowledge discovery and data mining. First edn. American Association for Artificial Intelligence, Menlo Park, CA, USA (1996)
2. Inmon, W.H.: Building the Data Warehouse. Second edn. John Wiley & Sons, Inc., New York, NY, USA (1996)
3. Object Management Group (OMG): Referring to the MDA, UML, CWM, OCL, and Mof2Text Specifications. `http://www.omg.org` (November 2007)
4. Data Mining Group: Predictive Model Markup Language (PMML), version 3.1. `http://www.dmg.org/pmml-v3-1.html` (Visited April 2007)
5. Rizzi, S., Bertino, E., Catania, B., Golfarelli, M., Halkidi, M., Terrovitis, M., Vassiliadis, P., Vazirgiannis, M., Vrachnos, E.: Towards a Logical Model for Patterns. In: ER. (2003) 77–90
6. Rizzi, S.: UML-Based Conceptual Modeling of Pattern-Bases. In: PaRMa. (2004)
7. Zubcoff, J., Trujillo, J.: A UML 2.0 profile to design Association Rule mining models in the multidimensional conceptual modeling of data warehouses. Data Knowl. Eng. **In Press** (2006) `doi:10.1016/j.datak.2006.10.007`
8. Zubcoff, J., Pardillo, J., Trujillo, J.: Integrating Clustering Data Mining into the Multidimensional Modeling of Data Warehouses with UML Profiles. In: DaWaK. (2007) 199–208
9. Box, G.E.P., Jenkins, G., Reinsel, G.: Time Series Analysis, Forecasting and Control. Third edn. Prentice Hall (1994)
10. Luján-Mora, S., Trujillo, J., Song, I.Y.: A UML profile for multidimensional modeling in data warehouses. Data Knowl. Eng. **59**(3) (2006) 725–769

Subtipado de Modelos: Una Definición Basada en la Sustitución entre Tipos y en la Aplicabilidad de Operaciones

Jose E. Rivera and Nathalie Moreno

Dept. Lenguajes y Ciencias de la Computación, Universidad de Málaga, España
{rivera,vergara}@lcc.uma.es

Resumen Los modelos y metamodelos son los artefactos claves en el *Desarrollo de Software Dirigido por Modelos (DSDM)*. Aunque varias son las notaciones existentes para su especificación, no existe acuerdo sobre la definición de un concepto tan básico como es el *tipo de un modelo*, aún siendo éste crucial en aspectos tan importantes como la interoperabilidad entre herramientas y la maximización de la reutilización. En este artículo proponemos el uso del metamodelo como el *tipo de un modelo* para así aprovechar los lenguajes y operaciones definidos sobre ellos, y presentamos una definición e implementación de subtipado de modelos (con sus respetivas variantes) que garantiza la seguridad de tipos (*type safety*) e introduce la noción de polimorfismo en el *DSDM*.

Palabras claves: Tipo de modelo, polimorfismo, DSDM, Subtipado

1. Introducción

Con la creciente aceptación del DSDM, son cada vez más las operaciones que se definen sobre los modelos: transformación, métricas, composición... La especificación de estas operaciones generalmente dependen de los metamodelos al cual los modelos operandos son conformes. Así, sería interesante definir otra operación, el *subtipado de modelos*, que se encargue de maximizar la reutilización de estas operaciones ya definidas. En este contexto, la definición del concepto *tipo de un modelo* pasaría a ser crucial, a pesar de que actualmente no existe un consenso sobre ella.

En este artículo proponemos el uso del metamodelo como el *tipo de un modelo*. Así mismo, introducimos una definición de la operación de subtipado de modelos que garantiza la seguridad de tipos e introduce la noción de polimorfismo en el *DSDM*. Concretamente, distinguimos entre cuatro clases de subtipados según el grado de relajación a la queramos someter a los metamodelos operandos: el *subtipado estricto*, el *subtipado plano*, el *subtipado con renombramiento*, y el *subtipado plano con renombramiento*.

El documento está estructurado de la siguiente forma. La Sección 2 introduce el concepto *tipo de modelo*. En la Sección 3 se presenta una posible definición del subtipado de modelos, junto con sus posibles variantes y los correspondientes algoritmos. Para finalizar, la Sección 4 compara nuestro trabajo con aquellos relacionados y en la Sección 5 se extraen las conclusiones y se exponen algunas líneas de trabajo futuro.

2. Tipo de un Modelo

Un tipo es un conjunto de valores que cumplen ciertas propiedades técnicas [1]. En general, estos valores se agrupan de forma que una serie de operaciones puedan ser aplicables sobre ellos.

Hasta ahora, se puede decir que no existe un consenso generalizado sobre la definición del *tipo de un modelo*, aun siendo un concepto crítico en ciertos aspectos del DSDM, como por ejemplo, en la descripción de los parámetros de entrada y salida de las operaciones y servicios de modelos.

La mayoría de los esfuerzos realizados en la definición de operaciones sobre modelos, tales como la *transformación*, han optado por usar sistemas de tipos desarrollados para el paradigma orientado a objetos, pues ciertas estructuras definidas en este paradigma son similares y se pueden aprovechar en el DSDM. En cambio, existen también diferencias, como es el caso de una mayor predominancia en el DSDM de dependencias cíclicas entre la conformidad de clases, y la aparición de ciertos aspectos menos comunes en los sistemas orientados a objetos como la jerarquía de meta-niveles y las asociaciones como elementos de modelado de primera clase [2].

Por lo tanto, esta adopción hace que los programas sean frágiles ante cambios en el metamodelo, aún cuando éstos, en principio, no deberían afectar en sí a la operación con la que se trabaje. Así, surge la necesidad de definir un *tipo de modelo* que se adapte mejor a las circunstancias. Son dos las opciones principales que podemos adoptar para resolver esta problemática: extender el sistema de tipos desarrollado para el paradigma orientado a objetos con los elementos necesarios para cubrir las necesidades de los modelos, o usar una estructura ya definida como es el metamodelo. Nosotros optaremos por esta última puesto que nos permite aprovechar las operaciones y los lenguajes de especificación sobre él ya definidos, y porque actualmente en las transformaciones entre modelos (la operación de modelos por excelencia) se usan para la descripción de sus parámetros de entrada y salida.

3. Subtipado de Modelos

Existen ciertas iniciativas para las que el subtipado de modelos puede llegar a ser crucial. Un claro ejemplo de ello es la conexión entre varios servicios de modelos, en la que hay que comprobar que el tipo de la entrada de un servicio sea sustituible por el tipo de la salida de otro. También es interesante en situaciones como en la búsqueda de un metamodelo en un repositorio, pues podríamos proveer un metamodelo inicial simple y buscar en el repositorio subtipos de él.

Además, los metamodelos, como cualquier otro artefacto software, evolucionan con el tiempo en cada una de las etapas de su vida. En estos casos la definición de subtipado de modelos también es útil para conocer qué clase de cambios invalidará (y cuales no) las operaciones sobre un metamodelo definidas.

Dado dos *tipos de modelos* M y M', consideraremos que M' es subtipo de M ($M' \leq M$) si podemos garantizar que al sustituir M por M', se puedan seguir aplicando las operaciones definidas sobre M a M', garantizando la seguridad de tipos.

A continuación introduciremos un algoritmo general de subtipado de modelos. Este algoritmo será sometido a distintos grados de relajación, originando cada uno de las variantes de subtipado de modelos. El algoritmo que presentamos está basado en la terminología de KM3 [3], un lenguaje textual especializado para la especificación de metamodelos. Esta elección no nos restringe a tener que definir los metamodelos desde un principio en KM3 puesto que existen transformaciones desde/hacia otros lenguajes de metamodelado, como por ejemplo Ecore. El metamodelo de KM3 puede observarse en la Fig. 1.

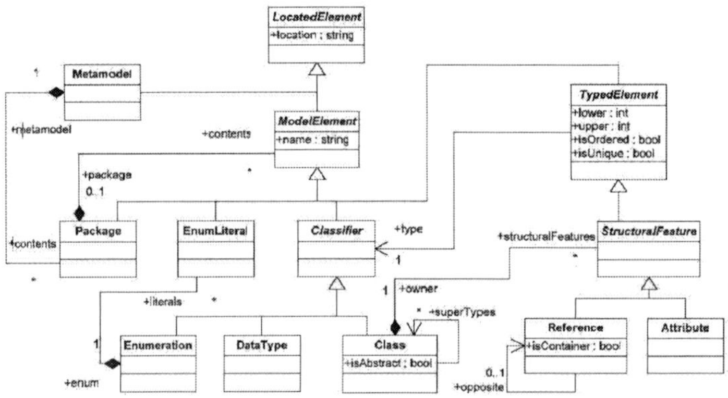

Figura 1. Metamodelo de KM3

Dado dos metamodelos M' y M, el subtipado se define de la siguiente forma:

- Un Metamodelo M' es subtipo de otro Metamodelo M ($M' \leq M$) si y sólo si:
  $\forall K \in \{M.Package\} \bullet \exists K' \in \{M'.Package\} \bullet (K' \leq K)$
- Un Paquete K' es subtipo de otro Paquete K ($K' \leq K$) si y sólo si:
  $isRelated(K'.name = K.name) \wedge$
  $\forall C \in \{K.Class\} \bullet \exists C' \in \{K'.Class\} \bullet (C' \leq C)$
- Una Clase C' es subtipo de otra Clase C ($C' \leq C$) si y sólo si:
  $isRelated(C'.name = C.name) \wedge (C'.isAbstract \Rightarrow C.isAbstract) \wedge$
  $\forall C \in \{C.superTypes\} \bullet \exists C' \in \{C'.superTypes\} \bullet (C' \leq C) \wedge$
  $\forall S \in \{C.structuralFeatures\} \bullet \exists S' \in \{C'.structuralFeatures\} \bullet$

$(S' \leq S)$

- Un Atributo P' es subtipo de otro Atributo P $(P' \leq P)$ si y sólo si:
$isRelated(P'.name = P.name) \wedge (P'.type \leq P.type) \wedge$
$(P'.isUnique = P.isUnique) \wedge (P'.lower \geq P.lower) \wedge$
$((P'.upper = P.upper) \vee (P'.upper \geq P.upper \geq 2)) \wedge$
$(P'.isOrdered = P.isOrdered)$
- Una Referencia R' es subtipo de otra Referencia R $(R' \leq R)$ si y sólo si:
$isRelated(R'.name = R.name) \wedge (R'.type \leq R.type) \wedge$
$(R'.isUnique = R.isUnique) \wedge (R'.lower \geq R.lower) \wedge$
$((R'.upper = R.upper) \vee (R'.upper \geq R.upper \geq 2)) \wedge$
$(R'.isOrdered = R.isOrdered) \wedge (R'.opposite \leq R.opposite)$

Tipos de datos. En KM3 sólo existen cuatro tipos de datos primitivos: *String*, *Boolean*, *Integer* y *Double*. Por lo tanto, la relación $\leq$ para los tipos de datos primitivos se cumplirá cuando ambos tipos de datos sean el mismo o en el caso *Double* $\leq$ *Integer*. En este último caso, a pesar de que podría existir alguna excepción como en la definición de la operación *módulo*, se verifica que todas las operaciones definidas para el tipo *Integer* están también definidas para el tipo *Double*. Nótese que nuestro contexto es el de reemplazamiento o sustitución frente a la aplicación de operaciones, y por ese motivo el sentido de la relación de subtipado es el contrario al usual (*Integer* $\leq$ *Double*).

Un enumerado $E1$ será subtipo de otro $E2$ siempre que este primero incluya todos los elementos del segundo.

Propiedades. La restricción entre los límites de las multiplicidades de las propiedades (atributos o referencias) surge por la diferencia en el modo de acceso sobre un elemento simple o sobre un conjunto de ellos. De la misma forma, obligamos a que las propiedades subtipo y supertipo sean ambas ordenadas o ambas no ordenadas, puesto que en general todas las operaciones definidas sobre colecciones no ordenadas (como los conjuntos) no tienen porqué estar definidas sobre colecciones ordenadas (como por ejemplo las listas). En cambio, no incluimos restricción alguna en cuanto a la característica contenedora de una referencia debido a que el modo de especificar el acceso a la referencia en cuestión varía.

La definición del subtipado para las referencias opuestas es exactamente igual al subtipado introducido para las referencias en general, salvo que no se comprueba que sus referencias opuestas sean a su vez subtipo, pues no es necesario en este caso.

Renombramiento. La operación $isRelated$ entre cadenas comprueba que exista cierta relación entre los nombres de los elementos. Según definamos esta operación, surgen dos variantes de subtipado: el *subtipo estricto*, si la definimos mediante la operación de igualdad; o el *subtipo con renombramiento*, si usamos uno de los siguientes métodos: (1) comprobar que los nombres sean sinónimos a partir de las correspondencias especificadas en un modelo *weaving* [4], u (2) obligar a que la diferencia entre los nombres sea menor a un error establecido. Este último caso es interesante tanto para detectar errores ortográficos, como para captar los casos de diferencias entre mayúsculas y minúsculas, espacios frente a guiones bajos, etc. Así, hemos implementado el algoritmo de la *distancia Levenshtein*, que devuelve el número total de manipulaciones que se necesitan realizar para transformar una cadena en otra.

Nótese que obligando a que exista cierta relación entre los nombres de los elementos del metamodelo (en lugar de definir un subtipado totalmente independiente de ellos) estamos promoviendo cierta conservación en la identidad de las clases.

Estructura de paquetes. Las restantes variantes de subtipado nacen al hacer éste independiente o no de la estructura de paquetes de los metamodelos, puesto que no siempre son relevantes en cuanto al *tipo de un modelo* se refiere. El algoritmo de *subtipado plano* (subtipado independiente de la estructura de paquete) difiere del algoritmo general de subtipado en que no se obliga a que exista para cada paquete otro paquete subtipo, si no que se comparan directamente las clases independientemente de los paquetes en los que estén albergadas.

Sustitución de metamodelos. Existen problemas asociados a la sustitución de un metamodelo por uno que sea subtipo plano o subtipo con renombramiento (o subtipo plano con renombramiento). En estos casos, las operaciones no se podrán aplicar directamente sobre el nuevo metamodelo, sino que necesitamos un acercamiento transformativo (totalmente automático) que nos adapte las operaciones realizando los cambios pertinentes: renombre de los elementos (en el caso de subtipado con renombramiento); o variación de los paquetes a los que pertenecen las clases (en el caso de subtipado plano), siempre y cuando haya sido necesario especificar explícitamente en la operación los paquetes en los que las clases están albergadas (en casos de posible ambigüedad).

Evolución de metamodelos. En resumen, y en cuanto a la evolución de metamodelos se refiere, a un metamodelo le podemos añadir cualquier tipo de elemento (paquetes, clases, atributos, referencias, relaciones de herencia...) y las operaciones definidas sobre él seguirán siendo aplicables. En cambio, no existe tal libertad en la realización de modificaciones, y nos tendremos que ceñir a las anteriormente mencionadas.

4. Trabajos Relacionados

Uno de los trabajos más importantes en este área es el realizado por Steel [2]. En él, se introduce una definición de *tipo de Modelo* como extensión al tipado de objetos. La única diferencia significante entre un metamodelo y el *tipo de Modelo* que en él se define es la estructura de paquetes. La razón de no escoger el metamodelo como el tipo de un modelo se la atribuyen a la existencia de referencias entre distintos modelos, que provoca que no se pueda garantizar que todos los objetos del modelo encuentren su tipo correpondiente en un sólo paquete. Nosotros, en cambio, pensamos que el problema radica en la definición que adoptan de un metamodelo, es decir, pensar en un metamodelo como en un único paquete MOF sin tener en cuenta las relaciones (fundamentalmente de importación) que pueden existir entre ellos. Además, el *subtipado plano* presentado en este artículo cubre la relación de subtipado que el autor propone.

Existen otros tipos de iniciativas que proponen comprobar la compatibilidad de tipo a partir de una serie de restricciones, como por ejemplo en [5] usando el lenguaje Alloy.

Por último, en [6] también se trata el problema de la evolución del metamodelo, pero centrándose en la adaptación de los modelos conformes a él en lugar de en las operaciones definidas sobre los metamodelos.

5. Conclusiones y Trabajo Futuro

En este artículo se ha propuesto el uso del metamodelo como el *tipo de un modelo* para aprovechar así los lenguajes y operaciones definidos sobre ellos. Basándose en esta consideracíon, se han definido distintas variantes del subtipado de modelos que garantizan la seguridad de tipos e introducen la noción de polimorfismo en el *DSDM*. Los algoritmos correpondientes a las distintas variantes han sido implementados e integrados en la herramienta Maudeling [7].

Actualmente, estamos trabajando en la incorporación directa de la terminología Ecore para así incluir en los algoritmos las relaciones de subtipado entre operaciones. Además, estamos implementando el acercamiento transformativo que adapta las operaciones definidas sobre un metamodelo a los metamodelos subtipos planos y/o con renombramiento.

Referencias

1. Cardelli, L., Wegner, P.: On understanding types, data abstraction, and polymorphism. ACM Computing Surveys **17**(4) (1985) 471–522
2. Steel, J.: Typage de modèles. PhD thesis, Université de Rennes 1 (2007)
3. Bézivin, J., Jouault, F.: KM3: a DSL for metamodel specification. In: Procs. of the 8th IFIP International Conference on Formal Methods for Open Object-Based Distributed Systems (FMOODS 2006). Volume 4037 of Lecture Notes in Computer Science., Bologna, Italy, Springer-Verlag (2006) 171–185
4. Fabro, M.D.D., Bezivin, J., Jouault, F., Breton, E., Gueltas, G.: AMW: a generic model weaver. In: Proceedings of the 1ère Journée sur l'Ingénierie Dirigée par les Modèles (IDM05). (2005) 105–114
5. Edwards, J., Jackson, D., Torlak, E.: A type system for object models. In: Proc. of the 12th International Symposium on Foundations of Software Engineering (SIGSOFT'04/FSE-12), ACM Press (2004) 189–199
6. Wachsmuth, G.: Metamodel adaptation and model co-adaptation. In: Proceedings of the 21st European Conference on Object-Oriented Programming (ECOOP'07). Volume 4069 of Lecture Notes in Computer Science., Springer-Verlag (2007)
7. Rivera, J.E., Durán, F., Vallecillo, A., Romero, J.R.: Maudeling: Herramienta de gestión de modelos usando Maude. In: Actas de XII Jornadas de Ingeniería del Software y Bases de Datos (JISBD'07), Zaragoza, Spain (2007) 409–410

AUTHOR INDEX

CIbSE - IberoAmerican Conference on Software Engineering
c/o Luca Cernuzzi
Universidad Católica "Nuestra Seóra de la Asunción",
Campus Universitario, Asunción
Barrio Santa Ana, C.C.1683, C.P. 1364
Asunción - Paraguay

ISBN 978-1-5108-4066-9

CURRAN ASSOCIATES INC.
proceedings.com

9 781510 840669